lonely

New England

Maine
p364

Vermont
p276

New Hampshire
p322

Central Massachusetts & the Berkshires
p175

Around Boston p88
◉ **Boston** p34

Connecticut
p241

Rhode Island
p208

Cape Cod, Nantucket & Martha's Vineyard
p124

THIS EDITION WRITTEN AND RESEARCHED BY

Gregor Clark,
Carolyn Bain, Mara Vorhees, Benedict Walker

PLAN
YOUR TRIP

FRANCONIA NOTCH STATE
PARK (P351)

JOE KLEMENTOVICH / GETTY IMAGES ©

BEACON HILL (P36)

S. GREG PANOSIAN / GETTY IMAGES ©

ON THE ROAD

Contents

UNDERSTAND

SPECIAL FEATURES

Welcome to New England

Mount spectacular summits and feel ocean breezes. Tantalize your taste buds with succulent seafood and sweet maple syrup. Relish history and high culture.

History

The history of New England is the history of America. It's the Pilgrims who came ashore at Plymouth Rock and the minutemen who fought for American independence. It's the ponderings of Ralph Waldo Emerson and the protests of Harriet Beecher Stowe. It's hundreds of years of poets and philosophers, progressive thinkers who dared to dream and dared to do. It is generations of immigrants who have shaped New England into the dynamic region that it is today.

Outdoor Adventure

New England undulates with the rolling hills and rocky peaks of the ancient Appalachian Mountains, from the beautiful birch-covered Berkshires in Western Massachusetts, to the lush Green Mountains in Vermont, to the towering White Mountains that stretch across New Hampshire and Maine.

Nearly 5000 miles of coastline means that New Englanders are into water sports: opportunities for fishing, swimming, surfing, sailing and sunbathing are unlimited. So pack your sunglasses and your sunblock and settle in for some quality time on the ocean.

Culture

At the cutting edge of culture, New England is home to two exciting, experimental contemporary-art museums, as well as myriad traditional art museums. Indie bands rock out in Boston, Portland and Burlington. The world-renowned Boston Symphony Orchestra takes its show on the road in summer, delighting audiences in the Berkshires. Meanwhile, there are blues jams in Maine, folk festivals in Newport and Lowell, and classical music in Rockport. Concert series, film festivals and theater productions mean the cultural calendar is jam-packed.

Food

To get a taste of New England, check out the calendar of events celebrating local delicacies, such as Maine lobsters, Wellfleet oysters and Vermont beer. Blessed with a burgeoning locavore movement and a wealth of international culinary influences, New England cuisine fuses the best of both worlds. A pile of pancakes drenched in maple syrup; fresh farm produce and sharp cheddar cheese; fish and shellfish straight from the sea; exotic dishes with influences of Portugal, Italy or Asia: this is just a sampling of the epicurean delights that travelers will find in New England.

Why I Love New England

By Mara Vorhees, Writer

For a place that is steeped in history, New England is ever moving forward. I am proud of the region's 18th-century revolutionary roots, but I'm even prouder that all six states embraced marriage equality in the 21st century. Emerson and Thoreau are inspiring, but it's Geraldine Brooks, Jhumpa Lahiri and Elizabeth Strout that keep me up reading late into the night. John Singer Sargent is iconic indeed, but even more intriguing is the art being created in the SoWa studios. New England's history is rich, to be sure, but the here and now is downright exhilarating.

For more about our writers, see p448.

Above: Kent Falls State Park (p274)

New England

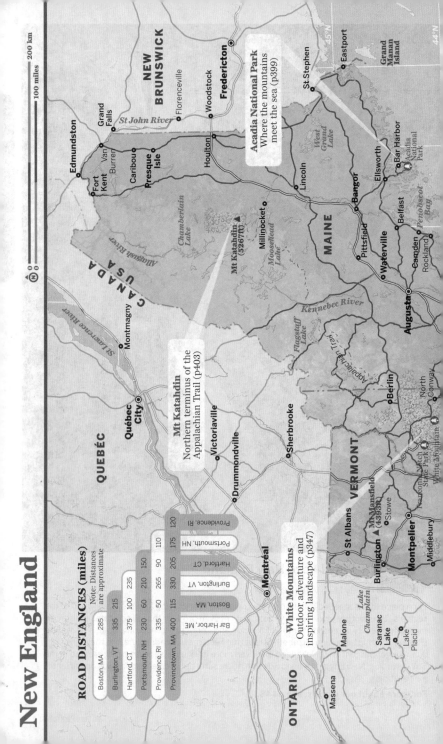

ROAD DISTANCES (miles)
Note: Distances are approximate

Boston, MA	285					
Burlington, VT	335	215				
Hartford, CT	375	100	235			
Portsmouth, NH	230	60	210	150		
Providence, RI	335	50	265	90	110	
Provincetown, MA	400	115	330	205	175	120
	Bar Harbor, ME	Boston, MA	Burlington, VT	Hartford, CT	Portsmouth, NH	Providence, RI

Mt Katahdin
Northern terminus of the Appalachian Trail (p403)

Acadia National Park
Where the mountains meet the sea (p399)

White Mountains
Outdoor adventure and inspiring landscape (p347)

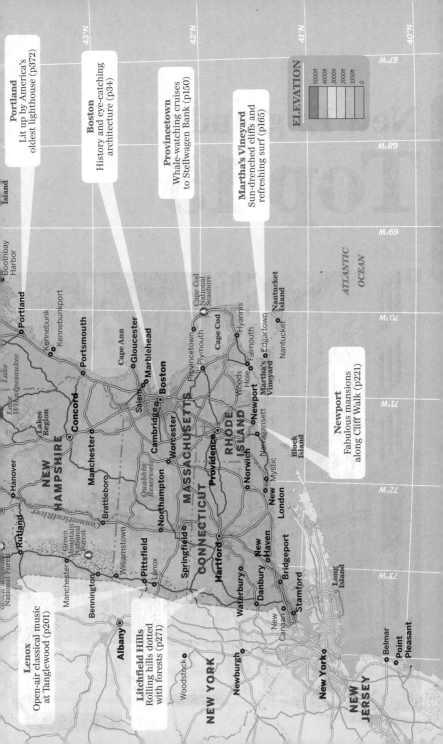

Portland
Lit up by America's oldest lighthouse (p372)

Boston
History and eye-catching architecture (p34)

Provincetown
Whale-watching cruises to Stellwagen Bank (p150)

Martha's Vineyard
Sun-drenched cliffs and refreshing surf (p165)

Newport
Fabulous mansions along Cliff Walk (p221)

Lenox
Open-air classical music at Tanglewood (p201)

Litchfield Hills
Rolling hills dotted with forests (p271)

ELEVATION

5000ft
4000ft
3000ft
2000ft
1000ft
0

ATLANTIC OCEAN

New England's
Top 15

Freedom Trail

1 The best introduction to revolutionary Boston is the Freedom Trail (p56). This walking trail winds its way past 16 sites that earned the town its status as the cradle of liberty. The 2.5-mile footpath follows the course of the conflict, from the Old State House – where British regulars killed five men in the Boston Massacre – to the Old North Church, where the sexton hung two lanterns to warn that the British troops would come by sea. Follow the red-brick road through American revolutionary history. Old State House (p41)

Fall Foliage

2 One of New England's greatest natural resources is seasonal change. Every fall the trees fling off that staid New England green and deck their boughs with flaming reds, light-bending yellows and ostentatious oranges. We're talking about the changing of the guard from summer to fall, better known as leaf-peeping season. Vermont is the star of the fall foliage show (p282). Drive north on historic Rte 100 to ogle the array of colors on the slopes of Mt Snow and among the bucolic hills of the Mad River Valley. Stowe (p310)

BOSTON © LITTLENY / SHUTTERSTOCK ©

DONLAND / SHUTTERSTOCK ©

SARA WINTER / SHUTTERSTOCK ©

White Mountains

3 The White Mountains are New England's ultimate destination for outdoor adventure and inspiring landscape, with 1200 miles of hiking trails and 48 peaks over 4000ft. Franconia Notch (p351) is a perfect place to start, with trailheads for dozens of different hiking routes, an aerial tramway that whisks passengers to the top of Cannon Mountain, and the spectacular rush of water through Flume Gorge. It's a destination for all seasons, with opportunities for hiking and biking, skiing and snowboarding, sitting fireside and sitting lakeside.

College Town, USA

4 From the Five Colleges to the Seven Sisters (well, four of them), New England is crowded with colleges and overrun with universities, making for a dynamic, diverse student scene (p420). More than 100 institutions of higher education are located in Boston and environs. But Boston is only the beginning of this college tour. Providence, Rhode Island, and New Haven, CT, are home to their own Ivy League institutions, while smaller towns around the region are dominated by lively leafy campuses of their own. Yale University (p261)

Acadia National Park

5 Acadia National Park (p399) is where the mountains meet the sea. Miles of rocky coastline and even more miles of hiking and biking trails make this wonderland Maine's most popular destination, and deservedly so. The high point (literally) is Cadillac Mountain, the 1530ft peak that can be accessed by foot, bike or vehicle. Early risers can catch the country's first sunrise from this celebrated summit. Later in the day, cool off with a dip in Echo Lake or take tea and popovers overlooking Jordan Pond.

5

Lobster Trap

6 Nowhere is more closely associated with this crustacean than Maine. The mighty lobster was once so plentiful it was fed to prisoners and used for fertilizer; now the state symbol is deservedly esteemed as a delicacy. Crack the shell of a freshly steamed lobster with drawn butter at one of Maine's many summertime lobster pounds (p369). Or catch (and eat) your own on board a do-it-yourself lobster boat. Either way, don't forget to tie on a plastic bib – Maine's most endearing and enduring fashion statement.

DANIEL GRILL / GETTY IMAGES / TETRA IMAGES RF ©

6

Mansions of Newport

7 Eleven fabulous mansions are vestiges of the 19th-century capitalist boom when the region's bankers and businesspeople built their summer homes overlooking the Atlantic. Now managed by the Preservation Society of Newport County, the mansions offer a glimpse into a world of unabashed wealth, and include grand homes modeled after an Italian Renaissance palace, an English manor and a Parisian chateau. See them all from the Cliff Walk (p228), a narrow footpath that snakes along the ocean's edge, offering stunning views all around.

Sailing Penobscot Bay

8 Explore the rugged coast of Maine the old-fashioned way – on board one of the grand, multimasted windjammers that fill the harbors of Camden and Rockport (p389). These majestic sailing ships offer cruises around the islands and coves of Penobscot Bay, all under the power of the wind. Feel the breeze through your hair and the spray on your face as you sail the high seas, stop for a lobster roll for lunch, venture a quick dip in the afternoon, and dine as the sun sets over the rocky Maine coastline.

Architecture

9 From Charles Bulfinch to Henry Hobson Richardson to IM Pei, the world's most renowned architects and designers have left their mark on the cityscape of Boston. See the city's signature buildings clustered around Copley Square (p48), including the Renaissance Revival Boston Public Library, the Richardsonian Romanesque Trinity Church and the modernist John Hancock Tower. Of course urban design is much more than just buildings. Some of Boston's most striking features are its green spaces, including the city's newest innovation in urban design, the Rose Kennedy Greenway. Copley Square (p48)

Beachy Keen

10 Summer in New England is humid, so it's no surprise that the region's entire population flocks to the coast for cool ocean breezes. Fortunately, it's a long coastline. In Massachusetts, the island of Martha's Vineyard (p165) is ringed with beaches, which means plenty of sea and sand for everyone. At Aquinnah Public Beach, the cliffs of Gay Head radiate incredible colors in the late-afternoon light, attracting serious sun worshippers and photographers. Alternately, Katama Beach (p171) is best for good old-fashioned sand and surf. Gay Head Cliffs (p173)

Litchfield Hills

11 With scenery to match the Green Mountains, pre-Colonial villages worthy of any movie set, and the finest food, culture and music in Connecticut, Litchfield Hills (p271) attracts a sophisticated crowd of weekending Manhattanites and celebrities escaping the limelight. No wonder it's often described as 'the Hamptons for people who like privacy.' Give yourself some time here and you'll be rewarded with classical concerts in Norfolk, colonial farmhouse breakfasts in Kent, vintage car races at Lime Rock Race Track and fly-fishing worthy of Brad Pitt's performance in *A River Runs Through It*.

Whale-Watching

12 Nothing matches the thrill of spotting a breaching humpback or watching a pod of dolphins play in the boat's wake. Off the coast of Massachusetts, Stellwagen Bank (p151) is an area of open ocean rich in marine life. The National Marine Sanctuary was designated to conserve the area's biological diversity and to facilitate research and other activity. Educational and informative whale-watching cruises are offered from Boston, Plymouth, Barnstable, Provincetown and Gloucester, MA. Onboard staff ensure that these rides do not interfere with the animals in any way.

Farm Fresh

13 New England cuisine is a treat, thanks in part to the abundance of fruits, vegetables and dairy products that come from local farms. Depending on the season, visitors can pick their own apples, cherries, berries and pumpkins, relishing the flavor of the produce. In winter, farmers tap the local trees for the incomparable flavor of maple syrup. Vermont is leading the regional movement toward artisanal cheeses, with a Cheese Trail (p281) mapping the route between dozens of local producers.

Tanglewood

14 Come summer, culture beckons in the Berkshires. At this renowned music festival (p201) in Lenox, you can spread a blanket on the lawn and uncork a bottle of wine as one of the finest symphony orchestras in the USA takes the stage. Not only does the Boston Symphony Orchestra summer in these cool hills, but guest musicians of every stripe, from James Taylor to jazz greats, make it onto the schedule. The setting of meadows and lawns, once part of a Gilded Age estate, is as sweetly refined as the music.

Shine the Light

15 Lighthouses have long served to communicate across dangerous waters, guiding ships through dark nights and darker storms. The image of the lonely beacon is borne out by hundreds of lighthouses up and down the New England coast. Nowadays, you can visit a lighthouse museum (p373), spend the night in a lighthouse, share a romantic dinner in a lighthouse, or even become a lighthouse keeper. Or you can just keep your camera handy and admire the stoic beauty of these iconic New England buildings. Sankaty Head lighthouse (p164)

Need to Know

For more information, see Survival Guide (p427)

Currency
US dollars ($)

Language
English

Visas
Citizens of many countries are eligible for the Visa Waiver Program, which requires prior approval via Electronic System for Travel Authorization (ESTA).

Money
ATMs are widely available, except in the smallest towns and most remote wilderness. Credit cards are accepted at most hotels and restaurants.

Cell Phones
Check with your service provider. For US travelers, Verizon, AT&T and Sprint have coverage throughout New England (except in rural and mountainous areas).

Time
Eastern Standard Time (GMT/UTC minus four hours)

When to Go

Stowe
GO Jul–Mar

Bar Harbor
GO Jun–Oct

Boston
GO May–Oct

Provincetown
GO May–Oct

Providence
GO May–Oct

■ Warm to hot summers, cold winters
■ Mild summers, cold winters
□ Polar climate

High Season
(May–Oct)

➡ Accommodation prices increase by 50% to 100%; book in advance.

➡ Temperate spring weather and blooming fruit trees. July/August are hot and humid, except in mountain areas.

➡ Cooler in September and October.

Shoulder
(Mar–Apr)

➡ Weather remains wintry throughout March; April sees some sunshine and spring buds.

➡ Less demand for accommodations; negotiate lower prices (also applies to beach areas in May/early June).

Low Season
(Nov–Feb)

➡ Significantly lower prices for accommodations.

➡ Some sights in seasonal destinations close.

➡ With snow comes ski season (December to March), meaning higher prices in ski resorts.

Useful Websites

Visit New England (www.visitnewengland.com) Listings for events, sights, restaurants and hotels in all six states.

New England Guide (www.boston.com/travel/newengland) Travel tips and itineraries from the *Boston Globe*.

Lonely Planet (www.lonelyplanet.com/usa/new-england) Destination information, hotel bookings, traveler forum and more.

Appalachian Mountain Club (www.outdoors.org) Fantastic resource for hiking, biking, camping, climbing and paddling in New England's great outdoors.

New England Lighthouses (www.lighthouse.cc) A list of lighthouses by state.

Important Numbers

USA country code	☑1
International access code from the USA	☑011 + country code
Emergency	☑911
Local directory	☑411

Exchange Rates

Australia	A$1	$0.75
Canada	C$1	$0.78
Euro zone	€1	$1.11
Japan	¥100	$0.97
New Zealand	NZ$1	$0.72
UK	UK£1	$1.33

For current exchange rates see www.xe.com.

Daily Costs

Budget: Less than $100

➡ Camping or dorm bed: $30–$60

➡ Bus tickets: $10–$20

➡ Street food: mains $8–$12

➡ NPS walking tours and free-admission days at museums: free

Midrange: $100–$200

➡ Double room in a midrange hotel: $100–$250

➡ Car rental for a portion of the trip: from $50 per day

➡ Admission to museums and parks: $10–$20

Top End: More than $250

➡ Double room in high-end hotel: from $250

➡ Eat at the region's finest restaurants: mains from $25

➡ Tickets to concerts, events and tours: $30–$100

Opening Hours

The following is a general guideline for operating hours. Shorter hours may apply during low seasons, when some venues close completely. Seasonal variations are noted in the listings.

Banks and offices 9am or 10am–5pm or 6pm Monday to Friday; sometimes 9am–noon Saturday

Bars and pubs 5pm–midnight, some until 2am

Restaurants Breakfast 6am–10am, lunch 11:30am–2:30pm, dinner 5pm–10pm daily

Shops 9am–7pm Monday to Saturday; some open noon–5pm Sunday, or until evening in tourist areas

Arriving in New England

Logan International Airport (Boston; p434) The subway (T) and the bus (silver line) connect the airport to city center from 5:30am to 12:30am; take a taxi for $25 to $40, which takes about 20 minutes.

Bradley International Airport (Hartford, CT; p434) A bus runs to the city center from 4:30am to midnight; a taxi is $45 and takes about 20 minutes to the center.

Getting Around

Simply put, the best way to get around New England is by car. The region is relatively small, the highways are good and public transportation is not as frequent or as widespread as it could be.

Car The most convenient option for seeing rural New England, exploring small towns and partaking of outdoor adventure. Driving and parking can be a challenge in Boston.

Train Amtrak travels up and down the Northeast Corridor, connecting Boston to coastal towns like Portland, Salem, Providence and New Haven.

Bus Regional bus lines connect bigger towns throughout the region.

For much more on **getting around**, see p436

If You Like...

Outdoor Activities

Sailing Take to the waters in an America's Cup yacht for thrilling sunset tours. (p228)

Cycling Pedal rail trails, including Cape Cod Rail Trail (p137), and Ashuwillticook Rail Trail (p204) in the Berkshires.

Hiking Make your way over the rocky precipices of Cadillac Mountain (p399) or through the narrow pass of the Flume Gorge (p351).

Kayaking Paddle your kayak around Nauset Marsh in the Cape Cod National Seashore. (p150)

Skiing Hit the slopes above Stowe, Vermont's coziest ski village. (p311)

Beaches

Cape Anne, Massachusetts Come to Wingaersheek Beach at low tide to investigate the tide pools. (p108)

Cape Cod, Massachusetts Race Point Beach (p151) in Provincetown and Nauset Beach (p144) in Orleans are spectacular beaches backed by sand dunes.

Block Island, Rhode Island Stroll north from Old Harbor to sink your feet into the sand at Benson Town Beach. (p237)

Ogunquit, Maine Frolic on the family-friendly 3-mile stretch of sand at Ogunquit Beach. (p368)

Shopping

Newbury St Boston's most famous shopping destination is lined with boutiques, galleries and high-fashion outlets. (p48)

Brimfield Antique Show The largest outdoor antiques fair in North America sprouts on farmers' fields in rural Brimfield. (p179)

Galleries Art aficionados will find plenty to catch their eye at galleries in Wellfleet (p147) and Provincetown (p150).

Artists colony Find handcrafted jewelry, Shaker rugs and ceramics at the rural artists colony in Tiverton. (p220)

Street markets In Burlington, the pedestrianized Church Street Marketplace offers easygoing shopping, Vermont-style. (p302)

LL Bean Head to the flagship store in Freeport, ME, for an amazing selection of outdoor gear and wear. (p381)

Scenic Byways

MA 127 Drive around Cape Ann for salt marshes, windswept beaches, art oases and countless clam shacks.

MA 6A The Old King's Hwy on Cape Cod is as antique as the shops along it.

Mohawk Trail (MA 2) Massachusetts' top fall foliage route. (p192)

CT 169 Tool around the Quiet Corner, between orchards and 200-year-old villages. (p254)

VT 100 Running along the base of the Green Mountains, this iconic road showcases farmland and foliage. (p299)

Kancamagus Highway The river hugs the road on this cruise through leafy mountain panoramas. (p349)

Park Loop Road This 27-mile loop circumnavigates the northeastern section of Mt Desert Island. (p399)

Historic Towns

Nantucket, Massachusetts Cobblestone streets and sea captains' mansions whisk you back to the island's whaling heyday. (p157)

Deerfield, Massachusetts This historic village is a museum of colonial living. (p190)

Newport, Rhode Island The 18th-century downtown was thankfully preserved by Doris Duke's millions. (p221)

Portsmouth, New Hampshire
A bustling port city with a fine
collection of historic houses
from the 17th and 18th centuries.
(p324)

Woodstock, Vermont Perfectly
preserved slice of old New England, with 18th- and 19th-century
architecture surrounding a village green. (p291)

Seafood

You might be tempted to go
on a self-directed lobster
tour of US 1 in Maine, stopping at every lobster pound
for fresh-steamed crusta-
ceans dripping with clari-
fied butter. But there's more
to life than lobster: there's
also scallops, crabs, clams,
oysters and fresh flaky fish.

Lobster Tie on a bib at Ford's
Lobster in Noank, CT (p260), or
any one of Maine's best lobster
pounds (p369).

Lobster rolls Pull up a picnic
table at Sesuit Harbor Cafe in
Dennis, MA. (p138)

Lobster bisque The perfect
beginning to any meal at
Brewster Fish House in Brewster,
MA. (p140)

Fried clams Go to Woodman's
and order Chubby's Original to
see how the fried-clam thing
started. (p113)

Oysters on the half shell
Slurp some down at Matunuck
Oyster Bar (p233) in Matunuck,
RI, or Neptune Oyster (p68) in
Boston.

Beer

Northampton Brewery Hoist a
microbrew at New England's oldest operating brewpub. (p187)

Top: Flume Gorge (p351)
Bottom: Newport (p221)

Long Trail Brewing Company Sip Vermont's number-one amber. (p296)

Shipyard Brewing Co Partake of tours and tastings in Portland, ME. (p378)

Mohegan Cafe & Brewery Sample the jalapeño pilsner at the Block Island brewery. (p239)

Cisco Brewers Imbibe island brew at this friendly, laid-back Nantucket spot. (p165)

Vermont Brewers Festival Sample dozens of local craft brews at this annual event in Burlington. (p305)

Lighthouses

Boston Light This historic lighthouse can be visited on special tours of the Boston Harbor Islands. (p43)

Portland Head Light Maine's oldest lighthouse was built by order of George Washington in 1791. (p373)

Gay Head Lighthouse Perched on the colorful cliffs of Martha's Vineyard. (p174)

Cape Cod Lighthouses Climb to the top of Cape Cod Highland Light in Truro for vast ocean views. (p149)

Beavertail Light Built in 1898, this Jamestown lighthouse is still signalling ships into Narragansett Bay. (p231)

Literature

In the mid-19th century – sometimes called the American Renaissance – New England was the epicenter of American literature and the region.

Robert Frost Pay a visit to the poet's former homes in Bennington (p285) and Franconia (p353).

Louisa May Alcott Visit Orchard House, where the author wrote *Little Women*. (p95)

Henry David Thoreau Follow the philosopher to his hideaway at Walden Pond. (p96)

Mark Twain Discover the irascible writer's penchant for opulence in his Gothic Revival mansion in Hartford. (p246)

Native American Culture

Peabody Essex Museum Complex, contemporary art is the highlight of the PEM's Native American exhibit. (p100)

Hood Museum of Art Dartmouth's art museum includes an extensive collection of Native American art and artifacts. (p338)

Mashpee Wampanoag Powwow Attend a live powwow, including dancing, drumming, games and more. (p144)

Mashantucket Pequot Museum The Mashantucket Pequot have reconstructed a 16th-century tribal village. (p257)

Fruitlands Museum The grounds contain a small, hands-on museum of Native American art and culture. (p93)

Abbe Museum This small museum displays thousands of artifacts from Maine's native peoples. (p394)

Graveyards

Sleepy Hollow Cemetery Ralph Waldo Emerson and others are buried on Authors' Ridge at this final resting place. (p94)

Granary Burying Ground Paul Revere and other revolutionary heroes are laid to rest in this Boston landmark. (p37)

Hope Cemetery Technically it's a cemetery, but it feels like a museum, replete with artistically designed headstones. (p316)

West Cemetery Emily Dickinson and other Amherst notables are buried here – and depicted in the colorful mural. (p188)

Mt Auburn Cemetery This beautiful, bucolic spot contains the graves of many 19th-century intellectuals. (p55)

Month by Month

January

Most of New England is snowed in by January. That's good news for skiers, who are well into their season by now.

February

The deepest, darkest part of winter; snow and cold temperatures continue. Many New Englanders retreat to warmer climes, making this an ideal time to enjoy the region's museums, restaurants, theaters and other indoor attractions.

🏃 Ski Season

Though the ski season extends from mid-December until the end of March, its peak is President's Day weekend (third weekend in February), when schools are closed for winter break. Book your accommodations well in advance if you plan to hit the slopes during this time.

March

New England is officially sick of winter. In Vermont and New Hampshire, ski season continues through to the end of the month.

✖ Maple Syrup Tasting

Vermont's maple-sugar producers open the doors for two days in late March during the Vermont Maple Open House Weekend (www.vermontmaple.org). Maine maple-syrup producers do the same on the last Sunday in March (www. mainemapleproducers.com).

April

Spring arrives, signaled by the emerging of crocuses and the blooming of forsythia. Baseball fans await Opening Day at Fenway Park. Temperatures range from 40°F to 55°F, although the occasional snowstorm also occurs.

🏃 Boston Marathon

At the country's 'longest running' marathon, tens of thousands of spectators watch runners cross the finish line at Copley Sq in Boston on the third Monday in April. (p60)

🎆 Patriots' Day

On the third Monday in April, companies of minutemen and regulars don Colonial dress and reenact the historic battles on Patriots' Day, April 19, on the greens in Lexington and Concord, MA. Arrive just after dawn. (p91)

May

The sun comes out on a semipermanent basis and the lilac and magnolia trees bloom all around the region. Memorial Day, the last Monday in May, officially kicks off beach season.

👁 College Graduations

As the academic year ends, students around the region celebrate their accomplishments. Boston, Cambridge, the Pioneer Valley and other university towns get overrun with students and their proud parents during graduation ceremonies, which might take place anytime in May or early June.

June

Temperatures range from 55°F to 75°F, with lots of rain. After graduation, students leave town, causing a noticeable decline in traffic and noise.

Celebration of Lupine

This little-known floral festival in early June in Franconia, NH, celebrates the annual bloom of delicious lupine with garden tours, art exhibits and concerts. (p353)

International Festival of Arts & Ideas

New Haven dedicates three weeks in June to dance, music, film and art. Besides the ticketed concerts and performances, there are free events and special programming for kids and families. (p263)

July

July is the region's hottest month and public beaches are invariably crowded. Temperatures usually range from 70°F to 85°F, but there's always a week or two when the mercury shoots above 90°F.

Berkshires Arts Festivals

The Berkshires are alive with the arts throughout the months of July and August. You can hear world-class music in the open air at Tanglewood (p201) in Lenox, take in mesmerizing dance performances at Jacob's Pillow (p199) in Lee, or see top-notch theater productions at the Williamstown Theatre Festival (p204).

Independence Day

Boston goes all out for Independence Day on July 4. The official Fourth of July festivities include a concert by the Boston Pops on the Esplanade, followed by magnificent fireworks. Smaller-scale celebrations take place all around the region. (p61)

Vermont Brewers Festival

The third weekend in July is dedicated to discussing beer, brewing beer and of course drinking beer, featuring Vermont's finest craft brews. (p305)

North Atlantic Blues Festival

If you're feeling blue, go to Rockland, ME, in mid-July for the region's biggest blues festival. Nationally known performers and local-brewed beers guarantee a good time.

Newport Folk Festival

One of the region's most exciting music events, this folk festival at Newport, RI, takes place in late July and attracts national stars as well as new names to perform all weekend long. (p228)

August

Summer continues unabated, with beaches packed to the gills. Only at the end of August do we begin to feel fall coming back on.

Maine Lobster Festival

If you love lobster like Maine loves lobster, come for the week-long Lobster Festival held in the first week in August in Rockland. King Neptune and the Sea Goddess oversee a week full of events and – of course – as much lobster as you can eat. (p388)

Rhode Island International Film Festival

The region's largest public film festival, held in the second week of August in Providence, RI, attracts interesting, independent films and sophisticated film-savvy audiences. (p215)

Provincetown Carnival

Carnival in P-town, held in the third week in August, is a week of crazy dance parties and streets filled with beautiful boys in colorful costumes (even more than usual). (p153)

Machias Wild Blueberry Festival

In its 41st year, this festival (www.machiasblueberry.com) includes pie-eating contests, cook-offs and hundreds of artisans hawking everything from blueberry jam to blueberry-themed artwork. Held on the third weekend in August.

September

The humidity disappears, leaving cooler temperatures and crisp air. Students return and streets are filled with U-Hauls during the first week. The first Monday in September is Labor Day, the official end of summer.

🎪 Big E

Officially known as the Eastern States Exposition, this fair in West Springfield, MA, in mid-September features animal shows, carnival rides, parades, concerts and more. (p182)

October

New England's best month. The academic year is rolling; the weather is crisp and cool; and the trees take on shades of red, gold and amber.

☉ Foliage Season

Witness Mother Nature at her most ostentatious. The colors all around the region are dazzling, but especially as they blanket the mountainsides in the Berkshires in Western Massachusetts, the Green Mountains in Vermont, and the White Mountains in New Hampshire and Maine.

🎪 Fryeburg Fair

There's something for everyone at this old-fashioned agricultural fair in Maine, from live animals to live music, from fun rides to fireworks. Held in the first week in October. (p356)

🍴 Wellfleet OysterFest

Who can be surprised that a food festival in Wellfleet celebrates oysters? Come to this huge event the weekend after Columbus Day for plenty of eating, drinking and slurping. (p147)

🎪 Haunted Happenings

The 'Witch City' of Salem celebrates Halloween all month long, with spooky tours, parades, concerts, pumpkin carvings and trick-or-treating. Pub crawls and costume parties keep the carousing going late into the evenings. (p103)

🏃 Head of the Charles

The world's largest rowing event takes place in Boston on the Charles River on the third weekend in October, attracting thousands of rowers and thousands more spectators. (p61)

🎪 New Hampshire Pumpkin Festival

Now held in Laconia, this annual event draws thousands of visitors to see the construction of a tower of jack-o'-lanterns as high as the sky. Held on the third or fourth weekend in October, there's also a craft fair, costume parade, seed-spitting contests and fireworks. (p336)

November

Winter is coming and you can feel it in the air. You may even see snow flurries. Thanksgiving Day – the third Thursday in November – kicks off the holiday season.

🎪 America's Hometown Thanksgiving Celebration

Plymouth, MA, is the birthplace of Thanksgiving, so it's appropriate that the town celebrates this heritage with a parade, concerts, crafts and – of course – food. Held the weekend before Thanksgiving. (p121)

December

Winter sets in, with at least one big snow storm in December to prove it. Christmas lights and holiday fairs make the region festive.

🎪 Boston Tea Party Remembered

New Englanders take their reenactments seriously. In the case of the Tea Party, on December 16, they dress up like Mohawk warriors and dump tea into the Boston Harbor, just like their forebears in 1773. (p61)

☆ First Night

It actually starts on the 'last night,' New Year's Eve, and continues into the wee hours of the New Year. Activities, performances and other events are held at venues all around Boston and Burlington. Buy a button and attend as many as you can. (p61)

Plan Your Trip
Itineraries

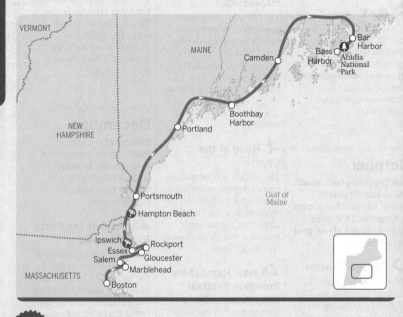

2 WEEKS Coastal New England

New England is intrinsically tied to the sea – historically, commercially and emotionally. To see this connection firsthand, just follow the coastline.

Start in **Boston**, a city that has recently rediscovered its connection to the sea. Follow the HarborWalk along the water's edge from Christopher Columbus Park, stopping at the New England Aquarium and the Institute for Contemporary Art. The following day, board a ferry out to the Harbor Islands.

Continue northward to **Marblehead** and **Salem**, both rich in maritime history. Don't miss the Peabody Essex Museum and its wonderful maritime exhibit. To glimpse New England's fishing industry at work – and to sample its culinary treats – journey to **Gloucester**. This is also your jumping-off point for a whale-watching cruise to Stellwagen Bank.

Circle around Cape Ann to discover the charms of **Rockport** and the mysteries of Dogtown. Then continue up the coast to frolic in the waves at Crane Beach in **Ipswich** and feast on fried clams in **Essex**.

Acadia National Park (p399)

The New Hampshire seacoast is scant, but not without merit: walk the boardwalk at **Hampton Beach** and admire the old houses in historic **Portsmouth**. Continuing into Maine, spend a day or two exploring **Portland**. Eat, drink and shop the Old Port District and check out the Portland Museum of Art. Don't leave town without snapping a photo of the Portland Head Light on Cape Elizabeth. Continuing north, stroll around lovely (but crowded) **Boothbay Harbor**, perhaps stopping for a seafood lunch on the harbor.

Don't miss a stop in pretty **Camden**, where you can take a windjammer cruise up the rocky coast. When you return to dry land, clamber to the top of Mt Battie in Camden Hills State Park for sweeping views of Penobscot Bay.

End your trip in beautiful **Bar Harbor** and **Acadia National Park**, which are highlights of the New England coast. You'll have no problem occupying yourself for a weekend or a week, exploring Mt Desert Island's beautiful scenery while hiking, biking, kayaking, camping and more. For a delicious detour, head to Thurston's Lobster Pound overlooking **Bass Harbor**. This is your last chance to get your fill of fresh Maine lobster, so tie on your bib and enjoy.

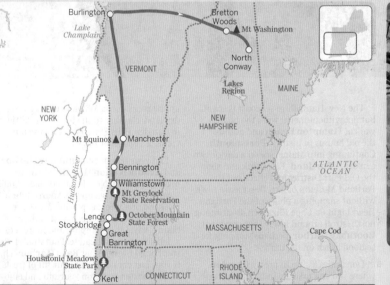

TISOPHOTOGRAPHY / GETTY IMAGES ©

10 DAYS Fall Foliage

The brilliance of fall in New England is legendary. Scarlet and sugar maples, ash, birch, beech, dogwood, tulip tree, oak and sassafras all contribute to the carnival of autumn color.

Start in Connecticut's **Kent**. Hike up Cobble Mountain in Macedonia Brook State Park for views of the forested hills against a backdrop of the Taconic and Catskill mountain ranges. Heading north on Rte 7, stop at **Housatonic Meadows State Park** to snap a photo of the Cornwall Bridge, then continue into Massachusetts.

Blanketing the westernmost part of the state, the rounded mountains of the Berkshires turn crimson and gold as early as mid-September. Set up camp in **Great Barrington**, a formerly industrial town now populated with art galleries and upscale restaurants. It's a good base for exploring **October Mountain State Forest**, a multicolored tapestry of hemlocks, birches and oaks. This reserve's name – attributed to Herman Melville – gives a good indication of when this park is at its loveliest.

Cruising north from Great Barrington, you'll pass through the Berkshires' most charming towns: **Stockbridge**, **Lenox** and **Williamstown**. Stop for a few hours or a few days for fine dining, shopping and cultural offerings. Dedicate at least one day to exploring **Mt Greylock State Reservation**: the summit offers a view stretching up to 100 miles across more than five states.

Cross into Vermont and continue north through the historic villages of **Bennington** and **Manchester**. For fall foliage views head to the top of **Mt Equinox**, where the 360-degree panorama includes the Adirondacks and the lush Battenkill Valley. Continue north to **Burlington**, your base for frolicking on Lake Champlain, and sail away on a schooner for offshore foliage views.

Head southeast through Montpelier and continue into New Hampshire. Your destination is **Bretton Woods**, where you can admire the foliage from the porch of the historic hotel or from a hanging sky bridge. Then make your way to the summit of **Mt Washington**, whether by car, by train or on foot. When you're ready to come down from the clouds, descend into **North Conway**. Many of the town's restaurants and inns offer expansive views of the nearby mountains, making it an ideal place to wrap up a fall foliage tour.

MICHAEL WARWICK / SHUTTERSTOCK ©

Top: Cornwall Bridge (p274)
Bottom: Fall foliage

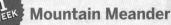

1 WEEK

Mountain Meander

PLAN YOUR TRIP ITINERARIES

If you're longing to breathe pure mountain air and gaze over mountain majesty, follow this route through the region's most glorious peaks.

Start your mountain meander at **Franconia Notch State Park**, where you can hike down the Flume, ride a tramway up Cannon Mountain and see what little remains of the Old Man of the Mountain. Spend a few nights at one of many welcoming inns in **Franconia** or **Bethlehem** and don't miss dinner at the creative Cold Mountain Cafe.

The next day, journey east on Rte 302, relishing the spectacular views of the White Mountains. Stop at the historic Mount Washington Hotel at **Bretton Woods**. This is the base for a ride on the Cog Railway to the top of **Mt Washington**, New England's highest peak. Or, if you prefer to make the climb on your own two feet, continue on Rte 302 to **Crawford Notch State Park**, the access point for many hikes in the area.

To give your legs a break, drive west across the White Mountain National Forest on the scenic **Kancamagus Highway**. This route offers countless opportunities for hiking, camping and other outdoor adventuring. Otherwise, just enjoy the scenery and motor through to I-93, continuing southwest into Vermont.

Expansive vistas unfold with abandon as you approach the Green Mountains on US 4. Continue on to **Killington**, for a day of wintertime skiing or summertime mountain biking.

Continue north on VT 100, which is often called 'the spine of the state.' Snaking north through the mountains, this classic route feels like a backcountry road, littered with cow-strewn meadows and white-steepled churches. Spend a few hours or a few days exploring, turning off on the gap roads and stopping in any number of tiny towns along the way. Don't miss **Warren** and **Waitsfield**, excellent for browsing art galleries and antique shops, while the nearby ski resorts offer mountain biking and horseback riding.

Sidle up to **Stowe**, where the looming **Mt Mansfield** is the outdoor capital of northern Vermont. After exerting yourself sledding or skiing, biking or hiking, indulge in some Ben & Jerry's ice cream from the factory in **Waterbury**. After climbing many peaks, skiing many slopes and snapping many photos, you've earned it.

Top: Cannon Mountain (p351)
Bottom: Mount Washington Cog Railway (p360), Bretton Woods

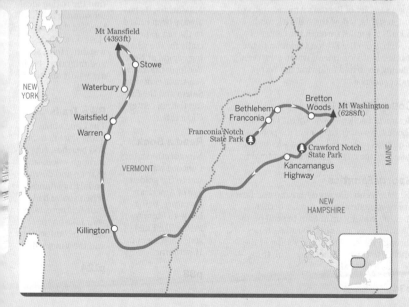

Regions at a Glance

Boston

History
Academia
Sports

Freedom Trail

For a sampler of Boston's American Revolution sights, follow the redbrick road. It leads 2.4 miles through the center of Boston, from the Boston Common to the Bunker Hill Monument, tracing the events leading up to and following the War of Independence.

College Town, USA

Boston is a college town; there's no doubt about it. No other element of the population is quite as influential as the students, who take over the city from September to May.

Sports Fanatics

'Fanatic' is no idle word here. Boston fans are passionate about sports, whether they are waking up at 5am to scull on the Charles River, running countless miles through the city streets or yelling at the pitcher to throw something – anything – besides a fast ball.

p34

Around Boston

History
Seafaring
Literature

Pilgrims & Presidents

From the Pilgrims' landing at Plymouth to witch hysteria in Salem, and from the first Revolutionary battle at Lexington to the presidents who were born and buried in Quincy, this region has shaped US history.

Ocean Economy

The fate of eastern Massachusetts has always been linked to the sea, especially for the whaling capital at New Bedford, the former sea-trade center at Salem and the fading fishing center at Gloucester.

Read a Book

Nineteenth-century Concord was central to the golden age of American literature, being home to literary greats like Emerson, Thoreau and Hawthorne.

p88

Cape Cod, Nantucket & Martha's Vineyard

Beaches
Wildlife
Cycling

Seashore

Surrounded by sea, it's hard to imagine a place with more world-class beaches: from tidal flats to gnarly open-ocean surf, and from soft sandy dunes to aeons-old clay cliffs.

Creature Features

Humpback whales find the region ideal for summering, too. See them up close on a whale-watching tour. Seals and migratory birds are wildly abundant as well.

Bike Trails

The Cape's bike paths skirt marshes and beaches, cut through woods and soar up and down undulating dunes. When you've had your fill there, take your bike on the ferry to Nantucket and the Vineyard.

p124

Central Mass & the Berkshires

Culture
Food
Hiking

Summer Performances

Each summer a major symphony orchestra, top-notch dance troupes and renowned theater performers land in the hills of the Berkshires, transforming this rural region into a cultural mecca.

Locavore Heaven

Apple orchards and farm fields are more than just scenery here. Their harvest is yours for the picking: menus are ripe with farm-to-table dishes, from organic veggies and cheeses to grass-fed meats.

Trails Galore

From the river valleys to the mountaintops, you're never far from a trailhead. Parks, forests and nature preserves offer everything from good birding to sweaty outings along the Appalachian Trail.

p175

Rhode Island

Nightlife
History
Beaches

Pumping Providence

Providence is positively hopping: from punk dives and hip art bars to loungy neighborhood joints with an art nouveau aesthetic, there's something for everyone.

History Writ Small

From Providence's drawing-room radicals and Bristol's slave-trading profiteers to the Colonial clapboards of Little Compton and the mansions of Newport's capitalist kings, the East Bay tells the American story in microcosm.

Ocean State

From South County's multi-mile stretches of white sand to the bluff-backed shores of Block Island, the 'Ocean State' has some of the most beautiful beaches in the northeast, perfect for swimming, surfing or building sand castles.

p208

Connecticut

Art
Wine
Hiking

Artistic Gems

Connecticut's reputation as a culturally barren NYC suburb is belied by its wonderful galleries and museums. See avant-garde installations at the Aldrich, American masterpieces in New Britain, and esteemed collections in Hartford and New Haven.

Wine Tasting

Connecticut's gently rolling hills may not be the most famous wine country, but among the state's two dozen or so wineries there are some real gems, including Hopkins Vineyard in New Preston.

Ponds & Peaks

With rolling hills and picturesque ponds, Connecticut is wonderful walking country. Hike to Caleb's Peak, amble along Squantz Pond or wander the trails of the Quiet Corner for the perfect antidote to big-city life.

p241

Vermont

Outdoors
Food & Drink
Villages

Outdoor Fun

Kayak Jamaica State Park's raging springtime rapids, mountain bike Kingdom Trails' 200-plus miles of cycling paths in summer, survey Mt Mansfield's kaleidoscopic colors on a fall hike or ski the best slopes in the east all winter long.

Local Produce

Vermont's classic patchwork of small farms is home to organic producers, sugar shacks, cheese-makers and microbreweries, whose products appear on menus and at farmers markets statewide.

Vintage Villages

Vermont values small towns: billboards and big box stores heavily restricted, allowing historic villages to show off their timeless charms. Among the most picturesque are Newfane, Grafton and Woodstock.

p276

New Hampshire

Lakes
Leaf-Peeping
Winter Sports

Lake Life

On Golden Pond didn't do it justice. Something about paddling in a kayak, cruising on a boat, taking a sunset dip or gazing out at the bobbing loons from a deck makes time stand still in the Lakes Region.

Scenic Drives

Enjoy Kancamagus Hwy's winding turns through state parks and past gushing gorges, or village-hop along state roads in the Monadnock region. During the fall foliage season, almost every road qualifies as a scenic byway.

Let It Snow

When winter lasts as long as it does in New Hampshire, you find something to do. Ski the magnificent slopes at White Mountain ski resorts, or cruise cross-country in Jackson XC.

p322

Maine

Boating
Lobsters
Antiquing

Take to the Sea

From the multi-masted windjammers of Camden and Rockport, to whale-watching cruises of Bar Harbor and kayak trips amid the islands of Penobscot Bay, Maine is paradise for those who feel at home on the water.

Lobster by the Pound

Maine's famous crustaceans come hot and fresh from the ocean at its many lobster pounds and seafood shacks. Tie on a bib, grab a metal cracker and go to town on these succulent beasties.

Antique Road Show

Trolling the antiques stores of Maine's pretty fishing villages and mountain towns is a summer visitors' tradition.

p364

On the Road

Boston

POP 636,000 / ☎ 617

Best Places to Eat

➜ Pomodoro (p67)
➜ El Pelon (p72)
➜ Row 34 (p69)
➜ Courtyard (p71)
➜ Life Alive (p73)
➜ Brewer's Fork (p68)

Best Places to Sleep

➜ Liberty Hotel (p63)
➜ Verb Hotel (p65)
➜ HI-Boston (p63)
➜ Gryphon House (p65)
➜ Kendall Hotel (p65)

Why Go?

The winding streets and stately architecture recall a history of revolution and renewal; and still today, Boston is among the country's most forward-looking and barrier-breaking cities.

For all intents and purposes, Boston is the oldest city in America. And you can hardly walk a step over its cobblestone streets without running into some historic site. But Boston has not been relegated to the past.

A history of cultural patronage means that the city's art and music scenes continue to charm and challenge contemporary audiences. Cutting-edge urban planning projects are reshaping the city even now, as neighborhoods are revived and rediscovered. Historic universities and colleges still attract scientists, philosophers and writers, who shape the city's evolving culture.

When to Go
Boston

April On Patriots' Day, hordes of sports fans attend the world's oldest marathon.

Summer Hot and humid; many locals make for the beach.

Fall The city comes alive in fall, when students fill the streets.

Boston Highlights

1 Freedom Trail (p56)
Following in the footsteps of patriots.

2 Boston Tea Party Ships & Museum (p46) Fomenting revolution among the exhibits.

3 Museum of Fine Arts (p53) Admiring the Art of the Americas collection.

4 North End (p67) Feasting on a plate of pasta and a bottle of wine, but remembering to save room for a cannoli for dessert.

5 Charles River Bike Path (p57) Riding a bicycle along this scenic stretch.

6 Fenway Park (p79) Watching the Red Sox spank the Yankees.

7 Beacon Hill (p36) Strolling the brick sidewalks and admiring the architecture.

8 Boston Symphony Orchestra (p78) Listening to the orchestra work its magic amid the grandeur of Symphony Hall.

History

Boston is rich in history, made by successive generations of political and social nonconformists inspired by the idea of a better way to live.

In 1630 a thousand Puritans made the treacherous transatlantic crossing to the New World. Upon arrival, John Winthrop gazed upon the Shawmut Peninsula and declared, 'we shall be as a city upon a hill, with the eyes of all people upon us.' Massachusetts Bay Colony was founded as a 'model Christian community,' where personal virtue and industry replaced aristocratic England's class hierarchy and indulgence. A spiritual elite governed in a Puritan theocracy. They established America's first public school and library. Harvard College was founded to supply the colony with homegrown ministers.

When Britain became entangled in expensive wars, it coveted Boston's merchant wealth. The Crown imposed trade restrictions and tariffs. Bostonians protested; Britain dispatched troops. In 1770 a mob provoked British regulars with slurs and snowballs until they fired into the crowd, killing five in the Boston Massacre. In 1773 the Tea Act incited further resentment. Local radicals disguised as Mohawks dumped 90,000 pounds of tea into the harbor in an event known as the Boston Tea Party. The king took it personally: the port was blockaded and the city placed under military rule.

Defiant colonists organized a militia. British troops marched to Concord to seize hidden arms. The Old North Church hung two signal lanterns in the steeple, and Paul Revere galloped into the night, and history. Next morning, Redcoats skirmished with minutemen on Lexington Green and Concord's Old North Bridge, beginning the War of Independence. Boston figured prominently in the early phase of the American Revolution. Finally, in March 1776, the British evacuated and Boston was liberated.

By the middle of the 19th century, industrial wealth transformed Boston. The hilltops were used as landfill, forming the Back Bay. The city acquired lush public parks and great cultural institutions. Boston was a center of Enlightenment, creating America's first homegrown intellectual movement, transcendentalism. Bostonians were at the forefront of progressive social movements, like abolitionism and suffrage. The city was a vibrant center for arts and science, earning the reputation as the Athens of America.

With industry came social change. The city was inundated with immigrants: Boston Brahmans were forced to mix with Irish, Italians and Portuguese. Anti-immigrant and anti-Catholic sentiments were shrill. Brahman dominance subsided. The Democratic Party represented the new ethnic working poor and featured flamboyant populist politicians.

A decline in manufacturing caused economic recession in the mid-20th century. But as a center of intellectual capital, the region rebounded, led by high technology and medicine. More recently, Boston was again a battle site for social reform, this time for gay rights. In 2004 the country's first legal gay marriage occurred in Cambridge. Meanwhile, Massachusetts elected its first (the nation's second) African American governor.

◎ Sights

◉ Beacon Hill & Boston Common

With an intriguing history, distinctive architecture and unparalleled neighborhood charm, Beacon Hill is Boston's most prestigious address. It's hard to beat the utter loveliness of the place: the narrow cobblestone streets lit with gas lanterns; the distinguished brick town houses decked with purple windowpanes and blooming flower boxes; and streets such as stately Louisburg Sq that capture the neighborhood's grandeur. The commercial street that traverses the flat of the hill – Charles St – is Boston's most enchanting spot for browsing boutiques and haggling over antiques.

★**Boston Common**   PARK
(Map p38; btwn Tremont, Charles, Beacon & Park Sts; ☺6am-midnight; P🚗; T Park St) The Boston Common has served many purposes over the years, including as a campground for British troops during the Revolutionary War and as green grass for cattle grazing until 1830. Although there is still a grazing ordinance on the books, the Common today serves picnickers, sunbathers and people-watchers. In winter, the Frog Pond (p57) attracts ice-skaters, while summer draws theater lovers for Shakespeare on the Common (p79). This is also the starting point for the Freedom Trail.

The Common is the country's oldest public park. If you have any doubt, refer to the plaque emblazoned with the words of the treaty between Governor Winthrop and William Blaxton, who sold the land for £30 in 1634.

The on-site information kiosk is a great source of information, maps and tour guides. Otherwise, wander freely about this 50-acre green, crisscrossed with walking paths and dotted with monuments. Bostonians hustle to and from the nearby T (subway) stations; others stroll leisurely, enjoying the fresh air or engaging in any number of Common activities, from free concerts to playground shenanigans to seasonal festivities.

★ **Massachusetts State House**   NOTABLE BUILDING
(Map p38; www.sec.state.ma.us; cnr Beacon & Bowdoin Sts; ⏲9am-5pm, tours 10am-3:30pm Mon-Fri; T Park St) **FREE** High atop Beacon Hill, Massachusetts' leaders and legislators attempt to turn their ideas into concrete policies and practices within the State House. John Hancock provided the land (previously part of his cow pasture); Charles Bulfinch designed the commanding state capitol; but it was Oliver Wendell Holmes who called it 'the hub of the solar system' (thus earning Boston the nickname 'the Hub'). Free 40-minute tours cover the history, artwork, architecture and political personalities of the State House.

Park Street Church   CHURCH
(Map p38; www.parkstreet.org; 1 Park St; ⏲9:30am-3pm Tue-Sat mid-Jun–Aug; T Park St) Shortly after the construction of Park St Church, powder for the War of 1812 was stored in the basement, earning this location the moniker 'Brimstone Corner.' But that was hardly the most inflammatory event that took place here. Noted for its graceful, 217ft steeple, this Boston landmark has been hosting historic lectures and musical performances since its founding.

Granary Burying Ground   CEMETERY
(Map p38; Tremont St; ⏲9am-5pm; T Park St) Dating to 1660, this atmospheric atoll is crammed with historic headstones, many with evocative (and creepy) carvings. This is the final resting place of all your favorite revolutionary heroes, including Paul Revere, Samuel Adams, John Hancock and James Otis. Benjamin Franklin is buried in

---

BOSTON FOR CHILDREN

Tours

Boston by Foot (p59) 'Boston by Little Feet' is the only Freedom Trail walking tour designed especially for children aged six to 12.

Boston Duck Tours (p59) Kids of all ages are invited to drive the duck on the raging waters of the Charles River. Bonus: quacking loudly is encouraged.

Freedom Trail Foundation Older kids will appreciate the guides in costume. Download a scavenger hunt or reading list for your child before setting out (www.thefreedomtrail.org).

Urban AdvenTours (p59) This bike tour is great for all ages. Kids' bikes and helmets are available for rent, as are bike trailers for toddlers.

Sights & Activities

Museum of Science (p55) More opportunities to combine fun and learning than anywhere in the city. The Discovery Center is specially designed for kids aged under eight.

New England Aquarium (p41) Kids can see eye to eye with thousands of sea species in the Giant Ocean Tank.

Boston Children's Museum (p48) Hours of fun climbing, constructing and creating. The museum is especially good for kids aged three to eight.

Franklin Park Zoo (p58) In addition to the many animal exhibits, the zoo has a wild and wonderful 10,000-sq-ft playground.

Harvard Museum of Natural History (p55) It's almost as good as the zoo. Sure, the stuffed animals don't move, but they let the kids get really close and look them in the eye.

MIT Museum (p57) It's too complicated for small kids, but teenagers will get a kick out of the robots, holograms and other interesting science stuff.

Beacon Hill & Downtown

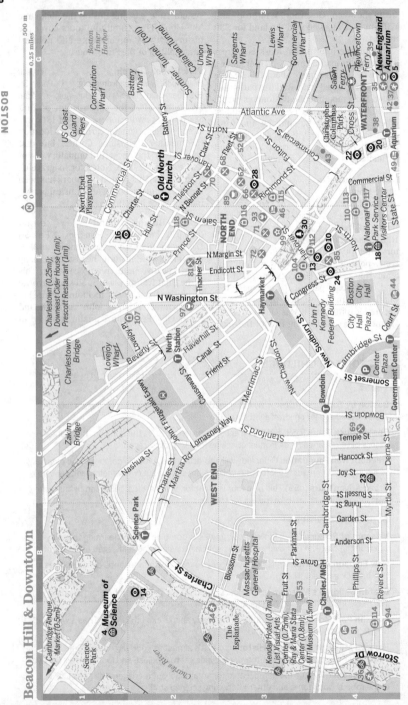

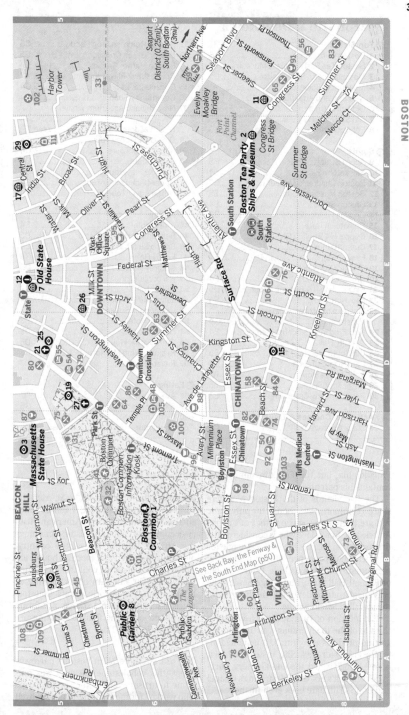

BOSTON

BEACON HILL

Massachusetts State House

Pinckney St
Louisburg Square
Mt Vernon St
Walnut St

Brimmer St
Lime St
Chestnut St
Byron St

Acorn St
Chestnut St

Embankment Rd

Beacon St

Joy St

Park St

Tremont St

Boston Common Information Kiosk

Boston Common 1

Charles St

Public Garden 8

Public Garden

The Lagoon

Commonwealth Ave
Newbury St
Boylston St
Berkeley St

Arlington St
Arlington

Park Plaza

BAY VILLAGE

Piedmont St
Winchester St
Church St
Melrose St

Stuart St
Isabella St
Columbus Ave

Marginal Rd

Charles St S

See Back Bay, the Fenway & the South End Map (p50)

Walnut St

DOWNTOWN

Downtown Crossing

Washington St
Temple Pl
Avery St
Boylston St

Tufts Medical Center

CHINATOWN

Chinatown
Essex St
Beach St
Kneeland St
Harrison Ave
Washington St
Tyler St
Ash St
May Pl
Marginal Rd

Milk St
Arch St
Otis St
Summer St
Chauncy St
Hawley St
Kingston St
Essex St
Lincoln St
South St
Atlantic Ave

Devonshire St
Federal St
High St
Congress St
Pearl St
Oliver St
Franklin St
Milk St
Water St
India St
Broad St
High St
Central St

Post Office Square

Surface Rd
Atlantic Ave

South Station
South Station

Boston Tea Party Ships & Museum 2
South Station

Fort Point Channel

Congress St Bridge
Summer St Bridge
Dorchester Ave

Evelyn Moakley Bridge

Northern Ave
Farnsworth St
Sleeper St
Congress St
Seaport Blvd
Thomson Pl
Summer St
Melcher St
Necco Ct
A St

Seaport District (0.25mi); South Boston (3mi)

Harbor Tower

7 Old State House
Old State House
State
12

17
29

26

21 25
19
27
3
87
9
45

108
109
77

102
33

11
56
65
91
83

59
41

102

80
54
55
79

64
105
48
86
75

32
31
101
40

100
96
98
50
92
103

60
78

57
73

90

15

58
84
82
74

106
94

88

Beacon Hill & Downtown

Philadelphia, but the Franklin family plot contains his parents.

The five victims of the Boston Massacre share a common grave, though the only name you are likely to recognize is that of Crispus Attucks, the freed slave who is considered the first person to lose his life in the struggle for American independence. Other noteworthy permanent residents include Peter Faneuil, of Faneuil Hall fame, and Judge Sewall, the only magistrate to denounce the hanging of the so-called Salem witches.

The location of Park St Church was once the site of the town granary; as the burying ground predates the church, it is named after the grain storage facility instead. While it is sometimes called the Old Granary Burying Ground, it's not the oldest; King's Chapel and Copp's Hill date back even further.

Museum of African American History   MUSEUM

(Map p38; http://maah.org; 46 Joy St; adult/child $5/free; ◎10am-4pm Mon-Sat; ⓣPark St, Bowdoin) The Museum of African American History occupies two adjacent historic buildings: the African Meeting House, the country's oldest black church and meeting house; and Abiel Smith School, the country's first school for blacks. The museum offers rotating exhibits about the historic events that took place here, and is also a source of information about – and the final destination of – the Black Heritage Trail.

Acorn Street   STREET

(Map p38; ⓣCharles/MGH) Boston's narrowest street, this cobblestone alleyway was once home to artisans and to the service people who worked for the adjacent mansion dwellers. The brick walls on the north side of the street enclose examples of Beacon Hill's hidden gardens.

⊙ Downtown & Waterfront

Much of Boston's business and tourist activity takes place in this central neighborhood. Downtown is a bustling district crammed with modern complexes and colonial buildings, including Faneuil Hall and Quincy Market. The Waterfront is home to the HarborWalk, the Harbor Islands ferries and the New England Aquarium.

★ **New England Aquarium**   AQUARIUM
(Map p38; www.neaq.org; Central Wharf; adult/child $27/19; ⊙9am-5pm Mon-Fri, to 6pm Sat & Sun, 1hr later Jul & Aug; P⛟; TAquarium) 🐾 Teeming with sea creatures of all sizes, shapes and colors, this giant fishbowl is the centerpiece of downtown Boston's waterfront. The main attraction is the three-story Giant Ocean Tank, which swirls with thousands of creatures great and small, including turtles, sharks and eels. Countless side exhibits explore the lives and habitats of other underwater oddities, as well as penguins and marine mammals.

★ **Old State House**   HISTORIC BUILDING
(Map p38; www.revolutionaryboston.org; 206 Washington St; adult/child $10/free; ⊙9am-6pm Jun-Aug, to 5pm Sep-May; TState) Dating from 1713, the Old State House is Boston's oldest surviving public building, where the Massachusetts Assembly used to debate the issues of the day before the revolution. The building is best known for its balcony, where the Declaration of Independence was first

read to Bostonians in 1776. Inside, the Old State House contains a small museum of revolutionary memorabilia, with videos and multimedia presentations about the Boston Massacre, which took place out front.

Boston Massacre Site MONUMENT
(Map p38; cnr State & Devonshire Sts; T State) Directly in front of the Old State House, encircled by cobblestones, the Boston Massacre site marks the spot where the first blood was shed for the American independence movement. On March 5, 1770, an angry mob of colonists swarmed the British soldiers guarding the State House. Sam Adams, John Hancock and about 40 other protesters hurled snowballs, rocks and insults. Thus provoked, the soldiers fired into the crowd and killed five townspeople, including Crispus Attucks, a former slave.

The incident sparked enormous anti-British sentiment. Paul Revere helped fan the flames by widely disseminating an engraving that depicted the scene as an unmitigated slaughter (an original print is on display inside the Old State House). Interestingly, John Adams and Josiah Quincy – both of whom opposed the heavy-handed authoritarian British rule – defended the accused soldiers in court, and seven of the nine were acquitted.

Design Museum Boston MUSEUM
(http://designmuseumboston.org) Redefining what it means to be a 'museum', Design Museum Boston brings the goods to you. This 'pop-up' museum launches exhibits in public spaces all around town, from shopping malls to public parks to airports. Keep your eyes open. Design is all around you.

King's Chapel & Burying Ground CHURCH, CEMETERY
(Map p38; www.kings-chapel.org; 58 Tremont St; donation $2, Bells & Bones tour $10; ⊙10am-5pm Mon-Sat, 1:30-5pm Sun; T State) Puritan Bostonians were not pleased when the original Anglican church was erected on this site in 1688. The chapel standing today – built in 1754 – houses the largest bell ever made by Paul Revere, as well as a historic organ. The adjacent burying ground is the oldest in the city. Besides the biweekly services, recitals are held here every week (12:15pm Tuesday).

Old South Meeting House HISTORIC BUILDING
(Map p38; www.osmh.org; 310 Washington St; adult/child $6/1; ⊙9:30am-5pm Apr-Oct, 10am-4pm Nov-Mar; ⊛; T Downtown Crossing, State)

'No tax on tea!' That was the decision on December 16, 1773, when 5000 angry colonists gathered here to protest British taxes, leading to the Boston Tea Party. Download an audio of the historic pre–Tea Party meeting from the museum website, then visit the graceful meeting house to check out the exhibit about the history of the building and the protest.

Faneuil Hall HISTORIC BUILDING
(Map p38; www.nps.gov/bost; Congress St; ⊙9am-5pm; T Haymarket, Government Center) **FREE** 'Those who cannot bear free speech had best go home,' said Wendell Phillips. 'Faneuil Hall is no place for slavish hearts.' Indeed, this public meeting place was the site of so much rabble-rousing that it earned the nickname the 'Cradle of Liberty.' After the revolution, Faneuil Hall was a forum for meetings about abolition, women's suffrage and war. On the 2nd floor, the historic hall is normally open to the public, who can hear about the building's history from National Park Service (NPS) rangers.

New England Holocaust Memorial MEMORIAL
(Map p38; www.nehm.org; btwn Union & Congress Sts; T Haymarket) Constructed in 1995, the six luminescent glass columns of the New England Holocaust Memorial are engraved with six million numbers, representing those killed in the Holocaust. Each tower – with smoldering coals sending plumes of steam up through the glass corridors – represents a different Nazi death camp. The memorial sits along the Freedom Trail, a sobering reminder of its larger meaning.

Rose Kennedy Greenway PARK
(Map p38; www.rosekennedygreenway.org; ⊛; T Aquarium, Haymarket) The gateway to the newly revitalized waterfront is the Rose Kennedy Greenway. Where once was a hulking overhead highway, now winds a 27-acre strip of landscaped gardens and fountain-lined greens, with the artist market, Greenway Open Market (p80), for Saturday shoppers, and food trucks for weekday lunchers. Cool off in the whimsical **Rings Fountain**, walk the calming **labyrinth**, or take a ride on the custom-designed Greenway **carousel** (per ride $3; ⊙11am-7pm Apr-Dec; ⊛).

Custom House HISTORIC BUILDING
(Map p38; www.marriott.com; 3 McKinley Sq; observation deck $5-7.50; ⊙observation deck 2pm & 6pm Sat-Thu; T Aquarium) Begun in 1837, the

ARNOLD ARBORETUM

Under a public/private partnership with Harvard University, the 265-acre Arnold Arboretum (www.arboretum.harvard.edu; 125 Arborway; ☉dawn-dusk; 🚴; Ⓣ Forest Hills) is planted with over 15,000 exotic trees and flowering shrubs. This gem is pleasant year-round, but it's particularly beautiful in the bloom of spring. Dog walking, Frisbee throwing, bicycling, sledding and general contemplation are encouraged (but picnicking is not allowed). The southern Forest Hills gate is located on the Arborway just west of the metro station.

A visitor center (☉10am-5pm Thu-Tue; Ⓣ Forest Hills) is located at the main gate, just south of the rotary at Rte 1 and Rte 203. Free one-hour walking tours are offered several times a week from April to November.

lower portion of the Custom House resembles a Greek temple. But the federal government wanted something grander, so in 1913 it exempted itself from local height restrictions and financed a 500ft tower. Nowadays there are many taller buildings, but the 22ft illuminated clock makes this gem the most recognizable part of the city skyline. Twice a day (weather permitting), the 26th-floor observation deck opens up for fabulous views.

Blackstone Block   HISTORIC SITE

(Map p38; cnr Union & Hanover Sts; Ⓣ Haymarket) Named after Boston's first settler, this tiny warren of streets dates to the 17th and 18th centuries. Established in 1826, Union Oyster House (Map p38; www.unionoysterhouse.com; 41 Union St; mains lunch $15-20, dinner $22-32; ☉11am-9:30pm; Ⓣ Haymarket) is Boston's oldest restaurant. Around the corner in Creek Sq, the c 1767 Ebenezer Hancock House was the home of John Hancock's brother. At the base of the shop next door, the 1737 Boston Stone (Marshall St) served as the terminus for measuring distances to and from 'the Hub.' (The State House dome now serves this purpose.)

◉ Boston Harbor Islands

If you're dreaming of an island vacation, you've come to the right place. The Boston Harbor Islands (www.bostonharborislands.org) consist of 34 islands, many of which are open for trail-walking, bird-watching, camping, kayaking and swimming. Explore a 19th-century fort at Georges Island; walk the trails and lounge on the beach at Spectacle Island; or climb to the top of Boston's iconic oldest lighthouse at Little Brewster. Mostly operated by the National Park Service (NPS), the Harbor Islands offer a unique opportunity for outdoor adventure – and they're a quick boat ride from downtown Boston.

Little Brewster Island   ISLAND, LIGHTHOUSE

(☎617-223-8666; adult/youth/non-climber $41/32/30; ☉9:30am & 1pm Fri-Sun Jun-Sep; 🚢from Long Wharf) Little Brewster is the country's oldest light station and site of the iconic Boston Light, dating from 1783. To visit Little Brewster, you must take an organized tour (reservations required). Learn about Boston's maritime history during a one-hour sail around the harbor, then spend two hours exploring the island. Adventurous travelers can climb the 76 steps to the top of the lighthouse for a close-up view of the rotating light and a far-off view of the city skyline.

Tours depart from the Boston Harbor Islands Pavillion on the Rose Kennedy Greenway.

Spectacle Island   ISLAND

(☉dawn-dusk early May–mid-Sep; 🚴; 🚢from Long Wharf) 🚩 A Harbor Islands hub, Spectacle Island has a large marina, a solar-powered visitors center, a healthy snack bar and sandy, supervised beaches. Five miles of walking trails provide access to a 157ft peak overlooking the harbor. Special events include Saturday-morning yoga classes, Sunday-afternoon jazz concerts and Thursday-evening clam bakes. Spectacle Island is relatively close to the city and a ferry runs here directly from Long Wharf (hourly in July and August, less frequently in June and September).

Georges Island   ISLAND, FORT

(☉early May–mid-Sep; 🚴; 🚢from Long Wharf or Hull) Georges Island is one of the transportation hubs for the islands. It is also the site of Fort Warren, a 19th-century fort and Civil War prison. While NPS rangers give guided tours of the fort and there is a small museum, it is largely abandoned, with many dark tunnels, creepy corners and magnificent lookouts to discover. Weekends on Georges are packed with kids programs, Civil War–era baseball games and jazz concerts.

This is one of the only islands with facilities like a snack bar and restrooms. There's also an 'after-hours' barbecue on Wednesday nights (see website for details).

Lovells Island   ISLAND
(☉mid-Jun–early Sep; 🚢from Georges) Two deadly shipwrecks may bode badly for seafarers, but that doesn't seem to stop recreational boaters, swimmers and sunbathers from lounging on Lovells' long rocky beach. Some of the former uses of Lovells are evident: European settlers used the island as a rabbit run, and descendent bunnies are still running this place; Fort Standish dates from WWI but has yet to be excavated. With facilities for camping and picnicking, Lovells is one of the most popular Harbor Islands destinations.

Thompson Island   ISLAND
(🕿617-328-3900; www.thompsonisland.org; ☉noon-5pm Sat & Sun Jun-Aug; 🚢from EDIC Pier) Thompson Island was settled as early as 1626 by a Scotsman, David Thompson, who set up a trading post to do business with the Neponset Indians. Today this island is privately owned by Thompson Island Outward Bound, a nonprofit organization that develops fun and challenging physical adventures, especially for training and developing leadership skills. As such, the public can explore its 200-plus acres only on weekends, when it's wonderful for walking, fishing and birding.

A dedicated ferry leaves from EDIC Pier in the Seaport District; see the website for details.

Grape Island   ISLAND
(☉mid-Jun–early Sep; 🚢from Georges or Hingham) Grape Island is rich with fruity goodness – not grapes, but raspberries, bayberries and elderberries, all growing wild amid the scrubby wooded trails. The wild fruit attracts abundant birdlife. Unlike many of the Harbor Islands, Grape Island has no remains of forts or military prisons, but during the Revolutionary War, it was the site of a skirmish over hay, known as the Battle of Grape Island.

Peddocks Island   ISLAND
(☉mid-Jun–early Sep; 🚢from Georges or Long Wharf) One of the largest Harbor Islands, Peddocks consists of four headlands connected by sandbars. Hiking trails wander through marsh, pond and coastal environs. But the dominant feature of Peddocks Island is the remains of Fort Andrews, a large facility with more than 20 buildings. Peddocks' proximity to the mainland ensured its use as a military stronghold, from the Revolutionary War right through WWII.

Bumpkin Island   ISLAND
(☉early May–mid-Sep; 🚢from Georges or Hull) This small island has served many purposes over the years, first farming then fish drying and smelting. In 1900 it was the site of a children's hospital, but it was taken over for navy training during WWI. You can still explore the remains of a stone farmhouse and the hospital. The beaches are not the best for swimming, as they are slate and seashell. A network of trails leads through fields overgrown with wildflowers. It's one of three islands with camping facilities.

◉ West End & North End

Although the West End and North End are physically adjacent, they are atmospherically worlds apart. The West End is an institutional area without much zest. By contrast, the North End is delightfully spicy, thanks to the many Italian *ristoranti* and *salumeria* that line the streets.

★Old North Church   CHURCH
(Map p38; www.oldnorth.com; 193 Salem St; requested donation $3, tour adult/child $6/4; ☉9am-5pm Mar-Dec, to 6pm Jun-Oct, 10am-4pm Nov-Feb; Ⓣ Haymarket, North Station) 'One if by land, Two if by sea...'. Longfellow's poem 'Paul Revere's Ride' has immortalized this graceful church. It was here, on the night of April 18, 1775, that the sexton hung two lanterns from the steeple, as a signal that the British would advance on Lexington and Concord via the sea route. Also called Christ Church, this 1723 place of worship is Boston's oldest church.

The 175ft steeple houses the oldest bells (1744) still rung in the US. Today's steeple is a 1954 replica, since severe weather toppled two prior ones, but the 1740 weather vane is original. All visitors are invited to enjoy a 10-minute presentation about the history of the Old North Church. For more detailed information, a 30-minute Behind the Scenes tour takes visitors up into the belfry and down into the crypt.

Behind the church, several hidden brick courtyards offer quiet respite for a moment of peaceful meditation. Heading down the hill, shady **Paul Revere Mall** perfectly frames the Old North Church. Often called 'the Prado' by locals, it is a lively meeting place for North Enders of all generations.

Copp's Hill Burying Ground   CEMETERY
(Map p38; Hull St; ⊙ dawn-dusk; T North Station) The city's second-oldest cemetery – dating to 1660 – is the final resting place for an estimated 10,000 souls. It is named for William Copp, who originally owned this land. While the oldest graves belong to Copp's children, there are several other noteworthy residents.

Near the Charter St gate you'll find the graves of the Mather family – Increase, Cotton and Samuel – all of whom were politically powerful religious leaders in the colonial community. Front and center is the grave of Daniel Malcolm, whose headstone commemorates his rebel activism. British soldiers apparently took offense at this claim

and used the headstone for target practice. The small plot of land also contains more than a thousand free blacks, many of whom lived in the North End.

Paul Revere House   HISTORIC SITE
(Map p38; www.paulreverehouse.org; 19 North Sq; adult/child $3.50/1; ⊙ 9:30am-5:15pm mid-Apr–Oct, to 4:15pm Nov–mid-Apr, closed Mon Jan-Mar; ♿; T Haymarket) When silversmith Paul Revere rode to warn patriots of the British march to Lexington and Concord, he set out from this home on North Sq. This small clapboard house was built in 1680, making it the oldest house in Boston. A self-guided tour through the house and courtyard gives a glimpse of what life was like for the Revere family (which included 16 children!).

⊙ Charlestown

The site of the original settlement of the Massachusetts Bay Colony, Charlestown is the terminus for the Freedom Trail. Many tourists tromp across these historic

KENNEDY FAMILY SITES

John F Kennedy Library & Museum (www.jfklibrary.org; Columbia Point; adult/child $14/10; ⊙ 9am-5pm; T JFK/UMass) The legacy of JFK is ubiquitous in Boston, but the official memorial to the 35th president is the presidential library and museum – a striking, modern, marble building designed by IM Pei. The architectural centerpiece is the glass pavilion, with soaring 115ft ceilings and floor-to-ceiling windows overlooking Boston Harbor. The museum is a fitting tribute to JFK's life and legacy. The effective use of video re-creates history for visitors who may or may not remember the early 1960s.

A highlight is the museum's treatment of the Cuban Missile Crisis: a short film explores the dilemmas and decisions that the president faced, while an archival exhibit displays actual documents and correspondence from those 13 gripping days.

John F Kennedy National Historic Site (www.nps.gov/jofi; 83 Beals St; ⊙ 9:30am-5pm Wed-Sun mid-May–Oct; T Coolidge Corner) Four of the nine Kennedy children were born and raised in this modest house, including Jack, who was born in the master bedroom in 1917. Matriarch Rose Kennedy oversaw the restoration of the house in the late 1960s; today her narrative sheds light on the Kennedys' family life. Guided tours allow visitors to see furnishings, photographs and mementos that have been preserved from the time the family lived here.

A self-guided walking tour of the surrounding neighborhood sets the scene for the Kennedy family's day-to-day life, including church, school and shopping.

Edward Kennedy Institute for the US Senate (EMK Institute; www.emkinstitute.org; Columbia Point; adult/child $16/8; ⊙ 9am-5pm Tue-Sat, 10am-5pm Sun; T JKF/UMass) Ted Kennedy served in the US Senate for nearly half a century. It is fitting, therefore, that his legacy should include an institute and museum designed to teach the public about the inner workings of democracy. New in 2015, this state-of-the-art facility uses advanced technology, multimedia exhibits and interactive designs to engage visitors and demonstrate the functioning (and sometimes non-functioning) of the legislative process. The museum centerpiece is a full-scale replica of the Senate chamber.

cobblestone sidewalks to admire the USS *Constitution* and climb to the top of the Bunker Hill Monument, which towers above the neighborhood.

★ **Bunker Hill Monument** MONUMENT
(www.nps.gov/bost; Monument Sq; ⊘9am-5pm mid-Mar–Nov, 1-5pm Mon-Fri, 9am-5pm Sat & Sun Dec–mid-Mar; 🚹; 🚌93 from Haymarket, ⊤Community College) FREE This 220ft granite obelisk monument commemorates the turning-point battle that was fought on the surrounding hillside on June 17, 1775. Ultimately, the Redcoats prevailed, but the victory was bittersweet, as they lost more than one-third of their deployed forces, while the colonists suffered relatively few casualties. Climb the 294 steps to the top of the monument to enjoy the panorama of the city, the harbor and the North Shore.

★ **Charlestown Navy Yard** HISTORIC SITE
(www.nps.gov/bost; ⊘visitor center 9am-5pm daily mid-Mar–Nov, Thu-Sun Dec–mid-Mar; 🚌93 from Haymarket, ⊛Inner Harbor Ferry from Long Wharf, ⊤North Station) FREE Besides the historic ships docked here and the museum dedicated to them, the Charlestown Navy Yard is a living monument to its own history of shipbuilding and naval command. Visit the NPS visitor center located here, with a free film, guided tours and other info about the Navy Yard and Freedom Trail sites.

USS Constitution HISTORIC SITE
(www.oldironsides.com; Charlestown Navy Yard; ⊘2:30-6pm Tue-Fri, 10am-6pm Sat & Sun Apr-Oct, 2:30-4pm Thu-Fri, 10am-4pm Sat & Sun Nov-Mar; 🚹; 🚌93 from Haymarket, ⊛Inner Harbor Ferry from Long Wharf, ⊤North Station) FREE 'Her sides are made of iron!' So cried a crewman as he watched shot bounce off the thick oak hull of the USS *Constitution* during the War of 1812. This bit of irony earned the legendary ship her nickname. Indeed, she has never gone down in a battle. The USS *Constitution* is still the oldest commissioned US Navy ship, dating to 1797, and she is normally taken out onto Boston Harbor every July 4 in order to maintain her commissioned status.

Make sure you bring a photo ID to go aboard the *Constitution*. Currently undergoing restoration, the USS *Constitution* is now in dry dock until approximately 2018. She is still open to the public, but tours (given by Navy personnel) are limited to the top deck. You'll still learn lots of fun facts, like

how the captain's son died on her maiden voyage (an inauspicious start).

USS Constitution Museum MUSEUM
(www.ussconstitutionmuseum.org; First Ave, Charlestown Navy Yard; donation adult/child from $5/3; ⊘9am-6pm Apr-Oct, 10am-5pm Nov-Mar; 🚹; 🚌93 from Haymarket, ⊛Inner Harbor Ferry from Long Wharf, ⊤North Station) For a play-by-play of the USS *Constitution*'s various battles, as well as her current role as the flagship of the US Navy, head indoors to the museum. Most interesting is the exhibit on the Barbary War, which explains the birth of the US Navy during this relatively unknown conflict – America's first war at sea. Upstairs, kids can experience what it was like to be a sailor on the USS *Constitution* in 1812.

On the ground floor of the museum, the Model Shipwright Guild operates a workshop, where visitors can see volunteer modelers working on fantastically detailed miniatures of the USS *Constitution* and other ships.

⊙ Seaport District & South Boston

The Seaport District is a section of South Boston that is fast developing as an attractive waterside destination, thanks to the dynamic contemporary-art museum and the explosion of new dining options. Travel deeper into Southie for seaside breezes, a little history and a lot of beer.

★ **Boston Tea Party Ships & Museum** MUSEUM
(Map p38; www.bostonteapartyship.com; Congress St Bridge; adult/child $26/16; ⊘10am-5pm; 🚹; ⊤South Station) 'Boston Harbor a teapot tonight!' To protest unfair taxes, a gang of rebellious colonists dumped 342 chests of tea into the water. The 1773 protest – the Boston Tea Party – set into motion the events leading to the Revolutionary War. Nowadays, replica Tea Party Ships are moored at Griffin's Wharf, alongside an excellent experiential museum dedicated to the catalytic event. Using reenactments, multimedia and other fun exhibits, the museum addresses all aspects of the Boston Tea Party and events that followed.

Visitors can board the fully rigged *Eleanor* and the whaler *Beaver* to experience life aboard an 18th-century vessel. Would-be rebels can throw crates of tea into the harbor, in solidarity with their fiery forebears. To hear both sides of the story, visitors can witness a virtual debate between Sam Adams

Walking Tour
Freedom Trail

START BOSTON COMMON
END BUNKER HILL MONUMENT
LENGTH 2.5 MILES; THREE HOURS

Start at ① **Boston Common** (p36), America's oldest public park. On the northern side, you can't miss the gold-domed ② **Massachusetts State House** (p37) sitting atop Beacon Hill. Walk north on Tremont St, passing the soaring steeple of ③ **Park Street Church** (p37) and the Egyptian revival gates of the ④ **Granary Burying Ground** (p37).

At School St, the columned ⑤ **King's Chapel** (p42) overlooks the adjacent burying ground. Turn east on School St, and take note of the plaque commemorating this spot as the ⑥ **site of the first public school**.

Continue down School St past the ⑦ **Old Corner Bookstore**. Diagonally opposite, the ⑧ **Old South Meeting House** (p42) saw the beginnings of the Boston Tea Party.

Further north on Washington St, the ⑨ **Old State House** (p41) was the scene of the city's first public reading of the Declaration of Independence. Outside the Old State House a ring of cobblestones marks the ⑩ **Boston Massacre site** (p42), yet another uprising that fueled the revolution. Across the intersection, historic ⑪ **Faneuil Hall** (p42) has served as a public meeting place and marketplace for over 250 years.

From Faneuil Hall, follow Hanover St across the Rose Kennedy Greenway. One block east, charming North Sq is the site of the ⑫ **Paul Revere House** (p45). Back on Hanover St, the Paul Revere Mall offers a lovely vantage point to view the ⑬ **Old North Church** (p44). From the church, head west on Hull St to ⑭ **Copp's Hill Burying Ground** (p45), with grand views across the river to Charlestown.

Across the Charlestown Bridge, Constitution Rd brings you to the Charlestown Navy Yard, home of the world's oldest commissioned warship, the ⑮ **USS Constitution** (p46). Finally, wind your way through the historic streets of Charlestown center to the ⑯ **Bunker Hill Monument** (p46), site of the devastating American Revolution battle.

PUBLIC GARDEN

Adjoining Boston Common, the **Public Garden** (Map p38; www.friendsofthepublicgarden. org; Arlington St; ☉ 6am–midnight; ⊞; Ⓣ Arlington) is a 24-acre botanical oasis of Victorian flower beds, verdant grass and weeping willow trees shading a tranquil lagoon. The old-fashioned pedal-powered Swan Boats (p59) have been delighting children for generations. The most endearing statue in the Public Garden is *Make Way for Ducklings*, depicting Mrs Mallard and her eight ducklings, the main characters in the beloved book by Robert McCloskey.

Until it was filled in the early 19th century, the Public Garden was (like Back Bay) a tidal salt marsh. Now, at any time of the year, it is an island of loveliness, awash with seasonal blooms, gold-toned leaves or untrammeled snow.

and King George III (though in reality they never met). The museum's one actual artifact – a tea crate known as the Robinson Half Chest – is highlighted with an audio presentation. Tickets are expensive, considering it's a small museum. Save a couple of dollars by purchasing tickets online.

★ **Institute of Contemporary Art**　　MUSEUM
(ICA; www.icaboston.org; 100 Northern Ave; adult/child $15/free; ☉ 10am–5pm Tue, Wed, Sat & Sun, to 9pm Thu & Fri; ⊞; 🚌 SL1, SL2, Ⓣ South Station) Boston has become a focal point for contemporary art in the 21st century, with the Institute of Contemporary Art leading the way. The building is a work of art in itself: a glass structure cantilevered over a waterside plaza. The vast light-filled interior allows for multimedia presentations, educational programs and studio space, as well as the development of the permanent collection.

Boston Children's Museum　　MUSEUM
(Map p38; www.bostonchildrensmuseum.org; 300 Congress St; $16, Fri 5-9pm $1; ☉ 10am–5pm Sat-Thu, to 9pm Fri; ⊞; Ⓣ South Station) 🚼 The interactive, educational exhibits at the delightful Children's Museum keep kids entertained for hours. Highlights include a bubble exhibit, rock-climbing walls, a hands-on construction site and intercultural immersion experiences. The light-filled atrium features an amazing three-story climbing maze. In nice weather kids can enjoy outdoor eating and playing in the waterside park. Look for the iconic Hood milk bottle on Fort Point Channel.

◉ South End & Chinatown

Chinatown, the Theater District and the Leather District are overlapping areas, filled with glitzy theaters, Chinese restaurants and the remnants of Boston's shoe and leather

industry (now converted lofts and clubs). Nearby, the Victorian manses in the South End have been reclaimed by artists and gays, who have created a vibrant restaurant and gallery scene.

SoWa Artists Guild　　GALLERY
(Map p50; www.sowaartistsguild.com; 450 Harrison Ave; ☉ 5-9pm 1st Fri of month; 🚌 SL4, SL5, Ⓣ Tufts Medical Center) The brick-and-beam buildings along Harrison Ave were originally used to manufacture goods ranging from canned food to pianos. Now these factories turn out paintings and sculptures instead. The SoWa Artists Guild houses about 70 artist studios and more than a dozen galleries. This is the epicentre of the South End art district. There is a SoWa Open Studios event on the first Friday of every month, while many artists also welcome visitors during the SoWa Sundays (p82).

Chinatown Gate　　LANDMARK
(Map p38; Beach St; Ⓣ Chinatown) The official entrance to Chinatown is the decorative gate *(paifong)*, a gift from the city of Taipei. It is symbolic – not only as an entryway for guests visiting Chinatown, but also as an entryway for immigrants who are still settling here, as they come to establish relationships and put down roots in their newly claimed home.

Surrounding the gate and anchoring the southern end of the Rose Kennedy Greenway is the new **Chinatown Park**. A bamboo-lined walkway runs through the modern gardens. The plaza is often populated by local residents engaged in *Xiangqi* (Chinese chess).

◉ Back Bay

Back Bay includes the city's most fashionable window-shopping, latte-drinking and people-watching area, on **Newbury St**, as well as its most elegant architecture around **Copley Sq**.

★ **Boston Public Library** LIBRARY
(Map p50; www.bpl.org; 700 Boylston St; ⊘9am-
9pm Mon-Thu, to 5pm Fri & Sat year-round, also
1-5pm Sun Oct-May; ⊤Copley) Dating from
1852, the esteemed Boston Public Library
lends credence to Boston's reputation as the
'Athens of America.' The old McKim building
is notable for its magnificent facade and exquisite interior art. Pick up a free brochure
and take a self-guided tour; alternatively,
free guided tours depart from the entrance
hall (times vary).

★ **Trinity Church** CHURCH
(Map p50; www.trinitychurchboston.org; 206 Clarendon St; adult/child $7/free; ⊘10am-5pm Tue-
Sat, 1-5pm Sun; ⊤Copley) A masterpiece of
American architecture, Trinity Church is the
country's ultimate example of Richardsonian Romanesque. The granite exterior, with a
massive portico and side cloister, uses sand-
stone in colorful patterns. The interior is an
awe-striking array of vibrant murals and
stained glass, most by artist John LaFarge,
who cooperated closely with architect Henry
Hobson Richardson to create an integrated
composition of shapes, colors and textures.
Free architectural tours are offered following Sunday service around 11:15am.

★ **Charles River Esplanade** PARK
(Map p50; www.esplanadeassociation.org; ⛲;
⊤Charles/MGH, Kenmore) The southern bank
of the Charles River Basin is an enticing urban escape, with grassy knolls and cooling
waterways, all designed by Frederick Law
Olmsted. It stretches almost 3 miles along
the Boston shore of the Charles River, from
the Museum of Science to Boston University
Bridge. The park is dotted with public art,
including an oversized bust of Arthur Fiedler, longtime conductor of the Boston Pops.
Paths along the river are ideal for bicycling,
jogging or walking.

There are several children's playgrounds
along the Esplanade, including the **Charles-
bank Playground** (Map p38; ⊤Science Park),
near the Museum of Science, and the **Stone-
man Playground** (Map p50; ⊤Hynes), near
Massachusetts Ave.

Commonwealth Avenue STREET
(Map p50; ⊤Arlington, Copley, Hynes) The grandest of Back Bay's grand boulevards is Commonwealth Ave (more commonly Comm
Ave). The Champs-Élysées of Boston, the
dual carriageway connects the Public Garden with the Back Bay Fens, a green link

in Olmsted's Emerald Necklace. The grassy
mall is dotted with grand elms and lined
with stately brownstones.

Prudential Center
Skywalk Observatory VIEWPOINT
(Map p50; www.skywalkboston.com; 800 Boylston
St; adult/child $18/13; ⊘10am-10pm Mar-Oct, to
8pm Nov-Feb; ℙ⛲; ⊤Prudential) Technically
called the Shops at Prudential Center, this
landmark Boston building is not much more
than a fancy shopping mall. But it does
provide a bird's-eye view of Boston from
its 50th-floor skywalk. Completely enclosed
by glass, the Skywalk offers spectacular
360-degree views of Boston and Cambridge,
accompanied by an entertaining audio tour
(with a special version catering to kids). Alternatively, enjoy the same view from **Top of
the Hub** (Map p50; ☑617-536-1775; www.topof
thehub.net; 800 Boylston St; ⊘11:30am-1am; ☎;
⊤Prudential) for the price of a drink.

Mary Baker Eddy
Library & Mapparium LIBRARY
(Map p50; www.marybakereddylibrary.org; 200
Massachusetts Ave; adult/child $6/4; ⊘10am-4pm
Tue-Sun; ⛲; ⊤Symphony) The Mary Baker
Eddy Library houses one of Boston's hidden treasures. The intriguing Mapparium
is a room-size, stained-glass globe that visitors walk through on a glass bridge. It was
created in 1935, which is reflected in the
globe's geopolitical boundaries. The acous-
tics, which surprised even the designer, allow everyone in the room to hear even the
tiniest whisper.

John Hancock Tower NOTABLE BUILDING
(Map p50; 200 Clarendon St; ⊤Copley) Constructed with more than 10,000 panels of
mirrored glass, the 62-story John Hancock
Tower was designed in 1976 by Henry Cobb.
It is the tallest and most beloved skyscraper
on the Boston skyline – despite the precari-
ous falling panes of glass when it was first
built. The Hancock offers an amazing perspective on Trinity Church, reflected in its
facade.

◉ **Kenmore Square & Fenway**
Kenmore Sq and Fenway attract club-goers
and baseball fans to the streets surrounding Fenway Park, as well as art lovers and
culture vultures to the artistic institutions
situated along the Avenue of the Arts (Huntington Ave).

BOSTON SIGHTS

Back Bay, the Fenway & the South End

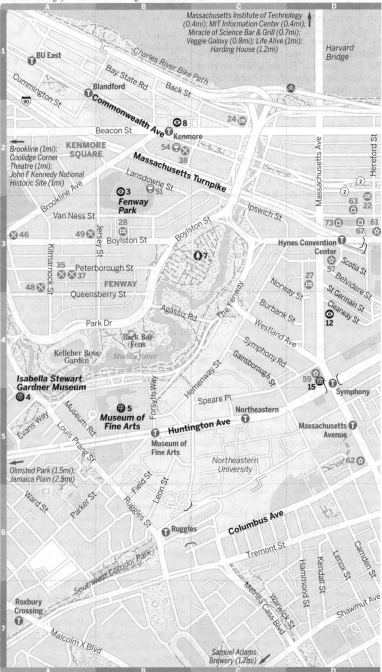

Massachusetts Institute of Technology
(0.4mi); MIT Information Center (0.4mi);
Miracle of Science Bar & Grill (0.7mi);
Veggie Galaxy (0.8mi); Life Alive (1mi);
Harding House (1.2mi)

Harvard
Bridge

BU East

Cummington St

Charles River Bike Path

Bay State Rd

Back St

Blandford

Commonwealth Ave

Beacon St

Kenmore

8

24

54
38

KENMORE
SQUARE

Massachusetts Turnpike

Brookline (1mi);
Coolidge Corner
Theatre (1mi);
John F Kennedy National
Historic Site (1mi)

Brookline Ave

Lansdowne St

51

3
Fenway
Park

Van Ness St

28

Boylston St

Boylston St

Ipswich St

Massachusetts Ave

Hereford St

2
2

63
22

73
67
61

46

49

Jersey St

7

Hynes Convention
Center

Scotia St

35
37

48

Peterborough St

FENWAY

Queensberry St

Kilmarnock St

Park Dr

Agassiz Rd

The Fenway

Norway St

27

Burbank St

Westland Ave

Symphony Rd

Gainsborough St

57

Belvidere St

St Germain St

Clearway St

12

Kelleher Rose
Garden

Back Bay
Fens

Muddy River

Isabella Stewart
Gardner Museum

4

Museum Rd

5
Museum of
Fine Arts

Forsyth Way

Hemenway St

Speare Pl

Northeastern

Huntington Ave

59
15

Symphony

Massachusetts
Avenue

Evans Way

Louis Prang St

Museum of
Fine Arts

Field St

Leon St

Northeastern
University

62

Olmsted Park (1.5mi);
Jamaica Plain (2.5mi)

Ward St

Parker St

Ruggles St

Ruggles

Columbus Ave

Tremont St

Hammond St

Kendall St

Lenox St

Camden St

Southwest Corridor Park

Shawmut Ave

Warwick St

Melnea Cass Blvd

Roxbury
Crossing

Malcolm X Blvd

Samuel Adams
Brewery (1.7mi)

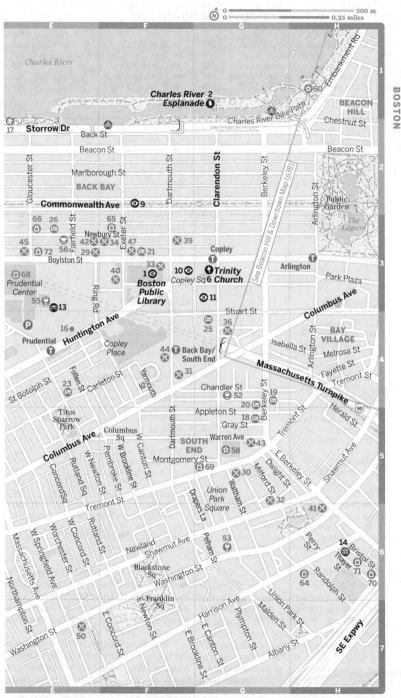

0 — 500 m
0 — 0.25 miles

Charles River

Charles River 2
Esplanade

60

BEACON
HILL

Charles River Bike Path

Chestnut St

17 **Storrow Dr**

Back St

Beacon St

Beacon St

Marlborough St

BACK BAY

Commonwealth Ave 9

Gloucester St

Fairfield St

Exeter St

Dartmouth St

Clarendon St

Berkeley St

Arlington St

Public
Garden

The
Lagoon

66 26

65

45

42 34

Newbury St

47

72 56

29

21

Boylston St

33

39

Copley

40

1
**Boston
Public
Library**

10

6 Trinity
Copley Sq Church

11

Arlington

Park Plaza

See Beacon Hill & Downtown Map (p38)

68

Prudential
Center

55 13

Huntington Ave

Ring Rd

16

Stuart St

52

25

36

Columbus Ave

BAY
VILLAGE

Isabella St

Melrose St

Prudential

Copley
Place

44 Back Bay/
South End

31

Arlington St

Fayette St

Tremont St

Massachusetts Turnpike

90

St Botolph St

Follen St

Carleton St

Yarmouth St

Chandler St

52

19

Herald St

23

Appleton St

20

18

Gray St

Berkeley St

Tremont St

Shawmut Ave

Titus
Sparrow
Park

Columbus Ave

Columbus
Sq

W Canton St

Dartmouth St

Warren Ave

43

SOUTH
END

58

W Newton St

W Brookline St

Montgomery St

69

30

Dwight St

E Berkeley St

Concord Sq

Rutland Sq

Pembroke St

Tremont St

Drapers La

Union
Park
Square

Waltham St

Milford St

32

41

Massachusetts Ave

W Springfield St

W Concord St

Rutland St

Worcester St

Newland

Shawmut Ave

Pelham St

53

Perry St

14
Thayer St

Bristol St

71

Northampton St

Blackstone
Sq

Washington St

64

Randolph St

70

Franklin
Sq

E Newton St

Harrison Ave

Plympton St

Malden St

Union Park St

Washington St

50

E Concord St

E Canton St

E Brookline St

Albany St

SE Expwy

Back Bay, the Fenway & the South End

★ **Isabella Stewart Gardner Museum** MUSEUM

(Map p50; www.gardnermuseum.org; 280 The Fenway; adult/child $15/free; ⊙11am-5pm Wed-Mon, to 9pm Thu; 🚻; ⊤Museum) The magnificent Venetian-style palazzo that houses this museum was home to 'Mrs Jack' Gardner herself until her death in 1924. A monument to one woman's taste for acquiring exquisite art, the Gardner is filled with almost 2000 priceless objects, primarily European, including outstanding tapestries and Italian Renaissance and 17th-century Dutch paintings. The four-story greenhouse courtyard is a masterpiece and a tranquil oasis that alone is worth the price of admission.

The most striking room on the 1st floor is the Spanish Cloister, with its Moorish arch framing John Singer Sargent's picture of a Gypsy dance. On the 2nd floor, the Dutch room contains a self-portrait by Rembrandt and another portrait by Rubens. The majestic Tapestry Room evokes a castle hall, hung with 10 allegorical tapestries.

The 3rd floor contains the highlights of this rich collection, including the sumptuous Veronese Room. The museum's most celebrated gallery is the Titian Room, which is centered on the artist's famous rendition of *Europa.* Your final stop is the Gothic Room, featuring Sargent's remarkable portrait of Mrs Gardner herself.

★**Museum of Fine Arts**   MUSEUM
(MFA; Map p50; www.mfa.org; 465 Huntington Ave; adult/child $25/free; ☉10am-5pm Sat-Tue, to 10pm Wed-Fri; 🚗; 🚆Museum, Ruggles) Since 1876, the Museum of Fine Arts has been Boston's premier venue for showcasing art by local, national and international artists. Nowadays the museum's holdings encompass all eras, from the ancient world to contemporary times, and all areas of the globe, making it truly encyclopedic in scope. Most recently, the museum has added gorgeous new wings dedicated to the Art of the Americas and to contemporary art, contributing to Boston's emergence as an art center in the 21st century.

The centerpiece of the MFA is the four-story Americas wing, which includes 53 galleries exhibiting art from the pre-Columbian era up through the 20th century. The 2nd level is, perhaps, the richest part of the wing. An entire gallery is dedicated to John Singer Sargent, including his iconic painting *The Daughters of Edward Darley Boit.*

Located in the museum's northern wing, the MFA's collection of European art spans the centuries from the Middle Ages to the 20th century. The highlight of the European exhibit is no doubt the Impressionists and post-Impressionists, with masterpieces by Degas, Gauguin, Renoir and Van Gogh, as well as the largest collection of Monets outside Paris.

In the southwestern wing, the collection of Asian art includes the exhibits in the serene Buddhist Temple room. In the southeastern part of the museum, the MFA's ancient-art collection also covers a huge geographic spectrum, including two rooms of mummies in the Egyptian galleries.

The Linde Wing for Contemporary Art is full of surprises. The darling of museum patrons is *Black River,* a fantastic woven tapestry of discarded bottle caps by Ghanaian artist El Anatsui.

Back Bay Fens   PARK
(Map p50; Park Dr; ☉dawn-dusk; 🚆Museum) The Back Bay Fens, or the Fenway, follows the Muddy River, an aptly named creek that is choked with tall reeds. The Fens features well-cared-for community gardens, the elegant Kelleher Rose Garden, and plenty of space to toss a Frisbee, play pick-up basketball or lie in the sun.

Citgo Sign   LANDMARK
(Map p50; 🚆Kenmore) London has Big Ben, Paris has the Eiffel Tower and Boston has the Citgo sign. It's an unlikely landmark in this high-minded city, but Bostonians love the bright-blinking 'trimark' that has towered over Kenmore Sq since 1965. Every time the Red Sox hit a home run over the left-field wall at Fenway Park, Citgo's colorful logo is seen by thousands of fans. It also symbolizes the end of the Boston Marathon, as it falls at Mile 25 in the race.

◉ Cambridge

Stretched out along the north shore of the Charles River, Cambridge is a separate city that boasts two distinguished universities, a host of historic sites, and artistic and cultural attractions galore. The streets around Harvard Sq and Central Sq are home to restaurants, bars and clubs that rival their counterparts across the river.

★**Harvard University**   UNIVERSITY
(Map p54; www.harvard.edu; Massachusetts Ave; tours free; 🚆Harvard) Founded in 1636 to educate men for the ministry, Harvard is America's oldest college. The original Ivy League school has eight graduates who went on to be US presidents, not to mention dozens of Nobel laureates and Pulitzer Prize winners. The geographic heart of Harvard University – where redbrick buildings and leaf-covered paths exude academia – is Harvard Yard. Free historical tours of Harvard Yard depart from the Smith Campus Center (www.harvard.edu/visitors; 1350 Massachusetts Ave; ☉9am-5pm Mon-Sat); self-guided tours are also available.

Flanking Johnston Gate are the two oldest buildings on campus. South of the gate, Massachusetts Hall (Harvard Yard) houses the offices of the president of the university. Dating to 1720, it is the oldest building at Harvard and the oldest academic building in the country. North is Harvard Hall (Harvard Yard), which dates to 1766 and

Cambridge

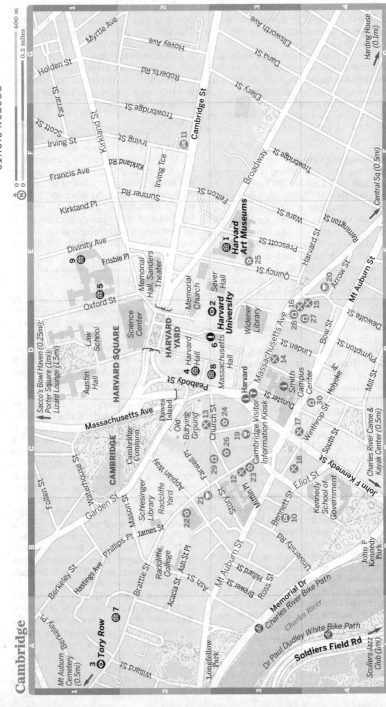

Cambridge

originally housed the library. The focal point of the yard is the John Harvard statue (p56), where every Harvard hopeful has a photo taken (and touches the statue's shiny shoe for good luck).

★**Harvard Art Museums** MUSEUM
(Map p54; www.harvardartmuseums.org; 32 Quincy St; adult/child/student $15/free/10; ⊙10am-5pm; Ⓣ Harvard) The recent renovation and expansion of Harvard's art museums allowed the university's massive 250,000-piece collection to come together under one very stylish roof, designed by architect extraordinaire Renzo Piano. The artwork spans the globe, with separate collections devoted to Asian and Islamic cultures (formerly the Arthur M Sackler Museum), northern European and Germanic cultures (formerly the Busch-Reisinger Museum) and other Western art, especially European modernism (formerly the Fogg).

Harvard Museum of Natural History MUSEUM
(Map p54; www.hmnh.harvard.edu; 26 Oxford St; adult/child/student $12/8/10; ⊙9am-5pm; Ⓜ 86, Ⓣ Harvard) This institution is famed for its botanical galleries, featuring some 3000 pieces of handblown glass flowers and plants. At the intersection of art and science, the collection of intricately crafted flora is pretty amazing. Now, there is a

smaller, complementary exhibit of Sea Creatures in Glass, by the same artists. Nearby, the zoological galleries house an enormous number of stuffed animals and reassembled skeletons, as well as an impressive fossil collection. Other cool exhibits feature climate change, sparkling gemstones and arthropods (yes, cockroaches).

★**Mt Auburn Cemetery** CEMETERY
(www.mountauburn.org; 580 Mt Auburn St; ⊙8am-7pm May-Sep, to 5pm Oct-Apr; Ⓜ; Ⓠ71, 73, Ⓣ Harvard) FREE This delightful spot at the end of Brattle St is worth the 30-minute walk west from Harvard Sq. Developed in 1831, it was the first 'garden cemetery' in the US. Maps pinpoint the rare botanical specimens and notable burial plots. Famous long-term residents include Mary Baker Eddy (founder of the Christian Science Church), Isabella Stewart Gardner (socialite and art collector), Winslow Homer (19th-century American painter), Oliver Wendell Holmes (US Supreme Court Justice) and Henry W Longfellow (19th-century writer).

★**Museum of Science** MUSEUM
(Map p38; www.mos.org; Charles River Dam; adult/child $23/20; ⊙9am-7pm Sat-Thu Jul & Aug, to 5pm Sep-Jun, to 9pm Fri year-round; Ⓟ Ⓜ; Ⓣ Science Park/West End) ✔ This educational playground has more than 600 interactive exhibits. Favorites include the world's largest

LOCAL KNOWLEDGE

THE STATUE OF THREE LIES

Daniel Chester French's sculpture (Map p54; Harvard Yard; T Harvard), inscribed 'John Harvard, Founder of Harvard College, 1638,' is known as the statue of three lies. It does not actually depict Harvard (since no image of him exists), but a random student. Plus, John Harvard was not the founder of the college, but its first benefactor in 1638. Finally, the college was actually founded two years earlier in 1636. The Harvard symbol hardly lives up to the university's motto, *Veritas* (Truth).

lightning-bolt generator, a full-scale space capsule, a world population meter and an impressive dinosaur exhibit. The amazing array of exhibits and presentations explores computers and technology, maps and models, the human body and human evolution, and the birds and the bees (both literally and figuratively). The newest addition is the Hall of Human Life, where visitors can witness the hatching of baby chicks.

The Discovery Center is a hands-on play area for kids under the age of eight. The museum also houses the Charles Hayden Planetarium and Mugar Omni Theater (p77).

Charles Hayden Planetarium   PLANETARIUM

(Map p38; www.mos.org; Museum of Science, Charles River Dam; adult/child $10/8; ⊙9am-5pm Sat-Thu, to 9pm Fri) Housed in the Museum of Science, the planetarium boasts a state-of-the-art projection system that casts a heavenly star show, as well as programs about black holes and other astronomical mysteries. Watch out for late-night laser light shows set to Pink Floyd.

Peabody Museum of
Archaeology & Ethnology   MUSEUM

(Map p54; www.peabody.harvard.edu; 11 Divinity Ave; adult/child/student $12/8/10; ⊙9am-5pm; ♿; ☒86, T Harvard) The centerpiece of the Peabody is the impressive Hall of the North American Indian, which traces how native peoples responded to the arrival of Europeans from the 15th to the 18th centuries. Other exhibits examine indigenous cultures throughout the Americas, including a fantastic comparison of cave paintings and murals of the Awatovi (New Mexico), the Maya (Guatemala) and the Moche (Peru).

The price of admission includes entry to the neighboring Harvard Museum of Natural History.

★ Tory Row   STREET

(Map p54; Brattle St; T Harvard) Heading west out of Harvard Sq, Brattle St is the epitome of colonial posh. Lined with man-

sions that were once home to royal sympathizers, the street earned the nickname Tory Row.

Longfellow House   HISTORIC BUILDING

(Map p54; www.nps.gov/long; 105 Brattle St; ⊙tours 9:30am-5pm Wed-Sun Jun-Oct, grounds dawn-dusk year-round; ☒71, 73, T Harvard) FREE Brattle St's most famous resident was Henry Wadsworth Longfellow, whose stately manor is now a National Historic Site. The poet lived here for 45 years, from 1837 to 1882, writing many of his most famous poems, including *Evangeline* and *The Song of Hiawatha*. Accessible by guided tour, the Georgian mansion contains many of Longfellow's belongings as well as lush period gardens.

🏃 Activities

Walking

★ Freedom Trail   WALKING

(T Park) FREE For a sampler of Boston's revolutionary sights, follow the redbrick road. It leads 2.5 miles through the center of Boston, from Boston Common to the Bunker Hill Monument, and traces the events leading up to and following the War of Independence. The Freedom Trail is well marked and easy to follow on your own.

Otherwise, there are plenty of tours that follow this trail, including the National Park Service's free option.

Boating

Charles River Canoe
& Kayak Center   CANOEING, KAYAKING

(www.ski-paddle.com; 500 Broad Canal Way; per hour canoe $20, kayak $15-20; ⊙noon-8pm Mon-Fri, 9am-8pm Sat & Sun May-Oct; ♿; T Kendall/MIT) Besides canoe and kayak rental, Charles River Canoe & Kayak offers classes and organized outings. Experienced kayakers can venture out to the harbor, but the river and basin are lovely for skyline views and fall foliage. There is another outlet in Allston (www.ski-paddle.com; Soldier's Field Rd; per hour canoe $20, kayak $15-20; ⊙10am-8pm Mon-Fri,

9am-8pm Sat & Sun May-Oct; T Harvard Sq), near Harvard Sq, which allows for an excellent one-way 5-mile trip between the two rental centers.

Community Boating   WATER SPORTS
(Map p38; www.community-boating.org; Charles River Esplanade; kayak/SUP/sailboat per day $40/40/79; ☺1pm-dusk Mon-Fri, 9am-dusk Sat & Sun Apr-Oct; T Charles/MGH) Offers experienced sailors unlimited use of sailboats and kayaks on the Charles River, but you'll have to take a test to demonstrate your ability. A 30-day 'learn to sail' package costs $99, while a 60-day boating pass is $239.

Codzilla   BOATING
(Map p38; www.bostonharborcruises.com; 1 Long Wharf; adult/child $29/25; ☺hours vary May-Sep; ♿; T Aquarium) 'Boating' may not be the proper word to describe this activity, which takes place on a 2800HP speedboat that cruises through the waves at speeds of up to 40mph. Painted like a shark with a big toothy grin, the boat has a unique hull design that enables it to do the ocean version of doughnuts. Warning: you will get wet.

Cycling
★**Minuteman Bikeway**   CYCLING
(www.minutemanbikeway.org; ♿; T Alewife, Davis) The best of Boston's bicycle trails starts near Alewife station and leads 5 miles to historic Lexington Center, then traverses an additional 4 miles of idyllic scenery and terminates in the rural suburb of Bedford. The wide, straight, paved path gets crowd-ed on weekends. Rent a bike at the Bicycle Exchange (www.cambridgebicycleexchange.com; 2067 Massachusetts Ave; rental 1 day $25, additional days $10; ☺9am-6pm Tue-Sat, noon-5pm Sun; T Porter). The Minuteman Bikeway is also accessible from Davis Sq in Somerville (Davis T station) via the 2-mile Community Path to Alewife.

Charles River Bike Path   CYCLING
(Storrow Dr & Memorial Dr; ♿; T Harvard, Kendall/MIT, Charles/MGH, Science Park) A popular cycling circuit runs along both sides of the Charles River between the Museum of Science and the Mt Auburn St Bridge in Watertown center (5 miles west of Cambridge). The round trip is 17 miles, but 10 bridges in between offer ample opportunities to turn around and shorten the trip. Rent a bike at Cambridge Bicycle (www.cambridge bicycle.com; 259 Massachusetts Ave; per day $30; ☺10am-7pm Mon-Sat, noon-6pm Sun; T Central) or Back Bay Bicycles (www.papa-wheelies. com; 362 Commonwealth Ave; city/road bike per day $35/65; ☺11am-7pm Mon-Fri, 10am-6pm Sat, noon-5pm Sun; T Hynes).

Ride carefully! This trail is not particularly well maintained (watch for roots and narrow passes) and is often crowded with pedestrians.

Skating
Boston Common Frog Pond   SKATING
(Map p38; www.bostonfrogpond.com; Boston Common; adult/child $6/free, rental $12/6; ☺10am-4pm Mon, to 9pm Tue-Sun mid-Nov–mid-Mar; ♿; T Park St) When temperatures

---

DON'T MISS

MASSACHUSETTS INSTITUTE OF TECHNOLOGY

The Massachusetts Institute of Technology (MIT; www.mit.edu; 77 Massachusetts Ave; ☺tours 11am & 3pm Mon-Fri; T Kendall/MIT) offers a completely novel perspective on Cambridge academia: proudly nerdy, but not quite as tweedy as Harvard. A recent frenzy of building has resulted in some of the most architecturally intriguing structures you'll find on either side of the river. Tours depart from the MIT Information Center (www. mit.edu; 77 Massachusetts Ave; ☺9am-5pm Mon-Fri; T Central).

Of all the funky buildings on the MIT campus, none has received more attention than the Ray & Maria Stata Center (CSAIL; www.csail.mit.edu; 32 Vassar St; T Kendall/MIT), an avant-garde edifice that was designed by architectural legend Frank Gehry. Other worthwhile stops on campus include the MIT Museum (www.web.mit.edu/museum; 265 Massachusetts Ave; adult/child $10/5; ☺10am-6pm Jul & Aug, to 5pm Sep-Jun; P ♿; T Central) and the List Visual Arts Center (http://listart.mit.edu; 20 Ames St, Weisner Bldg; donation $5; ☺noon-6pm Tue, Wed & Fri-Sun, to 8pm Thu; T Kendall/MIT). You can pick up or download a map of MIT's public art, proof enough that this university supports artistic as well as technological innovation.

BOSTON'S GLORIOUS GREENWAYS

The Emerald Necklace (www.emeraldnecklace.org; T Forest Hills) is an evocative name for a series of parks and green spaces that weave some 7 miles through Boston, from the Boston Common to Franklin Park. Designed by Frederick Law Olmsted in the late 19th century, the Emerald Necklace treats city residents to a bit of fresh air, green grass and flowing water, right within the city limits. It's well suited for cycling, so hop on a bike and go for the green.

Olmsted Park (T Riverway) features a paved path that hugs the banks of Leverett Pond and Ward's Pond in Jamaica Plain. The idyllic spring-fed Jamaica Pond (www.jamaicapond.com; 507 Jamaica Way; boat rental per hour $15; boathouse noon-sunset Mon-Thu, 10am-sunset Fri-Sun Apr-Oct; ; T Green St), on the west side of the Jamaicaway, is more than 50ft deep and great for boating, fishing, jogging and picnicking. Beautifully landscaped and wonderfully serene, the Arnold Arboretum (p43) will appeal not only to green thumbs and plant lovers, but also to anyone who can take time to smell the roses. Check the website to see what's blooming when you're visiting.

Franklin Park (T Stony Brook, Green St, Forest Hills), at 500-plus acres, is an underutilized resource – partly because it borders a sketchy neighborhood, and partly because it is so huge. Still, on weekend afternoons the park is full of families from the nearby neighborhoods of Jamaica Plain, Dorchester and Roxbury. Take the orange line to Stony Brook, Green St or Forest Hills and walk about a half-mile east to the park's edge. The Franklin Park Zoo (www.zoonewengland.com; 1 Franklin Park Rd; adult/child $20/14; 10am-5pm Mon-Fri, 10am-6pm Sat & Sun Apr-Sep, to 4pm daily Oct-Mar; P ; 22, 28, T Ruggles) is also contained within the park.

North of Jamaica Plain, other green links in the Emerald Necklace include the Back Bay Fens (p53), the Commonwealth Ave mall (p49) and the Public Garden (p48), with the terminus at the Boston Common (p36).

---

drop, the Boston Common becomes an urban winter wonderland, with slipping and sliding, swirling and twirling on the Frog Pond. Weekends are often crowded, as are weekdays around noon, as local skate fiends spend their lunch break on the ice. In warmer weather, the Frog Pond becomes a wet and wild spray pool where kids can cool off.

The nearby Tadpole Playground (Map p38; T Park) is another fun place for the kids to expend some extra energy.

Other Activities

★ New England
Aquarium Whale Watch   WHALE WATCHING
(Map p38; www.neaq.org; Central Wharf; adult/child/infant $49/33/16; times vary Apr-Oct; ; T Aquarium) Board the *Voyager III* for the journey out to Stellwagen Bank, a rich feeding ground for whales, dolphins and marine birds. Onboard naturalists can answer all your questions, plus they have keen eyes. Whale sightings are guaranteed, otherwise you'll receive a coupon for a free trip at a later date.

Boat captains and onboard naturalists are trained by New England Aquarium experts to ensure that the tours do not interfere with the animals or harm them in any way.

Sacco's Bowl Haven   BOWLING
(www.flatbreadcompany.com; 45 Day St, Somerville; per lane per hour $25; 9am-midnight Mon-Sat, to 10:30pm Sun; ; T Davis) Founded in 1939, Sacco's Bowl Haven is a Somerville institution – old-time candlepin bowling lanes that managed to survive into the 21st century. The place was overtaken and updated by Flatbread Co, who brightened the space and added clay ovens, but preserved most of the lanes and the good-time atmosphere. Now you can enjoy delicious organic pizzas and cold craft beers with your candlepins.

Downeast Cider House   BREWERY
(http://downeastcider.com; 200 Terminal St; 3-7pm Fri, 11am-10pm Sat, 1-6pm Sun; 93 from Haymarket, T Inner Harbor Ferry from Long Wharf) FREE It's not much of a tour: since the facility is small, you'll see most of it standing in place. But you will see the cider being produced, sample some seasonal variations and learn a bushel about the process. Staff is enthusiastic and the tour is enlightening. Located under the Tobin Bridge.

📌 Tours

Boat Tours

Swan Boats   BOATING

(Map p38; www.swanboats.com; Public Garden; adult/child $3.50/2; ⊙10am-5pm Jun-Aug, to 4pm mid-Apr–May, noon-4pm Sep; T Arlington) A relic of Boston's bygone days, a ride on the swan boats offers 15 minutes of serenity.

On the tranquil lagoon of the Public Garden, the story of the slow-going swan boats goes back to 1877. Robert Paget developed a catamaran with a pedal-powered paddlewheel. Inspired by the opera *Lohengrin,* in which a heroic knight rides across a river in a swan-drawn boat, Paget designed a graceful swan to hide the boat captain.

While today's swan boats are larger than the 1877 original, they still utilize the same technology and they are still managed by Paget's descendants.

Boston Green Cruises   CRUISE

(Map p38; www.bostongreencruises.com; 60 Rowes Wharf; adult/child from $28/24; �foot; T Aquarium, South Station) 🚤 See the sights and hear the sounds of the city from Boston's first super-quiet, zero-emissions electric boat. Spend an hour floating in the Boston Harbor or cruising on the Charles River (or upgrade to a 90-minute combo trip for $39/35 per adult/child).

Boston Harbor Cruises   CRUISE

(Map p38; www.bostonharborcruises.com; 1 Long Wharf; adult/child $27/23; 🚶; T Aquarium) Boston Harbor Cruises offers a slew of options for those who want to get out on the water, such as a Historic Sightseeing Tour around the Inner Harbor. The Charles River & Locks Tour is a 90-minute loop around the whole of the Shawmut Peninsula. Other special events include sunset cruises and weekend lighthouse cruises (prices vary).

Boston Duck Tours   BOATING

(Map p50; ☑ 617-267-3825; www.bostonducktours.com; adult/child $37.50/26; 🚶; T Aquarium, Science Park, Prudential) These ridiculously popular tours use WWII amphibious vehicles that cruise the downtown streets before splashing into the Charles River. The 80-minute tours depart from the Museum of Science, the Prudential Center or the New England Aquarium. Reserve in advance.

Super Duck Tours   BOATING

(Map p38; www.bostonsupertours.com; Long Wharf; adult/child/infant US$33/22/11; T Aquarium)

This 90-minute duck tour is super because it goes in the Boston Harbor, offering views of the Charlestown Navy Yard, the North End and the waterfront. The tour departs from the Charlestown Navy Yard, but you can get there via a free shuttle from Long Wharf.

Cycling Tours

★Urban AdvenTours   CYCLING

(Map p38; ☑ 617-670-0637; www.urbanadventours.com; 103 Atlantic Ave; tours from $55; ⊙9am-8pm; 🚶; T Aquarium) 🚲 Founded by avid cyclists who believe the best views of Boston are from a bicycle. And they are right! The City View Ride provides a great overview of how to get around by bike, including ride-bys of some of Boston's best sites. Other specialty tours include Bikes at Night and the Emerald Necklace tour. Bicycles, helmets and water are all provided.

Trolley Tours

Beantown Trolley   TROLLEY TOUR

(☑ 617-720-6342, 800-343-1328; www.brushhilltours.com; adult/child/senior $35/15/33; ⊙9am-4:30pm) Trolley color: red. Take an 80-minute tour or hop off and hop on at 11 different stops around the city. The price includes a harbor cruise from the New England Aquarium or admission to the Mapparium.

Upper Deck Trolley Tours   TROLLEY TOUR

(Map p38; www.bostonsupertours.com; basic adult/child $37/19, 2-day tickets $56/32; 🚶; T Aquarium) Super-tall trolleys give passengers a view over the traffic. This is the only trolley tour that goes to Cambridge. The two-day ticket includes a harbor or river cruise, as well as admission to the Institute of Contemporary Art (ICA) or one of the Cambridge museums.

Old Town Trolley Tours   TROLLEY TOUR

(Map p38; www.historictours.com; Long Wharf; adult/child $41/20; 🚶; T Aquarium) Tour around the city, hopping on and off all day long. Save 10% when you book online. This ticket also includes admission to the Old State House and a short harbor cruise, as well as a discount at the Boston Tea Party Ships & Museum.

Walking Tours

Boston by Foot   WALKING

(www.bostonbyfoot.com; adult/child $15/10; 🚶) This fantastic nonprofit organization offers 90-minute walking tours, with neighborhood-specific walks and specialty theme tours, like Literary Landmarks, the Dark Side of Boston and Boston for Little Feet – a kid-friendly version of the Freedom Trail.

Black Heritage Trail WALKING
(Map p38; www.nps.gov/boaf; ☉tours 2pm Tue-Thu Jun, Mon-Sat Jun-Oct, plus 10am & noon Jun-Aug; T Park St) FREE This 1.6-mile walking tour explores the history of the abolitionist movement and African American settlement on Beacon Hill. The NPS conducts excellent, informative guided tours, but maps and descriptions for self-guided tours are available at the Museum of African American History. Departs from the Robert Gould Shaw memorial.

Hahvahd Tour WALKING
(Trademark Tours; www.harvardtour.com; adult/child $10/7; T Harvard) This company was founded by a couple of Harvard students who shared the inside scoop on history and student life at the university. Now the company offers a whole menu of Boston tours, but the funny, offbeat Hahvahd Tour is the trademark. Tour guides are still students – broke students, presumably – who aren't afraid to ask for tips.

Photo Walks WALKING
(☑ 617-851-2273; www.photowalks.com; adult/youth $40/20; 🕭) A walking tour combined with a photography lesson. Different routes cover Boston's most photogenic neighborhoods.

North End Market Tour WALKING
(☑ 617-523-6032; www.bostonfoodtours.com; tours $57; ☉tours 10am & 2pm Wed & Sat, 10am & 3pm Fri) A three-hour tour around the North End that includes shopping in a *salumeria,* sampling pastries at the local *pasticceria,* smelling the herbs and spices that flavor Italian cooking, and sampling spirits at an *enoteca* (wine bar). Guests have the opportunity to chat with local shopkeepers and other longtime North End residents to reminisce about eating and living in this food-rich neighborhood.

NPS Freedom Trail Tour WALKING
(Map p38; www.nps.gov/bost; Faneuil Hall; ☉hourly 10am-3pm Sat & Sun Apr-Jun, daily Jul-Oct; T State) FREE Show up at least 30 minutes early to snag a spot on one of the free, ranger-led Freedom Trail tours provided by the National Park Service. Tours depart from the visitor center in Faneuil Hall, and follow a portion of the Freedom Trail (not including Charlestown), for a total of 90 minutes. Each tour is limited to 30 people.

📷 Festivals & Events

★ Boston Marathon SPORTS
(www.baa.org; ☉3rd Mon Apr) One of the country's most prestigious marathons takes runners on a 26.2-mile course ending at Copley Sq on Patriots' Day, a Massachusetts holiday on the third Monday in April.

Patriots' Day HISTORY
(www.battleroad.org; ☉3rd Mon Apr) On the third Monday in April, history buffs commemorate the start of the American Revolution, with a re-enactment of the battle on Lexington Green (11 miles west of Boston) and a commemoration ceremony at the North Bridge in Concord (17 miles west of Boston).

GAY & LESBIAN BOSTON

Out and active gay communities are visible all around Boston, especially in the South End and Jamaica Plain. Stop by **Calamus Bookstore** (Map p38; www.facebook.com/calamusbooks; 92 South St; ☉11:30am-6:30pm Mon-Sat, 12:30-5:30pm Sun; T South Station), which is an excellent source of information about community events and organizations.

There is no shortage of entertainment options catering to LGBTQ travelers. From drag shows to dyke nights, this sexually diverse community has something for everybody.

The biggest event of the year for the Boston gay and lesbian community is June's Boston Pride, a week of parades, parties, festivals and flag-raisings.

There are excellent sources of information for the gay and lesbian community:

Bay Windows (www.baywindows.com) A weekly newspaper for LGBTQ readers. The print edition is distributed throughout New England, but the website is also an excellent source of news and information.

Edge Boston (www.edgeboston.com) The Boston branch of the nationwide network of publications offering news and entertainment for LGBTQ readers. Includes a nightlife section with culture and club reviews.

SoWa Art Walk ART
(www.sowaartwalk.com; ⊙11am-6pm, 1st Sun in May; ⊤New England Medical Center) There's more to SoWa than Open Markets and Open Studios. The biggest event of the year is the annual SoWa Art Walk, which draws thousands of visitors (and visiting artists) to the neighborhood. Many artists (in the Artists Guild and elsewhere) open their studios, while others set up booths at the outdoor art market. Local galleries also get in on the festive event.

Hidden Gardens of Beacon Hill GARDENS
(www.beaconhillgardenclub.org; $45-55; ⊙9am-5pm on 3rd Thursday in May) Sponsored by the Beacon Hill Garden Club, here's your chance to get a peek at a dozen of the neighborhood's urban gardens. Hidden courtyards and secret passageways are opened up to visitors to marvel at the beautiful blooms and other lovely landscaping. The tour is self-guided.

Boston Calling MUSIC
(www.bostoncalling.com; Harvard Athletic Complex, Allston; ⊙May) Independent-music lovers take over a large outdoor Boston venue for three days of all-out, rock-out music. The festival occurs during the last weekend in May.

Boston Pride Festival LGBTQ
(☑617-262-9405; www.bostonpride.org; ⊙Jun) During the first full week in June, Boston does its part for this now-national celebration, kicking off with the raising of a rainbow flag on City Hall Plaza. Events occur throughout the week. The highlight is the Pride Parade and Festival on the second Sunday in June.

The parade attracts tens of thousands of participants, decked out in outrageous costumes and showing off their gay pride, culminating in a huge party on the Boston Common.

Fourth of July HOLIDAY
(www.july4th.org; ⊙Jul 4) Boston hosts one of the biggest Independence Day bashes in the USA, with a free Boston Pops concert on the Esplanade and a fireworks display that's televised nationally.

Head of the Charles Regatta SPORTS
(www.hocr.org; ⊙mid-Oct) Spectators line the banks of the Charles River on a weekend in mid-October to watch the world's largest rowing event.

Boston Tea Party Reenactment HISTORY
(www.oldsouthmeetinghouse.org; ⊙Dec) On the Sunday prior to December 16, costumed actors march from Old South Meeting House to the waterfront and toss crates of tea into the harbor. Nowadays, the event takes place on the newly rebuilt Griffin's Wharf, where the Tea Party ships are docked.

First Night First Day NEW YEAR
(www.firstnightboston.org; ⊙Dec 31) New Year celebrations begin early and continue past midnight, culminating in fireworks over the harbor. The fun continues on New Year's Day, with more activities and exhibitions. Purchase a special button (see the website for button vendors) that permits entrance into events citywide.

🛏 Sleeping

Boston offers a wide range of accommodations, from inviting guesthouses in historic quarters to swanky hotels with all the amenities. Considering that Boston is a city filled with students, there are surprisingly few accommodations options targeting budget travelers and backpackers.

Beacon Hill & Boston Common

John Jeffries House HOTEL $$
(Map p38; ☑617-367-1866; www.johnjeffries house.com; 14 David Mugar Way; s/d $135/164, ste $189-199; ℗❋⊛; ⊤Charles/MGH) Reproduction furnishings, original molding, hardwood floors and mahogany accents recall the era when Dr John Jeffries founded what is now the world-renowned Massachusetts Eye & Ear Infirmary. Many patients reside here when they come to town for treatment, as do travelers. Complimentary breakfast is served in the parlor, but you can also whip up your own meal in your in-room kitchenette.

Beacon Hill
Hotel & Bistro BOUTIQUE HOTEL $$$
(Map p38; ☑617-723-7575; www.beaconhill hotel.com; 25 Charles St; r $269-349; ℗❋⊛; ⊤Charles/MGH) This upscale European-style inn blends into its namesake neighborhood without flash or fanfare. Carved out of former residential buildings typical of Beacon Hill, the hotel has 12 very small but stylish rooms, decorated with contemporary furniture, louvered shutters and a designer's soothing palette of paint choices. Added

ℹ BOSTON ACCOMMODATIONS BOOKING SERVICES

Even the highest-end hotels post promotions and off-season sales on their websites. Several agencies manage B&Bs and apartments for short-term rental.

LonelyPlanet (www.lonelyplanet.com/usa/boston/hotels) Includes reviews and booking service.

B&B Agency of Boston (www.boston-bnbagency.com) Fully furnished vacation rentals, available for daily, weekly or monthly let.

Bed & Breakfast Associates Bay Colony (www.bnbboston.com) A huge database of unhosted, furnished rooms and apartments.

Inn Boston Reservations (www.innbostonreservations.com) Studios and apartments for rent in Boston's best neighborhoods.

perks include the exclusive roof deck, and complimentary breakfast at the urbane, on-site bistro.

🛏 Downtown & Waterfront

Godfrey Hotel HOTEL $$$
(Map p38; ☑617-804-2000; www.godfreyhotel boston.com; 505 Washington St; d from $339; P🅿✳🛜; T Downtown Crossing) In the heart of downtown Boston, the Godfrey is a recent addition to this revitalized area. The all-new boutique facilities are super-sleek, with lobby and rooms decked out in contemporary whites and golds. Smartphone room entry, smart TVs (with web-streaming capabilities) and Bose speakers are some of the high-tech perks. The on-site George Howell coffee offers a different kind of perk.

Ames Hotel BOUTIQUE HOTEL $$$
(Map p38; ☑617-979-8100; www.ameshotel.com; 1 Court St; r from $369; P✳🛜; T State) It's easy to miss this understated hotel, tucked behind the granite facade of the historic Ames Building (Boston's first skyscraper). Starting in the lobby and extending to the guest rooms, the style is elegant but eclectic, artfully blending modern minimalism and old-fashioned ornamental details. The upper floors yield wonderful views over the city.

Nine Zero BOUTIQUE HOTEL $$$
(Map p38; ☑617-772-5810; www.ninezero.com; 90 Tremont St; r from $309; P✳🛜🐾; T Park St) 🐾 This chic boutique hotel appeals to a broad audience, courting business travelers with a complimentary shoe-shine service and ergonomic workspace; active travelers with complimentary bikes and in-room yoga mats; and animal lovers with Kimpton's signature pet service. All of the above enjoy

excellent customer service and marvelous views of the State House and the Granary from the upper floors.

Harborside Inn BOUTIQUE HOTEL $$$
(Map p38; ☑617-723-7500; www.harborsideinn boston.com; 185 State St; r from $269; P✳@🛜; T Aquarium) Steps from Faneuil Hall and the waterfront, this boutique hotel inhabits a respectfully renovated 19th-century mercantile warehouse. The 116 rooms are on the small side, but are comfortable and appropriately nautically themed. Note that Atrium Rooms face the atrium (ahem) and Cabin Rooms have no windows at all. Add $20 for a city view (worth it).

Omni Parker House HISTORIC HOTEL $$$
(Map p38; ☑617-227-8600; www.omnihotels.com; 60 School St; r from $340; P✳🛜🐾; T Park St) History and Parker House go hand in hand like JFK and Jackie O (who got engaged here). Malcolm X was a busboy here; Ho Chi Minh was a pastry chef here; and Boston cream pie, the official state dessert, was created here. The lovely guest rooms are decorated in rich red and gold tones and equipped with all the high-tech gadgetry.

🛏 West End & North End

La Cappella Suites B&B $$
(Map p38; ☑617-523-9020; www.lacappella suites.com; 290 North St; ste $170-225; ✳🛜; T Haymarket) 'La Cappella' refers to the small chapel of La Societá di San Calogero di Sciacca that previously occupied this redbrick building. Now it is a private home with three spacious guest suites on the upper floors, topped off by a shared roof deck. Look for Italian marble flooring, skyline views and access to a kitchen and common areas.

★ **Liberty Hotel**   HOTEL **$$$**
(Map p38; ☑ 617-224-4000; www.libertyhotel.com;
215 Charles St; r from $350; ℗ ➲ ❋ 🛜; Ⓣ Charles/
MGH) It is with intended irony that the noto-
rious Charles Street Jail has been convert-
ed into the classy Liberty Hotel. Today, the
spectacular lobby soars under a 90ft ceiling.
Guest rooms boast floor-to-ceiling windows
with amazing views of the Charles River and
Beacon Hill, not to mention luxurious linens
and high-tech amenities, such as LCD televi-
sions and iPod docking stations.

Over the years, the jail housed many fa-
mous residents, including the anarchists
Sacco and Vanzetti, black liberationist Mal-
colm X and Boston's own James Michael
Curley. Check out the small exhibit on the
building's history, which is just off the lobby.

Bricco Suites   APARTMENT **$$$**
(Map p38; ☑ 617-459-1293; www.bricco.com; 241
Hanover St; d/ste from $311/350; ❋ 🛜; Ⓣ Hay-
market) Immerse yourself in the Italian
American Boston experience with a stay in
a lovely, light-filled apartment in the heart
of the North End. The DePasquales rent 15
studios and apartments – all of them decked
out with polished hardwood floors, marble
bathrooms, Italian linens and gas fireplaces.
There's no elevator, but it's worth the climb.

🛏 Charlestown

Constitution Inn   HOTEL **$$**
(☑ 617-241-8400; www.constitutioninn.org; 150
Third Ave; d $189-229; ℗ ❋ 🛜 🏊; 🚌 93 from
Haymarket, 🚢 F4 from Long Wharf) Housed in a
granite building in the historic Charlestown
Navy Yard, this excellent, affordable hotel
accommodates active and retired military
personnel, but you don't have to have a crew
cut to stay here. Somewhat institutional, the
rooms are clean and crisp, freshly paint-
ed, and furnished with cherry-wood beds
and desks. Some have kitchenettes. Guests
gain free access to the Olympic-class fitness
center.

🛏 Seaport District & South Boston

Envoy Hotel   DESIGN HOTEL **$$$**
(Map p38; ☑ 617-338-3030; www.theenvoyhotel.
com; 70 Sleeper St; r $303-380; ❋ 🛜 🏊; Ⓣ South
Station) Here's a gorgeous new boutique
hotel perched at the corner where the Fort
Point Channel meets the sea. In the rooms,
floor-to-ceiling windows optimize the van-

tage point, offering wonderful water views.
The interior design is sophisticated and stylish, keeping it simple with colors, but playing with textures, materials and even words.
The rooftop bar is an obvious draw.

Residence Inn Marriott   BOUTIQUE HOTEL **$$$**
(Map p38; ☑ 617-478-0840; www.marriott.com/
hotels/travel/bosfp-residence-inn-boston-down
town-seaport/; 370 Congress St; r $304-364;
℗ ❋ 🛜 🏊; 🚇 SL1, SL2, Ⓣ South Station) This
is not your typical Marriott. Housed in a
historic, brick warehouse, this boutique
hotel now features an old-style atrium and
glass elevators leading up to spectacular,
spacious suites. Twelve-foot ceilings and
enormous windows are in every room, as is
a floor-to-ceiling cityscape mural. King-size
beds, fully equipped kitchens and up-to-
date gadgetry ensure optimal comfort and
convenience.

Seaport Boston Hotel   HOTEL **$$$**
(☑ 617-385-4000; www.seaportboston.com; 1 Sea-
port Lane; r from $314; ℗ ❋ 🛜 🏊; 🚇 SL1, SL2,
Ⓣ South Station) 🌿 With glorious views of the
Boston Harbor, this business hotel is up to
snuff when it comes to high-tech amenities
and creature comforts (eg you decide on
what to lay your head, with a selection from
the 'pillow library'). Soothing tones, plush
linens and robes, and a unique no-tipping
policy guarantee a relaxing retreat.

🛏 South End & Chinatown

HI-Boston   HOSTEL **$**
(Map p38; ☑ 617-536-9455; www.bostonhostel.
org; 19 Stuart St; dm $45-75, d with bath $220;
❋ @ 🛜; Ⓣ Chinatown, Boylston) 🌿 HI-Boston
sets the standard for urban hostels, with
its modern, ecofriendly facility in the historic Dill Building. Purpose-built rooms
are comfortable and clean, as are the
shared bathrooms. Community spaces are
numerous, from fully equipped kitchen
to trendy ground-floor cafe, and there's a
whole calendar of activities on offer. The
place is large, but it books out, so reserve
in advance.

Dorms vary in size (sleeping four to eight
people) and guest gender (male, female or
mixed); prices vary accordingly.

40 Berkeley   HOSTEL **$**
(Map p50; ☑ 617-375-2524; www.40berkeley.
com; 40 Berkeley St; d/tr/q from $110/120/130;
🛜; Ⓣ Back Bay) Straddling the South End
and Back Bay, this safe, friendly hostelry

was the first YWCA in the country. It's no longer a Y, but it still rents some 200 basic rooms (some overlooking the lovely garden) to guests on a nightly and long-term basis. Bathrooms are shared, as are other useful facilities, such as telephone, library, TV room and laundry.

Chandler Inn
HOTEL $$

(Map p50; ✆ 617-482-3450; www.chandlerinn.com; 26 Chandler St; r from $239; ❄ ☎; T Back Bay) Small but sleek rooms show off a designer's touch, giving them a sophisticated, urban glow. Travelers appreciate the plasma TVs and iPod docks, all of which come at relatively affordable prices. As a bonus, congenial staff provide super service. Across the street, the inn rents out 11 newly renovated, modern apartments of various sizes, under the moniker Chandler Studios.

Hotel 140
HOTEL $$

(Map p50; ✆ 617-585-5440; www.hotel140.com; 140 Clarendon St; r from $203; ❄ @ ☎; T Copley, Back Bay) Still something of a hidden hotel bargain, Hotel 140 has gone upscale with a complete overhaul of its classic brick building. Rooms are small but stylish and filled with light. Despite all the upgrades, the best thing about this place is still the friendly, conscientious staff.

Revere Hotel
DESIGN HOTEL $$$

(Map p38; ✆ 617-482-1800; www.reverehotel.com; 200 Stuart St; d from $374; ❄ ☎ ⛱ ❄; T Boylston) It's hard to enter the circular lobby without contemplating the centerpiece Serra-inspired sculpture. But that's just the beginning of the artistic flare at the Revere Hotel, as the rooms are replete with furniture, light fixtures and other contemporary design elements that marry form and function. City views are wonderful, especially from the rooftop lounge.

Chandler Studios
APARTMENT $$$

(Map p50; ✆ 617-482-3450; www.chandlerstudiosboston.com; 54 Berkeley St; ste from $329; ❄ ☎; T Back Bay) Managed by Chandler Inn (p64), these 11 newly renovated, modern apartments are located opposite the hotel. The lodgings are urban chic, with modern wood-and-chrome furniture and B&W wall murals. In-room kitchenettes make the place ideal for longer-term stays. The accommodations are technically unhosted, although reception is right across the street.

🛏 Back Bay

★ Newbury Guest House
GUESTHOUSE $$

(Map p50; ✆ 617-437-7666/8; www.newburyguesthouse.com; 261 Newbury St; d from $239; ❄ ☎; T Hynes, Copley) Dating to 1882, these three interconnected brick and brownstone buildings offer a prime location in the heart of Newbury St. A recent renovation has preserved charming features like ceiling medallions and in-room fireplaces, but now the rooms feature clean lines, luxurious linens and modern amenities. Each morning, a complimentary continental breakfast is laid out next to the marble fireplace in the salon.

Charlesmark Hotel
BOUTIQUE HOTEL $$

(Map p50; ✆ 617-247-1212; www.thecharlesmark.com; 655 Boylston St; r from $239; ❄ ☎; T Copley) The Charlesmark's small but sleek rooms are at the crossroads of European style and functionality. The design is classic modernism, and the effect is urbane and relatively affordable. This hip hotel is backed by a small group of warmly efficient staff that see to every detail. The downstairs lounge spills out onto the sidewalk where the people-watching is tops. Complimentary continental breakfast.

Commonwealth Court Guest House
GUESTHOUSE $$

(Map p50; ✆ 617-424-1230; www.commonwealthcourt.com; 284 Commonwealth Ave; r per night $99-140, per week $400-600; ❄; T Hynes) These 20 rooms with kitchenettes are not super spiffy, but the price is right for this great location. The Euro-style guesthouse is located in a turn-of-the-20th-century brownstone in the heart of Back Bay. Once a private residence, it retains a homey feel and lots of lavish architectural details.

The service is pleasant, but not overly attentive (maid service occurs only twice a week and the office closes in the evenings).

Copley House
APARTMENT $$

(Map p50; ✆ 617-236-8300; www.copleyhouse.com; 239 W Newton St; d/ste from $190/210; ❄ ☎; T Prudential) Straddling the Back Bay and the South End, Copley House occupies four different buildings, offering significant variability between rooms. Generally, antique wood trim and big windows beaming with light make this Queen Anne–style inn a place of respite, while the location makes it a handy base for exploring Boston. The simple kitchenette rooms are not large, but they offer exceptional value.

🛏 Kenmore Square & Fenway

**Oasis Guest House
& Adams B&B** GUESTHOUSE **$$**
(Map p50; ☑ 617-267-2262, 617-230-0105; www.
oasisguesthouse.com; 22 Edgerly Rd; r from $199,
s/d without bath $119/169; P✳✲🛜; T Hynes,
Symphony) These homey side-by-side (joint-
ly managed) guesthouses offer a peace-
ful, pleasant oasis in the midst of Boston's
chaotic city streets. Thirty-odd guest rooms
occupy four attractive, brick, bow-front
town houses on this tree-lined lane. The
modest, light-filled rooms are tastefully and
traditionally decorated, most with queen
beds, floral quilts and nondescript prints.

The common living room does not exactly
encourage lingering, but outdoor decks and
kitchen facilities are nice touches. Compli-
mentary continental breakfast.

★**Verb Hotel** BOUTIQUE HOTEL **$$$**
(Map p50; ☑ 855-695-6678; www.theverbho
tel.com; 1271 Boylston St; r from $250-280;
P✳🛜✲🐾; T Kenmore) The Verb Hotel
took a down-and-out HoJo property and
turned it into Boston's most radical, retro,
rock-and-roll hotel. The style is mid-Century
Modern; the theme is music. Memorabilia is
on display throughout the joint, with a juke-
box cranking out tunes in the lobby. Classy,
clean-lined rooms face the swimming pool
or Fenway Park. A-plus for service and style.

★**Gryphon House** B&B **$$$**
(Map p50; ☑ 617-375-9003; www.innboston.com;
9 Bay State Rd; r $258-305; P✳🛜; T Kenmore)
A premier example of Richardson Roman-
esque, this beautiful five-story brownstone
is a paradigm of artistry and luxury over-
looking the picturesque Charles River.
Eight spacious suites have different styles,
including Victorian, Gothic and arts-and-
crafts, but they all have 19th-century period
details. And they all have home-away-from-
home perks such as entertainment centers,
wet bars and gas fireplaces. Prices include a
delicious breakfast.

🛏 Cambridge

Kendall Hotel BOUTIQUE HOTEL **$$**
(☑ 617-566-1300; www.kendallhotel.com; 350 Main
St; r $198-248; P✳🛜; T Kendall/MIT) Once
the Engine 7 Firehouse, this city landmark
is now a cool and classy all-American hotel.
The 65 guest rooms exhibit a firefighter riff,
alongside the requisite creature comforts.

The place could use some extra help at the
front desk, but at least there's no scrimping
at the breakfast table. The on-site Black
Sheep restaurant is worth visiting for lunch
or dinner, too.

Harding House B&B **$$**
(☑ 617-876-2888; www.harding-house.com; 288
Harvard St; r $210-260, without bath $155-165;
P✳@🛜; T Central) This treasure blends re-
finement and comfort, artistry and efficien-
cy. Old wooden floors toss back a warm glow
and sport throw rugs, with antique furnish-
ings to complete the inviting atmosphere.
Noise does travel in this old house, but the
place is quite comfortable. Other perks:
free parking (!), a thoughtfully designed
continental breakfast and complimentary
museum passes.

Irving House at Harvard GUESTHOUSE **$$**
(Map p54; ☑ 617-547-4600; www.irvinghouse.com;
24 Irving St; r from $225, without bath from $135;
P✳@🛜; T Harvard) 🍃 Call it a big inn or
a homey hotel, this property welcomes the
world-weariest of travelers. The 44 rooms
range in size, but every bed is covered with a
quilt, and big windows let in plenty of light.
There is a bistro-style atmosphere in the
brick-lined basement, where you can browse
its books, plan your travels or munch on free
continental breakfast.

Charles Hotel HOTEL **$$$**
(Map p54; ☑ 617-864-1200; www.charleshotel.com;
1 Bennett St; r from $299; P✳🛜✲; T Harvard)
Calling itself 'the smart place to stay,' this
institution has hosted the university's most
esteemed guests, ranging from Bob Barker
to the Dalai Lama. Guest rooms have been
recently renovated to include sleek Shaker-
style furnishings, Italian marble bathrooms
with TV mirrors, and all the luxuries and
amenities one would expect from a highly
rated hotel. Prime location overlooking the
Charles River.

🍴 Eating

🍴 Beacon Hill
& Boston Common

★**Paramount** CAFETERIA **$**
(Map p38; www.paramountboston.com; 44 Charles
St; mains breakfast & lunch $8-14, dinner $15-
23; ⊙ 7am-10pm Mon-Fri, from 8am Sat & Sun;
🍴♿; T Charles/MGH) This old-fashioned
cafeteria is a neighborhood favorite. A-plus

diner fare includes pancakes, home fries, burgers and sandwiches, and big, hearty salads. Banana and caramel French toast is an obvious go-to for the brunch crowd. Don't sit down until you get your food! The wait may seem endless, but patrons swear it is worth it.

At dinner, add table service and candlelight, and the place goes upscale without losing its down-home charm.

Piperi Mediterranean Grill　MIDDLE EASTERN $
(Map p38; www.piperi.com; 1 Beacon St; mains $6-8; ⊙11am-6pm Mon-Fri, noon-4pm Sat & Sun; 🍴🦽; T Government Center) The concept is simple. Decide whether you want a flat-bread sandwich, salad or meze plate. Choose chicken, steak or veggies as a main ingredient. Then add fresh toppings such as hummus, tabouleh, slaw, cheese etc. Hungry Boston workers line up out the door for this quick, healthy, fresh and affordable lunch; service is efficient so you won't wait long.

Grotto　ITALIAN $$
(Map p38; ☎617-227-3434; www.grottorestaurant.com; 37 Bowdoin St; mains $21-26, 3-course prix-fixe dinner $40; ⊙11:30am-3pm Mon-Fri & 5-10pm daily; T Bowdoin) In a word: romantic. Tucked into a basement on the back side of Beacon Hill, this cozy, cave-like place lives up to its name. The funky decor – exposed-brick walls decked with rotating art exhibits – reflects the innovative menu. Reservations recommended, as the place is tiny.

No 9 Park　EUROPEAN $$$
(Map p38; ☎617-742-9991; www.no9park.com; 9 Park St; mains $42, 3-course prix-fixe dinner $76; ⊙5:30-9pm Sun & Mon, to 10pm Tue-Sat; T Park St) This swanky place has been around for years, but it still tops many fine-dining lists. Chef-owner Barbara Lynch has been lauded by food and wine magazines for her delecta-

ble French and Italian culinary masterpieces and her first-rate wine list. She has now cast her celebrity-chef spell all around town, but this is the place that made her famous. Reservations recommended.

✗ Downtown & Waterfront

Grass Roots Cafe　KOREAN, SANDWICHES $
(Map p38; 101 Arch St; mains $8-10; ⊙6:30am-7pm Mon-Fri; T Downtown Crossing) Here is a surprising hole-in-the-wall Korean gem, where two brothers are serving up traditional deliciousness from their ancestral homeland. Favorites include the Triple B (bi bim bop) and Porky's Nightmare (spicy marinated pork). For less adventurous palates, the all-American sandwiches are well-stuffed and tasty. Fresh ingredients and personable service make this a sure win.

Pedro's Tacos　MEXICAN $
(Map p38; www.pedrostacos.com; 55 Bromfield St; tacos $4-8; ⊙7am-6pm Mon-Fri; 🍴🦽; T Park St) Imagine a sweet, surfside taco shop in Southern California, transplanted to downtown Boston. That's Pedro's, complete with boards on the wall, chilled-out ambience and to-die-for tacos and burritos. The potato taco is one of the cheapest, best lunches around.

Gene's Chinese Flatbread　CHINESE $
(Map p38; 86 Bedford St; sandwiches $4.50, mains $6-11; ⊙11am-6:30am Mon-Sat; T Chinatown) It's not often that we recommend leaving Chinatown for Chinese food, but it's only a few blocks away. And it's worth the detour to this unassuming storefront for chewy Xi'an-style noodles. No 9 (Cumin lamb hand-pulled noodles) seems to be the fan favorite. Seating is limited and credit cards are not accepted.

Chacarero　SANDWICHES $
(Map p38; www.chacarero.com; 101 Arch St; mains $7-10; ⊙11am-6pm Mon-Fri; T Downtown Crossing) A *chacarero* is a traditional Chilean sandwich made with grilled chicken or beef, Muenster cheese, fresh tomatoes, guacamole and the surprise ingredient – steamed green beans. Stuffed into homemade bread, the sandwiches are a longtime favorite for lunch around downtown.

Falafel King　MIDDLE EASTERN $
(Map p38; 48 Winter St; mains $7-9; ⊙11am-8pm Mon-Fri, to 4pm Sat; 🍴; T Downtown Crossing) Two words: free falafels. That's right,

---

TOP PICKS FOR VEGETARIANS

Veggie Galaxy (p73) Your favorite diner fare – all animal-free.

Sweetgreen (p71) Caters to every kind of special diet, as well as people who enjoy fresh, delicious food.

Life Alive (p73) Smoothies, salads and sandwiches that are good for body and soul.

Clover Food Lab (p73) Clover's chickpea fritter is a thing of beauty.

everyone gets a little free sample before ordering. There is no disputing that this carry-out spot is indeed the falafel king of Boston. The food is fast, delicious and cheap, and you're only half a block from a picnic on the Common. If you prefer to sit inside, there's another location nearby on **Summer St** (Map p38; 62 Summer St; mains $7-9; ⊙11am-7:30pm Mon-Fri; ✐; ⊤Downtown Crossing).

Yvonne's MODERN AMERICAN $$$
(Map p38; http://yvonnesboston.com; 2 Winter Pl; ⊙5-11pm, bar to 2am; ✐; ⊤Park) Staff will usher you discreetly through closed doors into this hidden 'modern supper club'. The spectacular space artfully blends old-school luxury with contemporary eclecticism. The menu of mostly small plates does the same, with items from hush puppies to baked oysters to chicken and quinoa meatballs. Yvonne's has revived this historic space, which housed the venerated Lock-Ober restaurant for some 137 years.

🍴 West End & North End

Galleria Umberto PIZZA $
(Map p38; 289 Hanover St; mains $2-5; ⊙11am-2:30pm Mon-Sat; ✐🍴; ⊤Haymarket) Paper plates, cans of soda, Sicilian pizza: can't beat it. This lunchtime legend closes as soon as the slices are gone. And considering their thick and chewy goodness, that's often before the official 2:30pm closing time. Loyal patrons line up early so they are sure to get theirs. Cash only.

Pauli's SANDWICHES $
(Map p38; www.paulisnorthend.com; 65 Salem St; sandwiches $7-9, lobster rolls $16; ⊙8am-9pm Mon-Sat, 9am-5pm Sun; 🛜✐🍴; ⊤Haymarket) If you're in the mood for a 'lobsta roll,' head directly to Pauli's to be served up 7oz of pink succulent goodness, stuffed into a lightly grilled hot-dog roll – just the way it's meant to be. The menu of sandwiches is extensive and most of them are tasty; the California wrap is popular among the health conscious.

Pizzeria Regina PIZZA $
(Map p38; www.pizzeriaregina.com; 11½ Thacher St; pizzas $13-21; ⊙11am-11:30pm, to 12:30am Fri & Sat; ✐🍴; ⊤Haymarket) The queen of North End pizzerias is the legendary Pizzeria Regina, famous for brusque but endearing waitstaff and crispy, thin-crust pizza. Thanks to the slightly spicy sauce (flavored with aged Romano), Regina repeatedly wins accolades

BOSTON'S FOOD TRUCKS

The **Hub Food Trucks** (www.hubfood trucks.com) website is a labor of love of Steve Leibowitz, who loves to eat at food trucks and write about it. He's also got an interactive schedule and other info.

for its pies and pitchers of beer. Reservations are not accepted, so be prepared to wait.

★Pomodoro ITALIAN $$
(Map p38; ✆617-367-4348; 351 Hanover St; mains brunch $12, dinner $23-24; ⊙5-11pm Mon-Fri, noon-11pm Sat & Sun; ⊤Haymarket) Pomodoro has a new (only slightly larger) location, but it's still one of the North End's most romantic settings for delectable Italian. The food is simple but perfectly prepared: fresh pasta, spicy tomato sauce, grilled fish and meats, and wine by the glass. If you're lucky, you might be on the receiving end of a complimentary tiramisu for dessert. Cash only.

Locale PIZZA $$
(Map p38; www.localeboston.com; 352 Hanover St; pizzas $14-18; ⊙4-9:30pm Mon-Fri, noon-10pm Sat, noon-9pm Sun; ✐; ⊤Haymarket) Locale has recently started to appear on lists of Boston's best pizzas. It's a modern affair, with strikingly minimalist decor and some surprising pizza toppings (broccoli rabe, for one). But customers love the bubbly Neapolitan crusts, the specialty combinations and the affordable wines by the glass. The Cacio e Pepe (cheese and pepper) can't be beat.

Daily Catch SEAFOOD $$
(Map p38; www.thedailycatch.com; 323 Hanover St; mains $18-23; ⊙11am-10pm; ⊤Haymarket) Although owner Paul Freddura long ago added a few tables and an open kitchen, this shoebox fish joint still retains the atmosphere of a retail fish market (complete with wine served in plastic cups). Fortunately, it also retains the freshness of the fish. The specialty is *tinta de calamari* (squid-ink pasta). Cash only.

Giacomo's Ristorante ITALIAN $$
(Map p38; www.giacomosblog-boston.blogspot. com; 355 Hanover St; mains $14-19; ⊙4:30-10pm Mon-Thu, 5-11pm Fri & Sat, 4-9:30pm Sun; ✐; ⊤Haymarket) Customers line up before the doors open so they can guarantee themselves a spot in the first round of seating at this North End favorite. Enthusiastic

DON'T MISS

SWEET NORTH END

....

It wouldn't be a night in the North End if you didn't end it with a cannoli or some other sweet thang. Here's where to get yours:

Maria's Pastry (Map p38; www.mariaspastry.com; 46 Cross St; pastries $3-5; ⊙7am-7pm Mon-Sat, to 5pm Sun; ⏴; ⏀Haymarket) Three generations of Merola women are now working to bring you Boston's most authentic Italian pastries, especially *sfogliatelle* (layered, shell-shaped pastry filled with ricotta).

Modern Pastry Shop (Map p38; www.modernpastry.com; 257 Hanover St; sweets $2-4; ⊙8am-10pm Sun-Thu, to 11pm Fri, to midnight Sat; ⏀Haymarket) While crowds of tourists and suburbanites are queuing out the door at Mike's Pastry across the street, pop into the Modern Pastry for divine cookies and cannolis.

Lulu's Sweet Shoppe (Map p38; www.lulussweetshoppeboston.com; 57 Salem St; sweets $2.50-5; ⊙11:30am-9pm; ⏴; ⏀Haymarket) If you prefer cupcakes over cannolis. Red velvet? Boston cream cupcake? Don't take too long to decide or you will annoy the counter staff.

and entertaining waitstaff plus cramped quarters ensure that you get to know your neighbors. The cuisine is no-frills southern Italian fare, served in unbelievable portions. Cash only.

★**Neptune Oyster** SEAFOOD $$$
(Map p38; ☑617-742-3474; www.neptuneoyster.com; 63 Salem St; mains $19-32; ⊙11:30am-10pm Sun-Thu, to 10:30pm Fri & Sat; ⏀Haymarket) Neptune's menu hints at Italian, but you'll also find elements of Mexican, French, Southern and old-fashioned New England. The daily seafood specials and impressive raw bar (featuring several kinds of oysters, plus littlenecks, cherrystones, crabs and mussels) confirm that this is not your traditional North End eatery.

The retro interior offers a convivial – if crowded – setting, with an excellent option for solo diners at the marble bar.

✕ Charlestown

Prescott Restaurant LATIN AMERICAN $
(http://prescottboston.com; 50 Terminal St; mains $8-15; ⊙10am-4pm Mon-Fri, 8am-3pm Sat & Sun; ⏴; ⏹93 from Haymarket, ⏵Inner Harbor Ferry from Long Wharf, ⏀Bunker Hill Community College) Prescott wants to show you the *other* side of Charlestown – the hard-working, blue-collar C-town of immigrants and dock workers. On this menu, fish tacos and breakfast burritos sit alongside banana bread French toast and Caprese omelets. It's all prepared to perfection. You'll find this unexpected gem in a manufacturing

building on the working waterfront. The patio overlooks the loading docks.

★**Brewer's Fork** PIZZA $$
(www.brewersfork.com; 7 Moulton St; small plates $8-14, pizzas $14-18; ⊙5-11:30pm; ⏹93 from Haymarket, ⏵Inner Harbor Ferry from Long Wharf, ⏀North Station) This casual hipster hangout has quickly become a local favorite, thanks to its enticing menu of small plates and pizzas, not to mention the excellent, oft-changing selection of about 30 craft beers. The wood-fired oven is the star of the show, but this place also does amazing things with its cheese and charcuterie boards.

Navy Yard Bistro & Wine Bar FRENCH $$
(www.navyyardbistro.com; cnr Second Ave & Sixth St; mains $18-28; ⊙5-10pm; ⏹93 from Haymarket, ⏵Inner Harbor Ferry from Long Wharf, ⏀North Station) Dark and romantic, this hideaway is tucked into an off-street pedestrian walkway, allowing for comfortable outdoor seating in summer months. Inside, the cozy, carved-wood interior is an ideal date destination – perfect for roasted quail or braised short ribs and other old-fashioned favorites. The menu also features seasonal vegetables and excellent wines.

✕ Seaport District & South Boston

Flour BAKERY, CAFE $
(Map p38; www.flourbakery.com; 12 Farnsworth St; pastries $2-4, salads & sandwiches $7-10; ⊙7am-8pm Mon-Fri, 8am-6pm Sat, 9am-5pm Sun; ⏴⏴; ⏀South Station) ✎ Flour implores patrons

to 'make life sweeter...eat dessert first!' It's hard to resist at this pastry-lover's paradise. If you can't decide – and it can be a challenge – go for the melt-in-your-mouth brioche sticky buns. But dessert is not all: delicious sandwiches, soups, salads and pizzas are also available. Flour is a Certified Green Restaurant.

Yankee Lobster Co
SEAFOOD $

(www.yankeelobstercompany.com; 300 Northern Ave; mains $11-20; ⊘10am-9pm Mon-Sat, 11am-6pm Sun; 🚇SL1, SL2, Ⓣ South Station) The Zanti family has been fishing for three generations, so they definitely know their stuff. A relatively recent addition is this retail fish market, scattered with a few tables in case you want to dine in. And you do. Order something simple like clam chowder or a lobster roll, accompany it with a cold beer, and you will not be disappointed.

★ Row 34
SEAFOOD $$

(Map p38; ☑617-553-5900; www.row34.com; 383 Congress St; oysters $2.50-3, mains lunch $14-18, dinner $16-27; ⊘11:30am-10pm Sun-Thu, to 11pm Fri & Sat; Ⓣ South Station) In the heart of the new Seaport District, this is a 'workingman's oyster bar' (by working man, they mean yuppie). Set in a sharp, post-industrial space, the place offers a dozen types of raw oysters and clams, alongside an amazing selection of craft beers. There's also a full menu of cooked seafood, ranging from the traditional to the trendy.

Legal Harborside
SEAFOOD $$

(www.legalseafoods.com; 270 Northern Ave; mains $13-25; ⊘11am-midnight Fri & Sat; 👪; 🚇SL1, SL2, Ⓣ South Station) This vast glass-fronted waterfront complex offers three different restaurant concepts on three floors. Our favorite is the 1st floor – a casual restaurant and fish market that is a throwback to Legal's original outlet from 1904. The updated menu includes a raw bar, small plates, seafood grills and plenty of international influences. There is outdoor seating in the summer months.

Barking Crab
SEAFOOD $$

(Map p38; www.barkingcrab.com; 88 Sleeper St; sandwiches from $9, mains $17-27; ⊘11:30am-10pm; 🚇SL1, SL2, Ⓣ South Station, Aquarium) Big buckets of crabs (bairdi, king, snow, Dungeness etc), steamers dripping in lemon and butter, paper plates piled high with all things fried, pitchers of ice-cold beer... Devour your feast at communal picnic tables

overlooking the water. Service is slack, noise levels are high, but the atmosphere is jovial. Be prepared to wait for a table if the weather is warm.

✗ South End & Chinatown

Mike & Patty's
SANDWICHES $

(Map p38; www.mikeandpattys.com; 12 Church St; sandwiches $5-10; ⊘7:30am-2pm Wed-Sun; ☑; Ⓣ New England Medical Center, Arlington) Tucked away in Bay Village, this tiny gem of a corner sandwich shop does amazing things between two slices of bread. There are only eight options and they're all pretty perfect, but the hands-down favorite is the Fancy (fried egg, cheddar cheese, bacon and avocado on multigrain). There's always a line but it moves quickly.

Avana Sushi
SUSHI $

(Map p38; www.avanasushi.com; 42 Beach St; sushi & sashimi $4-6; ⊘11am-10pm; Ⓣ Chinatown) This place is essentially unmarked from the street, tucked into a tiny, cramped food court, next to a cell-phone store. There's only a handful of seats, and the tableware is all plastic and styrofoam. But the sushi is fresh and affordable, and service is personable. It's hard to beat.

My Thai Vegan Café
THAI $

(Map p38; 3 Beach St; mains $8-15; ⊘11am-10pm; ☑; Ⓣ Chinatown) This welcoming cafe is up a sketchy staircase, tucked into a sunlit second-story space. It's an animal-free zone – but good enough that meat eaters will enjoy eating here, too. The menu has a Thai twist, offering noodle soups, dumplings, excellent spring rolls and pad thai. The bubble tea gets raves.

Picco
PIZZA $

(Map p50; www.piccorestaurant.com; 513 Tremont St; mains $10-15; ⊘11am-10pm Sun-Wed, to 11pm Thu-Sat; ☑👪; Ⓣ Back Bay) The crust of a Picco pizza undergoes a two-day process of cold fermentation before it goes into the oven and then into your mouth. The result is a thin crust with substantial texture and rich flavor. You can add toppings to create your own pizza, or try the specialty Alsatian (sautéed onions, shallots, garlic, sour cream, bacon and Gruyère cheese).

★ Q Restaurant
ASIAN $$

(Map p38; www.thequsa.com; 660 Washington St; hot pot $12-25; ⊘11:30am-11pm Sun-Thu, to 1am Fri & Sat; 🛜☑👪; Ⓣ Chinatown) Hip and hungry patrons flock to this trendy hot-pot spot in Chinatown. Q is unusual for its spacious interior and upscale atmosphere, but it's also a unique, interactive eating experience. Choose your broth, choose your morsels of meat and veggies, cook them in the pot and eat them as you go.

Toro
TAPAS $$

(Map p50; ☎617-536-4300; www.toro-restaurant. com; 1704 Washington St; tapas $10-15; ☺noon-10pm Mon-Thu, noon-midnight Fri, 5pm-midnight Sat, 10:30am-10pm Sun; ☑; ☐SL4, SL5, ⊤Massachusetts Ave) ✪ True to its Spanish spirit, Toro is bursting with energy, from the open kitchen to the lively bar to the communal butcher-block tables. The menu features simple but sublime tapas – grilled chilies with sea salt, corn on the cob dripping with lemon and butter, and delectable, garlicky shrimp. For accompaniment, take your pick from rioja, sangria or its spiced-up mojitos and margaritas.

Shōjō
ASIAN, FUSION $$

(Map p38; www.shojoboston.com; 9a Tyler St; small plates $7-15; ☺5:30-11pm Mon-Wed, 11am-11pm Thu, 11am-2am Fri & Sat; ⊤Chinatown) Clean, contemporary and super cool, Shōjō is unique in Chinatown for its trendy vibe (and unfortunately loud music). The menu picks and chooses from all over Asia and beyond,

---

BREW HA HA

A few national brews originate right here in Boston. Visit the facilities to see how your favorite beer is made and to partake of free samples.

Samuel Adams (www.samueladams. com; 30 Germania St; donation $2; ☺10am-3pm Mon-Thu & Sat, to 5:30pm Fri; ⊤Stony Brook) One-hour tours depart every 45 minutes. Learn about the history of Sam Adams the brewer and Sam Adams the beer.

Harpoon Brewery (www.harpoon brewery.com; 306 Northern Ave; tours $5; ☺beer hall 11am-7pm Sun-Wed, to 11pm Thu-Sat, tours noon-5pm Sun-Wed, to 6pm Thu-Sat; ☐SL1, SL2, ⊤South Station) Very popular weekend tours of the brewery include a free souvenir beer mug. Alternatively, come during the week for free samples in the tasting room, which offers a view into the brewery at work.

---

effortlessly blending disparate elements into original, enticing, shareable fare. If you're not afraid for your arteries, the duck fat fries are highly recommended.

Myers & Chang
ASIAN $$

(Map p50; ☎617-542-5200; www.myersandchang. com; 1145 Washington St; small plates $10-18; ☺11:30am-10pm Sun-Thu, to 11pm Fri & Sat; ☑; ☐SL4, SL5, ⊤Tufts Medical Center) This superhip Asian spot blends Thai, Chinese and Vietnamese cuisines, which means delicious dumplings, spicy stir-fries and oodles of noodles. The kitchen staff does amazing things with a wok, and the menu of small plates allows you to sample a wide selection of dishes. Dim sum for dinner? This is your place.

Bistro du Midi
FRENCH $$

(Map p38; ☎617-426-7878; www.bistrodumidi. com; 272 Boylston St; mains cafe $12-25, dining room $26-42; ☺cafe 11am-10pm Sun-Wed, to 11pm Thu-Sat, dining room 5-10pm; ⊤Arlington) The upstairs dining room is exquisite, but the downstairs cafe exudes warmth and camaraderie, inviting casual callers to linger over wine and snacks. In either setting, the Provençal fare is artfully presented and simply delicious. Reservations are required for dinner upstairs, but drop-ins are welcome at the cafe all day.

Coppa
ITALIAN $$

(Map p50; ☎617-391-0902; www.coppaboston. com; 253 Shawmut Ave; small plates $10-16, pasta $16-27; ☺noon-10pm, to 11pm Fri & Sat, from 11am Sat & Sun; ☐SL4, SL5, ⊤Back Bay) This South End *enoteca* (wine bar) recreates an Italian dining experience with authenticity and innovation, serving up *salumi* (cured meats), antipasti, pasta and other delicious small plates. Wash it all down with an Aperol spritz and you might be tricked into thinking you're in Venice.

★ O Ya
SUSHI $$$

(Map p38; ☎617-654-9900; www.oyarestaurant boston.com; 9 East St; nigiri & sashimi pieces $8-20; ☺5-10pm Tue-Sat; ☑; ⊤South Station) Who knew that raw fish could be so exciting? At O Ya, each piece of nigiri or sashimi is dripped with something unexpected but exquisite, from honey truffle sauce to banana pepper mousse. Salmon *tataki* is topped with a torched tomato. Foie gras is drizzled in balsamic chocolate *kabayaki* (sweet, soy glaze).

B&G Oysters SEAFOOD $$$

(Map p50; ☑617-423-0550; www.bandgoysters. com; 550 Tremont St; single oysters $3, mains $19-33; ⊙11:30am-11pm Mon-Sat, noon-10pm Sun; ☎; ⊤Back Bay) Patrons flock to this casually cool oyster bar to get in on the raw delicacies offered by chef Barbara Lynch. Sit inside at the marble bar or outside on the peaceful terrace, and indulge in the freshest shellfish from local waters. An extensive list of wines and a modest menu of mains and appetizers (mostly seafood) are ample accompaniment for the oysters.

🍴 Back Bay

Luke's Lobster SEAFOOD $

(Map p50; www.lukeslobster.com; 75 Exeter St; mains $9-16; ⊙11am-9pm Sun-Wed, to 10pm Thu-Sat) Luke Holden took a Maine seafood shack and put it smack-dab in the middle of the Back Bay, so that all the hungry shoppers could get a classic lobster roll for lunch. The place looks authentic, complete with weathered wood interior and nautical decor, but more importantly, the lobster rolls are the real deal – and affordable too. Only lacking sea breezes.

Dirty Water Dough Co PIZZA $

(Map p50; www.dirtywaterdough.com; 222 Newbury St; slices $3-4, pizzas $11-13; ⊙11am-10am Sun-Thu, to 11pm Fri & Sat; ☑📶; ⊤Copley) If there's anything that Bostonians love more than the Standells, it's pizza. That explains why the kids are lining up to get theirs from Dirty Water Dough, where they can get a big slice and a soda for $5. Other perks: locally sourced ingredients, unusual topping combos and gluten-free options, not to mention the Dirty Water IPA.

Flour BAKERY $

(Map p50; www.flourbakery.com; 131 Clarendon St; pastries $3-5, sandwiches $9; ⊙7am-8pm Mon-Fri, 8am-6pm Sat, 9am-5pm Sun; ☎☑📶; ⊤Back Bay/South End) Joann Chang's beloved bakery is taking over Boston. This outlet – on the edge of Back Bay – has the same flaky pastries and rich coffee that we have come to expect, not to mention sandwiches, soups, salads and pizzas. And just to prove there is something for everybody, Flour also sells homemade dog biscuits for your canine friend.

Sweetgreen VEGETARIAN $

(Map p50; www.sweetgreen.com; 659 Boylston St; mains $6-10; ⊙10:30am-10:30pm; ☑📶; ⊤Copley) Vegetarians, gluten-free eaters, health nuts and all human beings will rejoice in the goodness that is served at Sweetgreen. Choose salad or wrap, then custom-design your own; or choose one of the unexpected, delicious, fresh combos that have already been invented, including seasonal specialties. So healthy. So satisfying. So good.

Parish Café SANDWICHES $

(Map p38; www.parishcafe.com; 361 Boylston St; sandwiches $12-15; ⊙11:30-1am, bar to 2am; ☑; ⊤Arlington) Sample the creations of Boston's most famous chefs without exhausting your expense account. The menu at Parish features a rotating roster of salads and sandwiches, each designed by a local celebrity chef, including Jody Adams, Ken Oringer and Tony Maws. The place feels more 'pub' than 'cafe' with a long bar backed by big TVs and mirrors.

★Courtyard MODERN AMERICAN $$

(Map p50; www.thecateredaffair.com/bpl; 700 Boylston St; mains $19-22, tea $32; ⊙lunch 11:30am-2:30pm Mon-Fri, tea 2-4pm Wed-Fri & 11:30am-3pm Sat; ⊤Copley) The perfect destination for an elegant luncheon with artfully prepared food is – believe it or not – the Boston Public Library. Overlooking the beautiful Italianate courtyard, this grown-up restaurant serves seasonal, innovative and exotic dishes (along with a few standards). After 2pm, the Courtyard serves a delightful afternoon tea, with a selection of sandwiches, scones and sweets.

★Lolita Cocina MEXICAN $$

(Map p50; www.lolitatequilabars.com; 271 Dartmouth St; tacos $11-15, mains $17-26; ⊙5pm-1am, bar to 2am; ☑; ⊤Copley) This spicy little Mexican number is full of surprises (which we won't ruin for you). We will reveal that the menu is packed with unusual and enticing Mexican fare that does not disappoint: lobster enchiladas, charred sweet corn and decadent garlic shrimp. Oh, and there's all-you-can-eat tacos for $9 on Monday nights.

By the way, there are no less than eight different margaritas on offer, including the eye-popping Diablo. You'd be forgiven if you skipped dinner and just came here to drink.

Salty Pig ITALIAN $$

(Map p50; www.thesaltypig.com; 130 Dartmouth St; charcuterie $7, mains $13-21; ⊙11:30am-midnight; ⊤Back Bay) With prosciutto, pâté, rillettes, *testa* (head cheese), *sanguinaccio* (blood sausage), *porchetta* (pork shoulder) and more, you'll feel like you're in one of those cultures that eats every part of the animal. The 'Salty Pig Parts' get paired with stinky cheeses and other accompaniments for amazing charcuterie plates. There's pizza and pasta for the less adventurous, and cocktails and craft beers for the thirsty.

Coda
PUB FOOD $$

(Map p50; www.codaboston.com; 329 Columbus Ave; mains lunch $9-13, dinner $13-22; ⊙11:30am-11pm Sun-Thu, to 1am Fri & Sat, from 10:30am Sat & Sun; 🛜; Ⓣ Back Bay) Coda does the essentials, and does them right. The menu changes seasonally, but you'll often find grilled salmon, *steak frites* and bone-in chicken breast, all prepared to perfection. The Coda burger (offered with add-ons to please epicureans) does not disappoint. Understated interior. Hip clientele. Potent cocktails. Good times.

Piattini
ITALIAN $$

(Map p50; www.piattini.com; 226 Newbury St; small plates $9-15, mains $18-25; ⊙11:30am-10pm Sun-Thu, to 11pm Fri & Sat; 🖋; Ⓣ Copley) If you have trouble deciding what to order, Piattini can help. The name means 'small plates,' so you don't have to choose just one. The list of wines by the glass is extensive, each accompanied by tasting notes and fun facts. This intimate *enoteca* and its pleasant patio are delightful settings to sample the flavors of Italy. (Bonus: *gelateria* next door!)

Select Oyster Bar
SEAFOOD $$$

(Map p50; www.selectboston.com; 50 Gloucester St; mains $29-38; ⊙11:30am-9:30pm Sun-Thu, to 10:30pm Fri & Sat; Ⓣ Hynes Convention Center) New England seafood meets Mediterranean flavors at this trendy little oyster bar off Newbury St. The space is delightfully cozy and the menu is innovative and amazing. Unfortunately, it's too expensive to be the 'neighborhood spot' that Chef Michael Serpa is going for, but it's still a charmer. Note the 20% gratuity included on all tabs.

Atlantic Fish Co
SEAFOOD $$$

(Map p50; www.atlanticfishco.com; 761 Boylston St; mains lunch $12-22, dinner $28-38; ⊙11:30am-11pm Sun-Thu, to midnight Fri & Sat; Ⓣ Copley) New England clam chowder in a bread bowl: for a perfect lunch here, that's all you need to know. For nonbelievers, we will add seafood *fra diavolo*, lobster ravioli and local Jonah crabcakes. There's more, of course, and the menu is printed daily to showcase

the freshest ingredients. Enjoy it in the seafaring dining room or on the flower-filled sidewalk patio.

🍴 Kenmore Square & Fenway

★El Pelon
MEXICAN $

(Map p50; www.elpelon.com; 92 Peterborough St; mains $6-8; ⊙11am-11pm; 🖋🖲; Ⓣ Museum) If your budget is tight, don't miss this chance to fill up on Boston's best burritos, tacos and tortas, made with the freshest ingredients. The *tacos de la casa* are highly recommended, especially the *pescado*, made with Icelandic cod and topped with chili mayo. Plates are paper and cutlery is plastic.

Tasty Burger
BURGERS $

(Map p50; www.tastyburger.com; 1301 Boylston St; burgers $5-6; ⊙11am-2am; 🖲; Ⓣ Fenway) Once a Mobil gas station, it's now a retro burger joint, with picnic tables outside and a pool table inside. The name of the place is a nod to *Pulp Fiction,* as is the poster of Samuel L Jackson on the wall. You won't find a halfpound of Kobe beef on your bun, but you will have to agree, 'That's a tasty burger.'

Gyro City
GREEK $

(Map p50; www.gyrocityboston.com; 88 Peterborough St; mains $7-10; ⊙11am-11pm; 🖋🖲; Ⓣ Museum) This authentic *gyrotico* fits right in on Peterborough St (aka Fenway's restaurant row), with cheap, scrumptious, filling food. There are a variety of gyros, each with a delightful twist (eg french fries on the traditional pork gyro) – as well as baklava made by a real live Greek mama. Counter seating inside, patio seating outside.

Sweet Cheeks
BARBECUE $$

(Map p50; www.sweetcheeksq.com; 1381 Boylston St; mains $18-26; ⊙11:30am-10pm Sun-Thu, to 11pm Fri & Sat; 🖲; Ⓣ Kenmore) Fun, casual, noisy and supremely tasty, Sweet Cheeks consistently ranks among Boston's best barbecue places. Besides the recommended pulled pork and beef brisket, there's also crispy fried chicken, creamy mac 'n' cheese and the heavenly Bucket o' Biscuits, served hot and ready for slathering with honey butter. Outdoor seating is pleasant. The place gets packed on game nights.

Tapestry
PIZZA $$

(Map p50; www.tapestry.restaurant; 69 Kilmarnock St; pizzas $16-20, mains $18-28; ⊙5pm-midnight; Ⓣ Museum, Kenmore) A Fenway newcomer, Tapestry is a dual-concept restaurant – two-in-one. In the Expo Kitchen, the chefs are tossing pizzas and shucking oysters in a sharp but casual setting. Meanwhile, the Club Room is a higher-end lounge where guests are sampling innovative New American dishes – most of which will probably require looking up at least one ingredient.

★ **Island Creek Oyster Bar** SEAFOOD $$$
(Map p50; ☑ 617-532-5300; www.islandcreek oysterbar.com; 500 Commonwealth Ave; oysters $2.75-3.50, mains lunch $12-21, dinner $26-38; ☺ 4pm-1am; Ⓣ Kenmore) Island Creek has united 'farmer, chef and diner in one space' – and what a space it is. ICOB serves up the region's finest oysters, along with other local seafood, in an ethereal new-age setting. The specialty – lobster roe noodles topped with braised short ribs and grilled lobster – lives up to the hype.

✕ Cambridge

★ **Life Alive** VEGETARIAN $
(www.lifealive.com; 765 Massachusetts Ave; mains $8-10; ☺ 8am-10pm Mon-Sat, 11am-7pm Sun; ☑ 🖟; Ⓣ Central) ✈ Life Alive offers a joyful, healthful, purposeful approach to fast food. The unusual combinations of animal-free ingredients yield delicious results, most of which come in a bowl (like a salad) or in a wrap. There are also soups, sides and smoothies, all served in a funky, colorful, light-filled space.

Hokkaido Ramen Santouka JAPANESE $
(Map p54; www.santouka.co.jp; 1 Bow St; mains $10-14; ☺ 11am-9:30pm Sun-Thu, to 10:30pm Fri & Sat; Ⓣ Harvard) 'Have a bowl of ramen we dedicated ourselves to.' This worldwide chain is bringing a bit of Japanese simplicity and subtlety to Harvard Sq. Service is pleasant and fast, while the noodles are perfectly satisfying. If you're wondering why the staff occasionally shouts out, they are greeting and sending off their guests.

Night Market ASIAN $
(Map p54; www.nightmkt.com; 75 Winthrop St; dishes $6-12; ☺ 5-10pm Sun-Thu, to 11pm Fri & Sat; ☑) This super-hip, seemingly 'secret', subterranean spot serves up skewers, noodles and other smallish servings that you might find at an Asian market. There's an interesting selection of beers, as well as irresistible sake slushies. The food gets mixed reviews for consistency and authenticity, but everyone loves the clever concept, the graffiti-covered walls and the spot-on service.

Clover Food Lab VEGETARIAN $
(Map p54; www.cloverfoodlab.com; 1326 Massachusetts Ave; mains $8-10; ☺ 7am-midnight Mon-Sat, 9am-10pm Sun; 🖥☑🖟; Ⓣ Harvard) ✈ Clover is on the cutting edge. It's all high-tech with its 'live' menu updates and electronic ordering system. But it's really about the food – local, seasonal, vegetarian food – that is cheap, delicious and fast. How fast? Check the menu. Interesting tidbit: Clover started as a food truck (and still has trucks making the rounds).

Veggie Galaxy DINER $
(www.veggiegalaxy.com; 450 Massachusetts Ave; mains $9-15; ☺ 7am-10pm Mon-Fri, 9am-10pm Sat & Sun; ☑🖟; Ⓣ Central) What does the word 'diner' mean to you? All-day breakfast? Check. Burgers and milkshakes? Check. Counter seating and comfy booths? Got those, too. A circular glass display case showing off desserts? Yes, complete with tangy, delicious lemon-meringue pie. In short, Veggie Galaxy does everything that a diner is supposed to do, but it does it without meat. There's also an amazing vegan bakery – now that's going above and beyond diner duty!

Mr Bartley's Burger Cottage BURGERS $
(Map p54; www.mrbartley.com; 1246 Massachusetts Ave; burgers $10-15; ☺ 11am-9pm Mon-Sat; 🖟; Ⓣ Harvard) Packed with small tables and hungry college students, this burger joint has been a Harvard Sq institution for more than 50 years. Bartley's offers some 30 different burgers; sweet-potato fries, onion rings, thick frappés and raspberry-lime rickeys complete the classic American meal. Be aware that this place is old school: credit cards not accepted; no bathroom on-site.

Miracle of Science Bar & Grill AMERICAN $
(www.miracleofscience.us; 321 Massachusetts Ave; mains $10-14; ☺ 11am-midnight, bar to 1am; Ⓣ Central) With all the decor of your high-school science lab, this bar and grill was a pioneer of chic-geek. The menu takes the form of the periodic table posted on the wall, so you get the idea. Join the MIT wannabes for burgers, kebabs and other grilled fare, as well as a choice selection of beers on tap.

A recent article in *Science News* states that 'service with a smile' is hard on employees and does not increase sales; so don't expect it here.

Cambridge, 1 PIZZA $$

(Map p54; www.cambridge1.us; 27 Church St; pizzas $19-24; ⊙11:30am-midnight; ⊘; ⊤Harvard) Set in the old fire station, this pizzeria's name comes from the sign chiseled into the stonework out front. The interior is sleek, sparse and industrial, with big windows overlooking the Old Burying Ground in the back. The menu is equally simple: pizza, soup, salad, dessert. These oddly shaped pizzas are delectable, with crispy crusts and creative topping combos.

Alden & Harlow MODERN AMERICAN $$$

(Map p54; ☑617-864-2100; www.aldenharlow.com; 40 Brattle St; small plates $13-17; ⊙10:30am-2pm Sat & Sun, 5pm-midnight Sun-Wed, to 1am Thu-Sat; ⊘; ⊤Harvard) This subterranean space is offering a brand-new take on American cooking. The small plates are made for sharing, so everyone in your party gets to sample the goodness. By the way, it's no secret that the 'Secret Burger' is amazing. Reservations are essential. Unfortunately, service suffers when the place get busy, which is often.

Red House MODERN AMERICAN $$$

(Map p54; ☑617-576-0605; www.theredhouse. com; 98 Winthrop St; lunch $13-19, dinner $24-29; ⊙3-11pm Mon, noon-11pm Tue-Sun; ⊘; ⊤Harvard) Formerly known as the Cox-Hicks House, this quaint clapboard house dates to 1802. Reminiscent of an old-fashioned inn, it retains its historic charm with its wide-plank wood floors, cozy layout and functioning fireplace. In summer, the patio overlooks a quiet corner of Harvard Sq. The menu is mostly seafood and pasta; half-portions available. Oysters are two for $1 from noon to 6pm.

♀ Drinking & Nightlife

♀ Beacon Hill & Boston Common

Pressed JUICE BAR

(Map p38; http://pressedboston.com; 120 Charles St; shakes $10, mains $10; ⊙7am-6pm Mon-Fri, 9am-6pm Sat & Sun; ☎; ⊤Charles/MGH) We'll call it a juice bar, since it does make its own juices (out of every fruit and vegetable imaginable) as well as delicious vegan 'superfood shakes.' But the sandwiches and salads also deserve mention. Both your body and your tastebuds will thank you for eating this tasty, healthy fare. Pepita smashed avocado toast is our new favorite food.

21st Amendment PUB

(Map p38; www.21stboston.com; 150 Bowdoin St; ⊙11:30am-2am; ⊤Park St) Named for one of the US Constitution's most important amendments – the one repealing Prohibition – this quintessential tavern has been an ever-popular haunt for overeducated and underpaid statehouse workers to meet up and whinge about the wheels of government. The place feels especially cozy during winter, when you'll feel pretty good about yourself as you drink a stout near the copper-hooded fireplace.

♀ Downtown & Waterfront

Thinking Cup CAFE

(Map p38; www.thinkingcup.com; 165 Tremont St; ⊙7am-10pm Mon-Wed, to 11pm Thu-Sun; ⊤Boylston) ✐ There are a few things that make the Thinking Cup special. One is the French hot chocolate – ooh la la. Another is the Stumptown Coffee, the Portland brew that has earned accolades from coffee drinkers around the country. But the best thing? It's across from the Boston Common, making it a perfect stop for a post–Frog Pond warm-up.

Sip Café CAFE

(Map p38; www.sipboston.com; Post Office Sq; ⊙6:30am-6pm Mon-Fri Apr-Nov, to 5pm Dec-Mar; ⏰; ⊤Downtown Crossing) Enclosed by glass and surrounded by the greenery of Post Office Sq, Sip Café is a delightful place to stop for lunch or a caffeinated beverage. There's outdoor seating in warm weather, but even in winter, the high ceilings and streaming sunlight will warm your heart. As will the George Howell coffee, fresh daily-changing soups and yummy sandwiches.

Highball Lounge COCKTAIL BAR

(Map p38; www.highballboston.com; 90 Tremont St; ⊙5pm-2am; ⊤Park St) Go out to play! Well stocked with board games, the Highball Lounge has yours, whether you're on a date (Connect Four) or in a group (Jenga). The Viewmaster is for looking at the menu, which features local beers, creative cocktails and intriguing snack foods (Tater tot nachos, crispy brussel sprouts). This place will make you feel like a kid again. Except you can drink.

Caffe Nero CAFE

(Map p38; http://us.caffenero.com; 560 Washington St; ⊙6:30am-9:30pm; ☎; ⊤Chinatown, Downtown Crossing) Italian coffee. Antique

Alsatian bar. Comfy couches and cozy fireplace. Cosmopolitan clientele. This place is oozing Old World ambience, and we mean that in the most modern, sophisticated way. Espresso drinks are top-notch, and there's sidewalk seating in warm weather.

West End & North End

Parla COCKTAIL BAR
(Map p38; ☑ 617-367-2824; www.parlaboston. com; 230 Hanover St; ☺ 4pm-midnight Mon-Sat, 11am-midnight Sun; T Haymarket) If you have a hankering for something a little different, duck into this tiny hole-in-the-wall with a retro, Prohibition-era theme. The atmosphere is super-hip and somehow secretive, even though the place is on busy Hanover St. The talented bartender mixes up inventive cocktails, as you would expect in a speakeasy.

The food menu features some intriguing Italian fusion flavors, but the results don't always live up to expectations.

Ward 8 COCKTAIL BAR
(Map p38; www.ward8.com; 90 N Washington St; ☺ 11:30-1am, to 2am Fri & Sat, from 10am Sat & Sun; T North Station) The bartenders at this throwback know their stuff, mixing up a slew of specialty cocktails (including the namesake Ward 8) and serving them in clever thematic containers. The menu also features craft beers and tempting New American cuisine (try the duck wings). The atmosphere is classy but convivial – an excellent addition to the North End–West End scene.

Caffé Vittoria CAFE
(Map p38; www.caffevittoria.com; 290-96 Hanover St; ☺ 7am-midnight; ☎; T Haymarket) A delightful destination for dessert or aperitifs. The frilly parlor displays antique espresso machines and black-and-white photos, with a pressed-tin ceiling reminiscent of the Victorian era. Grab a marble-topped table, order a cappuccino and enjoy the romantic setting. Cash only, just like the olden days.

Charlestown

Pier Six BAR
(www.pier6boston.com; 1 Eighth St, Pier 6; ☺ 11am-1am; ☐ 93 from Haymarket, ☐ Inner Harbor Ferry from Long Wharf, T North Station) Set at the end of the pier behind the Navy Yard, this understated tavern offers one of the loveliest views of the Boston Harbor and city skyline. The food is not that memorable, but it's a fine

place to go to catch some rays on your face, the breeze off the water and to enjoy an ice-cold one from behind the bar.

Warren Tavern PUB
(www.warrentavern.com; 2 Pleasant St; ☺ 11am-1am Mon-Fri, 10am-1am Sat & Sun; T Community College) One of the oldest pubs in Boston, the Warren Tavern has been pouring pints for its customers since George Washington and Paul Revere drank here. It is named for General Joseph Warren, a fallen hero of the Battle of Bunker Hill (shortly after which – in 1780 – this pub was opened). Also recommended as a lunch stop.

Seaport District & South Boston

★**Drink** COCKTAIL BAR
(Map p38; www.drinkfortpoint.com; 348 Congress St; ☺ 4pm-1am; ☐ SL1, SL2, T South Station) There is no cocktail menu at Drink. Instead you have a chat with the bartender, and he or she will whip something up according to your specifications. It takes seriously the art of drink mixology – and you will too, after you sample one of its concoctions. Critics complain about long waits to enter and pretension from the staff, but the ambience is fantastic.

Lookout Rooftop Bar BAR
(Map p38; http://theenvoyhotel.com; Envoy Hotel, 70 Sleeper St; ☺ 4pm-1am seasonal; ☐ SL1, SL2, T South Station) This trendy bar starts filling up almost as soon as it opens, as hotel guests and local workers ascend to the rooftop to take in potent drinks and spectacular views. There's a good chance you'll have to wait to get in, but you can leave your phone number and you'll get a text when you're up.

South End & Chinatown

★**Gallows** PUB
(Map p50; www.thegallowsboston.com; 1395 Washington St; ☺ 5-10pm Mon-Wed, 11:30am-11pm Thu-Sat, 11am-10pm Sun; ☐ SL4, SL5, T Tufts Medical Center) It's a relative newcomer, but already a South End favorite. The dark woody interior is inviting and the bartenders are truly talented. The gastropub grub includes such interesting fare as the 'carpet burger' topped with fried oysters and pickles, the enticing Scotch egg, and scrumptious vegetarian poutine. Solid beer selection, delectable cocktails.

★ **Beehive** COCKTAIL BAR

(Map p50; ☑ 617-423-0069; www.beehiveboston. com; 541 Tremont St; ⊗ 5pm-midnight Mon-Thu, 5pm-2am Fri, 9:30am-2am Sat, 9:30am-noon Sun; T Back Bay) The Beehive has transformed the basement of the Boston Center for the Arts into a 1920s Paris jazz club. This place is more about the scene than the music, which is often provided by students from Berklee College of Music. But the food is good and the vibe is definitely hip. Reservations required if you want a table.

Delux Café BAR

(Map p50; ☑ 617-338-5258; 100 Chandler St; ⊗ 5pm-1am Mon-Sat; T Back Bay) The South End's best – and perhaps only – hipster dive bar. Now under new ownership, this long-standing favorite has been cleaned up (a little), but the decor is still mainly Christmas lights and the atmosphere is still totally laid-back. The kitchen still turns out an incredible grilled cheese sandwich, and it still doesn't accept credit cards.

Jacob Wirth BEER HALL

(Map p38; ☑ 617-338-8586; www.jacobwirth.com; 31-37 Stuart St; ⊗ 11:30am-last guest; ▣; T Boylston) Boston's second-oldest eatery is this atmospheric Bavarian beer hall. The menu features Wiener schnitzel, sauerbraten, potato pancakes and pork chops, but the highlight is the beer – almost 30 different drafts, including Jake's House Lager and Jake's Special Dark. From Thursday to Saturday (from 8pm), Jake hosts a sing-along that rouses the *haus*.

Whisky Saigon CLUB

(Map p38; www.whiskysaigon.com; 116 Boylston St; cover free-$15; ⊗ 9pm-2am Fri & Sat; T Boylston) Whisky Saigon is probably the hottest dance spot in Boston at the time of writing, and with good reason. Who can resist bubbles and fog on the dance floor? It's classy, with upscale decor, good-looking patrons and a top-notch sound system playing mostly electronic dance music. The bottled-water-only policy is a big bone of contention, but the coat check is free.

🍷 Back Bay

Wired Puppy CAFE

(Map p50; www.wiredpuppy.com; 250 Newbury St; ⊗ 6:30am-7:30pm; 🛜; T Hynes) Delicious organic coffee, welcoming atmosphere and free wi-fi or computer use. Surely that's all you need. But there's also the cozy,

exposed-brick interior and the awesome outdoor patio. Plus, lots of love for your four-legged friends.

Club Café GAY

(Map p38; www.clubcafe.com; 209 Columbus Ave; ⊗ 11am-2am; T Back Bay) It's a club! It's a cafe! It's cabaret! Anything goes at this glossy, gay nightlife extravaganza. There is live cabaret in the Napoleon Room five nights a week, while the main dance and lounge area has tea parties, salsa dancing, trivia competitions, karaoke, bingo and good old-fashioned dance parties.

🍷 Kenmore Square & Fenway

★ **Bleacher Bar** SPORTS BAR

(Map p50; www.bleacherbarboston.com; 82a Lansdowne St; ⊗ 11am-1am Sun-Wed, to 2am Thu-Sat; T Kenmore) Tucked under the bleachers at Fenway Park, this classy bar offers a view onto center field. It's not the best place to watch the game, as the place gets packed, but it's a fun way to experience America's oldest ballpark, even when the Sox are not playing. Gentlemen: enjoy the view from the loo!

If you want a seat in front of the window, get your name on the waiting list an hour or two before game time; once seated, diners have 45 minutes in the hot seat.

Hawthorne COCKTAIL BAR

(Map p50; www.thehawthornebar.com; 500a Commonwealth Ave; ⊗ 5pm-2am; T Kenmore) Located in the basement of the Hotel Commonwealth, this is a living room–style cocktail lounge that attracts the city's sophisticates. Sink into the plush furniture and sip a custom cocktail.

🍷 Cambridge

★ **Café Pamplona** CAFE

(Map p54; http://cafepamplona.weebly.com; 12 Bow St; ⊗ 11am-midnight; 🛜; T Harvard) Located in a cozy cellar on a backstreet, this no-frills European cafe is the choice among old-time Cantabrigians. In addition to tea and coffee drinks, Pamplona has light snacks, such as gazpacho, sandwiches and biscotti. The tiny outdoor terrace is a delight in summer.

★ **Beat Brasserie** BAR

(Map p54; www.beatbrasserie.com; 13 Brattle St; ⊗ 11am-midnight Mon-Thu, 11am-2am Fri, 10am-2am Sat, 10am-midnight Sun; T Harvard) This vast, underground bistro packs in

---

LET'S GO OUT TO THE MOVIES!

Catch a flick at one of Boston's historic theaters or academic institutions.

Brattle Theatre (p78) This film lover's *cinema paradiso* features repertory series showcasing particular directors or series.

Coolidge Corner Theatre (www.coolidge.org; 290 Harvard St; tickets $9-11; Ⓣ Coolidge Corner) An art-deco neighborhood palace, this old theater blazes with exterior neon and a line-up of indie fare.

Harvard Film Archive Cinematheque (Map p54; www.hcl.harvard.edu/hfa; 24 Quincy St; tickets $9-12; ⊙ screenings Mon, Wed & Fri-Sun; Ⓣ Harvard) Housed in the esteemed Carpenter Center (designed by Le Corbusier), the Cinematheque presents thoughtful film events, often featuring the filmmakers themselves.

---

good-looking patrons for international food, classy cocktails and live jazz and blues. It's inspired by the Beat Generation writers – and named for a rundown Parisian motel where they hung out – but there's nothing down-and-out about this hot spot.

LA Burdick CAFE
(Map p54; www.burdickchocolate.com; 52d Brattle St; ⊙ 8am-9pm Sun-Thu, to 10pm Fri & Sat; Ⓣ Harvard) This boutique chocolatier doubles as a cafe, usually packed full of happy patrons drinking hot cocoa. Whether you choose dark or milk, it's sure to be some of the best chocolate you'll drink in your lifetime. There are only a handful of tables, so it's hard to score a seat when temperatures are chilly.

☆ Entertainment

Comedy

★ Comedy Studio COMEDY
(Map p54; www.thecomedystudio.com; 1238 Massachusetts Ave; $10-15; ⊙ show 8pm Tue-Sun; Ⓣ Harvard) The 3rd floor of the Hong Kong noodle house contains a low-budget comedy house with a reputation for hosting cutting-edge acts. This is where talented future stars (such as Brian Kiley, who became a writer for Conan O'Brien) refine their racy material. Each night has a different theme; on Tuesday, for instance, you can usually see a weird magic show.

Improv Asylum COMEDY
(Map p38; www.improvasylum.com; 216 Hanover St; tickets $7-27; ⊙ shows 8pm Sun-Thu, 7:30pm, 10pm & midnight Fri & Sat; ♿; Ⓣ Haymarket) A basement theater is somehow the perfect setting for the dark humor spewing from the mouths of this offbeat crew. No topic is too touchy, no politics too correct. While the shows vary from night to night, the standard Mainstage Show mixes up the improv with comedy sketches that are guaranteed to make you giggle.

Laugh Boston COMEDY
(www.laughboston.com; 425 Summer St; $8-25; ⊙ times vary Wed-Sun; ▣ SL1, SL2, Ⓣ South Station) The funny guys over at Improv Asylum decided that Boston needed a few more laughs, so they opened this premier, stand-up comedy club in the Westin Hotel. The place has a swanky, happy atmosphere, and there's programming five nights a week. In addition to local and national acts, there's the legendary, true-story slam, known as The Moth.

Wilbur Theatre COMEDY
(Map p38; www.thewilbur.com; 246 Tremont St; tickets $20-50; Ⓣ Boylston) The colonial Wilbur Theatre dates to 1914, and over the years has hosted many prominent theatrical productions. These days it is Boston's premier comedy club. The smallish house hosts nationally known cut-ups, as well as music acts and other kinds of hard-to-categorize performance. The theater itself could use a refresher but the talent is good.

Cinema

Mugar Omni Theater CINEMA
(Map p38; www.mos.org; Science Museum, Charles River Dam; adult/child $10/8; ♿; Ⓣ Science Park) For total IMAX immersion, check out the space-themed and natural-science-oriented flicks at the Museum of Science's theater. A sweet sound system will have you believing you're actually roving around Mars or being attacked by sharks. Yikes.

Simons IMAX Theatre CINEMA
(Map p38; www.neaq.org; Central Wharf; adult/child $10/8; ⊙ 10am-10pm; ♿; Ⓣ Aquarium) At

the New England Aquarium, this IMAX bad boy plays mostly educational 3-D films on a six-story screen (the largest in the region). Many shows have an underwater theme, so you might find yourself swimming with tropical penguins, breaching with whales or fleeing from hungry sharks.

Brattle Theatre
CINEMA

(Map p54; www.brattlefilm.org; 40 Brattle St; T Harvard) The Brattle is a film lover's *cinema paradiso*. Film noir, independent films and series that celebrate directors or periods are shown regularly in this renovated 1890 repertory theater. Some famous (or infamous) special events include the annual Valentine's Day screening of *Casablanca* and occasional cartoon marathons.

Live Music

★Club Passim
LIVE MUSIC

(Map p54; ☑617-492-7679; www.clubpassim.org; 47 Palmer St; tickets $15-30; T Harvard) Folk music in Boston seems to be endangered outside of Irish bars, but the legendary Club Passim does such a great job booking top-notch acts that it practically fills in the vacuum by itself. The colorful, intimate room is hidden off a side street in Harvard Sq, just as it has been since 1969.

★Wally's Café
BLUES, JAZZ

(Map p50; www.wallyscafe.com; 427 Massachusetts Ave; ⊙noon-2am; T Massachusetts Ave) When Wally's opened in 1947, Barbadian immigrant Joseph Walcott became the first African American to own a nightclub in New England. Old-school, gritty and small, it still attracts a racially diverse crowd to hear jammin' jazz music 365 days a year. Berklee students love this place, especially the nightly jam sessions (6pm to 9pm).

★Red Room @ Café 939
LIVE MUSIC

(Map p50; www.cafe939.com; 939 Boylston St; T Hynes) Run by Berklee students, the Red Room @ 939 has emerged as one of Boston's least predictable and most enjoyable music venues. It has an excellent sound system and a baby grand piano; most importantly, it books interesting, eclectic up-and-coming musicians. Check out wicked local Wednesdays to sample the local sound. Buy tickets in advance at the Berklee Performance Center (p80).

Sinclair
LIVE MUSIC

(Map p54; www.sinclaircambridge.com; 52 Church St; tickets $15-30; ⊙5pm-1am Mon, 11am-1am Tue-Sun; T Harvard) Top-notch small venue to hear live music. The acoustics are excellent and the mezzanine level allows you to escape the crowds on the floor. The club attracts a good range of local and regional bands and DJs.

★Lizard Lounge
LIVE MUSIC

(www.lizardloungeclub.com; 1667 Massachusetts Ave; cover $7-15; ⊙8pm-1am Sun-Wed, 8:30pm-2am Thu-Sat; T Harvard) The underground Lizard Lounge doubles as a jazz and rock venue. The big drawcard is the Sunday-night poetry slam, featuring music by the jazzy Jeff Robinson Trio. Also popular are the Monday open-mic challenge and regular appearances by local favorite Club d'Elf. The bar stocks an excellent list of New England beers, which are complemented by the sweet-potato fries.

★Boston Symphony Orchestra
CLASSICAL MUSIC

(BSO; Map p50; ☑617-266-1200; www.bso.org; 301 Massachusetts Ave; tickets $30-115; T Symphony) Flawless acoustics match the ambitious programs of the world-renowned Boston Symphony Orchestra. From September to April, the BSO performs in the beauteous Symphony Hall (Map p50; www.bso.org; 301 Massachusetts Ave; ⊙tours 4pm Wed & 2pm Sat, reservation required), featuring an ornamental high-relief ceiling and attracting a fancy-dress crowd. In summer months the BSO retreats to Tanglewood in Western Massachusetts.

ⓘ CLASSIC ON THE CHEAP

The Boston Symphony Orchestra (BSO) often offers various discounted ticket schemes, which might allow you to hear classical music on the cheap:

➡ Same-day 'rush' tickets ($9) are available for Tuesday and Thursday evening performances (on sale from 5pm), as well as Friday afternoon performances (on sale from 10am).

➡ Check the schedule for open rehearsals, which usually take place in the afternoon midweek. Tickets are $18 to $30.

➡ Occasionally, discounted tickets are offered for certain segments of the population (eg $20 for under 40s).

Hatch Memorial Shell   CONCERT VENUE
(Map p50; www.hatchshell.com; Charles River Esplanade; T Charles/MGH, Arlington) Free summer concerts take place at this outdoor bandstand on the banks of the Charles River. Most famously, there's Boston's biggest annual music event, the Boston Pops' July 4 concert. But throughout the summer, there are also Friday-night movies, Wednesday-night orchestral ensembles and the occasional oldies concert.

Sports

★ **Fenway Park**   BASEBALL
(Map p50; www.redsox.com; 4 Yawkey Way; bleachers $25-40, grandstand $29-78, box $50-75, tours adult/child $18/12, premium tour $30; T Kenmore) From April to September you can watch the Red Sox play at Fenway Park, the nation's oldest and most storied ballpark. Unfortunately, it is also the most expensive – not that this stops the Fenway faithful from scooping up the tickets. There are sometimes game-day tickets on sale starting 90 minutes before the opening pitch.

New England Patriots   SPECTATOR SPORT
(www.patriots.com) The four-time Super Bowl champs play football in the state-of-the-art Gilette Stadium, which is just 50 minutes south of Boston, but it's hard to get a ticket (most seats are sold to season-ticket holders). From I-93, take I-95 south to Rte 1. Otherwise, direct trains go to Foxborough from South Station.

Boston Celtics   SPECTATOR SPORT
(www.nba.com/celtics) The NBA Boston Celtics play basketball from October to April at TD Garden (www.tdgarden.com).

Performing Arts

★ **Shakespeare on the Common**   THEATER
(Map p38; www.commshakes.org; Boston Common; ☉ 8pm Tue-Sat, 7pm Sun Jul & Aug; T Park St) Each summer, the Commonwealth Shakespeare Company stages a major production on the Boston Common, drawing crowds for (free) Shakespeare under the stars. Productions often appeal to the masses with a populist twist. Thus *The Taming of the Shrew*, set in a North End restaurant.

American Repertory Theater   PERFORMING ARTS
(ART; Map p54; ☑ 617-547-8300; www.american repertorytheater.org; 64 Brattle St; tickets $40-75; T Harvard) There isn't a bad seat in the house at the Loeb Drama Theater, where the

---

> ### ⓘ THEATER DISCOUNTS
>
> **BosTix kiosks** (www.bostix.org; ☉ 10am-6pm Tue-Sat, 11am-4pm Sun) offers discounted tickets to theater productions citywide. Discounts up to 50% are available for same-day purchase: check the website to see what's available. Some (but not all) purchases must be made in person, in cash, at outlets on Copley Sq or at Quincy Market.

prestigious ART stages new plays and experimental interpretations of classics. Artistic Director Diane Paulus encourages a broad interpretation of 'theater,' staging interactive murder mysteries, readings of novels in their entirety and robot operas. The ART's musical productions, in particular, have been racking up the Tonies.

Opera House   LIVE PERFORMANCE
(Map p38; www.bostonoperahouse.com; 539 Washington St; T Downtown Crossing) This lavish theater has been restored to its 1928 glory, complete with mural-painted ceiling, gilded molding and plush velvet curtains. The glitzy venue regularly hosts productions from the Broadway Across America series, and is also the main performance space for the Boston Ballet.

Boston Ballet   DANCE
(☑ 617-695-6950; www.bostonballet.org; tickets $40-100) Boston's skillful ballet troupe performs both modern and classic works at the Opera House. The program varies every year, but during the Christmas season they always put on a wildly popular performance of the *Nutcracker*. Student and child 'rush' tickets are available for $25 two hours before the performance; seniors get the same deal, but only for Saturday and Sunday matinees.

Boston Center for the Arts   THEATER
(Map p50; www.bcaonline.org; 539 Tremont St; T Back Bay) There's rarely a dull moment at the BCA, which serves as a nexus for excellent small theater productions. Over 20 companies present more than 45 separate productions yearly, from comedies and drama to modern dance and musicals. The BCA occupies a complex comprising several buildings, including a cyclorama from 1884 built to display panoramic paintings, a former organ factory and the Mills Gallery.

Berklee Performance Center BLUES, JAZZ
(Map p50; www.berklee.edu/bpc; 136 Massa-chusetts Ave; tickets $8-45; T Hynes) The performance hall at this notable music college hosts a wide variety of performers, from high-energy jazz recitals to songs by smoky-throated vocalists to oddball sets by keyboard-tapping guys who look like their day job is dungeon master.

Shopping

Beacon Hill & Boston Common

December Thieves FASHION & ACCESSORIES
(Map p38; www.decemberthieves.com; 88 Charles St; ⊙11am-7pm Mon-Fri, 10am-6pm Sat, noon-5pm Sun; T Charles/MGH) The intriguing window dressing will lure you into this tiny shop, which showcases designer pieces from Boston and abroad. In addition to stylish women's clothing, handbags and jewelry, you'll also find an eclectic assortment of finely crafted household goods. There's only a few of each item stocked, guaranteeing that your special find will always feel unique.

Eugene Galleries ANTIQUES
(Map p38; www.eugenegalleries.com; 76 Charles St; ⊙11am-6pm Mon-Sat, noon-6pm Sun; T Charles/MGH) This tiny shop has a re-markable selection of antique prints and maps, especially focusing on old Boston. Follow the history of the city's development by examining 18th- and 19th-century maps

and witness the filling-in of Back Bay and the greening of the city. Historic prints highlight Boston landmarks, making for excellent old-fashioned gifts.

Downtown & Waterfront

Brattle Book Shop BOOKS
(Map p38; www.brattlebookshop.com; 9 West St; ⊙9am-5:30pm Mon-Sat; T Park St) Since 1825, the Brattle Book Shop has catered to Bos-ton's literati: it's a treasure trove crammed with out-of-print, rare and first-edition books. Ken Gloss – whose family has owned this gem since 1949 – is an expert on anti-quarian books, moonlighting as a consultant and appraiser (see him on *Antiques Road-show*). Don't miss the bargains on the out-side lot.

Greenway Open Market ARTS & CRAFTS
(Map p38; www.newenglandopenmarkets.com; Rose Kennedy Greenway; ⊙11am-5pm Sat & Sun May-Oct; ☎; T Aquarium) This weekend artist market brings dozens of vendors to display their wares in the open air. Look for unique, handmade gifts, jewelry, bags, paintings, ce-ramics and other arts and crafts – most of which are locally and ethically made. Food trucks are always on hand to cater to the hungry.

Boston Public Market MARKET
(BPM; Map p38; www.bostonpublicmarket.org; 136 Blackstone St; ⊙8am-8pm Wed-Sun May-Jun, daily Jul-Nov, tours 6:30pm Thu & 10:30am Sat; ☎; T Haymarket) A locavore's long-

---

BOOKSTORES OF HARVARD SQUARE

Harvard Sq has long been famous for its used and independent bookstores. There are not as many as there used to be, but there are still enough to fill up your afternoon with browsing. Some of the more unusual bookstores:

Grolier Poetry Bookshop (Map p54; www.grolierpoetrybookshop.org; 6 Plympton St; ⊙11am-7pm Tue & Wed, to 6pm Thu-Sat; T Harvard) Founded in 1927, Grolier is the oldest – and perhaps the most famous – poetry bookstore in the USA.

Harvard Bookstore (Map p54; www.harvard.com; 1256 Massachusetts Ave; ⊙9am-11pm Mon-Sat, 10am-10pm Sun; T Harvard) The university community's favorite place to come to browse (though not officially affiliated with the university).

Raven Used Books (Map p54; www.ravencambridge.com; 23 Church St; ⊙10am-9pm Mon-Sat, 11am-8pm Sun; T Harvard) Its 16,000 books focus on scholarly titles, especially in the liberal arts.

Schoenhof's Foreign Books (Map p54; www.schoenhofs.com; 76a Mt Auburn St; ⊙10am-6pm Mon-Wed, Fri & Sat, to 8pm Thu; T Harvard) Since 1856, Schoenhof's has been pro-viding Boston's foreign-language-speaking literati with reading material in some 700 languages.

time dream-come-true, this daily farmers market – housed in a brick-and-mortar building – gives shoppers access to fresh foodstuffs, grown, harvested and produced right here in New England. Come for seasonal produce, fresh seafood, meats and poultry from local farms, artisan cheeses and dairy products, maple syrup and other sweets. Don't miss the local brews found in Hopsters' Alley.

Haymarket
MARKET

(Map p38; Blackstone & Hanover Sts; ⊗7am-5pm Fri & Sat; Ⓣ Haymarket) Touch the produce at Haymarket and you risk the wrath of the vendors, but nowhere in the city matches these prices on ripe-and-ready fruits and vegetables. And nowhere matches Haymarket for local charm. Operated by the Haymarket Vendors Association, this outdoor market is an outlet for discount produce that was purchased from wholesalers.

Quincy Market
MALL

(Map p38; www.faneuilhallmarketplace.com; ⊗10am-9pm Mon-Sat, to 6pm Sun; 🔊; Ⓣ Haymarket) Once a meat and produce market, now a festive shopping center. The three historic market buildings are home to dozens of shops, some that are national chains and others that are Boston originals. Top spots for souvenirs include **Lucy's League** (Map p38; www.rosterstores.com/lucysleague; North Market, Faneuil Hall; ⊗10am-9pm Mon-Sat, to 6pm Sun; Ⓣ Government Center) for stylish sports gear, **Geoclassics** (Map p38; www.geoclassics.com; North Market, Faneuil Hall; ⊗10am-9pm Mon-Sat, noon-6pm Sun; Ⓣ State) for unique jewelry, and **Make Way for Ducklings** (Map p38; www.makewayforducklings.com; North Market, Faneuil Hall; ⊗10am-9pm Mon-Sat, noon-6pm Sun; Ⓣ Haymarket) for children's books and games.

🏠 West End & North End

William Carlton Workshop
FASHION & ACCESSORIES

(Map p38; www.williamcarltonboston.com; 148a Salem St; ⊗hours vary; Ⓣ Haymarket) Like something out of another era, this old-timey hat shop is littered with artifacts and antiques (including a sewing machine that is actually used to make the hats). The headgear – some of which is custom-made – includes stylish but simple flat caps, baseball caps and work caps, all with retro flare.

North Bennet Street School
ARTS & CRAFTS

(Map p38; www.nbss.org; 150 North St; ⊗9am-3pm Mon-Fri; Ⓣ Haymarket) The North Ben-

---

> ### ℹ️ PAY YOUR SALES TAX – NOT!
>
> There is no sales tax in Massachusetts on clothing up to $175 because – get this – it's a necessity! Now, if we could only convince our frugal partner of the *necessity* of those designer jeans...

---

net Street School has been training craftspeople for over 100 years. Established in 1885, the school offers programs in traditional skills like bookbinding, woodworking and locksmithing. The school's on-site gallery sells incredible handcrafted pieces made by students and alumni. Look for unique jewelry, handmade journals, and exquisite wooden furniture and musical instruments.

Converse Flagship Store
SHOES

(Map p38; converse.com; 140 N Washington St; ⊗10am-7pm Mon-Sat, 11am-6pm Sun; Ⓣ North Station) Occupying the ground level of the Converse world headquarters, this flagship store has a sweet selection of its classic sneakers, including some true originals. Look for a handful of styles with Boston themes – 'Exclusive at Lovejoy Wharf' as they say. Or, you can customize a pair with your own colors and images.

Upstairs is Rubber Tracks, a recording studio where emerging musicians can apply to do their stuff for free.

Salumeria Italiana
FOOD & DRINKS

(Map p38; www.salumeriaitaliana.com; 151 Richmond St; ⊗8am-7pm Mon-Sat, 10am-4pm Sun; Ⓣ Haymarket) Shelves stocked with extra-virgin olive oil and aged balsamic vinegar; cases crammed with cured meats, hard cheeses and olives of all shapes and sizes; boxes of pasta; jars of sauce: this little store is the archetype of North End specialty shops.

Inquire about the Rubio aged balsamic vinegar, produced exclusively for this shop by an artisan in Modena, Italy. Made from Trebbiano grapes and aged in oak barrels, this is the secret ingredient of many North End chefs.

Polcari's Coffee
FOOD & DRINKS

(Map p38; www.polcariscoffee.com; 105 Salem St; ⊗10am-6:30pm Mon-Fri, 9am-6pm Sat; Ⓣ Haymarket) Since 1932, this corner shop is where North Enders have stocked up on their beans. Look for 27 kinds of imported coffee, over 150 spices, and an impressive selection of legumes, grains, flours and loose teas.

DON'T MISS

BOSTON'S BEST ANTIQUE SHOPPING

Cambridge Antique Market (www.marketantique.com; 201 Monsignor O'Brien Hwy; ⊙11am-6pm Tue-Sun; ⓣLechmere) An old warehouse crowded with trash and treasures.

SoWa Vintage Market (Map p50; www.sowavintagemarket.com; 450 Harrison Ave; ⊙10am-4pm Sun, also 5-9pm 1st Fri of month; ⬚SL4, SL5, ⓣTufts Medical Center) Intriguing indoor flea market, open on Sundays.

Marika's Antique Shop (Map p38; 130 Charles St; ⊙10am-5pm Tue-Sat; ⓣCharles/MGH) Beacon Hill classic, hawking antiques for more than 50 years.

Eugene Galleries (p80) Maps, magazines and other old printed matter.

🔒 Seaport District & South Boston

Society of Arts & Crafts　　ARTS & CRAFTS
(www.societyofcrafts.org; 100 Pier 4 Blvd, Suite 200; ⊙10am-6pm Tue-Sat; ⬚SL1, SL2) After spending over a century in its Newbury St location, this prestigious nonprofit gallery has moved to new digs along the South Boston waterfront. With three times as much space, the SAC now has room for a craft library, lectures and workshops, and even more retail and exhibit space, including an outdoor civic plaza.

🔒 South End & Chinatown

★**Bobby From Boston**　　CLOTHING, VINTAGE
(Map p50; http://bobby-from-boston.com; 19 Thayer St; ⊙noon-6pm Tue-Sun; ⬚SL4, SL5, ⓣTufts Medical Center) Bobby is one of Boston's coolest cats. Men from all over the greater Boston area come to the South End to peruse Bobby's amazing selection of classic clothing from another era. This is stuff that your grandfather wore – if he was a very stylish man. Smoking jackets, bow ties, bomber jackets and more.

SoWa Open Market　　HANDICRAFTS, MARKET
(Map p50; www.sowaboston.com; Thayer St; ⊙10am-4pm Sun May-Oct; ⬚SL4, SL5, ⓣTufts Medical Center) Part flea market and part artists' market, this weekly outdoor event is a fabulous opportunity for strolling, shopping and people-watching. More than 100 vendors set up shop under white tents. It's never the same two weeks in a row, but there's always plenty of arts and crafts, as well as edgier art, vintage clothing, jewelry, local farm produce and homemade sweets.

Heist　　FASHION & ACCESSORIES
(Map p50; www.decemberthieves.com; 524 Harrison Ave; ⊙10am-5pm Sun) Well placed to lure in Sunday foot traffic, Heist is a cool collection of designer duds, bags, jewelry and other attractive gear. Carefully sourced from local, national and international designers, the common denominator is quality craftmanship and unique styles. If you can't get here on a Sunday, head to its store December Thieves (p80) on Beacon Hill.

SoWa Sundays　　MARKET
(Map p50; www.sowaboston.com; Harrison Ave; ⊙10am-4pm Sun May-Oct; ⬚SL4, SL5, ⓣTufts Medical Center) Summer Sundays are lively in the South End, which hosts SoWa Sundays from May to October. Three different markets fill the art district's parking lots, hosting the SoWa Open Market for arts and crafts, SoWa Farmers Market for fresh produce and SoWa Vintage Market for antiques and treasures (year-round).

Sault New England　　CLOTHING, GIFTS
(Map p50; www.saultne.com; 577 Tremont St; ⊙10am-7pm Mon-Sat, to 5pm Sun; ⓣBack Bay) Blending prepster and hipster, rustic and chic, this little basement boutique packs in a lot of intriguing stuff. The eclectic mix of merchandise runs the gamut from new and vintage clothing to coffee-table books and homemade terrariums. A New England theme runs through the store, with nods to the Kennedys, *Jaws* and LL Bean.

🔒 Back Bay

Three Wise Donkeys　　CLOTHING
(Map p50; www.facebook.com/ThreeWiseDonkeys; 51 Gloucester St; ⊙11am-6pm Mon-Wed, 11am-8pm Thu-Sat, noon-5pm Sun; ⓣHynes Convention Center) Cool concept, awesome designs and quality product add up to a win. Three Wise Donkeys works directly with artists (some local) who have created the unique artwork that lines the walls. Find a design that you like and they'll print

it on an organic cotton T-shirt in the color and style of your choosing. Made to order in 15 minutes.

International Poster Gallery ART
(Map p50; www.internationalposter.com; 205 Newbury St; ⊘10am-6pm Mon-Sat, noon-6pm Sun; ⊤Copley) This niche gallery stocks thousands of vintage posters from around the world. Thousands. The posters span the globe, with themes ranging from food and drink to travel to political propaganda. They are all there for the browsing, though it's easier to scroll through the online archive, which also offers all kinds of useful information and tips for would-be collectors.

Lunarik Fashions FASHION & ACCESSORIES
(Map p50; www.facebook.com/Lunarik-Fashions -239512945292/; 279 Newbury St; ⊘11am-7pm Mon-Fri, 10am-8pm Sat, noon-6pm Sun; ⊤Hynes) Like a modern woman's handbag, Lunarik is packed with useful stuff, much of it by local designers. Look for whimsical collage-covered pieces by Jenn Sherr, beautiful handcrafted jewelry by Dasken Designs, and the best-selling richly colored leather handbags by Saya Cullinan. Who wouldn't want to pack their stuff into that!

Converse SHOES, CLOTHING
(Map p50; www.converse.com; 348 Newbury St; ⊘10am-7pm Mon-Fri, to 8pm Sat, 11am-6pm Sun; ⊤Hynes) Converse started making shoes right up the road in Malden, MA, way back in 1908. Chuck Taylor joined the 'team' in the 1920s and the rest is history. This retail store carries sneakers, denim and other gear. The iconic shoes come in all colors and patterns; make them uniquely your own at the in-store customization area.

Trident Booksellers & Café BOOKS
(Map p50; www.tridentbookscafe.com; 338 Newbury St; ⊘8am-midnight; 🛜; ⊤Hynes) Pick out a pile of books and retreat to a quiet corner of the cafe to decide which ones you really want to buy. You'll come away enriched, as Trident's stock tends toward New Age titles. But there's a little bit of everything here, as the 'hippie turned back-to-the-lander, turned Buddhist, turned entrepreneur' owners know how to keep their customers happy.

Newbury Comics MUSIC
(Map p50; www.newburycomics.com; 332 Newbury St; ⊘10am-10pm Mon-Sat, 11am-8pm Sun; ⊤Hynes) How does a music store remain rel-evant in the digital world? One word: vinyl. In addition to the many cheap CDs and DVDs, there's a solid selection of new release vinyl. Incidentally, it does sell comic books, as well as action figures and other silly gags. No wonder everyone is having such a wicked good time.

❶ Information

EMERGENCY
Ambulance, Fire & Police (🖉911)

INTERNET ACCESS
Boston Public Library (www.bpl.org; 700 Boylston St; ⊘9am-9pm Mon-Thu, to 5pm Fri & Sat year-round, 1-5pm Sun Oct-May; 🛜; ⊤Copley) Internet access free for 15-minute intervals. Or get a visitor courtesy card at the circulation desk and sign up for one hour of free terminal time. Arrive first thing in the morning to avoid long waits.

Cambridge Public Library (www.cambridge ma.gov/cpl; 449 Broadway; ⊘9am-9pm Mon-Thu, to 5pm Fri & Sat, plus 1-5pm Sun Sep-Jun only; 🛜; ⊤Harvard) The sparkling new glass library has dozens of zippy computers that are free to the public. It's a busy place so you may have to wait your turn.

Wired Puppy (www.wiredpuppy.com; 250 Newbury St; ⊘6:30am-7:30pm; 🛜; ⊤Hynes) Free wireless access and free computer use in case you don't have your own. This is also a comfortable, cozy place to just come and drink coffee.

MEDIA
Boston Globe (www.bostonglobe.com) One of two major daily newspapers, the *Globe* publishes extensive lifestyle and arts coverage, with plenty of entertainment listings.

Boston Herald (www.bostonherald.com) A right-wing daily, competing with the *Globe;* has its own entertainment section.

Boston Magazine (www.bostonmagazine.com) The city's monthly glossy magazine.

Improper Bostonian (www.improper.com) A sassy biweekly distributed free from sidewalk dispenser boxes.

MEDICAL SERVICES
Massachusetts General Hospital (🖉617-726-2000; www.massgeneral.org; 55 Fruit St; ⊘24hr; ⊤Charles/MGH) Arguably the city's biggest and best. It can often refer you to smaller clinics and crisis hotlines.

TOURIST INFORMATION
Boston Common Information Kiosk (GBCVB Visitors Center; Map p38; www.bostonusa.com; Boston Common; ⊘8:30am-5pm; ⊤Park St)

Starting point for the Freedom Trail and many other walking tours.

Cambridge Visitor Information Kiosk (Map p54; www.cambridge-usa.org; Harvard Sq; ⊙9am-5pm Mon-Fri, to 1pm Sat & Sun; ⊤Harvard) Detailed information on current Cambridge happenings and self-guided walking tours.

Greater Boston Convention & Visitors Bureau (GBCVB; ☑888-733-2678; www.bostonusa.com) Has visitor centers at Boston Common and Prudential Center (Map p50; www.prudentialcenter.com; 800 Boylston St; ⊙10am-9pm Mon-Sat, 11am-8pm Sun; ☎; ⊤Prudential).

National Park Service Visitor Center (NPS; www.nps.gov/bost) Downtown (Map p38; Faneuil Hall; ⊙9am-6pm; ⊤State) and Charlestown (p46). Free tours of the Freedom Trail depart from the downtown location. First come first served; arrive at least 30 minutes early.

USEFUL WEBSITES

Boston.com (www.boston.com) The online presence of the *Boston Globe*, with event listings, restaurant reviews, local news, weather and more.

Universal Hub (www.universalhub.com) Bostonians talk to each other about whatever is on their mind (sometimes nothing).

❶ Getting There & Away

Most travelers arrive in Boston by plane, with many national and international flights in and out of Logan International Airport. Two smaller regional airports – Manchester Airport (p434) in New Hampshire and TF Green Airport (p434) near Providence, RI – offer alternatives that are also accessible to Boston and are sometimes less expensive.

Flights, cars and tours can be booked online at lonelyplanet.com/bookings.

AIR

On Massachusetts Route 1A in East Boston, **Logan International Airport** (☑800-235-6426; www.massport.com/logan) has five separate terminals that are connected by the frequent shuttle bus 11. Downtown Boston is just a few miles from the airport and is accessible by bus, subway, water shuttle and taxi.

BOAT

Bay State Cruise Company (www.boston-ptown.com; Commonwealth Pier, Seaport Blvd; round-trip adult/child $88/65; ⬜SL1, SL2, ⊤South Station) Bay State Cruise Company operates ferries between Boston and Provincetown. The 90-minute trip runs three times a day.

Provincetown Ferry (Map p38; www.bostonharborcruises.com; 1 Long Wharf; round-trip adult/child $88/65; ⊙May-Oct; ⊤Aquarium) Boston Harbor Cruises operate ferries between Boston and Provincetown (90 minutes). The schedule varies throughout the season, but it runs three times a day at peak times.

Salem Ferry (Map p38; www.salemferry.com; Central Wharf; round-trip adult/child $45/35; ⊙7am-7pm Mon-Fri, 8am-8pm Sat & Sun May-Oct; ⊤Aquarium) A commuter service between Boston Central Wharf and Salem. The boat docks in Salem, leaving early enough so commuters are in Boston before 8am on weekdays. Check the time of the last return to Boston.

BUS

Buses are most useful for regional destinations, although **Greyhound** (☑617-526-1800, 800-231-2222; www.greyhound.com) operates services around the country. In recent years, there has been a spate of new companies offering cheap and efficient service to New York City (four to five hours).

---

❶ GETTING TO NEW YORK CITY

The infamous 'Chinatown Buses' originated in the late 1990s as an affordable way for Chinese workers to travel to and from jobs. They offered super-cheap tickets between Boston and New York, traveling from Chinatown to Chinatown. Young, savvy travelers caught wind of the bargain transportation, and the phenomenon began to spread. It was crowded and confusing and probably not that safe, but it sure was cheap.

In recent years, more and more companies are running buses on this route; however, they don't always start and end in Chinatown. With competition has come improved service and better safety records, and many offer free wireless service on board. But the prices remain blissfully low, especially if you book well in advance.

Go Bus (www.gobuses.com; Alewife Brook Pkwy; 1 way $18-42; ☎; ⊤Alewife) Buses to New York City depart from Alewife station in Cambridge.

Lucky Star Bus (www.luckystarbus.com; South Station; 1 way $25; ☎) Ten daily departures. Tickets must be purchased at least one hour before departure time.

LOCAL KNOWLEDGE

TRAVEL CHEAPER WITH A CHARLIE CARD

The Charlie in question is a fictional character from the Kingston Trio hit *Charlie on the MTA*. Charlie's sad story was that he could not get off the Boston T (then known as the Metropolitan Transit Authority) because he did not have the exit fare.

Now Charlie has been immortalized – yet again – by the MBTA's fare system: the Charlie Card. The plastic cards are available from the attendant at designated T stations. Once you have a card, you can add money at the automated fare machines; at the turnstile you will be charged $2.25 per ride.

The system is designed to favor commuters and cardholders. If you do not request a Charlie Card, you can purchase a paper fare card from the machine, but the turnstile will charge you $2.75 per ride. Similarly, Charlie Card–holders pay $1.70 to ride the bus, but for those paying cash it's $2.

South Station (Map p38; www.south-station. net; 700 Atlantic Ave; T South Station) For intercity travel, Boston has a modern, indoor, user-friendly bus station at Summer St, conveniently adjacent to the South Station train station and above the red-line T stop.

C&J Trailways (www.ridecj.com; ☎) Runs buses to Newburyport, MA, as well as Portsmouth and Dover, NH.

Concord Coach Lines (www.concordcoachlines. com; ☎) Buses run from Boston up to various destinations in New Hampshire and Maine.

Megabus (www.megabus.com; South Station; 1 way $10-30; ☎) Rates vary depending on the time of day of travel and how far in advance tickets are purchased. In addition to New York, buses go to Burlington and Montpelier, VT; Hartford and New Haven, CT; and Portland, ME.

Peter Pan Bus Lines (www.peterpanbus.com) Peter Pan Bus Lines serves 52 destinations in the northeast, as far north as Concord, NH, and as far south as Washington, DC, as well as Western Massachusetts (where Peter Pan operates on behalf of Greyhound). Fares are comparable to Greyhound.

TRAIN

Most trains operated by **Amtrak** (☎ 800-872-7245; www.amtrak.com; South Station; T South Station) go in and out of South Station. Boston is the northern terminus of the Northeast Corridor, which sends frequent trains to New York (4½ hours), Philadelphia (six hours) and Washington, DC (eight hours). The *Lakeshore Express* goes daily to Buffalo (12 hours) and Chicago (23 hours), while the *Downeaster* goes from North Station to Portland, ME (2½ hours).

ℹ Getting Around

Boston is geographically small and logistically manageable. The sights and activities of principal interest to travelers are contained within an area that's only about 1 mile wide by 3 miles long.

This makes Boston a wonderful walking or cycling city. Otherwise, most of the main attractions are accessible by subway. Some outlying sites require a bus ride. And a few – namely the Boston Harbor Islands – require a boat ride or two.

Incidentally, Boston is a waterside city, and riding in boats is part of the fun. Water shuttles are a convenient transportation option for a few harborside destinations, including the airport.

TO/FROM THE AIRPORT

Bus

The silver line is the MBTA's 'bus rapid transit service.' It travels between Logan International Airport and South Station, with stops in the Seaport District. Silver-line buses pick up at the airport terminals and connect directly to the subway station, so you don't have to buy another ticket for the T.

This is the most convenient way to get into the city if you are staying in the Seaport District or anywhere along the red line (Downtown, Beacon Hill, Cambridge). Prices and hours are the same as the T.

Car & Motorcycle

If you're driving from the airport into Boston or to points north of the city, the Sumner Tunnel ($3.50 toll) will lead you to Storrow Dr or over the Zakim Bridge to I-93 North. To points south of Boston, use the Ted Williams Tunnel ($3.50) to I-93 South. To or from points west, the Mass Pike connects directly with the Ted Williams Tunnel. When you're heading to the airport from downtown Boston, take the Callahan Tunnel. All three tunnels are off I-93 and free when heading inbound.

Subway

The T, or the MBTA subway (p86), is a fast and cheap way to reach the city from the airport. From any terminal, take a free, well-marked shuttle bus (22 or 33) to the blue-line T station called Airport and you'll be downtown within 30 minutes.

ℹ️ BRING YOUR BIKE ON THE T

You can bring bikes on the T (subway), the bus and the commuter rail for no additional fare. Bikes are not allowed on green-line trains or silver-line buses, nor are they allowed on any trains during rush hour (7am to 10am and 4pm to 7pm, Monday to Friday). Bikes are not permitted inside buses, but most MBTA buses have bicycle racks on the outside.

Taxi

Taxi fare from Logan is approximately $25 to downtown Boston, $30 to Kenmore Sq and $35 to Harvard Sq.

Water Shuttle

Water shuttles operate between Logan and the Boston waterfront. In both cases, fares to the North End and Charlestown are twice as much as fares to downtown. Take the free water transportation shuttle bus 66 from the airport terminal to the ferry dock.

BICYCLE

In recent years, Boston has made vast improvements in its infrastructure for cyclists, including painting miles of bicycle lanes, upgrading bike facilities on and around public transportation, and implementing an excellent bike-share program. Boston drivers are used to sharing the roads with their two-wheeled friends (and they are used to arriving *after* their two-wheeled friends, who are less impeded by traffic snarls). Cyclists should always obey traffic rules and ride defensively.

Boston's bike-share program is the **Hubway** (www.thehubway.com; 24/72hr membership $6/12, per 30/60/90min free/$2/4; ⏱24hr). There are more than 160 Hubway stations around Boston, Cambridge, Brookline and Somerville, stocked with 1600 bikes that are available for short-term loan. Purchase a temporary membership at any bicycle kiosk, then pay by the half-hour for bike use (free under 30 minutes). Return the bike to any station in the vicinity of your destination.

The Hubway pricing is designed so a bike ride can substitute for a cab ride (eg to make a one-way trip or run an errand), not for leisurely riding or long trips, which would be expensive. Check the website for a map of Hubway stations.

Helmets are not legally required – except for children under age 17 – but they are recommended and available for purchase at reduced rates through the Hubway website.

BOAT

City Water Taxi (www.citywatertaxi.com; ⏱8am-10pm Mon-Sat, 10am-8pm Sun) Makes on-demand taxi stops at about 15 waterfront points, including Logan International Airport, the Barking Crab, the Seaport District, Long Wharf, Sargents Wharf in the North End and the Charlestown Navy Yard. Call to order a pick-up.

Inner Harbor Ferry (www.mbta.com; 1 way $3.25; ⏱6:30am-8:30pm Mon-Fri, 10am-6:30pm Sat & Sun; ⓣAquarium) The MBTA runs the Inner Harbor Ferry every 15 to 30 minutes between the Charlestown Navy Yard and Long Wharf on the Boston waterfront.

BUS

The **MBTA** (☎617-222-5215; www.mbta.com; per ride $1.70-2.75) operates bus routes within the city. These can be difficult to figure out for the short-term visitor, but schedules are posted on its website and at some bus stops along the routes. The standard bus fare is $2, or $1.70 with a Charlie Card. If you're transferring to the T on a Charlie Card, the bus fare is free.

The silver line, a so-called 'rapid' bus, starts at Downtown Crossing and runs along Washington St in the South End to Roxbury's Dudley Sq. Another route goes from South Station to the Seaport District, then under the harbor to Logan International Airport. This waterfront route costs $2.75 ($2.25 with a Charlie Card), instead of the normal bus fare.

The silver line is different from the regular MBTA buses because it drives in a designated lane (supposedly reducing travel time). More importantly, the silver line starts/terminates inside the South Station or Downtown Crossing subway terminal, so you can transfer to/from the T without purchasing an additional ticket.

SUBWAY (THE T)

The MBTA operates the USA's oldest **subway** (☎617-222-3200; www.mbta.com; per ride $2.25-2.75; ⏱5:30am-12:30am), built in 1897 and known locally as the 'T.' There are four lines – red, blue, green and orange – that radiate from the principal downtown stations: Downtown Crossing, Government Center, Park St and State. When traveling away from any of these stations, you are heading 'outbound.'

Although the MBTA might like you to believe otherwise, the silver line is a bus line with a dedicated traffic lane – not a subway line.

Tourist passes with unlimited travel (on subway, bus or water shuttle) are available for periods of one day ($12) or one week ($21.50). Kids under 11 years ride for free. Passes may be purchased at the Boston Welcome Center on Tremont St and at the following T stations: Park St, Government Center, Back Bay, Alewife, Copley, Quincy Adams, Harvard, North Station,

South Station, Hynes and Airport. For longer stays, you can buy a monthly pass allowing unlimited use of the subway and local bus ($84.50). Otherwise, buy a paper fare card ($2.75 per ride) at any station or a Charlie Card ($2.25 per ride) at designated stations.

At night, the last red-line trains pass through Park St around closing time (depending on the direction), but all T stations and lines are different: check the posting at the station.

TAXI

Cabs are plentiful but expensive. Rates are determined by the meter, which calculates miles. Expect to pay about $15 to $20 between most tourist points within the city limits, without much traffic. If you have trouble hailing a cab, head to any nearby hotel, where they congregate.

TRAIN

The **MBTA commuter rail** (☏ 800-392-6100, 617-222-3200; www.mbta.com) services destinations in the metropolitan Boston area. Trains heading west and north of the city, including to Concord and Salem, leave from bustling North Station on Causeway St. Trains heading south, including to Plymouth and TF Green Airport in Providence, leave from South Station.

Around Boston

📞 781, 978, 508, 339 / POP 4.7 MILLION

Best Places to Eat

➡ Blue Blinds Bakery (p122)

➡ Glenn's Food & Libations (p116)

➡ JT Farnham's (p113)

➡ Life Alive (p99)

➡ Roy Moore Lobster Co (p111)

Best Places to Sleep

➡ Blue (p115)

➡ Inn at Castle Hill (p113)

➡ Lizzie Borden Bed & Breakfast (p117)

➡ Longfellow's Wayside Inn (p97)

➡ Rocky Neck Accommodations (p107)

Why Go?

Boston may be the state capital, but it's not the only town in eastern Massachusetts with traveler appeal. Many nearby places with rich histories, vibrant cultural scenes and unique events merit a visit. Easily accessible from Boston, most of these are ideal day-trip destinations.

The towns surrounding Boston represent every aspect of New England history: Colonial, revolutionary, maritime, literary and industrial. Inspired by intriguing events of the past and spectacular seascapes in the present, writers, artists and filmmakers continue to enrich the region's cultural life. Miles of pristine coastline draw beachcombers and sunbathers. Hikers and cyclists, canoeists and kayakers, bird-watchers and whale-watchers have myriad opportunities to engage with the local active lifestyle.

When to Go
Gloucester

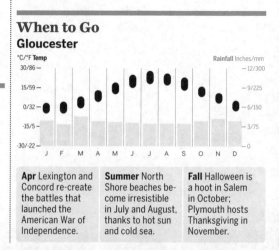

Apr Lexington and Concord re-create the battles that launched the American War of Independence.

Summer North Shore beaches become irresistible in July and August, thanks to hot sun and cold sea.

Fall Halloween is a hoot in Salem in October; Plymouth hosts Thanksgiving in November.

Around Boston Highlights

1 Minuteman Commuter Bikeway (p92) Cycling through history, from Cambridge to Lexington.

2 Gloucester (p105) Hitting the beaches, admiring the art and feasting on seafood.

3 Minute Man National Historic Park (p91) Traversing the park and recalling the beginnings of American independence.

4 Peabody Essex Museum (p100) Admiring the collection of treasures from around the world.

5 Parker River National Wildlife Refuge (p114) Spying on birds and frolicking in the waves at this island sanctuary.

6 Plimoth Plantation (p118) Experiencing the realities of Pilgrim life.

7 Lowell Folk Festival (p98) Enjoying the cultural diversity and lively music in this vibrant immigrant town.

History

The original inhabitants of Massachusetts belonged to several different Algonquian tribes, including the Wampanoag and the Pennacook.

After running aground off the coast of Cape Cod, the Pilgrims established their permanent settlement at Plymouth Colony in 1620. The Puritans followed them in 1628, establishing the Massachusetts Bay Colony on the sites of present-day Boston and Salem. In the following years, daring souls in search of religious freedom or economic opportunity settled all along the coast of Massachusetts.

In the 18th century, discontent simmered in the American colonies, with the independence movement most active in the area around Boston. The War of Independence started with battles in Lexington and Concord.

Eastern Massachusetts also played a crucial role in the country's economic development. During the age of sails and whales, towns such as Salem, Newburyport and New Bedford amassed great wealth from maritime trade, shipbuilding and whaling. Later, Lowell was an exemplary textile town, instigating the industrial revolution. Villages on Cape Ann – especially Gloucester – were leaders in the fishing industry.

With the decline of these sectors in the 20th century, the area has turned to tourism to pick up the economic slack, with varying degrees of success. In an attempt to revitalize their aging city centers, Salem, Lowell and New Bedford have created National Historic Sites, turning old industrial buildings into museums and opening restaurants and cafes to cater to tourists. Gloucester, too, touts its working waterfront as a heritage center, where visitors can book a whale-watching tour or learn about marine life.

National & State Parks

The region around Boston includes several diverse sites – significant to the region's revolutionary, mercantile and industrial past – that have been designated National Historic Parks by the National Park Service (NPS).

Adams National Historic Park (p116) Includes the birthplace of two US presidents (John Adams and John Quincy Adams), as well as the Adams family homestead in Quincy.

Minute Man National Historic Park (p91) Incorporates Battle Rd between Lexington and Concord, where the first skirmishes of the American Revolution developed into full-blown fighting. This area remains much as it was 200 years ago.

Lowell National Historic Park (p98) A leader in the industrial revolution, Lowell now hosts museums and tours dedicated to its history.

Salem Maritime National Historic Site (p100) This North Shore town shows off its maritime roots, with ships, docks, captains' homes and a customs house, all preserved from the 18th century.

State efforts to limit intrusive development and preserve ecosystems include the following:

Sandy Point State Reservation (p115) A delightfully pristine beach located at the southern tip of Plum Island, most of which is protected by the federally managed Parker River Wildlife Refuge.

Walden Pond (p96) An inspirational, wonderful natural resource managed by the Commonwealth of Massachusetts; the acres of undisturbed woods around it are protected by the efforts of private institutions.

Blue Hills Reservation Just a few miles south of Boston, this little-known but much-appreciated park is the work of the Massachusetts Department of Conservation and Recreation.

ⓘ Getting There & Away

Many of the sights around Boston are accessible by the **Massachusetts Bay Transportation Authority commuter rail** (MBTA; ☑ 800-392-6100, 617-222-3200; www.mbta.com). Trains depart from Boston's North Station to destinations on the North Shore, including Gloucester, Rockport, Newburyport and Salem. North Station is also the departure point for trains heading west to Concord and Lowell. Plymouth is served by trains departing from South Station in Boston. Other destinations can be reached by bus, but it's preferable to use a private vehicle to get the most from a trip out of the city.

WEST OF BOSTON

Some places might boast about starting a revolution, but Boston's western suburbs can actually make the claim that two revolutions were launched here. Most famously, the American Revolution – the celebrated War of Independence that spawned a nation – started with encounters on the town greens at Lexington and Concord. And the industrial revolution – the economic transformation that would turn this new nation from agriculture to manufacturing – began in the textile mills of Lowell.

Lexington

📞 781, 339 / POP 31,400

This upscale suburb, about 18 miles from Boston's center, is a bustling village of white churches and historic taverns, with tour buses surrounding the village green. Here, the skirmish between patriots and British troops jump-started the War of Independence. Each year on April 19, historians and patriots don their 18th-century costumes and grab their rifles for an elaborate re-enactment of the events of 1775.

While this history is celebrated and preserved, it is in stark contrast to the peaceful, even staid, community that is Lexington today. If you stray more than a few blocks from the green, you could be in Anywhere, USA, with few reminders that this is where it all started. Nonetheless, it is a pleasant enough Anywhere, USA, with restaurants and shops lining the main drag, and impressive Georgian architecture anchoring either end.

◉ Sights

★ Minute Man National Historic Park   PARK

(www.nps.gov/mima; 250 North Great Rd, Lincoln; ☺9am-5pm Apr-Oct; 🚼) FREE The route that British troops followed to Concord has been designated the Minute Man National His-toric Park. The visitors center at the eastern end of the park shows an informative multimedia presentation depicting Paul Revere's ride and the ensuing battles. Within the park, Battle Rd is a 5-mile wooded trail that connects the historic sites related to the battles – from Meriam's Corner, where gunfire erupted while British soldiers were retreating, to the Paul Revere capture site.

Minute Man National Historical Park is about 2 miles west of Lexington center on Rte 2A.

Battle Green   HISTORIC SITE

(Massachusetts Ave) The historic Battle Green is where the skirmish between patriots and British troops jump-started the War of Independence. The Lexington Minuteman Statue (crafted by Henry Hudson Kitson in 1900) stands guard at the southeastern end of Battle Green, honoring the bravery of the 77 minutemen who met the British here in 1775, and the eight who died.

The Parker Boulder, named for their commander, marks the spot where the minutemen faced a force almost 10 times their strength. It is inscribed with Parker's instructions to his troops: 'Stand your ground. Don't fire unless fired upon. But if they mean to have a war, let it begin here.' Across the street, history buffs built a replica of the Old Belfry that sounded the alarm signaling the start of the revolution.

Buckman Tavern   MUSEUM

(www.lexingtonhistory.org; 1 Bedford Rd; adult/child $8/5; ☺9:30am-4pm mid-Mar–Nov) Facing the Battle Green, the 1709 Buckman Tavern was the headquarters of the minutemen. Here, they spent the tense hours between the midnight call to arms and the dawn arrival of the Redcoats. Today, the tavern has been

AROUND BOSTON LEXINGTON

PATRIOTS' DAY

The Patriots' Day (www.battleroad.org) celebration in Lexington starts early – really early. On the third Monday in April, as dawn breaks, local history buffs are assembled on the village green, some decked out in 'redcoats', while others sport the scruffy attire of minutemen, firearms in hand, ready to reenact the fateful battle that kicked off the American War of Independence.

Later in the day, the conflict at Old North Bridge in Concord is reenacted, as are skirmishes at Meriam's Corner and Hartwell Tavern in Minute Man National Historic Park. Spectators can witness the arrival of Paul Revere in Lexington, as well as his capture along Battle Rd.

Massachusetts is one of only two states in the USA that recognize Patriots' Day as a public holiday. This is where the action went down on April 19, 1775. And this is where it goes down every year on the third weekend of April. See the website for a complete schedule of events.

restored to its 18th-century appearance, complete with bar, fireplace and bullet holes resulting from British musket fire.

A combined ticket with Munroe Tavern and Hancock-Clarke House (p92) is $15/8 per adult/child.

Munroe Tavern   HISTORIC SITE
(www.lexingtonhistory.com; 1332 Massachusetts Ave; adult/child $8/5; ⊗ noon-4pm Jun-Oct) One mile east of the Battle Green, this historic tavern is named for the 18th-century proprietor, William Munroe, who was also an orderly sergeant in the minuteman brigade that fought on April 19, 1775. Later that day, the tavern was occupied by British troops, who raided the provisions and used the dining room as a field hospital. Nowadays, many Munroe family heirlooms and other Revolution-era relics are on display.

Hancock-Clarke House   HISTORIC SITE
(www.lexingtonhistory.org; 36 Hancock St; adult/child $8/5; ⊗ 10am-4pm Jun-Oct) This 1737 house was the home of Reverend John Hancock (grandfather of *the* John Hancock, the Declaration signer). On the night of April 18, 1775, the good Reverend hosted John Hancock and Samuel Adams in this parsonage. The house now has an exhibit of the personal items of Reverend Hancock and his successor, Reverend Jonas Clarke.

🏃 Activities

★ Minuteman
Commuter Bikeway   CYCLING
The Minuteman Commuter Bikeway follows an old railroad right-of-way from near the Alewife Red Line subway terminus in Cambridge through Arlington to Lexington and Bedford, a total distance of about 14 miles. From Lexington center, you can also ride along Massachusetts Ave to Rte 2A, which parallels the Battle Rd trail, and eventually leads into Concord center.

👉 Tours

Liberty Ride   BUS
(www.libertyride.us; adult/child $28/12; ⊗ 10am-4pm daily Jun-Oct, Sat & Sun Apr & May) If you don't have your own wheels, consider catching the Liberty Ride, a hop-on, hop-off trolley, which includes all of the major sites in both Lexington and Concord. Buy tickets at the Lexington Visitors Center.

🍴 Eating & Drinking

Via Lago Café   CAFE $
(www.vialagocatering.com; 1845 Massachusetts Ave; mains $6-10; ⊗ 7am-8pm Mon-Sat; 🚲 🛗) This cafe has high ceilings, intimate tables, a scent of fresh-roasted coffee and a great deli case. You'll often see cyclists in here kicking back with the daily paper, a cup of exotic java or tea, and a sandwich of roast turkey, Swiss cheese and sprouts.

Rancatore's Ice Cream   ICE CREAM $
(www.rancs.com; 1752 Massachusetts Ave; ⊗ 10am-11pm; 🚲) Cool off with a scoop of homemade ice cream or sorbet from this family-run place. Some of Ranc's flavors inspire worshipful devotion, such as bourbon butter pecan and classic coconut. The hot-fudge sundaes are also legendary.

Ride Studio Cafe   CAFE
(www.ridestudiocafe.com; 1720 Massachusetts Ave; ⊗ 7am-7pm Mon-Fri, 8am-6pm Sat & Sun) Part bike store, part cafe, this is a novel concept. Come hang out with other cyclists, browse the gear and drink invigorating coffee. A perfect stop pre-, post- or midride.

ℹ Information

Lexington Visitors Center (Lexington Chamber of Commerce; www.lexingtonchamber. org; 1875 Massachusetts Ave; ⊗ 9am-5pm) Opposite Battle Green, next to Buckman Tavern.

ℹ Getting There & Away

BICYCLE
The most enjoyable way to get to Lexington – no contest – is to come by bicycle via the Minuteman Commuter Bikeway. It's about 6.5 miles from Cambridge to Lexington, and another 5 miles to Bedford.

BUS
MBTA (www.mbta.com) buses 62 (Bedford VA Hospital) and 76 (Hanscom Field) run from the Red Line Alewife subway terminus through Lexington center at least hourly on weekdays, less frequently on Saturday; there are no buses on Sunday.

CAR & MOTORCYCLE
Take MA 2 west from Boston or Cambridge to exit 54 (Waltham St) or exit 53 (Spring St). From I-95 (MA 128), take exit 30 or 31.

Concord

☑ 978 / POP 17,700

On April 18, 1775, British troops marched out of Boston, searching for arms that colonists had hidden west of the city. The following morning, they skirmished with Colonial minutemen in Lexington, then continued on to Concord, where the rivals faced off at North Bridge, in the first battle of the War of Independence.

Today, tall, white church steeples rise above ancient oaks, elms and maples, giving Concord a stateliness that belies the revolutionary drama that occurred centuries ago. Indeed it's easy to see how writers such as Ralph Waldo Emerson, Nathaniel Hawthorne, Henry David Thoreau and Louisa May Alcott found their inspiration here. Concord was also the home of famed sculptor Daniel Chester French (who went on to create the Lincoln Memorial in Washington, DC).

These days travelers can relive history in Concord. Patriots' Day (p91) is celebrated with gusto, and many significant literary sites are open for visitors.

◎ Sights

★ **Old North Bridge**   HISTORIC SITE
(www.nps.gov/mima; Monument St; ⊙ dawn-dusk)
FREE A half-mile north of Memorial Sq in Concord center, the wooden span of Old North Bridge is the site of the 'shot heard around the world' (as Emerson wrote in his poem *Concord Hymn*). This is where enraged minutemen fired on British troops, forcing them to retreat to Boston. Daniel Chester French's first statue, *Minute Man,* presides over the park from the opposite side of the bridge.

On the far side of the bridge, the Buttrick mansion contains the visitor center (p97), where you can see a video about the battle and admire the Revolutionary War brass cannon, the Hancock. On your way up to Old North Bridge, look for the yellow **Bullet Hole House** (Elisha Jones House; 262 Monument St), at which British troops purportedly fired as they retreated from North Bridge.

Concord Museum   MUSEUM
(www.concordmuseum.org; 200 Lexington Rd; adult/child $10/5; ⊙ 9am-5pm Mon-Sat, noon-5pm Sun Apr-Dec, 11am-4pm Mon-Sat, 1-4pm Sun Jan-Mar; ⊕) Southeast of Monument Sq, Concord Museum brings the town's diverse history under one roof. The museum's prized possession is one of the 'two if by sea' lanterns that hung in the steeple of the Old North Church in Boston as a signal to Paul Revere. It also has the world's largest collection of Henry David Thoreau artifacts, including his writing desk from Walden Pond. Scavenger hunts and other activities make this little museum a great destination for kids.

WORTH A TRIP

FRUITLANDS MUSEUMS

Fruitlands Museums (www.fruitlands.org; 102 Prospect Hill Rd, Harvard; adult/child $14/6, grounds only $6/3; ⊙ 11am-4pm Mon & Wed-Fri, 10am-5pm Sat & Sun Apr-Oct) is a beautifully landscaped, 210-acre property that was the site of Bronson Alcott's short-lived experiment in communal living. The original hillside farmhouse was used by Alcott and his utopian 'Con-Sociate' (communal) family. Other museums have since been moved to the estate, including the 1794 Shaker House, a Native American museum and a gallery featuring paintings by 19th-century itinerant artists and Hudson River School landscape painters. There are also several miles of walking trails through picturesque woods and farmland.

In the early 19th century, Concordian thinkers were at the forefront of transcendentalism, a philosophical movement that espoused that God 'transcends' all people and things. Bronson Alcott (1799–1888), educational reformer and father of Louisa May Alcott, was a leader among this group pursuing transcendental ideals. Toward this end, he founded Fruitlands, an experimental vegetarian community (read: commune).

Nowadays, Fruitlands hosts all kinds of special events, including a summer concert series. One of the highlights is the Fruitlands Tearoom. Dine alfresco, and soak up the fresh air and fabulous scenery.

Fruitlands is in Harvard, about 30 miles west of Boston. Take Rte 2 to exit 38A, Rte 111, then take the first right onto Old Shirley Rd.

Concord

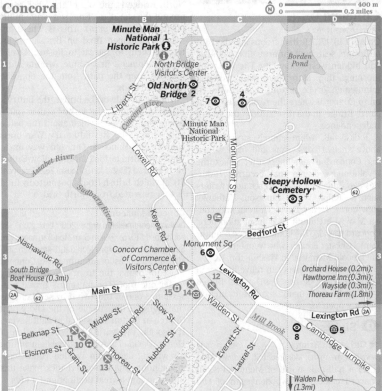

★ **Sleepy Hollow Cemetery** CEMETERY
(www.friendsofsleepyhollow.org; Bedford St;
☉7am-6pm) This is the final resting place
for the most famous Concordians. Though
the entrance is only a block east of Monument Sq, the most interesting part, **Authors' Ridge**, is a 15-minute walk along
Bedford St. Henry David Thoreau and
his family are buried here, as are the Alcotts and the Hawthornes. Ralph Waldo
Emerson's tombstone is a large, uncarved
rose-quartz boulder, an appropriate transcendentalist symbol.

★ **DeCordova Museum
& Sculpture Park** MUSEUM
(www.decordova.org; 51 Sandy Pond Rd, Lincoln;
adult/child $14/free; ☉10am-5pm; ⓜ) The
magical DeCordova Sculpture Park encompasses 35 acres of green hills, providing a
spectacular natural environment for a con-
stantly changing exhibit of outdoor artwork.

As many as 75 pieces are on display at any
given time. Inside the complex, a museum
hosts rotating exhibits of sculpture, painting, photography and mixed media. From
Concord, drive east on Rte 2 and turn right
on Bedford Rd.

Discovery Museums MUSEUM
(www.discoverymuseums.org; 177 Main St, Acton;
$12.50; ⓜ) The Discovery Museums consist
of two unique side-by-side museums – both
great for children. Occupying an old Victorian house, the **Children's Museum** (☉9am-
4:30pm Jun-Aug, closed Mon Sep-May) invites
kids to play make-believe, cooking up some
eats in a bite-size diner, hunting for wildlife
on safari, conducting a toy train and more.

The **Science Museum** (☉1-4:30pm Tue-
Sun Sep-May, 10am-4:30pm Jun-Aug) is for
slightly older kids, but it's equally playful,
with hands-on exhibits such as earth science
and an inventor's workshop.

Concord

Wayside   HOUSE
(455 Lexington Rd; adult/child $7/5; ⊙10am-
4:30pm Mon & Thu-Sat, 1-4:30pm Sun Jun-Aug,
Mon, Fri & Sun only Sep & Oct) Also known as
the 'Home of Authors,' this gracious colonial
mansion was home to three writers of note
during the 19th century. Louisa May Alcott,
Nathaniel Hawthorne and Harriet Lothrop
(Margaret Sidney) all stayed here at different times. The tour focuses on the history
of the house, with an eye to ways that these
socially conscious writers sustained the spirit of the revolution, eg the Alcotts' role in the
abolitionist movement at the Underground
Railroad.

Orchard House   HISTORIC SITE
(www.louisamayalcott.org; 399 Lexington Rd;
adult/child $10/5; ⊙10am-4:30pm Mon-Sat,
1-4:30pm Sun Apr-Oct, 11am-3pm Mon-Fri, 10am-
4:30pm Sat, 1-4:30pm Sun Nov-Mar) Louisa May
Alcott (1832–88) was a junior member of
Concord's august literary crowd, but her
work proved to be durable: *Little Women* is
among the most popular young-adult books
ever written. The mostly autobiographical
novel is set in Concord. Take a tour of Alcott's childhood home, Orchard House, to
see how the Alcotts lived and where the
novel was actually written.

**Ralph Waldo Emerson
Memorial House**   HISTORIC SITE
(28 Cambridge Turnpike; adult/child $9/7; ⊙10am-
4:30pm Thu-Sat, 1-4:30pm Sun mid-Apr–Oct) This
house is where the philosopher lived for almost 50 years (1835–82). Emerson was the
paterfamilias of literary Concord, one of
the great literary figures of his age and the
founding thinker of the transcendentalist
movement. The house often hosted his renowned circle of friends and still contains
many original furnishings.

Old Manse   HISTORIC SITE
(www.thetrustees.org; 269 Monument St; adult/child
$10/5; ⊙noon-5pm Tue-Sun May-Oct, Sat & Sun
only Mar, Apr, Nov & Dec) Right next to Old North
Bridge, the Old Manse was built in 1769 by
Ralph Waldo's grandfather, Reverend William Emerson. Today it's filled with mementos, including those of Nathaniel and Sophia
Hawthorne, who lived here for a few years.
The highlight of Old Manse is the gorgeously
maintained grounds – the fabulous organic
garden was planted by Henry David Thoreau
as a wedding gift to the Hawthornes.

Monument Square   SQUARE
The grassy center of Monument Sq is a favorite resting and picnicking spot for cyclists touring Concord's scenic roads. At the
southeastern end of the square is **Wright
Tavern**, one of the first places the British
troops searched in their hunt for arms on
April 19, 1775. It became their headquarters
for the operation.

Old Hill Burying Ground, with graves
dating from colonial times, is on the hillside
at the southeastern end of Monument Sq.

Thoreau Farm   HISTORIC SITE
(www.thoreaufarm.org; 341 Virginia Rd; adult/child
$6/free; ⊙tours 11am, 1pm & 3pm Sat May-Oct)
Fans of Thoreau can travel off the beaten
path to the house where he was born, which
is about 4 miles east of Concord center.
Henry David lived in his grandmother's
farmhouse for only a few months after his
birth, but the rural retreat would prove influential and inspirational throughout his
life. The grounds are still an inviting place
for exploration and reflection.

🏃 Activities

The placid Concord River and the country
roads are excellent for canoeing and cycling. The 90-minute Liberty Ride (p92)
covers the town's major minuteman sites as

well as some of Concord's places of literary importance.

South Bridge Boat House
CANOEING

(☑978-369-9438; www.southbridgeboathouse.com; 502 Main St; rental per hour $16-18, tours adult/child $65/55; ☉10am-dusk Apr-Oct) A mile west of Monument Sq, you can rent canoes or kayaks for paddling the Concord and Assabet Rivers. The favorite route is downstream to Old North Bridge, and back past the many fine riverside houses and the campus of prestigious Concord Academy – a paddle of about two hours. The tour follows a similar route and includes a picnic lunch.

🐦 Tours

Concord Bike Tours
CYCLING

(www.concordbiketours.com; adult/child $50/35) Highly recommended bicycle tours explore different themes of Concord's history, such as revolutionary sites, Concord authors or the Underground Railroad. This is a great way to see Battle Rd. Guides are knowledgeable and entertaining, the scenery is marvelous and the riding is not too rigorous for novice cyclists.

Concord Guides
HISTORY

(☑978-369-3120; www.concordguides.com; adult/child/student/youth $19/7/15/12; ☉1pm Fri, 11am & 1pm Sat, noon Sun Apr-Oct) The chamber of commerce offers tours of revolutionary, literary and colonial Concord. Tours depart from the Colonial Inn; reservations required.

🛏 Sleeping

While there is a paucity of hotels and motels in Concord, travelers will find dozens of B&Bs in the area. Get a complete list from the Concord Chamber of Commerce.

North Bridge Inn
INN $$

(☑888-530-0007; www.northbridgeinn.com; 21 Monument St; ste $200-235, apt $300; 🅿❄🤖) Six suites are decked out with down comforters, plush pillows, tiled bathrooms and kitchenettes. A hearty breakfast is served in the sun-filled morning room. All guests are warmly welcomed by the resident corgi.

Hawthorne Inn
B&B $$$

(☑978-369-5610; www.concordmass.com; 462 Lexington Rd; r $279-359; 🅿❄🤖) The artist owners here have put their passion and skill into turning their home into a creative sanctuary, with gardens filled with flowers and figures, china cabinets packed with kitschy collectibles and rooms adorned in luxury. Homemade gourmet breakfasts served on hand-painted pottery are a highlight.

🍴 Eating

Concord Cheese Shop
DELI $

(www.concordcheeseshop.com; 29 Walden St; sandwiches $8-12; ☉10am-5:30pm Tue-Sat; ☑) This is a cheese shop, as it claims, with an excellent selection of imported and local cheese, as well as wine and other specialty food items. But the folks behind the counter can whip those ingredients into an amazing sandwich

---

DON'T MISS

WALDEN POND

I went to the woods because I wished to live deliberately, to front only the essential facts of life, and see if I could not learn what it had to teach, and not, when I came to die, discover that I had not lived.

So wrote Henry David Thoreau about his time at **Walden Pond** (www.mass.gov/dcr/parks/walden; 915 Walden St; parking $8-10; ☉dawn-dusk) **FREE**. Thoreau took the naturalist beliefs of transcendentalism out of the realm of theory and into practice when he left the comforts of the town and built himself a rustic cabin on the shores of the pond. His famous memoir of his time spent there, *Walden; or, Life in the Woods* (1854), was full of praise for nature and disapproval of the stresses of civilized life – sentiments that have found an eager audience ever since.

The glacial pond is now a state park, surrounded by acres of forest preserved by the Walden Woods project, a nonprofit organization. It lies about 3 miles south of Monument Sq, along Walden St (MA 126) south of MA 2. There's a swimming beach and facilities on the southern side, and a footpath that circles the large pond (about a 1.5-mile stroll). The **site of Thoreau's cabin** is on the northeastern side, marked by a cairn and signs. The park gets packed when the weather is warm; the number of visitors is restricted, so arrive early in summer.

(or soup or salad) – perfect for a picnic on Memorial Sq. Or you can find a spot in the cozy (but comfortable) seating area.

Bedford Farms   ICE CREAM $
(www.bedfordfarmsicecream.com; 68 Thoreau St; ice cream from $4; ☺11am-9:30pm Mar-Nov, noon-6pm Dec-Feb; 🚻) Dating to the 19th century, this local dairy specializes in delectable ice cream, and frozen yogurt that tastes like delectable ice cream. If prices seem a tad high, it's because the scoops are gigantic. Its trademark flavor is Moosetracks (vanilla ice cream, chocolate swirl, peanut-butter cups). Conveniently located next to the train depot.

Haute Coffee   CAFE $
(www.myhautecoffee.com; 12 Walden St; mains $6-10; ☺7am-5pm Mon-Fri, from 8am Sat & Sun; 🛜✏) Here's a sweet coffee shop serving rich Counter Culture coffee, ground and brewed to order. If you're hungry, there are simple, delicious soups, sandwiches and tartines. The baked goods and pastries are made inhouse and they're pretty irresistible.

Country Kitchen   SANDWICHES $
(www.facebook.com/Country-Kitchen-160160267379702/; 181 Sudbury Rd; sandwiches $5-10; ☺6am-4pm Mon-Fri; 🚻) At lunchtime, this little yellow house often has a line out the door, which is testament to its tiny size, as well as its amazing sandwiches. The Thanksgiving sandwich is the hands-down favorite, with roast turkey carved straight off the bird. It doesn't accept credit cards and there's no seating, save the picnic table out front.

80 Thoreau·   MODERN AMERICAN $$$
(✏978-318-0008; www.80thoreau.com; 80 Thoreau St; mains $23-32; ☺5:30-10:30pm Mon-Thu, 5-11:30pm Fri & Sat) Understated and elegant, this modern restaurant is an anomaly in historic Concord – but that's a good thing. The menu – short but sweet – features deliciously unexpected combinations of flavors, mostly using seasonal, local ingredients. There's also a busy bar area, which offers a concise selection of classic cocktails and long list of wines suitable for pairing.

🛍 Shopping

Concord Bookshop   BOOKS
(www.concordbookshop.com; 65 Main St; ☺9:30am-6pm Mon-Sat, noon-5pm Sun) An independent bookstore packed with good reads and especially featuring local authors.

WORTH A TRIP

LONGFELLOW'S WAYSIDE INN

Made famous by Longfellow's collection of poems *Tales of a Wayside Inn*, Longfellow's Wayside Inn (✏978-443-1776; www.wayside.org; 76 Wayside Inn Rd, Sudbury; d incl breakfast $140-185; ❋🛜) offers 10 period rooms and lovely landscaped grounds. Also on-site is an extensive archive of the history of the inn, which has been operating since 1716, making it the oldest functioning inn in the country. It's 13 miles south of Concord on US 20.

The on-site restaurant is also recommended for old-fashioned New England cuisine, including Indian pudding for dessert.

ℹ Information

Concord Chamber of Commerce & Visitors Center (www.concordchamberofcommerce.org; 58 Main St; ☺10am-4pm Apr-Oct) Concord Chamber of Commerce has full details on sites, including opening hours for the homes, which vary with the season.

North Bridge Visitor's Center (www.nps.gov/mima; Liberty St; ☺9am-5pm Apr-Oct, to 3pm Tue-Sat Mar & Nov-Dec) On the far side of the bridge, the Buttrick mansion contains the NPS visitor center, where you can see a video about the Battle of Concord and admire the Revolutionary War brass cannon, the Hancock. Along with the skirmish at Lexington, the face-off at North Bridge was the first major clash between British regulars and Colonial minutemen.

ℹ Getting There & Away

CAR & MOTORCYCLE

Driving west on MA 2 from Boston or Cambridge, it's some 20 miles to Concord. Coming from Lexington, follow signs from Lexington Green to Concord and Battle Rd, the route taken by the British troops on April 19, 1775.

TRAIN

MBTA commuter rail (p90) trains run between Boston's North Station and Concord ('the Depot'; $8.50, 40 minutes, 12 daily) in either direction on the Fitchburg/South Acton line.

Lowell

✏978 / POP 108,900

In the early 19th century, textile mills in Lowell churned out cloth by the mile, driven by the abundant waterpower of Pawtucket

Falls. Today, the city at the confluence of the Concord and Merrimack Rivers doesn't have such a robust economy, but its historic center recalls the industrial revolution glory days – a working textile mill, canal boat tours and trolley rides evoke the birth of America as an industrial giant.

In modern Lowell, 25 miles north of Boston, an influx of Southeast Asian immigrants has diversified the culture (and cuisine) of this classic New England mill town. A short walk from the historic center into the ethnic neighborhood known as the Acre reveals that Lowell has definitely changed from the city it was 150 years ago.

Lowell was the birthplace of two American cultural icons: painter James Abbott McNeill Whistler and writer Jack Kerouac.

◎ Sights

Lowell National Historic Park   HISTORIC SITE
(✚) The historic buildings in the city center – connected by the trolley and canal boats – constitute the national park, which gives a fascinating peek at the workings of a 19th-century industrial town. Stop first at the Market Mills Visitors Center to pick up a map and check out the general exhibits. An introductory multimedia video on historic Lowell is shown every half-hour.

Five blocks northeast along the river, the fascinating **Boott Cotton Mills Museum** (www.nps.gov/lowe; 115 John St; adult/child/student $6/3/4; ⊘9:30am-5pm; ✚) has exhibits that chronicle the rise and fall of the industrial revolution in Lowell, including technological changes, labor movements and immigration. The highlight is a working weave room, with 88 power looms. A special exhibit on **Mill Girls & Immigrants** (40 French St; ⊘11am-5pm Jun-Sep, 1:30-5pm Oct-Nov) **FREE** examines the lives of working people.

Whistler House Museum of Art   MUSEUM
(www.whistlerhouse.org; 243 Worthen St; adult/child $10/7; ⊘11am-4pm Wed-Sun) James McNeill Whistler's birthplace, built in 1823, is the home of the Lowell Art Association. It houses a small collection of work by New England artists, including some etchings by Whistler himself. Outside, an 8ft bronze statue of the artist by sculptor Mico Kaufman is the centerpiece of the Whistler Park and Gardens.

Whistler House is on the western side of the Merrimack Canal, two blocks west of the Market Mills Visitors Center.

Jack Kerouac Commemorative   MEMORIAL
(Bridge St) Dedicated in 1988, the Jack Kerouac Commemorative features a landscaped path where excerpts of the writer's work are posted, including opening passages from his five novels set in Lowell. They are thoughtfully displayed with Catholic and Buddhist symbols, representing the belief systems that influenced him. The memorial is northeast of the visitor center along the Eastern Canal.

Edson Cemetery   CEMETERY
(cnr Gorham & Saratoga Sts) Two miles south of Lowell center, Kerouac is buried in the Sampas family plot at Edson Cemetery. His grave remains a pilgrimage site for devotees who were inspired by his free spirit.

New England Quilt Museum   MUSEUM
(www.nequiltmuseum.org; 18 Shattuck St; adult/senior & student $7/5; ⊘10am-4pm Tue-Sat, noon-4pm Sun May-Oct, 10am-4pm Wed-Sat Nov-Apr) This little museum has found its niche. The friendly, knowledgeable staff members show off a collection of over 150 antique and contemporary quilts from around New England. Rotating exhibits highlight thematic work such as Japanese quilts, appliqué quilts and the Red Sox (of course). Great gift shop.

Brush Art Gallery & Studios   GALLERY
(www.thebrush.org; 256 Market St; ⊘11am-4pm Tue-Sat, noon-4pm Sun) This gallery and studio space was founded by the local historical commission – with support from the federal government – as part of the city's ongoing revitalization efforts. Stop by to see exhibits and meet the resident artists.

☞ Tours

NPS Tours   BOATING
(www.nps.gov/lowe; canal tours adult/child $12/8, walking tours free; ⊘10am-3pm Jun-Oct) Canal tours are offered throughout summer, with themes such as Engineering Innovations and Working the Water. The schedule varies according to season and water level. Park rangers also lead free walking tours of Lowell Cemetery, the Acre and the Riverwalk.

★⁵ Festivals & Events

Lowell Folk Festival   MUSIC
(www.lowellfolkfestival.org; ⊘Jul) Three days of food, music (on six stages!), parades and other festivities honoring the diverse multicultural community that Lowell has become.

Lowell Celebrates Kerouac   LITERATURE
(LCK; www.lowellcelebrateskerouac.org; ⊙Oct) A
local nonprofit organization hosts four days
of events dedicated to Beat writer Jack Kerouac, featuring tours of many places in his
novels, as well as panel discussions, readings,
music and poetry. Literature buffs travel
from around the world for this unique event.

🛏 Sleeping

There aren't many places to stay in Lowell,
or reasons to stay here. However, if you must
spend the night, a few options meet standard needs.

**UMass Lowell Inn
& Conference Center**   HOTEL $
(📞877-886-5422; www.acc-umlinnandconference
center.com; 50 Warren St; r from $129; ❈🔊🏊)
Located in the heart of downtown Lowell
overlooking the canals. Some rooms have
scenic views of the Merrimack, and all
rooms are freshly renovated with standard
amenities.

🍴 Eating & Drinking

⭐**Life Alive**   VEGETARIAN $
(www.lifealive.com; 194 Middle St; meals $8-10;
⊙10am-8pm Mon-Sat, to 6pm Sun; 🍴) 🌿
Scrumptious salads, fresh, fantastic food and
jubilant juices fill out the menu at this funky
cafe. The choices can be overwhelming, but
you can't go wrong with the signature dish
known as 'The Goddess': veggies and tofu
served over rice with a zinger ginger nama

shoyu sauce. The food is healthy and veg
friendly; the setting is arty and appealing.

Arthur's Paradise Diner   DINER $
(112 Bridge St; meals $6-10; ⊙7am-noon; 🚹) The
epitome of 'old school,' this place is open
only for breakfast and lunch and specializes
in something called the Boot Mill sandwich
(egg, bacon, cheese and home fries on a
grilled roll). Housed in an authentic Worcester Diner Car #727.

Worthen House   PUB
(www.worthenhousecafe.com; 141 Worthen St;
⊙11am-2am) This brick tavern (Lowell's oldest, dating to 1834) is famed for its amazing pulley-driven fan system (which is still
operational). The pressed-tin ceiling and
wooden bar remain from the early days,
giving this place an old-fashioned neighborhood feel. Stop by for a pint of Guinness
and a burger.

ℹ Information

Market Mills Visitors Center (www.nps.gov/
lowe; 246 Market St, Market Mills; ⊙9am-5pm)
Starting place for Lowell National Historical
Park.

ℹ Getting There & Around

BUS
The **Lowell Regional Transit Authority** (www.
lrta.com) runs a shuttle bus that departs every
15 minutes from the Downtown Transit Center,
stopping near the museums and visitor center.

LOCAL KNOWLEDGE

CAMBODIAN CUISINE IN LOWELL

Adventurous eaters can delve into Lowell's interior to discover authentic, delicious
Khmer cuisine.

Heng Lay (www.facebook.com/HengLayRestaurant/; 153 Liberty St; mains $8-15; ⊙8am-8pm
Thu-Tue) A half-mile west of the train station, this is Lowell's newest favorite family-run
Cambodian restaurant, serving up big bowls of Phnom Penh noodles to satisfied cus-
tomers. Accommodating service with a smile is a hallmark of this place.

Red Rose Restaurant (716 Middlesex St; mains $8-15; ⊙8am-8pm) In a word: authentic.
As in Khmer-speaking waitstaff and delicious, adventurous food straight from Phnom
Penh. If you don't know what to order, try the *loc lac:* cubes of beef marinated in soy
sauce, grilled or fried, and served with a lime dipping sauce. The Red Rose is about three
blocks west of the train station.

Simply Khmer (www.simplykhmerrestaurant.com; 26 Lincoln St; mains $10-18; ⊙4-9pm
Tue, 10am-9pm Wed-Sun) When TV personality Andrew Zimmern wanted to sample some
Bizarre Foods from Cambodia, this is where he came. The place was popular before
that, though, thanks to its approachable menu. The restaurant is southwest of the train
station, off Chelmsford St.

CAR & MOTORCYCLE
From I-495, follow the Lowell Connector to its end at exit 5-C to reach the city center.

TRAIN
MBTA commuter rail (p90) trains depart Boston's North Station for Lowell ($9.25). Trains go in either direction 10 times a day during the week, four times on weekends. Trains from Boston terminate at the Gallagher Transportation Terminal on Thorndike St, a 15-minute walk southwest of the city center (or take the shuttle).

NORTH SHORE

The entire coast of Massachusetts claims a rich history, but no part offers more recreational, cultural and dining diversions than the North Shore of Boston. Salem was among America's wealthiest ports during the 19th century; Gloucester is the nation's most famous fishing port; and Marblehead remains one of the premier yachting centres. Trade and fishing have brought wealthy residents, sumptuous houses, and great collections of art and artifacts to the area. Explore the region's rich maritime history and spectacular coastal scenery, and don't miss the opportunity for a seafood feast.

Salem

📣 978 / POP 42,500

This town's very name conjures up images of diabolical witchcraft and people being burned at the stake. The famous Salem witch trials of 1692 are ingrained in the national memory. Indeed, Salem goes all out at Halloween, when the whole town dresses up for parades and parties, and shops sell all manner of Wiccan accessories.

These incidents obscure Salem's true claim to fame: its glory days as a center for clipper-ship trade with the Far East. Elias Hasket Derby, America's first millionaire, built Derby Wharf, which is now the center of the Salem Maritime National Historic Site.

Today Salem is a middle-class commuter suburb of Boston with an enviable location on the sea. Its rich history and culture, from witches to ships to art, continue to cast a spell of enchantment on all those who visit.

◎ Sights

The 1.7 mile **Heritage Trail** is a route connecting Salem's major historic sites. Follow the red line painted on the sidewalk.

★**Peabody Essex Museum** MUSEUM
(www.pem.org; 161 Essex St; adult/child $20/free; ◷10am-5pm Tue-Sun; ▣) All of the art, artifacts and curiosities that Salem merchants brought back from the Far East were the foundation for this museum. Founded in 1799, it is the country's oldest museum in continuous operation. The building itself is impressive, with a light-filled atrium, and it's a wonderful setting for the vast collections, which focus on New England decorative arts and maritime history.

Predictably, the Peabody Essex is particularly strong on Asian art, including pieces from China, Japan, Polynesia, Micronesia and Melanesia. The collection from preindustrial Japan is rated as the best in the world. **Yin Yu Tang** (adult/child $5/free) is a Chinese house that was shipped to the museum from China's southeastern Huizhou region.

The interactive **Art & Nature Center** has games and exhibits specifically designed for children, while age-specific 'Gallery Discovery Kits' make the other exhibits intriguing for little ones.

Salem Maritime
National Historic Site HISTORIC SITE
(www.nps.gov/sama; 193 Derby St; ◷9am-5pm) **FREE** This National Historic Site comprises the Custom House, the wharves and other buildings along Derby St that are remnants of the shipping industry that once thrived along this stretch of Salem. Of the 50 wharves that once lined Salem Harbor, only three remain, the longest of which is **Derby Wharf**. Check the website for a schedule of guided tours of the various buildings, or download an audio walking tour of the whole area.

The most prominent building along Derby St is the **Custom House**, where permits and certificates were issued and, of course, taxes paid. Other buildings at the site include warehouses, the scale house and **Elias Hasket Derby's home**. Climb aboard the **tall ship Friendship** on Derby Wharf and stop by the **West India Goods Store**, a working store with spices and other items similar to those sold two centuries ago.

Chestnut Street HISTORIC SITE
Lovers of old houses should venture to Chestnut St, which is among the most architecturally lovely streets in the country. (Alternatively, follow the McIntire Historic District Walking Trail.) One of these stately homes is the **Stephen Phillips Memorial**

DON'T MISS

WITCH CITY

The city of Salem embraces its witchy past with a healthy dose of whimsy. But the history offers a valuable lesson about what can happen when fear and frenzy are allowed to trump common sense and compassion.

By the time the witch hysteria of 1692 had finally died down, a total of 156 people had been accused, 55 people had pleaded guilty and implicated others to save their own lives, and 14 women and six men who would not confess had been executed. Stop by the **Witch Trials Memorial** (Charter St), a simple but dramatic monument that honors the innocent victims.

Now for the whimsy. After remembering this very real tragedy, you can head over to the **TV Land statue** (cnr Washington & Essex Sts) to have your picture taken with Samantha Stephens, the spell-casting, nose-twitching beauty from the classic show *Bewitched*.

Trust House (www.phillipsmuseum.org; 34 Chestnut St; adult/child/senior & student $8/4/7; ⊙11am-4pm Tue-Sun Jun-Oct, Sat & Sun Nov-May), which displays the family furnishings of Salem sea captains, including a collection of antique carriages and cars.

House of the Seven Gables HISTORIC SITE
(www.7gables.org; 54 Turner St; adult/child/teen $13/8/10; ⊙10am-7pm Jul-Oct, to 5pm Nov-Jun) 'Halfway down a by-street of one of our New England towns stands a rusty wooden house, with seven acutely peaked gables facing towards various points of the compass, and a huge clustered chimney in their midst.' So wrote Nathaniel Hawthorne in his 1851 novel *The House of Seven Gables*.

The novel brings to life the gloomy Puritan atmosphere of early New England and its effects on the people's psyches; the house does the same. Look for wonderful seaside gardens, many original furnishings and a mysterious secret staircase.

★ **Witch House** HISTORIC SITE
(Jonathan Corwin House; www.witchhouse.info; 310 Essex St; adult/child $8.25/4.25, tour extra $2; ⊙10am-5pm Mar-Nov) Of more than a score of witchy attractions in town, this is the only actual historic site. The house was once the home of Jonathan Corwin, a local magistrate who was called on to investigate witchcraft claims. He examined several accused witches, possibly in the 1st-floor rooms of this house. The house demonstrates the family's daily life at the time of the witch hysteria, providing historical context for the episode. Open longer hours in October.

☞ Tours

Due to Salem's witch history, there is an unusual interest in the paranormal, as evidenced by the many spooky tours on offer.

Hocus Pocus Tours HISTORY
(www.hocuspocustours.com; adult/child $16/8) It's called Hocus Pocus, but it's not hokey (or pokey). This is an informative, historically accurate overview of Salem's sordid past, given by an enthusiastic and entertaining couple.

Spellbound Tours TOURS
(www.spellboundtours.com; adult/child/senior & student $15/8/11; ⊙8pm daily, plus 2pm Fri-Sun) Guided by a professional paranormal investigator, this 75-minute nighttime tour covers the darkest and scariest episodes of Salem's history. Visit actual sites from the witch hysteria, but also learn about voodoo, haunted houses and modern-day vampires. Apparently, some visitors have reported seeing ghosts on this tour. Now *that's* scary.

Salem Night Tour HISTORY
(www.salemnighttour.com; 127 Essex St; adult/child $15/10; ⊙tours 8pm) Lantern-led tours offer insights into Salem's haunted history. The tour covers a dozen historic sites, thus providing a pretty good overview of the witch hysteria of 1692. Guides are well informed and super enthusiastic, although the tour groups are perhaps too big for comfort.

Salem Trolley BUS
(www.salemtrolley.com; adult/child $18/8; ⊙10am-5pm Apr-Oct) This one-hour tour starts at the NPS visitor center (p105) and covers most of the town's places of interest. Tickets are good for the whole day, which means you can get on and off at will. Catch the courtesy shuttle from the MBTA commuter rail station.

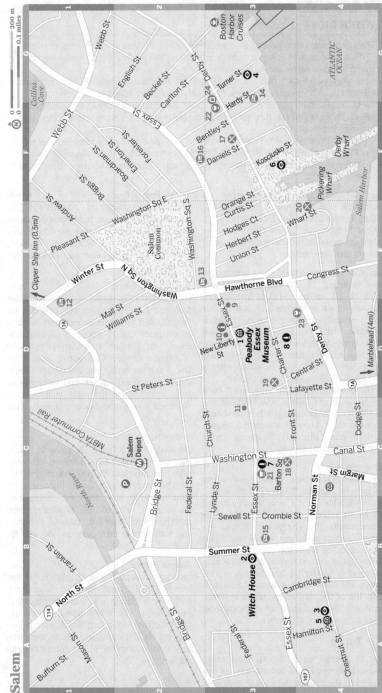

Salem

🎊 Festivals & Events

★ Haunted Happenings
Halloween CULTURAL
(www.hauntedhappenings.org; ☉Oct) Everyone in Salem celebrates Halloween, not just the witches. And they celebrate for much of the month of October with special exhibits, parades, concerts, pumpkin carvings, costume parties and trick-or-treating. It all culminates on October 31 with the crowning of the King and Queen of Halloween. Book your lodging way in advance and expect to pay more.

🛏 Sleeping

Many of Salem's historic houses have been converted into B&Bs and guesthouses, some of which claim a resident ghost. Prices increase dramatically during the Haunted Happenings Halloween festival in October.

★ Stephen Daniels House B&B $$
(☎978-744-5709; www.thedanielshouse.com; 1 Daniels St; r $125-150; P🖀) This must be Salem's oldest lodging, with parts dating from 1667. Two walk-in fireplaces grace the common area, and the rooms are filled with period antiques. It's appropriate in this spooky town that such an old house be haunted: rumor has it that a ghost cat roams the ancient halls, and it's even been known to jump into bed with guests.

Morning Glory B&B $$
(☎978-741-1703; www.morninggloryybb.com; 22 Hardy St; d $175-185, ste $220; ☉Mar-Nov; P🖀@🖀) ⚡ Next to the House of Seven Gables, this glorious B&B is hard to beat. To make guests feel welcome, innkeeper and Salem native Bob Shea pulls out all the stops, not the least of which are the delectable homemade pastries prepared by his mother. Three frilly rooms and one sweet suite are named for Salem celebrities – that is, the witch victims of 1692.

Amelia Payson House B&B $$
(☎978-744-8304; www.ameliapaysonhouse.com; 16 Winter St; d $160-185; P🖀@🖀) Just steps from Salem Common, this Greek Revival home is graced with a grand foyer and a lovely parlor, complete with grand piano. The three guest rooms are decorated with floral wallpaper, oriental rugs, rich drapes and ornamental fireplaces. There's a decadent hot breakfast every morning.

Hawthorne Hotel HOTEL $$
(☎978-744-4080; www.hawthornehotel.com; 18 Washington Sq W; s/d from $174/194; P🖀@🖀🐾) This historic Federalist-style hotel is at the heart of Salem. For years it was the only full-service hotel, with 84 updated rooms, a fancy restaurant and a cozy pub. Rooms are decked out with reproduction 18th-century furnishings, so you can feel like a wealthy merchant from Salem's glory days.

AMERICA'S OLDEST CANDY COMPANY

For more than 200 years Ye Olde Pepper Companie (www.peppercandy.net; 122 Derby St; ⊙10am-6pm) has been making sweets – you gotta believe that it knows what it's doing. The current owners (for *only* four generations) continue to use original 19th-century recipes for old-fashioned delights like Black Jacks (flavored with blackstrap molasses) and Gibraltars (lemon and peppermint treats). Sweet!

In 1806, an Englishwoman named Mrs Spencer survived a shipwreck, and arrived in Salem with hardly a penny to her name. Her new neighbors were kind enough to lend her some cash to purchase a barrel of sugar. Mrs Spencer used the sugar to create 'Salem Gibraltar,' a candy that sated the sweet tooth of sea captains and sailing merchants. She sold the candy from the front steps of the local church, eventually earning enough to purchase a horse and wagon and sell her products in neighboring towns. In 1830, Mrs Spencer sold her by-then-successful company to John William Pepper, hence the current name.

Salem Inn INN $$

(☎978-741-0680; www.saleminnma.com; 7 Summer St; d $179-229, ste $239-309; P❋🐾🛜🐶) The inn's 40 rooms are located in three historic houses, including Captain West House, a large, brick sea captain's home from 1834. The rooms vary greatly, but they are all individually decorated with antiques, period detail and other charms, while still providing modern amenities. Suites are equipped with kitchenettes, making them ideal for families.

🍴 Eating

There are many restaurants and cafes sprinkled around the downtown area, especially along Essex St and on Pickering Wharf. The venues run the gamut from old-fashioned diners to newfangled fusion.

Derby Joe SANDWICHES $

(www.derbyjoe.co; 142 Derby St; sandwiches $9; ⊙6am-4pm Mon-Fri, 7:30am-5pm Sat & Sun; 🛜🍽️) Derby Joe has quickly become beloved in Salem for its friendly owners, strong coffee, tasty sandwiches and nonstop chess tournament in the house. Now on offer: picnic baskets packed with your favorite sandwiches.

New England Soup Factory SOUP $

(www.nesoupfactorysalem.com; 140 Washington St; soup $5-10, sandwiches $4-8; ⊙11am-8pm Mon-Fri, to 7pm Sat, noon-7pm Sun; 🍽️🖥️) When there's a chill in the air, nothing warms body and soul like a bowl of hot soup. It's not much to look at, but the New England Soup Factory offers 10 amazing, rotating options every day. Favorites include chicken-pot-pie soup (topped with puff pastry) and pumpkin lobster bisque. In summer, it serves cold soups, of course.

Red's Sandwich Shop DINER $

(www.redssandwichshop.com; 15 Central St; mains $5-8; ⊙5am-3pm Mon-Sat, 6am-1pm Sun) This Salem institution has been serving eggs and sandwiches to faithful customers for over 50 years. The food is hearty and basic, but the real attraction is Red's old-school decor, complete with counter service and friendly faces. It's housed in the old London Coffee House building (around since 1698).

Sea Level Oyster Bar SEAFOOD $$

(www.sealeveloysterbar.com; 94 Wharf St; sandwiches $10-17, mains $18-22; ⊙11:30am-midnight) With a snazzy interior and a wide porch overlooking the harbor, this upscale oyster bar is a fine spot for dinner or drinks. High marks for craft cocktails, generous lobster rolls and the small but choice selection of oysters.

🍸 Drinking & Nightlife

★Gulu-Gulu Café CAFE

(www.gulugulucafe.com; 247 Essex St; ⊙8am-1am; 🛜) *Gulu-gulu* means 'gulp, gulp' in French, and this place is named after a now-defunct cafe in Prague. That's an indication of how eclectic it is, featuring (in no particular order) delicious coffee, art-adorned walls, sinful crepes, live music, exotic liqueurs and board games.

In a Pig's Eye PUB

(www.inapigseye.com; 148 Derby St; mains $8-13; ⊙11:30am-10pm, bar to 1am) This dark, friendly pub boasts an eclectic menu of burgers and beef stroganoff, homemade soups and tasty salads, and 'Pig's Eye Favorites' like steak tips or pork chops. Despite the small space, it has live music (usually acoustic) six nights a week. The Friday-afternoon Blues Jam is legendary.

Salem Beer Works
MICROBREWERY

(www.beerworks.net; 178 Derby St; ⊙11am-midnight, to 1am Fri & Sat) Part of the Boston Beer Works family, this microbrewery serves 15 brews on tap, as well as a full menu of pub grub, sandwiches and more. The specialty seems to be things fried, which undoubtedly encourages more beer drinking. There are pool tables and outdoor seating.

❶ Information

Hawthorne in Salem (www.hawthorneinsalem. org) An extensive site with loads of articles about Nathaniel Hawthorne, his life in Salem and his writings about the town.

NPS Regional Visitor Center (www.nps.gov/sama; 2 New Liberty St; ⊙9am-5pm Wed-Sun) Offers information on Salem. For a good overview, catch a free screening of *Where Past Is Present*, a short film about Salem history. You can also pick up a map and description of several self-guided walking tours and other area attractions.

Official Guide (www.salem.org) A useful information site with links to local businesses, an up-to-date events calendar and an ongoing blog.

❶ Getting There & Away

BOAT

Boston Harbor Cruises (Salem Ferry; www.bostonharborcruises.com; 10 Blaney St; round-trip adult/child $45/35; ⊙May-Oct) operates the Salem ferry, which makes the scenic, one-hour trip between Salem Ferry Center and Long Wharf in Boston. Travels four or five times a day.

CAR & MOTORCYCLE

Salem is 20 miles northeast of Boston. From MA 128, take MA 114 east into Salem center.

TRAIN

The Rockport/Newburyport line of the MBTA commuter rail (p90) runs from Boston's North Station to Salem Depot ($7, 30 minutes). Trains run every 30 minutes during the morning and evening rush hours, hourly during the rest of day, and less frequently at weekends.

Gloucester

🗐 978 / POP 29,400

Founded in 1623 by English fisherfolk, Gloucester is one of New England's oldest towns. This port, on Cape Ann, has made its living from fishing for almost 400 years, and it has inspired books and films like Rudyard Kipling's *Captains Courageous* and Sebastian Junger's *The Perfect Storm*. And despite some recent economic diversification, the town still smells of fish. You can't miss the fishing boats, festooned with nets, dredges and winches, tied to the wharves or motoring along into the harbor, with clouds of hungry seagulls hovering expectantly above.

◉ Sights

Rocky Neck Art Colony
GALLERY

(www.rockyneckartcolony.org) The artistic legacy of Gloucester native Fitz Henry Lane endures, as Gloucester still boasts a vibrant artists community at Rocky Neck Art Colony. In addition to the cooperative **Gallery 53 on Rocky Neck** (53 Rocky Neck Ave; ⊙10am-6pm Sun-Thu, to 8pm Fri & Sat Jun–mid-Oct), there are about a dozen galleries and studios that open to visitors, as well as a couple of restaurants. Follow Main St east and south around the harbor to East Gloucester.

Pick up a map and walking tour at the **Cultural Center** (www.rockyneckartcolony. org; 9 Wonson St; ⊙noon-4pm Thu-Sun Sep-May, to 6pm Jun-Aug) or the Chamber of Commerce (p109).

Gloucester Maritime Heritage Center
MUSEUM

(www.maritimegloucester.org; 23 Harbor Loop; adult/child $6/4; ⊙10am-5pm Jun-Oct; ⊕) Visit Gloucester's working waterfront and see the ongoing restoration of wooden boats, watch the operation of a marine railway that hauls ships out of the water, and compare the different kinds of fishing boats that were used over the years. From the Grant Circle rotary, take Washington St to its terminus, then turn left on Rogers St to Harbor Loop.

Inside the museum, the interactive exhibit **Fitting Out** focuses on the many businesses that grew up around Gloucester's fishing industry. That doesn't sound so interesting until you chart your course through the local waters or try your hand at rope making. **Sea Pocket Lab** is a hands-on educational aquarium with exhibits on local marine habitats. It's a great chance for kids to get down and dirty with sea stars, sea urchins, snails, crabs and seaweed. The Stellwagen Bank Marine Sanctuary Exhibit provides an excellent introduction for whale-watchers heading out on an excursion.

Cape Ann Museum
MUSEUM

(www.capeannmuseum.org; 27 Pleasant St; adult/child $10/free; ⊙10am-5pm Tue-Sat, 1-4pm Sun) This tiny museum is a gem – particularly for its paintings by Gloucester native Fitz Henry

DON'T MISS

WHALE-WATCHING CRUISES TO STELLWAGEN BANK

Gloucester is perfectly situated to launch your whale-watching expedition, thanks to the proximity of **Stellwagen Bank** (www.stellwagen.noaa.gov), 842 sq miles of open ocean rich in marine life. The area was declared a National Marine Sanctuary in 1992 to conserve its biological diversity and facilitate research and other beneficial activity. Today it's a destination for whale-watching, diving and managed fishing.

Whale-watching cruises usually depart several times a day in summer, but only once a day or only at weekends in April, May, September and October. Reservations are recommended. Whale sightings are practically guaranteed.

Lane. Exhibits also showcase the region's granite-quarrying industry and – of course – its maritime history. The museum is in the heart of downtown Gloucester, just north of Main St.

Beauport   HISTORIC SITE
(www.historicnewengland.org; 75 Eastern Point Blvd, Eastern Point; adult/student $15/8; ⊙10am-4pm Tue-Sun Jun–mid-Oct) The lavish home of interior designer Henry Davis Sleeper is known as Beauport, or the Sleeper-McCann mansion. Sleeper scoured New England for houses that were about to be demolished and scavenged wood paneling, architectural elements and furniture. In place of unity, he created a wildly eclectic but artistically surprising – and satisfying – place to live.

Now in the care of Historic New England, Beauport is open to visitors for fascinating guided tours. The mansion also hosts specialized tours, weekend brunch and other events.

St Peter's Square   SQUARE
Don't leave Gloucester without paying your respects at St Peter's Sq, where Leonard Craske's famous statue *Gloucester Fisherman* is dedicated to 'They That Go Down to the Sea in Ships, 1623–1923.'

North Shore Arts Association   GALLERY
(www.nsarts.org; 11 Pirates Lane; ⊙10am-5pm Mon-Sat, noon-5pm Sun May-Oct) With some 600 members, this vibrant local arts association has been hosting exhibits and performances since 1922. Visit the lovely harborside setting to see one of the rotating exhibits, catch a lecture or workshop, or hobnob with local artists.

🏃 Activities

Seven Seas Whale Watch   WHALE WATCHING
(✆978-283-1776, 888-283-1776; www.7seaswhale watch.com; 63 Rogers St; adult/child $48/32; 🚤)

Three generations of sea captains have navigated the waters around Stellwagen Bank. Seven Seas vessels depart from Rogers St in the center of Gloucester, between St Peter's Sq and the Gloucester House Restaurant.

Capt Bill & Sons Whale Watch   WHALE WATCHING
(✆978-283-6995; www.captbillandsons.com; 24 Harbor Loop; adult/child $48/32; 🚤) The boat leaves from behind Captain Carlo's Seafood Market & Restaurant. Don't miss the on-site whale exhibit featuring a humpback skeleton.

Cape Ann Whale Watch   WHALE WATCHING
(✆978-283-5110; www.seethewhales.com; Rose's Wharf, 415 Main St; adult/child $48/33; 🚤) This long-standing company takes passengers out to Stellwagen Bank on the *Hurricane II*. Cruises depart from Rose's Wharf, east of Gloucester center (on the way to East Gloucester).

Yankee Fleet   FISHING
(www.yankeefleet.com; 1 Parker St; adult/child full day $68/59, half-day $49/38) Summon your inner Gloucester fisher and see what you can reel in. Boats go out to Stellwagen Bank, or to closer fishing grounds at Jeffreys Ledge or Tillies Bank (depending on whether you choose the half-day or full-day option). The crew is accommodating – yes, they will clean your catch!

Ryan & Wood Distillery   DISTILLERY
(www.ryanandwood.com; 15 Great Republic Dr; ⊙tours 10am & 1pm Mon, Wed, Fri & Sat) As you learn about the process of distilling fine spirits here, you will feel, hear and taste the passion that goes into this operation. Admire the shiny old-fashioned alembic copper pot that is still in use. Try your hand at filling and labeling bottles. And of course, sample the goods – gin, rum, whisky and vodka – and buy a bottle too! From

the second rotary on Rte 128, take the exit to Blackburn Industrial Park. Turn right on Blackburn Dr and left on Great Republic Dr.

Schooner Thomas E Lannon   BOATING
(📋978-281-6634; www.schooner.org; Rogers St; adult/child $40/27.50; 🚢) This 65ft ship is the spitting image of the Gloucester fishing schooners. It leaves on two-hour sails from the Seven Seas wharf. Sunset cruises feature live music, ranging from Celtic to classical to bluegrass. Bonus for families: on Saturday mornings one kid sails for free with the purchase of one adult fare.

🖊 Tours

Cape Ann Foodie Tours   TOURS
(📋617-902-8291; www.capeannfoodietours.com; $55; ☺tours 11:30am) If you're the type of person who likes to discover a place by taste, this could be for you. Eat your way around Gloucester, Rockport or Newburyport (or all three!). Fresh-caught seafood, locally brewed beers and handcrafted sweets are all served with a side of history.

🎊 Festivals & Events

St Peter's Festival   RELIGIOUS
(www.stpetersfiesta.org) Honoring the patron saint of fisherfolk, this carnival at St Peter's Sq takes place over five days in late June. Besides rides and music, the main event is the procession through the streets of a statue of St Peter. Customarily, the cardinal of the Catholic Archdiocese of Boston attends to bless the fishing fleet.

🛏 Sleeping

There are only a few places to stay in town, but the residential areas are peppered with gracious homes that are now B&Bs, while the coastlines are lined with grand old hotels and beachfront motels. The art colony at Rocky Neck is a unique part of town with an affordable lodging option.

Crow's Nest Inn   INN $
(📋978-281-2965; www.crowsnestgloucester.com; 334 Main St; r $75) If you want to wake to the sound of fisherfolk's cries and the smell of salt air, and you don't mind basic bunks, stay at the Crow's Nest, upstairs from the pub made famous by *The Perfect Storm*. Rooms are clean; the price is right.

★Rocky Neck Accommodations   APARTMENT $$
(📋978-381-9848; www.rockyneckaccommodations.com; 43 Rocky Neck Ave; r $155-165, ste $265-285; 🅿🤶) You don't have to be an artist to live the bohemian life in Gloucester. The colony association offers light-filled efficiencies – all equipped with kitchenettes – at the Rocky Neck Art Colony. The rooms are sweet and simple, most with beautiful views of Smith Cove. Weekly rates also available.

Cape Ann Motor Inn   MOTEL $$
(📋978-281-2900; www.capeannmotorinn.com; 33 Rockport Rd; r/ste $180/275; 🤶) The rooms are small and a bit dated, but you can't beat the location: directly on Long Beach. Balconies overlook the surf, sand and two lighthouses.

OFF THE BEATEN TRACK

DOGTOWN

Much of the interior of Cape Ann is wild and undeveloped, partially protected by reservations, but mostly left to the whims of nature and history. This vast territory is known as Dogtown.

Those who venture into Dogtown might discover the mysterious glacial rock formations that inspired artist Marsden Hartley; the ruins of an ancient, abandoned Colonial settlement; or strange, stern rock inscriptions that date to the Great Depression. It's a beautiful but forbidding place, which has seen more than its fair share of mystery and tragedy, as detailed in Elyssa East's award-winning book *Dogtown: Death and Enchantment in a New England Ghost Town*.

Dogtown contains miles and miles of trails, but they're poorly maintained and mostly unmarked. Simply put, it's not easy to navigate. Let a local expert show you the way with **Walk the Words** (www.walkthewords.com; adult/child $15/7; ☺9am daily), a two-hour hike to Dogtown's most intriguing spots. If you want to go it alone, pick up a map from the **Bookstore of Gloucester** (www.facebook.com/The-Bookstore-of-Gloucester-115872231806098/; 61 Main St; ☺9am-6pm Mon-Sat, 11am-5pm Sun). You can access Dogtown between Gloucester and Annisquam. From MA 127, take Reynaud St to Cherry St.

LIFE'S A BEACH ON CAPE ANN

Cape Ann has several excellent beaches that draw thousands of Boston-area sun-and-sea worshippers on any hot day in July or August.

Wingaersheek Beach (232 Atlantic Rd; parking weekdays/weekends $20/25; ☉ 8am-9pm) A wide swath of sand surrounded by Ipswich Bay, the Annisquam River and lots of sand dunes. At low tide a long sandbar stretches for more than half a mile out into the bay. Take Rte 128 to exit 13.

Good Harbor Beach (http://gloucester-ma.gov; Thatcher Rd/Rte 127A; parking weekdays/weekends $30/25; ☉ 8am-9pm) A spacious, sandy beach midway between Gloucester and Rockport. The parking lot fills up before the beach does, so if you get here early enough, you will enjoy the minimal crowds all day long.

Stage Fort Park (http://gloucester-ma.gov; parking weekdays/weekends $10/15) Includes two lovely small beaches: the picturesque Half-Moon Beach and the more remote Cressy's Beach. It's off MA 127, just south of the cut.

If you came to Cape Ann to go to the beach, here you are. Continental breakfast. Loquacious resident parrot.

Julietta House GUESTHOUSE $$
(☏ 978-281-2300; www.juliettahouse.com; 84 Prospect St; r $165-235; P ✳ 🖥) Steps from Gloucester Harbor, this grand Georgian house has eight spacious and elegant rooms with period furnishings and private bathrooms. The environment is quite luxurious, while service is purposefully hands off. This place promises privacy and comfort, without the overwrought frills and friendliness of some guesthouses.

Atlantis Oceanfront Inn MOTEL $$
(☏ 978-283-0014; www.atlantisoceanfrontinn.com; 125 Atlantic Rd; d $160-255; P ✳ 🖥 🏊) The institutional but comfortable rooms at this large motel-style facility are spruced up with private terraces and exceptional ocean views. This place takes full advantage of its oceanfront setting, with its lovely rocky waterside walkway and a light-filled breakfast cafe. From the terminus of MA 128, take Bass Ave east to Atlantic Rd.

✗ Eating

Virgilio's Italian Bakery DELI $
(www.facebook.com/Virgilios-Bakery-333299 483409677; 29 Main St; sandwiches $5-8; ☉ 9am-5pm) Primarily a takeout joint, Virgilio's has excellent sandwiches and other Italian treats. Try the famous St Joseph sandwich – like an Italian sub on a fresh-baked roll. Pick one up and head down to the waterfront for a picnic.

Two Sisters Coffee Shop DINER $
(www.facebook.com/TwoSistersCoffeeShop; 27 Washington St; mains $5-8; ☉ 6:30am-1pm; 🚗) This local place is where the fisherfolk go for breakfast when they come in from their catch. They're early risers, so you may have to wait for a table. Corned-beef hash, eggs in a hole and pancakes all get rave reviews. Service is a little salty.

Franklin Cape Ann AMERICAN $$
(www.franklincafe.com; 118 Main St; mains $15-20; ☉ 5-10:30pm Sun-Thu, to midnight Fri & Sat; 🚗) The North Shore branch of a South End favorite in Boston, this cool place has an urban atmosphere and an excellent, modern New American menu. More often than not, daily specials feature fresh seafood and seasonal vegetables, always accompanied by an appropriate wine. Regulars rave about the cocktails too.

Causeway Restaurant SEAFOOD $$
(www.thecausewayrestaurant.com; 78 Essex St; mains $12-25; ☉ 11am-8pm Sun-Thu, to 9pm Fri & Sat) Gloucester's favorite seafood shack is about a mile west of town, on the mainland. It's a convivial, crowded place serving irresistible clam chowder, heaping portions of fried clams and twin lobster specials. Expect to wait for a table and don't forget to BYOB.

Duckworth's Bistrot AMERICAN $$$
(☏ 978-282-4426; www.duckworthsbistrot.com; 197 E Main St; mains $22-28; ☉ 5-9:30 Tue-Sat; 🚗) Half-portions and wines by the glass (or carafe) mean that Duckworth's won't break the bank. But the menu of fresh seafood and local produce means you will dine like a gourmand. Specialties include the oysters of the

day – served with two special sauces – and to-die-for lobster risotto, which features an ever-changing seasonal vegetable. Reservations recommended.

🍷 Drinking & Entertainment

Crow's Nest   PUB
(www.crowsnestgloucester.com; 334 Main St; ⊘11am-1am) The down-and-dirty fisherfolk bar made famous in *The Perfect Storm*. But this is the real deal, not the set the movie folks threw up for a few weeks during filming. Come early if you want to drink with the fishing crews. It gets crowded with tourists in summer.

Gloucester Stage Company   THEATER
(www.gloucesterstage.com; 267 E Main St; $20-40) This company stages excellent small-theater productions of classics and modern works. It's a small venue known for top-notch acting. Excellent summer theater.

Rhumb Line   LIVE MUSIC
(www.therhumbline.com; 40 Railroad Ave; ⊘11:30am-1am) This club across from the train station is the best place on Cape Ann to hear live music, with performances six nights a week, plus an 'open jam' on Monday night. Acts range from mellow acoustic and blues to high-energy rock. Definitely a local scene, but it's friendly.

🔒 Shopping

Dogtown Books   BOOKS
(www.dogtownbooks.com; 132 Main St; ⊘10am-10pm) A crowded store with narrow aisles and shelves packed with new and used books. There's lots of local history here. There are also a lot of rules: watch yourself.

ℹ️ Information

Cape Ann Chamber of Commerce (www.capeannchamber.com; 33 Commercial St; ⊘9am-5pm Mon-Fri, 10am-5pm Sat, 11am-4pm Sun) South of St Peter's Sq.

ℹ️ Getting There & Away

BUS
The **Cape Ann Transportation Authority** (www.canntran.com) runs five routes around Cape Ann to destinations such as Good Harbor Beach, Rockport and other villages.

CAR & MOTORCYCLE
You can reach Cape Ann quickly from Boston or North Shore towns via the four-lane Rte 128, but the scenic route along MA 127 follows the coastline through the prim villages of Prides Crossing, Manchester-by-the-Sea and Magnolia.

TRAIN
Take the Rockport line of the MBTA commuter rail (p90) from Boston's North Station to Gloucester ($10.50, one hour).

ℹ️ Getting Around

Gloucester Harbor Water Shuttle (www.CapeAnnHarborTours.com; adult/child $10/5; ⊘noon-6pm daily Jun-Aug, noon-4pm Sat & Sun Apr, May, Sep & Oct) The M/V *Lady Jillian* makes stops at the Heritage Center (Harbor Loop), in downtown Gloucester (Gloucester House Restaurant), on Rocky Neck and at St Peter's Landing. You can hop on and off to visit local sights, or stay on board for a tour.

Rockport

☑ 978 / POP 6950

At the northern tip of Cape Ann, Rockport is a quaint contrast to gritty Gloucester. The town takes its name from its 19th-century role as a shipping center for granite cut from the local quarries. The stone is still ubiquitous: monuments, building foundations, pavements and piers remain as testament to Rockport's past.

That's about all that remains of this industrial history, however. A century ago, Winslow Homer, Childe Hassam, Fitz Henry Lane and other acclaimed artists came to Rockport's rugged shores, inspired by the hearty fisherfolk who wrested a hard-won but satisfying living from the sea. Today Rockport earns a crust from the tourists who come to look at the artists. The artists themselves have long since given up looking for hearty fisherfolk because the descendants of the fishers are all running boutiques and B&Bs.

👁 Sights

Halibut Point Reservation   WILDLIFE RESERVE
(www.thetrustees.org; ⊘dawn-dusk; 🅿) **FREE**
Only a few miles north of Dock Sq along MA 127 is Halibut Point Reservation. A 10-minute walk through the forest brings you to yawning, abandoned granite quarries, huge hills of granite rubble, and a granite foreshore of tumbled, smoothed rock perfect for picnicking, sunbathing, reading or painting. The surf can be strong here, making swimming unwise, but natural pools can be good for wading or cooling your feet. A map is available at the entrance; parking costs $5 to $6.

Bearskin Neck
STREET

(www.bearskinneck.net) Bearskin Neck is the peninsula that juts into the harbor, lined with galleries, lobster shacks and souvenir shops. The name Bearskin Neck apparently comes from the legend of a young boy who was attacked by a bear. In an attempt to save the boy, his uncle, Ebenezer Babson, went after the bear with his fish knife. Babson managed to kill the bear and save the child, and then he skinned the bear and laid the pelt on the rocks to dry.

Dock Square
SQUARE

Dock Sq is the hub of Rockport. Visible from here, the red fishing shack decorated with colorful buoys is known as **Motif No 1**, since it has been captured by so many artists for so many years. (Actually, it should be called Motif No 1-B, as the original shack vanished during a great storm in 1978 and a brand-new replica was erected in its place.)

Paper House
NOTABLE BUILDING

(www.paperhouserockport.com; 52 Pigeon Hill St; adult/child $2/1; ⊙10am-5pm Apr-Oct) In 1922, long before there was any municipal recycling program, Elis F Stenman decided that something useful should be done with all those daily newspapers lying about. He and his family set to work folding, rolling and pasting the papers into suitable shapes as building materials. Twenty years and 100,000 newspapers later, they had built the Paper House.

The walls are 215 layers thick, and the furnishings – table, chairs, lamps, sofa, even a grandfather clock and a piano – are all made of newspaper. Some pieces even specialize: one desk is made from *Christian Science Monitor* reports of Charles Lindbergh's flight, and the fireplace mantel is made from rotogravures drawn from the *Boston Sunday Herald* and the *New York Herald Tribune*. The text is still legible on all of the newspapers, so there's built-in reading material (literally).

The Paper House is inland from Pigeon Cove. From MA 27, take Curtiss St to Pigeon Hill St.

🏃 Activities

Long Beach
BEACH

(Thatcher Rd) Some claim that Long Beach, which straddles the Rockport–Gloucester border, is the best beach on the North Shore. It is lovely indeed – ideal for swimming, surfing, snorkeling and sunbathing – with a unique view of the twin lighthouses on Thacher Island. Unfortunately, there's no parking unless you buy a sticker from the Chamber of Commerce.

North Shore Kayak Outdoor Center
KAYAKING

(☑978-546-5050; www.northshorekayak.com; 9 Tuna Wharf; tours adult/child $45/25, kayaks per day $45-70, bikes per day $30) Rockport is a perfect base for sea kayaking – a great way to explore the rocky coast of Cape Ann. Besides renting kayaks, this outfit offers kayak tours, starting at $40/25 per adult/child for a two-hour tour.

🎉 Festivals & Events

★ Rockport Chamber Music Festival
MUSIC

(☑978-546-7391; www.rockportmusic.org; 37 Main St; ⊙Jun & Jul) This festival hosts concerts by internationally acclaimed performers. Concerts take place at the Shalin Liu Performance Center, a gorgeous hall overlooking the ocean. Most concerts sell out, so it's advisable to order tickets in advance.

🛏 Sleeping

★ Tuck Inn
B&B $$

(☑978-546-7260; www.tuckinn.com; 17 High St; r $165-175, ste $195; P❄@🞧🏊) Despite the unfortunate name, this inn offers excellent value. The renovated 1790s Colonial home has nine rooms and a four-person suite. Elegant communal rooms feature period decor. Local artwork and homemade quilts are some of the little touches that make the rooms special. The breakfast buffet – with seasonal fruit salads, and fresh-baked bread and pastries – will be a highlight of your stay.

Addison Choate Inn
B&B $$

(☑978-546-7543; www.addisonchoateinn.com; 49 Broadway; r $189-199, ste $205; P❄🞧) This Greek Revival residence stands out among Rockport's historic inns. The traditional decor includes canopy beds, wide-plank hardwood floors and period wallpaper. The 3rd-floor suite overlooks Rockport harbor. New innkeepers Jen and Ted do their utmost to make guests feel welcome and even pampered. The gourmet breakfast (think homemade waffles or French toast) doesn't hurt in that regard.

Captain's Bounty on the Beach
MOTEL $$

(☑978-546-9557; www.captainsbountymotorinn. com; 1 Beach St; r from $215, ste $225; P❄🞧) The draw here is the prime location, right on

Front Beach and a short stroll from Dock Sq. The 24 simple rooms all have lovely views of the beach, where lobster folk check their traps at dawn. All rooms have refrigerators and microwaves, and some are equipped with full kitchens.

Bearskin Neck Motor Lodge
MOTEL $$

(☑978-546-6677; www.bearskinneckmotorlodge. com; 64 Bearskin Neck; d $205-235; P 🕾) The only lodging on Bearskin Neck is this motel-style lodge near the end of the strip. Needless to say, every room has a great view and a balcony from which you can enjoy it. The recently upgraded rooms are quite spiffy, with traditional wooden furniture, striking new light fixtures and intriguing sea-glass artwork on the walls.

Inn on Cove Hill
B&B $$

(Caleb Norwood Jr House; ☑978-546-2701; www. innoncovehill.com; 37 Mt Pleasant St; r $160-175, ste $250; P) This is a Federal-style house built in 1791 with, so they say, pirates' gold that was discovered nearby. It has been lovingly restored down to the tiniest detail. Doubles have wide-plank hardwood floors, ornate moldings and canopy beds; there's fresh fruit and homemade muffins for breakfast. The location, a block from Dock Sq, is hard to beat.

Eden Pines Inn
B&B $$

(☑978-546-2505; www.edenpinesinn.com; 48 Eden Rd; r $225; P ✳🕾) Eden Pines is all about the view: it's spectacular. Perched up on the rocks, the inn faces Loblolly Cove, the Thacher Island lighthouses and the big blue beyond. It's gorgeous no matter where you're standing – your private balcony, the breakfast nook, or the wide, breezy front porch. Rooms are spacious and comfortable and service is impeccable.

Sally Webster Inn
B&B $$

(☑978-546-9251, 877-546-9251; www.sallywebster. com; 34 Mt Pleasant St; r $150-170; P ✳@🕾) This handsome brick Colonial place, built in 1832, offers eight rooms with early-American decor. Many have working fireplaces, and all have authentic architectural details and period furniture. Well-groomed flower beds and cool ocean breezes make the terrace a wonderful respite.

✗ Eating

Dock Sq has several cafes, while Bearskin Neck is crowded with ice-cream stores, cafes and cozy restaurants – and plenty of seafood. Many places reduce their hours or close completely in winter.

Helmut's Strudel
BAKERY $

(www.helmuts-strudel.com; 69 Bearskin Neck; desserts $5-8; ⊙7am-5:30pm Mon-Thu, to 7pm Fri-Sun; ☑🖍) For dessert, try this Austrian bakery, almost near the outer end of the Neck. Helmut's serves strudels, filled croissants, pastries, cider and coffee. Four shaded tables overlook the yacht-filled harbor.

Top Dog
HOT DOGS $

(www.topdogrockport.com; 2 Doyle's Cove Rd; dogs $6-10; ⊙11am-4pm Mon-Thu, to 7pm Fri-Sun Apr-Oct; 🖍) More than a dozen kinds of dogs, from a German Shepherd (with fresh sauerkraut) to a Chihuahua (with jalapeños, salsa and cheese). Located on the Neck.

★ Roy Moore Lobster Company
SEAFOOD $$

(www.facebook.com/Roy-Moore-Lobster-Co-12528 7641097/; 39 Bearskin Neck; lobsters $15; ⊙9am-6pm) This takeout kitchen has the cheapest lobster-in-the-rough on the Neck. Your beast comes on a tray with melted butter, a fork and a wet wipe for cleanup. Find a seat at a picnic table on the back patio and dig in. Don't forget to bring your own beer or wine.

Red Skiff
SEAFOOD $$

(www.facebook.com/Red-Skiff-Restaurant-15285 6038086274/; 15 Mount Pleasant St; breakfast $5-10, mains $10-20; ⊙6:30am-3pm Mon-Sat, 7am-2pm Sun; 🖍) Be prepared to wait for a table at this old-fashioned seafood shack, in the heart of Rockport, close to the T Wharf. Come for pancakes and eggs for breakfast, or clam chowder and lobster rolls for lunch. It doesn't look like much, but the service is friendly and the fish is fresh.

Ellen's Harborside
DINER $$

(www.ellensharborside.com; 1 Wharf Rd; sandwiches $10-12, mains $13-30; ⊙11:30am-9pm May-Oct; 🖍) By the T Wharf in the town center, Ellen's has grown famous serving a simple menu of American breakfasts, chicken, ribs and lobster since 1954. Consider the award-winning clam chowder. It's all very old school – from the quaint dining room to the warm service to the classic New England cuisine – except for the gluten-free menu (pretty newfangled, and much appreciated by some).

🍷 Drinking & Nightlife

Rockport is a dry town, meaning that alcohol is not sold in stores and rarely sold in restaurants, and there are no bars. However, most restaurants allow you to bring your own drinks (though they may charge a corkage fee). You can buy liquor outside

Rockport at **Lanesville Package Store** (1080 Washington St/MA 127, Lanesville; ⊙8am-9pm Mon-Sat, noon-6pm Sun) and **Liquor Locker** (www.liquorlockergloucester.com; 287 Main St, Gloucester; ⊙8am-10pm Mon-Sat, noon-6pm Sun).

Brothers Brew Coffee Shop   CAFE
(27 Main St; ⊙7am-4pm)   Two words: coffee and doughnuts. There are other (perhaps healthier) options for breakfast, but go for the doughnuts. You won't regret it.

❶ Information

Rockport Chamber of Commerce (www.rockportusa.com; Upper Main St; ⊙9am-5pm Mon-Sat Apr-Oct) Located about 1 mile out of town on Rte 127.

See Cape Ann (www.seecapeann.com) Cape Ann's online information booth.

❶ Getting There & Away

BUS
The Cape Ann Transportation Authority (p109) operates bus routes between the towns of Cape Ann. Fares are $1 to $1.25.

CAR & MOTORCYCLE
MA 127/127A loops around Cape Ann, connecting Magnolia and Gloucester to Rockport. Driving the entire loop is worth it for the seaside scenery in East Gloucester, Lanesville and Annisquam.

Street parking in Rockport is in short supply in summer, but you can park for free in the **Blue Gate Parking Lot** (Upper Main St; ⊙11am-7pm mid-May–Sep), then take the trolley ($1) or walk the three-quarters of a mile to Dock Sq.

TRAIN
Take the MBTA commuter rail (p90) from Boston's North Station to Rockport ($10.50, one hour).

Ipswich & Essex

⤴978 / POP IPSWICH 13,200, ESSEX 3500

North of Cape Ann, Ipswich and Essex are pretty New England towns surrounded by rocky coast and sandy beaches, extensive marshland, forested hills and rural farmland.

Ipswich and Essex are examples of New England towns that are pretty today because they were poor in the past. There was no harbor, and no source of waterpower for factories, so commercial and industrial development went elsewhere in the 18th and 19th centuries. As a result, the 17th-century houses were not torn down to build grander residences. Today the towns are famous for their ample antique shops and succulent clams. Formerly the home of novelist John Updike, Ipswich is also the setting for some of his novels and short stories like *A&P*, which is based on the local market.

⊙ Sights

Essex Shipbuilding Museum   MUSEUM
(www.essexshipbuildingmuseum.org; 66 Main St, Essex; guided tour adult/child $10/5, self-guided tour $7; ⊙10am-5pm Wed-Sun Jun-Oct, Sat & Sun Nov-May; ♿) This unique museum was established in 1976 as a local repository for all of the shipbuilding artifacts of Essex residents. The fascinating collections of photos, tools and ship models came from local basements and attics, allowing the village to preserve its history. Most of the collections are housed in the town's **1835 schoolhouse** (check out the **Old Burying Ground** behind it). Docents are well informed and passionate about local history.

The historical society also operates the **Waterline Center** in the museum shipyard, a section of waterfront property where shipbuilding activities have taken place for hundreds of years (and still do!). The historic Essex-built schooner *Evelina M Goulart* is moored here.

Appleton Farms   FARM
(www.thetrustees.org; 219 County Rd, Ipswich; $3; ⊙8am-dusk; ♿) 🐾 Six miles of trails wind along old carriageways, past ancient stonewall property markers and through acres of grasslands. Farm friends dot the pastures, while wilder animals are spotted in the woodlands. The store sells fresh, organically grown produce, not to mention tantalizing jams, spreads and sauces made with said produce. This is bucolic New England at its best. From MA 128 take MA 1A north. Turn left on Cutler Rd and drive 2 miles to the intersection with Highland Rd.

Crane Beach   BEACH
(www.thetrustees.org; Argilla Rd, Ipswich; pedestrian & cyclist $2, car weekday/weekend $25/30; ⊙8am-dusk; ♿) One of the longest, widest, sandiest beaches in the region is Crane Beach, with 5.5 miles of fine-sand barrier beach on Ipswich Bay. It is set in the midst of the Crane Wildlife Refuge, so the entire surrounding area is pristine and beautiful. Five miles of trails traverse the dunes. The only downside is the pesky greenhead flies that buzz around (and bite) in late July and early August.

Castle Hill on the Crane Estate HISTORIC SITE
(www.thetrustees.org; Argilla Rd, Ipswich; house tours $15-20, grounds car/bike $10/2; ☉house 10am-4pm Tue-Sun Jun-Oct, plus Sat & Sun Apr & May, grounds 8am-dusk year-round; P 🖭) High atop Castle Hill sits the 1920s estate of Chicago plumbing-fixture magnate Richard T Crane. The 59-room Stuart-style Great House is open for guided tours and special events. Check the website for a variety of thematic tours that show off the history, architecture and extensive grounds of the estate home. The lovely landscaped grounds, which are open daily, contain several miles of walking trails.

Cogswell's Grant HISTORIC HOUSE
(www.historicnewengland.org; 60 Spring St, Essex; adult/senior/student $10/9/8; ☉11am-4pm Wed-Sat Jun–mid-Oct) This Colonial-era farmhouse dates to 1728, and is furnished and decorated with all manner of 'country arts' from the era. The home is the product of six decades of redecorating and refurbishing by Bertram and Nina Fletcher Little. In the early 20th century, the couple were renowned collectors and scholars of American folk art, and their home remains largely as it was when the family lived there. From Main St, Essex, take Rte 22, then turn right on Spring St.

Ipswich Museum MUSEUM
(www.ipswichmuseum.org; 54 S Main St, Ipswich; 1/3 houses $10/15; ☉10am-4pm Thu-Sat Apr & May, plus Wed & Sun Jun-Oct) Three houses comprise this village historical museum, including the 'first period' Whipple House (www.ipswichmuseum.org; 1 South Village Green, Ipswich; adult/child $10/5; ☉10am-4pm Thu-Sat Apr & May, plus Wed & Sun Jun-Oct), which dates to 1677. The bulk of the collection is in the 1800 Heard House, which also contains historic furnishings, textiles and decorative arts, as well as an excellent collection of paintings by Ipswich artists from the 19th and 20th centuries.

⌲ Tours

Essex River Basin Adventures KAYAKING
(🖉978-768-3722; www.erba.com; 1 Main St, Essex; tours $47-78; ☉10am-5pm Mon-Sat, noon-5pm Sun) Explore the tidal estuaries of the Essex River. Tours include basic kayak instruction, as well as plenty of opportunities for bird-watching. Romantics will have a hard time choosing between a sunset paddle around the Essex River Basin and a moonlight paddle to Crane's Beach.

⌴ Sleeping & Eating

★Inn at Castle Hill INN $$$
(🖉978-412-2555; innatcastlehill.thetrustees.org; 280 Argilla Rd, Ipswich; r woodland view $235-285, ocean view $395-515; P 🖭 🛜) 🌿 On the beautiful grounds of the Crane Estate, this inn is an example of understated luxury, its 10 rooms each uniquely decorated with subtle elegance. Turndown service, plush robes and afternoon tea are some of the perks. Instead of televisions (of which there are none), guests enjoy a wraparound veranda and its magnificent views of sand dunes and salt marshes.

★JT Farnham's SEAFOOD $$
(88 Eastern Ave, Essex; mains $15-25; ☉11am-8pm; 🖭) When the Food Network came to Essex to weigh in on the fried-clam debate for the show *Food Feud,* the winner was JT Farnham, thanks to the crispiness of his clams. Pull up a picnic table and enjoy the amazing estuary view.

Clam Box SEAFOOD $$
(www.clamboxipswich.com; 246 High St/MA 133, Essex; mains $15-32; ☉11am-8pm) You can't miss this classic clam shack, just north of Ipswich center. Built in 1938, it actually looks like a clam box, spruced up with striped awnings. Folks line up out the door for crispy fried clams and onion rings – some claim they're the best in the land.

★Woodman's SEAFOOD $$$
(www.woodmans.com; 121 Main St/MA 133, Essex; sandwiches $8-20, mains $15-32; ☉11am-8pm Sun-Thu, to 9pm Fri & Sat) This roadhouse is the most famous spot in the area to come for clams, any way you like them. The specialty is Chubby's original fried clams and crispy onion rings, but this place serves everything from boiled lobsters to homemade clam cakes to a seasonal raw bar.

❶ Getting There & Away

CAR & MOTORCYCLE
From Gloucester, MA 133 heads north to Essex and on to Ipswich. If you're coming from Boston, get off I-95 at Topsfield Rd, which takes you into Ipswich.

TRAIN
Ipswich is on the Newburyport line of the MBTA commuter rail (p90). Trains leave Boston's North Station for Ipswich ($9.25, 50 minutes) about 12 times each weekday and five times on Saturday (no trains Sunday).

Marblehead

📍 781 / POP 19,800

First settled in 1629, Marblehead is a maritime village with winding streets, brightly painted Colonial houses, and 1000 sailing yachts bobbing at moorings in the harbor. This is the Boston area's premier yachting port and one of New England's most prestigious addresses. Clustered around the harbor, Marblehead center is dotted with historic houses, art galleries and waterside parks.

◎ Sights

Abbott Hall HISTORIC BUILDING
(Washington Sq, Washington St; ⊘9am-4pm)
FREE Every American is familiar with *The Spirit of '76*, the patriotic painting (c 1876) by Archibald M Willard, depicting three American Revolution figures – a drummer, a fife player and a flag bearer. The painting hangs in the selectmen's meeting room in Abbott Hall, home of the Marblehead Historical Commission.

The redbrick building with a lofty clock tower is the seat of Marblehead's town government, and houses artifacts of Marblehead's history, including the original title deed to Marblehead from the Nanapashemet Native Americans, dated 1684.

❶ Information

Marblehead Chamber of Commerce (📍781-639 8469; www.marbleheadchamber.org; cnr Pleasant, Essex & Spring Sts; ⊘noon-5pm Mon-Fri, 10am-5pm Sat & Sun) The booth near the town's main intersection has information about local B&Bs, restaurants and a weekly gallery walk.

❶ Getting There & Away

From Salem, MA 114 – locally called Pleasant St – passes through modern commercial Marblehead en route to the Marblehead Historic District (Old Town).

Newburyport & Plum Island

📍 978 / POP 17,800

At the mouth of the Merrimack River, Newburyport prospered as a shipping port and silversmith center during the late 18th century. Not too much has changed in the last 200 years, as Newburyport's brick buildings and graceful churches still show off the Federal style that was popular back in those days. Today the center of this town is a model of historic preservation and gentrification. Newburyport is also the gateway to the barrier Plum Island, a national wildlife refuge with some of the best bird-watching in New England.

◎ Sights

Parker River National Wildlife Refuge WILDLIFE RESERVE
(www.fws.gov/refuge/parker_river; Plum Island; car/bike & pedestrian $5/2; ⊘dawn-dusk) This 4662-acre sanctuary occupies the southern three-quarters of Plum Island. More than 800 species of bird, plant and animal reside in its many ecological habitats, including beaches, sand dunes, salt pans, salt marshes, freshwater impoundments and maritime forests. This is prime bird-watching territory, with a few miles of foot trails and several observation areas set up specifically for spotting shorebirds and waterfowl. Stop at the visitors center (p116) for maps, bird lists and loads of informative exhibits and programs.

The beaches are also pristine and lovely. But much of the beachfront is closed in summer because it is an important habitat for the endangered piping plover. During spring and fall, you can observe migrating songbirds, including magnificent wood warblers in the forest. In winter the refuge is a good place to see waterfowl, the rough-legged hawk and the snowy owl.

Custom House Maritime Museum MUSEUM
(www.customhousemaritimemuseum.org; 25 Water St; adult/senior & child $7/5; ⊘10am-4pm Tue-Sat, noon-4pm Sun May-Dec, 10am-4pm Sat & Sun only Jan-Apr) The 1835 granite Custom House, built by Robert Mills (of Washington Monument fame), is an excellent example of Classical Revival architecture. It now houses the Maritime Museum, which exhibits artifacts from Newburyport's maritime history as a major shipbuilding center and seaport. Seafaring folk will have a field day in the Moseley Gallery with its collection of model clipper ships.

Cushing House Museum & Garden HISTORIC SITE
(www.newburyhistory.com; 98 High St; adult/child $5/free; ⊘10am-4pm Tue-Fri, noon-4pm Sat & Sun Jun-Oct) This 21-room Federal home is decked out with fine furnishings and decorative pieces from the region. Collections of portraits, silver, needlework, toys and

clocks are all on display, not to mention the impressive Asian collection from Newburyport's early Chinese trade. The museum offers guided tours, exhibits, special events and lectures.

Sandy Point State Reservation BEACH
(www.mass.gov/dcr; ⊙dawn-8pm; 🚻) At the southern tip of Plum Island, Sandy Point is a 77-acre state park that is popular for swimming, sunning and tide-pooling. Walking trails and an observation tower also make for good bird-watching. Access Sandy Point through the Parker River National Wildlife Refuge, but note that parking is limited, so you'd best get an early start. Also, beware the blood-thirsty greenhead flies, which buzz and bite in July and August.

🏃 Activities

Newburyport Whale Watch BOATING
(☎800-848-1111; www.newburyportwhalewatch.com; 54 Merrimac St; adult/child $48/33; 🚻) Offers bird- and whale-watching tours, as well as occasional cruises to the Isle of Shoals. All cruises are on the cushy, custom-built *Captain's Lady*.

Plum Island Kayak KAYAKING
(☎978-462-5510; www.plumislandkayak.com; 38 Merrimac St; tours $45-55, single/tandem kayaks per day $65/85; ⊙9am-5pm Sat & Sun May & Oct, 9am-5pm Mon-Thu, to 8pm Fri-Sun Jun-Sep) Rent a kayak and explore Plum Island on your own, or join one of several tours during the day (or night) exploring the islands, mud bars, salt marshes and shoreline. Expect to see lots of birds, or for a truly unique experience, paddle among the resident seals.

🛏 Sleeping

Clark Currier Inn GUESTHOUSE $$
(☎978-465-8363; www.clarkcurrierinn.com; 45 Green St; r $185-210; P🅿❄@🛜) Travelers in search of a genteel experience can luxuriate in this 1803 Federal mansion, with its stately parlor and welcoming library. Details such as fireplaces and canopy beds make the seven guest rooms extra charming. A continental breakfast – fresh fruit and pastries – is served.

★Blue INN $$$
(☎855-255-2583; www.blueinn.com; 20 Fordham Way, Plum Island; d from $460; P❄🛜♨) In a drop-dead-gorgeous location on a beautiful beach, this sophisticated inn is quite a surprise on unassuming Plum Island. Rooms

DINING ATOP NEWBURYPORT'S LIGHTHOUSE

At **Rear Range Lighthouse** (☎800-727-2326; www.lighthousepreservation.org; 61½ Water St; meal for 2 $450), you'll have to climb five flights of stairs, plus a 6ft ladder. And you'll have to bring your own bottle of wine. At the top, you'll dine in complete privacy, surrounded by views of city, sea and sky. The food comes from one of four local restaurants, but the lighthouse location is what makes this a unique and supremely romantic experience.

The price includes a $350 tax-deductible donation to the Lighthouse Preservation Society.

feature high ceilings, contemporary decor, fresh white linen and streaming sunlight. Private decks, shared hot tubs and in-room fireplaces are a few of the perks – all steps from the surf. Breakfast is delivered to your room.

Garrison Inn BOUTIQUE HOTEL $$$
(☎978-499-8500; www.garrisoninn.com; 11 Brown Sq; d $260-340, ste from $300; P❄🛜♨) Once a private mansion, this gracious redbrick building is named for William Lloyd Garrison, the abolitionist who was born in Newburyport. Its 24 luxurious beige-and-black 'boudoirs' are done up in an elegant, eclectic mix of contemporary and classic. Original architectural features such as exposed-brick walls, cathedral ceilings and spiral staircases are highlighted. Made-to-order breakfast.

🍴 Eating

Revitalive Cafe & Juice Bar VEGAN $
(www.revitalive.com; Tannery Mall, 50 Water St; mains $8-10; ⊙7am-7pm Mon-Fri, 9am-5pm Sat & Sun; 🌱) Vegan, gluten-free, raw – whatever your dietary restriction, this sweet little cafe has got you covered. Even if you're an omnivore, you'll drool over the fresh salads, fresh-made soups and cold-pressed juices. Or feast on a deliciously healthy 'bowl', built on quinoa or rice. Also: smoothies. It's located inside the Tannery shopping mall.

Loretta AMERICAN $$
(☎978-463-0000; www.lorettarestaurant.com; 15 Pleasant St; sandwiches $7-15, dinner $16-28; ⊙11am-9:30pm, bar to 11pm or midnight) With

memorabilia on the walls and ribs and burgers on the menu, Loretta specializes in all-American goodness. This classic restaurant is a longtime favorite in Newburyport, but it recently moved to a bigger, swankier space. More to love.

★ Glenn's Food & Libations
INTERNATIONAL, SEAFOOD $$$

(☑ 978-465-3811; www.glennsrestaurant.com; 50 Water St; mains $25-35; ⊙ 5-10pm Tue-Sun) Now in a snazzy new location, Glenn is still out to spice up your life. He's got the seafood you're looking for, but he's serving it in ways you never imagined. Oysters might come baked with chili and pumpkin-seed pesto. Tuna is encrusted with sesame seeds and served with a blackberry-ginger sauce. The menu changes frequently, but it's always exciting.

Aside from the creative cooking, there's an excellent wine list, and live jazz on Sunday evening.

Plum Island Grille
SEAFOOD $$$

(☑ 978-463-2290; www.plumislandgrille.com; Sunset Blvd, Plum Island; mains lunch $14-23, dinner $25-34; ⊙ 4-8pm Mon-Fri, noon-8pm Sat & Sun) Cross the bridge to Plum Island to find this sophisticated seafood grill, serving up grilled fish and a specialty oyster menu. The food is inconsistent, but the setting is spectacular. Watch the sun set over the salt marsh and feast on the fruits of the sea. Reservations are recommended in season.

ⓘ Information

Greater Newburyport Chamber of Commerce (www.newburyportchamber.org; 38 Merrimac St; ⊙ 9am-5pm Mon-Fri, 10am-4pm Sat, noon-4pm Sun) Seasonal information booth in Market Sq from June to October.

Parker River Visitors Center (www.fws.gov/refuge/parker_river; 6 Plum Island Turnpike; ⊙ 11am-4pm) On the mainland, just east of the causeway. Stop by for maps, exhibits and other information about the refuge.

ⓘ Getting There & Away

BUS
C&J Trailways (www.ridecj.com; Storey Ave) runs hourly buses from Logan International Airport (adult/child $21/10.50) and Boston's South Station (adult/child $32/16).

CAR & MOTORCYCLE
From I-95 north, take exit 57 and follow signs to downtown Newburyport. There are free parking lots on Green and Merrimack Sts.

TRAIN
MBTA commuter rail (p90) runs a line from North Station to Newburyport ($10.50, one hour). There are more than 10 trains daily on weekdays, six on weekends.

SOUTH SHORE

As with much of the Massachusetts coast, the South Shore is blessed with historic sites and natural beauty. Seeing firsthand the challenges faced by the Pilgrims who first landed at Plymouth Rock is a vivid reminder of the value of religious tolerance and stubborn endurance – both at the core of the nation's foundation. Generations later, these values were lived out by founding father John Adams and his son John Quincy Adams.

Quincy
☑ 617 / POP 93,500

Like all good New England towns, Quincy, about 10 miles south of Boston, is not pronounced the obvious way: say 'Quin-zee' if you want to talk like the locals.

What makes Quincy notable – and earns this town the nickname 'The City of Presidents' – is that it is the birthplace of the second and sixth presidents of the United States: John Adams and John Quincy Adams. The collection of houses where the Adams family lived now makes up the Adams National Historic Park.

In more recent history, Quincy is the birthplace of the Dropkick Murphys and Dunkin' Donuts.

⊙ Sights

Adams National Historic Park
HISTORIC SITE

(www.nps.gov/adam; 1250 Hancock St; adult/child $10/free; ⊙ 9am-5pm mid-Apr–mid-Nov; ⓣ Quincy Center) The Adams family sights are accessible by guided tours departing from the Adams National Historic Park Visitor Center. Every half-hour (until 3:15pm), trolleys travel to the **John Adams and John Quincy Adams Birthplaces**, the oldest presidential birthplaces in the United States. The half-hour film *Enduring Legacy* is also shown at the visitor center.

The two 17th-century saltbox houses stand side by side along the old Coast Rd, which connected Plymouth to Boston. The houses are furnished as they would have

NEW ENGLAND'S CREEPIEST SLEEP?: LIZZIE BORDEN B&B

Lizzie Borden took an axe
And gave her mother forty whacks.
And when she saw what she had done
She gave her father forty-one.

This children's rhyme is just one of many inconsistencies in the account of what happened in Fall River on the night of 1892. Actually, Abby Borden was assaulted with 18 blows to the head with a hatchet, while Andrew Borden received 11. Ouch.

Although Lizzie Borden was acquitted of this crime, her story was rife with contradictions. That nobody else was ever accused was enough for Lizzie Borden to go down in popular history as America's most famous murderess.

Today, the Greek Revival Borden House in Fall River is the **Lizzie Borden Bed & Breakfast** (☑508-675-7333; www.lizzie-borden.com; 230 Second St; r $200-250). Decked out with period furnishings and decor, the eight rooms are named for the family members that actually stayed there. It's artfully and accurately remodeled, which makes it all the creepier.

If you don't care to spend the night in the room where Abby Borden was found murdered, you can just come for a **tour** (www.lizzie-borden.com; 230 Second St; adult/child $18/10; ⊙11am-3pm). You might meet one of the resident ghosts (according to paranormal investigators).

been in the 18th century, so visitors can see where John Adams began his law career, started his family and wrote the Massachusetts Constitution (which was later used as the basis for the US Constitution).

From here, the trolley continues to the **Old House**, also called Peacefields, which was the residence of four generations of the Adams family from 1788 to 1927. The house contains original furnishings and decorations from the Adams family, including the chair in which John Adams died on July 4, 1826, the 50th anniversary of the Declaration of Independence (and, spookily, the same day that Thomas Jefferson died on his estate in Virginia). In the grounds, the spectacular two-story library and the lovely formal gardens are highlights.

Presidential Crypt   CHURCH
(www.ufpc.org; 1306 Hancock St; donation adult/child/senior & student $5/free/3; ⊙11am-4pm Mon-Fri, noon-4pm Sat & Sun mid-Apr–mid-Nov; Ⓣ Quincy Center) John and Abigail Adams and John Quincy and Louisa Catherine Adams are all interred in the basement of the handsome granite United First Parish Church, in the center of Quincy. The crypt is open by guided tour.

Hancock Cemetery   CEMETERY
(1307 Hancock St; ⊙dawn-dusk; Ⓣ Quincy Center) Opposite the church, Hancock Cemetery is

the final resting place of many notable Quincy residents, including most of the Quincy and Adams families. The Adams family vault, near the street, was the original site of the graves of the presidents and their wives, before they were interred in the Presidential Crypt in the church across the street. A map to Hancock Cemetery is available from the church.

World's End   PARK
(www.thetrustees.org; 250 Martin's Lane, Hingham; adult/child $6/free; ⊙8am-dusk) This 251-acre peninsula was designed by Frederick Law Olmsted for residential development in 1889. Carriage paths were laid out and trees were planted, but the houses were never built. Instead, wide, grassy meadows attract butterflies and grass-nesting birds. Today, management by the Trustees of Reservations guarantees continued serenity and beauty. The more than 4 miles of tree-lined paths are perfect for walking, mountain biking or cross-country skiing – download a map from the Trustees website. World's End is accessible by car from Hingham.

🍴 Eating & Drinking

Craig's Cafe   CAFE $
(www.craigscafe.com; 1354 Hancock St; mains $8-10; ⊙7am-3pm Mon & Tue, 7am-3pm & 5-9pm Wed-Fri, 7am-1pm & 5-10pm Sat, 7am-1pm Sun;

T Quincy Center) Now under new ownership, this simple cafe serves soups, salads and sandwiches with a smile. Breakfast is a highlight, with a half a dozen Benedicts and no shortage of omelets, pancakes and more. Daily specials guarantee a fresh and delicious lunch. This place is a local favorite.

Townshend   MODERN AMERICAN $$$
(☑ 617-481-9694; www.thetownshend.com; 1250 Hancock St; mains lunch $12-17, dinner $24-29; ☺ 11am-1am Mon-Fri, 4pm-1am Sat) Quincy isn't exactly known for fine dining and cocktails, but the Townshend might just change that. The menu is broad (and frequently changing), but specialties like golf-ball-sized arancini and handmade pasta give it an Italian bent. Local beers on tap and craft cocktails make this a fine place to come for a drink, too.

Paddy Barry's   IRISH PUB
(www.paddybarrys.com; 1574 Hancock St; ☺ from 1pm Mon-Thu, from noon Fri-Sun; T Quincy Center) No food, just friendly folks, inviting atmosphere and perfectly poured Guinness. You might catch some live music, but the good craic is guaranteed.

❶ Information

Adams National Historic Park Visitor Center (www.nps.gov/adam; 1250 Hancock St; ☺ 9am-5pm mid-Apr–mid-Nov, 10am-4pm Tue-Fri mid-Nov–mid-Apr; T Quincy Center) Directly opposite the T station. Tours of the national park start here, and plenty of information about the surrounding area is also available.

❶ Getting There & Away

CAR

Drive south from Boston on I-93 to exit 12 and follow the signs over the Neponset Bridge. Take Hancock St into Quincy Center.

SUBWAY

The easiest way to reach the Adams National Historic Park from Boston is to take the Red Line to Quincy Center (Braintree line).

Plymouth

📞 508 / POP 58,300

Plymouth calls itself 'America's Home Town.' It was here that the Pilgrims first settled in the winter of 1620, seeking a place where they could practice their religion as they wished, without interference from government. An innocuous, weathered ball of granite – the famous Plymouth Rock – marks the spot where they supposedly first stepped ashore in this foreign land, and many museums and historic houses in the surrounding streets recall their struggles, sacrifices and triumphs.

◉ Sights

★**Plimoth Plantation**   MUSEUM
(www.plimoth.org; 137 Warren Ave; adult/child $28/16; ☺ 9am-5pm Apr-Nov; ♿) Three miles south of Plymouth center, Plimoth Plantation authentically re-creates the Pilgrims' settlement in its primary exhibit, entitled **1627 English Village**. Everything in the village – costumes, implements, vocabulary, artistry, recipes and crops – has been painstakingly researched and remade. Costumed interpreters, acting in character, explain the details of daily life and answer your questions as you watch them work and play.

During the winter of 1620–21, half of the Pilgrims died of disease, privation and exposure to the elements. But new arrivals joined the survivors the following year, and by 1627 – just before an additional influx of Pilgrims founded the colony of Massachusetts Bay – Plymouth Colony was on the road to prosperity. Plimoth Plantation provides excellent educational and entertaining insight into what was happening in Plymouth during that period.

In the **crafts center**, you can help artisans as they weave baskets and cloth, throw pottery and build fine furniture using the techniques and tools of the early 17th century. Exhibits explain how these manufactured goods were shipped across the Atlantic in exchange for Colonial necessities.

The **Wampanoag Homesite** replicates the life of a Native American community in the same area during that time. Homesite huts are made of wattle and daub (a framework of woven rods and twigs covered and plastered with clay); inhabitants engage in crafts while wearing traditional garb. Unlike the actors at the English Village, these individuals are not acting as historic characters but are indigenous people speaking from a modern perspective.

★**Mayflower II**   SHIP
(www.plimoth.org; State Pier, Water St; adult/child $12.50/8.50; ☺ 9am-5pm Apr-Nov; ♿) If Plymouth Rock tells us little about the Pilgrims, *Mayflower II* speaks volumes: it is a replica of the small ship in which they made the fateful voyage. Actors in period costume are on board, recounting harrowing tales from the journey.

As you climb aboard, you have to wonder how 102 people – with all the household effects, tools, provisions, animals and seed to establish a colony – could have lived together on this tiny vessel for 66 days, subsisting on hard, moldy biscuits, dried peas and beer as the ship passed through the stormy North Atlantic waters. But they did, landing on this wild, forested shore in the frigid months of December 1620 – testament to their courageous spirit and the strength of their religious beliefs.

★ **Pilgrim Hall Museum**   MUSEUM
(www.pilgrimhall.org; 75 Court St; adult/child $10/6; ⊘9:30am-4:30pm Feb-Dec; 🖤) Claiming to be the oldest continually operating public museum in the country, Pilgrim Hall Museum was founded in 1824. Its exhibits are not reproductions but real objects that the Pilgrims and their Wampanoag neighbors used in their daily lives – from Governor Bradford's chair to Constance Hopkins' beaver hat.

The exhibits are dedicated to correcting the misrepresentations about the Pilgrims that have been passed down through history.

Plimoth Grist Mill   MUSEUM
(☑508-746-1622; www.plimoth.org/mill; 6 Spring Lane; adult/child $7/5; ⊘9am-5pm Apr-Nov; 🖤) In 1636, local leaders constructed a gristmill on Town Brook so that the growing community could grind corn and produce cornmeal. Today, the replica mill is on the site of the original, still grinding corn the old-fashioned way.

A few days a week, you can see the waterwheel at work, hear the crackling of corn and smell the cornmeal as it is produced. On other days, tours demonstrate the process of grinding whole corn into cornmeal and discuss the ecology of the area.

Plymouth
Antiquarian Society   HISTORIC SITE
(www.plymouthantiquariansociety.org; 126 Water St) Maintains three historic houses from three different centuries. The oldest is the **1677 Harlow Old Fort House** (119 Sandwich St; ⊘11am-3pm Tue Jun-Aug), one of the few remaining 'First Period' structures in Plymouth. On pretty North St, the **1749 Spooner House** (27 North St; adult/child $6/3; ⊘2-6pm Thu & Sun Jun-Aug) showcases 200 years of domestic life, complete with original furniture and housewares. Finally, the **1809 Hedge House** (126 Water St; adult/child $6/3;

⊘2-6pm Wed-Sun Jun-Aug) is a grand, Federal edifice overlooking Plymouth Harbor.

The society also oversees **Sacrifice Rock** (394 Old Sandwich Rd) [FREE], the oldest of its historic sites. 'The other rock' is an ancient landmark where Wampanoag travelers would place branches and stones as offerings in exchange for safe travels. It's about 6 miles south of Plymouth center.

Myles Standish State Forest   PARK
(www.mass.gov/dcr; Cranberry Rd, South Carver; parking $8-10; ⊘dawn-dusk; 🖤) About 6 miles south of Plymouth, this 16,000-acre park is the largest public recreation area in southeastern Massachusetts. It contains 15 miles of biking and hiking trails and 16 ponds – two with beaches. It's a wonderful wilderness for picnicking, fishing, swimming and camping. From MA 3, take exit 5 to Long Pond Rd.

1667 Jabez Howland House   HISTORIC SITE
(www.pilgrimjohnhowlandsociety.org; 33 Sandwich St; adult/child/senior & student $6/5/3; ⊘10am-4:30pm late May-Nov) This is the only house in Plymouth that was home to a known *Mayflower* passenger. John Howland lived here with his wife, Elizabeth Tilley, and their son Jabez and his family. The house has been restored to its original appearance, complete with period furnishings and many artifacts and documents from the family.

Richard Sparrow House   HISTORIC SITE
(www.sparrowhouse.com; 42 Summer St; adult/child $2/1; ⊘10am-5pm) Plymouth's oldest house was built by one of the original Pilgrim settlers in 1640. Today there is a small art gallery in the more recent addition, while the oldest, original part of the house is maintained to 17th-century standards as a small museum.

Plymouth

Plymouth Rock   MONUMENT

(Water St) Thousands of visitors come each year to look at this weathered granite ball and consider what it was like for the Pilgrims who stepped ashore on a foreign land in the autumn of 1620. We don't really know that the Pilgrims landed on Plymouth Rock, as it's not mentioned in any early written accounts. But the story gained popularity during Colonial times.

In 1774, 20 yoke of oxen were harnessed to the rock to move it – splitting it in the process. Half of the cloven boulder went on display in Pilgrim Hall from 1834 to 1867. The sea and wind lashed at the other half, and innumerable small pieces were chipped off and carried away by souvenir hunters over the centuries. By the 20th century the rock was an endangered artifact, and steps were taken to protect it. In 1921 the reunited halves were sheltered in the present granite enclosure. In 1989 the rock was repaired and strengthened to withstand weathering. And

so it stands today, relatively small, broken and mended, an enduring symbol of the quest for religious freedom.

Mayflower Society Museum   HISTORIC SITE

(www.themayflowersociety.com; 4 Winslow St; adult/child $7/5; ☺11am-4pm May-Oct) The offices of the General Society of Mayflower Descendants are housed in the magnificent 1754 house of Edward Winslow, the great-grandson of Plymouth Colony's third governor. Guided tours show off antique furniture, family portraiture and stunning architectural details.

👉 Tours

Dead of Night Ghost Tours   HISTORY

(☎508-866-5111, 508-277-2371; www.deadofnight ghosttours.com; $15-20) Here's where you'll learn about the dark side of Plymouth history. As the sun sets, hoist a gas lantern and set out to explore the city's age-old streets and ancient burial grounds. You can choose

Plymouth

◎ Top Sights
1 Mayflower II	D2
2 Pilgrim Hall Museum	B2

◎ Sights
3 1667 Jabez Howland House	C4
4 1749 Spooner House	C3
5 1809 Hedge House	B1
6 Mayflower Society Museum	C2
7 Plimoth Grist Mill	C4
Plymouth Antiquarian Society	(see 5)
8 Plymouth Rock	D2
9 Richard Sparrow House	C4

✪ Activities, Courses & Tours
10 Capt John Boats	B1

🛏 Sleeping
11 By the Sea B&B	C2
12 Seabreeze Inn	B2

✕ Eating
13 Blue Blinds Bakery	C3
14 Blue-Eyed Crab	B1
15 KKatie's Burger Bar	C4

to end by visiting two haunted houses. There is no guarantee that you'll witness paranormal activity on the tour, but there's no guarantee that you won't!

Capt John Boats   BOATING
(🖉 508-746-2643; www.captjohn.com; Town Wharf; adult/child $48/29; ⏱ tours Apr-Oct; 🐾) Offers loads of options to get you out on the water, including whale-watching cruises and fishing trips. The whale-watching is a four-hour journey out to Stellwagen Bank (p106), the primary feeding grounds for five species of whale, not to mention dolphins and sea birds.

Pilgrim Path   HISTORY
(www.pilgrimpathtours.com) The Plymouth Area Chamber of Commerce offers this free audio tour. Pick up a headset at the Destination Plymouth visitor center (p122) or use the QR codes and listen on your phone. You'll hear about all the town's major historic sites, as well as some lesser-known sites and statues of 17th-century personalities that are scattered around town.

Plymouth Trolley Tours   BUS
(www.p-b.com; 1 ride adult/child $10/5, all-day pass $15/7.50; ⏱ 10am-5pm Jul & Aug) This traditional trolley tour covers the history of Plymouth from the Pilgrims to the fisherfolk. It includes all of the major sites – the all-day pass allows you to hop off to check them out, then hop back on the next trolley.

★ Festivals & Events

**America's Hometown
Thanksgiving Celebration**   CULTURAL
(www.usathanksgiving.com; ⏱ Nov) The weekend before Thanksgiving, historic Plymouth comes to life as pilgrims, pioneers and patriots parade the streets of 'America's Hometown.' The event features a food festival, a concert series, a craft show and the ongoing festivities at the 'historic village.' Have some fun, then stop by Plimoth Plantation to see how the Pilgrims really celebrated (or rather, didn't celebrate) Thanksgiving.

🛏 Sleeping

There are two sorts of accommodations options in Plymouth: beach motels, offering easy access to the sand and good amenities for families, and B&Bs, offering central locations and romantic, historic digs. You'll also find some more affordable but less appealing motels near the highway.

By the Sea B&B   B&B $$
(🖉 508-830-9643; www.bytheseabedandbreakfast.com; 22 Winslow St; ste $135-190; ⏱ May-Nov; 🅿✳🛜) There are two luxurious suites in this Victorian home overlooking Plymouth Harbor. Both offer lovely ocean views, which you might even enjoy from bed. There is also a wide front porch, should you care to feel the breeze – or shoot the breeze with your friendly hosts. Breakfast is served at a nearby restaurant.

Seabreeze Inn   B&B $$
(🖉 866-746-0282, 508-746-0282; www.seabreezeinnbandb.com; 20 Chilton St; ste $150-175; 🅿✳🛜) A grand Victorian with ocean views, this beauty was built in 1885 as the home of a sea captain. Now it is a delightful place to stay. Three pastel-painted suites have ornamental fireplaces, hardwood floors and lacy curtains. Breakfast is made to order, featuring bacon and eggs and homemade breads and pastries.

Pilgrim Sands   HOTEL $$
(🖉 800-729-7263; www.pilgrimsands.com; 150 Warren Ave; d without ocean view $139-189, with ocean view $219-229; 🅿✳@≋) This mini resort is a good option for families as it's right on a private beach and directly opposite Plimoth Plantation. The exterior is

not much to look at, but most of the rooms are recently refurbished and quite smart, while service is top notch.

✗ Eating

★ Blue Blinds Bakery   BAKERY $

(www.blueblindsbakery.com; 7 North St; ⏱6am-9pm Mon-Thu, 7am-3pm Fri & Sun; 🖋🖶) Blue Blinds is a cozy house – it feels like a home, really – with plants in the windows and a fire in the fireplace and folks sipping coffee on the shady front porch. The baked goods are out of this world, including fresh-baked organic breads, muffins and pastries. Breakfast is served all day, but the sandwiches and homemade soups are also divine.

KKatie's Burger Bar   BURGERS $

(www.kkaties.com; 38 Main St Extension; burgers $11-13; ⏱11:30am-11pm Sun-Thu, to midnight Fri & Sat; 🖶) Legend has it that when the Pilgrims landed at Plymouth Rock, they were dying for a burger. Finally, after 400 years, KKatie is fulfilling this wish. And apparently the Pilgrims all wanted different kinds of burger, because she's got more than 20 varieties on offer. Your accompaniments are sweet-potato fries, truffle fries or green fries (deep-fried green beans).

Lobster Hut   SEAFOOD $$

(www.lobsterhutplymouth.com; 25 Town Wharf; mains $10-20; ⏱11am-9pm) There's nothing fancy going on at the Lobster Hut, but who needs 'fancy' when you've got fresh seafood and breezy harbor views? It's a classic seafood shack, where you place your order at the counter and listen for your number. Preparations are straightforward and delicious. The dining room has not a speck of atmosphere, but there's plenty of outdoor seating.

Blue-Eyed Crab   SEAFOOD $$

(www.blue-eyedcrab.com; 170 Water St; sandwiches $12-16, dinner mains $21-29; ⏱11:30am-9pm Sun-Thu, to 10pm Fri & Sat) There are a few tried-and-true seafood restaurants clustered around Town Wharf. But if you like some Caribbean flavor with your fish (and perhaps a cocktail), head to this fun and funky joint, with tropical fish floating around its sunny-yellow walls.

ⓘ Information

Destination Plymouth (www.seeplymouth. com; 130 Water St; ⏱9am-8pm Jun-Aug, to 5pm Apr, May & Sep-Nov) Located at the rotary across from Plymouth Harbor; provides loads of information about local attractions, as well as assistance with B&B reservations.

Plymouth Guide Online (www.plymouthguide. com) Lots of information about tourist attractions and local events.

ⓘ Getting There & Away

BOAT

The **Plymouth-to-Provincetown Express Ferry** (www.captjohn.com; State Pier, 77 Water St; ⏱round-trip adult/child $45/30) deposits you on the tip of Cape Cod faster than a car would. From late June to early September, the 90-minute journey departs Plymouth at 10am and leaves Provincetown at 4:30pm.

BUS

Buses operated by **Plymouth & Brockton** (P&B; www.p-b.com) travel hourly to South Station ($15, one hour) or Logan International Airport ($22) in Boston. The Plymouth P&B terminal is at the commuter parking lot, exit 5 off MA 3. Hop on a PAL bus into Plymouth center.

CAR & MOTORCYCLE

Plymouth is 41 miles south of Boston via MA 3; it takes an hour with some traffic. From Providence, it's the same distance and time, but you'll want to head west on US 44.

TRAIN

You can reach Plymouth from Boston by MBTA commuter rail (p90) trains, which depart from South Station three or four times a day ($10.50, 90 minutes). From the station at Cordage Park, PAL buses connect to Plymouth center.

ⓘ Getting Around

GATRA (Plymouth Area Link; www.gatra.org; 1 way/day pass $1/3) operates several shuttle buses. The Freedom Link runs from the train depot to Plymouth center, while the Mayflower Link runs from Plymouth center to Plimoth Plantation.

New Bedford

♫ 508 / POP 95,100

During its heyday as a whaling port (1765–1860), New Bedford commanded as many as 400 whaling ships. This vast fleet brought home hundreds of thousands of barrels of whale oil for lighting America's lamps. Novelist Herman Melville worked on one of these ships for four years, and thus set his celebrated novel, *Moby-Dick; or, The Whale*, in New Bedford. Nowadays, the city center constitutes the New Bedford Whaling

National Historic Park, which encompasses an excellent whaling museum, some other historic buildings and the gritty working waterfront.

Sights

New Bedford Whaling Museum   MUSEUM
(www.whalingmuseum.org; 18 Johnny Cake Hill; adult/child/senior/student $16/6/14/9; ⊙9am-5pm Apr-Dec, 9am-4pm Tue-Sat, 11am-4pm Sun Jan-Mar) The centerpiece of New Bedford, this excellent, hands-on museum remembers the town's heyday as a whaling port. The museum occupies seven buildings situated between William and Union Sts. A 66ft skeleton of a blue whale and a smaller skeleton of a sperm whale welcome you at the entrance. To learn what whaling was all about, you need only tramp the decks of the *Lagoda,* a fully rigged, half-size replica of an actual whaling bark.

Seamen's Bethel   CHURCH
(www.seamensbethel.org; 15 Johnny Cake Hill; admission by donation; ⊙8am-4pm Mon-Fri May-Oct) Across from the Whaling Museum, this small chapel was a refuge from the rigors and stresses of maritime life. Melville immortalized it in *Moby-Dick,* where he wrote 'In this same New Bedford there stands a Whaleman's Chapel, and few are the moody fishermen...who fail to make a Sunday visit to the spot.'

This is where the marathon, nonstop reading of the novel takes place every year on January 3, the anniversary of Melville's embarkation from New Bedford harbor.

Eating

Quahog Republic Whaler's Tavern   SEAFOOD $$
(www.quahogrepublic.com; 24 North Water St; mains $8-20; ⊙11:30am-11pm, bar to 1am) You're in Whaling City; why not grab lunch at this friendly whaler's tavern, where you can feast on a well-stocked raw bar, yummy cod cakes or 'monsta lobsta rolls'? To complement the food (or not), there are a dozen mostly local beers on tap, enticing craft cocktails and dangerous rum flights.

Information

Your starting point for the New Bedford National Historic Park is the **Park Visitor Center** (www.nps.gpv/nebe; 33 Williams St; ⊙9am-5pm, closed Mon & Tue Jan-Mar), which offers lots of information, including a map for a self-guided walking tour and activity books for kids.

Getting There & Away

BOAT
Sea Streak fast ferry (www.seastreak.com; round-trip adult $50-70, child $35-40) runs from New Bedford to Vineyard Haven and Oak Bluffs on Martha's Vineyard (one hour, four to six daily) from mid-May to mid-October.

BUS
Peter Pan Bus (p85) offers bus services to/from Providence ($15, one hour, six daily) from the New Bedford ferry dock. **Dattco** (www.dattco.com) runs buses to Boston South Station ($15, 1½ hours, 12 daily), departing from the Southeastern Regional Transit Authority (SRTA) station at the corner of Elm and Pleasant Sts.

CAR & MOTORCYCLE
From I-195 take MA 18 south to exit 18S.

Cape Cod, Nantucket & Martha's Vineyard

✅ 508, 774

Best Places to Eat

➡ Chatham Fish Pier Market (p143)

➡ BlackFish (p150)

➡ Canteen (p154)

➡ Proprietors (p162)

➡ Sesuit Habor Cafe (p138)

Best Places to Sleep

➡ Inn at the Oaks (p146)

➡ Wequassett Resort (p140)

➡ Anchor-In (p133)

➡ Summercamp (p169)

➡ Roux (p154)

Why Go?

When summer comes around, New England's top seashore destination gets packed to the gills. Cars stream over the two bridges that connect Cape Cod to the mainland, ferries shuttle visitors to and from the islands, and sun-seeking bodies plop down on towels all along the shore.

This trio of destinations offers a beach for every mood. You can surf a wild Atlantic wave or dip a paddle into a quiet cove. Or just chill out and watch the kids build sandcastles.

But there's much more than sun, sand and surf. You'll find lighthouses to climb, clam shacks to frequent and beach parties to revel in. The Cape and Islands have scenic cycling paths and hiking trails, excellent art galleries and summer theater – and any one of them alone would be reason enough to come here. In combination, the appeal is undeniable.

When to Go
Barnstable

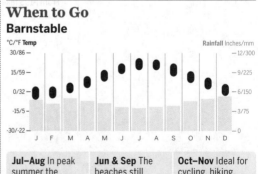

Jul–Aug In peak summer the ocean's warmest, the partying's hardest and the festivities maxed.

Jun & Sep The beaches still dazzle but crowds are thinner, hotel rates cheaper and traffic jams fewer.

Oct–Nov Ideal for cycling, hiking, kayaking – even a little swimming.

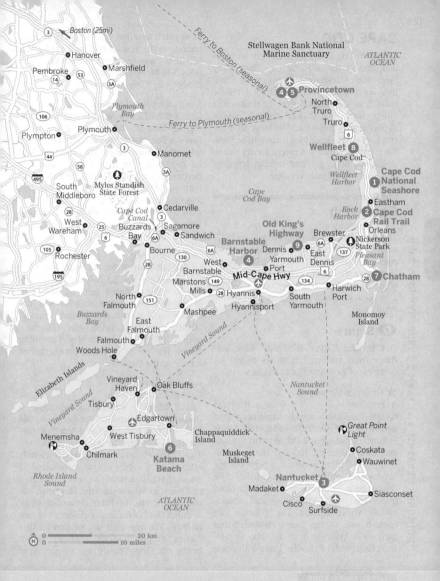

Cape Cod, Nantucket & Martha's Vineyard Highlights

1 Cape Cod National Seashore (p150) Climbing dunes and bodysurfing waves.

2 Cape Cod Rail Trail (p137) Cycling the bicycle trail and discovering your own swimming hole.

3 Nantucket (p157) Wandering the cobbled, Moby Dick–era streets of this town.

4 Whale-watching (p153) Ogling humpbacks from a boat out of Provincetown or Barnstable.

5 Provincetown (p150) Dining superbly and reveling in the carnival street scene.

6 Katama Beach (p171) Riding a wave on the Vineyard's south coast.

7 Chatham Fish Pier Market (p143) Eating fresh-off-the-boat seafood and scouting for seals.

8 Beachcomber (p148) Joining the party scene at the Cape's hottest nightspot.

9 Old King's Highway (p139) Admiring sea captains' mansions and antiquing.

CAPE COD

Quaint fishing villages, kitschy tourist traps and genteel towns – the Cape has many faces. Each attracts a different crowd. Families seeking calm waters perfect for little tykes favor Cape Cod Bay on the peninsula's quieter north side. College students looking to play hard in the day and let loose after the sun goes down set out for Falmouth or Wellfleet. Provincetown is a mecca for art lovers, whale-watchers, gay and lesbian travelers and...well, just about everyone.

Sandwich

📞 508 / POP 20,600

The Cape's oldest town (founded in 1637) makes a perfect first impression as you cross over the canal from the mainland. Head straight to the village center, where white-steepled churches, period homes and a working grist mill surround a picturesque swan pond.

◉ Sights

Pick up the *Village Walking Guide* brochure from various businesses to get an overview of local services and sights.

★**Heritage Museums
& Gardens** MUSEUM, GARDENS
(📞508-888-3300; www.heritagemuseumsand gardens.org; 67 Grove St; adult/child $18/8; ☺9am-5pm mid-Apr–mid-Oct; 🖼) Fun for kids and adults alike, the 100-acre Heritage Museums & Gardens sports a superb vintage automobile collection in a Shaker-style round barn, an authentic 1908 carousel (rides free with admission) and unusual folk art collections. The grounds also contain one of the finest rhododendron gardens in America; from mid-May to mid-June thousands of 'rhodies' blaze with color.

Here you'll also find ways to get your heart racing, via the new **Adventure Park** (📞508-866-0199; www.heritageadventurepark.org; 2hr ticket $34-44; ☺8am-8pm Jun-Aug, hours vary mid-Apr–May & Sep–mid-Nov; 🖼).

Sandwich Glass Museum MUSEUM
(📞508-888-0251; www.sandwichglassmuseum. org; 129 Main St; adult/child $9/2; ☺9:30am-5pm Apr-Dec, to 4pm Wed-Sun Feb-Mar) Sandwich glass, now prized by collectors, had its heyday in the 19th century, and this heritage is artfully displayed in this excellent, sprawling museum. But it's not just a period glass collection – there are also glass-blowing demonstrations given hourly throughout the day and a cool contemporary gallery.

Dexter Grist Mill HISTORIC BUILDING
(📞508-888-4361; Water St; adult/child $4/3; ☺11am-4:30pm Mon-Sat, 1-4pm Sun mid-Jun–mid-Oct) The restored mill on the edge of Shawme Pond dates to 1654 and has centuries-old gears that still grind cornmeal (available to buy). Bring your camera – with its spinning waterwheel and paddling swans, it's one of the most photographed scenes on the Cape.

**Green Briar Nature
Center & Jam Kitchen** MUSEUM
(📞508-888-6870; www.thorntonburgess.org; 6 Discovery Hill Rd; suggested donation adult/child $2/1; ☺10am-4pm Mon-Sat, 1-4pm Sun mid-Apr–Dec, 10am-4pm Tue-Sat Jan–mid-Apr; 🖼) This is a lovely mixed bag of family-friendly attractions: a nature center surrounded by walking trails; a small museum dedicated to Thornton W Burgess, the Sandwich native who wrote the Peter Cottontail series of children's books; and a century-old jam kitchen. You can sign up for jam-making classes, or purchase the kitchen's output in the gift shop. There's also a program of

---

LOCAL KNOWLEDGE

SANDWICH BOARDWALK

A local favorite that's missed by most visitors, the wooden-plank **Sandwich Boardwalk** (Boardwalk Rd) extends a scenic 1350ft across an expansive marsh to **Town Neck Beach**. The beach itself is a bit rocky – so-so for swimming but perfect for walks and beachcombing. Once you reach the beach, turn right to make a 1.5-mile loop along the shoreline and then follow the creek back to the boardwalk. There's a $15 parking fee in July and August; at other times it's free.

You won't find any signs: to get there, take MA 6A to the center of Sandwich, turn north onto Jarves St at the lights, then left on Factory St and right onto Boardwalk Rd.

CAPE COD BEACH GUIDE

The crowning glory of the Cape is its stunning beaches. Each has its own personality and there's one that's bound to fit yours. The top beaches for...

Surfing White Crest Beach (p146) in Wellfleet; Coast Guard Beach (p145) in Eastham

Windsurfing Kalmus Beach (p132) in Hyannis; West Dennis Beach (p137) in West Dennis

Sunsets First Encounter Beach (p145) in Eastham; Herring Cove Beach (p151) in Provincetown

Sunrises Nauset Beach (p144) in Orleans

Tidal flats Skaket Beach (p144) in Orleans; First Encounter Beach (p145) in Eastham

Fishing Race Point Beach (p151) in Provincetown; Sandy Neck Beach (p132) in Barnstable

Families Chapin Memorial Beach (p137) in Dennis; Old Silver Beach (p129) in Falmouth

Singles Craigville Beach (p132) in Barnstable; Cahoon Hollow Beach in Wellfleet

Seclusion Long Point Beach (p151) in Provincetown

Long walks Sandy Neck Beach (p132) in Barnstable; Chapin Memorial Beach (p137) in Dennis

Picnics Gray's Beach (p136) in Yarmouth Port; Veterans Beach (p133) in Hyannis

Sunbathing Take your pick!

events for kids and adults, from gardening to nature walks. It's east of town, signposted off Rte 6A.

Hoxie House HISTORIC BUILDING
(☑508-888-4361; 18 Water St; adult/child $4/3; ☉11am-4:30pm Mon-Sat, 1-4:30pm Sun mid-Jun–mid-Oct) Get a feel for what life was like for early settlers by touring Hoxie House, the oldest house on Cape Cod (c 1640). The saltbox-style house has been faithfully restored to the colonial period, complete with antiques, brick-fire hearth and the like.

Cape Cod Canal CANAL
(www.capecodcanal.us; 🚻🚹) FREE Cape Cod isn't connected by land to the mainland, but it's not exactly an island, or at least wasn't until the Cape Cod Canal was dug in 1914. The 7-mile-long canal saves ships from having to sail an extra 135 miles around the treacherous tip of the Cape. The canal is also a great recreational resource.

It's bordered on both sides by **bike paths** that attract not only cyclists but also in-line skaters, power walkers and kids with fishing poles. On a sunny day it looks like a scene from a Norman Rockwell painting.

For the lowdown on the canal, stop by the **Cape Cod Canal Visitor Center** (☑508-833-9678; www.capecodcanal.us; 60 Ed Moffitt Dr; ☉10am-5pm May-Oct), near the Sandwich Marina.

🍴 Sleeping & Eating

In keeping with the old-fashioned nature of the town, there are a number of cozy downtown inns in period buildings. More motels and inns line MA 6A.

Shawme-Crowell
State Forest CAMPGROUND $
(☑508-888-0351; reservations 877-422-6762; www.reserveamerica.com; 42 Main St; tent sites $20; yurts $50-60; ☉May–mid-Oct; 🚻) You'll find 285 cool and shady campsites (none with hookups) in this 760-acre pine and oak woodland. It's just 1 mile from the Cape Cod Canal and is popular with cyclists. If you don't have a tent, there are a handful of yurts on-site. Winter weekend camping is available.

Isaiah Jones Homestead B&B $$$
(☑508-888-9115; www.isaiahjones.com; 165 Main St; r $199-329; 🚻🏠) There's primo main-street appeal to this Victorian house, with pretty gardens and a fish pond. Inside are five period rooms in the main house, and two in the carriage house. Luxury linens, porch rockers, evening port by the fireplace – this is Sandwich at its cushiest.

Cape Cod

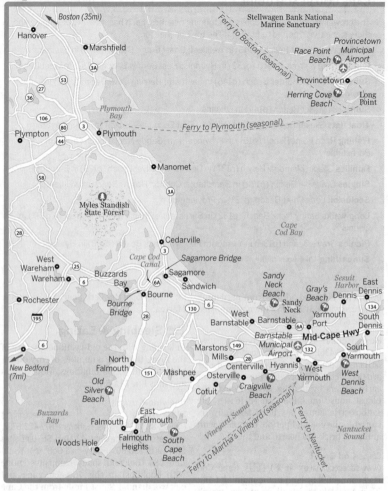

Brown Jug   DELI, CAFE **$**
(☑508-888-0053; www.thebrownjug.com; 1 Jarves St; sandwiches $7-9; ⊙10am-8pm Tue-Sat, noon-7pm Sun) Prime picnic supplies can be found at this specialty food store that also serves as wine purveyor and cafe. Wood-fired pizzas make for a perfect pit stop.

Dunbar House   CAFE **$$**
(☑508-833-2485; www.dunbarteashop.com; 1 Water St; mains $12-17; ⊙11am-5pm Sun-Wed, 11am-9pm Thu-Sat) Tucked amid gardens, a swan pond and period homes, the tea room resembles a Victorian-era movie set. The crumpets, cream teas and classical music

just add to the setting. Drop by for a spot of tea or enjoy a leisurely meal of ploughman's lunch, quiche or meat pie.

Belfry Inn & Bistro   MODERN AMERICAN **$$$**
(☑508-888-8550; www.belfryinn.com; 8 Jarves St; lunch $10-26, dinner mains $15-35; ⊙11:30am-3pm & 5-9pm Wed-Sun) If you like quirky, this restaurant (in the B&B of the same name) occupies the sanctuary of a former church and is one of the Cape's more unusual fine-dining spots. The changing menu of New American cuisine strays beyond the predictable, with options like ramen soup

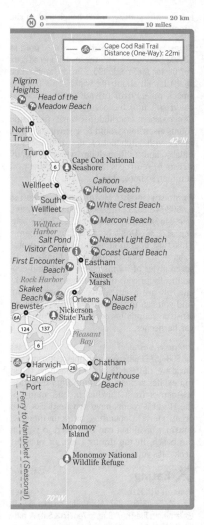

converge in the village center at Shawme Pond. Tupper Rd, off MA 6A, leads to the Cape Cod Canal.

Falmouth

📞 508 / POP 31,600

Crowd-pleasing beaches, a terrific bike trail and the quaint seaside village of Woods Hole are the highlights of the Cape's second-largest town. Falmouth puffs with pride over its most cherished daughter, Katharine Lee Bates, who wrote the words to the nation's favorite patriotic hymn, *America the Beautiful*.

⊙ Sights

Deeply indented Falmouth has 70 miles of coastline, with 10 beaches (nine saltwater, and one freshwater at Grew's Pond). From about mid-June to mid-September, all are attended by lifeguards in summer, and parking fees are charged ($10 to $20 per day). See more at www.falmouthmass.us/beach.

Old Silver Beach BEACH
(off MA 28A, North Falmouth; 🅿) Of all Falmouth's beaches, none is finer than Old Silver Beach. This long, sandy stretch of beach attracts scores of college students, families and day-trippers from the city. A rock jetty, sandbars and tidal pools provide lots of fun diversions for kids. The parking lot often fills up on hot days, so plan on getting there early. Facilities include changing rooms and a snack bar. Parking costs $20 in summer.

Highfield Hall & Gardens HISTORIC BUILDING
(📞508-495-1878; www.highfieldhallandgardens. org; 56 Highfield Dr; adult/child $5/free, 4-7pm Fri free; ⊙10am-4pm Mon-Thu, 10am-7pm Fri, 10am-2pm Sat & Sun mid-Apr–Oct) Saved from the wrecking ball in the 1990s and lovingly restored by the community, Highfield Hall dates from 1878 and was one of the early summer mansions to grace Cape Cod. It's now open to the public as a museum and cultural center; check the website for events and activities (art exhibitions, concerts on the lawn etc). **Beebe Woods**, the lovely surrounding gardens and trails, is open to visitors year-round.

Falmouth Museums on the Green MUSEUM
(📞508-548-4857; www.falmouthhistoricalsociety. org; 55 Palmer Ave; adult/child $5/free; ⊙10am-3pm Mon-Fri, to 1pm Sat Jun–mid-Oct) Falmouth's

and duck Bolognese. Sunday brunch combines church-like reverence with a delectable menu.

ⓘ Information

Sandwich Visitor Center (📞508-833-9755; www.sandwichchamber.com; 510 MA 130; ⊙10am-5pm Mon-Sat, to 4pm Sun mid-May–mid-Oct) Has local information. Operated by the local chamber of commerce.

ⓘ Getting There & Away

If you arrive on the Cape via US 6, take exit 2 (MA 130). Water (MA 130), Main and Grove Sts

quaint village green has an air of history about it – it's where members of the Colonial militia practiced in the 1700s and 19th-century sea captains built their homes. Today, two 18th-century houses are maintained here by the Falmouth Historical Society, and show period furniture and fine arts. The society also conducts **guided tours** ($5) at 10am Tuesday and Thursday mornings, from June to mid-October.

🏃 Activities

★ Shining Sea Bikeway CYCLING
(www.falmouthmass.us/bike; 🚲) A bright star among the Cape's stellar bike trails, this 10.7-mile beaut runs along the entire west coast of Falmouth, from County Rd in North Falmouth to Woods Hole ferry terminal, offering unspoiled views of salt ponds, marsh and seascapes. Completed in 2009, the bikeway follows an abandoned railroad bed, taking you places you'd never get a glimpse of otherwise.

🎊 Festivals & Events

Independence Day Celebration FIREWORKS
(www.falmouthfireworks.org; ⏰ Jul 4) The Cape's largest fireworks display explodes over Falmouth Harbor on the 4th of July.

🛏 Sleeping

Sippewissett
Campground & Cabins CAMPGROUND $
(✆ 508-548-2542; www.sippewissett.com; 836 Palmer Ave; 2-person campsites $38-53, cabins per week $310-1095; ⏰ mid-May–mid-Oct; 🛜) This well-organized, family-friendly place on the Shining Sea Bikeway has 100 wooded campsites and 11 cabins, plus fun tipis for hire. The cabins range from one to three rooms and can hold up to seven people; they're usually rented by the week. Perks include

---

DON'T MISS

LOBSTER ICE CREAM, ANYONE?

Lobster mania gets a new twist at **Ben & Bill's Chocolate Emporium** (✆ 508-548-7878; www.benandbills.com; 209 Main St; cones $5; ⏰ 9am-9pm summer, shorter hours rest of year), where the crustacean has crawled onto the ice cream menu. Forget plain vanilla: step up to the counter and order a scoop of lobster ice cream. Now there's one you won't find with the old 31 flavors, folks.

---

a free daily shuttle to the beach and to the Vineyard ferry.

Tides Motel of Falmouth MOTEL $$
(✆ 508-548-3126; www.tidesmotelcapecod.com; 267 Clinton Ave; r $115-195; ⏰ mid-May–mid-Oct; ❄️🛜) It's all about the water. This place is smack on its own private beach, and you could spit into the ocean from your deck. Otherwise, it's straightforward: the same rooms elsewhere would be a yawn (no-frills, many with kitchenette). Between the surf lullaby and million-dollar view, a steady stream of returnees keep the motel busy all summer, so book ahead.

Falmouth Heights Motor Lodge MOTEL $$
(✆ 508-548-3623; www.falmouthheightsresort. com; 146 Falmouth Heights Rd; r $59-269; ⏰ May-Oct; ❄️🛜🏊) Don't be fooled by the name. This tidy operation is no drive-up motor lodge – it's not even on the highway. All seven styles of rooms (some small and economically priced; others larger, with kitchenettes) are a cut above the competition. And you can throw your own party: the extensive grounds harbor a picnic grove with gas barbecues.

Inn on the Sound B&B $$$
(✆ 508-457-9666; www.innonthesound.com; 313 Grand Ave; r $159-449; ❄️🛜) Falmouth's finest inn exudes a clean, contemporary elegance. It's across from the beach, and many of the 11 guest rooms have private decks with ocean views. Depending on your mood, a gourmet breakfast can be served to you on the beach, in the dining room or on your deck – it's your call.

🍴 Eating

Maison Villatte CAFE $
(✆ 774-255-1855; 267 Main St; snacks $3-10; ⏰ 7am-5pm Tue-Thu & Sun, to 7pm Fri & Sat) A pair of French bakers crowned in toques work the ovens at this buzzing bakery-cafe, creating crusty artisan breads, flaky croissants and sinful pastries. Hearty sandwiches and robust coffee make it an ideal lunch spot.

Clam Shack SEAFOOD $
(✆ 508-540-7758; 227 Clinton Ave; mains $7-21; ⏰ 11:30am-7:30pm late May–mid-Oct) A classic of the genre, right on Falmouth Harbor. It's tiny, with picnic tables on the back deck and lots of fried seafood, as well as burgers and hot dogs. The clams – huge juicy bellies cooked to a perfect crisp – are the place to

ⓘ BEACH PARKING PERMITS

It's worth noting that visiting most Cape beaches at the height of summer (July and August, and often late June and early September) usually involves paying for a parking permit of between $15 and $25 per day. There may be a booth where payment is taken, or visitors may need to buy a permit from the town hall or a visitor center; weekly or seasonal passes are usually also available. Each town will have different dates, regulations etc, but it's a good idea to ask at your accommodation or at a visitor center for the rules that apply. Of course, there's always the option to save paying for parking by visiting the beach by bike or on foot.

start. Then eat up the spectacular view. You can bring your own alcohol; cash only.

★ **Añejo** MEXICAN $$
(☎508-388-7631; www.anejomexicanbistro.com; 188 Main St; mains $12-32; ⊘11:30am-late Mon-Sat, from 10am Sun) This buzzing bistro and tequila bar brings a little year-round heat to the main-street scene, with a big selection of margaritas and tequilas, and a menu of fab street food – enchiladas, tacos, tostadas – that spins fresh Mexican flavors Cape Cod–style, with lots of fish and local seafood.

Glass Onion MODERN AMERICAN $$$
(☎508-540-3730; www.theglassoniondining.com; 37 N Main St; mains $20-36; ⊘5-9pm Tue-Sat) The place to go to for one of those anniversaries ending in a zero. The menu stars New American cuisine with French and Italian influences. Top billing goes to the lobster strudel, brimming with chunks of succulent meat. Service and wine selections are as top-shelf as the food. No bookings taken.

ⓣ Drinking & Entertainment

Coffee Obsession COFFEE
(☎508-540-2233; www.coffeeobsession.com; 110 Palmer Ave; ⊘6am-5:30pm Mon-Sat, 7am-5pm Sun) This lo-fi cafe has an obsession many can relate to: coffee. Buy global beans by the pound or a toasted bagel to accompany your quality espresso, cappuccino or latte. It's a welcoming community spot.

Liam Maguire's Irish Pub & Restaurant IRISH PUB
(☎508-548-0285; www.liammaguire.com; 273 Main St; ⊘11:30am-1am Mon-Sat, from noon Sun) The perfect Irish pub: good food (from beef and Guinness stew to fish tacos), good *craic*, a good selection of draft beers, Irish bartenders, live music nightly and boisterous Irish songfests.

ⓘ Information

Falmouth Chamber of Commerce (☎508-548-8500; www.falmouthchamber.com; 20 Academy Lane; ⊘9am-5pm Mon-Fri, 10am-4pm Sat) In the center, just off Main St.

ⓘ Getting There & Away

Sitting at the southwest corner of the Cape, Falmouth is reached via MA 28, which becomes Main St in the center of town. Buses connect the town with Boston and other Cape destinations.

Ferries to Martha's Vineyard (p168) leave from Falmouth Harbor in summer, and year-round from Woods Hole, 4.5 miles southwest of downtown.

There is very limited parking in Woods Hole. Summer visitors are encouraged to ride the **WHOOSH Trolley** (☎800-352-7155; www.capecodtransit.org; one-way fare $2; ⊘9:45am-7:15pm Sun-Thu, to 7:45pm Fri & Sat mid-Jun–early Sep) from Falmouth.

Hyannis

☎508 / POP 14,100

Ferries, buses and planes all converge on Hyannis, the Cape's commercial hub (and part of the larger Barnstable township). So there's a good chance you will, too. The village center, especially the harborfront, has been rejuvenated, making it a pleasant place to break a journey.

In addition to being a jumping-off point for boats to Nantucket and Martha's Vineyard, Hyannis attracts Kennedy fans – JFK made his summer home here, and it was at the Kennedy compound that Teddy passed away in 2009. Hyannis Harbor, with its waterfront eateries and ferries, is a few minutes' walk from Main St.

⊙ Sights

★ **John F Kennedy Hyannis Museum** MUSEUM
(☎508-790-3077; www.jfkhyannismuseum.org; 397 Main St; adult/child $10/5; ⊘9am-5pm Mon-Sat, noon-5pm Sun Jun-Oct, 10am-4pm Mon-Sat,

WORTH A TRIP

WOODS HOLE

All eyes are on the sea in this tiny salty village with a huge reputation: ferries for Martha's Vineyard depart throughout the day, fishing boats chug in and out of the harbor and oceanographers ship off to distant lands from here.

Indeed, Woods Hole is home to one of the most prestigious marine research facilities in the world. Research at the private, non-profit **Woods Hole Oceanographic Institution** (WHOI, pronounced 'hooey') has run the gamut, from exploring the sunken *Titanic* to studying global warming. With dozens of buildings and laboratories, and staff and students numbering about 1000 (including world-class scientists and engineers, and Nobel laureates), it's the largest independent oceanographic institution in the US. A number of other scientific facilities and organizations have a presence in Woods Hole.

Free, guided 75-minute tours of some of the WHOI buildings and docks depart from the **WHOI information office** (☑ 508-289-2252; www.whoi.edu/visitus; 93 Water St; ◷ 8am-4pm Mon-Fri) at 10:30am and 1:30pm, Monday to Friday, in July and August; reservations are essential. The tours are aimed at an audience from teenagers to adults.

You'll gain insights into the work of the Woods Hole Oceanographic Institution at **WHOI Ocean Science Exhibit Center** (☑ 508-289-2663; www.whoi.edu/visitus; 15 School St; suggested donation $3; ◷ 10am-4:30pm Mon-Sat May-Oct, Mon-Fri Apr, Tue-Fri Nov-Dec; ♿), where interactive exhibits include a full-size model of the inner sphere of *Alvin*, WHOI's deep-sea submersible. In July and August, the exhibit center hosts a series of **public talks** (Tuesdays at 3pm) by WHOI scientists and engineers. Designed for a lay audience, they are a great opportunity to learn more about WHOI science.

Right at the ferry terminal, **Quicks Hole Tavern** (☑ 508-495-0048; www.quickshole wickedfresh.com; 29 Railroad Ave; lunch $11-26, dinner mains $23-33; ◷ 11:30am-close year-round) has a relaxed, casual feel that belies an accomplished menu. Options roam from quahog chowder to grilled Angus beef burger and seared rack of lamb. The 'pig candy' starter is a treat: house-smoked pork shoulder braised in maple syrup and house spices, served on guava puree. There's a summertime *taqueria*, too.

noon-4pm Sun mid-Apr–May & Nov) Hyannis has been the summer home of the Kennedy clan for generations. Back in the day, JFK spent his summers here – times that are beautifully documented at this museum with photographs and video, from JFK's childhood to the Camelot years of his presidency. The exhibits are poignantly done, and present a theme that changes annually (previous years have covered matriarch Rose and explored the brotherly bond between Jack and Bobby).

Sandy Neck Beach
BEACH

(☑ 508-362-8300; www.town.barnstable.ma.us/sandyneckpark; 425 Sandy Neck Rd, off MA 6A, West Barnstable; ◷ 8am-11pm) The barrier beach at Sandy Neck extends 6.5 miles along Cape Cod Bay, backed the entire way by undulating dunes and a scenic salt marsh. It's a destination for all sorts of recreational activities: brisk summer **swimming**, year-round **hiking**, and saltwater **fishing**. The dunes, which reach heights of 100ft, provide a habitat for red foxes, shorebirds and wildflowers. From four points along the beach, hiking trails cross inland over the dunes to a path skirting the salt marsh.

Craigville Beach
BEACH

(Craigville Beach Rd, Centerville) Looking for a warm-water swim? Craigville, like other south-side beaches, has warmer water than those on the north side of the Cape. This mile-long stretch of sand is a great swimming beach that attracts a college crowd.

With 450 parking spaces, the most of any Barnstable beach, you're unlikely to get shut out even on the sunniest midsummer day. Beach facilities include changing rooms, showers, lifeguards and snack bars. Parking costs $20 in summer.

Kalmus Beach
BEACH

(Ocean St) You'll find plenty of space in which to lay your towel on wide Kalmus Beach, at the south end of Ocean St in Hyannis. Thanks to its steady breezes, it's a haven for windsurfers. The warm summer waters also attract plenty of swimmers. Facilities include a snack bar, lifeguard and changing rooms. Parking costs $20 in summer.

Cape Cod Maritime Museum
MUSEUM

(📞508-775-1723; www.capecodmaritimemuseum.org; 135 South St; adult/child $6/free; ⊙10am-4pm Mon-Sat, from noon Sun mid-Mar–mid-Dec) Suitably close to Hyannis Harbor, this museum explores the Cape's seafaring connections, especially the local boat-building tradition.

HyArts District
ARTS CENTER

(📞508-862-4678; www.hyartsdistrict.com; 250 South St; ⊙shanties daily mid-Jun–mid-Oct, Fri-Sun mid-May–mid-Jun) Before you jump on that ferry, take a walk through the harborside HyArts District, which includes the Guyer Barn community art space and neighboring artist studios, the colorful artist shanties near the ferry docks, and the art-strewn Walkway to the Sea.

Veterans Beach
BEACH

(Ocean St; ♿) The closest beach to Hyannis' Main St, Veterans Beach is a favorite with families thanks to the playground facilities, picnic tables and shallow waters. Parking costs $20 in summer.

The north side of the beach is also the site of a **memorial to John F Kennedy**, and overlooks the harbor where JFK once sailed. There's free 30-minute parking at the memorial.

🜚 Tours

Hyannis Whale Watcher Cruises
WILDLIFE WATCHING

(📞800-287-0374; www.whales.net; 269 Millway Rd, Barnstable Harbor, Barnstable; adult/child $49/28; ⊙May–mid-Oct; ♿) All whale-watching boat cruises on Cape Cod leave from Provincetown except for this one, which makes for a longer boat ride out to **Stellwagen Bank National Marine Sanctuary**, where the whales hang out. On the plus side, if you're already here, it spares you the hour-long drive to Provincetown. The four-hour boat tours are narrated by well-informed naturalists.

Hy-Line Harbor Cruises
CRUISE

(📞508-790-0696; www.hylinecruises.com; 138 Ocean St Dock; adult/child $17/8; ⊙mid-May–Oct; ♿) Hy-Line, which is best known for its ferries to Martha's Vineyard and Nantucket, rolls out one of its old-fashioned steamboats each summer for harbor tours. These popular one-hour tours include a circle past the compound of Kennedy family homes. Kids ride free on morning trips all season.

🎉 Festivals & Events

Pops by the Sea
MUSIC

(www.artsfoundation.org; Hyannis Village Green, 367 Main St; ⊙mid-Aug) This concert on the village green on the second Sunday in August features the Boston Pops Orchestra and a celebrity guest conductor. It's the Cape's single largest cultural event. Tickets on the lawn are $20.

🛏 Sleeping

HI Hyannis
HOSTEL $

(📞508-775-7990; www.hiusa.org; 111 Ocean St; dm $35-40, d $79-99, q $109-129; ⊙mid-May–mid-Oct; 🅿@📶) 🍴 For a million-dollar view on a backpacker's budget, book yourself a bed at this hostel overlooking the harbor. It was built in 2010 by adding new wings to a period home and is within walking distance of the Main St scene, beaches and ferries. Now the caveat: there are only 42 beds, so book well in advance.

Captain Gosnold Village
COTTAGE $$

(📞508-775-9111; www.captaingosnold.com; 230 Gosnold St; studio $90-150, 2-bedroom cottage $180-350; 📶🏊) In a residential neighborhood, Captain Gosnold is a little community unto itself and just a sandal-shuffle from the beach. Choose from studios with kitchenettes, or fully equipped Cape Cod–style cottages. The homey cottages vary in size, from one to three bedrooms that sleep four to six people. Kids will find a pool, playground and plenty of room to romp.

SeaCoast Inn
MOTEL $$

(📞508-775-3828; www.seacoastcapecod.com; 33 Ocean St; r $79-259; ⊙Apr-Oct; ❄📶) This small, two-story motel offers neat, clean rooms just a two-minute walk from the harbor in one direction and Main St restaurants in the other. OK, there's no view or pool, but the rooms are thoroughly comfy, most have kitchenettes and the rates are a pretty good deal.

★ Anchor-In
HOTEL $$$

(📞508-775-0357; www.anchorin.com; 1 South St; r $94-374; ❄@📶🏊) This family-run boutique hotel puts the chains to shame. The harbor-front location offers a fine sense of place, and the heated outdoor pool is a perfect perch from which to watch fishing boats unload their catch. The rooms are bright and smart, with water-view balconies. If you're planning a day trip to Nantucket, the ferry is just a stroll away.

✗ Eating

Four Seas ICE CREAM $
(☑508-775-1394; www.fourseasicecream.com; 360 S Main St, Centerville; cones $5; ☺9am–10:30pm Jul-Aug, to 9:30pm late May–Jun & Sep–mid-Oct, 11am-5pm Fri-Sun mid-Oct–late May; ▣) This local institution near Craigville Beach has been dispensing homemade ice cream (and sandwiches) since 1934. Expect lines out the door, since everyone – including the Kennedy clan, whose Hyannisport home is nearby – comes here on hot summer nights.

In winter, Four Seas opens Friday to Sunday (but it's worth checking the website to confirm).

Pizza Barbone PIZZA $
(☑508-957-2377; www.pizzabarbone.com; 390 Main St; pizzas $10-15; ☺11am-9pm Sun-Thu, to 10pm Fri & Sat) Take a break from seafood at this stylishly rustic pizza palace, doling out delicious Neapolitan-style thin-crust pizzas from its wood-fired oven. Toppings are high-quality, like mushroom with rosemary, smoked mozzarella and truffle oil. Gluten-free and vegan options available.

★Pain D'Avignon BAKERY, BISTRO $$
(☑508-778-8588; www.paindavignon.com; 15 Hinckley Rd; lunch $8-17, dinner mains $19-32; ☺7am-4pm daily, plus 5-10pm Wed-Sun) It's not in the likeliest of locations (out by the airport, off MA 132), but seek this place out for a delectable slice of Paris. Patisserie favorites beckon in the morning, but more leisurely options like omelets and galettes (savory crepes) can be ordered. At lunch and dinner, classic French bistro fare shines: croque monsieur, quiche Lorraine, steak *frites*.

DON'T MISS

SNACK ATTACK

On your way into Hyannis, stop at the **Cape Cod Potato Chip Factory** (☑888-881-2447; www.capecodchips.com; 100 Breed's Hill Rd; ☺9am-5pm Mon-Fri) for a free, self-guided tour – in effect, it's just observing the chips march across the production and packaging lines through windows. The whole visit might take you 10 minutes, and you get free samples. From MA 132 (just west of the airport), take Independence Rd a half-mile north to the factory.

Tumi SEAFOOD $$
(☑508-534-9289; www.tumiceviche.com; 592R Main St; ceviche $9-15, mains $15-31; ☺11:30am-10pm; ▣) If you love seafood but you're hankering for something a little different, seek out this hidden Italian-Peruvian gem. Take your pick from nine kinds of ceviche (including vegetarian), as well as other raw shellfish, seafood pasta and some interesting Peruvian options. Hint: the 'R' in the address stands for 'rear'.

★Naked Oyster SEAFOOD $$$
(☑508-778-6500; www.nakedoyster.com; 410 Main St; lunch $8-19, dinner mains $16-36; ☺noon-10pm Mon-Sat) 🍃 Low food miles are key at this upmarket joint, where the eponymous bivalves come from the restaurant's oyster farm in Barnstable Harbor. They keep fine company in the raw bar: shrimp, littlenecks, lobster. The menu borrows global flavors to dress up fresh seafood – Thai shrimp, *moules frites*, fish tacos, curried scallops – with fine results.

🍷 Drinking & Entertainment

★Cape Cod Beer BREWERY
(☑508-790-4200; www.capecodbeer.com; 1336 Phinneys Lane; ☺10am-6pm Mon-Fri, 11am-3pm Sat) Not just a place for beer connoisseurs (although they'll be pretty happy), this brewery is a fun spot to while away some time. Free brewery tours happen daily (except Sunday) at 11am, but you can stop in for tastings ($5) any time. Check the website for events, from bring-your-pet 'yappy hour' to painting classes, live music and comedy nights.

Cape Cod Melody Tent LIVE MUSIC
(☑508-775-5630; www.melodytent.org; 21 W Main St; ☺late May–early Sep) The Melody Tent is just that – a giant tent, seating 2300 people – with nobody sitting more than 50ft from the revolving stage. From Memorial Day to Labor Day it headlines acts such as Aretha Franklin, Vince Gill and ZZ Top.

🛈 Information

Cape Cod Chamber of Commerce (☑508-362-3225; www.capecodchamber.org; 5 Patti Page Way, Centerville; ☺9am-5pm Mon-Sat, 10am-2pm Sun late May–mid-Oct, shorter hours rest of year) Provides Cape-wide information from its location just off US 6 (at MA 132).

Hyannis Area Chamber of Commerce (☑508-775-2201; www.hyannis.com; 768 Iyannough Rd/MA 132 (Kmart Plaza); ☺9am-5pm Mon-Sat, noon-5pm Sun late May–mid-Oct,

10am-4pm Mon-Sat, noon-4pm Sun rest of year) Provides tourist information for the Town of Barnstable, from a visitor center on MA 132.

ℹ Getting There & Away

AIR

Also known as Hyannis airport, the **Barnstable Municipal Airport** (☑ 508-775-2020; www.townofbarnstable.us/airport; 480 Barnstable Rd, off MA 132) sits only a mile or so north of Hyannis Main St. **Cape Air** (www.capeair.com) flies several times a day year-round between Hyannis and Boston and Nantucket, plus Martha's Vineyard from May to October. In summer, **JetBlue** (www.jetblue.com) has flights that connect Hyannis with New York's JFK airport.

BOAT

Hyannis is the jumping-off point for ferries to Nantucket (p163), operated by **Hy-Line Cruises** (☑ 508-778-2600; www.hylinecruises.com; Ocean St Dock) and **Steamship Authority** (☑ 508-477-8600; www.steamshipauthority.com; South St Dock). Parking lots near the docks cater to those traveling to the island (in peak season, there are large parking lots in town that are connected to the docks by shuttle). Parking costs from $5 to $20 per day, depending on the season.

BUS

Hyannis Transportation Center (HTC; ☑ 800-352-7155; www.capecodrta.org; 215 Iyannough Rd/MA 28) is Cape Cod's bus transportation hub. Frequent buses connect Hyannis with Boston (including Logan airport), or run further out to Provincetown (calling at Cape towns en route). Heading west, there are connections from Boston to Providence and New York City.

Sample one-way fares from Hyannis:
Boston ($20, 1¾ hours)
Logan airport ($26, two hours)
Provincetown ($11, 80 minutes)

Find schedules and fares at **Plymouth & Brockton** (www.p-b.com) and **Peter Pan** (www.peterpanbus.com).

TRAIN

The **Cape Flyer** (www.capeflyer.com) is a weekend train service operating from Memorial Day to Labor Day (late May to mid-October), connecting Boston's South Station with Hyannis. It operates on Friday evenings, Saturday and Sunday. From Boston to Hyannis takes about 2½ hours (one way/round-trip $22/40).

ℹ Getting Around

At summer's peak, the **Hyannis Trolley** (www.capecodrta.org/hyannis-trolley.htm; fare $2; ⊙10am-9:15pm mid-Jun–early Sep) provides

shuttle service from the Hyannis Transportation Center to Main St, the Ocean St docks and the Steamship Authority ferry docks. It can be flagged down on its route (wherever it's safe to do so).

Yarmouth
☑ 508 / POP 23,700

There are two Yarmouths, and the experience you have depends on what part of town you find yourself in. The north side of town, along MA 6A, called Yarmouth Port, is green and genteel, with shady trees, antique shops and gracious old homes. The second Yarmouth, to the south, where MA 28 crosses the villages of West Yarmouth and South Yarmouth, is a flat world of mini-golf, strip malls and endless motels.

◎ Sights

★**Captains' Mile** — HISTORIC BUILDING
(www.hsoy.org/thecaptainsmile-1-1/; along MA 6A, Yarmouth Port) Nearly 50 historic sea captains' homes are lined up along MA 6A (the Old King's Hwy) in Yarmouth Port, on a 1.5-mile stretch known as the Captains' Mile. Most of them are family homes these days (or genteel B&Bs), so you'll be doing much of your viewing from the sidewalk. You can download a walking tour brochure from the website of the Historical Society of Old Yarmouth (HSOY), which admirably outlines the history of many of the houses.

Edward Gorey House — MUSEUM
(☑ 508-362-3909; www.edwardgoreyhouse.org; 8 Strawberry Lane, Yarmouth Port; adult/child $8/2; ⊙11am-4pm Thu-Sat, noon-4pm Sun mid-Apr–Jun, 11am-4pm Fri-Sat, noon-4pm Sun mid-Oct–Dec) Near the post office on MA 6A sits the former home of the brilliant and somewhat twisted author and graphic artist Edward Gorey. He illustrated the books of Lewis Carroll, HG Wells and John Updike but is most widely recognized for his offbeat pen-and-ink animations used in the opening of the PBS *Mystery!* series. The museum honors Gorey, the artist and the person, with exhibits of fabulous works from his archives, plus details of his devotion to animal welfare.

Captain Bangs Hallett House — HISTORIC BUILDING
(☑ 508-362-3021; www.hsoy.org; 11 Strawberry Lane, Yarmouth Port; tour adult/child $3/free; ⊙1-4pm Fri-Sun mid-Jun–mid-Oct) The Historical Society of Old Yarmouth maintains this 1840

Greek Revival house, once home to a prosperous sea captain who made his fortune sailing to China and India. Access is by guided tour, which details the period furnishings and seafaring life; the last tour is at 3pm. Look for the house on the Common, behind the post office, just off MA 6A.

Gray's Beach
BEACH

(Center St, Yarmouth Port) Gray's Beach, also known as Bass Hole, is no prize for swimming, but a terrific 0.25-mile-long boardwalk extends over a tidal marsh and creek, offering a unique vantage for viewing all sorts of sea life. It's also a fine spot for picnics and sunsets, and the parking is free. To get there, take Center St off MA 6A, just west of the playground in the center of the village.

Seagull Beach
BEACH

(Seagull Rd, West Yarmouth) Long and wide Seagull Beach, off South Sea Ave from MA 28, is the town's best south-side beach. The scenic approach to the beach runs alongside a tidal river that provides a habitat for osprey and shorebirds; bring your binoculars. Facilities include a bathhouse and snack bar. Parking costs $15 in summer.

🛏 Sleeping & Eating

Big, family-friendly motels line MA 28 through West Yarmouth and South Yarmouth, including budget options. Old-world B&Bs and inns can be found along MA 6A in Yarmouth Port.

STAR PARTIES

What could be more cosmic than being outdoors on a warm summer night and staring up at the stars? How about gaping at Saturn's rings and Jupiter's moons?

Cape Cod Astronomical Society welcomes visitors to weekly summer 'star parties' at its **Werner Schmidt Observatory** (www.ccas.org; 210 Station Ave, South Yarmouth; ⊙ 8:30pm Thu late Jun–late Aug), behind the Dennis-Yarmouth Regional High School. Peer into the heavens through the observatory's telescope and through smaller scopes set up outdoors on the grounds. Club members put it all in focus and explain the celestial details – and they love to turn on newbies to the wonders of stargazing. Find more details online.

Village Inn
B&B $$

(☑ 508-362-3182; www.thevillageinncapecod.com; 92 MA 6A, Yarmouth Port; r $145-295; ❋ 🕸) New owners (an Irish brother-and-sister team) have taken over this relaxed B&B occupying a 200-year-old house that's on the National Register of Historic Places. Set on a one-acre lot, the inn provides lots of common space and eight guest rooms of varying sizes (including configurations for families). There's a two- or three-night minimum stay during summer's peak.

Happy Fish Bakery
BAKERY $

(☑ 774-994-8272; 173 MA 6A, Yarmouth Port; pastries $3-4; ⊙ 8am-4pm Wed-Sat, 8am-3pm Sun Jun-Sep, closed Wed rest of year) Follow your nose to the calorific French pastries, sticky buns and traditional loaves baked at this high-end bakery – and get in early or you may find favorites (like the almond croissant) sold out.

Inaho
JAPANESE $$$

(☑ 508-362-5522; www.inahocapecod.com; 157 MA 6A, Yarmouth Port; mains $15-35; ⊙ 5-10pm Tue-Sat) Beloved of locals, this serene year-round restaurant has an impeccable pedigree for putting seafood to great use. Sushi and sashimi are fresh and delicate, but teriyaki and tempura are also first-class. Reservations recommended.

ℹ Information

Yarmouth Chamber of Commerce (☑ 508-778-1008; www.yarmouthcapecod.com; 424 MA 28, West Yarmouth; ⊙ 9am-5pm Mon-Fri, plus Sat & Sun May-Oct)

ℹ Getting There & Away

Yarmouth town sprawls across three villages: Yarmouth Port on Cape Cod Bay (accessed via MA 6A) and West Yarmouth and South Yarmouth on the Cape's south side (accessed by MA 28). The most direct link between north and south is via Station Ave/Union St.

Dennis

☑ 508 / POP 14,100

Like neighboring Yarmouth, Dennis has a distinctly different character from north to south. Heavily trafficked MA 28, which cuts through the villages of West Dennis and Dennisport on the south side of town, is lined with motels, eateries and mini-golf. There are some scenic river-outlet areas for water sports like kayaking, too. The classier

DON'T MISS

UP FOR A PEDAL?: THE CAPE COD RAIL TRAIL

The mother of all Cape bicycle trails, the Cape Cod Rail Trail (CCRT) runs 22 glorious paved miles through forest, past cranberry bogs and along sandy ponds ideal for a dip. This rural route, formerly used as a railroad line, is one of the finest bike trails in all of New England.

The path begins in Dennis on MA 134 and continues through Nickerson State Park (p138) in Brewster, into Orleans and across the Cape Cod National Seashore (p150), all the way to South Wellfleet.

There's a hefty dose of Ye Olde Cape Cod scenery en route and you'll have opportunities to detour into villages for lunch or sightseeing. If you have only enough time to do part of the trail, begin at Nickerson State Park and head for the National Seashore – the landscape is unbeatable.

Bicycle rentals are available at the trailheads in Dennis and Wellfleet, at Nickerson State Park and opposite the National Seashore's visitor center in Eastham. There's car parking at all four sites (free except for a small charge at Nickerson).

---

north side, the village of Dennis, runs along MA 6A, with handsome old sea captains' homes sprouting second lives as inns, galleries and antique shops.

⊙ Sights

Chapin Memorial Beach   BEACH
(Chapin Beach Rd, Dennis; 🚻) Families will love the gently sloping waters at this dune-backed beach. Not only is it ideal for wading, but all sorts of tiny sea creatures can be explored in the tide pools. At low tide, you can walk way out onto the sandy tidal flats – it takes a hike just to reach water up to your knees. This mile-long beach is also perfect for sunsets and walks under the light of the moon.

West Dennis Beach   BEACH
(Lighthouse Rd, off MA 28, West Dennis) Extending one gorgeous mile along Nantucket Sound, this is the south side's mecca for swimmers, windsurfers and kiteboarders. It's a good bet for finding a parking space on even the sunniest of days, as the parking lot ($20 to $25) extends the full length of the beach, with room for 1000 cars.

Scargo Tower   TOWER
(Scargo Hill Rd, Dennis) **FREE** Built in 1902 on the highest spot in the area – 120ft above sea level – this 38-step, stone tower rising above Scargo Lake gives you grand views of Cape Cod Bay. On clear days you can see all the way to Sandwich and across to Provincetown. To get here, take MA 6A to Scargo Hill Rd.

🏃 Activities

Lobster Roll Cruises   CRUISE
(☑508-385-1686; www.lobsterrollcruises.com; 357 Sesuit Neck Rd, Dennis; cruises $30-45; ☺late May–mid-Oct) A different setting for a lobster dinner. Take the cute boat (the SS *Lobster Roll*) from Sesuit Harbor on a dinner cruise, or go light with the lobster-roll lunch cruise. The food, prepared by Sesuit Harbor Cafe (p138), is the real deal; there are non-seafood options. Reservations recommended (book online).

🛏 Sleeping & Eating

★Isaiah Hall Inn   B&B $$
(☑508-385-9928; www.isaiahhallinn.com; 152 Whig St, Dennis; r $120-250; ❄️🏠) Occupying an 1857 farmhouse, this year-round country-style inn offers homey comforts in a quiet yet central neighborhood. The house has sloping wood floors, canopied beds and a 12ft-long breakfast table ideal for convivial chatter with fellow guests. Prices reflect the season, room size and whether you opt for extras, like balconies or fireplaces. It's just behind the Cape Playhouse area.

Scargo Manor   B&B $$
(☑508-385-5534; www.scargomanor.com; 909 MA 6A, Dennis; r $150-310; ❄️🏠) The sea captain who built this grand house in 1895 scored a prime locale on Scargo Lake, and you're free to paddle off in the owner's canoe or kayaks whenever the mood strikes. For places you can't paddle to, you can pedal to, using the inn's loaner bikes. The antiques-laden house has seven rooms, each with its own character.

Captain Frosty's Fish & Chips
SEAFOOD $

(☑508-385-8548; www.captainfrosty.com; 219 MA 6A, Dennis; mains $7-20; ☺11am-8pm mid-Apr–Oct) Don't be misled by the 1950s ice-cream shack appearance: this simple seafood takeout joint does it right. Forget frozen food – there's none in this kitchen. Order fish and chips and you'll be munching on cod caught in nearby Chatham. And yes, there's still a dairy bar (soft-serve ice cream a specialty).

★ Sesuit Harbor Cafe
SEAFOOD $$

(☑508-385-6134; www.sesuit-harbor-cafe.com; 357 Sesuit Neck Rd, Dennis; mains $8-30; ☺7am-8:30pm May–mid-Oct) This is the Cape Cod you won't find on the highway: an idyllic shack tucked into Sesuit Harbor serving freshly caught seafood at picnic tables smack on the water. The scrumptious lobster rolls, like everything else, taste like they just crawled onto your plate. BYOB; cash only. Take Bridge St north off MA 6A.

Fin
SEAFOOD $$$

(☑508-385-2096; www.fincapecod.com; 800 MA 6A, Dennis; mains $24-32; ☺5-9pm Tue-Sun) Fin embodies the Cape's north-side character. Dining rooms over two floors of a gracious sea captain's home create an intimate dining experience. The chef-owner is a master with all things briny. Start with the rich house chowder, chock-full of Dennis oysters; then, if sea bass is on the menu, look no further. Meat-lovers have a few options, too. Reservations recommended.

Drinking & Entertainment

Harvest Gallery Wine Bar
WINE BAR

(☑508-385-2444; www.harvestgallerywinebar.com; 776 MA 6A, Dennis; ☺4:30pm-midnight) Tip your glass with class at this combo wine bar and art gallery behind the Dennis village post office. There's live music several nights a week (jazz, blues, folk etc), and a tempting grazing menu of tapas plates, oysters and pizza.

★ Cape Cinema
CINEMA

(☑508-385-2503; www.capecinema.com; 35 Hope Lane, off MA 6A, Dennis; tickets adult/child $9.50/6) On the grounds of the Cape Playhouse, this vintage movie theater shows foreign and independent films. It's a true art house: the entire ceiling is covered in an art-deco mural of the heavens painted by American realist painter Rockwell Kent.

Cape Playhouse
THEATER

(☑box office 508-385-3911; www.capeplayhouse.com; 820 MA 6A, Dennis; tickets $19-79; ☺early Jun–early Sep; ⓘ) The Cape Playhouse is the oldest operating professional summer theater (since 1927) in the US. Bette Davis once worked here as an usher, and some of the biggest names in showbiz have appeared on its stage. It hosts a different production every two weeks – everything from *Hairspray* to Hitchcock – and also has a children's theater, with classics, puppetry and more.

ⓘ Information

Dennis Chamber of Commerce (☑508-398-3568; www.visitdennis.com; 242 Swan River Rd, off MA 28 at MA 134, West Dennis; ☺10am-4pm Mon-Sat late May–mid-Oct, 9am-5pm Mon-Fri rest of year)

ⓘ Getting There & Away

Dennis town sprawls across five villages: the main Dennis village is on Cape Cod Bay (accessed via MA 6A), bordered by East Dennis and South Dennis. On the Cape's south side (accessed via MA 28) are West Dennis and Dennisport. The most direct link between north and south is via MA 134.

Brewster

☑508 / POP 9900

Woodsy Brewster, on the Cape's bay side, makes a good base for outdoorsy types. The Cape Cod Rail Trail cuts clear across town, and there's first-rate camping and water activities. Brewster also has fine restaurants, out of proportion to the town's small size. Everything of interest is on or just off MA 6A (also called Main St), which runs the length of the town.

◉ Sights

Nickerson State Park
STATE PARK

(☑508-896-3491; www.mass.gov/dcr; 3488 MA 6A; per car $10; ☺dawn-dusk; ⓘ) This 2000-acre oasis has eight freshwater ponds with sandy beaches ideal for swimming and boating, as well as miles of cycling and walking trails. Bring along a fishing pole to catch your own trout dinner or just pack a lunch and enjoy the picnic facilities; book ahead to camp. **Jack's Boat Rental** (☑508-896-8556; www.jacksboatrental.com; Flax Pond, Nickerson State Park; boat rentals per 30min $11-31; ☺10am-6pm mid-Jun–mid-Sep), within the park, rents canoes, kayaks and sailboats.

ANTIQUING HISTORIC 6A

Nearly anything you can imagine – from nautical antiques to art-deco kitsch – can be found on the tightly packed shelves of Cape Cod's 100-plus antique shops. The key to antiquing on the Cape is to follow MA 6A, also known as the Old King's Highway. The oldest continuous stretch of historic district in the USA, the road is lined with old sea-captains' homes, many of which have been converted to quality antique shops. You'll find the best hunting on the section between Barnstable and Brewster.

Then there are the auctions. The high roller on the scene, Eldred's (☑508-385-3116; www.eldreds.com; 1483 MA 6A, East Dennis; ☺8:30am-5pm Mon-Fri), specializes in fine arts and appraised antiques; five-figure bids here barely raise an eyebrow. More homespun is the Sandwich Auction House (☑508-888-1926; www.sandwichauction.com; 15 Tupper Rd, off MA 6A), which handles estate sales where you might find anything from antique Sandwich glass to old Elvis albums.

Cape Cod Museum of Natural History
MUSEUM

(☑508-896-3867; www.ccmnh.org; 869 MA 6A; adult/child $11/6; ☺9:30am-4pm Jun-Aug, 11am-3pm Sep, 11am-3pm Wed-Sun Oct-Dec & Apr-May, 11am-3pm Thu-Sun mid-Feb–Mar; ⚫) This family-friendly museum offers exhibits on the Cape's flora and fauna, including an aquarium and a butterfly house. It has a fine boardwalk trail across a salt marsh to a remote beach with tide pools. The museum has a calendar rich with naturalist-led walks, talks and kids' programs.

Brewster Store
HISTORIC BUILDING

(☑508-896-3744; www.brewsterstore.com; 1935 MA 6A, at MA 124; ☺6am-10pm Jun-Sep, shorter hours Oct-May) The Brewster Store, in the heart of town, is a sight in itself. The old-fashioned country store opened in 1866, and it's barely changed since: penny candy is still sold alongside the local newspaper. Don't miss the half-hidden stairs that lead to the 2nd floor, where you'll discover a stash of museum-quality memorabilia as old as the building.

Brewster Historical Society Museum
MUSEUM

(☑508-896-9521; www.brewsterhistoricalsociety. org; 739 Lower Rd, off MA 6A) FREE At the time of research, Brewster's active historical society was preparing to move into fine new premises, inside the restored 1799 Captain Elijah Cobb House. Its old museum was a treasure trove (treasures brought back by sea captains, colonial tools and other bits of Brewster's centuries-old history), so this new home will be worth a look. Check the website for details on opening hours.

🛏 Sleeping & Eating

★Nickerson State Park
CAMPGROUND $

(☑877-422-6762, 518-884-4959; www.reserve america.com; 3488 MA 6A; campsite $27, yurt $50-60; ☺mid-Apr–Oct; ⚫) Head here for Cape Cod's best camping, with more than 400 wooded campsites and a handful of yurts set in pond- and trail-filled grounds. It often fills up, so reserve your spot early. You can make reservations up to six months in advance.

★Old Sea Pines Inn
B&B $$

(☑508-896-6114; www.oldseapinesinn.com; 2553 MA 6A; r $120-170, ste $190-205; @🛜) Staying here is a bit like staying at Grandma's house: antique fittings, sleigh beds and sepia photographs on the bureau. This former girls' boarding school dating to 1840 has 24 rooms: some small; others commodious, with fireplace; some suited to families. Mosey out to the rocking chairs on the porch and soak up the yesteryear atmosphere.

Brewster by the Sea
B&B $$$

(☑508-896-3910; www.brewsterbythesea.com; 716 MA 6A; r $179-360; ❄🛜⚫) If your idea of a B&B stay is pure pampering, stop the search here. Spend the night in a room with a king-size brass bed, whirlpool bath and fireplace, then wake up to a gourmet farm-fresh breakfast. Spa treatments and deep-tissue massages take it to the next level; you can keep the serenity over 'afternoon repast' sweet treats.

Cobie's
SEAFOOD $$

(☑508-896-7021; www.cobies.com; 3260 MA 6A; mains $7-24; ☺11am-9pm mid-May–mid-Oct; ⚫) Just off the Cape Cod Rail Trail, this bustling roadside clam shack dishes out fried seafood

ℹ CAPE-WIDE INFO

For Cape-wide tourist information, stop at the Cape Cod Chamber of Commerce (p134).

Cape Cod Online (www.capecod online.com) is an excellent resource. If you're on the Cape for more than just the beaches, the Cape Cod Museum Trail (www.capecodmuseumtrail.com) has comprehensive info on natural, cultural and historic sights, plus a useful calendar of events.

that you can crunch and munch at outdoor picnic tables, as well as non-fishy fare like burgers and hot panini sandwiches. Great ice cream, too.

★ Brewster Fish House   SEAFOOD $$$
(☑ 508-896-7867; www.brewsterfishhouse.com; 2208 MA 6A; lunch $12-19, dinner $21-37; ☺ 11:30am-3pm & 5-9:30pm) It's not an eye-catcher from the outside, but it's heaven inside for seafood lovers. Start with the lobster bisque, naturally sweet and with chunks of fresh lobster. From there it's safe to cast your net in any direction; dishes are fresh and creative. Just a dozen tables, and no reservations, so try lunch or early dinner to avoid long waits.

ℹ Information

Brewster Chamber of Commerce (☑ 508-896-3500; www.brewster-capecod.org; 2198 MA 6A; ☺ 9am-3pm Jun–early Sep, noon-4pm Tue & Wed, 8:30am-12:30pm Thu & Fri mid-Sep–May) This office inside Brewster Town Hall has tourist information and sells beach parking permits in summer.

ℹ Getting There & Away

Brewster stretches along Cape Cod Bay between Dennis and Orleans. Access is best via MA 6A. From the Cape's south, take MA 124 or MA 137 from Harwich.

Harwich

☑ 508 / POP 12,200
Things move a little slower here in Harwich, and that's part of the appeal. It has good beaches and restaurants and one of the Cape's most photographed spots – yacht-packed Wychmere Harbor.

Most of what you'll need is along MA 28, which runs through the south side of town.

⊙ Sights

Sea Street Beach   BEACH
(Sea St, Harwich Port) Harwich has fine beaches, although many of them restrict parking to residents. But fret not: to get to one of the prettiest, park your car for free at the municipal lot behind the tourist office and then walk five minutes to the end of Sea St, which terminates at glistening Sea St Beach.

🛏 Sleeping & Eating

★ **Wequassett Resort**   RESORT $$$
(☑ 508-432-5400; www.wequassett.com; 2173 MA 28, East Harwich; r low/high season from $250/595; ❄@☂☀) The Cape's priciest, most prestigious lodging offers pretty much anything you could ask of a full-service, five-star resort: flower-filled gardens, private golf course, fine dining and a full menu of watery activities. On the grounds you'll be soothed with gorgeous views of Pleasant Bay, north of Chatham. The in-room Jacuzzis and fireplaces spell romance; families also welcome (kids' club on-site).

Brax Landing   SEAFOOD $$
(☑ 508-432-5515; www.braxrestaurant.com; 705 MA 28, Harwich Port; mains $8-25; ☺ 11:30am-10pm Mon-Sat, from 10am Sun) Head to this casual harborside gem for water-view dining and fresh seafood at honest prices. The menu's broad, but stick with the local catch, like the Chatham scrod or the hefty lobster rolls. Grab yourself a seat on the outdoor deck overlooking Saquatucket Harbor for the best drink-with-a-view in town.

Cape Sea Grille   SEAFOOD $$$
(☑ 508-432-4745; www.capeseagrille.com; 31 Sea St, Harwich Port; mains $24-38; ☺ 5-9pm or 10pm Apr–mid-Dec) Sit on the glass-enclosed porch of this old sea captain's house and savor some of the Cape's finest seafood. The crispy oysters and the seared lobster with pancetta are justifiably famous. Landlubbers won't be disappointed with steak and lamb. Reservations recommended. Check closing days online (it's open nightly late May to mid-September, closed a night or three outside those months).

Check Facebook for the location of the restaurant's ace summertime food truck, Salt Block, which roves from Harwich Port to Hyannis Harbor and other Cape picnic spots.

ℹ Information

Harwich Information Center (☑508-432-1600; www.harwichcc.com; cnr 1 Schoolhouse Rd & MA 28, Harwich Port; ⊙9am-5pm Mon-Fri, 10am-4pm Sat, 10am-2pm Sun Jun–early Sep, shorter hours rest of year)

ℹ Getting There & Away

BOAT

Freedom Cruise Line (☑508-432-8999; www.nantucketislandferry.com; 702 MA 28 at Saquatucket Harbor, Harwich Port; round-trip adult/child $74/51; ⊙late May–late Sep) operates a summer passenger ferry to Nantucket from Saquatucket Harbor in Harwich Port. It's conveniently scheduled for day-tripping, and offers free parking (for day-trippers only). Services operate one to three times daily in each direction (80 minutes), from late May to late September. Bookings advised.

CAR & MOTORCYCLE

MA 28 passes through the main tourist center of Harwich Port. MA 39 leads off it to reach East Harwich, which sits on Pleasant Bay north of Chatham.

Chatham

☑508 / POP 6130

The patriarch of Cape Cod towns, Chatham has a genteel reserve that is evident along its shady Main St: the shops are upscale; the lodgings, tony. That said, there's something for everyone here – families flock to town for seal-watching, birders migrate to the wildlife refuge. And then there are all those beaches. Sitting at the 'elbow' of the Cape, Chatham has an amazing 60 miles of shoreline along the ocean, the sound and countless coves and inlets.

MA 28 leads right to Main St, where the lion's share of shops and restaurants are lined up. Chatham is a town made for strolling. You'll find free parking along Main St and in the parking lot behind the Chatham Squire.

◎ Sights

Monomoy National Wildlife Refuge   WILDLIFE RESERVE
(☑508-945-0594; www.fws.gov/refuge/monomoy; 30 Wikis Way; ⊙sunrise-sunset) ⚑ Take Morris Island Rd beyond the Chatham Lighthouse to reach this 7600-acre wildlife refuge, spreading from Morris Island to encompass the shifting sands of the uninhabited North Monomoy and South Monomoy barrier islands. The refuge is a haven for shorebirds

and seabirds (nearly 300 species nest here; 10 times that number pass through on migrations). It's one of the most important ornithological stops on the Atlantic seaboard. There's a visitor center, a nature trail and access to the Morris Island shore.

North and South Monomoy Islands are accessible only by boat. Monomoy Island Ferry (p142) offers a **wildlife boat tour**.

Lighthouse Beach   BEACH
(Main St) Directly below Chatham Light is Lighthouse Beach, an endless expanse of sea and sandbars that offers some of the finest beach strolling on Cape Cod. Swimming isn't recommended – there are strong currents and no lifeguards. Plus, as signs warn, great white sharks live in these waters.

Chatham Shark Center   MUSEUM
(☑508-348-5901; www.atlanticwhiteshark.org; 235 Orleans Rd, North Chatham; $5; ⊙10am-4pm Sat & Sun Jun & Sep–mid-Oct, Wed-Sun Jul & Aug) Stop here for the lowdown on one of the Cape's most intriguing summer residents: the great white shark. Interactive exhibits and videos aimed at kids and adults attempt to demystify the animal given a good deal of bad PR in the Cape Cod–set movie, *Jaws*. It's under the auspices of the Atlantic White Shark Conservancy (motto: 'Awareness inspires conservation').

Chatham Marconi Maritime Center   MUSEUM
(☑508-945-8889; www.chathammarconi.org; 847 Orleans Rd/MA 28, North Chatham; adult/child $7.50/free; ⊙10:30am-4:30pm Tue-Sat, 1-4pm Sun late Jun–mid-Oct) Communication in all its guises is the focus at this museum dedicated to the history of WCC, a short-wave radio station that operated for many years in Chatham. WCC was the busiest coast station

---

LOCAL KNOWLEDGE

CHATHAM FISH PIER

In the mid-to-late afternoon, head to the **Chatham Fish Pier** (cnr Shore Rd & Barcliff Ave), about 1 mile north of Chatham Light, to watch the fishing fleet unload its daily catch from the visitors' viewing deck. If the tide's low, you'll get to see seals as well, which swim around the boats as the haul is brought in. Park in the upper parking lot and walk down behind the fish market.

SEAL-WATCHING

Gray and harbor seals gather in amazing hordes in Chatham's waters and haul out on the shoals. There are two ways to see them. When it's low tide, just go down to the Chatham Fish Pier and look due east to spot seals basking on the sandbars. To get closer to the action, join a boat tour: **Beachcomber** (✆508-945-5265; www.sealwatch.com; 174 Crowell Rd; seal-watching tours adult/child $29/25; ☉late May–late Sep) and **Monomoy Island Ferry** (✆508-237-0420; www.monomoyislandferry.com; Stage Harbor Marine, 80 Bridge St; seal-watching tour adult/child $35/30; ☉May-Oct) both have regular daily departures in summer.

in the public ship-to-shore radio service for most of the 20th century; during WWII it had the vital role of intercepting coded signals from German U-boats. An Enigma machine is part of a cool exhibit on coding and encryption.

Chatham Railroad Museum MUSEUM
(✆508-945-5100; www.chathamrailroadmuseum.com; 153 Depot Rd; by donation; ☉10am-4pm Tue-Sat mid-Jun–mid-Sep; 🚸) Train buffs won't want to miss the 1910 caboose and assorted memorabilia at Chatham's original 1887 railroad depot. The Victorian building is an architectural treasure worth a visit in itself.

🏃 Activities

Old Colony Trail CYCLING
(🚸) The Cape Cod Rail Trail (p137) is connected to Chatham by a spur called the Old Colony Trail, which runs 4.25 miles from the Harwich bike rotary to Depot Rd near the town center. In addition, Chatham's side streets and shady lanes are well suited to cycling. **Adventure Chatham** (✆800-809-1750; www.adventurechatham.com; 1150 Queen Anne Rd; bike/kayak rental per day from $25/50) can help with bike hire.

🛏️ Sleeping

Chatham Guest Rooms APARTMENT $$
(✆508-945-1660; www.chathamguestrooms.com; 1409 Main St/MA 28; ste $89-195; ❀🐾) 🐾 A top-shelf offering 1.5 miles west of downtown Chatham. Here, above the Maps of

Antiquity store, three suites are available at a bargain price. The Garden Suite and Main Suite can each sleep four: the Main Suite has a full kitchen and laundry facilities; the Garden Suite, a private porch. The owners are fonts of information, with commendable environmental policies.

Bow Roof House B&B $$
(✆508-945-1346; thebowroofhouse@gmail.com; 59 Queen Anne Rd; r $150; 🐾) It's hard to find places like this anymore. This homey, six-room, c 1780 house is delightfully old-fashioned in price and offerings, and within easy walking distance of the town center and Oyster Pond Beach. Except for a few modern-day conveniences, like the added private bathrooms, the house looks nearly the same as it did in colonial times.

Chatham Bars Inn RESORT $$$
(✆508-945-0096; www.chathambarsinn.com; 297 Shore Rd; r from $400; 🅿️❀🐾🏊) The grand dame of Cape lodging, century-old Chatham Bars sprawls over 25 seaside acres. A campus of cottages and buildings houses 217 sophisticated rooms and suites and loads of high-end trimmings: spa, restaurants, fitness center, children's programs, a boat to shuttle guests to the National Seashore, and a pool area directly on the private beach. Minimum stays in peak summer.

Captain's House Inn B&B $$$
(✆508-945-0127; www.captainshouseinn.com; 369 Old Harbor Rd; r $185-385; ❀🐾🏊) Everything about this inn, set in an 1839 Greek Revival mansion and its luxurious outbuildings, is gracious. The decor is sumptuous, most guest rooms have a fireplace, and a gourmet breakfast is served in style overlooking a bubbly fountain. It's open to the public for classic English high tea in the afternoon ($20); 24 hours' notice is essential.

🍴 Eating

Marion's Pie Shop BAKERY $
(✆508-432-9439; www.marionspieshopofchatham.com; 2022 Main St/MA 28; small pies $7-19; ☉8am-5pm) It's all about pie here (and a sign warns that well-behaved children are welcome, the rest will be made into pies). We're talking fresh fruit (wild blueberry, lemon meringue, strawberry peach) and savory (chicken, beef steak, clam). They're available in 6-inch and 9-inch sizes. Breakfast muffins and cinnamon nut rolls are huge and delicious.

Larry's PX   DINER $
(☑508-945-3964; 1591 Main St/MA 28; mains $6-16; ☺6am-2pm, from 5am in summer) True local flavor, with Formica tables, fishers' hours and service with a sassy smile. Join the townies for omelets and fried seafood. The sign on the door says 'Sorry, we're open.' Gotta love that.

★**Chatham Pier Fish Market**   SEAFOOD $$
(☑508-945-3474; www.chathampierfishmarket. com; 45 Barcliff Ave; mains $12-25; ☺10am-6pm May–mid-Nov) If you like it fresh and hyper-local, this salt-sprayed fish shack with its own sushi chef and day-boats is for you. The chowder's incredible, the fish so fresh it was swimming earlier in the day. It's takeout, but there are shady picnic tables where you can watch fishers unloading their catch and seals frolicking as you savor dinner.

Del Mar   AMERICAN $$
(☑508-945-9988; www.delmarbistro.com; 907 Main St; mains $15-34; ☺5-9pm Jun-Sep, short-er hours Oct-May) The creative menu at this stylish bistro swings from thin-crust fig-and-prosciutto pizza to maple-glazed duck and beyond. Global influences enhance fine local produce: Portuguese steamed littlenecks, seafood gumbo, wood-fired Wellfleet Bay scallops. The bar's a good place for solo diners, or simply for a cocktail.

🍷 Drinking & Entertainment

Chatham Bars Inn   COCKTAIL BAR
(☑508-945-0096; www.chathambarsinn.com; 297 Shore Rd) Drink in the seaside views from the veranda of this refined resort (built in 1914), or join the fun at the Beach House, where cocktails, clambakes and cookouts rock summer evenings.

Chatham Orpheum   CINEMA
(☑508-945-4900; www.chathamorpheum.org; 637 Main St; tickets adult/child $11/8) A beautifully restored, two-screen movie house dating from 1916. There's a cool cafe inside.

🔒 Shopping
Main St is lined with interesting shops and galleries.

Where the Sidewalk Ends   BOOKS
(☑508-945-0499; www.booksonthecape.com; 432 Main St; ☺10am-5pm, to 9:30pm summer) A beautiful barn full of books, and an adjacent children's annex – it's heaven for bibliophiles. Summertime kids' events (story times, etc) are very sweet. It's open later in summer.

ℹ️ Information
Chatham Chamber of Commerce (☑508-945-5199; www.chathaminfo.com; 2377 Main St/MA 28, cnr MA 137; ☺10am-2pm Mon-Sat Jun, 10am-5pm Mon-Sat Jul-Sep, closed Oct-May) For local info, stop at the chamber's

---

LOCAL KNOWLEDGE

CAPE COD FARMERS MARKETS

A homegrown movement of small-scale farms has taken root on Cape Cod. These days you're never far from a farmers market, where you can buy direct from growers. You'll find everything from organic arugula to Cape Cod honey and beach-plum jam at the following.

Falmouth (www.falmouthfarmersmarket.org; Marine Park, Scranton Ave; ☺noon-6pm Thu Jun-Sep)

Chatham (1652 Main St; ☺3-6:30pm Tue mid-May–mid-Oct)

Hyannis (www.capecodbeer.com; 1336 Phinneys Lane; ☺3-6pm Fri Jun-Sep)

Orleans (www.orleansfarmersmarket.com; 21 Old Colony Way; ☺8am-noon Sat Jun-Nov)

Wellfleet (www.wellfleetfarmersmarket.com; Wellfleet Preservation Hall, 335 Main St; ☺8am-noon Wed mid-May–mid-Oct)

Sandwich (www.sandwichfarmersmarket.com; Village Green, 164 MA 6A; ☺9am-1pm Tue May-Oct)

For more on food-focused events, plus farms, stores and restaurants that support local agriculture, visit www.buyfreshbuylocalcapecod.org.

A NATIVE AMERICAN FOURTH

Mashpee is a bit of a 'forgotten' Cape town, often overlooked by visitors who travel to the beaches of Falmouth or the ferry docks of Hyannis. This fast-growing Cape town is home to the Mashpee Wampanoag, the Native American tribe that welcomed the Pilgrims in 1620.

Over the July 4th weekend, the Wampanoag sponsor the **Mashpee Wampanoag Powwow** (www.mashpee wampanoagtribe.com/powwow; 220 MA 151, East Falmouth; ☉ early Jul), a big three-day event that includes Native American dancing, drumming, games, food and art, plus a very cool fireball ceremony after the sun sets on the Saturday evening. The event is open to the public, and is held at the Cape's fairgrounds in East Falmouth.

Bassett House Visitor Center as you drive into town.

Visitor Information Booth (www.chathaminfo. com; 533 Main St; ☉10am-5pm Jul-Sep, 11am-3pm late May, Jun & Oct) A handy info booth in downtown Chatham can answer questions. It's open Labor Day to Columbus Day.

❶ Getting There & Away

Chatham sits at the 'elbow' of the Cape. MA 28 is the main route through it; it becomes Main St in the downtown area.

MA 137 connects Chatham with US 6.

Orleans

☑ 508 / POP 5900

To many, Orleans is simply the place where MA 6A and MA 28 converge and US 6 continues onward as the sole road to Provincetown. Others know of the exhilarating surf at Nauset Beach and that untouched Nauset Marsh offers a unique kayaking experience through one of the Cape's richest ecosystems.

Atlantic-facing Nauset Beach is about 3 miles east of Orleans center. Skaket Beach is on the bay side about 1.5 miles west of the town center.

◉ Sights & Activities

Nauset Beach   BEACH
(Beach Rd, East Orleans) Dune-backed and gloriously wide and sandy, this wild barri-

er beach extends for miles along the open Atlantic. Nauset is one of the Cape's best beaches for surfing, bodysurfing, long walks, ace sunrises and just plain partying. You'll find a good clam shack and full facilities. Swing by on a Monday night in July and August for a rocking sunset concert.

Daily parking costs $20 in summer (late May to mid-September); tickets can be purchased at the parking lot gate.

Skaket Beach   BEACH
(Skaket Beach Rd; ⊞) On the bay side of town, calm Skaket Beach is a magnet for families – kids love wading in the shallow waters to dig for hermit crabs. Its generous sands triple in size when the tide goes out – at low tide you can walk the flats all the way to Brewster and back. Sunsets are often photo-worthy. To reach it, take West Rd off MA 6A. Daily parking costs $20 (late May to mid-September); buy tickets at the parking lot gate.

Goose Hummock Outdoor Center KAYAKING
(☑ 508-255-0455; www.goose.com; 15 MA 6A; kayak rental half/full day $25/50; ☉ 9am-5:30pm Mon-Fri, 8am-6pm Sat, 8am-4pm Sun) Right on Town Cove, this outfit rents kayaks, canoes and stand up paddle surfboards for use on the calm waters of the cove and Nauset Marsh. It's hard to imagine a prettier place to drop a paddle. Goose also offers lessons and **kayak tours** (from $50). Its store has oodles of fishing gear for sale and expert advice.

🛏 Sleeping & Eating

Cove Motel   MOTEL **$$**
(☑ 508-255-1203; www.thecoveorleans.com; 13 S Orleans Rd/MA 28; r $69-244; �} A good choice for those who want to be on the water but within strolling distance of the town center. Rooms are well equipped, but many are built motel-style around a parking lot. Others have a more Cape Cod–cottage look, set back overlooking a cove. For the best water views, request rooms 20 to 25.

Ship's Knees Inn   B&B **$$**
(☑ 508-255-1312; www.shipskneesinn.com; 186 Beach Rd, East Orleans; r shared bathroom $115-160, private bathroom $120-270; ☉ Apr-Dec; ☀ �} This place packs in excellent amenities and appealing period decor. Best of all, it's just a quarter-mile walk to Nauset Beach. The 17 rooms in this old sea captain's home have nautical themes. Sea captains were accustomed to close quarters: some of the rooms are tight on elbow room, others

are generous suites. Two rooms share a hall-way bathroom.

Hot Chocolate Sparrow
CAFE $

(☑508-240-2230; www.hotchocolatesparrow.com; 5 Old Colony Way; snacks $3-7; ⊙6:30am-9pm Sun-Thu, to 11pm Fri & Sat) One of the Cape's finest coffee bars brews heady espresso and cappuccino. Or, for a cool treat on a hot day, try the 'frozen hot chocolate.' Panini sandwiches, homemade pastries and fresh-from-the-oven cinnamon buns make perfect accompaniments, or a cabinet full of fudge and chocolates might tempt you.

ℹ Information

Orleans Chamber of Commerce (☑508-255-7203; www.orleanscapecod.org; 44 Main St; ⊙9am-5pm Mon-Fri) Dispenses information from its downtown location.

ℹ Getting There & Away

Orleans is where MA 6A and MA 28 converge; US 6 continues as the only road to Provincetown.

Eastham

☑508 / POP 4900
Eastham is not only the southern entrance to the Cape Cod National Seashore (p150), but it's also home to the Cape's oldest wind-mill and some well-known lighthouses. Don't be fooled by the bland commercial development along US 6 – slip off the high-way and you'll find an unspoiled world of beaches, marshes and trails.

◎ Sights

Coast Guard Beach
BEACH

(Ocean View Dr, off Doane Rd) All roads lead to the National Seashore's Coast Guard Beach. The main road from the Salt Pond Visi-tor Center (p150) deposits you here, as do cycling and hiking trails. And it's for good reason: this grand beach, backed by a classic coast guard station, is a stunner that attracts everyone from beachcombers to hard-core surfers. Bird-watchers also flock to Coast Guard Beach for the eagle-eye view of **Nau-set Marsh**.

Nauset Light Beach
BEACH

(Ocean View Dr) Cliff-backed Nauset Light Beach, north of Coast Guard Beach, is also the stuff of dreams. It's broad and sandy and its features and facilities are similar to Coast Guard Beach, but there's a large parking lot right at the beach. A photogenic **lighthouse** (☑508-240-2612; www.nausetlight.org; Ocean View Dr; ⊙tours Sun May-Oct, plus Tue & Wed Jul & Aug) **FREE** guards the shoreline.

Parking costs $20 in summer (ie the Cape Cod National Seashore per-vehicle admis-sion fee).

Fort Hill
VIEWPOINT

(Fort Hill Rd, off US 6) Don't miss the command-ing view of expansive Nauset Marsh from Fort Hill. It's a favorite place to be at dawn, but the view is memorable any time of the day. And bring your walking shoes for the 2-mile **Fort Hill Trail**. It leads down scenic Fort Hill toward the coast and then skirts inland to meander along raised boardwalks over a unique red-maple swamp. It's one of the nicest walks in the National Seashore, especially in fall.

First Encounter Beach
BEACH

(Samoset Rd; ♿) First Encounter Beach, where Samoset Rd meets Cape Cod Bay, is a fine place to watch the sunset. With its vast tidal flats and kid-friendly, calm, shal-low waters, it offers a night-and-day con-trast to the National Seashore beaches on

---

LOCAL KNOWLEDGE

BREAK OUT THE S'MORES!

That perfect day at the beach doesn't have to end when the sun goes down. Cape Cod National Seashore allows campfires on the sand at six of its beaches, though you'll need a free permit and there's a run on them in midsummer. Reservations can be made three days in advance at Salt Pond Visitor Center (p150) for Coast Guard, Nauset Light and Marconi Beaches, or the Province Lands Visitor Center (p151) for Race Point, Herring Cove and Head of the Meadow Beaches.

Tip: reservations go first to people lined up at the door when it opens at 9am; phone reservations are accepted if there are any left. Four permits are allowed each evening at each beach. Bring firewood (bundles are sold at grocery stores) and a bucket to douse the flames – and a big bag of marshmallows!

Eastham's wild Atlantic side. Parking costs $18 to $20 in summer.

And the name of the beach? It's the site of the first encounter between the Pilgrims and the local Native Americans, in 1620, prior to the Pilgrims settling in Plymouth.

Eastham Windmill   LANDMARK
(☑508-255-1798; 2515 US 6; ⊙10am-5pm Mon-Sat, 1-5pm Sun Jul-Aug) FREE Eastham's landmark windmill is the oldest structure in town, although it was actually built in Plymouth (MA) in 1680. It sits in a pretty park by the side of US 6.

🏃 Activities

Nauset Bike Trail   CYCLING
(www.nps.org/caco) The 1.6-mile Nauset Bike Trail traverses woods and a salt marsh en route from the Salt Pond Visitor Center to magnificent Coast Guard Beach. It passes the lovely Doane Rock picnic area, too.

🛏 Sleeping

HI Eastham   HOSTEL $
(☑508-255-2785; www.hiusa.org; 75 Goody Hallet Dr; dm $33-37, q $105-115; ⊙mid-Jun–mid-Sep; 🛜) 🧺 This summer hostel has 42 beds in a small colony of no-frills cabins set around a main building housing kitchen and lounge. Each basic cabin sleeps four to eight people (in bunk beds), and the place fills quickly. There are very few true budget options on the Cape, and this one is well placed for beaches and cycling trails.

★ Inn at the Oaks   B&B $$
(☑508-255-1886; www.innattheoaks.com; 3085 US 6; r $75-325; 🖾🛜🖾) This inn has 13 antique-filled guest rooms, set in a converted sea captain's house from 1870. There's a

---

SURFING WELLFLEET

You brought your surfboard, right? The adjacent town-run beaches of **Cahoon Hollow Beach** and **White Crest Beach** offer high-octane surfing. Backed by steep dunes, these long, untamed Atlantic beaches also make for memorable beach walks. Parking at either costs $20 in summer. If you need gear, **SickDay Surf Shop** (☑508-214-4158; www.sickday.cc; 361 Main St; surfboard rental per day $30; ⊙9am-9pm Mon-Sat May-Oct) can set you up.

---

room for every taste; the roomy suites in the carriage house are the pick. Expect a lot of stylishly relaxed charm: rockers on the wraparound porch, sprawling grounds and lots of common areas. It's not far from Salt Pond Visitor Center.

Eagle Wing Inn   MOTEL $$
(☑508-240-5656; www.eaglewingmotel.com; 960 US 6; r $119-179; 🖾🛜🖾) Spacious squeaky-clean rooms, comfy beds and quiet grounds are the draw at this boutique motel geared for adults. Opt for one of the rooms with a rear deck and watch the rabbits raid the backyard flowers. There's even a free laundry and complimentary bikes for guests – handy for covering the 2 miles to the National Seashore.

🍴 Eating

Karoo Restaurant   SOUTH AFRICAN $$
(☑508-255-8288; www.karoorestaurants.com; 3 Main St; mains $10-26; ⊙4:30-9pm Wed-Mon; 🌱) Home-style South African cooking is an unlikely find on the Cape, and an interesting option if your palate is growing weary of seafood. In a cool space with a splash of African color, sample *bobotie* (a mild curried meatloaf) or the spicy *peri-peri* chicken for a blast of tomato, garlic and chili. Good vegetarian options, too.

Arnold's Lobster & Clam Bar   SEAFOOD $$
(☑508-255-2575; www.arnoldsrestaurant.com; 3580 US 6; meals $5-25; ⊙11:30am-8pm mid-May–mid-Oct; 🎏) Fried seafood is the staple (plus renowned onion rings); there's also salads, baked cod and steamed lobster on the menu. Everything is fresh, and at night this place adds on a raw bar, separating it from other counter-service seafood shacks along the highway. It's super family-oriented, with kids' dishes served on Frisbees. Also has a mini-golf course and ice-cream stand.

Friendly Fisherman   SEAFOOD $$
(☑508-255-6770; www.friendlyfishermaneastham.com; 4580 US 6; meals $8-20; ⊙11:30am-8pm May-Sep; 🎏) This simple eatery, attached to a fish market, has outdoor picnic tables and serves the perfect lobster roll: huge, overflowing with sweet chunks of claw and tail meat, and with just enough mayo to hold it all together. The fried clams here are impressive, too. BYOB. Kids playground on-site.

ℹ Information

Eastham Visitor Information Booth (☎508-255-3444; www.easthamchamber.com; 1700 US 6, cnr Governor Prence Rd; ◷9am-6pm late May–mid-Oct) This summertime information booth is on US 6, just north of the Fort Hill turnoff. When it's closed, there are maps and guides available.

ℹ Getting There & Away

US 6 is the arterial through Eastham for cars; the Cape Cod Rail Trail is perfect for two-wheeled travel. A shuttle runs from Salt Pond Visitor Center to Coast Guard Beach in summer (it's free, but note that you must pay to access the National Seashore).

Wellfleet

☎508 / POP 3000

Art galleries, primo surfing beaches and those famous Wellfleet oysters lure visitors to this seaside village. Actually, there's not much Wellfleet doesn't have, other than crowds. It's a delightful throwback to an earlier era, from its drive-in movie theater to its unspoiled town center, which has barely changed in appearance since the 1950s.

◉ Sights

Marconi Beach   BEACH
(off US 6) Part of the Cape Cod National Seashore (p150), Marconi is a narrow Atlantic beach backed by sea cliffs and undulating dunes. Facilities include changing rooms, restrooms and showers. It's named for famous Italian inventor Guglielmo Marconi, who sent the first transatlantic wireless message from a station nearby in 1903. Parking costs $20 in summer (the permit fee to access the National Seashore). The **Atlantic White Cedar Swamp Trail** is a 1.5-mile nature trail that's worth exploring.

**Wellfleet Bay
Wildlife Sanctuary**   NATURE RESERVE
(☎508-349-2615; www.massaudubon.org; 291 US 6, South Wellfleet; adult/child $5/3; ◷trails 8am-dusk, nature center 8:30am-5pm; 🚻) 🦅 Birders flock to Mass Audubon's 940-acre sanctuary, where 5 miles of trails cross tidal creeks, salt marshes and beaches. The most popular is the **Goose Pond Trail** (1.5-mile round-trip), which leads out to a salt marsh and offers abundant opportunities for spotting marine and bird life. The sanctuary also offers guided walks and kayaking tours, seal cruises and summer kids' programs.

🏃 Activities

Little Capistrano Bike Shop   CYCLING
(☎508-349-2363; www.capecodbike.com; 1446 US 6, South Wellfleet; 24hr rental $23; ◷9am-4pm late May–mid-Oct) The northern end of the Cape Cod Rail Trail (p137) is at Lecount Hollow Rd near its intersection with US 6. You can rent bikes in summer here, right near the trailhead, and pedal south (grab some goodies from nearby PB Boulangerie & Bistro, p148, for the journey). Kids' bikes and trailers available.

🎊 Festivals & Events

Wellfleet OysterFest   FOOD
(www.wellfleetoysterfest.org; ◷mid-Oct) During the Wellfleet OysterFest, held on a weekend in mid-October, the entire town center becomes a food fair, with a beer garden, an oyster-shucking contest and, of course, belly-busters of the blessed bivalves. It's a wildly popular event and a great time to see Wellfleet at its most spirited.

🛏 Sleeping & Eating

Even'Tide Motel   MOTEL $$
(☎508-349-3410; www.eventidemotel.com; 650 US 6, South Wellfleet; r $89-207, cottages per week $1400-2800; ◷May-Oct; ❄🐕🏊) This highly regarded motel, set back from the highway in a grove of pine trees, has an assortment of options: regular motel rooms, plus 10 diverse cottages that can each accommodate two to 10 people (cottages generally rented by the week). Pluses include a large, indoor heated pool and 5 acres of wooded grounds that harbor sports and picnic facilities.

RETRO REVIVAL

For an evening of nostalgia, park at **Wellfleet Drive-In** (☑508-349-7176; www.wellfleetcin emas.com; 51 US 6, South Wellfleet; tickets adult/child $10/7.50; ☉ late May–mid-Sep; 🚗), one of a dwindling number of drive-in theaters surviving in the USA. Built in the 1950s, before the word 'cineplex' became part of the vernacular, everything except the movie being shown on the giant screen is true to the era. Yep, they still have those original mono speakers that you hook over the car window, there's an old-fashioned snack bar and, of course, it's always a double feature. Plastic – what's that? It's cash-only at the gate.

OK, there are a few accommodations to modern times. So as to not block anyone's view, the lot is now divided into two sections: one for SUVs, the other for cars. And you don't *need* to use those boxy window speakers: you can also listen by tuning your stereo car radio to an FM station. But other things remain unchanged – bring bug spray and a blanket!

Another time-honored throwback is **Wellfleet Flea Market** (☑508-349-0541; www. wellfleetcinemas.com/flea-market; 51 US 6, South Wellfleet; admission per car $3; ☉8am-3pm Sat & Sun late May–mid-Oct, also Wed & Thu Jul & Aug), held in summer at the drive-in. This is the largest flea market on the Cape, with 200 dealers selling everything from antiques to newly made objects, and from treasures to junk. Most vendors take cash only.

Surfside Cottages   COTTAGE **$$**
(☑508-349-3959; www.surfsidecottages.com; Ocean View Dr) This agency oversees the rental of a community of cottages just back from Lecount Hollow Beach (and full marks to the website, which specifies how many *steps* each place is to the beach!). Cottages vary in capacity and aesthetic, from simple old-school beach shack to a more modern fit-out and furnishings. Prices reflect this; rentals are generally by the week.

★PB Boulangerie & Bistro   BAKERY **$**
(☑508-349-1600; www.pbboulangeriebistro.com; 15 Lecount Hollow Rd, South Wellfleet; pastries $3-5, sandwiches $10-12; ☉bakery 7am-7pm, bistro 5-10pm Wed-Sun & 10am-2:30pm Sun) A Michelin-starred French baker setting up shop in tiny Wellfleet? You might think he'd gone to the line out the door. You can't miss PB: it's painted pink and set back from US 6. Scan the cabinets full of fruit tarts, chocolate-almond croissants and filled baguettes and you'll think you've died and gone to Paris.

The bistro menu (mains $19 to $45) is a high-end homage to French classics, mixed with some superlative local *fruits de mer*.

Mac's on the Pier   SEAFOOD **$$**
(☑508-349-9611; www.macsseafood.com; 265 Commercial St, Wellfleet Town Pier; mains $8-30; ☉11am-3:30pm Sun-Thu, to 8pm Fri & Sat Jun-Sep; ☑🚗) Head here for fish-market-fresh seafood at bargain prices. Fried-fish standards join the likes of oyster po'boys, sushi rolls

and grilled striped-bass dinners. You order at a window and chow down at picnic tables overlooking Wellfleet Harbor.

Wicked Oyster   AMERICAN **$$**
(☑508-349-3455; www.thewickedo.com; 50 Main St; dinner mains $15-33; ☉7:30am-noon & 5-9pm) Hang out here for the likes of filet mignon with a bourbon caramel sauce, buttermilk-fried calamari and, of course, several incarnations of Wellfleet oysters. Although the chef works his magic at dinner, you can also start your day here with a wicked omelet or smoked-salmon bagel.

Mac's Shack   SEAFOOD **$$$**
(☑508-349-6333; www.macsseafood.com; 91 Commercial St; mains $19-34; ☉11:30am-3pm & 4:30-9pm Apr-Oct) This is a fancier, full-service version of Mac's on the Pier, complete with cocktails, sushi chef and raw bar. The menu keeps the classic clam-shack favorites, but adds the likes of pasta *vongole,* tuna tartare, and shrimp and scallop dumplings.

🍷 Drinking & Entertainment

★Beachcomber   BAR
(☑508-349-6055; www.thebeachcomber.com; 1120 Cahoon Hollow Rd; ☉5pm-1am late May–early Sep) If you're ready for some serious partying, 'Da Coma' is *the* place to rock the night away. It's a bar. It's a restaurant. It's a dance club. It's the coolest summertime hangout on the entire Cape. It's set in a former lifeguard station right on Cahoon Hollow Beach, and you can watch the surf action till the sun goes down.

Wellfleet Harbor Actors Theater THEATER
(WHAT; ☑ 508-349-9428; www.what.org; 2357 US
6) WHAT's happening! The Cape's most celebrated theater always has something going
on in its state-of-the-art Julie Harris Stage.
The contemporary, experimental plays
staged here are always lively, occasionally
bawdy and often the subject of animated
conversation.

ℹ Information

Wellfleet Chamber of Commerce (☑ 508-
349-2510; www.wellfleetchamber.com; 1410 US
6, South Wellfleet; ⊙ 9am-6pm late May–mid-
Oct) Has an information booth by the South
Wellfleet post office at Lecount Hollow Rd.

ℹ Getting There & Away

Most of Wellfleet east of US 6 is part of the
Cape Cod National Seashore. To get to the town
center, turn west off US 6 at either Main St or
School St.

Truro

☑ 508 / POP 1740

Squeezed between Cape Cod Bay on the
west and the open Atlantic on the east, narrow Truro abounds with views of the water.
An odd collection of elements coexist here
peacefully: strip motels along the highway,
trophy homes in the hills and dales west of
US 6, and pine forests and beaches to the
east.

To reach Truro's historic sites, which are
on the ocean side, take Highland or South
Highland Rds off US 6. Or, for fun, just take
any winding road off the highway and let
yourself get a little lost, soaking in the distinctive scenery.

◎ Sights & Activities

Truro Vineyards WINERY, DISTILLERY
(☑ 508-487-6200; www.trurovineyardsofcapecod.
com; 11 Shore Rd/MA 6A, North Truro; tastings $10;
⊙ 11am-5pm Mon-Sat, noon-5pm Sun May-Oct,
Fri-Mon Apr, Nov & Dec) This boutique vineyard, the first on the Outer Cape, is worth a
stop. In recent times it has added a boutique
distillery, South Hollow Spirits, producing
amber rum and gin. From May to October,
tastings take place every half-hour (a pricey
$10 for five tastes); free **tours** are held at
1pm and 3pm. The grounds are a pretty spot
for a lazy afternoon, especially if the food
truck operated by BlackFish sets up.

Head of the Meadow Beach BEACH
(Head of the Meadow Rd, off US 6) Part of the
Cape Cod National Seashore (p150), this
wide, dune-backed beach has limited facilities, but there are lifeguards in summer.
If you happen to be there at low tide, you
might catch a glimpse of old shipwrecks
that met their fate on the shoals. There are
two entrances: the National Seashore beach
(parking $20) is to the left and open to the
public. The other entrance is for local residents only.

Cape Cod Highland Light LIGHTHOUSE
(☑ 508-487-1121; www.capecodlight.org; Highland
Light Rd; $4; ⊙ 10am-5:30pm mid-May–mid-Oct)
Sitting on the Cape's highest elevation (a
mere 120ft!), Cape Cod Highland Light dates
to 1797 and casts the brightest beam on the
New England coast. Admission includes a
10-minute video, an exhibit in the keeper's
house and a climb up the lighthouse's 69
steps to a sweeping vista. Children must be
at least 48in tall to make the climb.

The adjacent **Highland House Museum**
(☑ 508-487-3397; www.trurohistoricalsociety.org;
Highland Light Rd; adult/child $5/free; ⊙ 10am-
4:30pm Mon-Sat Jun-Sep) focuses on Truro's
farming and maritime past. It's packed with
all sorts of vintage goodies, from antique
dolls to shipwreck salvage.

🛏 Sleeping & Eating

★**North of Highland
Camping Area** CAMPGROUND $
(☑ 508-487-1191; www.capecodcamping.com; 52
Head of the Meadow Rd, North Truro; tent sites $40-
44; ⊙ late May–mid-Sep) 🏕 Little Truro harbors one of the most secluded campgrounds
on all of Cape Cod, with 237 sites spread
over 60 pine-fresh acres a short walk from
the beach. You don't have to worry about
setting up your tent next to an RV – it's tent
camping only. Amenities include metered
hot showers, camp store, laundry, a rec hall
and a kids' playground.

HI Truro HOSTEL $
(☑ 508-349-3889; www.hiusa.org; 111 N Pamet
Rd; dm $45-47; ⊙ late Jun–early Sep; P 🛜) 🏕
Budget digs don't get more atmospheric than this former coast-guard station
perched amid undulating dunes within
Cape Cod National Seashore (p150). It's so
remote that wild turkeys are the only traffic along the road – and it's but a stroll to a
quiet beach. There are just 42 beds, so book
early to avoid disappointment.

DON'T MISS

CAPE COD NATIONAL SEASHORE

Cape Cod National Seashore (www.nps.gov/caco) extends some 40 miles around the curve of the Outer Cape and encompasses the Atlantic shoreline from Orleans all the way to Provincetown. Under the auspices of the National Park Service, it's a treasure trove of unspoiled beaches, dunes, salt marshes, nature trails and forests. Thanks to the backing of President John F Kennedy, this vast area was set aside for preservation in the 1960s, just before a building boom hit the rest of his native Cape Cod.

Access to the park sights is easy: everything of interest is on or just off US 6. The year-round Salt Pond Visitor Center (☑508-255-3421; www.nps.gov/caco; 50 Nauset Rd, cnr US 6; ☺9am-5pm) in Eastham is the place to start. The Province Lands Visitor Center in Provincetown is smaller and open seasonally, but it has similar services to the Eastham center plus a fabulous ocean view.

Beach parking permits cost $20 per day or $60 per season and are valid at all National Seashore beaches, so you can use the same permit to spend the morning at one beach and the afternoon at another; pedestrians and cyclists pay $3, motorcyclists $10. The fees are collected only in summer – from late June through early September, when lifeguards are on duty – and on weekends and holidays from Memorial Day (late May) to the end of September. Outside these times, beach parking is free.

Chequessett Chocolate SWEETS $
(☑774-538-6249; www.chequessettchocolate.com; 8 Highland Rd, North Truro; ☺10am-5pm Mon-Tue, 8am-5pm Wed-Sun) Make a stop here to get a primo caffeine and choc fix. Chequessett makes delicious, artisanal bean-to-bar chocolate from sustainably grown cacao beans.

★ BlackFish MODERN AMERICAN $$
(☑508-349-3399; 17 Truro Center Rd; mains $15-35; ☺5-10pm mid-May–early Nov; ☑) Local ingredients meet urban sophistication at Truro's top dinner restaurant. From the nautical decor to the out-of-the-ordinary menu choices, everything clicks. Perhaps you'll want to start with the rabbit ragu and finish with the blackberry bread pudding and brandy ice cream. Try the house specialty, tuna Bolognese. There are always some creative vegetarian options as well. Bookings advised.

☆ Entertainment

Payomet Performing Arts Center LIVE MUSIC, THEATER
(☑508-487-5400; www.payomet.org; 29 Old Dewline Rd, North Truro; ☑) The center's theme – 'national talent on a local stage' – rings true, with performances by the likes of folk icon Arlo Guthrie and soul diva Sharon Jones. The setting, inside a large tent surrounded by woods, is as cool as the performers. Theater productions, circus classes and children's workshops also take place here in the summer.

❶ Information

Truro Chamber of Commerce (☑508-487-1288; www.trurochamberofcommerce.com; cnr US 6 & Head of the Meadow Rd, North Truro; ☺10am-4pm May–mid-Oct, 9am-6pm Jul & Aug) Has a visitor information booth on US 6, at the turning to Head of the Meadow Beach.

❶ Getting There & Away

From Truro, US 6 presses on to Provincetown and the tip of the Cape. A more scenic drive is via MA 6A, which follows the bay shore.

Provincetown
☑508 / POP 2950

This is it: Provincetown is as far as you can go on the Cape, and more than just geographically. The draw is irresistible. Fringe writers and artists began making a summer haven in Provincetown a century ago. Today this sandy outpost has morphed into the hottest gay and lesbian destination in the Northeast. Flamboyant street scenes, brilliant art galleries and unbridled nightlife paint the town center. But that's only half the show. Provincetown's untamed coastline and vast beaches also beg exploring. Sail off on a whale watch, cruise the night away, get lost in the dunes – but whatever you do, don't miss this unique, open-minded corner of New England.

◉ Sights

Start your exploration on Commercial St, the throbbing waterfront heart of Provincetown, where the lion's share of cafes, galleries and clubs vie for your attention.

★ Provincetown Art
Association & Museum   MUSEUM
(PAAM; ☑ 508-487-1750; www.paam.org; 460 Commercial St; adult/child $10/free; ⊙ 11am-8pm Mon-Thu, to 10pm Fri, to 6pm Sat, to 5pm Sun Jul & Aug, shorter hours rest of year, closed Mon-Wed Oct-May) Founded in 1914 to celebrate the town's thriving art community, this vibrant museum showcases the works of hundreds of artists who have found their inspiration on the Lower Cape. Chief among them are Charles Hawthorne, who led the early Provincetown art movement, and Edward Hopper, who had a home and gallery in the Truro dunes.

★ Pilgrim Monument
& Provincetown Museum   MUSEUM
(☑ 508-487-1310; www.pilgrim-monument.org; 1 High Pole Hill Rd; adult/child $12/4; ⊙ 9am-5pm Apr-May & Sep-Nov, to 7pm Jun-Aug) Climb to the top of the country's tallest all-granite structure (253ft) for a sweeping view of town, the beaches and the spine of the Lower Cape. The climb is 116 steps plus 60 ramps and takes about 10 minutes at a leisurely pace. At the base of the c 1910 tower is an evocative museum depicting the landing of the *Mayflower* Pilgrims and other Provincetown history.

Province Lands
Visitor Center   VISITOR CENTER
(☑ 508-487-1256; www.nps.gov/caco; 171 Race Point Rd, off US 6; ⊙ 9am-5pm May-Oct) Overlooking Race Point Beach, this Cape Cod National Seashore visitor center has displays on dune ecology and a rooftop observation deck with an eye-popping 360-degree view of the outermost reaches of Cape Cod. The park stays open to midnight, so even after the visitor center closes you can still climb to the deck for sunset views and unobstructed stargazing.

Race Point Beach   BEACH
(Race Point Rd) On the wild tip of the Cape, this Cape Cod National Seashore beach is a breathtaking stretch of sand, crashing surf and undulating dunes as far as the eye can see. Kick off your sandals, kids – the soft, grainy sand makes for a fun run. This is the kind of beach where you could walk for miles and see no one but the occasional angler casting for bluefish. Parking costs $20 in summer (the National Seashore fee).

Herring Cove Beach   BEACH
(Province Lands Rd) Swimmers favor the relatively calm (though certainly brisk) waters of Herring Cove Beach, part of the Cape Cod National Seashore. The long, sandy beach is popular with everyone. Though illegal, nude sunbathers head left to the south section of the beach; families usually break out the picnic baskets closer to the parking lot. The entire beach faces west, making it a spectacular place to be at sunset. Parking costs $20 in summer (the National Seashore fee).

East End Gallery District   GALLERY, AREA
(Commercial St) With the many artists who have worked here, it's no surprise that Provincetown hosts some of the finest art galleries in the region. For the best browsing, begin at PAAM and start walking southwest along Commercial St. Over the next few blocks every second storefront harbors a gallery worth a peek.

Pick up a copy of the *Provincetown Gallery Guide* (www.provincetowngalleryguide. com), or check out its website for gallery info, a map and details of events.

Long Point Beach   BEACH
Home to the Cape's most remote grains of sand, Long Point Beach is reached by a two-hour walk (each way) along the stone dike at the western end of Commercial St. There are no facilities, so bring water. Be sure to time your walk carefully, as the dike is submerged at extreme high tide. Or do it the easy way and hop on the **Long Point Shuttle** (☑ 508-487-0898; www.flyersboats.com; MacMillan Pier; one-way/round-trip $10/15; ⊙ 10am-5pm), which ferries sunbathers across the bay from June to September.

Stellwagen Bank National
Marine Sanctuary   WILDLIFE RESERVE
(www.stellwagen.noaa.gov) Provincetown is the perfect launch point for whale-watching, since it's the closest port to Stellwagen Bank National Marine Sanctuary, the summer feeding ground for humpback whales. Some 17 species have been seen at one time or another; many of the estimated 350 remaining North Atlantic right whales, one of the world's most endangered

CAPE COD, NANTUCKET & MARTHA'S VINEYARD PROVINCETOWN

Provincetown

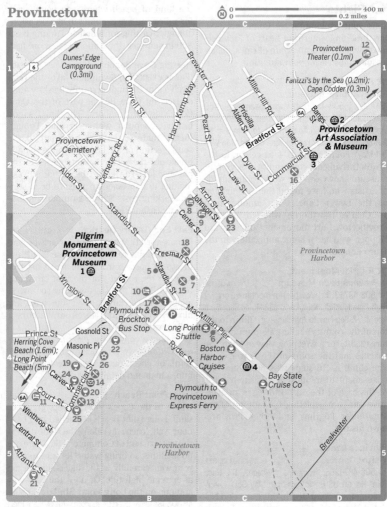

whale species, frequent these waters. Take a whale-watching boat tour to scour the sanctuary waters for life.

Whydah Pirate Museum MUSEUM
(☎508-487-8899; www.whydah.com; MacMillan Pier; adult/child $10/8; ☺10am-5pm May-Oct) Of the more than 3000 shipwrecks off the coast of the Cape, the *Whydah* is one of the best documented. Captained by 'Black Sam' Bellamy, the *Whydah* sank in 1717 and to this day remains the only authenticated pirate ship ever salvaged. A local expedition recovered more than 100,000 items of

booty – coins, jewelry, weapons – and some of these are on display at this museum on the wharf.

Note, however, that many of the prize pieces may be on loan and exhibited elsewhere by the National Geographic Society, which aided in the recovery. Argh, matey.

🏃 Activities

Province Lands Bike Trail CYCLING
(www.nps.gov/caco) An exhilarating 7.5 miles of paved bike trails crisscross the forest and undulating dunes of the Cape Cod National Seashore. As a bonus, you can cool off with a

Provincetown

swim: the main 5.5-mile loop trail has spur trails leading to both Herring Cove and Race Point Beaches.

There are a number of bike-rental places in central P-town.

Provincetown Aquasports KAYAKING
(☑508-413-9563; www.ptownaquasports.com; 333R Commercial St; 2hr tours $45-55) As well as offering kayak and stand up paddle surfboard rentals, this outfit has excellent tours running daily (weather permitting): two hours on a SUP or kayak sightseeing in Provincetown Harbor, or out to Long Point Lighthouse (the latter is for more experienced kayakers). There's also the unique tour 'Riding the Tide' at Herring Cove tidal lake. SUP yoga, too!

⌲ Tours

Check the offerings of the Province Lands Visitor Center (p151), which has a menu of guided walks and activities in the National Seashore.

★Dolphin Fleet Whale Watch WILDLIFE WATCHING
(☑800-826-9300; www.whalewatch.com; MacMillan Pier; adult/child $47/31; ⊙mid-Apr–Oct; ⚑) Dolphin Fleet offers as many as 10 whale-watch tours daily in peak season, each lasting three to four hours. You can expect a lot of splashy fun. Humpback whales have a flair for acrobatic breaching and come surprisingly close to the boats, offering great photo ops. The naturalists on board not only have all the skinny on these mammoth leviathans but also play a vital role in monitoring the whale population.

★Art's Dune Tours TOURS
(☑508-487-1950; www.artsdunetours.com; 4 Standish St; day tours adult/child $29/18, sunset tours adult/child $45/25) Art's offers 4WD tours that are surprisingly informative and scenic. And talk about local – the same family has been running these tours since 1946. The basic hour-long daytime tour takes you along a remote stretch of beach before heading off to explore the dunes. For more drama, take the two-hour sunset tour (add a clambake option for extra local flavor).

★ Festivals & Events

See www.ptownchamber.com/calendar-of-events for the lowdown.

Provincetown Carnival LGBT
(www.ptown.org/carnival; ⊙Aug) Mardi Gras, drag queens, flowery floats: this is the ultimate gay party event in this gay party town, attracting some 90,000 revelers over the entire third week of August.

⊨ Sleeping

Dunes' Edge Campground CAMPGROUND $
(☑508-487-9815; www.thetrustees.org; 386 US 6; tent sites $35-49, RV sites with hookups $47-64; ⊙mid-May–mid-Oct; P⚑) Camp amid the dunes and shady pines at this

family-friendly campground on the north side of US 6, between the National Seashore and town. With just 100 sites, it gets booked solid in midsummer, so reserve well in advance (book online). Facilities are decent: coin showers, coin laundry, camp store.

Cape Codder
GUESTHOUSE $

(☎508-487-0131; www.capecodderguests.com; 570 Commercial St; r with shared bathroom $50-90; ☺May-Oct; 🅿🎐🔰🐾) Definitely think budget – this is a very simple place that makes no pretense to be anything more. The 14 rooms share four bathrooms, there are no TVs or phones, and there's the occasional wall crack and threadbare bedspread. But heck, for these prices in this town it's a steal. You can't beat the private beach and sundeck.

Race Point Lighthouse
INN $$

(☎855-722-3959; www.mybnbwebsite.com/race pointlighthouse; Race Point; d with shared bathroom $115-205; ☺May-Nov) 🏄 Want to *really* get away? If unspoiled sand dunes and a 19th-century lighthouse sound like good company, book one of the three upstairs bedrooms in the old lighthouse-keeper's house. It's a cool place: totally off the grid, powered by solar panels and a wind turbine, and literally on the outer tip of the Cape, miles from the nearest neighbor.

You need to BYO linen and food (there is kitchen access); the price includes 4WD transport to the house. If you're traveling in a group, the Whistle House sleeps eight and is generally rented by the week. Full details are online.

Moffett House
GUESTHOUSE $$

(☎508-487-6615; www.moffetthouse.com; 296a Commercial St; d without bathroom $55-164, with bathroom $65-184; 🅿🎐@🔰) Set back on an alleyway, this guesthouse is not only quiet but has another bonus: every room comes with two bicycles for your stay. Rooms are basic – it's more like crashing with a friend than doing the B&B thing – but you get kitchen privileges, bagels and coffee in the morning (in summer), and lots of opportunities to meet fellow travelers.

Christopher's by the Bay
B&B $$

(☎508-487-9263; www.christophersbythebay. com; 8 Johnson St; r with shared bathroom $70-175, with private bathroom $90-285; 🅿🎐🔰🐾) Tucked away on a quiet side street, this welcoming inn is a top-value place. Local art on the walls and personal recommendations from the owners add a homey Provincetown

flavor. Rooms on the 2nd floor are the largest and snazziest, but the 3rd-floor rooms, which share a bathroom, get the ocean view.

★Roux
B&B $$$

(☎508-487-1717; www.rouxprovincetown.com; 210 Bradford St; r $145-425; 🅿🎐🔰) A fabulously warm welcome combines with a riot of color, art and animal print at this relative newcomer to the local scene. Owners Ali and Ilene oversee six character-filled rooms decked out with artistic flair, and their creativity extends to the excellent breakfast dishes. For unwinding, there are art-filled common areas, a garden and afternoon happy hour.

★Carpe Diem
BOUTIQUE HOTEL $$$

(☎508-487-4242; www.carpediemguesthouse. com; 12-14 Johnson St; r $139-549; 🅿🎐🔰🔰) Sophisticated yet relaxed, this boutique inn blends a soothing mix of smiling Buddhas, orchid sprays and artistic decor. Each guest room is inspired by a different gay literary genius; the room themed on poet Raj Rao, for example, has sumptuous embroidered fabrics and hand-carved Indian furniture. The on-site spa includes a Finnish sauna, hot tub and massage therapy.

Revere Guesthouse
B&B $$$

(☎508-487-2292; www.reverehouse.com; 14 Court St; r $115-359, apt $185-419; 🅿🔰🔰) Tasteful rooms, fresh-baked breakfast goodies and welcoming little touches will make you feel right at home here. The setting is peaceful, yet just minutes from all the action, and the garden's fire pit is a nice touch. There's a one-bedroom apartment with kitchen that's good for longer stays.

✖ Eating

Provincetown has one of the best dining scenes this side of Boston. Every third building on Commercial St houses some sort of eatery, so that's the place to start.

★Canteen
MODERN AMERICAN $

(☎508-487-3800; www.thecanteenptown.com; 225 Commercial St; mains $8-19; ☺11am-9pm; 🍴🖥) Cool and casual, but unmistakably gourmet – this is your optimal P-town lunch stop. Choose from classics like lobster rolls and barbecued pulled-pork sandwiches, or innovations like cod *bahn mi* and shrimp sliders. Accompany with crispy Brussels sprouts and cold beer. Take a seat at the communal picnic table on the sand, and devour.

Cafe Heaven
CAFE $

(☑ 508-487-9639; 199 Commercial St; mains $8-17; ☺ 8am-10pm; ✐) Light and airy but small and crowded, this art-filled storefront is an easy-on-the-wallet lunch and breakfast place. The menu ranges from sinfully good brioche French toast to healthy salads. Excellent sandwiches, too, like croque monsieur and chicken pesto melt. Don't be deterred by the wait: the tables turn over quickly.

Purple Feather
Cafe & Treatery
CAFE $

(☑ 508-487-9100; www.thepurplefeather.com; 334 Commercial St; panini $7-12; ☺ 11am-9pm Sun-Thu, to midnight Fri & Sat; ☎ ✿) You can't miss the *purpleness* of this place, a popular spot for coffee, killer panini sandwiches, a rainbow of gelatos and decadent desserts – all made from scratch.

Portuguese Bakery
BAKERY $

(☑ 508-487-1803; 299 Commercial St; snacks $2-5; ☺ 7am-11pm) This old-school bakery has been serving up *malassada* (sweet fried dough), spicy linguica (sausage) sandwiches and Portuguese soups for more than a century. True local flavor.

Lobster Pot
SEAFOOD $$

(☑ 508-487-0842; www.ptownlobsterpot.com; 321 Commercial St; mains $11-34; ☺ 11:30am-9pm Apr-Nov) True to its name, this busy fish house overlooking the harbor is *the* place for lobster, and many have been lured by its retro neon sign. Start with the lobster bisque, then put on a bib and crack open the perfect boiled lobster (there's a full gluten-free menu, too). The best way to beat the crowd is to come mid-afternoon.

Fanizzi's by the Sea
SEAFOOD $$

(☑ 508-487-1964; www.fanizzisrestaurant.com; 539 Commercial St; mains $9-29; ☺ 11:30am-9:30pm Mon-Sat, from 10am Sun; ✿) Consistent food, an amazing water view and reasonable prices make this restaurant a local favorite. The extensive menu has something for everyone, from fresh seafood and salads to comfort food; there's even a kids' menu. So why is it cheaper than the rest of the pack? It's less central – about a 15-minute walk northeast of the town center.

★ Mews
Restaurant & Cafe
MODERN AMERICAN $$$

(☑ 508-487-1500; www.mews.com; 429 Commercial St; mains bistro $13-21, restaurant $22-35; ☺ 5:30-10pm) A fantastic water view, the hottest martini bar in town and scrumptious food add up to Provincetown's finest dining scene. There are two sections. Opt to dine gourmet on lobster risotto and filet mignon downstairs, where you're right on the sand, or go casual with a juicy Angus burger from the bistro menu upstairs. Reservations recommended.

GAY & LESBIAN PROVINCETOWN

While other cities have their gay districts, in Provincetown the entire town is the gay district. The following are some of the highlights of the scene:

A-House (Atlantic House; ☑ 508-487-3169; www.ahouse.com; 4 Masonic Pl; ☺ bar noon-1am, club 10pm-1am) This landmark club has several faces: the Little Bar, an intimate pub; the Macho Bar; and the Big Room, the town's hottest DJ dance club.

Boatslip Beach Club (☑ 508-487-1669; www.boatslipresort.com; 161 Commercial St) Hosts wildly popular afternoon tea dances, often packed with gorgeous guys. DJs fire things up: visit on Thursdays for dance classics from the '70s and '80s. There's accommodations, too.

Crown & Anchor (www.onlyatthecrown.com; 247 Commercial St; ☺ hours vary) The queen of the scene, this multi-wing complex has a nightclub, a video bar, a leather bar and a fun, steamy cabaret that takes it to the limit, plus loads of shows and events – from Broadway concerts to drag revues and burlesque troupes. Accommodation and restaurant on-site, too.

Pied Bar (☑ 508-487-1527; www.piedbar.net; 193 Commercial St; ☺ noon-1am May-Oct) This woman-owned waterfront lounge is a popular dance spot for all genders, especially around sunset. The main event is the 'After Tea T-Dance,' to which folks head after the Boatslip.

🍷 Drinking & Nightlife

Nor'East Beer Garden   PUB
(☑508-487-2337; www.thenoreastbeergarden.
com; 206 Commercial St; ⊙11:30am-11:30pm
Mon-Fri, from 10am Sat & Sun May-Sep) The
cocktails always flow in P-town, but it's not
immune from the craft-brew explosion.
This delightful main-street oasis features 16
draft beers from all over the US, and adds
extra appeal with garden-inspired cocktails
(eg tequila with housemade rhubarb syrup
and lime juice), plus some impressive kitch-
en output.

Harbor Lounge   COCKTAIL BAR
(☑508-413-9527;   www.theharborlounge.com;
359 Commercial St; ⊙noon-10pm Apr-Dec) The
Harbor Lounge takes full advantage of its
seaside setting, with floor-to-ceiling windows and a boardwalk stretching out into
the bay. Candlelit tables and black leather
sofas constitute the decor – nothing else
is needed. The cocktails are surprisingly
affordable, with many martini concoctions
to sample.

Aqua Bar   BAR
(☑774-593-5106; 207 Commercial St; ⊙10am-
1am late Apr-Nov) Imagine a food court where
the options include a raw bar, sushi, gelato
and other international delights. Add a fully
stocked bar with generous bartenders pouring the drinks. Now put the whole place in a
gorgeous seaside setting, overlooking a little
beach and beautiful harbor. Now imagine
this whole scene at sunset. That's Aqua Bar.

☆ Entertainment

Provincetown is awash with gay fun, drag
shows and cabarets. Gay, straight or in-
between, everyone's welcome, and many
shows have first-rate performers. The
Crown & Anchor (p155) has a fat calendar
of events. Visit Provincetown on the Web
(www.provincetown.com) for the entertainment scoop.

Waters Edge Cinema   CINEMA
(☑508-413-9369;   www.watersedgecinema.org;
237 Commercial St; tickets adult/child $12/10) Up-
stairs at the Whaler's Wharf complex, this
recently restored cinema shows mainstream
and art-house films – a good option on a
rainy day.

Provincetown Theater   THEATER
(☑508-487-7487; www.provincetowntheater.org;
238 Bradford St) This stellar performing arts

center, 1 mile northeast of the town center,
always has something of interest happening – sometimes Broadway musicals, sometimes offbeat local shows.

Provincetown Art House   THEATER
(☑508-487-9222; www.ptownarthouse.com; 214
Commercial St) The Art House has two state-
of-the-art stages featuring a variety of edgy
theater   performances,   drag   shows   and
cabarets.

🛍 Shopping

Commercial St has the most creative and interesting specialty shops on the Cape.

ℹ Information

Provincetown Business Guild (www.ptown.
org) A website oriented towards the gay
community.

Provincetown Chamber of Commerce
(☑508-487-3424; www.ptownchamber.com;
307 Commercial St; ⊙9am-6pm) The town's
helpful tourist office is right at MacMillan Pier.

Provincetown Magazine (www.provincetown
magazine.com) Published weekly from April
through October. Pick up a free copy around
town or read online.

Provincetown on the Web (www.provincetown.
com) Comprehensive local info, from a services
directory to detailed events listings.

ℹ Getting There & Away

AIR

Provincetown Municipal Airport (☑508-487-
0241; www.provincetown-ma.gov; 176 Race
Point Rd) is northwest of town. It's connected
year-round to Boston via frequent flights with
Cape Air (www.capeair.com).

BOAT

From around May to October, boats connect
Provincetown's MacMillan Pier with Boston and
Plymouth. Schedules are geared to day-trippers,
with morning arrivals into Provincetown and
late-afternoon departures. No ferries carry cars,
but bikes can be transported for a fee (around
$12 round-trip). Advance reservations are rec-
ommended, especially on weekends and in peak
summer.

Bay State Cruise Co (☑877-783-3779; www.
boston-ptown.com; round-trip adult/child
$88/65; ⊙mid-May–mid-Oct) Fast ferry (1½
hours) operates three times daily from Boston's
World Trade Center Pier.

Boston Harbor Cruises (☑877-339-4253;
www.bostonharborcruises.com; round-trip
adult/child $88/65; ⊙mid-May–mid-Oct)

Fast-ferry service (1½ hours) from Long Wharf in Boston up to three times daily.

Plymouth to Provincetown Express Ferry (☎508-747-2400; www.p-townferry.com; 77 Water St, Plymouth; round-trip adult/child $45/34; ⌚late Jun–mid-Sep) Ferry from Plymouth (1½ hours, once daily). Arrives and departs from Fishermans Wharf, next to MacMillan Pier.

BUS

The **Plymouth & Brockton** (www.p-b.com) bus, which terminates at MacMillan Pier, runs several times a day from Boston (one way $31 to $37, three to 3½ hours), stopping at other Cape towns along the way. In Boston, it stops at Logan airport and South Station.

CAR & MOTORCYCLE

From the Cape Cod Canal via US 6, it takes about 1½ hours to reach Provincetown (65 miles), depending on traffic. Commercial St is narrow and crowded with pedestrians, so you'll want to do most of your driving along the more car-friendly Bradford St.

Getting Around

P-town is heaving in summer and on-street parking is next to impossible, but you may be able to find space in the town's main public parking lot at MacMillan Pier ($3 per hour, $30 for a 24-hour period). Town parking is free from November to March, but pricey at other times. It's a good idea to leave your car at your accommodation and walk or cycle – or ask advice from your accommodation on parking lots. There are a number of central bike-hire places.

From late May to late September, the **Provincetown Shuttle** (www.capecodtransit.org/ptown-route.htm; single trip/day pass $2/6) travels up and down Bradford St, and to MacMillan Pier, Herring Cove Beach, Province Lands Visitor Center and Race Point Beach, and North Truro. Bike racks are available.

Taxi fares are a set $7 per person anywhere within town, $9 between the airport or Race Point Beach and town. Call **Cape Cab** (☎508-487-2222; www.capecabtaxi.com).

NANTUCKET & AROUND

One need not be a millionaire to visit Nantucket, but it couldn't hurt. This compact island, 30 miles south of Cape Cod, grew rich from whaling in the 19th century. In recent decades it's seen a rebirth as a summer getaway for CEOs, society types and other well-heeled visitors from Boston and New York.

LOCAL KNOWLEDGE

ACK ATTACK

ACK! In Nantucket, the word adorns T-shirts, caps and logos. No, it's not a comment on the island's high cost of living, or reaction to the limerick 'There once was a man from Nantucket.' Instead, ACK is the code for Nantucket Memorial Airport (think 'nAntuCKet') and has been fondly adopted as an insider's moniker for all things Nantucket. Even the website for the island's daily newspaper, the *Inquirer and Mirror*, is www.ack.net.

It's easy to see why. Nantucket is New England at its most rose-covered, cobble-stoned, picture-postcard perfect, and even in the peak of summer there's always an empty stretch of sandy beach to be found. Outdoor activities abound, and there are fine museums, smart restaurants and fun bars.

Nantucket Town

☎508 / POP 10,400

The town of Nantucket (called 'Town' by the locals) is the island's only real population center. Once home port to the world's largest whaling fleet, the town's storied past is reflected in the gracious period buildings lining its leafy streets. It boasts the nation's largest concentration of houses built prior to 1850 and is the only place in the US where the entire town is a National Historic Landmark. It's a thoroughly enjoyable place to just amble about and soak up the atmosphere.

There are two ferry terminals: Straight Wharf and Steamboat Wharf. Walk off Straight Wharf and you're on Main St; Steamboat Wharf is just a few blocks north. The majority of restaurants, inns and other visitor facilities are within a 10-minute walk of the wharves.

Sights

★**Nantucket Whaling Museum** MUSEUM

(☎508-228-1894; www.nha.org; 13 Broad St; adult/child $20/5; ⌚11am-4pm Apr-May, 10am-5pm Jun-Oct, hours vary Sat & Sun Nov-Dec & mid-Feb–Mar) One of the island's highlights, this evocative museum occupies an 1847 spermaceti (whale oil) candle factory and the excellent exhibits relive Nantucket's 19th-century heyday as

Nantucket Island

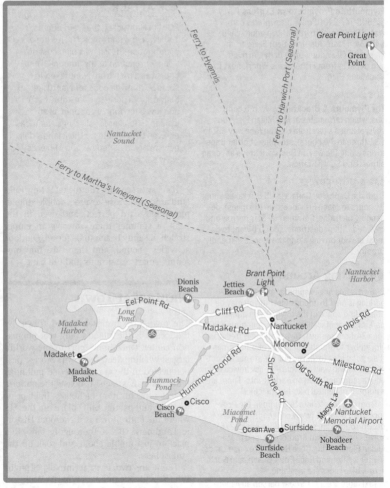

the whaling center of the world. There's a worthwhile, albeit long (54 minutes), documentary on the island, incredible scrimshaw exhibits (engravings and carvings done by sailors on ivory, whalebone or baleen), and a 46ft sperm whale skeleton rising above it all. Be sure to head to the rooftop deck for lovely views.

★ **Nantucket Atheneum**　HISTORIC SITE
(☑ 508-228-1110; www.nantucketatheneum.org; 1 India St; ⓒ 9:30am-1pm Mon, to 5pm Tue, Wed & Fri, to 7:30pm Thu, to 4pm Sat) **FREE** More than just the public library, this stately Greek

Revival edifice is a sight in itself. The 2nd-floor **Great Hall** has hosted such notables as Ralph Waldo Emerson and abolitionist Frederick Douglass. Nationally known opinion-makers still speak here today; ask about the summer **lecture series**, and look out for classes and concerts (there's a useful calendar online).

★ **Brant Point Light**　LIGHTHOUSE
(Easton St) Welcoming ferries into Nantucket Harbor, this lighthouse was established in 1746 and is still in operation. It's quite tiny (only 26ft), but impossibly photogenic – you

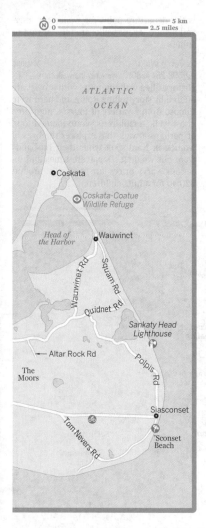

maintains dozens of historical sites covering everything from its farming beginnings to the prosperous whaling days. The NHA's most famous property is the Whaling Museum (p157), but there are others open to the public in summer, including an **old mill** (50 Prospect St; ⊙11am-4pm mid-May–mid-Oct), an **old jail** (15 Vestal St; ⊙11am-4pm mid-May–mid-Oct) and the island's **oldest house** (16 Sunset Hill; ⊙11am-4pm late May–mid-Oct). The entrance fee to the Whaling Museum includes access to the other properties; visiting each individually costs adult/child $6/3.

Nantucket Lightship Basket Museum
MUSEUM

(☑508-228-1177; www.nantucketlightshipbasketmuseum.org; 49 Union St; adult/child $5/3; ⊙10am-4:30pm Tue-Sat late May–early Oct) What the lighthouse is to the New England coast, the lightship was to the sea – essentially a floating lighthouse to warn of dangerous shoals or sandbars below. Sailors would stay aboard the lightships for weeks on end, and to combat boredom they created beautiful, intricate baskets that have become emblems of Nantucket. This small museum highlights these craftspeople and their products.

🏃 Activities

Cycling around Nantucket is an unbeatable way to savor the island's natural beauty. Bike paths connect the town with the main beaches and the villages of Madaket and 'Sconset – nowhere on the island is more than an hour's pedal away.

The other popular activity involves boating, and a stroll along Straight Wharf will present you with cruise or fishing excursion options.

Friendship Sloop Endeavor
BOATING

(☑508-228-5585; www.endeavorsailing.com; Straight Wharf; 1½hr sail $45-60; ⊙May-Oct) Feel the wind in your hair on a sail aboard the Friendship Sloop *Endeavor,* which runs numerous daily harbor sails and a popular sunset cruise. Bookings advised.

☞ Tours

Nantucket Bike Tours
CYCLING

(☑508-784-6690; www.nantucketbybike.com; 31 Washington St; tour incl bike $65-85) Garnering glowing reviews, this company helps you explore the bike paths and hidden gems of Nantucket, with a little history thrown in. Tours are generally 2½ to three hours;

may see many wedding parties using it as a backdrop. It's well worth the walk or cycle.

★ First Congregational Church
CHURCH

(☑508-228-0950; 62 Centre St; suggested donation adult/child $5/1; ⊙10am-4pm Mon-Sat May–mid-Oct) Everyone comes to this church, which traces its roots to the early 1700s, for the eagle-eye view from the top of the steeple. It's well worth the 94-step climb!

Nantucket Historical Association
HISTORIC SITE

(NHA; ☑508-228-1894; www.nha.org) The umbrella Nantucket Historical Association classic tours include a spin around Nantucket town or out to 'Sconset, a sunset tour (order a wine and cheese basket) or a pedal to Cisco Brewers (p165). Customized tours arranged.

Nantucket Historical Association Walking Tours WALKING
(📞508-228-1894; www.nha.org; 13 Broad St; adult/child $10/4; ⏰11:15am & 2:15pm mid-May–Oct) Guides from the Nantucket Historical Association lead 90-minute history-themed walking tours of the town twice daily. Confirm schedules and purchase tickets at the Nantucket Whaling Museum (p157), which is the departure point for walks (no reservations are taken; walks are offered rain or shine).

Raven's Walk WALKING
(📞508-257-4586; www.ravens-walk.com; ♿) History-filled walking tours with a twist are offered by story-telling Robin and her raven. Choose from a variety of tours: a nighttime ghost walk, a children's pirate-themed tour, or perhaps a walk that explores the lives of women in Nantucket while their husbands were out whaling. Departure times and locations vary; prices are generally around $20/10 for adults/children.

Nantucket Town

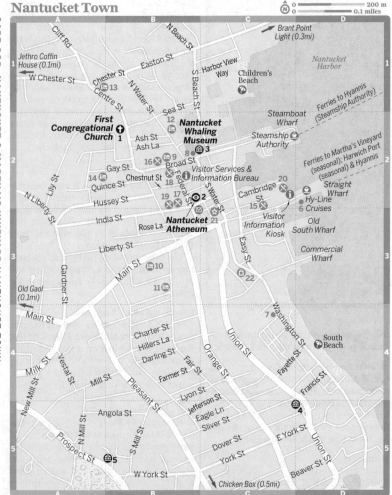

🎊 Festivals & Events

For more information on Nantucket festivals, go to www.nantucketchamber.org.

🛏 Sleeping

Unless you've got island friends with a spare room, a summer stay on Nantucket won't be cheap. Don't even look for a motel or campground – tony Nantucket is all about inns, and many of those are receiving dramatic makeovers to bring them to design-magazine standard.

Barnacle Inn   B&B $$
(📞508-228-0332; www.thebarnacleinn.com; 11 Fair St; r without bathroom $85-290, with bathroom $90-410; ⊗late Apr–early Nov; ❋🛜) This is what old Nantucket is all about: folksy owners and simple, quaint accommodations that hearken to earlier times. Rooms in this turn-of-the-19th-century inn don't have phones or TVs, but they do have good rates, particularly if you opt for a shared bath.

★76 Main   BOUTIQUE HOTEL $$$
(📞508-228-2533; www.76main.com; 76 Main St; r $149-719; ⊗late Apr–Dec; ❋🛜) In the ultra-refined neighborhood at the top of Main St, 76 Main shines with great design detail and nautical accents: elegant wallpapers, fabrics and bed headboards are a feature, and the courtyard with fire pit is a coveted retreat.

Facilities are first-rate and fun (including a cocktail mixer bar). We like the suites off the courtyard the most.

21 Broad   BOUTIQUE HOTEL $$$
(📞508-228-4749; www.21broadhotel.com; 21 Broad St; r $139-689; ⊗late Apr–Dec; ❋🛜) A summery, light-filled design is the result of this inn's extreme makeover. Fun splashes of seaside colors (blues and yellows) and glitzy common areas (including an alfresco deck with fire pit, and lounge with turntable) combine with well-equipped rooms featuring soft linens, guest iPads and fridges.

Brass Lantern Inn   B&B $$$
(📞508-228-4064; www.brasslanterninnnantucket.com; 11 N Water St; r $115-595; ❋🛜❋) A winning central location and elegant pastel-colored decor make this 1847 inn a firm favorite. The welcome is warm, the breakfast plentiful. Year-round opening and pet-friendly policies add to the appeal.

Centerboard Inn   B&B $$$
(📞508-228-9696; www.centerboardinn.com; 8 Chester St; r from $399-659; ❋@🛜) The pampering provided by the welcoming innkeeper here – with extras like spa-quality bath lotions and loaner iPads – give this chic B&B a leg-up on the competition. Rooms sport an upscale island decor, and the location is perfect for sightseeing. After a day on the town slip back to relax over cheese and wine at afternoon 'tea.'

Sherburne Inn   B&B $$$
(📞508-228-4425; www.sherburneinn.com; 10 Gay St; r $125-550; ❋🛜) Sit in the parlor by the Victorian fireplace and share travel tips with fellow guests at this gracious inn. Built in 1838, the inn flawlessly fuses period appeal

Nantucket Town

with modern amenities. Rooms are comfy, with four-poster beds. The street is quiet, yet the inn is just a two-minute stroll from the town center.

✗ Eating

★ Corner Table
CAFE $

(☑508-228-2665; www.nantucketculinary.com; 22 Federal St; mains $7-15; ⊗7am-9pm) 🍴 A real local gathering place, this sweet cafe has great coffee, a cabinet full of high-quality eats to eat in or takeaway (black bean and sweet potato salad, chicken ragu with pasta, mascarpone raspberry cheesecake), daily soups and sandwiches, a sofa or two, and a sustainable, community-minded ethos.

★ Proprietors
MODERN AMERICAN $$

(☑508-228-7747; www.proprietorsnantucket.com; 9 India St; plates $13-34; ⊗5:30pm-late Mon-Sat, 10:30am-2pm Sun Apr-Oct) 🍴 Creative, globally inspired cooking and fine cocktails go down a treat here, at this bar-restaurant that proudly flaunts local farm-to-table fare. Your eyes may be bigger than your belly when reading the small-plates-focused menu: the housemade charcuterie is a worthy choice, as are smoked-cod churros, roasted bone marrow and crispy tuna. Return on Sundays for the lauded brunch.

B-ACK Yard BBQ
BARBECUE $$

(☑508-228-0227; www.ackbackyard.com; 20 Straight Wharf; mains $15-30; ⊗11:30am-1am) Taking inspiration from the South, but wrapping it in a New England sensibility, BYB 'only smokes the good stuff.' Clam chowder comes with smoked bacon, mac 'n' cheese comes with lobster. Meats by the half-pound include pulled pork shoulder, beef burnt ends, and house-smoked kielbasa. It all pairs well with local beers, but there's a big selection of bourbon, too.

Brotherhood of Thieves
PUB FOOD $$

(☑508-228-2551; www.brotherhoodofthieves.com; 23 Broad St; mains $13-28; ⊗11:30am-10pm) A longtime favorite of locals, who come for the friendly tavern atmosphere (set off with brick and dark woods) and some of the island's best burgers. Not in a burger mood? How about a fish burrito made with local cod, or some broiled Nantucket scallops? The craft beers on tap, some island-brewed, go down easy.

★ Company of the Cauldron
MODERN AMERICAN $$$

(☑508-228-4016; www.companyofthecauldron.com; 5 India St; 4-course dinners $73; ⊗6:30-10pm Mon-Sat mid-May–mid-Oct) A splendid choice for a romantic dinner out, this intimate restaurant has attentive service and top-rated food. It offers only reserved seating times and four-course prix-fixe dinners, with the likes of rosemary-skewered shrimp followed by beef tournedos. As the chef concentrates his magic on just one menu each evening, it's done to perfection. Book early for Lobster Monday.

Straight Wharf Restaurant
SEAFOOD $$$

(☑508-228-4499; www.straightwharfrestaurant.com; 6 Harbor Sq, Straight Wharf; mains $30-45; ⊗11am-10pm mid-May–mid-Oct) The best place for fresh-caught seafood served up with a harbor view is the deck of this hot restaurant featuring New American fare. Start with iced oysters with lemon granita, then move on to the restaurant's very own clambake: buttered lobster, sweet corn, chorizo, potatoes and littleneck clams.

🍷 Drinking & Entertainment

Chicken Box
LIVE MUSIC

(☑508-228-5625; www.thechickenbox.com; 16 Dave St; ⊗noon-1am) This former fried-chicken shack has evolved into a roadhouse for live jazz and blues. Actually, depending on who's on the island, these days it can cover the full spectrum, especially rock and reggae. The college crowd meets here, too. It's located 1 mile south of town via Pleasant St. See the website for events.

Starlight Theatre
CINEMA

(☑508-228-4435; www.starlightack.com; 1 N Union St; tickets adult/child $10/7) Nantucket's 90-seat theater screens indie and other

---

LOCAL KNOWLEDGE

GO LANING

Go local, go laning. That's the 1930s term Nantucketers coined for wandering about the narrow streets of the town's historic district, especially in the early evening. For the finest stroll, walk up cobbled Main St, just past the c 1818 Pacific National Bank. There you'll find the grandest whaling-era mansions lined up in a row. Other laning favorites: Gardner and Liberty Sts and the honeycombed lanes between Federal and S Water Sts.

award-winning films. It's also a venue for live entertainment on summer weekends. It's attached to a cool cafe-bar.

🛍 Shopping

Nantucket has dozens of upmarket galleries, antique shops and clothing boutiques, as well as specialty shops that carry the island's signature lightship baskets. You'll find a collection of art galleries lined up like ducks in a row on Old South Wharf.

Artists Association of Nantucket ART
(☑508-228-0294; www.nantucketarts.org; 19 Washington St; 🖐) Browse the eclectic works of over 200 Nantucket artists who exhibit at this association gallery. Families with budding artists should inquire about the summer programs – art classes are arranged for adults (from painting to photography to printmaking, for beginners to advanced) and kids.

ℹ Information

Visitor Services & Information Bureau
(☑508-228-0925; www.nantucket-ma.gov; 25 Federal St; ⊙9am-5pm Jun-Sep, Mon-Sat rest of year) Has everything you'll need, including public restrooms and a list of available accommodations. The folks here also maintain a summertime kiosk (⊙9am-5pm Jun–mid-Oct) on Straight Wharf.

ℹ Getting There & Away

AIR

Nantucket Memorial Airport (www.nantucket airport.com; 14 Airport Rd) is 3 miles southeast of Nantucket town. It has year-round service to Boston, Hyannis, New Bedford and Martha's Vineyard, and seasonal services to New York. Check **Cape Air** (www.capeair.com) for schedules. Delta, American and JetBlue also offer seasonal services to/from New York and Washington, DC.

The airport is connected by local bus to town ($2) from mid-June to early September.

BOAT

The most common way to reach Nantucket is by the Steamship Authority and Hy-Line Cruises ferries from Hyannis.

The **Steamship Authority** (☑508-477-8600; www.steamshipauthority.com; South St Dock, Hyannis) runs frequent, year-round ferries between Hyannis and Nantucket (Steamboat Wharf). There are two options:
➡ The **traditional ferry** takes 2¼ hours and operates three to six times daily in each direction (one-way adult/child/bike $18.50/9.50/7).

It carries cars (one way $140 to $225 depending on size and season), but the high fares aim to discourage visitors from adding to traffic congestion on Nantucket's narrow streets. If you are bringing a car, book *well* in advance.
➡ The **high-speed ferry** carries passengers only, not vehicles, and operates four to five times daily from mid-April to early January (one-way adult/child/bike $36.50/18.75/7). Journey time is one hour. If you take the high-speed ferry as a same-day trip on Monday to Thursday, the return fare drops to $50/25 for adults/children.

Hy-Line Cruises (☑508-778-2600; www.hylinecruises.com; Ocean St Dock, Hyannis) operates a fast passenger ferry from Hyannis to Nantucket (Straight Wharf) year-round. The journey time is one hour; there are five to nine sailings daily (one-way adult/child/bike $41/29/7).

Hy-Line also operates a daily summer ferry between Nantucket and Oak Bluffs on Martha's Vineyard (one-way adult/child/bicycle $36/24/7); travel time is 70 minutes. Unfortunately the times don't allow an easy day trip to the Vineyard from Nantucket.

Seastreak (☑800-262-8743; www.seastreak.com) operates high-speed passenger ferries in the summer (mid-May to early September) to Nantucket daily from New Bedford, MA, and with weekend services from New Jersey and New York City.

ℹ Getting Around

BICYCLE

No destination on the island is more than 8 miles from town; thanks to Nantucket's relatively flat terrain and dedicated bike trails, cycling is an unbeatable way to explore. Bike paths connect the town with the main beaches and the villages of Madaket and 'Sconset (Siasconset) – no place is more than an hour's pedal away.

Rentals are available at **Young's Bicycle Shop** (☑ 508-228-1151; www.youngsbicycleshop.com; 6 Broad St; ⊗ 8:30am-5:30pm).

BUS

Getting around Nantucket is a snap. **Nantucket Regional Transit Authority** (NRTA; ☑ 508-228-7025; www.nrtawave.com; fares $1-2, 1-/3-/7-day passes $7/12/20; ⊗ late May–mid-Oct) runs handy shuttle buses (known as 'the Wave') all over the island, connecting Nantucket Town with 'Sconset in the east, Madaket in the west and beach destinations in between.

Most routes operate every 20 to 60 minutes throughout the day, from Memorial Day to Columbus Day. Fares are paid via electronic fare boxes; exact fare is advised. Buses have racks for two bikes.

CAR & MOTORCYCLE

In summer, the center of Nantucket town is choked with cars, so you probably won't want to join the congestion. However, several companies, including **Nantucket Island Rent A Car** (☑ 508-228-9989; www.nantucketisland rentacar.com; Nantucket Memorial Airport, 14 Airport Rd; ⊗ Apr–mid-Oct) at the airport and Young's Bicycle Shop in town, rent cars. **Affordable Rentals** (☑ 508-228-3501; www. affrentals.com; 6 South Beach St, Nantucket town), also in town, has cars, jeeps and mopeds for rent.

Prices start at around $75 per day for a car, but can easily be double that in peak season. It pays to book your rental in advance.

TAXI

Taxi rides from Nantucket Town cost $12 to the airport, and $21 to 'Sconset (prices for one passenger, additional passengers $2 each).

There are taxi stands near both boat wharves and at the airport. To order a taxi, call **All Point Taxi & Tours** (☑ 508-228-5779).

Around Nantucket

Siasconset

Although this village is barely 7 miles from town, it thinks of itself as worlds apart. Nantucket town may seem uncrowded and unhurried compared with the rest of the US, but Siasconset (aka 'Sconset) takes it to another level.

The petite village centers on a pair of cozy cafes, a tiny general store and a stamp-size post office. It's a wonderful place for lunch and a walk – but the secret's out, so get there early.

◉ Sights

'Sconset   VILLAGE

The old cottages in this seaside village are a watercolor artist's dream, with white-picket fences and climbing pink roses on gray cedar shingles. You'll find some of the loveliest cottages on **Broadway**, near the village center. Many of them, including the **Lucretia M Folger House**, at the corner of Main St and Broadway, date to the 18th century. All are private homes now, so do your peeking from a respectful distance.

'Sconset Beach   BEACH

East-facing 'Sconset Beach gets pounded by the open Atlantic, which has eroded much of the long, narrow beach in recent years. In fact, the erosion has been so severe that in 2007 the **Sankaty Head lighthouse** (Baxter Rd), at the north side of the village, was moved inland to prevent it from tumbling over a 90ft bluff.

🛏 Sleeping & Eating

Summer House Cottages   COTTAGE $$$

(☑ 508-257-4577;   www.summerhousecottages. com; 17 Ocean Ave; r & ste $275-695, cottages $450-1045; 🛜 ⛱) A refined getaway of low-key elegance. Stay in one of 'Sconset's signature rose-covered cottages (sizes vary, and include in-demand three-bedroom options) and relax by the pool or just drink in the ocean view. Some rooms have fireplace and Jacuzzi. Breakfast is included in the rates. A piano bar, bistro and fine-dining restaurant round out the high-class facilities.

Sconset Café   CAFE $$$

(☑ 508-257-4008; www.sconsetcafe.com; 8 Main St; mains $21-39; ⊗ 6-10pm Jun-Sep) This place is a village institution for its laid-back style as much as for its crab cakes. Pick up a bottle of wine at the store next door and enjoy it with your meal. No credit cards accepted; reservations recommended.

ℹ Getting There & Away

The nicest way to reach 'Sconset is by bike, but there's a summertime bus, too.

South Shore

The south shore communities of **Surfside** and **Cisco** consist almost entirely of private homes, but visitors head here for the long, broad beaches, which are among the island's best.

◉ Sights

Madaket Beach BEACH
There's not a lot to see at Nantucket's western outpost, but this beach, at the end of its namesake bike path, is the island's ace place to watch sunsets. The strong currents and heavy surf make it less than ideal for swimming, but there's some attractive beach walking to be done.

Surfside Beach BEACH
Surfside Beach, 3 miles from Nantucket town at the end of Surfside Rd, is a top draw with the college and 20-something set. It has full facilities, including a snack shack, and a moderate-to-heavy surf that can make for good bodysurfing.

Cisco Beach BEACH
You'll find some of the most consistently surfable waves at Cisco Beach, at the end of Hummock Pond Rd. Nantucket Island Surf School (☑508-560-1020; www.nantucketsurfing.com; 1hr lesson $50-75, surfboard/SUP half-day $35/70; ☺8am-8pm mid-Jun–mid-Sep) here can handle everything you'll need for hitting the waves.

🛏 Sleeping & Eating

★**HI Nantucket** HOSTEL $
(Star of the Sea; ☑508-228-0433; www.hiusa.org; 31 Western Ave; dm $37-45; ☺mid-May–mid-Oct; @🛜) 🏊 Known locally as Star of the Sea, this cool hostel has a million-dollar setting just minutes from Surfside Beach. It's housed in a former lifesaving station that dates to 1873 and is listed on the National Register of Historic Places. As Nantucket's sole budget option, its 49 beds are in high demand, so book as far in advance as possible.

★**Bartlett's Farm** MARKET $
(☑508-228-4403; www.bartlettsfarm.com; 33 Bartlett Farm Rd; ☺8am-6pm; 🏊) 🏊 From a humble farm stand this family operation has grown into a huge gourmet market, with salads, tempting desserts and sandwiches (including a great lobster roll). It's the perfect place to grab everything you'll need for a lunch or sunset picnic on the beach. Events are held here, too – like regular farm-to-table dinners and free **farm tours**.

🍷 Drinking

★**Cisco Brewers** BREWERY
(☑508-325-5929; www.ciscobrewers.com; 5 Bartlett Farm Rd; tours $20; ☺11am-7pm Mon-Sat, noon-6pm Sun, tours daily 1pm & 4pm) Enjoy a hoppy pint of Whale's Tale pale ale at the friendliest brewery you'll likely ever see. Cisco Brewers is the 'other' Nantucket, a laid-back place where fun banter loosens those stiff upper lips found in primmer quarters. In addition to the brewery, there's a small **distillery**, casual indoor and outdoor bars, regular food trucks and live music.

ℹ Getting There & Away

The nicest way to reach the south shore beaches is by bike, but there are summertime bus connections, too.

MARTHA'S VINEYARD

Bathed in scenic beauty, Martha's Vineyard attracts wide-eyed day-trippers, celebrity second-home owners, and urbanites seeking a restful getaway; its 15,000 year-round residents include many artists, musicians and back-to-nature types.

The Vineyard remains untouched by the kind of rampant commercialism found on the mainland – there's not a single chain restaurant or cookie-cutter motel in sight. Instead you'll find cozy inns, chef-driven restaurants and a bounty of green farms and grand beaches. And there's something for every mood here – fine dining in gentrified Edgartown one day and hitting the cotton candy and carousel scene in Oak Bluffs the next.

Martha's Vineyard is the largest island in New England, extending some 23 miles at its widest. Although it sits just 7 miles off the coast of Cape Cod, Vineyarders feel themselves such a world apart that they often refer to the mainland as 'America.'

Vineyard Haven

☑508 / POP 3950
Although it's the island's commercial center, Vineyard Haven is a town of considerable charm. Its harbor has more traditional wooden schooners and sloops than any harbor of its size in New England.

Central Vineyard Haven (aka Tisbury) is just four or five blocks wide and about a half-mile long. Main St, dotted with galleries and boutiques, is the main thoroughfare through town. Steamship Authority ferries

Martha's Vineyard

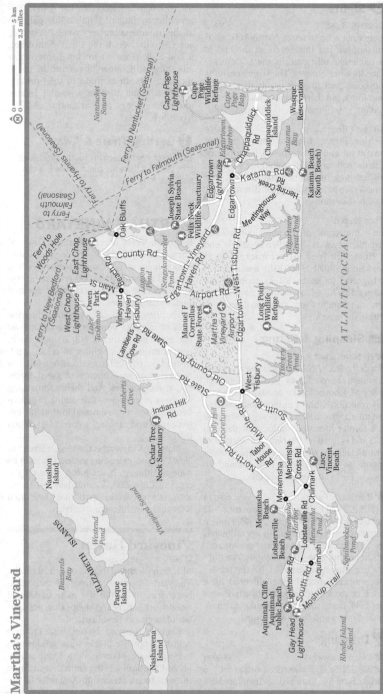

Nantucket Sound

Ferry to Nantucket (Seasonal)

Ferry to Falmouth (Seasonal)

Ferry to Hyannis (Seasonal)

Ferry to Falmouth (Seasonal)

Ferry to Woods Hole

Ferry to New Bedford (Seasonal)

Cape Poge Lighthouse

Cape Poge Wildlife Refuge

Cape Poge Bay

Chappaquiddick Rd

Chappaquiddick Island

Wasque Reservation

Katama Bay

Edgartown Harbor

Edgartown Lighthouse

Katama Rd

Herring Creek Rd

Katama Beach (South Beach)

Edgartown

Joseph Sylvia State Beach

Felix Neck Wildlife Sanctuary

Edgartown–Vineyard Haven Rd

Meetinghouse Way

Edgartown–West Tisbury Rd

Edgartown Great Pond

Oak Bluffs

County Rd

Sengekontacket Pond

Lagoon Pond

Airport Rd

Manuel F Correllus State Forest

Martha's Vineyard Airport

Long Point Wildlife Refuge

ATLANTIC OCEAN

East Chop Lighthouse

West Chop Lighthouse

Main St

Beach Rd

Owen Park

Vineyard Haven (Tisbury)

Lake Tashmoo

Lamberts Cove Rd

State Rd

Old County Rd

State Rd

West Tisbury

South Rd

Tisbury Great Pond

Lamberts Cove

Indian Hill Rd

Cedar Tree Neck Sanctuary

Naushon Island

ELIZABETH ISLANDS

Westend Pond

Vineyard Sound

Polly Hill Arboretum

Middle Rd

North Rd

Tabor House Rd

Menemsha Cross Rd

Chilmark

Lucy Vincent Beach

Menemsha Beach

Menemsha

Menemsha Harbor

Menemsha Pond

Squibnocket Pond

Buzzards Bay

Pasque Island

Lobsterville Beach

Lobsterville Rd

Aquinnah

Moshup Trail

Squibnocket Beach

Aquinnah Cliffs Aquinnah Public Beach

Gay Head Lighthouse

Lighthouse Rd

South Rd

Rhode Island Sound

Nashawena Island

5 km

2.5 miles

dock at the end of Union St, a block from Main St. From the terminal, Water St leads to the infamous 'Five Corners' intersection: five roads come together and no one really has the right of way. Good luck.

✈ Activities

Wind's Up   WATER SPORTS
(☑508-693-4252; www.windsupmv.com; 199 Beach Rd; 4hr rentals $35-55; ⊙9am-6pm Jul & Aug, shorter hours rest of year) Vineyard Haven has **windsurfing** action for all levels. Lagoon Pond, south of the drawbridge between Vineyard Haven and Oak Bluffs, has good wind and enclosed waters suitable for beginners and intermediates. Vineyard Harbor, on the ocean side, is good for advanced windsurfers. Wind's Up, at the drawbridge, rents windsurfing gear, stand up paddle surfboards and kayaks. Lessons also arranged.

🛏 Sleeping & Eating

Martha's Vineyard
Family Campground   CAMPGROUND $
(☑508-693-3772; www.campmv.com; 569 Edgartown Rd; tent/RV sites $58/64, cabins $145-165; ⊙mid-May–mid-Oct) This woodsy place offers the island's only camping and has basic cabins that sleep four to six people. Book early, especially for weekends. It's 2 miles south of the ferry terminal.

Mansion House   HOTEL $$$
(☑508-693-2200; www.mvmansionhouse.com; 9 Main St; r winter/summer from $99/309; ❄☕♨🅿) 🍴 With 48 rooms, Mansion House is a little big to be termed 'boutique,' but it's got a lot of personality and owners who care. The fresh citrus tones and the balconies appeal, plus there's an on-site spa and fitness center (the latter is free to guests). The icing on the cake is the rooftop deck with panoramic harbor views.

★ Art Cliff Diner   CAFE $
(☑508-693-1224; 39 Beach Rd; mains $8-20; ⊙7am-2pm Thu-Tue) 🍴 Hands-down the best place in town for breakfast and lunch. Chef-owner Gina Stanley, a grad of the prestigious Culinary Institute of America, adds flair to everything she touches, from the almond-encrusted French toast to the fresh fish tacos. The eclectic menu utilizes farm-fresh island ingredients. Expect a line, but it's worth the wait.

Net Result   SEAFOOD $$
(☑508-693-6071; www.mvseafood.com; 79 Beach Rd; mains $5-20; ⊙7am-7pm) On the west side of town, this fish market is fresh, fresh, fresh, with everything from sushi to award-winning chowder, lobster rolls and fish and chips. It's takeout, but there are picnic tables outside. Or better yet – take it to the beach.

ℹ Information

The main island **visitor center** (☑508-693-0085; www.mvy.com; 24 Beach Rd; ⊙9am-5pm Mon-Fri) is not far from the ferry dock.

At the ferry dock, there is a summertime **information booth** (⊙9am-noon & 4:30-7:30pm Mon-Fri, 9am-7:30pm Sat, 9am-5pm Sun late May–Aug, 9am-noon Sep–mid-Oct) across from the ferry terminal, open from Memorial Day to Columbus Day.

Oak Bluffs
📞508 / POP 4600

Odds are, this ferry-port town – where the lion's share of summer day-tripping boats arrive – will be your introduction to the island. Welcome to the Vineyard's summer fun mecca: a place to wander with an ice-cream cone in hand, poke around honky-tonk sights and go clubbing at night.

All ferries dock in the center of town; the Steamship Authority boats along Seaview Ave and the other ferries along Circuit Ave Extension. The two roads connect together as a single loop. The area between the two docks is filled with trinket shops, eateries and bike-rental outlets.

⊙ Sights

★ Campgrounds
& Tabernacle   HISTORIC SITE
(www.mvcma.org) Oak Bluffs started out in the mid-19th century as a summer retreat by a revivalist church, whose members enjoyed a day at the beach as much as a gospel service. They first camped out in tents, then built some 300 wooden cottages, each adorned with whimsical filigree trim.

From bustling Circuit Ave, slip into the alley between the Secret Garden and the Tibet store and you'll feel like you've dropped down the rabbit hole. Suddenly it's a world of gingerbread-trimmed houses, adorned with hearts and angels and Candy Land colors.

ℹ️ GETTING TO MARTHA'S VINEYARD

Air

Martha's Vineyard Airport (MVY; ☎508-693-7022; www.mvyairport.com; 71 Airport Rd, Vineyard Haven) is in the center of the island, about 6 miles south of Vineyard Haven, and is served by buses. It has year-round service to Boston and Nantucket and seasonal services to Hyannis, New Bedford (MA) and New York. Check **Cape Air** (www.capeair. com) for schedules. Delta and JetBlue also offer seasonal services from New York's JFK Airport.

Boat

Steamship Authority (☎508-477-8600; www.steamshipauthority.com; one-way adult/ child/bike $8.50/4.50/4) operates a frequent, year-round ferry service to Martha's Vineyard. It connects Vineyard Haven with Woods Hole, south of Falmouth on the Cape (a 45-minute voyage). This is the only ferry that carries vehicles – if you're bringing a car, book well in advance (one-way car passage is $43.50 to $78.50, depending on size and season). There are up to 14 services daily in each direction.

The are also summer connections to the Vineyard. Reservations are recommended:

Woods Hole to Oak Bluffs From mid-May to mid-October, Steamship Authority also has ferries from Woods Hole to Oak Bluffs (four or five daily, 45 minutes). The fares are the same as to Vineyard Haven.

Falmouth to Oak Bluffs From late May to mid-October, the passenger-only ferry **Island Queen** (☎508-548-4800; www.islandqueen.com; 75 Falmouth Heights Rd, Falmouth Harbor; ⊗round-trip adult/child/bike $20/10/8) sails up to seven times daily between Oak Bluffs and Falmouth Harbor (35 minutes).

Falmouth to Edgartown From late May to early September, the **Falmouth-Edgartown Ferry** (☎508-548-9400; www.falmouthedgartownferry.com; one-way adult/child/bike $25/15/5) operates from Falmouth Harbor to Edgartown. There are up to five services daily from mid-June to early September, and also weekend services from late May to mid-June.

Hyannis to Oak Bluffs From May to October, **Hy-Line Cruises** (☎508-778-2600; www. hylinecruises.com; Ocean St Dock, Hyannis; round-trip adult/child/bike $59/39/14) operates a high-speed ferry from Hyannis to Oak Bluffs (one hour) two to six times daily.

New Bedford to Oak Bluffs From mid-May to mid-October, **Seastreak** (☎800-262-8743; www.seastreak.com; 49 State Pier, New Bedford, MA; round-trip adult/child $70/40) runs a handful of times daily from New Bedford, MA (one hour), to Oak Bluffs. Tickets are cheaper for travel on a weekday.

Oak Bluffs to Nantucket From late May to early October, Hy-Line Cruises also operates an inter-island ferry up to three times a day in each direction (70 minutes), making a day trip possible in July and August (round-trip adult/child/bike $65/45/14).

These brightly painted cottages – known as the Campgrounds – surround emerald-green **Trinity Park** and its open-air Taber-nacle (1879), where the lucky descendants of the Methodist Camp Meeting Association still gather for community sing-alongs and concerts.

Cottage Museum MUSEUM
(☎508-693-0525; www.mvcma.org; 2 Trinity Park; adult/child $2/50¢; ⊗10am-4pm Mon-Sat, 1-4pm Sun late May–early Sep) You can visit a typical Campground cottage, complete with period furnishings, thanks to the Cottage Museum. It's filled with Camp Meeting Association history and artifacts.

Flying Horses Carousel HISTORIC SITE
(www.mvpreservation.org; 15 Lake Ave; $3; ⊗10am-10pm late May–mid-Sep, shorter hours rest of year; 👶) Take a nostalgic ride on this National Historic Landmark, which has been captivating kids of all ages since 1876. It's the USA's oldest continuously operating merry-go-round, and these antique horses have manes of real horse hair.

👉 Tours

MVCMA Walking Tours   WALKING
(📞508-693-0525; www.mvcma.org/walking-tours.
html; tours $10-12; ⊘10am Tue & Thu Jul & Aug)
Join a 90-minute walking tour around the
Campgrounds to hear the 160-year history
of this remarkable neighborhood. Meet at
the Tabernacle (p167). The price includes
admission to the Cottage Museum.

🎊 Festivals & Events

Grand Illumination Night   CULTURAL
(www.mvcma.org; ⊘mid-Aug) It's all about
lights. If you're lucky enough to be in
Oak Bluffs on the third Wednesday in August, you'll see the Campground cottages
adorned with colorful Chinese and Japanese lanterns; a sing-along and concert is
held in the Tabernacle. The lanterns are lit
at dusk – it's quite magical.

🛏 Sleeping

Want to stay in a Campground cottage? All
cottages are privately owned, and some are
rented by owners on a weekly basis in summer ($2500 to $3000 is the going rate). Some
listings can be found on the **Camp Meeting
Association** (www.mvcma.org) website.

Nashua House   INN $$
(📞508-693-0043; www.nashuahouse.com; 30
Kennebec Ave; r $79-239; 🌐🛜) The Vineyard
the way it used to be...but with some con-
cessions to modernity (some rooms have
TV, some have private bathroom). You'll
find simple, spotless, characterful accom-
modations at this quaint 1873 inn with
restaurants and pubs just beyond the front
door. It's good value in the summer; in the
off-season, when rates drop by nearly half,
it's a steal.

Narragansett House   B&B $$
(📞508-693-3627; www.narragansetthouse.com;
46 Narragansett Ave; d $120-300; ⊘May-Oct;
🌐🛜) This charming place comprises two
adjacent Victorian gingerbread-trimmed
houses on a quiet residential street that's
just a stroll from the center. It's old-
fashioned without being cloying, and all the
rooms have private baths.

★Summercamp   HOTEL $$$
(📞508-693-6611; www.summercamphotel.com;
70 Lake Ave; r $149-509; ⊘May-Oct; 🌐🛜) We
dare you not to smile in response to the
detail of this fun place, the brand-new
incarnation of an iconic 1879 hotel that

borders the Tabernacle area. The nostal-
gic summer-camp theme extends from the
Astroturfed games room to the canteen
selling retro snacks. And there's even a
twin room with bunks. Decor is fresh and
inspired, location is ace.

🍴 Eating & Drinking

Mad Martha's   ICE CREAM $
(📞508-693-9151; 12 Circuit Ave; cones from $5;
⊘11am-8pm late May–mid-Oct; 🍴) If the Oba-
mas are on the island and you want to snag
a photo, this is your best paparazzi hang:
they'll invariably swing by for a scoop of
award-winning homemade ice cream. If you
like it rich, order up a scoop of the coconut
cream. You'll find branches of Mad Martha's
in Vineyard Haven and Edgartown, too.

Linda Jean's   DINER $
(📞508-693-4093; www.lindajeansrestaurant.
com; 25 Circuit Ave; mains $6-17; ⊘6am-7pm;
🚗🍴) The town's best all-around inexpen-
sive eatery rakes in the locals with unbeat-
able blueberry pancakes, juicy burgers
and simple but filling dinners. Kids' menu
available.

**Martha's Vineyard
Gourmet Cafe & Bakery**   BAKERY $
(📞508-693-3688; www.mvbakery.com; 5 Post
Office Sq; baked goods $1-3; ⊘7am-5pm mid-
Apr–mid-Oct) This simple joint serves inex-
pensive coffee, famous apple fritters and
cannoli, but the time to swing by is from
7pm to 1am (when the shop itself is shut),
when you can go around the back, knock
on the door and buy hot, fresh doughnuts
straight from the baker. This, friends, is
MV's 'Back Door Donuts' – a much-loved
tradition here.

Slice of Life   CAFE $$
(📞508-693-3838; www.sliceoflifemv.com; 50
Circuit Ave; dinner mains $11-27; ⊘8am-9pm;
🚗) The look is casual; the fare is gourmet.
At breakfast, there's kick-ass coffee, porto-
bello scrambles and fab crab-cake bagels.
At dinner the roasted cod with sun-dried
tomatoes is a savory favorite. And the desserts – decadent crème brûlée and luscious
lemon tarts – are as good as you'll find
anywhere.

Sweet Life Café   MODERN AMERICAN $$$
(📞508-696-0200; www.sweetlifemv.com; 63 Cir-
cuit Ave; mains $28-44; ⊘5:30-10pm mid-May–
Oct) New American cuisine with a French
accent is offered by this stylish bistro, which

VINEYARD ROOTS

African Americans have deep, proud roots on the Vineyard. Arriving as slaves in the late 1600s, they broke the yoke here long before slavery ended on the mainland. In 1779 a freed slave named Rebecca Amos became a landowner when she inherited a farm from her Wampanoag husband. Her influence on the island was widespread – Martha's Vineyard's only black whaling captain, William Martin, was one of her descendants.

During the Harlem Renaissance, African American tourism to the Vineyard took off. Writer Dorothy West, author of *The Wedding*, was an early convert to the island's charms. Oak Bluffs soon became a prime vacation destination for East Coast African American movers and shakers.

The cadre of African Americans gathered on the Vineyard during the 1960s was so influential that political activist Joe Overton's Oak Bluffs home became known as the 'Summer White House' of the Civil Rights movement. His guest list ranged from Malcolm X to Jackie Robinson and Harry Belafonte. It was at Overton's home that Martin Luther King Jr worked on his famous 'I Have a Dream' speech. The term 'Summer White House' took on new meaning in 2009 when America's first black president, Barack Obama, took his summer vacation on the Vineyard.

Learn more about the Vineyard's black heritage at www.mvheritagetrail.org.

provides the town's finest dining. Tuna tartare, fried softshell crab and miso-glazed local cod are joined on the menu by other innovative dishes utilizing local produce (not just seafood). Reservations advised.

★ **Offshore Ale Co** MICROBREWERY, PUB
(☑508-693-2626; www.offshoreale.com; 30 Kennebec Ave; ☉11:30am-10pm) Join the throngs of locals and visitors at this popular microbrewery – enjoy a pint of Hop Goddess ale, some superior pub grub (including a knockout lobster roll) and the kind of laid-back atmosphere where boats are suspended from the ceiling and peanut shells are thrown on the floor.

ℹ Information

Visitor Information Booth (☑508-693-4266; cnr Circuit & Lake Aves; ☉9am-5pm late May–mid-Oct) The town hall staffs this convenient summertime info booth near the carousel.

Martha's Vineyard Hospital (☑508-693-0410; www.mvhospital.com; 1 Hospital Rd; ☉24hr) The island's only hospital is at the west side of Oak Bluffs, just off the Vineyard Haven–Oak Bluffs road.

Edgartown

☑508 / POP 4100

Perched on a fine natural harbor, Edgartown has a rich maritime history and a patrician air. At the height of the whaling era it was home to more than 100 sea captains,

whose fortunes built the grand old homes that still line the streets today. Unlike Oak Bluffs and Vineyard Haven, which have substantial ferries carting folks in and out, Edgartown has just a small, passenger-only ferry. It's the quietest of the three main towns and the one most geared to upmarket travelers.

All roads into Edgartown lead to Main St, which extends down to the harbor. Water St runs parallel to the harbor. Most restaurants and inns are on or near these two streets.

◉ Sights

Chappaquiddick ISLAND
Accessed by frequent ferry (the 'Chappy Ferry') from Edgartown harbor, Chappaquiddick is a small island with a big history, thanks to a fatal accident in 1969 that involved Senator Ted Kennedy. The island's population is around 180; it's a popular spot with visitors for its beaches, cycling, hiking, fishing and birding. Bring a bike and a picnic over on the ferry and go exploring (there are no shops or restaurants). Be sure to visit **Mytoi**, a beautiful Japanese-style garden.

It's worth looking into the summer tours of **Cape Poge Wildlife Reserve** (☑508-627-3599; www.thetrustees.org; Chappaquiddick; ⛵), offered by a nonprofit group called the Trustees. You must book ahead for tours that visit the remote lighthouse or enjoy naturalist-guided kayaking on Cape Poge Bay.

Katama Beach BEACH
(Katama Rd) Although they're convenient, Edgartown's in-town beaches are just kids' stuff. For the real deal head to Katama Beach, also called South Beach, about 3 miles south of Edgartown center. Kept in a natural state, this barrier beach stretches for three magnificent miles. Rugged surf will please surfers on the ocean side; many swimmers prefer the protected salt ponds on the inland side.

There's a bike path connecting Edgartown with Katama Beach – excellent for avoiding parking hassles.

Felix Neck
Wildlife Sanctuary NATURE RESERVE
(☑508-627-4850; www.massaudubon.org; off Edgartown–Vineyard Haven Rd; adult/child $4/3; ☺trails dawn-dusk; ⬛) Mass Audubon's Felix Neck Wildlife Sanctuary, 3 miles northwest of Edgartown center, is a birder's paradise, with miles of trails skirting fields, marshes and ponds. Because of the varied habitat, this 194-acre sanctuary harbors an amazing variety of winged creatures, including ducks, oystercatchers, wild turkeys, ospreys and red-tailed hawks. Bring your binoculars.

The sanctuary also offers **nature tours**, from family kayak trips to marine discovery outings – especially in July and August. See the website for details.

Martha's Vineyard Museum MUSEUM
(☑508-627-4441; www.marthasvineyardhistory.org; 59 School St; adult/child $10/5; ☺10am-5pm Mon-Sat, noon-5pm Sun late May–mid-Oct, 10am-4pm Mon-Sat rest of year) This well-done museum has a fascinating collection of whaling paraphernalia and scrimshaw, and puts the history of Martha's Vineyard into context. The campus includes a number of buildings, including a 1740s Colonial home. Don't miss the lighthouse display, which includes the huge, 1000-prism Fresnel lens that sat in the Gay Head Lighthouse for a century until electrical power arrived in 1951.

🛏 Sleeping & Eating

⭐**The Christopher** BOUTIQUE HOTEL $$$
(☑508-627-4784; www.thechristophermv.com; 24 S Water St; r $239-589; ☺May-Dec; 🅿❄🛜) The central Victorian Inn has been reborn as the Christopher, and the makeover has been quite something: bright, bold and boutique in the best possible way. Edgartown is just outside your doorstep, but inside it's

about high-tech gadgets, stylish nooks and a cool outdoor courtyard with fire pit. Fifteen rooms are spread over three floors (note: no elevator).

Edgartown Inn B&B $$$
(☑508-627-4794; www.edgartowninn.com; 56 N Water St; r $125-325; ☺mid-Apr–Oct; 🅿❄🛜) The best bargain in town, with 14 straightforward rooms spread across the main inn and garden house. The inn dates to 1798 and claims Nathaniel Hawthorne and Daniel Webster among its earliest guests. Rooms have changed only a bit since then, but most have private bathrooms. Ask about last-minute specials; you might score a discount if things are slow.

Espresso Love CAFE $
(☑508-627-9211; www.espressolove.com; 17 Church St; mains $7-14; ☺6:30am-8pm; 🛜) This year-round cafe serves the richest cup o' joe in town, sweet cinnamon rolls and good sandwiches, like curried chicken with walnuts and currants. The shady courtyard is a fine place to enjoy lunch on a sunny day, and the location near the bus terminal is handy.

Among the Flowers Café CAFE $$
(☑508-627-3233; www.amongtheflowersmv.com; 17 Mayhew Lane; lunch $7-19, dinner mains $22-34; ☺8am-4pm mid-Apr–Oct, to 10pm Jun-Aug; 🥄) Join the in-the-know crowd on the garden patio (under cute striped awnings and – yes – among the flowering plants) for homemade soups, waffles, sandwiches, crepes and even lobster rolls. Although everything's served on paper or plastic, it's still kinda chichi. In summer, it serves dinner as well, and the kitchen kicks it up a notch.

🍷 Drinking & Entertainment

Seafood Shanty BAR
(☑508-627-8622; www.theseafoodshanty.com; 31 Dock St; ☺11am-12:30am mid-May–Oct) The upstairs deck at this harborside seafood restaurant is *the* place in town for drinks with a view.

⭐**Flatbread Company** LIVE MUSIC
(☑508-693-1137; www.flatbreadcompany.com; 17 Airport Rd; ☺4pm-late Jun-Sep) Formerly the home of Carly Simon's legendary Hot Tin Roof, Flatbread continues the tradition, staging the hottest bands on the island. And it makes damn good organic pizzas too. It's adjacent to Martha's Vineyard Airport.

❶ Information

Edgartown Visitors Center (29 Church St; ⊙8:30am-6pm Jun-Sep) This operation at the bus terminal has rest rooms and a post office.

West Tisbury

📞 508 / POP 2740

The island's agricultural heart has a white church, calm ponds and a vintage general store, all evoking an old-time sensibility. West Tisbury also has some worthwhile artists' studios and galleries sprinkled throughout.

◉ Sights

Alley's General Store HISTORIC BUILDING
(📞508-693-0088; 1041 State Rd; ⊙7am-6pm Mon-Sat, to 5pm Sun) Part food shop ('dealers in almost everything'), part historic landmark, Alley's General Store is a favorite local gathering place and has been since 1858. Lots of souvenirs and gifts available.

Field Gallery & Sculpture Garden GALLERY
(📞508-693-5595; www.fieldgallery.com; 1050 State Rd; ⊙10am-5pm Mon-Sat, 11am-4pm Sun May-Oct) You can't miss the Field Gallery, a field of large white sculptures by local artist and gallery founder Tom Maley (1911–2000) that playfully pose while tourists mill around them. There's an indoor gallery, too, with works by artists of local and national renown.

Cedar Tree Neck Sanctuary NATURE RESERVE
(www.sheriffsmeadow.org; Indian Hill Rd, off State Rd; ⊙8:30am-5:30pm) **FREE** Cedar Tree Neck's inviting 2.5-mile hike crosses native bogs and forest to a coastal bluff with views of Cape Cod and the Elizabeth Islands. Be sure to take the short detour to **Ames Pond** to enjoy a meditative moment with painted turtles and peeping tree frogs. To get there, take State Rd to Indian Hill Rd and continue 1.8 miles.

Long Point Wildlife Refuge NATURE RESERVE
(📞508-693-7392; www.thetrustees.org; off Edgartown–West Tisbury Rd; adult/child $5/free; ⊙9am-5:30pm) Pond, cove and ocean views all open up on a mile-long trail that leads to a remote beach. Along the way birders can expect to spot nesting osprey and other raptors, from northern harriers to the more common red-tailed hawks. Kayaks and stand up paddle surfboards can be hired to explore **Long Cove Pond**. From mid-June to mid-September, there's a $10 fee to park at the refuge. It pays to check the website for directions.

Polly Hill Arboretum NATURE RESERVE
(📞508-693-9426; www.pollyhillarboretum.org; 809 State Rd; adult/child $5/free; ⊙grounds sunrise-sunset) This 60-acre refuge celebrates woodlands and wildflower meadows, and is particularly pretty in the fall. The **visitor center** is open from 9:30am to 4pm from Memorial Day to Columbus Day. You can explore on your own or join an hour-long **guided tour** (daily at 10am in July and August).

🛌 Sleeping & Eating

HI Martha's Vineyard HOSTEL $
(📞508-693-2665; www.hiusa.org; 525 Edgartown–West Tisbury Rd; dm $35-39, d/q $99/135; ⊙mid-May–early Oct; 🅿@🛜) 🧺 Reserve early for a bed at this popular, purpose-built hostel in the center of the island. It has everything you'd expect: a solid kitchen, games room, bike delivery, no curfew and friendly staff. The public bus stops out front and it's right on the bike path. Dorms and private rooms are available.

West Tisbury Farmers Market MARKET $
(www.thewesttisburyfarmersmarket.com; 1067 State Rd; ⊙9am-noon Sat Jun–mid-Oct, plus Wed Jul & Aug) 🧺 Be sure to head to the Grange Hall in the center of West Tisbury on market days for fresh-from-the-farm produce. The best time to go is Saturday, when it's a full-on community event, with live fiddle music and alpacas for the kids to pet.

Chilmark & Menemsha

📞 508 / POP 870

Occupying most of the western side of the island between Vineyard Sound and the Atlantic, Chilmark is a place of pastoral landscapes and easygoing people. Chilmark's chief destination is the picture-perfect fishing village of Menemsha, where you'll find shacks selling seafood fresh off the boat.

◉ Sights

★**Menemsha Harbor & Beach** BEACH
(Basin Rd, Menemsha) Virtually unchanged since it appeared in the movie *Jaws* 40 years ago, Menemsha is a relaxing outpost to explore. Basin Rd borders a harbor of fishing boats on one side and dunes on the other, ending at the public Menemsha Beach. Sunsets here are nothing short of spectacular.

ⓘ GETTING AROUND THE VINEYARD

Bicycle

The best bike trails on the Vineyard start in Edgartown. Some good options:

➡ Pedal 6 miles on a super-scenic bike route along the coastal road to Oak Bluffs.

➡ Take the trail that follows the Edgartown–West Tisbury Rd to Manuel F Correllus State Forest, the island's largest conservation tract. Within the forested area are some lovely loops you can cycle: one is 3 miles, on the northeast corner; the other is roughly 10 miles around the forest.

➡ Take the 3-mile bike path south for a swim at Katama Beach (p171).

➡ Take a bike on the Chappy ferry and explore Chappaquiddick (round-trip for bike and rider is $6).

Rent bikes at the following locations:

Martha's (☑ 800-559-0312; www.marthasbikerentals.com; 4 Lagoon Pond Rd; bike rental per day $27.50; ⊙ 9am-5:30pm) Vineyard Haven.

Anderson's (☑ 508-693-9346; www.andersonsbikerentals.com; 1 Circuit Ave Extension; bike rental per day/week $20/85; ⊙ 9am-6pm May-Oct) Oak Bluffs.

Martha's Vineyard Bike Rental (☑ 800-627-2763; www.marthasvineyardbike.com; 1 Main St; bike rental per day $25; ⊙ 9am-6pm Apr-Oct) Edgartown.

Bus

Year-round, the **Martha's Vineyard Regional Transit Authority** (☑ 508-693-9440; www.vineyardtransit.com; per ride from $2.50, 1-/3-day pass $8/18) operates a network of buses from the Vineyard Haven ferry terminal to villages throughout the island. It's a practical way to get around and even serves out-of-the-way destinations such as the Aquinnah Cliffs.

Bus 13 travels frequently between the three main towns (Vineyard Haven aka Tisbury, Oak Bluffs and Edgartown). Fares are $1.25 per town, each way, including town of origin (so Vineyard Haven to Oak Bluffs is $2.50, to Edgartown is $3.75).

Taxi

Without a car of your own, bikes make a great option, but you may also need taxi services: call **Martha's Vineyard Taxi** (☑ 508-693-8660; www.vineyardtransport.com).

✕ Eating

Menemsha Fish Market   SEAFOOD $$
(☑ 508-645-2282; www.menemshafishmarket.net; 54 Basin Rd, Menemsha; lobster meals $14-35; ⊙ 9am-8pm) On a cold day, warm up with some chowder or opt for a super-fresh lobster roll at this rustic, no-frills, year-round fish market in Menemsha. Or go the whole hog for sunset-watching and get a full lobster clambake feast ($55): two 1¼-pound cooked lobsters, soup, coleslaw and a choice of either mussels, steamers or shrimp.

Aquinnah

☑ 508 / POP 310

Apart from its isolation, the chief attraction of Aquinnah is the windswept cliffs that form a jagged face down to the Atlantic – astonishing in the colorful variety of sand, gravel, fossils and clay that reveal aeons of geological history.

Aquinnah also has a rich Native American history, and it's here more than anywhere else on the island that you'll notice the influence of the island's Wampanoag people.

Parking in the car park to access the cliffs and public beach costs $15.

◎ Sights

Aquinnah Cliffs   LANDMARK
Also known as the Gay Head Cliffs, these clay cliffs, overlooking a 5-mile-long beach, were formed by glaciers 100 million years ago. Rising 150ft from the ocean, they're dramatic any time of day but are at their very best in the late afternoon, when they glow in the most amazing array of colors.

The beach area directly below the cliffs is off-limits.

The clay cliffs are a National Historic Landmark owned by the Wampanoag tribe. To protect them from erosion, it's illegal to bathe in the mud pools that form at the bottom of the cliffs, to climb the cliffs, or to remove clay from the area.

Gay Head Lighthouse　　　LIGHTHOUSE
(☑508-645-2300; www.gayheadlight.org; adult/child $5/free; ☉11am-4pm Jul-Sep, plus Sat & Sun Jun & Oct) Built in 1844 with a state-of-the-art Fresnel lens, this red-brick structure on the Gay Head cliffs is arguably the most scenic lighthouse on the Vineyard. In 2015 it was carefully moved 134ft back from its eroding cliff-edge, buying at least 150 years before erosion may require another move inland. Islanders raised $3 million for the relocation.

In addition to daytime openings, the care-takers also open the lighthouse for two hours around sunset on Thursday evenings in July and August. See the website for details.

🛏 Sleeping

★**Outermost Inn**　　　　INN $$$
(☑508-645-3511; www.outermostinn.com; 81 Lighthouse Rd; r $310-430; ☉mid-May–mid-Oct; ❋🅟) Be a guest of Hugh Taylor (musician James Taylor's younger brother) at this at-tractive seven-room inn near Gay Head Lighthouse. The hilltop setting and ocean views are grand, and the Taylors make you feel at home. Dinner at the inn's **restaurant**, prepared by an accomplished chef, is open to the public and in hot demand, so phone reservations are essential.

Central Massachusetts & the Berkshires

📞 413, 508

Best Places to Eat

➜ Armsby Abbey (p178)

➜ Chef Wayne's Big Mamou (p183)

➜ Gould's Sugar House (p192)

➜ Marketplace Cafe (p203)

➜ Mezze Bistro & Bar (p205)

Best Places to Sleep

➜ Bascom Lodge (p207)

➜ Guest House at Field Farm (p205)

➜ Porches (p206)

➜ River Bend Farm B&B (p205)

➜ Starlight Llama B&B (p185)

Why Go?

Artfully blending the cultural and cosmopolitan with the rural and rustic, the Pioneer Valley and the Berkshires offer a tantalizing mix of artistic offerings, verdant hills and sweet farmland. Stretch your quads on hiking trails up Massachusetts' highest mountain and through nature preserves that blanket the surrounding hills. Alternatively, ramble through estate homes of the once famous, listen to world-class musicians from a picnic blanket on well-manicured lawn, and feast on farm-to-table cuisine at chef-driven restaurants. You could easily spend an entire summer hopscotching the patchwork of wilderness areas, while taking in a dance festival here, an illustrious music series there and summer theater all over the place.

At every turn, you'll come across peppy college towns with shady campuses, bohemian cafes and exceptional art museums. And those lucky enough to be here in autumn will find apples ripe for the picking and hillsides ablaze in brilliant fall foliage.

When to Go
Worcester

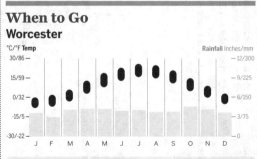

Jun–Aug Cultural attractions, summer theater, dance and concert festivals.

Sep–Oct Gorgeous colors, but traffic jams up on weekends.

Nov–May Prices are lower and college towns are still lively during these quieter months.

Central Massachusetts & the Berkshires Highlights

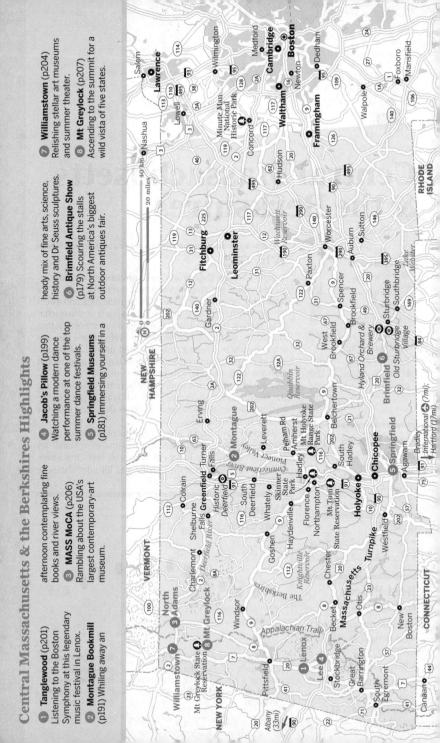

1 **Tanglewood** (p201) Listening to the Boston Symphony at this legendary music festival in Lenox.

2 **Montague Bookmill** (p191) Whiling away an afternoon contemplating fine books and river views.

3 **MASS MoCA** (p206) Rambling about the USA's largest contemporary-art museum.

4 **Jacob's Pillow** (p199) Watching a modern dance performance at one of the top summer dance festivals.

5 **Springfield Museums** (p181) Immersing yourself in a heady mix of fine arts, science, history and Dr Seuss sculptures.

6 **Brimfield Antique Show** (p179) Scouring the stalls at North America's biggest outdoor antiques fair.

7 **Williamstown** (p204) Relishing stellar art museums and summer theater.

8 **Mt Greylock** (p207) Ascending to the summit for a wild vista of five states.

ℹ Getting There & Around

AIR
Worcester has a regional **airport** (ORH; www.massport.com; 375 Airport Dr) but it sees very little service. Springfield and the Pioneer Valley towns are served by Bradley International Airport (p434), just over the line in Connecticut.

BUS
Peter Pan Bus Lines (www.peterpanbus.com) connects towns in the region with numerous points in New England.

CAR & MOTORCYCLE
The Massachusetts Turnpike (Mass Pike; I-90) and MA 2 are the major east–west roads connecting Boston with central and western Massachusetts. The Mass Pike is a toll road.

TRAIN
The *Lake Shore Limited,* operated by **Amtrak** (www.amtrak.com), departs from Boston, stopping at Worcester, Springfield and Pittsfield before reaching Albany, NY. The *Vermonter* runs from St Albans, Vermont, to Washington, DC, via Springfield.

CENTRAL MASSACHUSETTS

Also referred to as Worcester County, central Massachusetts marks a boundary between Boston's suburbs to the east and vast swatches of farm and hill country to the west. It lacks the visual charm of eastern and western Massachusetts, but it has a few attractions. The city of Worcester (say 'Wooster') dominates the area, offering a worthwhile art museum and classic diners for those who care to stop. A bigger draw is the re-created colonial village of Sturbridge and the enormous antiques market at Brimfield.

Worcester
☑ 508 / POP 182,500
Welcome to 'Worm Town,' as locals affectionately call their city. A wealthy manufacturing center during the industrial revolution, this place invented and produced barbed wire, the modern envelope and more. Worcester has struggled mightily since factories began shutting down after WWII, with scant urban-renewal victories in recent years. Nonetheless, the city's nine small colleges inject youth and creativity, though the biggest draw might be the numerous historic diners that have slung blue-collar eggs for generations.

Main St, four blocks west of I-290, is the central drag. The rest of the city sprawls in a confusing mess of streets, and a map will greatly help exploration efforts.

◉ Sights & Activities

EcoTarium MUSEUM
(www.ecotarium.org; 222 Harrington Way; adult/child $15/10, planetarium $5, canopy walk $10; ☉10am-5pm Tue-Sat, noon-5pm Sun; 🅿) 🌿 This museum and 'center for environmental exploration' presents an array of exhibits to intrigue young minds. The new outdoor exhibit area features many places to dig, build, climb, move and create – and that's in addition to the scenic walking trails. Other kid favorites include bubbles, dinosaurs, rocks and minerals, and a cool interactive exhibit about Mt Washington. Some of the most exciting offerings (tree-canopy walks, planetarium shows, explorer express train) cost extra.

Worcester Art Museum MUSEUM
(☑508-799-4406; www.worcesterart.org; 55 Salisbury St; adult/child $14/6; ☉11am-5pm Wed-Fri & Sun, 10am-5pm Sat; 🅿) During Worcester's golden age, its captains of industry bestowed largesse upon the town. The Worcester Art Museum, off Main St, remains a generous and impressive bequest. The museum's unexpected and comprehensive collection ranges from ancient Egyptian artifacts to European masterworks and contemporary American pieces, including Paul Revere silverwork. It also has a wild collection of Samurai and medieval armor.

🛏 Sleeping & Eating

Putnam House B&B B&B $
(☑508-865-9094; www.putnamhousebandb.com; 211 Putnam Hill Rd, Sutton; r/ste $95/105; 🅿) Dating to 1737, this hilltop farmstead was the home of Massachusetts senator David Putnam in the early 1800s. Restored by master carpenters, it has large fireplaces, exposed beams and an enormous red centennial barn. The hosts exemplify the term, preparing generous breakfasts. Find the place 10 miles southeast of Worcester.

Belmont Vegetarian VEGETARIAN $
(www.belmontvegetarian.com; 157 Belmont St; meals $6-12; ☉11am-8pm Tue-Sat; 🍴) Proof positive that beautiful flowers can bloom in the most unassuming of places, Belmont offers huge portions of Jamaican-inspired vegetarian fare with enough soulful flavor to convert the most hardened carnivore. You can't go wrong with soy pepper steak.

CENTRAL MASSACHUSETTS & THE BERKSHIRES STURBRIDGE

DON'T MISS

WORCESTER DINERS

Worcester nurtured a great American icon: the diner. Here, in this rust-belt city, you'll find a dozen old relics tucked behind warehouses, underneath old train trestles, and steps from dicey bars. Some were made by Worcester Lunch Car Company, which produced 650 prefabricated beauties from 1906 to 1961. Models from the '30s tend to incorporate rich wood trim and look like old train cars. Those from the '50s shoot for a sleek 'streamlined' aesthetic, with gleaming metal exteriors. Visit one of Worcester's finest:

Miss Worcester Diner (☑ 508-753-5600; 300 Southbridge St; mains $6-10; ⊙ 5am-2pm Mon-Fri, 6am-2pm Sat & Sun)

Corner Lunch (www.facebook.com/CornerLunchDiner; 133 Lamartine St; mains $4-11; ⊙ 6am-2pm Wed-Mon)

Boulevard Diner (www.facebook.com/Boulevard-Diner-106450722008; 155 Shrewsbury St; mains $5-10; ⊙ 24hr)

★ **Armsby Abbey**　　　　　　　AMERICAN $$
(☑ 508-795-1012; www.armsbyabbey.com; 144 Main St; sandwiches $15-18, mains $20-30; ⊙ 11:30am-10pm Mon-Fri, 10am-10pm Sat & Sun; 🛜) The Abbey rakes in all sorts of awards for its locally sourced, slow-food menu and stellar selection of craft beers on tap. Think comfort food with a gourmet twist. They are very big on farmstead cheeses here; choose from more than a dozen cheesy wedges, served with fresh-baked bread from the next-door bakery. The setting is hip, urban and welcoming.

❶ Information

Central Massachusetts Convention & Visitors Bureau (☑ 508-755-7400; 91 Prescott St; ⊙ 9am-5pm Mon-Fri) Has the skinny on Worcester and the rest of central Massachusetts.

❶ Getting There & Away

BUS

Peter Pan Bus Lines (☑ 800-343-9999; www.peterpanbus.com; Union Station, 2 Washington Sq) operates buses between Worcester and other destinations throughout New England.

CAR & MOTORCYCLE

Worcester stands at the junction of four interstate highways. About an hour's drive will bring you here from Boston, Providence or Springfield.

TRAIN

Amtrak trains (www.amtrak.com) stop here en route between Boston and Chicago. **MBTA** (www.mbta.com) runs frequent commuter trains to/from Boston ($10.50, 80 minutes). Trains for both rails leave from Union Station.

Sturbridge

☑ 508 / POP 9270

Sturbridge's main attraction – the living museum at Old Sturbridge Village – has preserved an example of a traditional Yankee community; at the same time, the town itself is lined with motor inns, fast-food chains, gas stations and roadside shops, which sprouted up to meet the needs of museum visitors. So while the town may not have the same historic atmosphere or rural charm as some of its westerly neighbors, at least we all can appreciate the irony here.

In any case, families and history buffs will enjoy the excellent museum. In town, there is no shortage of amenities for visitors, though traffic on Main St is often a nightmare. Welcome to the 21st century.

❍ Sights

Old Sturbridge Village　　　　　MUSEUM
(OSV; www.osv.org; US 20; adult/child $28/14; ⊙ 9:30am-5pm May-Oct, to 4pm Wed-Sun Nov, variable hours Dec; 🅿) Historic buildings from throughout the region have been moved to this site to re-create a New England town from the 1830s, with 40 restored structures filled with antiques. Rather than labeling the exhibits, this museum has 'interpreters' – people who dress in costume, ply the trades of their ancestors and explain to visitors what they are doing.

Although many historians find the layout of the village less than accurate, attention to detail is high. The country store displays products brought from throughout the world by New England sailing ships. Crafters and artisans use authentic tools and materials. The livestock has even been back-bred to approximate the animals that lived on New England farms a century-and-a-half ago. Expect to spend at least three hours here. Admission is good for two days.

Hyland Orchard & Rapscallion Brewery FARM

(www.hylandorchard.com; 195 Arnold Rd; ⊘farm 6-10pm Fri, noon-6pm Sat & Sun Jun-Oct, brewery 3-10pm Tue-Fri, noon-9pm Sat & Sun; 🖼) **FREE** In a picture-perfect red barn surrounded by bucolic farmland, this farm offers something for everyone. The craft brewery produces a dozen different beers, including three or four different IPAs (order by the flight or pitcher) and a tempting honey. There's live music on weekends and occasional special events, but no food is served. The kids will be flat out with the petting farm, wagon rides and ice-cream parlor. And come fall, peaches and apples are ripe for picking.

To find Hyland, go west on Main St/US 20, turn right on Arnold Rd and go 2 miles north.

Brimfield Antique Show ANTIQUES

(www.brimfieldshow.org; US 20, Brimfield; admission free-$8; ⊘6am-dusk Tue-Sun) Six miles west of Sturbridge is the Brimfield Antique Show, the largest outdoor antiques fair in North America. How big is it? This mecca for collectors of antique furniture, toys and tools takes place on 23 farmers' fields, where 6000 sellers and 130,000 buyers gather to do business. The town has shops open year-round, but the major antiques shows are held in mid-May, early July and early September, usually from Tuesday through Sunday.

🛌 Sleeping

Along a 1-mile stretch of US 20 just off exit 9 is a procession of chain hotels ranging from Super 8 to Hampton Inn. If you prefer to stay somewhere more atmospheric, and perhaps historic, you can find a few old-fashioned inns, too. Keep in mind, many lodgings fill up on weekends in summer and fall. When the Brimfield Antique Show is in progress, prices rise substantially and advance reservations are necessary.

Wells State Park CAMPGROUND $

(☎877-422-6762; www.mass.gov/dcr; MA 49; tent sites $17, yurts $45-55) This campground offers 60 wooded sites – some lakefront – on its 1470 acres. It's north of I-90, 5 miles from Old Sturbridge Village.

Old Sturbridge Inn INN, LODGE $$

(Reeder Family Lodges; ☎508-347-5503; www.osv. org/inn; 369 Main St; r $139-155; 🅿🗷🐾) Just outside the grounds of Old Sturbridge Village, this lodging facility is managed by the museum. It includes the 1789 Oliver Wight House, a charming home with 10 rooms decked out with canopy beds, floral wallpaper and enormous fireplaces. The remaining 29 units are more modern and more spacious. All include a generous breakfast buffet and discounted admission to the museum.

Nathan Goodale House B&B $$

(☎413-245-9228; www.brimfield.org; 11 Warren Rd/ MA 19N, Brimfield; r $90-100, during antique shows $125-200; 🐾) In a large and simple Victorian Italianate house, this B&B has tasteful rooms that are decked out with antiques, likely procured at the nearby Brimfield Antique Show. It's nicely situated in a residential area, just a few blocks from the show – an ideal base for your antiquing outing.

Publick House Historic Inn INN $$

(☎508-347-3313; www.publickhouse.com; 140 Main St/MA 131; motel r from $69, inn r/ste from $109/139; 🗷🐾🌊) Here is Sturbridge's most famous historic inn, the 1771 Publick House, near the village common. Three separate buildings make up the property: your best

CENTRAL MASSACHUSETTS & THE BERKSHIRES STURBRIDGE

WORTH A TRIP

SALEM CROSS INN

Built in 1705, **Salem Cross Inn** (☎508-867-2345; www.salemcrossinn.com; 260 W Main St/MA 9, West Brookfield; lunch $10-18, dinner $16-28; ⊘11:30am-9pm Tue-Fri, 5-9pm Sat, noon-8pm Sun Apr-Dec, Fri-Sun only Jan-Mar) is set on 600 green acres in a bucolic country landscape. Feast on specialties such as calf's liver with bacon and caramelized onions or lavender duck. In addition to the main dining room there's also the Hexmark Tavern, which cooks up comfort food like chicken pot pie and meatloaf at family-friendly prices.

Besides offering traditional New England meals, the inn hosts special events ranging from a colonial-style fireplace feast cooked on an open hearth to a theatrical murder-mystery dinner. To get there follow US 20 to MA 148 north; 7 miles along, turn left onto MA 9 and go 5 miles.

bet is the Publick Inn itself, with its canopy beds and 18th-century decor. For budget travelers, the on-site Country Motor Lodge looks like it sounds – generic – but affordable.

✕ Eating

Annie's Country Kitchen   BREAKFAST $
(www.anniescountrykitchen.com; 140 Main St/MA 131; mains $4-10; ⊙5am-2pm Mon-Tue, to 7pm Wed-Fri, to noon Sat & Sun; 🐾) If you're big on breakfast and nuts about home fries, this local shack is the place to jump-start your day. The omelets are huge, but it's the pancakes – filled with everything from wild blueberries to chocolate chips – that will bust your gut. You might not get hungry until dinner.

Thai Place   THAI $
(www.thaiplacerestaurant.net; 371 Main St; mains $6-12; ⊙11:30am-9pm; 🐾) Here you'll find real-deal home-style Thai fare with solid options for vegetarians and carnivores alike. Don't be misled by the wallet-friendly prices – everything, including the seafood offerings, is top-of-the-line fresh.

**Publick House
Historic Tap Room**   AMERICAN $$
(☑508-347-3313; www.publickhouse.com; 277 Main St/MA 131; mains $18-30; ⊙7:30am-8:30pm) The historic inn's original dining room features a rustic atmosphere, enhanced by the enormous wide-hearth fireplace. Here you can order a traditional Thanksgiving turkey dinner any day of the year, or turn it up a notch with classic pot roast or roast duck in cranberry glaze. While the food is fine, it isn't quite as good as the history.

❶ Information

Sturbridge Area Tourist Association (☑508-347-2761; www.sturbridgetownships.com; 380 Main St/US 20; ⊙9am-5pm Mon-Fri, 10am-4pm Sat & Sun) This helpful information office is conveniently situated opposite the entrance to Old Sturbridge Village.

❶ Getting There & Away

Most travelers arrive in Sturbridge by car via the Mass Pike, I-90. Take exit 9 onto I-84, and it will deposit you onto Main St (US 20), not far from the gate of Old Sturbridge Village.

PIONEER VALLEY

With the exception of gritty Springfield, the Pioneer Valley offers a gentle landscape of college towns, picturesque farms and old mills that have been charmingly converted into modern use. The uber-cool burg of Northampton provides the region's top dining, nightlife and street scenes, while the other destinations offer unique museums, geological marvels and a few unexpected roadside gems.

Springfield

☑413 / POP 153,700

Shoot. You're in Springfield. This recession-hit town has certainly seen better days, but there are some surprises here that might just make you glad you came.

Downtown, you'll find some striking reminders of the city's 19th-century wealth, including a handful of quality museums, a grand symphony hall and stately Romanesque Revival buildings at Court Sq. Up the hill there's an intriguing armory dating back to the American Revolution. And, as all local grade-schoolers know, basketball originated in Springfield, which explains the presence of the Hall of Fame.

While most of the business types who work here flee promptly at 5pm, Springfield somehow supports a lively night scene. Not to mention, one of the best Cajun eateries this side of New Orleans. Another surprise.

SPRINGFIELD'S MOTO MOJO

When Americans hear 'motorcycle,' they're most likely to think Harley-Davidson. But Springfield-based Indian was the first (1901) and was, many say, the best. Up until it disbanded in 1953, the Indian Motocycle Company produced its bikes in a sprawling factory complex on the outskirts of Springfield. The 'r' in 'motorcycle' was, by the way, dropped as a marketing gimmick. Through the merger of several bike companies, the Indian Motorcycle Corporation was created in 1999 to jump-start the manufacture of Indians again, but it's widely accepted that the new bikes couldn't hold a candle to the originals.

A mint collection of the original Indian bikes are now on display in the Museum of Springfield History, including a rare 1904 Indian that was apparently the ride of choice of the company's founder.

SPRINGFIELD MUSEUMS

The **Springfield Museums** (www.springfieldmuseums.org; 21 Edwards St; ⏺10am-5pm Tue-Sat, 11am-5pm Sun; P♿) surround Museum Quadrangle, two blocks northeast of Court Sq. Out front, look for the Augustus Saint-Gaudens statue *The Puritan*. One ticket (adult/child $18/10) grants entrance to all five museums, giving a surprisingly good dose of art, fine arts, history and science. Access to the grounds (and the Dr Seuss National Memorial Sculpture Garden) is free.

Amazing World of Dr Seuss Scheduled to open in 2017, this innovative museum is dedicated to the life and work of Springfield native Theodore Geisel, aka Dr Seuss. Exhibits use the stories of Dr Seuss to engage children with rhyming games, storytelling and building their vocabulary. More traditional exhibitions showcase the author's personal memorabilia and a reproduction of his studio.

Smith Art Museum This museum has exterior windows designed by Tiffany Studios and a fine collection of 19th-century American and European paintings, textiles, ceramics and more. The samurai armor collection is among the finest outside of Japan. In the Hasbro Discovery Center, kids can explore the art in a hands-on way (drawing and tracing, trying on costumes and armor, playing games).

Museum of Fine Arts The 20 galleries of this art deco–style building are filled with lesser paintings of the great European masters and better works of lesser masters. The impressionist collection includes works by Pissarro and Renoir, while the contemporary gallery includes pieces by Georgia O'Keeffe and Picasso. One of the best-known pieces is *The Historical Monument of the American Republic*, a grand work by Erastus Salisbury Field that depicts US history using architectural towers.

Museum of Springfield History Showcasing the city's distant heyday, this museum is home to the Esta Mantos Indian Motocycle collection (the world's largest). There's also a huge assortment of firearms, including more Smith & Wesson guns than you'll see anywhere else. And there's a fabulous automobile collection that includes a couple of early Rolls Royce roadsters that were built right here in Springfield.

Springfield Science Museum This museum possesses a respectable, if slightly outdated, range of natural-history and science exhibits. The Dinosaur Hall has a full-size replica of a *Tyrannosaurus rex*, the African Hall covers evolution and ecology and the **Seymour Planetarium** (adult/child $3/2) has shows daily.

◉ Sights

★**Naismith Memorial Basketball Hall of Fame** MUSEUM
(www.hoophall.com; 1000 W Columbus Ave; adult/child $23/16; ⏺10am-5pm; P♿) Though the emphasis at the basketball hall of fame seems to be more hoopla than hoops – there's an abundance of multiscreened TVs and disembodied cheering – true devotees of the game will be thrilled to shoot baskets, feel the center-court excitement and learn about the sport's history and great players.

One touted figure is James Naismith (1861–1939), inventor of the game, who came to Springfield to work as a physical-education instructor at the International YMCA Training School (later Springfield College). Naismith wanted to develop a good, fast team sport that could be played indoors during the long New England winters. In December of 1891, he had the idea of nailing two wooden peach baskets to opposite walls in the college gymnasium. He wrote down 13 rules for the game (12 of which are still used), and thus basketball was born.

Dr Seuss National Memorial Sculpture Garden PARK
(www.catinthehat.org; 21 Edwards St; ⏺dawn-dusk; ♿) FREE Your kids will insist on stopping at the Dr Seuss National Memorial Sculpture Garden, dedicated to Springfield's favorite native son. Life-size bronze sculptures of the Cat in the Hat and other wonky characters look beseechingly at passers-by. Oh me, oh my. Coming soon: the Amazing World of Dr Seuss, a museum dedicated to the children's author.

Springfield Armory National Historic Site HISTORIC SITE
(☏413-734-8551; www.nps.gov/spar; cnr State & Federal Sts; ⏺9am-5pm May-Oct, 9am-5pm

Springfield

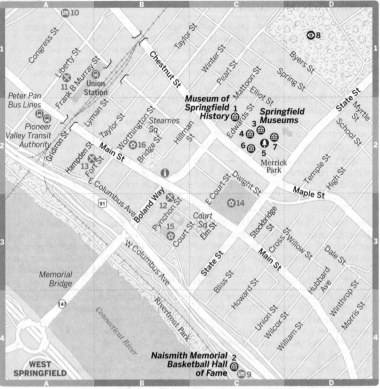

Wed-Sun Nov-Mar; [P]) FREE This national historic site preserves what remains of the USA's greatest federal armory, built under the command of General George Washington during the American Revolution. Nowadays, it holds one of the world's largest collections of firearms, including Remingtons, Colts, Lugers and even weapons from as early as the 1400s. In other words, guns galore. For the weirdest sculpture you might ever see, don't miss the *Organ of Muskets*, composed of 645 rifles.

🎪 Festivals & Events

Big E FAIR
(www.thebige.com; 1305 Memorial Ave/MA 147; adult/child 1-day pass $15/10, unlimited entry $40/20; ⊙mid-Sep) In mid-September, sleepy West Springfield explodes into activity with the annual Eastern States Exposition, better known as the Big E. It's 17 days of farm exhibits and horse shows, carnival rides and parades, concerts and circus performances, mass consumption of food on sticks, and one giant dairy-themed sculpture out of butter. It's the largest event of its kind in New England.

Discounts available for advance purchase; carnival rides cost extra.

Springfield Jazz & Roots Festival MUSIC
(www.springfieldjazzfest.org; ⊙Aug) FREE This free outdoor festival celebrates the diverse cultural heritage of Springfield's population, with a day of performances by mostly local and regional performers. The music runs the gamut, from Dixieland jazz to R & B to Latin rhythms. It all goes down on Court Sq on the first Saturday in August.

🛏 Sleeping

La Quinta Inn & Suites HOTEL $
(☎413-781-0900; www.lq.com; 100 Congress St; r from $109; [P][※][🛜][🖵]) Plain but practical, the

Springfield

◉ Top Sights
1 Museum of Springfield History...........C2
2 Naismith Memorial Basketball
   Hall of Fame....................................... C4
3 Springfield Museums C2

◉ Sights
4 Amazing World of Dr Seuss................C2
5 Dr Seuss National Memorial
   Sculpture Garden C2
6 Museum of Fine Arts C2
7 Smith Art Museum C2
8 Springfield Armory National
   Historic Site D1
   Springfield Science
   Museum .... (see 3)

🛏 Sleeping
9 Hilton Garden Inn................................. C4
10 La Quinta Inn & Suites......................... A1

🍽 Eating
11 Chef Wayne's Big Mamou................... A1
12 Nadim's Mediterranean Grill B3
13 Student Prince Cafe & Fort
   Restaurant...A2

✿ Entertainment
14 MassMutual Center C3
15 Symphony Hall.....................................B3
16 Theodore's...B2

freshly renovated rooms at this hotel offer the best value of any in-town hotel. Rates include a hot breakfast.

Naomi's Inn   B&B $$
(☏413-433-6019; www.naomisinn.net; 20 Springfield St; r $119-149; P❋🛜) With a broad porch and shady trees, this gracious home overlooks a hospital compound 1.5 miles northwest of the city center. The six rooms are ample and comfortable, each with a different decorating scheme. To get there, follow the signs to Bay State Medical Center; the inn is opposite the hospital. Prices include a full hot breakfast.

Hilton Garden Inn   HOTEL $$
(☏413-886-8000; www.hilton.com; 800 W Columbus Ave; r from $199; P❋🛜🏊) Just a hoop toss away from the Naismith Memorial Basketball Hall of Fame, this garden-variety hotel has advantages, particularly for families. Not only are the basketball sights right there, but the hall of fame complex also contains pizzerias and other low-key eateries. And when you've had your fill of basketball, you can retreat to the swimming pool.

🍴 Eating

There's a slew of lunch places, pubs and bistros in the vicinity of Court Sq and Union Station. If you're hungry, you're in luck, as there are a few gems here.

★Chef Wayne's Big Mamou   CAJUN $$
(www.chefwaynes-bigmamou.com; 63 Liberty St; mains $8-20; ⊙11am-8:30pm Mon-Fri, noon-9:30pm Sat, plus 10am-3pm Sun Oct-May) Don't be fooled by its meager appearance – this hole in the wall serves up fabulous home-style Cajun fare. Highlights include the barbecued pulled pork, crayfish quesadillas and blackened catfish. One caveat: you'll want to get there early at dinner, especially on weekends, when lines form outside the door. Reservations are not taken. You can BYO alcohol.

Nadim's Mediterranean Grill   MIDDLE EASTERN $$
(www.nadims.com; 1390 Main St; mains $15-25; ⊙11am-10pm Mon-Fri, 3-11pm Sat; 🖋) The upscale setting and Mediterranean menu attract a business crowd at this downtown restaurant. Lebanese standards are done well, including *fattoush, kafta* and kebabs. Fan favorites include hummachos (hummus dip with meat, feta and veggies), fried wings (drizzled with cilantro, garlic and lemon) and the 'famous' lentil soup. Service is friendly and efficient.

Student Prince Cafe & Fort Restaurant   GERMAN $$
(www.studentprince.com; 8 Fort St; mains $17-29; ⊙11am-9pm) The Student Prince has been scratching those schnitzel and sauerkraut itches since 1935 and shows no signs of slowing down. Even if you're not in the mood for heavy starches, come by anyway to admire the impressive beer steins lining the walls (one was owned by a Russian czar). You'll also find some satisfying brews on tap.

🍷 Drinking & Entertainment

Take a walk down Worthington St and you'll find a bunch of pubs and clubs crammed into these blocks, one of them likely to suit your taste.

Pick up a copy of the free *Valley Advocate* (www.valleyadvocate.com) for entertainment listings.

★Theodore's   BLUES
(www.theobbq.com; 201 Worthington St; ⊙11am-2am Mon-Fri, 5pm-2am Sat & Sun) Offering

DR SEUSS & FRIENDS

The writer and illustrator responsible for such nonsensically sensible classics as *The Cat in the Hat* was born Theodor Seuss Geisel in 1904 in Springfield, Massachusetts. Geisel credits his mother for inspiring his signature rhyming style; she would lull him and his sister to sleep by chanting pie lists she remembered from her bakery days back in Germany.

After graduating from Dartmouth College, Geisel made his living primarily as a political cartoonist and ad man. His first children's book, *And to Think That I Saw It on Mulberry Street*, was rejected by dozens of publishers before one bit. Geisel's first major success came with the publication of *The Cat in the Hat*, which he wrote after reading Rudolf Flesch's *Why Johnny Can't Read*, an article that asserted children's books of the day were boring and 'antiseptic,' and called upon people like Geisel (and, er, Walt Disney) to raise the standard of primers for young children. By the time he died in 1991, Geisel had published 44 books and his work had been translated into more than 20 languages. His classic *Green Eggs & Ham* is still ranked as one of the top-selling English-language books to date.

Forming part of the Springfield Museums complex, the Dr Seuss National Memorial Sculpture Garden (p181) was completed in 2002, featuring bronze pieces made by Geisel's step-daughter, the sculptor Lark Grey Dimond-Cates. As such, the courtyard at the Museum Quadrangle features life-size depictions of many of Seuss' characters, as well as the author himself. And now, a new project is underway. As early as 2017, the Springfield Museums will include The Amazing World of Dr Seuss (p181), an entire museum dedicated to the children's author and his books.

'booze, blues and BBQ,' this joint is a gem. Truly great blues and jazz acts get booked in the lively bar, and the barbecue is finger-lickin' good. There's music from Tuesday to Saturday; Wednesday is open-mike night but the others are guaranteed winners.

A jazzy mural captures its illustrious history (the Blues Foundation once named Theodore's the best blues club in the country).

Springfield Symphony Orchestra   CLASSICAL MUSIC
(www.springfieldsymphony.org; tickets $22-65) This respected symphony orchestra – New England's largest outside of Boston – does monthly performances at Symphony Hall (413-788-7033; www.symphonyhall.com; 34 Court St). The repertoire is diverse, including holiday extravaganzas, internationally themed concerts and special guests.

MassMutual Center   CONCERT VENUE
(www.massmutualcenter.com; 1277 Main St) A major venue for conventions, exhibits and big rock concerts.

❶ Information

Greater Springfield Convention Visitors Bureau (413-787-1548; www.valleyvisitor.com; 1441 Main St; ⊙8:30am-5pm Mon-Fri) A block and a half northwest of Court Sq.

❶ Getting There & Away

BUS

Peter Pan Bus Lines (800-343-9999; www.peterpanbus.com; 1776 Main St) connects Springfield with cities throughout New England. The bus station is a 10-minute walk northwest of Court Sq. In the same terminal, the **Pioneer Valley Transit Authority** (PVTA; www.pvta.com; 1776 Main St; ticket $1.25) runs routes to 23 communities in the region, including all of the five colleges.

CAR & MOTORCYCLE

To reach downtown Springfield, take I-91 exit 6 northbound or exit 7 southbound. Follow it to State St (east) then Main St (north), and you'll be at Court Sq in the heart of Springfield.

TRAIN

Amtrak (www.amtrak.com; 66 Lyman St, Union Station) operates between Boston and Springfield Union Station, which is a 10-minute walk northwest of Court Sq. The *Lake Shore Limited*, the once-a-day train running between Boston and Chicago, stops in Springfield, as does the once-a-day *Vermonter*, which runs between St Albans, VT, and Washington, DC.

Northampton

413 / POP 28,500

In a region famous for its charming college towns, you'd be hard-pressed to find anything more appealing than the crooked streets of downtown Northampton. Old red-brick buildings and lots of pedestrian traffic provide a lively backdrop for your wanderings, which will likely include cafes, rock clubs and bookstores (which explains why locals call their town 'NoHo'). Move a few steps outside of the picturesque commercial center and you'll stumble onto the bucolic grounds of Smith College. Northampton is a well-known liberal enclave in these parts. The lesbian community is famously outspoken, and rainbow flags wave wildly all over this town.

◎ Sights

★**Dinosaur Footprints** HISTORIC SITE
(www.thetrustees.org; US 5, Holyoke; ⊘ dawn-dusk Apr-Nov) FREE Around 190 million years ago, the Pioneer Valley area was a sub-tropical swamp inhabited by carnivorous, two-legged dinosaurs, and a large cluster of their footprints is preserved in situ on the west bank of the Connecticut River. The prints here, some 134 in all, represent three distinct species. It's a cool sight and just a two-minute walk from the road.

From Northampton, go south on Pleasant St/US 5 for about 5 miles. The small parking lot is on the left-hand side.

Smith College COLLEGE
(www.smith.edu; Elm St) Founded 'for the education of the intelligent gentlewoman' in 1875, Smith College is one of the largest women's colleges in the country, with 2600 students. The verdant 125-acre campus holds an eclectic architectural mix of nearly 100 buildings, set on a pretty pond. Notable alums of the college include Sylvia Plath, Julia Child and Gloria Steinem. After exploring the campus, take a stroll around Paradise Pond and snap a photo at the Japanese tea hut.

Smith College Museum of Art MUSEUM
(www.smith.edu/artmuseum; 20 Elm St; adult/child $5/free; ⊘10am-4pm Tue-Sat, noon-4pm Sun) This impressive campus museum boasts a 25,000-piece collection. The collection is particularly strong in 19th- and 20th-century European and North American paintings, including works by Degas, Winslow Homer, Picasso and James Abbott McNeill Whistler. Another highlight is the so-called 'functional art'; that is, the remarkable restrooms and the eclectic collection of benches (that you can actually sit on) – all designed and created by contemporary American artists.

Lyman Conservatory GARDENS
(www.smith.edu/garden; 15 College Lane; ⊘8:30am-4pm) FREE Visitors are welcome to explore Smith College's collection of Victorian greenhouses, set opposite Paradise Pond, which are packed to the brim with odd things in bloom. There's a popular 'bulb show' in spring and a 'mum show' in autumn. A handy campus map also shows the way to the campus arboretum and half a dozen other more formal gardens.

🛌 Sleeping

It's typically easiest to find a room during summer, when school's not in session. At other times, room price and availability depend largely on the college's schedule of ceremonies and events.

In addition to places to stay in Northampton, there's a run of midrange chain hotels along MA 9 in Hadley, midway between Northampton and Amherst.

★**Starlight Llama B&B** B&B $$
(☏413-584-1703; www.starlightllama.com; 940 Chesterfield Rd, Florence; r $115; 🐾) ✿ Five miles and a world away in neighboring Florence, Starlight offers the ultimate back-to-nature sleep. This off-the-grid solar-powered farm sits amid 65 acres of llama pastures, hiking trails and friendly barnyard creatures. Owner John Clapp built the house, and much of the Shaker-style furniture found in the three guest rooms. Breakfast features the farm's own free-range eggs and organic produce.

Autumn Inn MOTEL $$
(☏413-584-7660; www.hampshirehospitality.com; 259 Elm St/MA 9; r $119-129, ste from $149; 🅿🐾) More of a motel than an inn, this barn and raised-ranch combination presents an odd facade. But inside, the rooms are comfortable and spacious, while service is warm and accommodating. It's next to the Smith College campus, a 15-minute walk into town. Breakfast is included.

Hotel Northampton HISTORIC HOTEL $$
(☏413-584-3100; www.hotelnorthampton.com; 36 King St; r from $185-245; 🅿) This old-timer is perfectly situated smack in the center of Northampton and has been the town's best bet since 1927. The 100 rooms are airy and well-fitted, with traditional furnishings and floral quilts and curtains. There's a quiet grandeur to the place. And mailing a postcard via an antiquated letterbox system always feels good.

NORWOTTUCK RAIL TRAIL

The **Norwottuck Rail Trail** (www.mass.gov/eea/agencies/dcr/massparks/region-west/norwottuck-rail-trail.html; ☉ dawn-dusk), pronounced nor-wah-tuk, is a walking and cycling path that follows the former Boston & Maine Railroad right-of-way from Amherst to Hadley to Northampton, a total distance of 11 miles. For much of its length, the trail parallels MA 9, passing through open farms and crossing the broad Connecticut River on a historic 1500ft-long bridge.

Parking and access to the trail can be found on Station Rd in Amherst, at the Mountain Farms Mall on MA 9 in Hadley and at Elwell State Park on Damon Rd in Northampton. You can rent bikes from **Northampton Bicycle** (www.nohobike.com; 319 Pleasant St; per day from $25; ☉ 9:30am-7pm Mon-Fri, to 5pm Sat, noon-5pm Sun) in Northampton.

✗ Eating

Northampton is the region's dining epicenter, with a wide range of restaurants representing all price points and international tastes. Vegetarians will think they have died and gone to meat-free heaven, as all restaurants cater to their clientele with plenty of innovative, veggie fare. Most of the eateries are lined up along Main and surrounding streets.

Local Burger
BURGERS $

(www.localnorthampton.com; 16 Main St; mains $6-10; ☉ 11:30am-10pm Sun-Thu, to 3am Fri & Sat; ☑ 🐾) Locavores flock to this burger joint on Main St, where every effort is made to use locally sourced beef and produce. Burgermasters turn out eight tasty custom burgers (especially good for satisfying the late-night munchies), while the sweet-potato fries are an irresistible accompaniment. No alcohol is served but you can bring your own.

Herrell's Ice Cream
ICE CREAM $

(Thornes Marketplace, Old South St; cones $3-5; ☉ noon-11pm Sun-Thu, to midnight Fri & Sat) Steve Herrell began scooping out gourmet ice cream in this place in 1980. Even before that, he had invented 'Smoosh-ins', which is when a topping (any topping) is manually smushed into the ice cream (any flavor) using a scoop and spade and special board. Highly recommended.

Woodstar Cafe
CAFE $

(www.woodstarcafe.com; 60 Masonic St; mains $5-8; ☉ 7am-8pm Tue-Sat, to 6pm Sun-Mon; 🐾☑) Students flock to this family-run bakery/cafe, just a stone's throw from campus, for tasty sandwiches made on the freshest of bread and named after local towns and landmarks. Save room for dessert, as the pastries – made on-site – are divine.

Green Bean
CAFE $

(www.greenbeannorthampton.com; 241 Main St; mains $5-12; ☉ 7am-3pm; 🐾) ☑ Pioneer Valley farmers stock the kitchen at this cute, mostly vegetarian eatery that dishes up organic egg dishes all day long. There's also innovative tofu, tempeh and rice dishes that will make your mouth water. Locavores will love the prices, too, which are surprisingly easy on the wallet.

Bela
VEGETARIAN $

(☎ 413-586-8011; www.belaveg.com; 68 Masonic St; mains $8-13; ☉ noon-8:30pm Tue-Sat; ☑ 🐾) ☑ This cozy vegetarian restaurant puts such an emphasis on fresh ingredients that the chalkboard menu changes daily depending on what local farmers are harvesting. Think home-cooked comfort food and a setting that welcomes families – there's even a collection of toys for the kids! Cash only.

Haymarket Café
CAFE $

(☎ 413-586-9969; www.haymarketcafe.com; 185 Main St; dishes $5-10; ☉ 7am-10pm Mon-Sat, from 8am Sun; 🐾☑) Need a place where you can read an entire book in one go? Then try lounging around this bohemian cafe offering espresso, fresh juices, tempeh burgers and an extensive vegetarian menu. If students hunkered down over heated laptops and cooling coffee have snatched all the upstairs tables, look for the steps leading down to the cozy basement.

Paul & Elizabeth's
SEAFOOD $$

(☎ 413-584-4832; www.paulandelizabeths.com; 150 Main St; mains $11-17; ☉ 11:30am-9:30pm; 🐾☑🐾) ☑ This airy, plant-adorned restaurant, known locally as P&E's, sits on the top floor of Thornes Marketplace and is the town's premier natural-foods restaurant. It serves vegetarian cuisine and seafood, often with an Asian bent. Here's a rare opportunity to sample old-fashioned Indian pudding, so don't miss it!

India House
INDIAN $$

(www.indiahousenorthampton.com; 45 State St; mains $12-25; ⏱5-9:30pm; 🖉) This upscale Indian restaurant was the first in the Pioneer Valley. It is housed in an attractive house decked out with Jaipuri artwork and custom-made (in India) furniture. It's a perfect setting to sample the inspired tandoori, korma and curried dishes. Everything is made from scratch, so special requests are gladly accommodated. Vegetarians have plenty to choose from.

Sierra Grille
MODERN AMERICAN $$$

(☑413-584-1150; www.sierragrille.net; 41 Strong Ave; mains $17-33; ⏱3pm-1am) A smart setting, juicy steaks and a knockout brew selection make this the hottest omnivore dinner spot in town. The kitchen also does a stellar job with fish – the Ahi tuna topped with Thai hot basil sauce will awaken taste buds you didn't know existed. Reservations are a must on weekends.

🍷 Drinking & Nightlife

Besides its very own microbrewery, Northampton has a slew of pubs and wine bars catering to students and other tipplers.

Northampton Brewery
MICROBREWERY

(www.northamptonbrewery.com; 11 Brewster Ct; ⏱11:30am-1am; 🛜🖉) 🖉 This brewpub claims to be the oldest operating in New England. At any given time, there are about a dozen fresh and tasty beers on offer, along with a solid menu of pub grub and pizzas. The interior is warm and welcoming, but it's the generously sized rooftop deck that draws the crowds.

Con Vino
WINE BAR

(www.facebook.com/ConVinoNorthampton; 101 Armory St; ⏱5-11pm Mon-Thu, 3pm-1am Fri & Sat, 11am-10pm Sun) An extensive and expertly curated wine list features dozens of options available by the glass. If you can't decide, the staff is enthusiastic, knowledgeable and willing to make recommendations. As a complement to the vino, the food menu features cheese plates and tapas. Enjoy it all on a sweet little patio.

Dirty Truth
BAR

(www.facebook.com/dirtytruthbeerhall; 29 Main St; ⏱4pm-2am Mon-Fri, from 11am Sat & Sun) Slide into a high-top under some decent contemporary art to choose from the impressive list of available draft beers scrawled on the chalkboard menu. When the weather is fine, the front windows open up for fresh air and people-watching.

☆ Entertainment

Northampton is the top music destination in the Pioneer Valley, with two venues hosting lots of concerts. For listings of what's happening, pick up a copy of the free *Valley Advocate* (www.valleyadvocate.com).

New Century Theatre
THEATER

(☑413-585-3220; www.newcenturytheatre.org; 🖐) One of the best regional theater companies in the US stages works by playwrights such as Wendy Wasserstein and Northampton's own Sam Rush. Performances are held at the Mendenhall Center on the Smith College campus.

Calvin Theatre
CONCERT VENUE

(☑413-586-8686; www.iheg.com; 19 King St; tickets $35-65) This restored movie house hosts big-name performances with everything from hot rock and indie bands to comedy shows. The Gilded Era decor is pretty fancy, but the place could do with a fresh coat of paint.

Academy of Music Theatre
THEATER

(☑413-584-3220; www.academyofmusictheatre. com; 274 Main St) This gracious, balconied theater is one of the oldest movie houses in the USA (1890), and one of the most beautiful. It shows first-run independent films, plus books all sorts of music concerts from folk to cabaret as well as theatrical troupes.

Iron Horse Music Hall
CONCERT VENUE

(☑413-586-8686; www.iheg.com; 20 Center St; tickets $10-30) The town's prime venue for folk, rock and jazz with performers from Judy Collins to Dar Williams. Table seating means the atmosphere is pretty relaxed, though the food and drinks are overpriced and underwhelming.

ℹ Information

Greater Northampton Chamber of Commerce
(☑413-584-1900; www.explorenorthampton. com; 99 Pleasant St; ⏱9am-5pm Mon-Fri, plus 10am-2pm Sat & Sun May-Oct) Get all your questions answered at the local chamber.

ℹ Getting There & Around

Northampton is 18 miles north of Springfield on I-91. If you don't score a parking spot on Main St, you'll find public parking at **Thornes Marketplace** (www.thornesmarketplace.com; 150 Main

St; ⊙10am-6pm Mon-Wed, to 8pm Thu-Sat, noon-5pm Sun) in the town center.

Pioneer Valley Transit Authority (PVTA; www.pvta.com; ride/daily pass $1.25/3) provides bus services (with bike racks) throughout the Five College area, with the Northampton–Amherst route having the most frequent service.

Amherst

📞 413 / POP 37,800

This quintessential college town is home to the prestigious Amherst College, a pretty 'junior ivy' that borders the town green, as well as the hulking University of Massachusetts and the cozy liberal-arts Hampshire College. Start your explorations at the town green, at the intersection of MA 116 and MA 9. In the surrounding streets, you'll find a few funky galleries, a bookshop or two, countless coffeehouses, and a few small but worthwhile museums (several of which are associated with the colleges).

◉ Sights

Emily Dickinson Museum　MUSEUM
(www.emilydickinsonmuseum.org; 280 Main St; adult/child $10/5; ⊙11am-4pm Wed-Mon Mar-May & Sep-Dec, to 5pm Jun-Aug) During her lifetime, Emily Dickinson (1830–86) published only seven poems, but after her death more than 1000 of her poems were discovered and published, and her verses on love, nature and immortality have made her one of the most important poets in the US. She spent most of her life in near seclusion in this stately home near the center of Amherst. Tours of the Dickinson Homestead (40 minutes) focus on the poet and her works.

Eric Carle Museum of Picture Book Art　MUSEUM
(www.carlemuseum.org; 125 W Bay Rd; adult/child $9/6; ⊙10am-4pm Tue-Fri, to 5pm Sat, noon-5pm Sun; 👶) Co-founded by the author and illustrator of *The Very Hungry Caterpillar,* this superb museum celebrates book illustrations from around the world with rotating exhibits in three galleries, as well as a permanent collection. All visitors (grown-ups included) are encouraged to express their own artistic sentiments in the hands-on art studio.

Atkins Farms Country Market　FARM
(www.atkinsfarms.com; 1150 West St/MA 116; ⊙7am-8pm; 👶) ＦＲＥＥ This farm produce center and local institution, about 3 miles south of Amherst, offers maple-sugar products in spring, garden produce in summer and apple picking in the fall. Call about other activities, such as a scarecrow-making workshop in October, that take place throughout the year. A deli-bakery sells a full array of picnic supplies.

Amherst College　COLLEGE
(www.amherst.edu; 220 South Pleasant St) Founded in 1821, Amherst College has retained its character and quality partly by maintaining its small size (1600 students). The scenic campus lies just south of the town common. Get information on guided campus tours or pick up a self-guided walking-tour brochure at the admissions office. There are also a few museums on campus, including the small but fantastic **Mead Art Museum** (www.amherst.edu/museums/mead; Amherst College, 41 Quadrangle Dr; ⊙9am-5pm Tue-Sun, to 8pm Fri) ＦＲＥＥ and the equally fascinating **Beneski Museum of Natural History** (www.amherst.

LOCAL KNOWLEDGE

GHOSTS OF AMHERST

For a peek at Amherst's colorful past, make your way to the **West Cemetery** (Triangle St; ⊙dawn-dusk), between Triangle St and N Pleasant St. Here you'll find the graves of Amherst's notables, including Emily Dickinson. To spot her stone, follow the main paved path to the far end of the cemetery; the Dickinson family plot borders the left side of the path. Nearby, the ghosts of Amherst come alive on a brilliant mural, painted by David Fichter, which has overlooked the cemetery since 2005.

The mural depicts the history of Amherst, focusing mostly on the folks buried here. You'll see, painted larger than life, everyone from local farmer Howard Atkins to famed poet Robert Frost, a professor at Amherst College. And, of course, Emily herself. Due to new construction next to the cemetery, the original mural was slated for destruction in 2016. But all parties (developer, artist, historical commission) have agreed that the mural will be re-created – and improved – upon completion of the new building, estimated in 2018. Stay tuned.

edu/museums/naturalhistory; Amherst College, 11 Barrett Hill Rd; ⏱11am-4pm Tue-Fri, 10am-5pm Sat & Sun; 🅿) `FREE`.

🛏 Sleeping

Amherst's most appealing properties are well-located, smack in the center of town, while more affordable properties are near the UMass campus or on the outskirts of town. The Amherst Area Chamber of Commerce (p190) has a list of more than two-dozen member B&Bs.

Be aware of the college schedules when planning a visit. It's wise to book as far in advance as possible if planning a trip for late August or mid-May, when students and their families are coming and going.

★**Lord Jeffery Inn**   INN $$
(☎413-256-8200; www.lordjefferyinn.com; 30 Boltwood Ave; r from $200; ❄🏷) 🍴 The finest place to lay your head in Amherst is this boutique operation, in a classic setting overlooking Amherst Green. The Colonial-era inn masterfully fuses traditional fittings with mod conveniences, with additional welcome perks such as organic toiletries and farm-to-table menu.

Amherst Inn   B&B $$
(☎413-253-5000; www.allenhouse.com; 257 Main St; r $105-195; ❄🏷) A stately, three-story Victorian with handsome Tudor detailing, this classic B&B also offers plenty of appeal in price and comfort. It books heavily with return guests but a nearby sister operation, the Allen House, adds another half-dozen rooms to the mix. The rate includes a sumptuous five-course breakfast, served in the elegant dining room.

UMass Hotel   HOTEL $$
(☎877-822-2110; www.umasshotel.com; 1 Campus Center Way; d $155-170; ❄🏷) Staying at this hotel run by UMass' hospitality program provides all the pluses and minuses of campus life. Guests have plenty of contact with students and are smack in the heart of all the action UMass has to offer. After a recent renovation, the rooms are quite pleasant, though they lack individualized climate control. Continental breakfast – essentially, pastries – is included in the price.

🍴 Eating

Being a college town, Amherst has many places near the town green peddling pizza, sandwiches, burritos and fresh-brewed

---

ℹ FIVE COLLEGES CALENDAR

With five colleges in the area – Amherst, Hampshire, Mount Holyoke, Smith and UMass Amherst – the Pioneer Valley has a rich offering of concerts, lectures, performances and workshops. To see what's on the docket at the various campuses, check out the Five Colleges Calendar (www.fivecolleges.edu/calendar). Many of the offerings are free of charge.

---

coffee. Competition is fierce and quality is high, making the town a fun place to be at lunchtime.

Lone Wolf   CAFE $
(www.thelonewolfamherst.com; 63 Main St; mains $6-10; ⏱7am-2pm; 🥗🅿) Who says brunch is only for weekends? Thanks to the friendly waitstaff and its use of local, organic ingredients, the Lone Wolf has earned itself a strong fan base for its superb omelets, huevos rancheros and Benedicts. Vegans, take note: there are plenty of animal-free options too.

Antonio's Pizza by the Slice   PIZZA $
(www.antoniospizza.com; 31 N Pleasant St; slices $3; ⏱10am-2am) Amherst's most popular pizza place features excellent slices made with a truly vast variety of toppings. Bizarro as some offerings are (eg black bean avocado), the place comes across as authentic, set in an old brick building graced with a white-and-red awning.

Baku's African Restaurant   AFRICAN $$
(www.bakusafricanrestaurant.com; 197 N Pleasant St; lunch $6-7, mains $11-15; ⏱noon-8pm Mon-Thu, to 9pm Fri & Sat) Missing mama's cooking? The flavors may be a bit more exotic here, but with pots simmering on the stove and just five tables, this is real home cooking, Nigerian style. Chef-owner Chichi Ononibaku whips up everything from scratch. Think black-eyed peas with plantains, melon-seed soup and curried goat meat – oh, mama!

Chez Albert   FRENCH $$$
(☎413-253-3811; www.facebook.com/chezalbert amherst; 188 N Pleasant St; lunch $10-15, dinner mains $24-30; ⏱11:30am-2pm Tue-Fri, 5-9pm Mon-Sat) Want to impress a date? Take a seat at one of the copper-top tables at this chic bistro serving up the best French fare in the valley. The menu changes to take advantage of seasonal fare but includes all

PEACE PAGODA

The world can always do with a little more peace. A group of monks, nuns and volunteers are doing their part in an unexpected spot in the woods near the pea-sized town of Leverett. Run by the non-proselytizing Nipponzan Myohoji sect of Buddhism, the **Leverett Peace Pagoda** (www.newenglandpeacepagoda.org; 100 Cave Hill Rd, Leverett; ☉ dawn-dusk) was the first in the Western Hemisphere. The centerpiece is a stupa, a 100ft-tall white bell-shaped monument to Buddha – meant to be circumambulated, not entered. Nearby, prayer flags wave above a frog-filled pond.

To get to there from Amherst, take MA 9 west until MA 116 north, then turn onto MA 63 north and follow it 7 miles. Turn right onto Jackson Hill Rd and then right onto Cave Hill Rd. Parking is about half a mile up the road.

the traditional mainstays such as escargots, pâté and Boulonnais seafood stew, expertly prepared.

🍷 Drinking & Nightlife

With nearly 30,000 college students letting off steam when Friday rolls around, the pubs in Amherst overflow on the weekends.

Moan & Dove   BAR
(www.facebook.com/The-Moan-and-Dove-196421892196; 460 West St; ☉3pm-1am Mon-Fri, 1pm-1am Sat & Sun) The folks at this small, dark saloon near Hampshire College know their beer. Choose from 150 bottles and 20 draft beers. No food is served – unless you count free peanuts. The place attracts a good crowd, and sometimes the barkeepers have trouble keeping up, but if you order right, it's worth the wait.

Amherst Coffee   CAFE
(www.amherstcoffee.com; 28 Amity St; ☉6:30am-12:30am Mon-Sat, 8am-11pm Sun) Coffee shop by day, wine and whiskey bar by night, this place is surprisingly urbane for little Amherst. The limited menu features a delectable selection of charcuterie, cheese and other Italian-style snacks. Stop in for a drink before or after catching a flick at the on-site Amherst Cinema.

☆ Entertainment

Amherst Cinema   CINEMA
(www.amherstcinema.org; 28 Amity St; tickets $9-10; 🖭) 🎞 Here's an independent, nonprofit theater that's in the process of installing solar panels to power the films. That's all good, but the real reason to come here is for the cutting-edge programming – classic films, foreign flicks, art-house hits, documentaries and shorts, not to mention retrospectives and talks by contemporary filmmakers.

UMass Fine Arts Center   PERFORMING ARTS
(http://fac.umass.edu; UMass campus, 151 Presidents Dr) This striking concert hall is the region's largest venue, located on the University of Massachusetts campus. It offers a full program of classical and world-music concerts, theater and dance.

ℹ Information

Amherst Area Chamber of Commerce
(📞413-253-0700; www.amherstarea.com; 28 Amity St; ☉8:30am-4:30pm Mon-Fri) In the heart of town, just around the corner from Pleasant St and the town common.

ℹ Getting There & Around

Peter Pan Bus Lines (p184) runs long-distance buses to Springfield, Boston and New York. The **Pioneer Valley Transit Authority** (PVTA; www.pvta.com; ride/day pass $1.25/3) provides bus service around Amherst and to Northampton and other nearby towns.

Deerfield

📞 413 / POP 5100

While the modern commercial center is in South Deerfield, it's Historic Deerfield 6 miles to the north that history buffs swarm to, where zoning and preservation keep the rural village looking like a time warp to the 18th century – sleepy, slow and without much to do other than look at the period buildings.

Old Main St (as the old main street is called) runs parallel to US 5/MA 10. Follow the signs from I-91.

◉ Sights

Historic Deerfield Village   MUSEUM
(www.historic-deerfield.org; Old Main St; adult/child $14/5; ☉9:30am-4:30pm Apr-Dec; 🖭) The

main street of Historic Deerfield Village escaped the ravages of time and now presents a noble prospect: a dozen houses dating from the 1700s and 1800s, well preserved and filled with period furnishings that reflect their original occupants. There's also a museum stuffed with artifacts, several active workshops and a walking path through a working farm. In various buildings you might see (and try) old-fashioned cooking, woodworking or farming techniques.

If you're just passing through, it costs nothing to stroll Old Main St and admire the historic buildings from the outside, stroll through the farmland or visit the centuries-old cemetery.

Memorial Hall Museum　　　　MUSEUM
(www.americancenturies.mass.edu; cnr Memorial St, US 5 & MA 10; adult/child $6/3; ⊙ 11am-4:30pm Sat & Sun May, Tue-Sun Jun-Oct) Here's the original building of Deerfield Academy (1798), the prestigious preparatory school in town. It's now a museum of Pocumtuck Valley life and history. Puritan and Native American artifacts include carved and painted chests, embroidery, musical instruments and glass-plate photographs. Most dramatically, this is where you can see the so-called Indian House Door, a relic from the famous 1704 Deerfield Raid, when some 50 villagers were killed by French and Native American attackers.

🏃 Activities

Northfield Mountain Recreation & Environmental Center　　OUTDOORS
(http://h2opower-new.itwcorp.info/firstlightpower/recreation; ⊙ late Jun–mid-Oct; ♿) Stretching 7 miles along the Connecticut River, this attractive recreation area is maintained by the hydroelectric company that dammed the river (as per their federal license). Recreational opportunities include 26 miles of trails that are perfect for hiking, mountain biking and cross-country skiing. On the water, there's canoeing and kayaking, as well as an informative river-boat cruise.

Quinnetukut II　　　　BOATING
(☑ 800-859-2960; http://h2opower-new.itwcorp.info/firstlightpower/recreation; MA 63; adult/child $12/6; ⊙ cruises 11am, 1:15pm & 3pm Fri-Sun) For a junket on the Connecticut River, catch a riverboat cruise on the *Quinnetukit II*. A lecturer fills you in on the history, geology and ecology of the river and the region during the 12-mile, 1½-hour ride, and you'll pass under the elegant French King Bridge. Cruises are run by the Northfield Mountain Recreation & Environmental Center.

To get to the departure point, take I-91 north to exit 27, then MA 2 east, then MA 63 north. Reservations necessary.

🛏 Sleeping & Eating

Deerfield Inn　　　　INN $$
(☑ 413-774-5587; www.deerfieldinn.com; 81 Old Main St; tw from $150, d $160-200; ✳ 🐾 🛜 🍽) This inn, smack in the heart of the historic district, has 24 rooms furnished with antiques and housed in a gracious Greek Revival farmhouse. The included hot, hearty breakfast – as well as other meals – are served in the attached restaurant, which sources many ingredients from the surrounding farmland.

ℹ Information

Across from the Deerfield Inn, **Hall Tavern Visitor Center** (www.historic-deerfield.org; Old Main St; ⊙ 9:30am-4:30pm) has maps, brochures and handles ticket sales for the museum.

MONTAGUE BOOKMILL

Montague Bookmill (www.montaguebookmill.com; 440 Greenfield Rd, Montague; ⊙ 10am-6pm Sun-Wed, to 8pm Thu-Sat) promises 'books you don't need in a place you can't find.' Luckily, both claims are slightly exaggerated. Housed in a converted cedar gristmill from 1842, the bookmill's maze of rooms are packed with used books and comfy couches. Westward-facing walls are punctuated by large windows that overlook the roiling Sawmill River and its waterfall.

An art gallery and casual cafe share the same awesome river view, making it a fun place to join locals whiling away a lazy afternoon. From Amherst, take MA 63 to the Montague Center exit. Take a left off the exit and turn right onto Main St. Continue through the town center, bearing left after the village green onto Greenfield Rd; the mill is on the left.

CENTRAL MASSACHUSETTS & THE BERKSHIRES DEERFIELD

ⓘ Getting There & Away

Historic Deerfield is about 6 miles south of MA 2. Take US 5 heading south at Greenfield.

Shelburne Falls

♩ 413 / POP 1700

This artisan community's main drag – Bridge St – is tiny and charming, only three blocks long but with a passel of interesting galleries and craft shops. Forming the background are Massaemett Mountain, the Deerfield River and a pair of picturesque bridges that cross it – one made of iron, the other covered in flowers.

⦿ Sights

Bridge of Flowers   BRIDGE
(www.bridgeofflowersmass.org; ⊘ Apr-Oct) FREE
Since 1929, volunteers have maintained this bridge of blooms over the Deerfield River. One can't deny that it's one photogenic civic centerpiece. Over 500 varieties of flowers, shrubs and vines flaunt their colors on the 400ft-long span from early spring through late fall. Access to the bridge is from Water St.

Glacial Potholes   WATERFALL
(Deerfield Ave) FREE Stones trapped swirling in the roiling Deerfield River have been grinding into the rock bed at this location ever since the ice age. The result: 50 near-perfect circles in the riverbed, including the largest known glacial pothole (39ft diameter) in the world.

🏃 Activities

Deerfield Valley Canopy Tours   ADVENTURE
(☏ 800-532-7483; www.deerfieldzipline.com; 7 Main St/MA 2, Charlemont; zip $79-92; ⊘ 10am-5pm) Ready to fly? This zip line lets you unleash your inner Tarzan on a treetop glide above the Deerfield River Valley. The three-

DON'T MISS

MOHAWK TRAIL

For the finest fall foliage drive in Massachusetts, head west on MA 2 from Greenfield to Williamstown on the 63-mile route known as the **Mohawk Trail** (www.mohawktrail.com). The lively Deerfield River slides alongside, with roaring, bucking stretches of white water that turn leaf-peeping into an adrenaline sport for kayakers.

hour outing includes two hanging bridges, three rappels and 11 zips that get progressively longer. The hardest part is stepping off the first platform – the rest is pure exhilaration!

Children are welcome to join in the fun as long as they are at least 10 years old and weigh a minimum of 70 pounds. Charlemont is 7 miles west of Shelburne Falls.

Zoar Outdoor   RAFTING
(☏ 800-532-7483; www.zoaroutdoor.com; 7 Main St/MA 2, Charlemont; kayak from $33, rafting $61-89; ⊘ 9am-5pm; 🖫) This outfitter offers all sorts of splashy fun from Class II and III white-water rafting to canoeing and kayaking the Deerfield River. No experience? No problem. Zoar's enthusiastic guides adeptly provide newbies with all the ABCs. It's a family-friendly scene with several activities geared especially for kids.

🛏 Sleeping

Dancing Bear Guest House   GUESTHOUSE $$
(☏ 413-625-9281; www.dancingbearguesthouse.com; 22 Mechanic St; r $129-149; ❉ 🛜) Everything the town has to offer is within easy walking distance of this c 1825 guesthouse. The owners are welcoming, the breakfast home-cooked and the rooms squeaky clean. It's like staying with old friends – a perfect choice for travelers who truly want a local experience.

Bird's Nest   B&B $$
(☏ 413-625-9523; www.birdsnestbnb.com; 2 Charlemont Rd, Buckland; d $110-140) Located in the small village of Buckland, about 4 miles southwest of Shelburne Falls, this 1797 farmhouse offers three charming, comfortable rooms, as well as personable service and irresistible baked goods, served at breakfast and throughout the day.

🍴 Eating & Drinking

★ **Gould's Sugar House**   BREAKFAST $$
(www.goulds-sugarhouse.com; 270 Mohawk Trail; mains $8-12; ⊘ 8:30am-2pm Mar-Apr & Sep-Nov) The standard order at this family-run farm is fluffy pancake perfection, drizzled with maple heaven. Other unexpected highlights include the sugar pickles (yes, you read that right), maple ice cream and corn fritters. While you wait (and you will wait), you can watch the syrup being made. Located right on the Mohawk Hwy, east of the Shelburne Falls turnoff.

NEW ENGLAND NATIONAL SCENIC TRAIL

Formerly the Metacomet-Monadnock Trail (or M-M), the **New England National Scenic Trail** (NET; www.amcberkshire.org/netmm) is a 200-mile greenway and footpath that traverses some of the most spectacular scenery in Western Massachusetts (as well as Connecticut and New Hampshire). The trail enters Massachusetts from Connecticut near the Agawam/Southwick town line. It proceeds north up the Connecticut River valley, ascends Mt Tom, then heads east along the Holyoke Range, including **Skinner State Park** (www.mass.gov/dcr; 10 Skinner State Park Rd; ☺9am-8pm May-Aug, to 6pm Sep, to 4pm Oct-Nov), before bearing north again.

After entering New Hampshire, the trail ascends Mt Monadnock, where it joins the Monadnock-Sunapee Greenway. The easiest access for day hikes is in the state parks, where leaflets and simple local trail maps are available. For longer hikes, it's good to have the *New England Trail Map & Guide*, published by the Appalachian Mountain Club. Trail excerpts are posted on the website of the Appalachian Mountain Club Berkshire Chapter.

Gypsy Apple Bistro　　　FUSION $$
(☑413-625-6345; www.facebook.com/GypsyApple
-Bistro-139533602761476/; 65 Bridge St; mains
$20-30; ☺11am-9pm Tue-Sun) This is an un-
expected dining delight in Shelburne Falls.
The tiny place artfully blends New England
ingredients, French flavors, impeccable ser-
vice and a uniquely inviting atmosphere.
The menu is short and sweet – featuring
classic dishes like rack of lamb and roasted
chicken – but it's all perfectly prepared. The
place is tiny: be sure to reserve.

West End Pub　　　PUB FOOD $$
(www.westendpubinfo.com; 16 State St; lunch $7-10,
dinner $13-21; ☺11am-9pm Tue-Sun; ☻) Shel-
burne Falls' favorite place for a drink also
serves a varied menu of sandwiches, burgers, meat dishes and vegetarian options.
Best of all, it has a fantastic deck jutting out
above the Deerfield River and directly overlooking the Bridge of Flowers.

Mocha Maya's　　　CAFE
(☑413-625-6292; www.mochamayas.com; 417
Bridge St; ☺7am-6pm Mon-Sat, to 5pm Sun;
☻) ☞ No matter what your thirst, Mocha
Maya's is the place, pouring everything from
organic fair-trade coffee to locally crafted
beer. Occasional live music and poetry readings take place on Friday and Saturday evenings after hours.

🛍 Shopping

You'll make many artistic discoveries as you
wander through town. Otherwise, stop by
the visitor center for a complete list of the
artisans, from potters to quilters to weavers,
that call Shelburne Falls home.

ℹ Information

Shelburne Falls Visitor Center (☑413-625-
2526; www.shelburnefalls.com; 75 Bridge St;
☺10am-4pm Mon-Sat, noon-3pm Sun) Helps
with accommodations in the area.

ℹ Getting There & Away

Shelburne Falls is on the south side of MA 2, about
27 miles east of North Adams. Heading south, MA
112 turns into Main St, which runs into Bridge St.

THE BERKSHIRES

Few places in America combine culture and
country living as deftly as the Berkshire
hills, home to world-class music, dance and
theater festivals – the likes of Tanglewood
and Jacob's Pillow – as well as miles of hiking trails and acres of farmland.

Extending from the highest point in the
state – Mt Greylock – southward to the Connecticut state line, the Berkshires have been
a summer refuge for more than a century,
when the rich and famous arrived to build
summer 'cottages' of grand proportions.
Many of these mansions survive as inns
or performance venues. And still today, on
summer weekends when the sidewalks are
scorching in Boston and New York, crowds
of city dwellers jump in their cars and head
for the Berkshire breezes.

Great Barrington & Around

☑413 / POP 7100

Great Barrington's Main St used to consist of
Woolworth's, hardware stores, thrift shops
and a run-down diner. These have given way

to artsy boutiques, antique shops, coffee-houses and restaurants. Nowadays, the town boasts the best dining scene in the region, with easy access to hiking trails and magnificent scenery in the surrounding hills.

The Housatonic River flows through the center of town just east of Main St/US 7, the central thoroughfare.

◉ Sights & Activities

Most of your time in town will be spent strolling along the pedestrian-scaled Main St, with its mild bustle, handful of shops and dozen or so restaurants. After an hour or two's rest in small-town America, you might consider a hike in the hills.

Windy Hill Farm   FARM
(www.windyhillfarminc.com; 686 Stockbridge Rd/US 7; ⊙9am-5pm) If you hop in the car and drive, you're bound to find several farms where you can pick seasonal produce at harvest times. The setting can be overwhelmingly beautiful in the fall. A favorite is Windy Hill Farm, about 5 miles north of Great Barrington, where more than a score of apple varieties, from pucker-sour to candy-sweet, are yours for the autumn picking. Summer is blueberry-picking season.

Monument Mountain   HIKING
(www.thetrustees.org; US 7; parking $5; ⊙sunrise-sunset) Less than 5 miles north of Great Barrington center on US 7 is Monument Mountain, which has two hiking trails to the 1642ft summit of Squaw Peak. From the top you'll get fabulous views all the way to Mt Greylock in the northwestern corner of the state and to the Catskills in New York.

Housatonic River Walk   WALKING
(www.gbriverwalk.org) The picturesque Housatonic River flows through the center of Great Barrington, with the River Walk offering a perfect perch from which to admire it. Access the walking path from Main St (behind Rite-Aid) or from Bridge St.

Bartholomew's Cobble   HIKING
(www.thetrustees.org; US 7, Sheffield; adult/child $5/1; ⊙sunrise-sunset) South of Great Barrington, it's easy to kill a few hours at the 329-acre Bartholomew's Cobble, a 'cobble' being a high, rocky knoll of limestone, marble or quartzite. Five miles of hiking trails provide routes for enjoying the cobble and the woods, including the strenuous route to the top of Hurlbut's Hill and the Ledges Trail, which weaves along the Housatonic River.

The Berkshires

Keep your eyes peeled for some of the 200 species of birds who fly around here. Bartholomew's Cobble is 10 miles south of Great Barrington along US 7 and MA 7A toward Ashley Falls.

Beartown State Forest   OUTDOORS

(www.mass.gov/dcr; 69 Blue Hill Rd, Monterey; parking $8-10) This lovely state park is centered on Benedict Pond, a perfect spot for swimming, fishing, canoeing and kayaking. There are miles of hiking trails, including a piece of the Appalachian Trail. The furthest reaches of this forest are home to deer, bears, bobcats and fishers. Less ambitious hikers can stroll the 1.5-mile Benedict Pond Loop.

★ Festivals & Events

Aston Magna   MUSIC

(www.astonmagna.org; ☺Jun-Jul) Listen to Bach, Brahms, Buxtehude and other early classical music in Great Barrington during June and July. Now in its fifth decade!

⛏ Sleeping

Beartown State Forest   CAMPGROUND $

(☑413-528-0904; www.mass.gov/dcr; 69 Blue Hill Rd, Monterey; tent sites $22) It's mostly backpackers who stay at this quiet campground on the Appalachian Trail, 8 miles east of Great Barrington via MA 23. It has 12 basic sites that overlook 35-acre Benedict Pond.

Mt Washington State Forest   CAMPGROUND $

(☑413-528-0330; www.mass.gov/dcr; East St, Mt Washington) The forest contains the glorious Bash Bish Falls as well as 30 miles of trails and fantastic views from Alander Mountain. Wilderness camping is available for the adventurous.

Lantern House Motel   MOTEL $$

(☑413-528-2350; www.thelanternhousemotel. com; 256 Stockbridge Rd/MA 7; r $55-200; ✳🛜🐾🏊) The decor's a bit dated, for sure, but the cheerful operators of this independent family-run motel keep everything spotlessly clean and the place is darn comfortable. Most of the rooms are spacious, too, so if you've got kids, you won't be tripping over them here.

The 3-acre backyard with its saltwater pool and playground gear offers kid-centric diversions. Plus, there's a doughnut shop down the street.

Old Inn on the Green   INN $$$

(☑413-229-7924; www.oldinn.com; 134 Hartsville-New Marlborough Rd/MA 57, New Marlborough; Old Inn r $285, Thayer House r $385; ✳🛜🐾) Once a relay stop on a post road, the Old Inn, c 1760, is exactly what most people picture when they think New England country inn. The dining rooms are lit entirely by candlelight, and guest rooms are furnished with wideplank floors, four-poster beds and (some) fireplaces. Breakfast features treats such as homemade granola, fresh fruit and warm pastries.

Rooms in the nearby Thayer House are equally atmospheric but more spacious. This property shares welcoming common areas, a swimming pool and gorgeous views all around.

Wainwright Inn   B&B $$$

(☑413-528-2062; www.wainwrightinn.com; 518 S Main St; r $169-219; ✳🛜) Great Barrington's finest place to lay your head, this c 1766 inn exudes historical appeal from its wraparound porches and spacious parlors to the period room decor. Most of the eight guest rooms come with working fireplaces. Breakfast is a decadent experience. The inn is a short walk from the center of town on a busy road.

✖ Eating & Drinking

Surrounded by farms and favored by back-to-earthers, Great Barrington is a natural for the eat-local movement. You'd be forgiven for making a special trip here, just for a meal.

Berkshire Co-op Market Cafe   CAFE $

(www.berkshire.coop; 42 Bridge St; meals $6-10; ☺8am-8pm; ☑) ✿ You don't need to spend a bundle to eat green, wholesome and local. This cafe inside the Berkshire Co-op Market, just off Main St, has a crunchy farm-fresh salad bar, generous made-to-order sandwiches (both meat and veggie) and fairtrade coffees.

★Allium   MODERN AMERICAN $$

(☑413-528-2118; www.alliumberkshires.com; 42 Railroad St; small plates $9-16, mains $16-28; ☺5-9:30pm) ✿ Allium subscribes to the slow-food movement, with a seasonal menu that relies on fresh organic produce, cheeses and meats. Go for cocktails and small plates in the lounge area, with a window facing the street, or a more formal meal in the dining room, with a view into the kitchen. This stylish restaurant combines rustic and modern design elements to great effect.

Baba Louie's
PIZZA $$

(www.babalouiespizza.com; 286 Main St; pizzas $12-18; ⊙11:30am-9:30pm; 🐾🖊️) Baba's is known for its organic sourdough crust and for the guys with dreadlocks. There's a pizza for every taste, running the gamut from the fan-favorite Dolce Vita with figs, gorgonzola and prosciutto to the gluten-free Vegetazione with artichoke hearts, broccoli, tofu and soy mozzarella.

John Andrews Restaurant
MODERN AMERICAN $$$

(🖊️413-528-3469; www.jarestaurant.com; 224 Hillsdale Rd; mains $28-38; ⊙5-9pm Thu-Tue; 🖊️) 🍃 Raised in an Iowa farm family, chef Dan Smith was a pioneer of the farm-to-table movement in the Berkshires. His restaurant turns out a fine Italian–New American menu featuring Lila's delicious lamb and other items from nearby farms. The setting, a rustic 19th-century farmhouse overlooking a garden, makes a perfect match for the menu. Alfresco seating in summer, fireplace in winter.

The $35 prix-fixe specials (available Sunday to Thursday) offer three-courses, each highlighting an ingredient from a featured local farm.

Castle Street Café
MODERN AMERICAN $$$

(🖊️413-528-5244; www.castlestreetcafe.com; 10 Castle St; mains $22-32; ⊙5-9:30pm Wed-Mon; 🖊️) 🍃 Castle Street Café's menu reads like a who's who of local farms: Pineland Farm grass-fed natural beef, Rawson Brook chèvre and Equinox Farm mesclun greens. Chef-owner Michael Ballon's preparations range from innovative vegetarian fare to classics like rack of lamb. The setting is as engaging as the food, with both a jazzy bar with a pub menu and an art-filled dining room. Prime time to dine is on Friday or Saturday, when there's live jazz.

Barrington Brewery
MICROBREWERY

(www.barringtonbrewery.net; 420 Stockbridge Rd; ⊙11:30am-9:30pm; 🐾) 🍃 You can rest easy, knowing your beer was brewed with solar power. The frothy, hoppy brews are the star of the show here but the grass-fed beef burgers make a decent complement and the outdoor seating takes it up a notch on a balmy summer night.

☆ Entertainment

For up-to-date entertainment listings, pick up a copy of the free *Berkshires Week* (www.berkshireeagle.com/berkshiresweek) at bars and restaurants.

Guthrie Center
LIVE MUSIC

(🖊️413-528-1955; www.guthriecenter.org; 4 Van Deusenville Rd; ⊙May-Sep) The old church made famous in Arlo Guthrie's *Alice's Restaurant* hosts a beloved Troubadour series, featuring folk concerts by the likes of Tom Chapin, Steve Katz and, occasionally, local boy Arlo himself. It's a cozy setting with just 100 seats, so book in advance.

Mahaiwe Performing Arts Center
PERFORMING ARTS

(www.mahaiwe.org; 14 Castle St) Culture vultures will find an eclectic menu of events at this classic theater, from jazz vocals to classic movies to modern dance.

ℹ️ Information

Southern Berkshire Chamber of Commerce (🖊️413-528-1510; www.southernberkshirechamber.com; 362 Main St; ⊙10am-6pm Thu-Mon) Maintains a kiosk in front of the town

---

WORTH A TRIP

BASH BISH FALLS

In the very southwest corner of the state, near the New York state line, is **Bash Bish Falls** (www.mass.gov/dcr; Falls Rd, Mt Washington; ⊙sunrise-sunset), the largest waterfall in Massachusetts. The water feeding the falls runs down a series of gorges before the torrent is sliced in two by a massive boulder perched directly above a pool. There it drops as a picture-perfect double waterfall. These 60ft-high falls are a popular spot for landscape painters to set up their easels.

To get there from Great Barrington, take MA 23 west to South Egremont. Turn onto MA 41 south and then take the immediate right onto Mt Washington Rd (which becomes East St) and continue for 7.5 miles. Turn right onto Cross Rd, then right onto West St and continue 1 mile. Turn left onto Falls Rd and follow that for 1.5 miles. The parking lot and trailhead will be on your left. The hike takes about 20 minutes.

hall that's well stocked with maps, restaurant menus and accommodations lists.

ℹ️ Getting There & Away

Most travelers arrive by car on US 7, which runs through the center of town. Otherwise, **Peter Pan** (www.peterpanbus.com; 362 Main St) buses run to/from Pittsfield and Greenfield, MA, as well as Canaan, CT.

Tyringham

🕿 413 / POP 330

The village of Tyringham, between Lee and Monterey, is the perfect destination for an excursion into the heart of the countryside. Once the home of a Shaker community (1792–1874), Tyringham is now famous for its **Gingerbread House** (Santarella; www.santarella.us; 75 Main St). Surrounding the tiny village center, scenic back roads snake over gentle hills and past farmland. If you have time to wander, you'll discover some woodsy places to hike, a roadside pond that begs a dip and a couple of art studios.

🏃 Activities

Tyringham Cobble   HIKING
(www.thetrustees.org; Jerusalem Rd; ⏰ dawn-dusk) To get some perspective on this tiny village's pastoral splendor, take a 2-mile hike over the knobs of Tyringham Cobble, which offers wildflower-strewn hillsides and spectacular views. Look for wild berries growing in the meadows and the uniquely shaped Rabbit Rock perched along the trail.

ℹ️ Getting There & Away

The tiny village of Tyringham lies 4 miles southeast of Lee; follow the aptly named Tyringham Rd.

Stockbridge

🕿 413 / POP 1950

Take a good look down Stockbridge's wide Main St. Notice anything? More specifically, notice anything missing? Not one stoplight stutters the view, not one telephone pole blights the picture-perfect scene – it looks very much the way Norman Rockwell might have seen it.

In fact, Rockwell did see it – he lived and worked in Stockbridge during the last 25 years of his life. Nowadays, Stockbridge attracts summer and fall visitors en masse, who come to stroll the streets, inspect the

---

ℹ️ **BERKSHIRES SCOOP**

Berkshire Grown (www.berkshiregrown.org) Online directory of pick-your-own orchards, farmers markets and restaurants offering organic local ingredients.

Berkshires Visitors Bureau (www.berkshires.org) Has the scoop on accommodations and activities.

Berkshires Week (www.berkshireeagle.com/berkshiresweek) Look at this newspaper's site for updated arts and theater listings.

See the Berkshires (www.berkshires.com) Extensive recommendations for dining, lodging, activities, galleries and more.

---

shops and sit in the rockers on the porch of the historic Red Lion Inn. And they come by the busload to visit the Norman Rockwell Museum on the town's outskirts.

All that fossilized picturesqueness bears a price. Noticeably absent from the village center is the kind of vitality that you find in the neighboring towns.

👁 Sights

Norman Rockwell Museum   MUSEUM
(www.nrm.org; 9 Glendale Rd/MA 183; adult/child $18/6; ⏰ 10am-4pm May-Oct, to 5pm Nov-Apr) Born in New York City, Norman Rockwell (1894–1978) sold his first magazine cover illustration to the *Saturday Evening Post* in 1916. In the following half-century he did another 321 covers for the *Post*, as well as illustrations for books, posters and many other magazines on his way to becoming the most popular illustrator in US history. This excellent little museum has the largest collection of Rockwell's original art, as well as Rockwell's studio, which was moved here from his Stockbridge home.

Chesterwood   MUSEUM
(www.chesterwood.org; 4 Williamsville Rd; adult/child/student $18/free/13; ⏰ 10am-5pm late May–mid-Oct) This pastoral 122-acre plot was 'heaven' to its owner Daniel Chester French (1850–1931), the sculptor best known for his great seated statue of Abraham Lincoln in the Lincoln Memorial in Washington, DC. French's more than 100 public works, mostly monumental, made him a wealthy man. His house and studio are substantially as they

were when he lived and worked here, with nearly 500 pieces of sculpture, finished and unfinished, in the barnlike studio. There are also rotating contemporary-sculpture exhibits in the grounds.

Naumkeag HISTORIC SITE
(www.thetrustees.org; 5 Prospect St; adult/child $15/free; ◎10am-5pm Sat & Sun Apr-May, daily Jun-Oct) Designed by the renowned architect Stanford White in 1885, this 44-room Gilded Age 'cottage' was the summer retreat of Joseph Hodges Choate, a former US ambassador to England. The estate retains so much of its original character that you might expect Choate to be sitting at the breakfast table. The influence of his travels abroad are visible not only in the home's rich and eclectic interior but also in the acres of surrounding formal gardens with their fountains, sculpture and themed plantings.

The prominent landscape architect Fletcher Steele spent some three decades laying out the gardens and establishing the plantings. Strolling through the gardens alone is worth the price of admission. To get there, follow Pine St from the Red Lion Inn to Prospect St.

★✚ Festivals & Events

Berkshire Theatre Festival THEATRE
(☑413-997-9444; www.berkshiretheatre.org; 83 E Main St; ◎Jun-Oct) Experimental theater is held at venues in Stockbridge and Pittsfield, from June to October.

⌂ Sleeping

Red Lion Inn HISTORIC HOTEL $$
(☑413-298-5545; www.redlioninn.com; 30 Main St; r without/with bathroom from $169/265; ❄@🎧🐾🍽) This aging white-frame hotel is at the very heart of Stockbridge village, marking the intersection of Main St and MA 7. It's been the town's focal point since 1773, though it was completely rebuilt after a fire in 1897. Many rooms in the main building have fireplaces, old print wallpaper, classic moldings and white linens.

1862 Seasons on Main B&B $$$
(☑413-298-5419; www.seasonsonmain.com; 47 Main St; r $245-295, ste $345; ❄🎧) This gracious Greek Revival home was built – you guessed it – in 1862. Its five superlative guest rooms are named for the seasons and decked out with antique beds, working fireplaces, claw-foot tubs in the bathrooms, and many romantic touches. Breakfast is a three-course, made-to-order feast. Service is impeccable and the extra perks will delight and surprise you throughout your stay.

Stockbridge Country Inn INN $$$
(☑413-298-4015; www.stockbridgecountryinn.com; 26 Glendale Rd/MA 183; r $229-349; 🎧🍽) Occupying a 19th-century estate house, this is the closest inn to the Norman Rockwell Museum. Antique fittings, four-poster beds and 4 acres of pretty grounds set the tone. But it's the full country breakfast served on a sunny porch overlooking flowery gardens that sets it apart.

✖ Eating

Lion's Den PUB FOOD $$
(www.redlioninn.com; 30 Main St; mains $12-14; ◎4-10pm Mon-Fri, noon-10pm Sat & Sun) Downstairs at the Red Lion Inn, this dark, cozy bar serves daily pub specials like chicken pot pie, Hungarian goulash and turkey dinner. In fair weather you can dine in the courtyard out back. Friendly crowd, live music on weekends.

Once Upon a Table AMERICAN $$$
(☑413-298-3870; www.onceuponatablebistro.com; 36 Main St; mains lunch $10-14, dinner $20-30; ◎11am-8:30pm Mon-Sat, to 3pm Sun) This bright spot in the Mews shopping arcade serves upscale fare in a sunny dining room. It's the best place in town for lunch, with choices like daily-changing omelets and sophisticated sandwiches. The dinner menu features reliably delicious treats such as pecan-crusted rainbow trout and fine dessert pastries.

Red Lion Inn AMERICAN $$$
(☑413-298-5545; www.redlioninn.com; 30 Main St; tavern mains $16-24, dining room mains $26-42; ◎7am-9pm Mon-Fri, 7:30am-9:30pm Sat & Sun) The Red Lion is the main eating venue in Stockbridge. On the stodgy side is the formal dining room, where you can indulge in a roasted native turkey while sitting under a crystal chandelier. More relaxed is the Widow Bingham Tavern, a rustic Colonial pub that serves gourmet sandwiches and many variations on cow.

❶ Information

Stockbridge Chamber of Commerce (☑413-298-5200; www.stockbridgechamber.org; 50 Main St; ◎9am-5pm Mon, Wed & Fri) You can also pick up brochures at the small kiosk opposite the library on Main St in the town center. It's often unstaffed, but the door's always open.

❶ Getting There & Away

The center of Stockbridge is at the intersection of MA 102 and MA 7. In town, MA 102 becomes Main St.

Operated by the **Berkshire Regional Transit Authority** (BRTA; www.berkshirerta.com; ride $1.75), buses connect Stockbridge to the other towns in the region. Peter Pan Bus Lines (p177) goes to Great Barrington, Lenox and Sturbridge, as well as New York City.

Lee

📲 413 / POP 5900

Welcome to the towniest town in the Berkshires. A main street, both cute and gritty, runs through the center, curving to cross some railroad tracks. On it you'll find a hardware store, a bar and a few places to eat including a proper diner favored by politicians desiring photo ops with working-class folks. Most travelers pass through Lee simply because it's near a convenient exit off the Mass Pike. The main draw is the prestigious Jacob's Pillow dance festival on the outskirts of town.

⊙ Sights & Activities

October Mountain State Forest   FOREST
(www.mass.gov/dcr; 317 Woodland Rd) Most out-of-towners head to Mt Greylock, and thus leave October Mountain State Forest to the locals. This 16,500-acre state park is the largest tract of green space in Massachusetts, and it's rife with opportunities for outdoor adventure. Hidden amid the hardwoods, Buckley Dunton Reservoir – a small body of water stocked with bass – is a great spot for canoeing. For hikers, a 9-mile stretch of the Appalachian Trail pierces the heart of the forest through copses of hemlocks, spruces, birches and oaks.

The mountain was supposedly named by Herman Melville, who could see these hills from his home in Pittsfield. To get to the park from Lee, follow US 20 west for 3 miles and look for signs.

✯ Festivals & Events

★ **Jacob's Pillow**   DANCE FESTIVAL
(📲 413-243-9919; www.jacobspillow.org; 358 George Carter Rd, Becket; ⊙mid-Jun–Aug) Founded by Ted Shawn in an old barn in 1932, Jacob's Pillow is one of the premier summer dance festivals in the USA. Through the years, Alvin Ailey, Merce Cunningham, the Martha Graham Dance Company and other leading interpreters of dance have taken part.

A smorgasbord of free shows, classes and talks allows even those on tight budgets to join in the fun. Look especially for free performances on the Inside/Out stage. The festival theaters are in the village of Becket, 8 miles east of Lee along US 20 and MA 8.

🛏 Sleeping

Motels in Lee are clustered around I-90 exit 2, on heavily trafficked US 20. For a list of independent inns and guesthouses, visit the Lee Lodging Association (www.leelodging.org).

**October Mountain
State Forest**   CAMPGROUND $
(📲413-243-1778; www.mass.gov/dcr; Center St; tent sites $17) This state forest campground, near the shores of the Housatonic River, has 47 sites with hot showers. To find the campground, turn east off US 20 onto Center St and follow the signs.

Jonathan Foote 1778 House   B&B $$
(📲413-243-4545; www.1778house.com; 1 East St; r/ste from $220/235; ❄ 🐾) An old Georgian farmhouse set in spacious grounds with shady maple trees and stone walls. Stay here for antiquated fireplaces, four-poster beds and beautiful views of the Berkshire hills. The three-course breakfast is served on the covered patio.

✗ Eating

While Joe's Diner is the main draw, you'll also find a Chinese joint, a good bakery and a health-food store in the center of town. There are more, better options in neighboring Lenox.

Joe's Diner   DINER $
(📲413-243-9756; 85 Center St; mains $4-9; ⊙5:30am-8:30pm Mon-Sat, 7am-2pm Sun) There's no better slice of blue-collar Americana in the Berkshires than Joe's Diner, at the north end of Main St. Norman Rockwell's famous painting of a policeman sitting at a counter talking to a young boy, *The Runaway* (1958), was inspired by this diner. Joe's has barely changed a wink – not the bar stools and not the old-fashioned diner fare.

❶ Information

Lee Chamber of Commerce (📲413-243-1705; www.leechamber.org; 3 Park Pl; ⊙10am-4pm Mon-Sat Jun-Oct) Maintains an information booth on the town green in summer.

❶ Getting There & Away

Just off I-90 at exit 2, Lee is the gateway to Lenox, Stockbridge and Great Barrington. US 20 is Lee's main street, and leads right into Lenox, about a 15-minute drive away.

Lenox

✈ 413 / POP 5000

This gracious, wealthy town is a historical anomaly: firstly, its charm was not destroyed by the industrial revolution; and then, prized for its bucolic peace, the town became a summer retreat for wealthy families with surnames like Carnegie, Vanderbilt and Westinghouse, who had made their fortunes by building factories in other towns.

As the cultural heart of the Berkshires, Lenox's illustrious past remains tangibly present today. The superstar among its attractions is the Tanglewood Music Festival, an incredibly popular summer event drawing scores of visitors from New York City, Boston and beyond.

❍ Sights

The Mount HISTORIC SITE
(www.edithwharton.org; 2 Plunkett St; adult/child $18/free; ⏰10am-5pm May-Oct) Almost 50 years after Nathaniel Hawthorne left his home in Lenox, another writer found inspiration in the Berkshires. Edith Wharton (1862–1937) came to Lenox in 1899 and proceeded to build her palatial estate, the Mount. When not writing, she would entertain literary friends here, including Henry James. Wharton was also a keen horticulturist and many visitors come here just to wander the magnificent formal gardens. Thanks to a $3 million restoration effort, the gardens have regained much of their original grandeur.

The Mount is on the southern outskirts of Lenox at US 7 and Plunkett St.

Pleasant Valley Wilderness Sanctuary NATURE RESERVE
(✈413-637-0320; www.massaudubon.org; 472 W Mountain Rd; adult/child $5/3; ⏰10am-4pm Tue-Sun Nov-Apr, daily May-Oct, trails dawn-dusk year-round) This 1300-acre wildlife sanctuary has 7 miles of pleasant walking trails through forests and meadows, as well as a challenging hike to the summit of Lenox Mountain. It's not uncommon to see beavers on the viewing platform near Pike's Pond. A nature center is open daily, and you can arrange canoe trips on the Housatonic.

To reach the sanctuary, go north on US 7 or MA 7A. Three-quarters of a mile north of the intersection of US 7 and MA 7A, turn left onto W Dugway Rd and go 1.5 miles to the sanctuary.

Berkshire Scenic Railway Museum MUSEUM
(www.berkshirescenicrailroad.org; 10 Willow Creek Rd; ⏰10am-2pm Sat May-Oct; 🚼) **FREE** This museum of railroad lore is set up in Lenox's 1903 vintage railroad station. Its model-railroad display is a favorite with kids, as are the toy trains they can play with. The museum is 1.5 miles east of Lenox center, via Housatonic St.

🏃 Activities

Kripalu Center YOGA
(✈413-448-3400; www.kripalu.org; West St/MA 183; day pass $100-125) ❦ The premier yoga institute in the northeast, Kripalu breathes tranquillity. Set on a lush estate overlooking a calm cerulean lake, this former Jesuit monastery and its environmentally green annex offer a wonderful setting for those wanting to take some time off to pursue inner peace.

Although serious students spend weeks here at a time, the center offers visitor-friendly flexibility. A day pass allows guests to join the yoga classes, meditation sessions and other holistic offerings, including three healthy delicious meals. Or one might stay the night and use Kripalu as a base during a longer stay.

Jiminy Peak Mountain Resort SKIING
(✈413-738-5500; www.jiminypeak.com; 37 Corey Rd, Hancock; one-day pass adult/child $65/43, lift tickets from $71/53; ⏰9am-10pm) ❦ In keeping with the Berkshires' ecofriendly green vibe, Jiminy Peak proudly claims title to being the first wind-power-operated ski resort in the country. Its 253ft wind turbine generates up to half the resort's electrical usage. And with 45 trails, and a Left Bank run of 2 miles, Jiminy offers the area's finest skiing.

It's an activity center in summer as well, when mountain biking, a ropes course and Segway tours take over the slopes. Jiminy Peak is 18 miles north of Lenox via US 7.

Arcadian Shop OUTDOORS
(✈413-637-3010; www.arcadian.com; 91 Pittsfield Rd/US 7; rentals per day $25-45; ⏰9:30am-6pm Mon-Sat, 11am-5pm Sun) The Arcadian Shop rents high-end mountain and road bikes, kayaks, skis and snowshoes. Kennedy Park, just north of downtown Lenox on US 7, is

TANGLEWOOD MUSIC FESTIVAL

Dating from 1934, the Tanglewood Music Festival (☑888-266-1200; www.tanglewood. org; 297 West St/MA 183, Lenox; lawn tickets $15-22, kids free; ☺late Jun-early Sep) is among the most esteemed summertime music events in the world. Symphony, pops, chamber music, jazz and blues are performed from late June through early September. You can count on renowned cellist Yo-Yo Ma, violinist Joshua Bell and singer James Taylor to perform each summer, along with a run of world-class guest artists and famed conductors.

Performance spaces include the 'Shed,' which is anything but – a 6000-seat concert shelter with several sides open to the surrounding lawns. The weekend Boston Symphony Orchestra concerts pack the largest crowds. Most casual attendees – up to 8000 of them – arrive three or four hours before concert time, staking out good listening spots on the lawn outside the Shed, then break out picnics until the music starts. Pack a picnic from a local market (☑413-637-2221; www.nejaimeswine.com; 60 Main St; picnic basket for 2 people $55; ☺9am-9pm Mon-Sat) or order in advance from Tanglewood Cafe (p202).

Families should check out Kids Corner, offered on weekends, where children can participate in musical, arts and crafts projects.

Tanglewood is easy to find – just follow the car in front of you! From Lenox center, head west on West St/MA 183 for about 1.5 miles. Ample free concert parking is available, but remember that parking – and, more importantly, unparking – 6000 cars can take time. If your lodging is close, consider walking.

popular with mountain bikers in summer and cross-country skiers in winter. You might also explore the Berkshires' many miles of stunning back roads or paddle down the Housatonic River.

🛏 Sleeping

Lenox has no hotels and only a few motels, but it does have lots of inns, which provide gorgeous environs and memorable stays (if you can afford them). The Tanglewood festival means that many inns require a two- or three-night minimum stay on Friday and Saturday nights in summer. Many thrifty travelers opt to sleep in lower-priced towns like Great Barrington or Pittsfield.

Days Inn
MOTEL $

(☑413-637-3560; www.daysinn.com; 194 Pittsfield Rd/US 7; r from $69; ❄☞☲) Shoring up the budget end, this two-story motel on the northern outskirts of Lenox offers a comfortable, if bland, room at an affordable price. A continental breakfast is also included. It's about a mile from the historic center.

Cornell Inn, Lenox
B&B $$

(☑413-637-4800; www.cornellbb.com; 203 Main St; d from $165; @☞) Spread across three historic houses, this B&B offers good value in a pricey town. When it's not full, the manager might even bargain a little – so ask about specials. It's no gilded mansion, but the rooms are cozy with the expected amenities, staff is

friendly, and hot breakfast is served on the porch overlooking the picturesque pond.

Bordering Kennedy Park at the north side of town, it's well suited for hikers and guests itching for a morning jog before breakfast.

Hampton Inn & Suites Berkshires-Lenox
MOTEL $$

(☑413-499-1111; www.berkshirehampton.com; 445 Pittsfield Rd/US 7; r $169-249; @☞☲) Top choice among the area's motels, the Hampton Inn sits in a quiet location 2 miles north of town. The tasteful but traditional rooms are comfortable but not luxurious.

★ Stonover Farm B&B
B&B $$$

(☑413-637-9100; www.stonoverfarm.com; 169 Under Mountain Rd; ste $385-485; ❄@☞) If you're looking for a break from musty Victorians with floral wallpaper, you'll love this contemporary inn wrapped in a century-old farmhouse. The three suites in the main house groan with casual luxury. Oversized jacuzzis, marble bathrooms, wine and cheese in the evening – this is pampering fitting its Tanglewood neighborhood setting. There are also two private stand-alone cottages.

Breakfast – fresh, homemade, decadent – is served in the creamery overlooking the pond or outside in the courtyard.

Canyon Ranch
SPA HOTEL $$$

(☑413-637-4100; www.canyonranchlenox.com; 165 Kemble St; r per person from $825; ❄☞☲) The well-heeled come from around the world to unwind and soak up the spa facilities at this famed resort. The all-inclusive rates include healthy gourmet meals (including vegetarian options), luxury spa treatments, fitness classes, outdoor activities, cooking demonstrations, creativity workshops and oodles of saunas, pools and quiet paths.

Birchwood Inn INN $$$

(☑ 413-637-2600; www.birchwood-inn.com; 7 Hubbard St; r $239-269, deluxe r $359-379; ❄ ☎ ❄) A pretty hilltop inn a couple of blocks from the town center, Birchwood occupies the oldest (1767) home in Lenox. The 11 spacious rooms vary in decor; some swing with a vintage floral design, others are more country classic, but all are romantic and luxurious. Deluxe rooms feature king-size beds and wood-burning fireplaces.

Home-cooked breakfasts, perhaps fondue Florentine soufflé or blueberry cheese blintzes, are served in a fireside dining room.

✖ Eating & Drinking

The top spots to eat in Lenox are clustered around Franklin St and Church St. In fact, if it weren't for Tanglewood, many visitors would spend all their time in this two-block area.

Bagel & Brew SANDWICHES $

(www.facebook.com/BagelandBrew; 18 Franklin St; sandwiches $6-9; ⊙ 7am-2pm & 5-11pm) Bagels by day, brews by night. There's about 18 different tasty bagel sandwiches, half for breakfast and half for lunch. Then there's a dozen different beers on tap – most of them regional – which get served in the beer garden out back, starting around the dinner hour. Alas, the food that accompanies the brew is not bagels, but slightly unexpected and truly delicious pub grub. This place has a great vibe.

Haven Cafe & Bakery CAFE $$

(☑ 413-637-8948; www.havencafebakery.com; 8 Franklin St; mains $8-15; ⊙ 7:30am-3pm; ☎ ✎) It looks like a cafe, but the sophisticated food evokes a more upscale experience. For breakfast, try croissant French toast or inventive egg dishes like salmon scramble; for lunch there are fancy salads and sandwiches – all highlighting local organic ingredients. Definitely save room for something sweet from the bakery counter.

Tanglewood Cafe CAFETERIA $$

(☑ 413-637-5240; Lion's Gate Entrance, Hawthorne Rd, Tanglewood campus; meals from $22; ✎ ♿) On the Tanglewood campus, the eponymous cafe has a menu of sandwiches, salads and other light fare. Alternatively, place an order 48 hours in advance for a picnic basket, which might include individual sandwiches and salads, a two-person fried-chicken dinner, or a four-person spread with crackers, cheese and charcuterie. The cafe opens when performances are on.

★ Nudel AMERICAN $$$

(☑ 413-551-7183; www.nudelrestaurant.com; 37 Church St; mains $22-26; ⊙ 5:30-9:30pm Tue-Sun) Nudel is a driving force in the area's sustainable-food movement, with just about everything on the menu seasonally inspired and locally sourced. The back-to-basics approach rings through in inventive dishes, which change daily but never disappoint. Incredible flavors. Nudel has a loyal following, so reservations are recommended in season.

Bistro Zinc FRENCH $$$

(☑ 413-637-8800; www.bistrozinc.com; 56 Church St; mains lunch $12-16, dinner $22-30; ⊙ 11:30am-3pm & 5:30-10pm) The postmodern decor here is all metal surfaces and light woods, with tin ceilings, black-and-white tile floors and wine-crate doors. Tempting French offerings include steak frites, beef bourguignonne and trout meunière, all with a nouveau twist.

★ Bookstore WINE BAR

(Get Lit Wine Bar; www.bookstoreinlenox.com; 11 Housatonic St; ⊙ 9am-6pm Mon-Thu, to 9pm Fri & Sat, 10am-3pm Sun) We've all been to bookstores that serve coffee, but this one serves wine. Good wine. Which is a perfect complement to the good books that are also on sale here. The proprietor, Matt, is a charming host who loves to talk about books and other important things.

☆ Entertainment

Shakespeare & Company THEATER

(☑ 413-637-1199; www.shakespeare.org; 70 Kemble St; ⊙ late Jun-early Sep) This renowned company often updates the Bard's plays to a contemporary setting, which is a fun twist. The company stages plays at a variety of locations, including a tented, outdoor theater which is a replica of Shakespeare's first London playhouse.

❶ Information

Lenox Chamber of Commerce (☑ 413-637-3646; www.lenox.org; 4 Housatonic St; ⊙ 10am-4pm Wed-Sat Sep-Jun, to 6pm daily Jul-Aug) This office, inside the public library, is a clearinghouse of information on everything from inns to what's going on.

ℹ️ Getting There & Away

Lenox is on MA 7A, just off US 7. The nearest airports are Bradley International in Connecticut and Albany International in New York. **Peter Pan Bus Lines** (www.peterpanbus.com; 5 Walker St) operates between Lenox and Boston. Amtrak trains stop in nearby Pittsfield.

Pittsfield

📋 413 / POP 44,000

Welcome to the service city of the Berkshires, where the trains stop and and the people shop (for things like vacuum cleaners, not art). Jokes about the name of this town are easy to make, and not without a modicum of accuracy. Still, travelers who pause here are often delighted by the unique and interesting museums, and they eat well while they are here, too.

That said, you probably don't need to spend the night.

◉ Sights

Crane Museum of Papermaking　　MUSEUM
(www.crane.com; 40 Pioneer St, Dalton; ⊙1-5pm Tue-Fri year-round, plus Mon Jun–mid-Oct) FREE
Since 1879 every single American bill has been printed on paper made by the Crane Company, based in the small mill town of Dalton. The Crane Museum of Papermaking, housed in the original stone mill room built in 1844, traces the history of Zenas Crane's enterprise, which is still family-run after seven generations. To get here from Pittsfield, take MA 9 northeast for 5 miles.

Berkshire Museum　　MUSEUM
(www.berkshiremuseum.org; 39 South St; adult/child $13/6; ⊙10am-5pm Mon-Sat, noon-5pm Sun; 👪) This surprisingly impressive museum has a solid collection of Hudson River

School artworks and a permanent Alexander Calder exhibit, as well as kid-friendly attractions like a touch-tank aquarium and a hands-on science center.

🍴 Eating

Marketplace Cafe　　SANDWICHES $
(www.ourmarketplacecafe.com; 53 North St; sandwiches $8-10; ⊙8am-8pm Mon-Sat, 9am-5pm Sun; 🐾) If you like sandwiches, you'll love this lunch spot near the Berkshire Museum. There's something about a funny local name that makes a sandwich taste better. Case in point: Bartholomew's Gobble is not a turkey sandwich, but a turkey dinner, complete with stuffing and cranberry, which happens to come between bread.

Shay's Rebellion is a roast-beef sammie, but the beef is roasted in-house, and served with sweet peppers, caramelized onions and Vermont cheddar. Also, French onion grilled cheese. Yes, please. Many vegetarian, vegan and gluten-free options.

Elizabeth's　　ITALIAN $$
(📋413-448-8244; 1264 East St; mains $20; ⊙5-9pm Wed-Sat; 🐾) Don't be put off by the location across the street from a vacant General Electric plant, nor by the deceptively casual interior. Folks travel from New York and Boston to sample Tom and Elizabeth Ellis' innovative Italian fare. Super-fresh ingredients and lots of love go into these dishes, most of which are vegetarian friendly.

ℹ️ Information

Berkshire Chamber of Commerce (📋413-499-1600; www.1berkshire.com; 66 Allen St; ⊙9am-5pm Mon-Fri) Has information on Pittsfield and the rest of the Berkshires.

WORTH A TRIP

HANCOCK SHAKER VILLAGE

Hancock Shaker Village (www.hancockshakervillage.org; US 20; adult/child/youth $20/free/8; ⊙10am-4pm, to 5pm Jul-Oct; 👪) is an evocative museum that illustrates the lives of the religious sect that founded the village in 1783. The Shakers believed in communal ownership, the sanctity of work and celibacy, the latter of which proved to be their demise. Known as the City of Peace, the village was occupied by Shakers until 1960. At its peak in 1830, the community numbered some 300 members.

Twenty of the original buildings have been restored and are open to view, most famously the Round Stone Barn (1826). You're free to wander about on your own, watch demonstrations of Shaker crafts, visit the heirloom gardens and hike up to Mt Sinai where the Shakers went to meditate. The village is 5 miles west of Pittsfield on US 20.

CYCLING THE HOOSIC

When Boston and Maine Railroad gave up on the corridor between Lanesborough and Adams in 1990, citizens agitated to have it recast as a universally accessible walk/bike path, and thus the 11-mile Ashuwillticook Rail Trail (www.mass.gov/dcr) was born. The trail cuts between Mt Greylock and the Hoosac Range, closely following the Hoosic River and the Cheshire Reservoir through glorious wetlands.

It's perfect for cycling, in-line skating, or just taking a stroll. The southern access is on the eastern outskirts of Pittsfield. At the intersection of MA 9 and MA 8, continue 1.5 miles north on MA 8 to the Lanesborough–Pittsfield line. Turn left at the Berkshire Mall Rd entrance to reach the rail-trail parking. The northern access is behind the Berkshires Visitors Bureau in Adams.

❶ Getting There & Away

Pittsfield is 7 miles north of Lenox on US 7, at the intersection with MA 9. Peter Pan Bus Lines operates out of the **Pittsfield Bus Terminal** (1 Columbus Ave), traveling south to Lenox or north to Williamstown and North Adams. Longer-distance buses go to Boston and New York. Amtrak (www.amtrak.com) trains also stop here, headed to Boston or Albany, New York.

Williamstown

📍 413 / POP 7750

Small but gracious Williamstown is nestled within the heart of the Purple Valley, so named because the surrounding mountains often seem shrouded in a lavender veil at dusk. Folks congregate in the friendly town center, which is only two blocks long, while dogs and kids frolic in the ample green spaces.

Williamstown is a quintessential New England college town, its charming streets and greens dotted with the stately brick and marble buildings of Williams College. Cultural life is rich, with a pair of exceptional art museums and one of the region's most respected summer theater festivals.

◉ Sights

★ **Clark Art Institute** MUSEUM
(www.clarkart.edu; 225 South St; adult/child $20/free; ⊙10am-5pm Tue-Sun) Even if you're not an avid art lover, don't miss this gem, set on 140 gorgeous acres of expansive lawns, flower-filled meadows and rolling hills. The building – with its triple-tiered reflecting pool – is a stunner. The collections are particularly strong in the impressionists, with significant works by Monet, Pissarro and Renoir. Mary Cassatt, Winslow Homer and John Singer Sargent represent contemporary American painting.

Robert Sterling Clark (1877–1956), a Yale engineer whose family made a fortune in the sewing-machine industry, began collecting art in Paris in 1912. He and his wife eventually housed their impressive collection in Williamstown in a white marble temple built expressly for the purpose. 'The Clark,' as everyone in town calls it, is less than 1 mile south of the intersection of US 7 and MA 2.

Williams College Museum of Art MUSEUM
(www.wcma.org; 15 Lawrence Hall Dr; ⊙10am-5pm, to 8pm Thu, closed Wed Sep-May) FREE This sister museum of the Clark Art Institute graces the center of town and has an incredible (free!) collection of its own. Around half of its 13,000 pieces comprise the American Collection, with substantial works by notables such as Edward Hopper (*Morning in a City*), Winslow Homer and Grant Wood, to name only a few. The photography collection is also noteworthy, with representation by Man Ray and Alfred Stieglitz. Did we mention it's free?

✪ Festivals & Events

Williamstown Theatre Festival THEATER
(📞413-597-3400; www.wtfestival.org; 1000 W Main St; ⊙Jun-Aug; 👪) Stars of the theater world descend upon Williamstown every year from the third week in June to the third week in August. Widely considered the best summer theater in the area, the Williamstown Theatre Festival was the first to win the Regional Theatre Tony Award.

The festival mounts the region's major theatrical offerings with a mix of classics and contemporary works by up-and-coming playwrights. Kevin Kline, Richard Dreyfuss and Gwyneth Paltrow are but a few of the well-known thespians who have performed here.

Besides the offerings on the Main Stage and Nikos Stage, there are cabaret performances in area restaurants and family nights when kids can attend performances for free.

🛏 Sleeping

In addition to Williamstown's handful of historic lodgings, you'll find several motels on the outskirts of town on MA 2 east and US 7 north.

Clarksburg State Park   CAMPGROUND $
(✆413-664-8345; www.mass.gov/dcr; 1199 Middle Rd, Clarksburg; tent sites $17) With views of the Berkshire hills and the Green Mountains, this is a scenic spot to pitch your tent. There are about 10 miles of walking trails, as well as kayaking, canoeing and swimming in Mauserts Pond. Follow MA 2 to MA 8 to reach these 45 campsites.

River Bend Farm B&B   B&B $$
(✆413-458-3121; www.riverbendfarmbb.com; 643 Simonds Rd/US 7; r $120; ⊙Apr-Oct; ❋☎) Step back in time to 1770, when this Georgian Colonial was a local tavern owned by Benjamin Simonds. The house owes its painstaking restoration to hosts Judy and Dave Loomis. Four simple, comfortable doubles share two bathrooms with claw-foot tubs. Breakfast is served in the wood-paneled tap room, next to the wide stone fireplace.

Despite the name, it's not on a farm but along US 7 on the north side of the little bridge over the Hoosic River.

Maple Terrace Motel   MOTEL $$
(✆413-458-9677; www.mapleterrace.com; 555 Main St; d $99-139; ☎❋) The Maple Terrace is a simple yet cozy 15-room place on the eastern outskirts of town. The Swedish innkeepers have snazzed up the grounds with gardens that make you want to linger. There's nothing fancy going on here, but the place is comfortable and service is warmly attentive.

★ Guest House at Field Farm   INN $$$
(✆413-458-3135; www.thetrustees.org/field-farm; 554 Sloan Rd; r $195-295; @☎❋) About 6 miles south of Williamstown, this one-of-a-kind inn offers an artful blend of mid-20th-century modernity and timeless mountain scenery. The six rooms are spacious and fitted with handcrafted furnishings that reflect the modernist style of the house. The sculpture-laden grounds feature miles of lightly trodden walking trails and a pair of Adirondack chairs set perfectly for unobstructed stargazing.

The building was built in 1948 in spare, clean-lined Bauhaus style on 300 acres of woods and farmland facing Mt Greylock. The original owners, art collectors Lawrence and Eleanor Bloedel, bequeathed the estate to the Trustees of Reservations, which now operates it.

🍴 Eating & Drinking

Williamstown has some quick and tasty options for eating, mostly lined up along Spring St.

Pappa Charlie's Deli   DELI $
(28 Spring St; mains $5-8; ⊙7:30am-8pm; ✍) Here's a welcoming breakfast spot where locals really do ask for 'the usual.' The stars themselves created the lunch sandwiches that bear their names. The Mary Tyler Moore is a favorite (bacon, lettuce, tomato and avocado), but the actress has since gone vegetarian, so you can get that too. Or order a Politician and get anything you want on it.

★ Mezze Bistro & Bar   FUSION $$
(✆413-458-0123; www.mezzerestaurant.com; 777 Cold Spring Rd/US 7; mains $14-28; ⊙5-9pm) You don't know exactly what you're going to get at this contemporary chic restaurant – as the menu changes frequently – but you know it's going to be good. Situated on 3 spectacular acres, Mezze's farm-to-table approach begins with an edible garden right on site. Much of the rest of the seasonal menu, from small-batch microbrews to organic meats, is locally sourced as well.

Tunnel City Coffee   CAFE
(www.tunnelcitycoffee.com; 100 Spring St; ⊙6am-6pm; ☎) A bustling den of cramming students and mentoring professors. Besides liquid caffeine, some seriously delicious desserts like triple-layer chocolate mousse cake will get you buzzing.

ℹ Information

Williamstown Chamber of Commerce (✆413-458-9077; www.williamstownchamber.com; 100 Spring St; ⊙11am-6pm Mon-Sat Jun-Aug) Operates a seasonal information booth in the B&L Building.

ℹ Getting There & Away

The bus station is in the lobby of the Williams Inn, at the intersection of US 7 and MA 2. Peter Pan Bus Lines runs buses to North Adams (23 minutes), Albany (one hour, 40 minutes) and New York City (five hours).

North Adams

413 / POP 13,500

At first glance, North Adams' beautiful and bleak 19th-century downtown seems out of sync with the rest of the Berkshires. It's not so lively and the amenities are limited. But it doesn't take long to discover the appeal – mainly, Mass MoCA, an exemplary contemporary-art museum of staggering proportions. Indeed, the place is big enough to be its own village, and its grounds do in fact contain some of the city's best dining, drinking and shopping.

◉ Sights & Activities

MASS MoCA MUSEUM
(Massachusetts Museum of Contemporary Art; www.massmoca.org; 87 Marshall St; adult/child $18/8; ⊙10am-6pm Jul & Aug, 11am-5pm Wed-Mon Sep-Jun; 🖈) MASS MoCA sprawls over 13 acres of downtown North Adams – one-third of the entire business district. After the Sprague Electric Company closed in 1985, some $31 million was spent to modernize the property into 'the largest gallery in the United States.' The museum encompasses 222,000 sq ft in 25 buildings, including art construction areas, performance centers and 19 galleries. One gallery is the size of a football field, giving installation artists the opportunity to explore a whole new dimension. Make sure you bring your walking shoes!

In addition to carrying the bread-and-butter rotation of description-defying installation pieces, the museum has evolved into one of the region's key venues for theater, documentary films and avant-garde dance performances. Families with budding artists should check out the museum's Kidspace, where children can create their own masterpiece.

Hoosac Range Trail HIKING
Near North Adams, there is an easy 1.6-mile trail to Sunset Rock, where you can pick blueberries in season. If you have more time, take the moderate 6.2-mile trail to Spruce Hill, where you'll be rewarded with open ledges and long views. The trail is known for rocky glacial cliffs and creepy tree formations, caused by wind and ice.

The trailhead is at the Western Summit of the Mohawk Trail, located on MA 2 about 4 miles east of North Adams.

🛏 Sleeping

Savoy Mountain State Forest CAMPGROUND $
(413-663-8469; www.mass.gov/dcr; 260 Central Shaft Rd, Florida; tent sites/cabins $17/50; 🐾) This wooded campground has 45 sites and four very rustic log cabins in one of the best state parks for mountain biking. From the center of town, head south on MA 8 and east on MA 116.

★Porches BOUTIQUE HOTEL $$
(413-664-0400; www.porches.com; 231 River St; d/ste from $239/279; 🖵🗘🎵🐾) Across the street from MASS MoCA, the artsy rooms here combine well-considered color palettes, ample lighting and French doors into a pleasant sleeping experience. It seems pricey for North Adams, but they got all the details right (and they are the only game in town).

🍴 Eating & Drinking

Lickety Split CAFE $
(www.licketysplitatmassmoca.com; 1040 Mass Moca Way; mains $5-10; ⊙8:30am-6pm) A convenient place for museum-goers to eat is at this pretty cafe inside MASS MoCA. Surprisingly good homemade soups and sandwiches, as well as breakfast fare and free-trade coffee. Alert: premium ice cream made in-house is served on-site.

Public Eat & Drink PUB FOOD $$
(www.publiceatanddrink.com; 34 Holden St; mains $10-22; ⊙11:30am-10pm; 🖵) With exposed-brick walls and big windows overlooking the street, this cozy pub is the most popular dinner spot in North Adams. Come for an excellent selection of craft beers and gourmet pub fare, like brie burgers, flatbread pizzas and bistro steak. Some decent vegetarian options as well.

Gramercy Bistro MODERN FRENCH $$
(413-663-5300; www.gramercybistro.com; 87 Marshall St; mains lunch $10-15, dinner $20-27; ⊙5-10pm Wed-Mon, plus noon-2pm Wed-Sun Jun-Aug) Located in one of MASS MoCA's outer buildings, this light-filled bistro is the fanciest place in town. Highlighting foods from local farms, the wide-ranging menu leans French, featuring dishes such as veal schnitzel à la holstein (with a fried egg, anchovies and capers) and sweet breads au beurre noir (with preserved lemon and artichoke). Brunch is recommended – stop in before visiting the museum.

Bright Ideas Brewing   BREWERY
(www.brightideasbrewing.com; 111 Mass MoCA Way; ☺4-10pm Thu, to 11pm Fri, 2-11pm Sat, noon-6pm Sun) Beer and art go together perfectly, as it turns out. They'll prove it to you at this brand new brewery in the Mass MoCA compound. Exposed-brick walls, cement floors and radical artwork constitute the decor in the former industrial space. There are a few tasty sandwiches and snacks for noshing, and the beer is fresh, cold and delicious. What a bright idea!

❶ Getting There & Away

North Adams sits along MA 2, about 6 miles east of Williamstown. The Berkshire Regional Transit Authority (p199) buses stop here along their loop around the Berkshire towns. Peter Pan buses (p177) also stop here, en route to Shelburne Falls, Williamstown and Pittsfield, as well as Albany, NY.

Mt Greylock State Reservation

At a modest 3491ft, the state's highest peak can't hold a candle altitude-wise to its western counterparts, but a climb up the 92ft-high **War Veterans Memorial Tower** at its summit rewards you with a panorama stretching up to 100 verdant miles, across the Taconic, Housatonic and Catskill ranges, and over five states. Even if the weather seems drab from the foot, a trip to the summit may well lift you above the gray blanket, and the view with a layer of cloud floating between tree line and sky is simply magical.

The reservation has some 45 miles of hiking trails, including a portion of the **Appalachian Trail**. Frequent trail pulloffs on the road up – including some that lead to

waterfalls – make it easy to get at least a little hike in before reaching the top of Mt Greylock.

🛏 Sleeping & Eating

At the summit of Mt Greylock, the rustic Bascom Lodge offers food and lodging in season. There are also a few primitive campsites in the park that are not accessible by car; call the visitor center for information and reservations.

★**Bascom Lodge**   LODGE $
(☎413-743-1591; www.bascomlodge.net; 1 Summit Rd; dm/d/q without bath $40/125/150, mains $8-12; ☺restaurant 8am-4:30pm Sat & Sun May & daily Jun-Oct, dinner by reservation; ℗) High atop Mt Greylock, this truly rustic hostelry was built as a federal work project in the 1930s. In the lobby, inviting leather sofas are arranged around a stone fireplace. Room have shared bathrooms, comfortable beds and wonderful views. The meals – fresh, hot and individually prepared – are excellent and filling, providing perfect sustenance for hikers.

❶ Information

Mt Mount Greylock State Reservation Visitor Center (☎413-499-4262; www.mass.gov/dcr, mount.greylock@state.ma.us; 30 Rockwell Rd, Lanesborough; ☺9am-5pm Jun-Aug, to 4.30pm Sep-May) Stop in at the visitor center for trail maps, bird lists and answers to any of your other questions.

❶ Getting There & Away

You can get to Mt Greylock from either Lanesborough (follow the signs 2 miles north of town) or North Adams (from MA 2 west, and again, follow the signs). Either way, it's 10 slow miles to the summit, where you can park for $5. The Greylock visitor center is halfway up via the Lanesborough route.

Rhode Island

📍 401 / POP 1.05 MILLION

Best Places to Eat

➜ birch (p216)
➜ Chez Pascal (p216)
➜ Champlin's Seafood (p233)
➜ Boat House (p220)
➜ Matunuck Oyster Bar (p233)

Best Places to Sleep

➜ Fishermen's Memorial State Park (p233)
➜ The Dean Hotel (p215)
➜ Castle Hill Inn (p229)
➜ The Chanler at Cliff Walk (p229)
➜ Ocean House (p235)

Why Go?

Rhode Island, the smallest of the US states, isn't actually an island. Although it takes only 45 minutes to traverse, this little wonder packs in over 400 miles of coastline with some of the finest white-sand swimming beaches in the northeast, deserted coves, rugged seaside cliffs and isolated lighthouses.

Hugging the shoreline before heading inland, delightful resorts, quaint colonial villages and extravagant mansions give way to lush fields of berry farms, vineyards, and the horse studs of Middletown and Portsmouth. Rhode Island's two cities, Providence, of working-class roots, and Newport, born of old money the likes of which most cannot conceive, are each among New England's finest, brimming with fantastic museums, neighborhoods boasting utterly gorgeous historic homes, and an urban fabric of top-notch restaurants and seriously cool bars. It's no wonder the *nouveau riche* continue to flock here for summer shenanigans.

When to Go
Providence

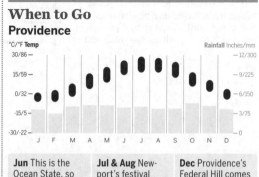

Jun This is the Ocean State, so hit the beach. In Newport, Rosecliff hosts the flower show.

Jul & Aug Newport's festival season is in full swing with classical, jazz and folk music.

Dec Providence's Federal Hill comes alive for the Christmas holiday.

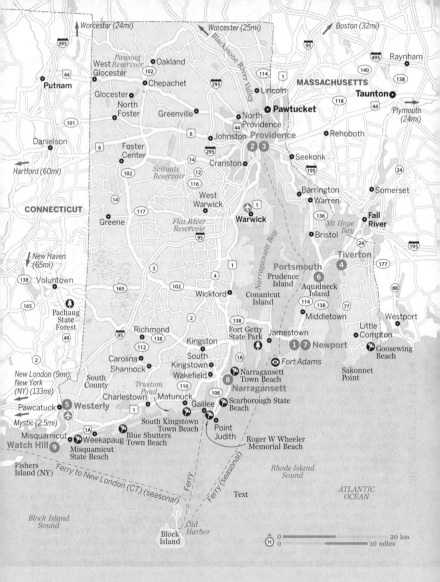

Rhode Island Highlights

1 Cliff Walk (p228) Gawp between the roaring Atlantic and stoic mansions of Newport's Bellevue Ave.

2 Providence (p211) Wandering in and around the city's happening downtown core.

3 WaterFire (p215) Witnessing the urban-revival spectacle of Providence's hugely popular festival.

4 Tiverton (p220) Touring the historic charm of the scenic East Bay.

5 Westerly (p234) Hitting the beach with the bronzed locals at Misquamicut State Beach.

6 Portsmouth (p227) Sipping champagne while taking in a polo match.

7 Newport Folk Festival (p228) Kicking back with a keg of locally brewed beer (not by yourself!) at this fab fest.

8 Champlin's Seafood (p233) Gorging on fresh lobster in Narragansett before boarding the Block Island Ferry.

9 Watch Hill (p235) Relishing the exquisite historic homes and architecture.

History

Ever since it was founded in 1636 by Roger Williams, a religious outcast from Boston, Providence has enjoyed an independent frame of mind. Williams' guiding principle, the one that got him ostracized from Massachusetts, was that all people should have freedom of conscience. He put his liberal beliefs into practice when settling Providence, remaining on friendly terms with the local Narragansett Native Americans after purchasing from them the land for a bold experiment in tolerance and peaceful coexistence.

Williams' principles would not last long. As Providence and Newport grew and merged into a single colony, competition and conflict with area tribes sparked several wars, leading to the decimation of the Wampanoag, Pequot, Narragansett and Nipmuck peoples. Rhode Island was also a prolific slave trader and its merchants would control much of that industry in the years after the Revolutionary War.

The city of Pawtucket birthed the American industrial revolution with the establishment of the water-powered Slater Mill in 1790. Industrialism impacted the character of Providence and surrounds, particularly along the Blackstone River, creating urban density. As with many small East Coast cities, these urban areas went into a precipitous decline in the 1940s and '50s as manufacturing industries (textiles and costume jewelry) faltered. In the 1960s, preservation efforts salvaged the historic architectural framework of Providence and Newport. Today, Newport has flourished into one of the nation's most attractive historical centers.

Providence also re-routed its destiny to emerge as a lively and stylish city with a dynamic economy and vibrant downtown core, largely due to the work of Buddy Cianci, twice-convicted felon and twice-elected mayor (1975–84, 1991–2002). Cianci is credited with saving the city from industrial and urban decline with a large-scale revitalization project that uncovered and rerouted previously subterranean river tributaries into a central artificial pond. The spectacle of today's wildly popular Waterfire festival is a powerful symbol of the city's phoenix-like rebirth along the confluence of the three rivers that gave it life. Cianci died in 2016, aged 74.

❶ Getting There & Around

Providence has excellent transportation options. Elsewhere in the state, things can be tricky unless you have your own wheels.

AIR

Green Airport (☑ 888-268-7222; www.pvdairport.com; 2000 Post Road, Warwick) Twenty minutes' drive south of downtown Providence, this airport is served by major US airlines and car-rental companies. The airport is connected to road and rail arteries via the Interlink transportation hub.

Westerly State Airport (☑ 401-596-2357; www.pvdairport.com; 56 Airport Rd, Westerly) Managed by the Green Airport Authority, this small airport operates flights to and from Block Island.

BOAT

Block Island Ferry (☑ 401-783-4613; www.blockislandferry.com) Runs a high-speed ferry from Point Judith in Narragansett (adult/child $38/22, 30 minutes) and a traditional ferry (adult/child $26/13, one hour). The latter is the only car ferry: vehicle reservations are essential and additional fees apply. There are also high-speed ferries from Newport (adult/child $51/26, one hour) and Fall River, MA (adult/child $60/30, two hours). Rates listed are for round-trip fares on different dates. Same-day round-trip fares are marginally cheaper.

Block Island Express (☑ 860-444-4624; www.goblockisland.com) Operates services from New London, CT, to Old Harbor, Block Island (round-trip adult/child $45/23, 75 minutes) between May and September.

BUS

Providence and Newport are well serviced, and some buses depart direct from Green Airport.

Peter Pan Bus Lines (☑ 800-343-9999; www.peterpanbus.com) Operates routes that connect Providence with New York City (from $30, 3¾ hours) and Boston (from $15, one hour), as well as Newport to Boston (from $24, 1½ hours).

Greyhound (☑ 800-231-2222; www.greyhound.com) Services similar routes at similar rates.

Rhode Island Public Transit Authority (RIPTA; ☑ 401-781-9400; www.ripta.com; one-ride/day pass/weekly pass $4/6/25) Rhode Island's regional transportation network links Providence's Kennedy Plaza with most towns and cities around the state.

CAR & MOTORCYCLE

I-95 cuts diagonally across the state, providing easy access from coastal Connecticut to the south and Boston to the north. From Worcester take Rte 146 to Providence. A variety of car-rental companies operate in Providence and Newport.

TRAIN

Amtrak (☑ 800-872-7245; www.amtrak.com) Trains operate between New York's Penn Station and Boston Back Bay Station, stopping in Westerly (five daily), Kingston (eight daily) and Providence (eight daily). The additional high-speed *Acela Express* train stops only in Providence.

Massachusetts Bay Transportation Authority (MBTA; ☑ 617-222-3200; www.mbta. com) Operates a commuter train between Providence and Boston ($10.50, one hour), and Providence and Green Airport ($11, 1½ hours).

PROVIDENCE

POP 178,000

Atop the confluence of the Providence, Moshassuck and Woonasquatucket Rivers, Rhode Island's capital city offers some of the finest urban strolling in New England: around Brown University's historic campus on 18th-century College Hill, along the landscaped Riverwalk trail, and among downtown's handsome streets and lanes with their hipster-y cafes, art-house theaters, fusion restaurants and trendsetting bars.

Once destined to become an industrial relic, Providence's fate was spared when Buddy Cianci, its then controversial two-time mayor, rolled out a plan to revitalize the downtown core by rerouting subterranean rivers, reclaiming land and restoring historic facades. It created a city where history's treasures are integrated into a creative present, not simply memorialized; where three centuries of architectural styles are unified in colorful urban streetscapes that are at once bold, beautiful and cooler than cool.

A large student population here helps keep the city's social and arts scenes lively and current.

⊙ Sights

★ **Rhode Island School of Design** UNIVERSITY, GALLERY
(RISD; ☑ 401-454-6300; www.risd.edu; 20 N Main St) Perhaps the top art school in the USA, RISD's imprint on Providence is easily felt, with students' creativity extending across the cityscape. Open to the public, the extraordinary collections of the **Museum of Art** (☑ 401-454-6500; www.risdmuseum.org; 224 Benefit St; adult/youth $12/3; ⊙ 10am-5pm Tue-Sun, to 9pm Thu; ﹢) include 19th-century French paintings; classical Greek, Roman and Etruscan art; medieval and Renaissance works; and examples of 19th- and 20th-century American painting, furniture and decorative arts.

PROVIDENCE ARCHITECTURE

Come to Providence and you'll find an urban assemblage of unsurpassable architectural merit – at least in the USA. It's the only American city to have its *entire* downtown listed on the National Registry of Historic Places. The beaux arts **City Hall** (25 Dorrance St) makes an imposing centerpiece to Kennedy Plaza, and the stately white dome of the **Rhode Island State House** remains visible from many corners of the city. The **Arcade** is modeled after Parisian antecedents. These impressive structures, along with the art-deco **Industrial Trust** (Bank of America; 55 Exchange Pl, Fleet Bldg), are only a few of many showcase buildings. The more ordinary 19th-century brick structures that fill in the space between their more famously designed neighbors work together to create a landscape of harmonious scale, beauty and craftsmanship.

Immediately east of downtown, you'll find College Hill, where you can see the city's colonial history reflected in the multihued 18th-century houses that line **Benefit St** on the East Side. These are, for the most part, private homes, but many are open for tours one weekend in mid-June during the annual Festival of Historic Homes (p214). Benefit St is a fitting symbol of the Providence renaissance, rescued by local preservationists in the 1960s from misguided urban-renewal efforts that would have destroyed it. Its treasures range from the 1708 **Stephen Hopkins House** (☑ 401-421-0694; 15 Hopkins St; donations accepted; ⊙ 1-4pm Wed-Sat May-Oct, otherwise by appointment), named for the 10-time governor and Declaration of Independence signer, to the clean Greek Revival lines of William Strickland's 1838 **Providence Athenaeum** (☑ 401-421-6970; www.providenceathenaeum. org; 251 Benefit St; ⊙ 9am-7pm Mon-Thu, to 5pm Fri & Sat, 1-5pm Sun) **FREE**. This is a library of the old school, with plaster busts and oil paintings filling in spaces not occupied by books. Edgar Allen Poe used to court ladies here.

Also on College Hill, the brick **John Brown House** (☑ 401-273-7507; www.rihs.org; 52 Power St; adult/child $10/6; ⊙ tours 1:30pm & 3pm Tue-Fri, 10:30am, noon, 1:30pm & 3pm Sat Apr-Dec), called the 'most magnificent and elegant mansion that I have ever seen on this continent' by John Quincy Adams, was built in 1786.

Providence

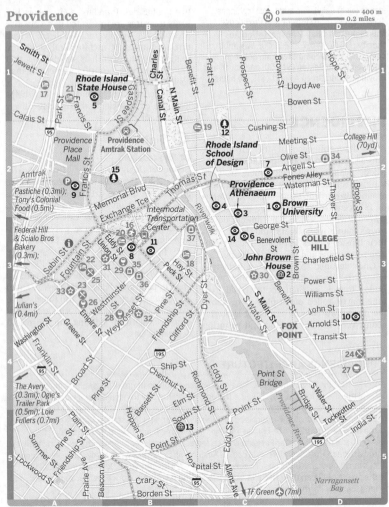

★**Rhode Island**
State House   NOTABLE BUILDING
(☑401-222-2357; www.rilin.state.ri.us; 82 Smith St; ☺tours by appointment) **FREE** Designed by McKim, Mead and White in 1904, the Rhode Island State House rises above the Providence skyline, easily visible from miles around. Modeled in part on St Peter's Basilica in Vatican City, it has the world's fourth-largest self-supporting marble dome and houses one of Gilbert Stuart's portraits of George Washington, which you might want to compare to a dollar bill from your wallet.

★**Brown University**   UNIVERSITY
(www.brown.edu) Dominating the crest of the College Hill neighborhood on the East Side, the campus of Brown University exudes Ivy League charm. **University Hall**, a 1770 brick edifice used as a barracks during the Revolutionary War, sits at its center. To explore the campus, start at the wrought-iron gates opening from the top of College St and make your way across the green toward Thayer St.

Free tours of the campus begin from the **Brown University Admissions Office** (☑401-863-2378; Corliss Brackett House, 45 Prospect St). Call or drop by for times.

Providence

RHODE ISLAND PROVIDENCE

College Hill AREA

East of the Providence River, College Hill contains over 100 Colonial, Federal and Revival houses dating from the 18th century. Stroll down Benefit St's 'Mile of History' for the best examples. Amid them you'll find the clean lines of William Strickland's 1838 Providence Athenaeum (p211), inside which plaster busts of Greek gods and philosophers preside over a collection that dates to 1753.

Culinary Arts Museum MUSEUM

(☑ 401-598-2805; www.culinary.org; 315 Harborside Blvd; adult/child $7/2; ◷ 10am-5pm Tue-Sat; ℗) Johnson & Wales' oddity of a museum displays about 300,000 objects connected in some way to the culinary arts. Ogle a cookbook collection dating back to the 15th century, resist fingering presidential cutlery and peruse over 4000 menus from around the world. To reach the museum, it's a straight shot south on Rte 1 toward Pawtuxet.

Fox Point AREA

South of Providence's College Hill neighborhood is Fox Point, the waterfront area where the city's substantial Portuguese pop-

ulation resides. Though gentrification has brought influxes of professors and artists, you can still find an old-world-style grocery like the **Friends Market** (☑ 401-861-0345; 126 Brook St; ◷ 9:15am-6:15pm Tue-Sat) tucked in among the trendy coffeehouses, salons and galleries. Most activity in Fox Point centers on Wickenden St.

Federal Hill AREA

Among the most colorful of Providence's neighborhoods is fervently Italian Federal Hill (when Tony Soprano's crew needed a special job done, they came here). West of the center, it's a great place to wander, taking in the aromas of sausages, peppers and garlic from neighborhood groceries such as Tony's Colonial Food (p218). Many of Providence's best restaurants are on Atwells Ave.

Roger Williams Park PARK

(1000 Elmwood Ave) **FREE** In 1871, Betsey Williams, great-great-great-granddaughter of the founder of Providence, donated her farm to the city as a public park. Today this 430-acre expanse of greenery, only a short drive south of Providence, includes lakes and ponds, forest copses and broad lawns, picnic grounds, the **Planetarium and Museum of Natural History** (☑401-785-9457; www.providenceri.com/museum; 1000 Elmwood Ave; museum/planetarium $2/3; ☉10am-4pm, planetarium shows 2pm Sat & Sun; ♿), an operating Victorian carousel, greenhouses and Williams' cottage.

The park's main attraction is the **Roger Williams Park Zoo** (www.rwpzoo.org; adult/child $15/10; ☉10am-4pm Oct-Mar, to 5pm Apr-Sep; P♿), which is home to more than 600 animals (polar bears, giraffes, lemurs) and performs some interesting conservation work.

Prospect Terrace Park
PARK

(184 Pratt St) A great spot from which to get an overview of Providence is the elevated, compact green space known as Prospect Terrace Park. In warm weather, you'll find students throwing Frisbees, office workers picnicking and, if you arrive at the transitional point between day and the arrival of night, a sunset view. The monumental statue facing the city is that of Providence founder Roger Williams, whose remains were moved to this site in 1939.

Waterplace Park
PARK

(☑401-621-1992; 1 Financial Way) The landscaped cobblestone paths of Providence's **Riverwalk** lead along the Woonasquatucket River to Waterplace Park's central pool and fountain, overlooked by a stepped amphitheater where outdoor artists perform in warm weather. Take a look at the historical maps and photos mounted on the walls of the walkway beneath Memorial Blvd.

DON'T MISS

EAST BAY BIKE PATH

Starting at India Point Park on the Narragansett Bay waterfront in Providence, this scenic path winds 14.5 miles south along a former railroad track. The mostly flat, paved route follows the shoreline to the pretty seaport of Bristol. State parks along the way make good spots for picnics.

Check out www.dot.ri.gov/bikeri, a website devoted to bicycling in Rhode Island. It has a downloadable map of bikeways throughout the state and other useful information.

Waterplace Park also serves as a nucleus for WaterFire, a summer festival.

Providence Children's Museum
MUSEUM

(☑401-273-5437; www.childrenmuseum.org; 100 South St; $9; ☉9am-6pm Tue-Sun, daily Apr-Labor Day; P) This well-designed, hands-on museum genuinely delights its intended guests, who can enter a giant kaleidoscope, do experiments with water fountains, pretend to be a veterinarian or play with marionettes made by some renowned puppeteers. It's aimed at kids aged one to 11.

🏃 Activities

Providence Rink
ICE SKATING

(☑401-331-5544; www.alexandanicitycenter.com; 2 Kennedy Plaza, Bank of America City Center; adult/child $6/3, skate rental $4; ☉10am-10pm Mon-Fri, 11am-10pm Sat & Sun mid-Nov–mid-Mar; ♿) This outdoor rink at the Bank of America City Center occupies prime downtown real estate. While the Biltmore hotel and Fleet Building provide a nice architectural backdrop, you might have to skate to some seriously loud pop songs. College students skate for $3 on Wednesday night.

🧭 Tours

★ Rhode Island Historical Society
WALKING

(RIHS; ☑401-273-7507; www.rihs.org; tours $5-14; ☉Jun-Oct) The historical society runs guided tours of College Hill's premier historic home, the John Brown House (p211). Other tours include Benefit St's 'Mile of History,' an informed amble on Riverwalk and summer walks along S Main St. All tours leave from outside the John Brown House.

Savoring Rhode Island
FOOD

(☑401-934-2149; www.savoringrhodeisland.com; tours $60; ☉tours 9am) Meet the chefs, bakers and ravioli makers of Federal Hill's historic restaurant row on chef Cindy Salvato's three-hour, behind-the-scenes walking tour. See the tiny kitchen where Venda Ravioli handcrafts hundreds of its namesake ravioli and visit Scialo Bros Bakery, which makes its *sfogliatelle* pastries from scratch each day. Take along a cooler so you can shop as you go.

🎉 Festivals & Events

Festival of Historic Homes
ARCHITECTURE

(www.ppsri.org; ☉Jun) Tour some of Providence's fabulous 18th-century homes during this annual shindig.

WATERFIRE

Over 15 summer nights, beginning at sunset, Providence's landscaped riverfront promenades spring to life with scheduled (and unscheduled) street performers, vendors, food trucks and throngs of onlookers who come to view the spectacle of 100 anchored, flaming braziers illuminating the water, marking the convergence of the Providence, Moshassuck and Woonasquatucket Rivers.

Created by Barnaby Evans in 1994, WaterFire (www.waterfire.org; ⊘ dates vary) has become locals' most loved annual event, celebrating the resurrection of sections of the river and Providence's phoenix-like transformation from a once certain fate of death by industry. Check the homepage for upcoming dates.

Rhode Island International Film Festival FILM
(www.film-festival.org; ⊘ Aug) For five days in August, cool kids from Rhode Island School of Design and beyond screen hundreds of independent shorts and feature-length films.

Gallery Night ART
(www.gallerynight.info) Held every third Thursday of the month from March to November from 5pm to 9pm. Twenty-three galleries and museums around the city open their doors for free viewings. Check out the website before you go and find out where to hop on the shuttle, hook up with a guide or sign up for a free celebrity-guided tour.

🛏 Sleeping

Providence is devoid of hostels and has a limited number of midrange options. The summer months represent peak season, while the big universities' parents' weekends and graduations fill rooms up to a year in advance.

★ The Dean Hotel BOUTIQUE HOTEL $$
(🗹 401-455-3326; www.thedeanhotel.com; 122 Fountain St; d from $109) New kid on the block, The Dean epitomizes all that is design in Providence. A one stop shop with beer hall, karaoke bar, cocktail den and beer hall downstairs, upstairs has eight quirky, personalized design-themed rooms that will be your stylish urban oasis from the fun and frivolity downstairs and beyond. One for the hipsters and the funsters.

★ Hampton Inn & Suites Providence Downtown HOTEL $$
(🗹 401-608-3500; www.hamptoninn.hilton.com; 58 Weybosset St; r $109-249; P 🕾) Occupying the historic Old Colony House on Weybosset St, the Hampton Inn has a superlative Providence location. Although the stand-

ard rooms are comfortable enough, it's the suites that are the winners here, set up like one-bedroom apartments. And you might want to bring your cookbook: each suite has a full refrigerator and microwave. Wi-fi is complimentary.

Providence Biltmore HISTORIC HOTEL $$
(🗹 401-421-0700; www.providencebiltmore.com; 11 Dorrance St; r from $169; P 🕾) The grand-daddy of Providence's hotels, the Biltmore dates to the 1920s. The lobby, both intimate and regal, nicely combines dark wood, twisting staircases and chandeliers, while well-appointed rooms stretch many stories above the old city. Ask for one of the 292 rooms that are on a high floor.

Christopher Dodge House B&B $$
(🗹 401-351-6111; www.providence-hotel.com; 11 W Park St; r $129-189; P) This 1858 Federal-style house is furnished with early American reproduction furniture and marble fireplaces. Austere on the outside, it has elegant proportions, large, shuttered windows and wooden floors.

Old Court B&B INN $$
(🗹 401-751-2002; www.oldcourt.com; 144 Benefit St; r weekday $135-185, weekend $165-215) Well positioned among the historic buildings of College Hill, this three-story, 1863 Italianate home has stacks of charm. Enjoy eccentric wallpaper, good jam at breakfast and occasional winter discounts.

Renaissance Providence Hotel HISTORIC HOTEL $$$
(🗹 401-276-0010; www.marriott.com; 5 Ave of the Arts; r $189-279; P ✳ 🕾) Built as a Masonic temple in 1929, this monster stood empty for 77 years before it opened in 2007 as a hotel. Some rooms overlook the Rhode Island State House and are decorated in forceful colors that attempt, with limited success, to evoke

Masonic traditions. The graffiti artist who once tagged the vacant building was hired to do his thing in the 'Masonic' hotel bar.

✗ Eating

Thanks to RISD and Johnson & Wales University culinary programs, Providence's restaurant scene is booming. The large student population on the East Side ensures plenty of good, inexpensive places exist around Thayer St, College Hill's main drag, and at Fox Point. To experience old Providence, head over to the restaurant district along Atwells Ave in Federal Hill.

Pastiche CAFE $
(☑ 401-861-5190; www.pastichefinedesserts.com; 92 Spruce St; cakes $3-6; ⊙ 8:30am-11pm Tue-Thu, 8:30am-11:30pm Fri & Sat, 10am-10pm Sun) Warmed by a fire in winter, this tiny cafe has a robin's-egg-blue facade, beyond which you'll find the cakes, tarts, pies and desserts for which it is famed.

Scialo Bros Bakery ITALIAN $
(☑ 401-421-0986; www.scialobakery.com; 257 Atwells Ave; sweets $1-3; ⊙ 8am-7pm Mon-Thu & Sat, to 8pm Fri, to 5pm Sun) Since 1916, the brick ovens at this Federal Hill relic have turned out top-notch butterballs, *torrone* (a nougat and almond combo), amaretti, and dozens of other kinds of Italian cookies and pastries. Avoid the mediocre cannoli.

Haven Brothers Diner DINER $
(☑ 401-603-8124; www.havenbrothersmobile.com; cnr Dorrance & Fulton Sts; meals $5-12; ⊙ 5pm-3am) Parked next to City Hall, this diner sits on the back of a truck that has rolled into the same spot every evening for decades. Climb up a rickety ladder to get basic diner fare alongside everyone from prominent politicians to college kids pulling an all-nighter to drunks. The murder burger ($4.50) comes highly recommended.

★Loie Fullers MODERN AMERICAN $$
(☑ 401-273-4375; www.loiefullers.com; 1455 Westminster St; mains $15-21; ⊙ 5-11pm Mon-Sat, 10am-2pm & 5-11pm Sun) This wonderfully original, atmospheric little bistro on the outskirts of the Federal Hill neighborhood is an oasis of fun and deliciousness on an otherwise drab trunk road. Inside, candles, ornate polished woods, frescoes and art nouveau elements transport you to another time, another place. On the French-inspired Modern American menu, comfort is King. Somebody had to let the cat outta the bag...

Local 121 MODERN AMERICAN $$
(☑ 401-274-2121; www.local121.com; 121 Washington St; mains $14-36; ⊙ 5pm-midnight Mon-Fri, from 10am Sat & Sun) Locavore mania comes to Providence with this opulent, old-school restaurant with contemporary aspirations. Housed in the old Dreyfus hotel (built in the 1890s), a building owned by the arts organization AS220, Local 121 has an easy, unpretentious grandeur – and some damn fine food. The menu is seasonal, but recent options include a perfect (local) scallop po'boy and (local) duck ham pizza.

Julian's MODERN AMERICAN $$
(☑ 401-861-1770; www.juliansprovidence.com; 318 Broadway; brunch $6-14, mains $16-28; ⊙ 9am-1am; 🛜📃♿) A messy combination of neon, exposed brick and ductwork in Federal Hill; come here for tattooed cooks preparing a stellar brunch (served until 5pm) changing blackboard specials (goat's cheese, caper, tomato and mushroom hash), along with a variety of poached eggs and plenty of vegetarian- and vegan-friendly options.

★birch MODERN AMERICAN $$$
(☑ 401-272-3105; www.birchrestaurant.com; 200 Washington St; 4-course dinner $49, beverage pairings $35; ⊙ 5-10pm Thu-Mon) With a background at Noma in Copenhagen and the fabulous Dorrance at the Biltmore, chef Benjamin Sukle and his wife, Heidi, have their own place, the understated, but fabulously good birch. Its intimate size and style (seating is around a U-shaped bar) means attention to detail is exacting in both the decor and the food, which focuses on underutilized, small-batch and hyperseasonal produce.

★Chez Pascal FRENCH $$$
(☑ 401-421-4422; www.chez-pascal.com; 960 Hope St; mains $23-30, 3-course bistro menu $40; ⊙ 5:30-9pm Mon-Thu, to 10pm Fri & Sat, Wurst Window 11:30am-2:30pm Tue-Sat) This friendly French bistro welcomes diners with inspiring homemade pâtés and charcuterie, escargots à la bourguignonne, and slow-roasted duck with a golden raisin and red-wine sauce. Sourcing ingredients from local growers, tuck in safe in the knowledge that you'll not only eat well but keep it in the neighborhood. At lunchtime keep it real with a hot dog ($8.50) from the Wurst Window.

🍸 Drinking & Nightlife

A sizable student population courtesy of several high-profile educational institutions ranks Providence's nightlife as second in

New England only to Boston. Finding out what's hot and what's not for yourself is half the fun.

★ **Ogie's Trailer Park** BAR
(☑ 401-383-8200; www.ogiestrailerpark.com; 1155 Westminster St; ☺ 4pm-1am Mon-Sat, noon-1am Sun) This place is just so awesome and unexpected that we almost want to keep it to ourselves. Let's just say that in terms of thematics and design, if you crossed the Brady Bunch with Mad Men with Breaking Bad, you'd be somewhere in the vicinity. Eat, drink and love. If you're boring or rude – go elsewhere.

★ **The Avery** BAR
(www.averyprovidence.com; 18 Luongo Sq; ☺ 4pm-midnight Mon-Fri, 5pm-midnight Sat & Sun) Tucked into a quiet residential neighborhood in West Providence, the Avery is easy to miss. But once inside there's a jaw-droppingly gorgeous varnished wood interior, with backlit art nouveau wood cuttings and an elegant, curved bar that's lit from beneath and lined with black-vinyl stools.

Providence Eagle GAY
(☑ 401-421-1447; www.providenceeagle.com; 124 Snow St; ☺ 5pm-late) For gay men who like their men wearing leather, riding into town on a steer, drinking beer and not talking about changing the curtains because the fabric is just all wrong.

The Salon BAR, CLUB
(www.thesalonpvd.com; 57 Eddy St; ☺ 5pm-1am Tue-Thu, to 2am Fri & Sat) The Salon mixes ping-pong tables and pinball machines with 1980s pop and pickleback shots (whiskey with a pickle juice chaser) upstairs, with live shows, open mike, DJs and dance parties downstairs. If you get hungry, there are PB&J sandwiches.

AS220 CLUB
(☑ 401-831-9327; www.as220.org; 115 Empire St; ☺ bar 5pm-1am) A longstanding outlet for all forms of Rhode Island art, AS220 (say 'A-S-two-twenty') books experimental bands, hosts readings and provides gallery space for a very active community. If you need a cup of coffee, vegan cookie or spinach pie, it also operates a cafe (noon to 10pm) and bar: hours vary.

Coffee Exchange COFFEE
(☑ 401-273-1198; www.sustainablecoffee.com; 207 Wickenden St; ☺ 6:30am-11pm; 🛜) Drink strong coffee at one of the many small tables in this college-town coffeehouse, with thick layers of flyers tacked to the walls and a large roaster lurking behind bean bins (there are 40 or so varieties available).

☆ Entertainment

Check the 'Lifebeat' section in the *Providence Journal* or the *Providence Phoenix* for listings of live music performers, venues and schedules.

Providence Performing Arts Center PERFORMING ARTS
(☑ 401-421-2787; www.ppacri.org; 220 Weybosset St) This popular venue for touring Broadway musicals and other big-name performances is in a former Loew's Theater dating from 1928. It has a lavish art-deco interior.

Cable Car Cinema CINEMA
(☑ 401-272-3970; www.cablecarcinema.com; 204 S Main St; tickets $9) This theater screens offbeat and foreign films. Inside, patrons sit on couches. The attached sidewalk cafe brews excellent coffee and serves sandwiches and baked goods. It's a good place to hang out, even if you aren't catching a flick.

Lupo's Heartbreak Hotel LIVE MUSIC
(☑ 401-331-5876; www.lupos.com; 79 Washington St) Providence's legendary music venue, Lupo's occupies digs in a converted theater, whose age adds historic charm. It hosts national acts (Regina Spektor, Tiger Army, Blonde Redheads) in a relatively small space.

Trinity Repertory Company THEATER
(☑ 401-351-4242; www.trinityrep.com; 201 Washington St; tickets $30-60) Trinity offers classic and contemporary plays *(Some Things are Private, A Christmas Carol)* in the stunning and historic Lederer Theater downtown. It's a favorite try-out space for Broadway productions, and it's not unusual for well-known stars to turn up in a performance. Student discounts available.

🛍 Shopping

Brown University Bookstore BOOKS
(☑ 401-863-3168; http://bookstore.brown.edu; 244 Thayer St; ☺ 9am-6pm Mon-Fri, 10am-6pm Sat, 11am-5pm Sun) Providence's most comprehensive bookstore.

Craftland ARTS & CRAFTS
(☑ 401-272-4285; www.craftlandshop.com; 235 Westminster St; ☺ 11am-6pm; 🛗) Craftland is a great place to shop for souvenirs given that its inventory consists of one-of-a-kind finds from over 150 local artists. Ceramics and jewelry sit alongside handmade soap, prints and kids' toys. Classes and workshops are offered from time to time. Check out the website for details.

Queen of Hearts   FASHION & ACCESSORIES
(☑401-421-1471; www.queenofheartsri.com; 222 Westminster St; ☺11am-6pm Mon-Wed, 11am-8pm Thu-Sat, noon-5pm Sun) Feel the love amid the vibrant and stylish threads in Queen of Hearts, where pieces with individuality and personality are the order of the day. Owned by designer Karen Beebe, the boutique stocks unique footwear (like the hot-pink Adele gladiator sandal), super-cute dresses, sunglasses and belts, many of them locally made and all well priced.

risd|works   ART, HOMEWARES
(☑401-277-4949; www.risdworks.com; 10 Westminster St; ☺10am-5pm Tue-Sun; ☒) RISD maintains several fine galleries. A design showcase is risd|works, a shop displaying an assortment of goods (jewelry, photographic prints, flatware, coffee tables, children's books) made by faculty members and alumni.

Tony's Colonial Food   FOOD
(☑401-621-8675; www.tonyscolonial.com; 311 Atwells Ave; ☺8:30am-6pm) Wander Providence's Federal Hill neighborhood and take in the aromas of sausages, peppers and garlic from neighborhood groceries such as Tony's. Imported olive oil, gourmet pastas and specialty cheeses have kept cooks happy since 1952.

ℹ Information

Providence Visitor Information Center
(☑401-751-1177; www.goprovidence.com; Rhode Island Convention Center, 1 Sabin St; ☺9am-5pm Mon-Sat) Stop by for maps and glossy print propaganda.

ℹ Getting There & Around

Providence is small, pretty and walkable, so once you arrive you'll probably want to get around on foot.

AIR

Green Airport (p210) is in Warwick, about 20 minutes south of Providence. Green is served by most major airlines.

Taxi services include **Airport Taxi** (☑401-737-2868; www.airporttaxiri.com) and **Checker Cab** (☑401-273-2222; www.checkercabri.com).

RIPTA buses 12, 20 and 66 ($2, 20 to 30 minutes) run to the Intermodal Transportation Center in Providence. Service is frequent on weekdays until 11pm. On Saturday and Sunday it is significantly reduced.

BUS

All long-distance buses and most local routes stop at the central **Intermodal Transportation Center** (Kennedy Plaza; ☺6am-8pm). Greyhound (p210) and Peter Pan Bus Lines (p210) have ticket counters inside, and there are maps outlining local services.

RIPTA (www.ripta.com; one way/day pass $2/6) operates two 'trolley' routes. The Green Line runs from the East Side through downtown to Federal Hill. The Gold Line runs from the Marriott hotel south to the hospital via Kennedy Plaza, and stops at the Point St Ferry Dock.

Peter Pan Bus Lines connects Providence and Green Airport with Boston's South Station ($9, one hour, 12 daily) and Boston's Logan International Airport ($21, 70 minutes, 12 daily).

Greyhound buses depart for Boston (from $12, 70 minutes, five daily), New York City (from $39, 3½ to six hours, six daily) and elsewhere.

CAR & MOTORCYCLE

With hills, two interstates and two rivers defining its downtown topography, Providence can be a confusing city to find your way around. Parking can be difficult downtown and near the train station. For a central lot, try the huge garage of the Providence Place mall and get a merchant to validate your ticket. On the East Side, you can usually find street parking easily.

Major car-rental companies have airport and downtown locations.

TRAIN

Amtrak (p210) trains connect Providence with Boston (from $16, 50 minutes) and New York (from $59, three hours). High-speed Acela trains also service Boston and New York.

MBTA commuter rail (p437) connects to Boston ($7, 70 minutes).

BLACKSTONE VALLEY

This attractive river valley in the northeast corner of the state is named for its first European settler, the Reverend William Blackstone, who arrived here in 1635. But it wasn't until the invention of the water-powered spinning jenny, which was brought to the area in the 1790s, that the region really began to boom. Fueled by the Blackstone River, small wool and cotton textile mills proliferated, becoming the valley's dominant industry. Be sure to check out Slater Mill, credited with beginning the Industrial Age.

After the decline of the Rhode Island textile plants, the area fell on hard economic times, but recently, after communities banded together in a concerted effort to repair the natural beauty of the region, Blackstone has become an increasingly popular destination for outdoor enthusiasts.

For the lowdown on this hard-to-pin-down area just outside Providence, focused around Pawtucket, and sections of which are in Massachusetts, visit www.tourblackstone.com.

◎ Sights

★Slater Mill   HISTORIC SITE
(☑401-725-8638; www.slatermill.org; 67 Roosevelt Ave, Pawtucket; adult/child 6-12yr $12/8.50; ☉10am-4pm Tue-Sun May-Oct) Slater Mill has been dubbed the 'Birthplace of the Industrial Revolution' – with good cause. It was here that, in 1793, Samuel Slater built the first successful water-powered cotton-spinning mill in North America, which effectively shaped the world we live in today.

Lincoln Woods State Park   STATE PARK
(☑401-723-7892; www.riparks.com; 2 Manchester Print Works Rd, Lincoln; ☉sunrise-sunset) A short drive (or bike ride) north of Providence, Lincoln Woods State Park has 627 acres of beautifully maintained grounds, extensive hiking trails, 92 picnic sites and two game fields. The lake-sized Olney Pond has a wide sandy beach and rocky outcroppings for diving into the water or lounging in the sun. There are also boat and kayak rentals, and a lifeguard's on duty during swimming season. In winter, ice skating, snowmobiling and ice fishing are popular.

❶ Information

Blackstone Valley Visitor Center (☑401-724-2200; www.tourblackstone.com; 175 Main St, Pawtucket; ☉10am-5pm Mon-Fri, to 4pm Sat & Sun) The Blackstone Valley Visitor Center is a good resource for information on the area, including events, maps and information on the 48-mile Blackstone River Bikeway, which will eventually lead all the way to Worcester, MA.

❶ Getting There & Away

The Blackstone Valley is centered around Pawtucket, which feels like a suburb of Providence (5 miles). From Newport (38 miles) take I-95 north.

THE EAST BAY

Rhode Island's jagged East Bay captures the early American story in microcosm, from the graves of early settlers in Little Compton, to the farmsteads and merchant homes of whalers and farmers in Warren and Barrington, and the mansions of slave traders in Bristol.

Aside from Barrington's historic and picturesque Tyler Point Cemetery, set between the Warren and Barrington Rivers, and Warren's clutch of early stone and clapboard churches (built in the 18th and 19th centuries), the most interesting of the three communities is Bristol. Further south is Sakonnet, the Wampanoag's 'Place of Black Geese,' a rural landscape of pastures and woods centred around the two tiny communities of Tiverton and Little Compton.

Bristol
POP 22,954

One fifth of all slaves transported to the USA were brought in Bristol ships and by the 18th century the town was one of the country's major commercial and shipbuilding ports. Today it's somewhere you drive through between Providence and Newport, though it does have some interesting museums and the highly regarded Colt State Park.

◎ Sights

Colt State Park   STATE PARK
(www.riparks.com; RI 114; ☉8:30am-4:30pm; Ⓟ) Bristol's Colt State Park is Rhode Island's most scenic park, with its entire western border fronting Narragansett Bay, fringed by 4 miles of cycling trails and shaded picnic tables.

Blithewold Mansion   HISTORIC BUILDING
(☑401-253-2707; www.blithewold.org; 101 Ferry Rd; adult/child $11/3; ☉10am-4pm Tue-Sun mid-Apr–Oct; Ⓟ) Local resident Angustus Van Wickle bought a 72ft Herreshoff yacht for his wife Bessie in 1895, but having nowhere suitable to moor it, he then had to build Blithewold Mansion. The arts-and-crafts mansion sits in a peerless position on Narragansett Bay and is particularly lovely in spring, when the daffodils line the shore.

Herreshoff Marine Museum   MUSEUM
(☑401-253-5000; www.herreshoff.org; 1 Burnside St; adult/child $10/free; ☉10am-5pm May-Oct; ♿) The world-class Herreshoff Marine Museum showcases some of the country's finest yachts, including eight built for the America's Cup. Featuring the America's Cup Hall of Fame and a fascinating display of boat-building techniques, there's something of interest here, even if you aren't much of a mariner.

Linden Place   HISTORIC BUILDING
(☑401-253-0390; www.lindenplace.org; 500 Hope St; adult/child $8/6; ☉10am-4pm Thu-Sat May-Oct; Ⓟ) Built by General George DeWolf,

this beautiful Federal-style historic home houses a small local history museum and is a popular spot for weddings. It gained popular attention after featuring in the 1974 classic *The Great Gatsby* and has been visited by four presidents of the USA.

ℹ️ Getting There & Away

RI 114 links Providence and Newport. Bristol is smack bang in the middle.

Tiverton

POP 15,780

The sprawling community of Tiverton stretches out lazily alongside the Sakonnet River, with views of distant sailing vessels and Aquidneck Island. The further south you explore on RI 77, the prettier the landscape becomes with ramshackle farm stands selling fresh produce, rolling fields extending in all directions and tantalizing flashes of the ocean in the distance.

A rare traffic light marks Tiverton's historic Four Corners (www.tivertonfourcorners.com). This crossroads represents the hub of the community where shops, restaurants and provision stores cluster.

🍴 Eating

Gray's Ice Cream   ICE CREAM $
(📞 401-624-4500; www.graysicecream.com; 16 East Rd; scoops from $3; ⊘ 7am-7pm) In business since 1923, Gray's Ice Cream makes over 40 flavors of fresh dairy ice cream, onsite daily. Stop by for a coffee cabinet (milkshake with ice cream), as beachgoers have been doing for decades.

★ Boat House   SEAFOOD $$
(📞 401-624-6300; www.boathousetiverton.com; 227 Schooner Dr; mains $18-42; ⊘ 11:30am-9pm; P) If you're looking for a good all-rounder, it's hard to fault the boat house for its fresh,

locally sourced and inventively prepared seafood and produce, reasonable prices and a magnificent setting on the banks of the Sakonnet River. Indoor and alfresco diners all enjoy the fantastic views and killer sunsets. A classic New England experience.

🛍️ Shopping

As a long-established artists colony, Tiverton has some lovely boutiques and galleries where you might just find that special one-off item to memorialize your trip.

ℹ️ Getting There & Away

To reach Tiverton from Providence (26 miles) take I-95 south and connect with RI 24. For Newport (15 miles), take RI 24 over the Sakonnet Bridge, then follow RI 114 south.

Little Compton

POP 3492

Fiercely protected by its close-knit community, and often overlooked for its lack of 'attractions,' Little Compton is one of the oldest and loveliest villages in New England.

As you drive south from Tiverton, the large wood-framed homes become older, grayer and statelier, just as an increasing number of stone walls crisscross the green landscape with its hand-hewn clapboard houses and the white-steepled United Congregational Church overlooking the Old Commons Burial Ground. Here, Elizabeth Padobie, daughter of *Mayflower* pilgrims Priscilla and John Alden and the first settler born in New England, is buried.

Though many are content just driving or biking around town, a pair of beaches also competes for your attention. To find them, turn right after arriving at the United Congregational Church, continue to Swamp Rd, make a left and head for the water.

RHODE ISLAND TIVERTON

WORTH A TRIP

PRUDENCE ISLAND

Idyllic **Prudence Island** (📞 401-683-0430; www.prudencebayislandstransport.com; ⊘ 6am-6pm Mon-Fri, to 4pm Sat & Sun) sits in the middle of Narragansett Bay, an easy 25-minute ferry ride (adult/child $5.40/1.90) from Bristol. Originally used for farming and later as a summer vacation spot for families from Providence and New York, who traveled here on the Fall River Line Steamer, the island now has only 88 inhabitants. There are some fine Victorian and beaux-arts houses near Stone Wharf, a lighthouse and a small store, but otherwise it's wild and unspoiled. Perfect for mountain biking, barbecues, fishing and paddling.

COFFEE MILK & CABINETS

In 1993, two popular beverages battled each other for the honor of becoming Rhode Island's official state drink: coffee milk and Del's frozen lemonade.

Though Del's tastes great, no one really doubted that coffee milk would come out on top. Rhode Island kids have guzzled this mixture of coffee syrup and milk since before the Great Depression. To try it, head to a grocery store, pick up a bottle and go to town.

While we've got your attention, please note this crucially important distinction: in Rhode Island, a milkshake is traditionally syrup and milk blended together without ice cream. Rhode Islanders call the version with ice cream a 'cabinet' or 'frappe.' (The term 'cabinet' is pretty much specific to Rhode Island, while 'frappe' gets thrown around by folks as far away as Boston.)

🛏 Sleeping & Eating

Stone House Inn　　　　　HISTORIC INN $$$
(☑ 401-635-2222; 122 Sakonnet Point Rd; d from $295; P🐾) When this unashamedly up-market inn opened its doors in 2016, Little Compton's notoriously private elite feared it meant the out-of-towners were coming. With only 13 rooms (lavish as they may be), it's hardly cause for an invasion. If you have cash and the inclination, this is your chance to take a peek at how the other half live.

Listed on the National Register of Historic Places, the building once housed an inn and speakeasy before it fell by the wayside. Today, with its own private yacht, luxurious spa, taproom and service from the good-ole-days, the unique inn is a destination in itself, within a very special, very sheltered and beautiful historic New England cloister.

★ Commons Lunch　　　　　DINER $$
(☑ 401-635-4388; 48 Commons; mains $10-20; ☺ 6am-7pm) Serving local old-world classics such as New England corned beef and cabbage and quahog stuffies (stuffed clams), New Englanders come from far and wide for the Johnny cakes (a kind of flat cornmeal pancake), which have been a Little Compton breakfast staple for centuries.

ⓘ Getting There & Away

Little Compton is at the end of the road. Take RI 77 south from Tiverton (10 miles).

NEWPORT

POP 24,700

Established by religious moderates, 'new port' flourished in the independent colony of Rhode Island, which declared itself a state here in 1776. Downtown, shutterbugs snap excitedly at immaculately preserved Colonial-era architecture and landmarks at seemingly every turn.

Fascinating as Newport's early history is, the real intrigue began in the late 1850s, when wealthy industrialists began building opulent summer residences along cliff-top Bellevue Ave. Impeccably styled on Italianate palazzos, French châteaus and Elizabethan manor houses, these gloriously restored mansions filled with priceless antiques and their breathtaking location must be seen to be believed. The curiosity, variety, extravagance and uniqueness of this spectacle is unrivaled.

Honoring its maritime roots, Newport remains a global center for yachting. Put simply, summers here go off: locals have excellent taste and know how to throw a shindig. There's always something going on, including a series of cross-genre festivals that are among the best in the US.

⦿ Sights

◉ Downtown

Downtown Newport's main north–south commercial streets are America's Cup Ave and Thames (that's 'thaymz,' not 'temz') St, which teems with restaurants, bars and weekend crowds. There are public toilets at the entrance to the parking lot at Bowen's Wharf. While downtown, be sure to notice the lanterns on Pelham St, the first street in the USA illuminated by gas (1805).

Bannister's Wharf　　　　　WATERFRONT
(Map p224) This quaint olde-y worlde-y wharf and marina has the added excitement of a small mall touting souvenirs and tourist 'stuff,' blending in to the old city by virtue of its liberal use of grey shingles.

Newport Area

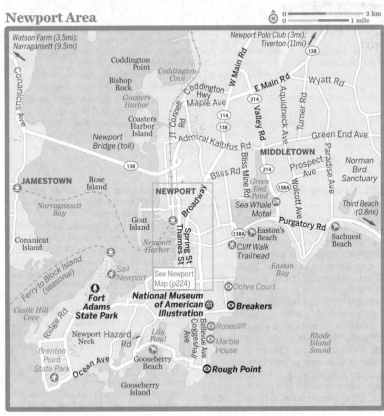

Bowen's Wharf WATERFRONT
(Map p224) Typifying Newport's transformation from working seaport to tourist town, this outdoor mall houses fudge shops and clothing stores alongside fishing boats and pleasure vessels.

Wanton-Lyman-Hazard House HISTORIC SITE
(Map p224; ☑ 401-841-8770; www.newporthistorical.org; 17 Broadway; tours $8) For some serious timber framing, visit the oldest surviving house in Newport, constructed c 1697. Used as a residence by colonial governors and well-to-do residents, it's now a museum of colonial Newport history operated by the Newport Historical Society. Check the online schedule for guided tours.

Touro Synagogue
National Historic Site SYNAGOGUE
(Map p224; ☑ 401-847-4794; www.tourosynagogue.org; 85 Touro St; adult/child $12/free; ⊙noon-1.30pm Sun-Fri May-Jun, 10am-4pm Sun-Fri Jul & Aug, to 1:30pm Sun-Fri Sep-Oct, noon-1.30pm Sun Nov-Apr) Designed by Peter Harrison (architect of the Athenaeum and King's Chapel, Boston), this synagogue is the finest example of 18th-century Georgian architecture in Newport. Its large glass windows illuminate an interior that treads the line between austere and lavish. Built by the nascent Sephardic Orthodox Congregation Yeshuat Israel in 1763, it has the distinction of being North America's oldest synagogue.

Trinity Church CHURCH
(Map p224; ☑ 401-846-0660; www.trinitynewport.org; Queen Anne Sq; suggested donation $5; ⊙10am-4pm Mon-Fri, to 3pm Sat mid-Jun–mid-Oct, 11am-2pm May–mid-Jun) On Queen Anne Sq, Trinity follows the design canon of Sir Christopher Wren's Palladian churches in London. Built between 1725 and 1726, it has a fine wineglass-shaped pulpit, Tiffany stained glass, traditional box pews (warmed by the bottoms of many celebrity guests including

George Washington, Queen Elizabeth II and Archbishop Desmond Tutu) and an organ once played by Handel.

Tours also run year-round right after the Sunday service (around 11am).

Whitehorne Museum
MUSEUM

(Map p224; ☑401-847-2448; www.newportrestoration.org; 416 Thames St; guided/self-guided tour/child $12/6/free; ⊙11am-3pm Thu-Mon May-Oct) A few decades ago, colonial Newport was decaying and undervalued. Enter Doris Duke, who used her huge fortune to preserve many of the buildings that now attract people to the city. One of them is Whitehorne, a Federal period estate. Rooms contain a collection of extraordinary furniture crafted by Newport's famed cabinetmakers, including pieces by Goddard and Townsend.

Museum of Yachting
MUSEUM

(Map p224; MoY; ☑401-848-5777; www.iyrs.edu; 449 Thames St; ⊙noon-5pm Tue-Sat May-Oct) Head inside this bad-boy museum in the 1831 Aquidneck Mill for a collection of model yachts, a handful of craft being restored by an on-site restoration school, and pictures of the New York Yacht Club winning the America's Cup regatta for 130 consecutive years until Australia ruined sporting history's longest winning streak in 1983.

Museum of Newport History
MUSEUM

(Map p224; ☑401-841-8770; www.newporthistory.org; 127 Thames St; adult/child $4/2; ⊙10am-4pm) Newport's excellent local history museum brings the city's fascinating history to life.

◉ Bellevue Avenue

During the 19th century, the wealthiest New York bankers and business families chose Newport as their summer playground, building their fabulous mansions along Bellevue Ave. Ten of the mansions (not including Rough Point or Ochre Court) are under the management of the **Preservation Society** (Map p224; ☑401-847-1000; www.newportmansions.org; 424 Bellevue Ave; 5-site ticket adult/child $33/11), and are open seasonally between June and November. Some are open year-round. Combination tickets are better value if you intend visiting several of the properties, and some tours require advance booking, which is advisable during high season. Tickets can be purchased online or on-site. The society also offers a range of food- and wine-themed events.

Alternatively, hire a bike and cruise along Bellevue Ave enjoying the view of the man-

sions and their grounds or saunter along the famed Cliff Walk (p228), a pedestrian path that runs along the headland between the mansions and their sea view.

★ Redwood Athenaeum
LIBRARY

(Map p224; ☑401-847-0292; www.redwoodlibrary.org; 50 Bellevue Ave; ⊙9:30am-5:30pm Mon-Wed, Fri & Sat, to 8pm Thu, 1-5pm Sun; P) FREE Founded by Abraham Redwood in 1747 as an important archive of American history and architecture, the neoclassical structure was built by Peter Harrison who the library honors with a room devoted to priceless American portraiture. There's also a gallery with revolving exhibits and a quiet reading room, and a series of genteel concerts and garden parties is held here. Guided tours run at 2pm every day (adult/child $5/free).

Newport Museum of Art
GALLERY

(Map p224; ☑401-848-8200; www.newportartmuseum.org; 76 Bellevue Ave; adult/child $10/free; ⊙10am-4pm Tue-Sat) This vibrant city art museum holds changing exhibitions and workshops throughout the year.

International Tennis Hall of Fame
MUSEUM

(Map p224; ☑401-849-3990; www.tennisfame.com; 194 Bellevue Ave; adult/child $15/free; ⊙10am-5pm) To experience something of the American aristocracy's approach to 19th-century leisure, visit this museum. It lies inside the historic Newport Casino building (1880), which served as a summer club for Newport's wealthiest residents. The US National Lawn Tennis Championships (forerunner of today's US Open tennis tournament) were held here in 1881. A scavenger hunt, available at reception, gets kids engaged with eight centuries of tennis.

If you brought your whites, playing on one of its 13 grass courts (closed in winter) remains a delightful throwback to earlier times ($110 for two people for one hour). Otherwise have a drink lawnside at the La Forge Casino Restaurant (lunch menu $30 to $35).

Audrain Automobile Museum
MUSEUM

(Map p224; ☑401-856-4420; www.audrainautomuseum.org; 222 Bellevue Ave; adult/student $12/8; ⊙10am-4pm) Little kids and big kids alike ooh and ahh at this museum, which from the outside looks like a luxury car dealership. A rotating selection from the museum's collection of over 160 of history's rarest vehicles, from Hummers to Lamborghinis, is displayed inside.

Newport

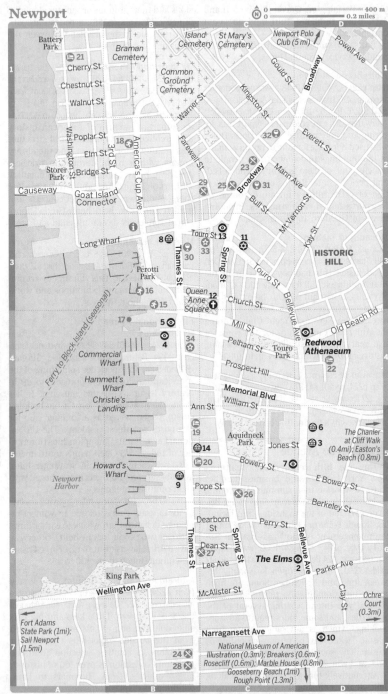

Newport

Kingscote
MANSION

(Map p224; ☑ 401-847-1000; 253 Bellevue Ave; adult/child $16/7; ☻10am-5pm Jul–mid-Oct; P) An Elizabethan fantasy complete with Tiffany glass, Kingscote was Newport's first 'cottage' strictly for summer use, designed by Richard Upjohn in 1841 for George Noble Jones of Savannah, GA. It was later bought by China-trade merchant William H King, who gave the house its name.

★ The Elms
MANSION

(Map p224; ☑ 401-847-1000; www.newportmansions.org; 367 Bellevue Ave; adult/child $16/7, servant life tour adult/child $15/5; ☻9am-5pm Apr–mid-Oct, hours vary mid-Oct–Mar; P♿) Designed by Horace Trumbauer in 1901, the Elms is a replica of Château d'Asnières, built near Paris in 1750. Here you can take a 'behind-the-scenes' tour that will have you snaking through the servants' quarters and up onto the roof. Along the way you'll learn about the activities of the army of servants and the architectural devices that kept them hidden from the view of those drinking port in the formal rooms.

Taking the regular tour in addition to the behind-the-scenes variant will give you the best idea of how a Newport mansion functioned, although it is exhausting. Advance reservations are required.

Ochre Court
MANSION

(Map p222; ☑ 401-847-6650; www.salve.edu; 100 Ochre Point Ave; ☻9am-4pm Mon-Fri) FREE Designed by Richard Morris Hunt and built in 1892, Ochre Court offers a grand view of the sea from its soaring three-story hallway. Elsewhere you can find a rainbow of stained glass, pointed arches, gargoyles and other emblems of an architecture inspired by a medieval (and mythical) French Gothic. Ochre Court now houses the administration of Salve Regina University, and as such provides an interesting example of the repurposing of a Newport mansion.

★ National Museum of American Illustration
MUSEUM

(Map p222; ☑ 401-851-8949; www.americanillustration.org; 492 Bellevue Ave; adult/child $18/8; ☻11am-5pm Thu-Mon May-Sep, 11am-5pm Fri & by reservation Mon-Thu Oct-Apr; P) This acclaimed museum features an impressive collection of Maxfield Parrish's impossibly luminous works in color, NC Wyeth prints, Norman Rockwell's nostalgia and the illustrations of other American graphic heavyweights. If you can, take the free guided tour on Friday (3pm; available year-round), which sheds light on the stories behind the images and how they molded American culture through the decades.

DON'T MISS

NEWPORT'S BEST BEACHES

Newport's public beaches are on the eastern side of the peninsula along Memorial Blvd. All are open 9am to 6pm in summer and charge a parking fee of $10/20 on weekdays/weekends (except for Gooseberry Beach, which charges $20 all week for parking).

Easton Beach (Map p222; First Beach; Memorial Blvd) This is the largest beach with a pseudo-Victorian pavilion containing bathhouses and showers, a snack bar and a large carousel. You can rent umbrellas, chairs and surf boards at the pavilion.

Sachuest Beach (Map p222; Second Beach; ☑ 401-846-6273) The most beautiful beach on Aquidneck Island curves around Sachuest Bay and is backed by the 450-acre Norman Bird Sanctuary.

Third Beach (☑ 401-847-1993) Popular with families because it is protected from the open ocean. Third Beach also appeals to windsurfers because the water is calm and the winds steady.

Gooseberry Beach (Map p222; 130 Ocean Ave; ☺ 9am-5pm) Calm waters, white sand and a restaurant.

The museum is housed within the palatial Vernon Court (yet another mansion, this one from 1898) set within Olmstead-designed grounds.

★ **Breakers** MANSION
(Map p222; ☑ 401-847-1000; www.newportmansions.org; 44 Ochre Point Ave; adult/child $21/7; ☺ 9am-5pm Apr–mid-Oct, hours vary mid-Oct–Mar; P) A 70-room Italian Renaissance mega-palace inspired by 16th-century Genoese palazzos, Breakers is the most magnificent Newport mansion. At the behest of Cornelius Vanderbilt II, Richard Morris Hunt did most of the design (though craftsmen from around the world perfected the decorative program). The building was completed in 1895 and sits at Ochre Point, on a grand oceanside site. The furnishings, most made expressly for the Breakers, are all original. Don't miss the **Children's Cottage** on the grounds.

Admission also includes entry into the **Breakers' Stable & Carriage House** (53 Coggeshall Ave; ☺ 9am-5pm Apr–mid-Oct, hours vary mid-Oct–Mar), also designed by Hunt, on the west side of Bellevue Ave.

Rosecliff MANSION
(Map p222; ☑ 401-847-1000; 548 Bellevue Ave; adult/child $16/7; ☺ 9am-4pm Apr–mid-Oct, hours vary mid-Oct–Mar; P) Built for Mrs Hermann Oelrichs, an heiress of the Comstock Lode silver treasure, Stanford White designed Rosecliff to look like the Grand Trianon at Versailles, and its palatial ballroom (Newport's largest) and landscaped grounds quickly became the setting for some truly enormous parties. Houdini entertained at one.

If the building seems oddly familiar during your visit, that might be because it has appeared in films such as the 1974 *Great Gatsby, Amistad* and *High Society*. In June the Newport Flower Festival is held here.

Marble House MANSION
(Map p222; ☑ 401-847-1000; 596 Bellevue Ave; adult/child $16/7; ☺ 10am-5pm; P) Designed by Richard Morris Hunt and built in 1892 for William K Vanderbilt, the younger brother of Cornelius II, the gaudy Marble House – built of many kinds of garishly colored marble – is a whorish building whose inspiration was drawn from the palace of Versailles. It comes complete with custom furnishings styled after the era of Louis XIV.

★ **Rough Point** MANSION
(Map p222; ☑ 401-849-7300; www.newportrestoration.com; 680 Bellevue Ave; adult/child $25/free; ☺ 10am-2pm Thu-Sat mid-Apr–mid-May, 10am-3:45pm Tue-Sun mid-May–mid-Nov; P) While the peerless position and splendor of the grounds alone are worth the price of admission, this faux-English manor house also contains heiress and philanthropist Doris Duke's impressive art holdings, including medieval tapestries, furniture owned by French emperors, Ming dynasty ceramics, and paintings by Renoir and Van Dyck.

Built in 1889 by Frederick W Vanderbilt on a rocky bluff jutting out into the ocean, Rough Point was later purchased by tobacco baron James B Duke, and passed to his only daughter, Doris (then aged 12), in 1925 along with his $80 million fortune. Throughout her teenage years Doris spent her summers here, and as an adult Rough Point was one of her favorite houses.

The contents of the house are exactly as she left them at the time of her death in 1993, when she bequeathed the house to the Newport Restoration Society (which she founded) with the directive that it be opened as a museum. Particularly interesting is a glassed-in sunroom containing just about the only pedestrian furniture (the couch appears to be from a department store). Also on hand are mannequins wearing some of Duke's eight decades of bizarro clothing.

◎ Parks

★ Fort Adams State Park   STATE PARK
(Map p222; www.fortadams.org; Harrison Ave; fort tours adult guided/self-guided $12/6, child $6/3; ☺ sunrise-sunset) Fort Adams is America's largest coastal fortification and is the centerpiece of this gorgeous state park, which juts out into Narragansett Bay. It's the venue for the Newport jazz and folk festivals and numerous special events. A beach, picnic and fishing areas and a boat ramp are open daily.

Brenton Point State Park   STATE PARK
(Map p222; ☑ 401-849-4562; Ocean Ave; ☺ dawn-dusk) On the southwesternmost tip of Aquidneck Island (now officially known as Rhode Island, although both names are used), this park is a prime place for exploring rocky outcrops, feeling like you're on the periphery and for flying kites.

Norman Bird Sanctuary   WILDLIFE RESERVE
(Map p222; ☑ 401-846-2577; www.normanbird sanctuary.org; 583 Third Beach Rd; adult/child $6/3; ☺ 9am-5pm) Established in 1949, this nature sanctuary works to protect the habitat of the area's abundant bird and plant life and runs various educational tours throughout the year.

☩ Activities

Newport is a great place to cycle, with only a few gentle slopes. A scenic and satisfying ride is the 10-mile loop around Ocean Ave, which includes Bellevue Ave and its many beautiful mansions.

Ten Speed Spokes   CYCLING
(Map p224; ☑ 401-847-5609; www.tenspeed spokes.com; 18 Elm St; hybrid per hr/3 days/week $7/65/90; ☺ 10am-6pm Mon-Fri, 10am-5pm Sat, noon-5pm Sun, shorter hours winter) Rents regular bikes as well as hybrids and offers free use of helmets and locks.

Newport Vineyards   WINE
(☑ 401-848-5161; www.newportvineyards.com; 909 East Main Rd, Middletown; ☺ tours 1pm & 3pm daily) Tours of the vineyards aren't only the main reason to stop by. There are wine tastings, a marketplace, a restaurant and bakery.

⬙ Courses

★ Sail Newport   BOATING
(Map p222; ☑ 401-846-1983; www.sailnewport.org; 60 Fort Adams Dr; instruction 6hr from $150, sailboat rental per 3hr from $79; ☺ 9am-7pm; ⬛) As you'd expect in the hometown of the prestigious America's Cup, the sailing in breezy Newport is phenomenal. Sail Newport offers intermediate and advanced youth and adult courses. The minimum age is seven years.

⬐ Tours

If you'd rather go on your own, the Newport Historical Society (www.newporthistorical. org) has devised a plethora of self-directed walking tours corresponding to mapped, QR coded signs describing many of the prominent and historic buildings at each location.

RHODE ISLAND NEWPORT

LOCAL KNOWLEDGE

POLO IN PORTSMOUTH

Drab though the urban environs may seem, in-the-know locals rate Portsmouth as a family-friendly destination. Not least because the polo matches hosted at Glen Farm make for a great family day out. Home to the **Newport Polo Club** (☑ 401-846-0200; www.nptpolo.com; 250 Linden Lane, Portsmouth; lawn seats adult/child $12/free; ☺ gates open 1pm), the 700-acre 'farm' was assembled by New York businessman Henry Taylor, who sought to create a gentleman's country seat in the grand English tradition. Every Saturday between June and September, the farm is host to the club's polo matches, which make a perfect way to enjoy the property and get an authentic taste of Newport highlife.

Bring a picnic basket for a field-side tailgate and watch the US team take on Egypt, Jamaica and other Olympic-caliber squads. Crowds aren't large and you'll be close enough to hear snorting horses and walloping mallets.

CLIFF WALK

In 1975, eager to protect their privacy, Newport's mansion owners sought to close Cliff Walk (www.cliffwalk.com), the public footpath that snakes along the cliff top overlooking their front lawns. The move was prevented by local fishermen and the 3.5-mile path was designated a National Recreation Trail. The best section runs from Ledge Rd near Rough Point to the Forty Steps (each one named for someone lost at sea) on Narragansett Ave.

There is metered parking on Narragansett Ave from 6am to 9pm ($1.25 per hour). There's a four-hour limit. Many favor this entry point because it shaves the first half-mile off the walk (which is pretty, but lacks mansions).

Newport History Tours   WALKING
(☑ 401-841-8770; www.newporthistorytours.org; Brick Market Museum & Shop, 127 Thames St; tours adult/child $12/5; ⊙ tour times vary; ▥) Newport History Tours will guide you on a walking tour of Historic Hill. Periodically, the society offers themed heritage tours, where you'll learn about 'Pirates & Scoundrels,' or Jewish or African American history. Tours begin at 10am or 11am at the Museum of Newport History (p223).

★ America's Cup Charters   BOATING
(Map p224; ☑ 401-846-9886; www.americascup charters.com; 49 America's Cup Ave, Newport Harbor Hotel Marina; sunset tour per adult/child $75/40; ⊙ May-Sep; ▥) Take the ultimate waterborne tour aboard a 12m, America's Cup racing yacht. Ticketed, two-hour sunset sails and private charters are available daily in season and offer an unforgettably thrilling experience.

Classic Cruises of Newport   BOATING
(Map p224; ☑ 401-847-0298; www.cruisenewport. com; Bannister's Wharf; adult/child from $25/20; ⊙ mid-May–mid-Oct) Runs excursions on the *Rum Runner II,* a Prohibition-era bootlegging vessel, and *Madeleine,* a 72ft schooner. The narrated tour will take you past mansions and former speakeasies.

Adirondack II   CRUISE
(Map p224; ☑ 401-217-0044; www.sail-newport. com; Bowen's Wharf; 1½hr cruise from $32; ⊙ 11am-7pm) This schooner sails from Bowen's Wharf five times a day.

★☆ Festivals & Events

If you plan to attend any of Newport's major festivals, make sure you reserve accommodations and tickets in advance (tickets usually go on sale in mid-May). For a full schedule of events, see www.discovernew port.org.

Newport Music Festival   MUSIC
(www.newportmusic.org; tickets $30-45; ⊙ mid-Jul) This internationally regarded festival offers classical music concerts in many of the great mansions.

**International Tennis
Hall of Fame Championships**   SPORTS
(☑ 401-849-6053; www.halloffametennischampion ships.com; tickets from $55; ⊙ Jul) For a week in July, Wimbledon comes to Newport with top athletes competing on the famed grass courts.

Newport Folk Festival   MUSIC
(www.newportfolk.org; Fort Adams State Park; 1-/3-day pass $49/120, parking $18; ⊙ late Jul) Big-name stars and up-and-coming groups perform at Fort Adams State Park and other venues around town. Bring sunscreen.

Newport Jazz Festival   JAZZ
(www.newportjazzfest.org; Fort Adams State Park; tickets $40-85, 3 days $155; ⊙ Jul/Aug) This classic festival usually takes place on an August weekend, with concerts at the Newport Casino and Fort Adams State Park. Popular shows can sell out a year in advance.

Newport International Boat Show   SAILING
(www.newportboatshow.com; Newport Yachting Center, 4 Commercial Wharf; adult $18-27, child free, parking $15; ⊙ Sep) Held in mid-September, this is one of the largest in-water boat shows in the country featuring 850 exhibitors.

⊨ Sleeping

Downtown accommodations often require a two-night minimum stay on summer weekends and a three-night minimum on holidays, when rates are at the high end of expensive. Off-season, excellent discount rates can be found if you can be flexible.

As rooms can be scarce in summer, you might want to use a reservation service. B&B of Newport (www.newporttribed andbreakfast.com) and Taylor-Made Reservations (☑ 401-847-6820; www.citybythesea. com) together represent about 400 establishments in the Newport area.

Bay Willows Inn
MOTEL **$**

(☑401-847-8400; 1225 Aquidneck Ave, Middletown; d from $55; ℗⊜) The friendly, most recent managers of this privately operated mid-last-century motel have done an excellent job in bringing it back to respectability. Rooms have had basic updates and are spacious, tastefully furnished, feature minimal chintz and lack cheap shortcuts. Bedding, shower pressure and wi-fi all make the grade. Great rates make it worth checking out.

Newport International Hostel
HOSTEL **$**

(Map p224; William Gyles Guesthouse; ☑401-369-0243; www.newporthostel.com; 16 Howard St; dm $40-70; ⊜Apr-Dec; ⊜) Book as early as you can to get in to Rhode Island's only hostel, run by an informal and knowledgeable host. The tiny guesthouse contains fixings for a simple breakfast, a laundry machine and spare, clean digs in a dormitory room.

Sea Whale Motel
MOTEL **$$**

(Map p222; ☑888-257-4096; www.seawhale.com; 150 Aquidneck Ave, Middletown; d $109-279; ℗⊜) This owner-occupied motel is a lovely place to stay with rooms facing Easton's Pond and flowers hung about the place everywhere. Rooms have little style, but are comfortable and neat with fridges, microwaves, and tea and coffee provided. Everything is within easy walking distance and the owner is a fount of information and recommendations.

Stella Maris Inn
INN **$$**

(Map p224; ☑401-849-2862; www.stellamarisinn.com; 91 Washington St; d $125-255; ℗) This quiet, stone-and-frame inn has numerous fireplaces, heaps of black-walnut furnishings, Victorian bric-a-brac and some floral upholstery. Rooms with garden views rent for less than those overlooking the water. The owner can be a bit gruff, but the prices are good (for Newport, that is). Oddly, it doesn't accept credit cards.

Francis Malbone House
INN **$$**

(Map p224; ☑401-846-0392; www.malbone.com; 392 Thames St; d $155-275; ℗⊜) This grand brick mansion was designed by the Touro Synagogue's architect and built in 1760 for a shipping merchant. Now beautifully decorated and immaculately kept with a lush garden, it is one of Newport's finest inns. Some guest rooms have working fireplaces, as do the public areas. Afternoon tea is included.

★Castle Hill Inn
INN **$$$**

(☑888-466-1355; www.castlehillinn.com; 590 Ocean Ave; d $385-845) Occupying a landmark Victorian mansion with 40 acres of waterfront land overlooking the mouth of Narragansett Bay, a short drive from Newport, this celebrated upscale inn has a variety of luxurious rooms and suites individually furnished in New England country chic. Lovelier still are the handful of secluded, semi-private cottages on the water's edge, great for romancin'.

★The Chanler at Cliff Walk
BOUTIQUE HOTEL **$$$**

(www.thechanler.com; r $300-660; ℗⊜❋⊜) Don't pull up in less than a BMW at this beautiful boutique hotel, worthy of its place on any 'Best Hotels' list. Affording a remarkable cliff-top position, the Chanler is a gorgeous 19th-century restored mansion boasting 20 sumptuous and exclusive guest rooms, immaculate gardens and first-class service; truly a destination hotel worth every penny.

★The Attwater
BOUTIQUE HOTEL **$$$**

(Map p224; ☑401-846-7444; www.theattwater.com; 22 Liberty St; r from $269; ℗❋⊜) Newport's newest hotel has the bold attire of a mid-summer beach party with turquoise, lime green and coral prints, ikat headboards and snazzily patterned geometric rugs. Picture windows and porches capture the summer light and rooms come furnished with thoughtful luxuries, like iPads, Apple TV and beach bags. There's no in-house restaurant, but the bistro serves French press coffee all day and the breakfast buffet is heaped with *brioche au chocolat*, corn muffins and ginger molasses cookies.

✖ Eating

From June through September make reservations and show up on time or lose your spot. Many Newport restaurants don't accept credit cards; ask about payment when you reserve. The widest selection of restaurants is along lower Thames St.

★Rosemary & Thyme Cafe
BAKERY, CAFE **$**

(Map p224; ☑401-619-3338; www.rosemaryandthymecafe.com; 382 Spring St; baked goods $2.50-5, sandwiches & pizza $6-12; ⊜7:30am-3pm Tue-Sat, to 11:30am Sun; ⊞) With a German baker in the kitchen it's hardly surprising that the counter at Rosemary & Thyme is piled high with buttery croissants, apple and cherry tarts, and plump muffins. At lunchtime gourmet sandwiches feature herbed goat's cheese and Tuscan dried tomatoes, an Alsatian cheese mix and a Havana Cuban pork loin outlier. A children's menu is also thoughtfully provided.

Mission
BURGERS $

(Map p224; ☑401-619-5560; www.missionnpt. com; 29 Marlborough St; hot dogs from $3.50, burgers from $7.25; ⊗11am-9pm) Don't hold it against the proprietors that this 'gourmet' burger bar is a hit with local hipsters. House-ground burgers, hot dogs and home-cut fries don't come any better than this.

Corner Cafe
CAFE $

(Map p224; ☑401-846-0606; www.cornercafe newport.com; 110 Broadway; items $6-18; ⊗7am-2:30pm Mon-Thu, to 10pm Fri & Sat, to 8pm Sun) This cheery cafe has good coffee and the best breakfasts in Newport, including a memorable eggs Benedict.

★Scales & Shells
SEAFOOD $$

(Map p224; ☑401-846-3474; www.scalesandshells. com; 527 Thames St; mains $14-34; ⊗5-9pm) Only opening for dinner and only serving seafood has allowed this casual, often packed eatery to hone its skills. This is one of the best places in town to have your seafood almost any way you like it.

Anthony's Seafood
SEAFOOD $$

(☑401-846-9620; www.anthonysseafood.net; 963 Aquidneck Ave; mains $12-32; ⊗11am-8pm Mon-Sat, from noon Sun) Lauded by locals, this wholesale, take-out and dine-in seafood joint tucked away from the main drag in Middletown is always hopping, testament to the quality and freshness of the seafood. It's a great place to try a quahog (stuffie). Order at the counter for dine in and takeout. Portions are enormous!

Mamma Luisa
ITALIAN $$

(Map p224; ☑401-848-5257; www.mammaluisa. com; 673 Thames St; mains $14-32; ⊗5-10pm Thu-Tue) This cozy restaurant serves authentic Italian fare to its enthusiastic customers, who recommend the low-key pasta house as a place to escape the Newport crowds. There are classic pasta dishes (cheese ravioli with fava beans, spaghetti *alle vongole*), as well as meat and fish dishes. Upstairs feels like eating at grandma's house.

★Fluke Wine Bar
SEAFOOD $$$

(Map p224; ☑401-849-7778; www.flukewinebar. com; 41 Bowen's Wharf; mains $40-60; ⊗5-11pm Wed-Sat Nov-Apr, daily summer) Fluke's Scandinavian-inspired dining room, with its blond wood and picture windows, offers an accomplished seafood menu featuring roasted monkfish, seasonal striped sea bass and plump scallops. Upstairs, the bar serves a rock-and-roll cocktail list.

Thames St Kitchen
MODERN AMERICAN $$$

(Map p224; ☑401-846-9100; www.thamesstreet kitchen.com; 677 Thames St; mains $16-36; ⊗5:30-11pm Tue-Sat) ✿ This BYOB restaurant is the baby of two New York chefs who are devoted to field-to-fork dining and craft their limited menu with exciting seasonal ingredients and unexpected flavor combinations, like monkfish and grapefruit, skirt steak with seaweed salad and lots of bright, fresh greens. Portions are small and flavors are big so savor them slowly.

White Horse Tavern
TAVERN $$$

(Map p224; ☑401-849-3600; www.whitehorse newport.com; 26 Marlborough St; meals $28-58; ⊗11:30am-9pm) If you'd like to eat at a tavern opened by a 17th-century pirate that once served as an annual meeting place for the colonial Rhode Island General Assembly, try this historic, gambrel-roofed beauty. Menus for dinner (at which men should wear a jacket) might include baked escargot, truffle-crusted Atlantic halibut or beef Wellington. Service is hit or miss. It opened in 1673, making it one of America's oldest taverns.

🍷 Drinking & Nightlife

Compared with quiet times of the year, Newport looks very different in July and August when it's teeming with crowds looking for a good time. Over these months, Thames St can at times feel like either a cobblestone obstacle course or sorority party gone bad.

Pour Judgement
BAR

(Map p224; ☑401-619-2115; www.pourjudgement newport.com; 32 Broadway; ⊗11am-1am) This little local bar serves homebrews and tasty pub-style fare for those who'd rather a more authentic atmosphere in their downtime than the tourism face presented by many other establishments.

Brick Alley Pub
PUB

(Map p224; ☑401-849-6334; www.brickalley.com; 140 Thames St; ⊗11:30am-9pm Sun-Thu, to 10pm Fri & Sat) With its wood-panelled booths, exposed brick wall and vintage memorabilia, the Brick Alley Pub is a fun and friendly place. Lounge on the large patio and order one of Newport's locally brewed beers or a frozen Mudslide (equal parts vodka, Kahlua and Baileys). If the munchies strike, its lobster rolls once won an award from *Bon Appetit* for best in the US.

Salvation Café
BAR

(Map p224; www.salvationcafe.com; 140 Broadway; ⊗5pm-midnight) With its outdoor tiki lounge, corduroy-velvet couches, stylish Formica tables and wood-paneled walls, this bar-cum-restaurant (mains $18 to $24) is indeed a salvation from Newport's tourist hordes. Here, you'll find creative cocktails served alongside grass-fed hanger steak *frites*, organic tandoori chicken and the like.

☆ Entertainment

Newport Blues Café   LIVE MUSIC
(Map p224; www.newportblues.com; 286 Thames St; ⊙7pm-1am Tue-Sat) This popular rhythm and blues bar and restaurant draws top acts to an old brownstone that was once a bank. It's an intimate space with many enjoying quahogs, house-smoked ribs or pork loins at tables adjoining the small stage. Dinner is offered from 6pm to 10pm; the music starts at 9:30pm.

Jane Pickens Theater   CINEMA
(Map p224; ☑401-846-5252; www.janepickens. com; 49 Touro St) This beautifully restored one-screen art house used to be an Episcopalian church, built around 1834. Simple, pretty and old, the theater contains an organ and a balcony. It screens both popular and art-house films.

ℹ Information

Newport Visitor Center (☑401-845-9123; www. discovernewport.com; 23 America's Cup Ave; ⊙9am-5pm) Offers maps, brochures, local bus information, tickets to major attractions, public restrooms and an ATM. There's free parking for 30 minutes adjacent to the center.

ℹ Getting There & Around

BICYCLE
Scooter World (☑401-619-1349; www.scooter worldri.com; 11 Christie's Landing; ⊙9am-7pm) Scooters are available by the hour ($35 for first hour, $15 each additional hour) or by the day ($150), as are bicycles ($10/40 per hour/day), kayaks ($25/50 per hour/half-day) and jet skis ($175 per hour).

BOAT
Block Island Ferry (www.blockislandferry. com) Between June and September high-speed ferries depart three times daily from a dock near Fort Adams to Block Island.

The **Jamestown Newport Ferry** (☑401-423-9900; www.jamestownnewportferry.com; Conanicut Marina, Jamestown; return adult/child $24/10; ⊙May-Oct) sails to Newport with stops at Fort Adams and Rose Island. It is the best deal going for a harbor cruise. If you want to make more of a stop on Rose Island, landing fees are adult/child $5/4 and you can spend the day beachcombing, fishing, touring the lighthouse and swimming before being picked up on the return journey.

BUS
Bonanza Bus Lines operates buses to Boston ($27, 1¾ hours, four to five daily) from the Newport Visitor Center.

RIPTA (www.ripta.com) bus 60 serves Providence ($2, one hour) almost every hour. For the South Kingstown Amtrak station, take bus 64 or 66 ($2, 90 minutes, five buses Monday to Friday, three on Saturday). Bus 14 serves TF Green airport (70 minutes) in Wickford.

Most RIPTA buses arrive and depart from the Newport Visitor Center.

CAR & MOTORCYCLE
Parking can be tough in Newport. Free street parking spaces do pop up, but check to make sure any non-metered spots aren't reserved for Newport residents.

JAMESTOWN & CONANICUT ISLAND

Merely miles away from neighboring Newport, rural Conanicut Island feels world's apart. Its first inhabitants were Quaker farmers, shepherds and pirates. Captain Kidd spent considerable time here and is said to have buried his treasure on the island – but it's never been found.

The island's real treasure is low-key, relaxed and rustic **Jamestown**, whose waterfront beckons you to stroll along it, admiring the excellent views of the **Claiborne Pell Newport Bridge**.

At the southernmost tip of the island you'll come to **Beavertail State Park**, where you can enjoy one of the best vistas – and sunsets – in the Ocean State. Many vacationers bring lawn chairs, barbecues and picnics and spend the day walking trails and enjoying the clifftop views.

◉ Sights

Beavertail Light   LIGHTHOUSE
(☑401-423-3270; www.beavertaillight.org; Beavertail State Park, Jamestown; donations welcome; ⊙10am-4:30pm Jun-Sep) If you make a donation and come in season, you can climb the tower of this picturesque lighthouse. Built in 1749, it's one of the oldest along the Atlantic coast, and still signals ships into Narragansett Bay.

Watson Farm HISTORIC SITE

(☑401-423-0005; www.historicnewengland.org; 455 North Rd, Jamestown; adult/child $4/free; ⊙1-5pm Tue, Thu & Sun Jun–mid-Oct; P) Explore Rhode Island's last operational windmill when you wander around Watson Farm, a 200-year-old working farm that continues to practice traditional farming methods, grazing Red Devon cattle across its seaside pastures. A self-guided walking map is provided.

🍴 Sleeping & Eating

There are only two hotels in Jamestown and an excellent campground. Both are a quiet alternative to the hustle and bustle of popular Newport, especially in peak tourist season.

Fort Getty State Park CAMPGROUND $

(☑401-423-7211; www.jamestownri.gov/residents/fort-getty; Fort Getty, Jamestown; tent/RV sites $27/40) This pleasant park lies on Conanicut Island in Jamestown, with 100 RV sites, 25 tent sites on a grassy field, a dock for fishing and a view of the squat Dutch Lighthouse. Follow RI 138 over the Newport Bridge and take the Jamestown exit, making your way to Mackerel Cove Beach and Fort Getty Rd. The park is open mid-May to September.

Wyndham Bay Voyage Inn HOTEL $$

(☑401-423-2100; www.wyndhambayvoyageinn.com; 150 Conanicus Ave; r from $149) On the waterfront overlooking Narragansett Bay toward Newport, this former late 1800s inn-cum-tourist hotel has a variety of room types, predominantly studios and suites. Although the decor is a bit chintzy, the location is perfect if you're looking for tranquility, just 10 minutes' drive from downtown Newport.

Village Hearth Artisan Bakery BAKERY $

(☑401-423-9282; www.villagehearthbakerycafe.com; 2 Watson Ave; items $4-12; ⊙7am-4pm Fri & Sat, 7am-2pm & 4:30-7pm Sun) This low-slung yellow shack is situated a block north of the Jamestown village centre. It houses a community bakery and, on Sundays only, a pizzeria. It's a good pit stop for picnic fare, selling excellent country loaves and pastries. The bakery accepts cash only.

ⓘ Getting There & Away

Jamestown and Conanicut Island are connected to Newport (6 miles) via the Claiborne Pell Newport Bridge. There's a $4 toll each way to cross the bridge. Heading west, over the Verrazzano Bridge, also an impressive feat of engineering for which there is no toll, you can pick up RI 1A and drop south to reach Narragansett (12 miles).

The Jamestown Newport Ferry (p231) sails between Jamestown and Newport with stops at Fort Adams and Rose Island. It is the best deal going for a harbor tour.

NARRAGANSETT & POINT JUDITH

Named after one of the most powerful Native American tribes in New England, Narragansett, meaning literally 'People of the Small Point,' is the essence of Rhode Island. Surrounded by miles of sandy beaches and punctuated by salt ponds and mudflats, it became a popular beach resort at the end of the 19th century. At this time, large oceanfront hotels were constructed alongside a holiday pier (which was rebuilt in the 1970s) and the Stanford White–designed Towers Casino, of which only the twin towers remain standing. But you're not here for the architecture.

After you've plunged your person in the chilly Atlantic and baked yourself bronze, head on down Ocean Rd to the pretty village of Point Judith, where there's not much to do other than gorge yourself on the freshly caught bounty of the deep. Sound like a tough day?

⊙ Sights

While the beach is free, parking isn't: all-day parking in all the beach lots costs $10.

Scarborough State Beach BEACH

(970 Ocean Rd) Scarborough (sometimes written as 'Scarboro') is considered by many to be the best in the state. A massive, castle-like pavilion, generous boardwalks, a wide and long beachfront, on-duty lifeguards and great, predictable surf make Scarborough special. On a hot summer day, expect hordes of beachgoers.

Roger W Wheeler State Beach BEACH

(100 Sand Hill Cove Rd; ♿) Locally known as Sand Hill Cove, the Roger W Wheeler State Beach, just south of Galilee, is the spot for families with small children. Not only does it have a playground and other facilities, it also has an extremely gradual drop-off and little surf because of protection afforded by the rocky arms of the Point Judith breakwater.

Narragansett Town Beach
BEACH

(39 Boston Neck Rd; entry/season pass $6/25; ⊙admission office 8:30am-5:30pm) This mile-long stretch of beach tends to be crowded because it's an easy walk from Narragansett Pier. It's popular with surfers thanks to its soft curling waves, and is serviced by two pavilions, changing rooms and restrooms. It's the only beach in Rhode Island that charges a per-person admission fee on top of parking.

🛏 Sleeping

★Fishermen's
Memorial State Park
CAMPGROUND $

(☑401-789-8374; www.riparks.com; 1011 Point Judith Rd; tent sites RI residents/nonresidents $14/20; ⊙May-Oct) Fishermen's Memorial State Park in Galilee is so popular that many families return year after year to the same site. There are only 180 campsites at Fishermen's, so it's wise to reserve early by requesting the necessary form from the park management or the Division of Parks & Recreation.

Admiral Dewey Inn
B&B $$

(☑401-783-2090; www.admiraldeweyinn.com; 668 Matunuck Beach Rd, South Kingstown; r from $139; P🐾) Near the beachy town of Matunuck, this 10-room 1898 National Historic Register building offers reasonable rates and a two-minute walk to the beach. Most of the rooms in the gray-shingled inn have water views, and there's a broad porch that catches the ocean breeze.

The Richards
B&B $$

(☑401-789-7746; www.therichardsbnb.com; 144 Gibson Ave, Narragansett; d/ste from $175/200; P🐾) Built of locally quarried granite, this Gothic English manor (c 1884) has just four rooms, each named after the color in which the room is painted. There are fireplaces and a tranquil garden on the grounds.

🍴 Eating

Fronted by commercial seafood warehouses, Point Judith is a great place to get the freshest of the fresh delights from the deep.

★Champlin's Seafood
SEAFOOD $

(☑401-783-3152; 256 Great Rd; dishes $3-15; ⊙11am-9pm summer, shorter hours off-season) At Champlin's Seafood, order a lobster roll, stuffed clams, scallops or one of many sea critters breaded and fried, and hang out on its 2nd-floor deck, which sits inches from

the harbor's channel. The swaying masts of rusty fishing vessels keep you company.

★Matunuck Oyster Bar
SEAFOOD $$

(☑401-783-4202; www.rhodyoysters.com; 629 Succotash Rd, Matunuck; mains $18-28, oysters each $1.85; ⊙11:30am-9pm) This small, indoor-outdoor seafood-centric restaurant sits on a spit of land opposite Galilee on Point Judith Pond. Considering that the parking lot is carpeted in shells, it's no surprise that this oyster bar specializes in local bivalves – all ultra-fresh and some raised in the restaurant's own farm at Potter Pond Estuary out back. The oyster sampler ($20) lets you try 12 varieties, all from Rhode Island and its immediate environs.

ⓘ Information

Narragansett Chamber of Commerce (☑401-783-7121; www.narragansettcoc.com; 36 Ocean Rd, Narragansett; ⊙9am-5pm Mon-Fri) For information on the town of Narragansett and its vicinity. It also operates a very useful free shuttle from an out-of-town parking lot to the downtown and pier areas during summer weekends.

South County Tourism Council (☑800-548-4662; www.southcountyri.com) For in-depth coverage of the entire South County area, including beaches and attractions, contact this office.

ⓘ Getting There & Away

Narragansett is 25 miles east of Westerly on US 1 and 15 miles from Newport (via Jamestown) on the other side of Narragansett Bay.

Rhode Island's port for car ferries to Block Island is at Galilee State Pier, at the southern end of RI 108 in the village of Galilee, near Point Judith.

SOUTHERN RHODE ISLAND

South of Matunuck the tribal lands of the Narragansett Nation spread south across 1800 acres of woods and fields encompassing Charlestown on the coast and, to the north, Richmond with its white-clapboard mill villages of Carolina and Shannock. In the westernmost corner of the state, Westerly sits on the Pawcatuck River, which marks the boundary between Rhode Island and Connecticut. Once a wealthy 19th-century town, it's now a quiet commuter community, upstaged by the wealthy Watch Hill resort.

Charlestown

POP 7800

Situated on the coast, Charlestown is framed by beaches and salt ponds rich in crabs and quahogs (clams), which locals love to eat minced with breadcrumbs, baked and stuffed back into the shell: stuffies!

The largest of these wetlands, Ninigret (or Charlestown) Pond is surrounded by the 1711-acre Ninigret State Conservation Area (50 Bend Rd, Charlestown; P), a coastal lagoon bounded by barrier beaches and fed by freshwater springs. A 2.5 mile beach (also known as East Beach) fronts the ocean and

DON'T MISS

FANTASTIC UMBRELLA FACTORY

A sprawling collection of 19th-century farm buildings and elaborate, unkempt gardens, Fantastic Umbrella Factory (☑401-364-6616; www.fantasticumbrella factory.com; 4820 Old Post Rd, Charlestown; ☺10am-6pm) got its start in 1968. A series of shacks and sheds are filled with a wide variety of gift items: from flower bulbs and perennials to greeting cards, toys, jewelry, junk and scads of stuff hippies love like drums and hemp clothing.

There's an organic cafe, and exotic birds and farm animals roam around freely to the delight of children.

offers fishing (striped bass, flounder, bluefish and tautog), a 10-speed bicycle course and well-marked walking trails, while the landside Ninigret Wildlife Refuge shelters deer and birds.

◉ Sights & Activities

Blue Shutters Town Beach BEACH
(⊕) A Charlestown-managed beach, this is a good choice for families. There are no amusements other than nature's own, but there are convenient facilities, a watchful staff of lifeguards, generally mild surf and smaller crowds.

🛏 Sleeping

Burlingame State Park Campsites CAMPGROUND $
(☑401-322-7337; www.riparks.com; off US 1 N, Charlestown; tent sites RI residents/nonresidents $14/20; ☺mid-Apr–mid-Oct) This lovely campground has more than 750 spacious wooded sites near crystal-clear Watchaug Pond, which provides a good beach for swimming. The park occupies 3100 acres. First-come, first-served is the rule, but you can call ahead to check on availability.

❶ Getting There & Away

From Charlestown, take US 1 west to Westerly (12 miles) or east to Narragansett (13 miles).

Westerly

POP 22,800

Westerly sits on Rhode Island's western border sharing the banks of the Pawcatuck River with Connecticut. In the 19th century it was a town of some wealth thanks to its high-grade granite quarries and textile mills. That heyday is long gone, although the area's beaches still draw huge weekend crowds in season.

◉ Sights & Activities

Misquamicut State Beach BEACH
With good surf and close proximity to the Connecticut state line, Misquamicut draws huge crowds. It offers families low prices and convenient facilities for changing, showering and eating. Misquamicut is situated just south of Westerly.

Atlantic Beach Park BEACH
(☑401-322-0504; www.atlanticbeachpark.com; 321-338 Atlantic Ave, Misquamicut; ⊕) This antique amusement area ranges between

charming and derelict. Here you'll find plenty to enjoy or avoid – miniature golf, batting cages, and rides for the kiddies, which, although worn and rickety, we are told are perfectly safe. Use your own judgment.

ⓘ Getting There & Away

Westerly is to the east of Mystic (8 miles) on US 1 and it's 5 miles south to the mansions of Watch Hill.

New England Airlines (p240) flies from Westerly airport to Block Island.

Watch Hill

POP 154

One of the tiniest summer colonies in the Ocean State, Watch Hill occupies a spit of land at the southwesternmost point of Rhode Island. Drive into the village along winding RI 1A and your jaw might drop slightly as you're met by huge, shingled, Queen Anne summerhouses commanding the rolling landscape from their perches high on rocky knolls. Unlike Newport's magnificent mansions, most of Watch Hill's equally grandiose but less extravagant homes remain privately owned – previous and current residents include Clarke Gable, Henry Ford and Taylor Swift.

Visitors spend their time at the beach and browsing in the shops along the two-block-long main drag, Bay St. For children, an ice-cream cone and a twirl on the carousel provide immediate gratification and fodder for fond memories.

◉ Sights & Activities

East Beach   BEACH

FREE This fine beach is in front of the Ocean House hotel. It stretches for several miles from the Watch Hill lighthouse all the way to Misquamicut, with the open ocean crashing on one side and large, gray-shingled homes rising behind grassy dunes on the other. The public access path to the beach is on Bluff Ave near Larkin Rd and neighboring property owners are vigilant about restricting beachgoers to the public area below the high-tide line.

Watch Hill Beach   BEACH

(adult/child $6/4; ⊙10am-7pm Mon-Fri, 9am-6pm Sat & Sun) This small beach is behind the Flying Horses Carousel.

Flying Horses Carousel   CAROUSEL

(Bay St; rides $1; ⊙11am-9pm Mon-Fri, 10am-9pm Sat & Sun; 🚼) This antique ride dates from 1883. Besides being perhaps the oldest carousel in the country, it boasts a unique design: its horses are suspended on chains so that they really do 'fly' outward as the carousel spins around. The flying horses have a mane of real horsehair and real leather saddles. No riders over 12 years old.

Napatree Point   WALKING

For a leisurely beach walk, the half-mile stroll to the westernmost tip of Watch Hill is unbeatable. With the Atlantic on one side and the yacht-studded Little Narragansett Bay on the other, Napatree is a protected conservation area, so walkers are asked to stay on the trails and off the dunes.

🛏 Sleeping

Consider Watch Hill if you're looking for somewhere truly memorable (and expensive) to stay. Peak season (summer) sees huge rate hikes on already hugely pricey rooms, and weekends are higher still. Midweek prices are often discounted by 25% or more, while off-season rates bring the price down another 25% or so.

★Ocean House   HOTEL $$$

(☑401-584-7000; www.oceanhouseri.com; 1 Bluff Ave; r from $495; 🅿✳🛜🐾) This visually striking hotel sits like a frosted yellow wedding cake, dominating the bluffs above East Beach. Though designed to emulate the grandeur of a previous era, the Ocean House is a recent construction with ultra-luxe modern amenities, including fireplaces, private terraces, Italian-woven linens and on and on. All rooms include complimentary 'resort activities' from yoga to cooking classes.

Watch Hill Inn   INN $$$

(☑401-348-6300; www.watchhillinn.com; 38 Bay St; r $200-375; 🅿✳🛜) The wood-floored rooms of this mostly modern (and well-equipped) inn contain Victorian-ish furnishings and overlook the bobbing boats floating in the harbor across the street. It sells out early and hosts a lot of wedding parties. There's also an annex, which offers studio, one- and two-bedroom apartments right on the beach.

🍴 Eating

You can count your dining options on one hand, save for the dining rooms of the finer hotels. Neighboring Westerly offers more to tempt hungry folks.

★ St Clair's Annex
ICE CREAM $

(📱401-348-8407; www.stclairannexrestaurant.com; 41 Bay St; cones from $3; ⊙7:45am-9pm summer, 8am-5pm winter) This ice-cream shop has been run by the same family since 1887, and features several dozen flavors of homemade ice cream. On top of traditional light breakfast fare (omelets and the like), it serves seaside specialties like lobster rolls, hot dogs and lemonade.

Allie's Donuts
DOUGHNUTS $

(📱401-295-8036; 3661 Quaker Lane/RI 2; ⊙5am-3pm Mon-Fri, 6am-1pm Sat & Sun) Allie has been turning out hot-to-trot homemade doughnuts from her roadside shack on RI 2 for over 40 years and Rhode Islanders travel from across the state to take them away by the dozen ($7.20). Light as air, they are filled and topped with delectable condiments, such as flaked coconut, chocolate and lemon cream, and cherry jelly.

The Cooked Goose
CAFE $

(📱401-348-9888; www.thecookedgoose.com; 92 Watch Hill Rd, Westerly; lunches $8-14; ⊙7am-7pm May-Sep, to 3pm Oct-Apr) With its appealing selection of Benedicts, omelets, baked goods (pain au chocolat, house-made doughnuts) and exotic sandwiches (consider the Nirvana, with baked tofu, honey ginger dressing, cheddar cheese and sprouts on whole wheat), this is a favorite of the Watch Hill elite. Prices are reasonable and the location, across from the harbor, is good for watching the boats.

84 High Street Café
AMERICAN, ITALIAN $$$

(📱401-596-7871; www.84highstreet.com; 84 High St, Westerly; mains $14-32; ⊙11am-late Mon-Sat, 9am-3pm Sun) With big plates of well-prepared Italian-influenced American classics (seafood Parmesan, for example, or baked Ritz cracker–stuffed shrimp), 84 High prides itself on massive portions of hearty, heavy but delicious fare. The lounge bar hosts local bands on Friday and Saturday nights.

Olympia Tea Room
BISTRO $$$

(📱401-348-8211; www.olympiatearoom.com; 74 Bay St; mains $14-38; ⊙11:30am-9pm) The most atmospheric restaurant in town, the Olympia is an authentic 1916 soda-fountain-turned-bistro. Varnished wooden booths, pink walls, black-and-white checkered tiles on the floor and the antique marble-topped soda fountain help to ease calf livers, broiled flounder, and little necks and sausages past your esophagus.

ⓘ Getting There & Away

Watch Hill is a scenic 5 miles drive southwest of Westerly. Continuing east along the coast for 13 miles you'll come to Charlestown.

Parking in Watch Hill is a real hassle. Most curb parking is vigorously reserved for town residents. If you're lucky, you can snag a free spot (strict three-hour limit) on Bay St. Otherwise, expect to shell out $10 to $15 in a private lot.

People with this much money might tend not to patronize public transport: services range from scarce to nonexistent.

BLOCK ISLAND
POP 1050

From the deck of the ferry, a cluster of mansard roofs and gingerbread houses rises picturesquely from the commercial village of Old Harbor, where little has changed since 1895, short of adding electricity and flush toilets! If you remain after the departure of the masses on the last ferry, the scale and pace of the island will delight or derange you: some find it blissfully quiet, others get island fever fast.

Block Island's simple pleasures center upon strolling the beach, which stretches for miles to the north of Old Harbor, biking around the island's rolling farmland and getting to know the calls of the many bird species that make the island home. During off-season, when the population dwindles to a few hundred, the landscape has the spare, haunted feeling of an Andrew Wyeth painting, with stone walls demarcating centuries-old property lines and few trees interrupting the spectacular ocean vistas.

◉ Sights

You're apt to find Block Island's **Old Harbor** hub simultaneously charming and annoying (during peak season at least). Antiquated buildings form the backdrop of a lively scene, with pedestrian traffic spilling off sidewalks and inexperienced moped riders wobbling around them. If you're keen to acquire some saltwater taffy, souvenir T-shirts or beach sandals, you'll be spoilt for choice. On a slow day, there's something really satisfying about sipping a beer on a patio and watching the ferries come and go.

North Light
LIGHTHOUSE

(⊙museum 10am-5pm Jun-Labor Day) At **Sandy Point**, the northernmost tip of the island, scenic North Light stands at the end of a

ℹ BLOCK ISLAND FERRY SERVICE

Block Island Ferry (www.blockislandferry.com) runs a high-speed ferry from Point Judith in Narragansett (round-trip adult/child $38/22, 30 minutes) from Memorial Day to mid-October, and a year-round traditional ferry (adult/child $26/13, one hour), which carries vehicles too.

You don't need a car to get around Block Island and, aside from hotel parking lots, there aren't many places to put one. You'll save a ton of money by leaving it behind in the well-organised parking lots at Point Judith ($10 per day). Besides, why mess with the island's pristine ecology and laid-back, bike-riding vibe (there are tons of bike and scooter rentals on the island).

If you simply can't live without your car, a one-way ticket costs $39.60, excluding driver. Bikes cost $3.20. Reservations for vehicle crossings are essential.

long sandy path lined with beach roses. At the trailhead, you'll find Settler's Rock, a small monument that lists the names of the island's original English settlers at the spot where they landed in 1661. The 1867 lighthouse contains a small **maritime museum** with information about famous island wrecks.

Southeast Light LIGHTHOUSE

You'll likely recognize the red-brick lighthouse called Southeast Light from postcards of the island. Set dramatically atop 200ft red-clay cliffs called Mohegan Bluffs south of Old Harbor, the lighthouse had to be moved back from the eroding cliff edge in 1993. With waves crashing below and sails moving across the Atlantic offshore, it's probably the best place on the island to watch the sunset. Just south of it a steep stairway descends to a narrow beach backed by the bluffs.

🏃 Activities

Bicycles and mopeds are available for rental at many places in Old Harbor (bikes are the noise-friendly option). A dozen outfits compete for your custom, all with similar prices.

Bird-watching opportunities abound, especially in spring and fall when migratory species make their way north or south along the Atlantic Flyway.

Block Island State Beach BEACH

The island's east coast, north of Old Harbor, is lined with this glorious, 3-mile beach. The southern part, **Benson Town Beach**, sits closest to Old Harbor, and is supplied with changing and showering stalls, a snack stand, and umbrella and boogie-board rentals. Heading north, you'll next hit **Crescent Beach**, then **Scotch Beach** and finally **Mansion Beach**.

★ Greenway Trail HIKING

Explore Block Island's unique ecosystems (dune fields, morainal grasslands, salt ponds and kettle hole ponds) along 15 miles of Greenway walking trails. The trails meander over the southern half of the island through Nathan Mott Park, the Enchanted Forest and Rodman's Hollow Natural Area. Access can be found on Lakeside Dr, and along Old Mill, Cooneymus, West Side and Beacon Hill Rds.

Rodman's Hollow Natural Area HIKING

(entrance off Cooneymus Rd) In the south of the island, this 100-acre wildlife refuge is laced with trails that end at the beach – perfect for a picnic.

Clay Head Nature Trail HIKING

(off Corn Neck Rd) To the north of Old Harbor, this trail follows high clay bluffs along the beachfront, then veers inland through a maze-like series of paths cut into low vegetation that attract dozens of bird species.

Block Island Fishworks FISHING

(☑ 401-466-5392; www.sandypointco.com; Ocean Ave, New Harbor; half-/full-day charters from $350/750) Fishing charters on a small boat with Coast Guard–licensed captain. Possible prey includes striped bass, bluefish, bonito, false albacore, tuna, shark, scup, sea bass and fluke.

🛏 Sleeping

Many places have a two- or three-day minimum stay in summer and close between November and April. Advance reservations are essential. Peak season runs roughly from mid-June to Labor Day. Off-season prices can be far cheaper than those listed here. Camping is not allowed on the island.

RHODE ISLAND BLOCK ISLAND

Block Island

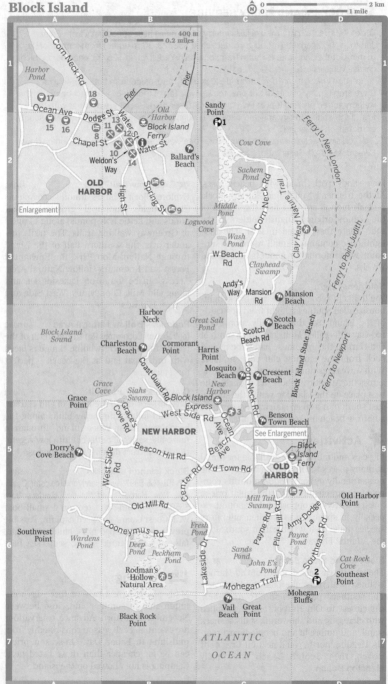

0 — 2 km
0 — 1 mile

Enlargement

0 — 400 m
0 — 0.2 miles

Harbor Pond

Corn Neck Rd

17
Ocean Ave
15 16
18
Dodge St
Water St
13
8 11
12
Chapel St
10
Weldon's Way
14

Pier

Old Harbor
Block Island Ferry
i
Water St

Ballard's Beach

OLD HARBOR

High St
Spring St
6
9

Sandy Point
1

Cow Cove

Sachem Pond

Middle Pond

Corn Neck Rd

Clay Head Nature Trail

4

Logwood Cove

Wash Pond

W Beach Rd

Clayhead Swamp

Andy's Way

Mansion Rd
Mansion Beach

Scotch Beach
Scotch Beach Rd

Ferry to New London

Ferry to Point Judith

Ferry to Newport

Harbor Neck

Great Salt Pond

Block Island Sound

Charleston Beach
Cormorant Point
Harris Point

Coast Guard Rd

Mosquito Beach
New Harbor
Block Island Express
Ocean Ave
3

Crescent Beach

Block Island State Beach

Grace Cove
Siahs Swamp
Grace's Cove Rd
Grace Point

West Side Rd

NEW HARBOR

Beach Ave

Benson Town Beach

See Enlargement

Block Island Ferry
OLD HARBOR

Dorry's Cove Beach
West Side Rd
Beacon Hill Rd
Center Rd
Old Town Rd

7

Old Harbor Point

Old Mill Rd

Mill Tail Swamp

Payne Rd
Pilot Hill Rd
Amy Dodge La

Southwest Point

Wardens Pond

Cooneymus Rd

Fresh Pond

Lakeside Dr

Sands Pond

Payne Pond

Southeast Rd

Cat Rock Cove

Deep Pond
Peckham Pond

Rodman's Hollow Natural Area
5

John E's Pond

Mohegan Trail
2
Mohegan Bluffs
Southeast Point

Black Rock Point

Vail Beach
Great Point

ATLANTIC OCEAN

Block Island

◉ Sights

⊕ Activities, Courses & Tours

⊜ Sleeping

⊗ Eating

◉ Drinking & Nightlife

The Visitor Center (p240) near the ferry dock keeps track of vacancies, and will try to help should you arrive sans reservation.

★ Sea Breeze Inn INN $$
(☑401-466-2275; www.seabreezeblockisland.com; Spring St, Old Harbor; r without bath $95-180, d $230-310; ℗) Some rooms in these charming hillside cottages have uninterrupted views over a tidal pond and the ocean beyond. Others face inward toward a country garden. Inside, airy rooms have eccentric, rustic furnishings, cathedral ceilings, and no electronic distractions like TVs and clocks. Breakfast comes served in a basket, which can be enjoyed on the porch.

Gables Inn INN $$
(☑401-466-2213; Dodge St, Old Harbor; r $145-220) A wood-framed Victorian, the friendly Gables features high beds and small rooms with a variety of lace and wallpaper, often of a vivid floral pattern. Guests have free access to beach supplies (towels, chairs, coolers, umbrellas) and a parlor of velvet furniture, although there's no view.

1661 Inn INN $$$
(☑401-466-2063; www.blockislandresorts.com; Spring St, Old Harbor; r $149-480; ℗⊜) Set on a sunset-facing hill overlooking the sea, the 1661 Inn has one of the best locations on the island. Its nine rooms are decorated in antique style with charming floral wallpaper, brass and four-poster beds, and some stunning private decks. You can just walk across the road for one of the island's finest dinners.

Atlantic Inn INN $$$
(☑401-466-5883; www.atlanticinn.com; High St, Old Harbor; d low season $195-235, high season $235-360; ℗) This 1879 establishment commands a gentle perch on a grassy hilltop, with ocean and town vistas. The gracefully appointed Victorian inn features a wide porch, a fine-dining restaurant and Adirondack chairs strewn across a spacious lawn. The 21 rooms vary in size, with some on the small side, but all are quaintly decorated with quilts and lace curtains.

✗ Eating

Most places are open for lunch and dinner during summer; many close off-season. Make dinner reservations in the high season or risk hour-long waits.

Aldo's Bakery & Homemade Ice Cream ICE CREAM $
(☑401-466-2198; www.aldosbakery.com; 130 Weldon's Way; ice cream from $3; ⊘6am-11pm May–mid-Oct; ⊞) Family friendly Aldo's has been serving homemade ice cream and pastries, including the delicious Portuguese sweetbread, to Block Island tourists for over 40 years. It even operates a 'pastry boat' so you can have fresh baked muffins delivered right to your deck.

Rebecca's SEAFOOD $
(☑401-466-5411; Water St, Old Harbor; mains from $5, fried fish $6-16; ⊘7am-2am Thu-Mon, to 8pm Tue & Wed) This snack stand serves burgers, chowder, grilled-cheese sandwiches, grease and deep-fried clams, fish, scallops and more to hungry tourists seated at picnic tables under umbrellas.

Mohegan Cafe & Brewery PUB FOOD $$
(☑401-466-5911; Water St, Old Harbor; mains $12-22; ⊘11:30am-9pm Sun-Thu, to 10pm Fri & Sat; ⊞) Besides brewing its own beer, this atmospheric pub with large picture windows offers a select menu of local fish specials

alongside more standard pub fare of steaks and barbecued brisket. The lunchtime lobster bisque and Cajun catfish sandwiches go down nicely with a hand-crafted beer.

★**Eli's**   MODERN AMERICAN **$$$**
(☑401-466-5230; www.elisblockisland.com; 456 Chapel St, Old Harbor; mains $18-36; ⊙from 5:30pm; ✍) The locally caught sea-bass special (tender fillets over scallions, grapes and beans) tastes so fresh and mildly salty and sweet that its memory will haunt you for weeks. For real. The room is cramped, crowded and casual with lots of pine wood and some well-conceived art.

Finn's Seafood   SEAFOOD **$$$**
(☑401-466-2473; www.finnsseafood.com; 212 Water St, Old Harbor; mains $12-34; ⊙11:30am-10pm) Finn's is an island institution, its bunting-draped deck the first cheerful sight that greets arrivals at the dock. Come here for New England–style chowder, clams, lobster rolls, steamers and broiled fish that still taste of the ocean. There's a takeout window, too.

🍷 Drinking & Nightlife

The fiercely beating heart of Block Island's nightlife centers on the crossroads between Ocean Ave and Corn Neck Rd. There's live music virtually every night of the week, in season.

★**The Oar**   BAR
(☑401-466-8820; Jobs Hill Rd, New Harbor; sushi $7-15; ⊙mid-May–Columbus Day; ♿🚲) Sitting on the lawn, cold Mudslide in hand, overlooking the boats bobbing in the Great Salt Pond, the Oar is quintessential Block Island and its open-sided, wraparound bar can't be beat. What's more, it serves a surprisingly decent sushi menu (although remember this is Block Island, not New York) alongside regular plates of fish and burgers.

Poor People's Pub   PUB
(☑401-466-8533; www.pppbi.com; 33 Ocean Ave, Old Harbor; ⊙11:30am-late) Poor People's Pub with its barbecue, beer and bands is a hit with everyone, not just the handful of visitors with a budget!

Captain Nick's   BAR
(☑401-466-5670; www.captainnicks.com; 34 Ocean Ave, Old Harbor; ⊙4pm-1am) Built of reclaimed wood, this is the island's most raucous bar. It has live music six days a week, sometimes acoustic, often rock (there's even

a weekly disco night). There's sushi Thursday through Sunday.

Yellow Kittens   BAR, CLUB
(☑401-466-5855; www.yellowkittens.com; Corn Neck Rd; ⊙11am-late) Just north of Old Harbor, Yellow Kittens attracts bands from around New England and keeps rowdy patrons happy with pool, table tennis and darts. It's been called Yellow Kittens since 1876!

ℹ Information

Visitor Center (☑401-466-2982; www.blockislandchamber.com; Water St, Old Harbor; ⊙9am-5pm summer, shorter hours rest of year) The Block Island Chamber of Commerce operates this visitor center next to the ferry dock, where you'll also find public restrooms.

ℹ Getting There & Away

AIR
New England Airlines (☑800-243-2460; www.block-island.com/nea; 56 Airport Rd, Westerly; one way/round-trip $54/99) Flies between Westerly State Airport, on Airport Rd off RI 78, and Block Island State Airport (12 minutes).

BOAT
In addition to services from Point Judith described on p237, Block Island Ferry operates high-speed ferries from Newport (adult/child $51/26, one hour) and Fall River, MA ($60/30, two hours).

Block Island Express (www.goblockisland.com) operates services from New London, CT, to Old Harbor, Block Island (round-trip adult/child $45/23, 75 minutes) between May and September.

ℹ Getting Around

Because of its size, Block Island doesn't use normal US street addresses, with each house assigned a fire number: useful if you're delivering mail or tracking down a blaze, but not much help to travelers. Be sure you grab the island map from the ferry!

BICYCLE & SCOOTER
Island Moped and Bike Rentals (☑401-741-2329; www.bimopeds.com; 41 Water St, Old Harbor; per day bikes/mopeds from $20/45; ⊙9am-8pm) Mountain bikes, tandems, hybrids and mopeds for rent, as well as beach chairs and umbrellas.

TAXI
Mig's Rig Taxi (☑401-480-0493; www.migsrigtaxi.com) A friendly and reliable taxi service that also offers island tours.

Connecticut

POP 3.6 MILLION / ☎ 203, 860, 959

Best Places to Eat

➜ Community Table (p272)

➜ Captain Daniel Packer Inne (p259)

➜ Trumbull Kitchen (p248)

➜ The Whelk (p268)

➜ ZINC (p265)

Best Places to Sleep

➜ Inn at Stonington (p260)

➜ Inn at Kent Falls (p274)

➜ Boardman House Inn (p250)

➜ Silas W. Robbins House (p248)

➜ Study at Yale (p264)

Why Go?

Known for its commuter cities, New York's neighbor is synonymous with the affluent lanes and mansions of *The Stepford Wives* and TV's *Gilmour Girls*. In old-moneyed Greenwich, Litchfield Hills and the Quiet Corner, these representations ring true, although many regard the state as a mere stepping stone to the 'real' New England, of whose tourist boom Connecticut was spared.

The upside is that Connecticut retains a more 'authentic' feel. The downside is a slow decaying of former heavyweights like Hartford and New London, where visitors can ponder the price of progress and get enthused about urban renewal. New Haven, home of Yale University, is one such place rewiring itself as a vibrant cultural hub.

Dense with historical attractions and the kind of bucolic nature that continues to inspire artists as it has for over a century, Connecticut begs for your attention and a well-deserved spot on your New England itinerary.

When to Go
Hartford

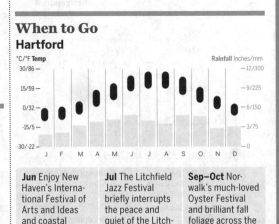

Jun Enjoy New Haven's International Festival of Arts and Ideas and coastal beach-going.

Jul The Litchfield Jazz Festival briefly interrupts the peace and quiet of the Litchfield Hills.

Sep–Oct Norwalk's much-loved Oyster Festival and brilliant fall foliage across the state.

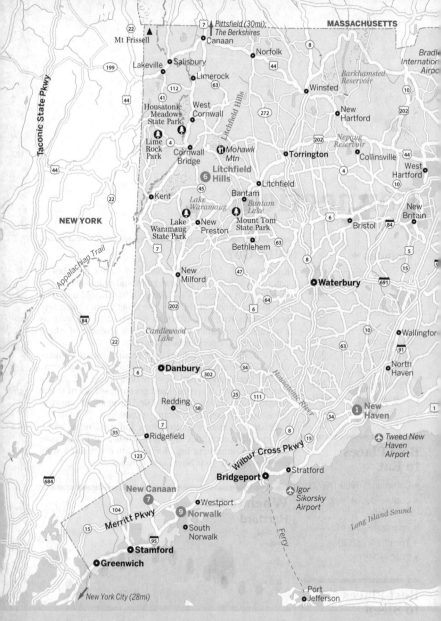

Connecticut Highlights

1 Yale University (p261) Exploring world-class museums and New Haven's student scene.

2 Mystic Seaport Museum (p256) Delighting budding mariners with Mystic's marvellous maritime world.

3 Wadsworth Atheneum (p245) Gawking at this magnificent historic collection of art and artifacts in Hartford.

4 New London (p253) Marveling at faded architectural gems and pondering progress before dining by the waterfront.

5 Essex Steam Train & Riverboat Ride (p252) Jumping on board for the romance of steam along the Connecticut River in Essex.

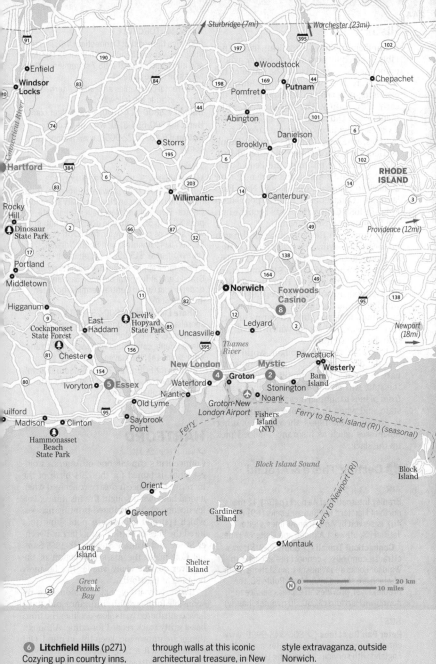

6 **Litchfield Hills** (p271) Cozying up in country inns, hiking forested hills and fishing the lazy Housatonic.

7 **Philip Johnson Glass House** (p270) Peering through walls at this iconic architectural treasure, in New Canaan, north of Greenwich.

8 **Foxwoods Casino** (p257) Getting lost in the excitement of this gargantuan Vegas-style extravaganza, outside Norwich.

9 **Norwalk** (p268) Slurping down the freshest oysters within a stone's throw of Manhattan.

History

A number of Native American tribes (notably the Pequot and the Mohegan, whose name for the river became the name of the state) were here when the first European explorers, primarily Dutch, appeared in the early 17th century. The first English settlement was at Old Saybrook in 1635, followed a year later by the Connecticut Colony, built by Massachusetts Puritans under Thomas Hooker. A third colony was founded in 1638 in New Haven. After the Pequot War (1637), the Native Americans were no longer a check to colonial expansion in New England, and Connecticut's English population grew. In 1686 Connecticut was brought into the Dominion of New England.

The American Revolution swept through Connecticut, leaving scars with major battles at Stonington (1775), Danbury (1777), New Haven (1779) and Groton (1781). Connecticut became the fifth state in 1788. It embarked on a period of prosperity, propelled by its whaling, shipbuilding, farming and manufacturing industries (from firearms to bicycles to household tools), which lasted well into the 19th century.

The 20th century brought world wars and the depression but, thanks in no small part to Connecticut's munitions industries, the state was able to fight back. Everything from planes to submarines were made in the state, and when the defense industry began to decline in the 1990s, the growth of other businesses (such as insurance) helped pick up the slack.

ℹ Getting There & Around

AIR

Bradley International Airport (p434), 12 miles north of Hartford in Windsor Locks (I-91 exit 40), is served by American Airlines, Delta, JetBlue, Southwest Airlines and United Airlines.

Connecticut Transit (✐ 860-525-9181; www.cttransit.com) buses connect the airport with Windsor Locks and Windsor train stations, both of which are served by Amtrak. Route 30, the Bradley Flyer, provides an express service to downtown Hartford ($1.50, 30 minutes, hourly).

BUS

Peter Pan Bus Lines (✐ 800-343-9999; www.peterpanbus.com) operates routes across New England with services connecting Hartford with New Haven (from $14, one hour) and Boston (from $20, two to 2½ hours). **Greyhound** (✐ 800-231-2222; www.greyhound.com) offers similar prices and some advance purchase discounts.

CAR & MOTORCYCLE

I-95 hugs the coast of Connecticut. I-91 starts in New Haven and heads north through Hartford and into Massachusetts. US 7 shimmies up the west side of the state.

Car-rental companies at Bradley International Airport include the following:

Budget (✐ 800-527-0700; www.budget.com)

Hertz (✐ 800-654-3131; www.hertz.com)

National (✐ 877-222-9058; www.nationalcar.com)

TRAIN

Metro-North (✐ 212-532-4900, 800-223-6052, 800-638-7646; new.mta.info/mnr) trains make the run between New York City's Grand Central Terminal and New Haven (peak/off-peak $22/16.50, from one hour 50 minutes), with services to Greenwich (peak/off-peak $13/9.75, 45 minutes) and South Norwalk (peak/off-peak $15.50/11.75, one hour).

Peak fares apply to weekday trains arriving in Grand Central Terminal between 5am and 10am or departing Grand Central Terminal between 4pm and 8pm.

Shore Line East (✐ 800-255-7433; www.shorelineeast.com), Connecticut's commuter rail service, travels along the shore of Long Island Sound, connecting with Metro-North and Amtrak lines at New Haven.

Amtrak (✐ 800-872-7245; www.amtrak.com) trains depart New York City's Penn Station for Connecticut on three lines.

HARTFORD

✐ 860 / POP 125,020

Connecticut's capital, one of America's oldest cities, is famed for the 1794 birth of the lucrative insurance industry, conceived when a local landowner sought fire insurance. Policy documents necessitated printing presses, which spurned a boom in publishing that lured the likes of Mark Twain, Harriet Beecher Stowe and Wallace Stevens. In 1855 Samuel Colt made the mass production of the revolver commercially viable. Big business boomed in Hartford.

It's an easy irony that the industries responsible for its wealth (insurance and guns) have contributed to its slow decline: Hartford has a gritty track record for crime. Although things are improving, keep this in mind. Old money has left a truly impressive legacy of fine historic attractions worthy of any New England itinerary. Visit during spring when the darling buds burst to life or in summer when trees are green and skies are blue and you're likely to be pleasantly surprised.

Hartford

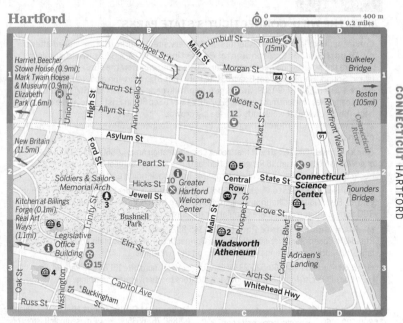

◉ Sights

The easiest way to take in most attractions is on foot. From Main St, it's also an easy walk down to the **riverfront**, where the not-for-profit **Riverfront Recapture** (📞 860-713-3131; www.riverfront.org) project encompasses landscaped walkways through a series of interlinked parks. Along here you can wander through the **Lincoln Financial Sculpture Park**, take rowing lessons or take a cruise down the river.

★ **Wadsworth Atheneum** MUSEUM
(📞 860-278-2670; www.thewadsworth.org; 600 Main St; adult/child $15/5; ⊙ 11am-5pm Wed-Fri, from 10am Sat & Sun) On September 19, 2015, the nation's oldest public art museum completed a five-year, $33-million renovation, renewing 32 galleries and 15 public spaces. The Wadsworth houses nearly 50,000 pieces of art in a castle-like Gothic Revival building. On display are paintings by members of the Hudson River School, including some by Hartford native Frederic Church; 19th-century impressionist works; 18th-century New England furniture; sculptures by Connecticut artist Alexander Calder; and an outstanding array of surrealist, postwar and contemporary works.

INTO THE WILD: CONNECTICUT'S STATE PARKS

Connecticut has a bevy of wonderful – and undervisited – parks that are looked after by the **Department of Environmental Protection** (☑ 860-424-3200; www.ct.gov/deep).

There are several fine beach state parks where you can view the sunset over Long Island Sound. Hammonasset Beach State Park (p253) in Madison and **Rocky Neck State Park** (☑ 860-739-1339; www.ct.gov/deep/rockyneck; 244 West Main St/CT 156, East Lyme; campsites resident/nonresident $20/30; ⊙ May 1-Sep 30) in East Lyme are two of the best, though summer weekends can see big crowds.

For weekend adventure in the rough, the Lower Connecticut River Valley has several options:

Cockaponset State Forest (Pattaconk Lake Recreation Area; ☑ 860-663-2030; www. ct.gov/deep/cockaponset; 18 Ranger Rd, Haddam) The second-biggest state forest in Connecticut offers fishing, hiking and swimming, horseback riding and more.

Devil's Hopyard State Park (☑ 860-873-8566; www.ct.gov/deep/devilshopyard; 366 Hopyard Rd, East Haddam) Chapman Falls tumbles more than 60ft over a series of steps. The 860 acres that surround it are popular for mountain biking and hiking.

Haddam Meadows State Park (☑ 860-345-8521; www.ct.gov/deep/haddammeadows; Rte 154, Haddam; ⊙ sunrise-sunset) Once a Connecticut River floodplain and agricultural land, this park is now a fine place to picnic on the riverbank.

Hurd State Park (☑ 860-526-2336; www.ct.gov/deep/hurd; Rte 151 & Hurd Park Rd, East Hampton) This car-free park is beloved by boaters for its riverside camping.

★**Connecticut Science Center** MUSEUM
(☑ 860-520-2160; www.ctsciencecenter.org; 250 Columbus Blvd; adult/child $22/15, movie $7/6; ⊙ 10am-5pm Tue-Sun; P) Designed by Italian architect Cesar Pelli, the Connecticut Science Center is both an exciting architectural space and an absorbing museum for adults and kids alike. Innovative, interactive exhibits and programs abound, there's a dedicated KidsZone on the 1st floor, films, stage shows and special events, and always a fascinating world-class visiting themed exhibition. You could easily spend a whole day here, but its best to arrive after 2pm when the school groups clear out. Check the website for what's on.

★**Mark Twain House & Museum** MUSEUM
(☑ 860-247-0998; www.marktwainhouse.org; 351 Farmington Ave, parking at 385 Farmington Ave; adult/child $19/11; ⊙ 9:30am-5:30pm, closed Tue Jan-Mar; P) For 17 years, encompassing the most productive period of his life, Samuel Langhorne Clemens (1835–1910) and his family lived in this striking orange-and-black brick Victorian house, which then stood in the pastoral area of the city called Nook Farm. Architect Edward Tuckerman Potter lavishly embellished it with turrets, gables and verandahs, and some of the interiors were done by Louis Comfort Tiffany. Admission to the house and museum is by guided tour only. Advance purchase is recommended.

Museum of Connecticut History MUSEUM
(☑ 860-757-6535; www.museumofcthistory.org; 231 Capitol Ave; ⊙ 9am-4pm Mon-Fri, to 2pm Sat) **FREE** This museum housed in the **Connecticut State Library** on Capitol Hill and renowned for its impressive genealogy library packs a punch for US history buffs. It also holds Connecticut's original royal charter of 1662, a prime collection of Colt firearms (which were manufactured in Hartford), coins and the table at which Abraham Lincoln signed the Emancipation Proclamation.

Elizabeth Park Rose Gardens GARDENS
(☑ 860-231-9443; www.elizabethparkct.org; cnr Prospect Ave & Asylum Ave; ⊙ dawn-dusk daily, concert times vary) Known for its collection of 15,000 rose bushes, the 102-acre Elizabeth Park was donated to the city by a wealthy industrialist, who asked that it be named for his wife. Planted with more than 900 varieties, the gardens are covered in blooms in June and July, but they flower, if less profusely, well into fall. During the summer months, **concerts** are held at the park.

State Capitol HISTORIC BUILDING
(☑ 860-240-0222; www.cga.ct.gov/capitoltours; cnr Capitol Ave & Trinity St; ⊙ hourly tours 9:15am-1:15pm Mon-Fri Sep-Jun, plus 2:15pm Jul-Aug) **FREE** Built of New England granite and white marble and topped by an ostentatious gold-leaf dome, the Gothic palace that is Connecticut's State Capitol (1879) was de-

signed by Richard Upjohn and took over a decade to complete. Because of the variety of architectural styles it reflects, it's been called 'the most beautiful ugly building in the world.' Frank Lloyd Wright dismissed it as 'ridiculous.' You be the judge. Guided tours depart from the southwest entrance of the Legislative Office Building (☑ 860-240-1000; 300 Capitol Ave).

Bushnell Park   PARK
(☑ tour 860-232-6710; www.bushnellpark.org; tours by donation; ☉ dawn-dusk) The Capitol overlooks the 37-acre Bushnell Park, the first public park in the US built with taxpayers' money. It was designed by Jacob Weidenmann and opened in 1861. Weidenmann's unique vision – an informal, natural style – broke from the traditional New England central green, and included 157 varieties of trees and shrubs from around North America, Europe and East Asia. In July, the park hosts the nation's longest running free jazz concert series (www.hartfordmondaynight jazz.com).

Travelers Tower   VIEWPOINT
(☑ 860-277-4208; 1 Tower Sq; ☉ 10am-3pm mid-May–Oct) FREE The best views of the city and the Connecticut River can be found on the observation deck of the newly restored, 34-story Travelers Tower, named after its tenant, the Travelers Insurance Company. When it was built, in 1919, the tower was the tallest in New England and the seventh tallest in the USA. To reach the observation deck, you have to climb 70 steps along a spiral staircase from the elevator to the deck.

Old State House   HISTORIC BUILDING
(☑ 860-522-6766; www.ctoldstatehouse.org; 800 Main St; adult/child $8/4; ☉ 10am-5pm Tue-Sat Jul–mid-Oct, Mon-Fri mid-Oct–Jul; ◈) Connect-icut's original capitol building (from 1797 to 1873) was designed by Charles Bulfinch, who also designed the Massachusetts State House in Boston, and was the site of the trial of the *Amistad* prisoners. Gilbert Stuart's famous 1801 portrait of George Washington hangs in the senate chamber. The newly expanded space houses interactive exhibits aimed at kids, as well as a Museum of Curiosities that features a two-headed calf, a narwhal's horn and a variety of mechanical devices.

Harriet Beecher-Stowe Center   MUSEUM
(☑ 860-522-9258; www.harrietbeecherstowe.org; 77 Forest St; adult/child $14/8; ☉ 9:30am-5pm Mon-Sat, noon-5pm Sun; P) As well as literary titan Mark Twain, Hartford was also home to Harriet Beecher Stowe, author of the antislavery book *Uncle Tom's Cabin*. Upon meeting Stowe, Abraham Lincoln is alleged to have said, 'So this is the little lady who made this big war.' The facility centers around the Stowe House, built in 1871, which reflects the author's strong ideas about decorating and domestic efficiency, as she expressed in her bestseller *American Woman's Home,* which was nearly as popular as her famous novel.

At the time of writing, restoration of the Stowe House was underway, with an estimated completion date of late 2017. The 1873 Visitor Center building and 1884 Katharine Seymour Day House will host guests until works are completed. Staff aim to show guests through parts of the Stowe House where construction permits.

✦ Festivals & Events

Greater Hartford Festival of Jazz   MUSIC
(www.hartfordjazz.org; ☉ Jul) The largest free jazz event in New England is held at venues throughout town.

DINOSAUR STATE PARK

Connecticut's answer to Jurassic Park, Dinosaur State Park (☑ 860-529-8423; www.dinosaurstatepark.org; 400 West St, Rocky Hill; adult/6-12yr $6/2; ☉ grounds 9am-4:30pm, exhibition center 9am-4:30pm Tue-Sun; P) lets you view dinosaur footprints left 200 million years ago on mudflats near Rocky Hill, 10 miles due south of Hartford along I-91. The tracks hardened in the mud and were only uncovered by road-building crews in the early 20th century. Today, they're preserved beneath a geodesic dome and you can tour an 80ft-long diorama that shows how the tracks were made. The park also has a picnic area and 2 miles of interesting nature trails.

Outside, there are several on-site dino prints where visitors can make plaster casts. The casting site is free, open from May through October, and the park provides everything you need but the plaster of paris, 25lb of which is recommended to make several decent-sized casts.

🛏 Sleeping

Sadly, it's slim pickings for decent hotels in Hartford's downtown core and prices can be steep for what you get. Better value may be found in chain offerings outside the city center.

★ **Hartford Marriott Downtown**　HOTEL $$
(☑ 860-249-8000; www.marriott.com; 200 Columbus Blvd; d/ste from $159/279; 🅿 @ 🛜 🛎) This colossal Marriott hotel is in the Adriaen's Landing District overlooking the Connecticut River and linked to the convention center. There are 401 stylish rooms spread over 22 stories alongside an indoor rooftop pool and fitness center. There's also an affiliated spa, an upscale restaurant and a slick bar on the ground floor.

★ **Silas W. Robbins House**　B&B $$$
(185 Broad St, Wethersfield; d $195-325; 🅿 😊 🛜) About 6 miles south of downtown Hartford in the charming historic village of Wethersfield, you'll find this beautiful and opulent 1873 French Second Empire home. Its common areas and five plush rooms with their soaring ceilings and light-filled windows overlooking the manicured grounds have been refurbished in the style of the period.

🍴 Eating & Drinking

Hartford has some noteworthy restaurants for a city of its size. Many participate in the biannual **Taste of Hartford** (www.ctnow.com/food-drink/restaurants/taste-of-hartford; ⊙ dates vary) festival.

Kitchen at Billings Forge　CAFE $
(☑ 860-727-8066; www.billingsforgeworks.org/the-kitchen; 559 Broad St; items $6-10; ⊙ 8am-4pm Mon-Fri) 🌿 Providing training and employment opportunities for the Billings Forge/Hartford community, this bright, forward-thinking cafe works with local farmers to source fresh seasonal produce in addition to what is grown in the community garden and farmers market to create a truly sustainable dining experience. The menu of salads, soups, sandwiches and fresh baked goods is usually under $10.

★ **Trumbull Kitchen**　MODERN AMERICAN $$
(www.maxrestaurantgroup.com/trumbull/; 150 Trumbull St; mains $13-30; ⊙ noon-11pm Mon-Sat, 4-10pm Sun) TK's smart-yet-casual fine-dining atmosphere awaits, with excellent service and a wonderfully executed, truly diverse menu making it a great alternative to some of Hartford's classier joints. Drop in for a cocktail and some fabulous appetizers, or save that appetite for fish, chicken, burgers and steak, freshly prepared and presented like works of art.

Salute　ITALIAN $$
(☑ 860-899-1350; www.salutehartford.com; 100 Trumbull St; lunch mains $9-16, dinner $16-33; ⊙ 11:30am-11pm Mon-Thu, to midnight Fri & Sat, 3-10pm Sun; 🌿) Charming service is the hallmark of this urban gem, which offers a contemporary take on Italian flavors. Regulars rave about the cheesy garlic bread, but other offerings are a tad more sophisticated. The pleasant patio overlooks Bushnell Park.

★ **ON20**　FUSION $$$
(☑ 860-722-5161; www.ontwenty.com; 400 Columbus Blvd; mains $25-35; ⊙ 11:30am-1:30pm Mon-Fri, plus 5:30-9:30pm Wed-Sat) On the 20th floor of the Hartford Steam Boiler Inspection and Insurance Co, contemporary ON20 serves an elegant fusion menu with peerless views of the city. An ever-evolving menu with dishes like lemongrass-scented loin with white bean chili, and laughing-bird shrimp with roasted grape are executed with precision and immaculately presented with bright drizzles, micro greens and flowers.

★ **City Steam Brewery Café**　BREWPUB
(☑ 860-525-1600; http://citysteam.biz; 942 Main St; ⊙ 11:30am-1am Mon-Sat, 4-10pm Sun) This big and boisterous place has housemade beers on tap. The Naughty Nurse Pale Ale is a bestseller, but the seasonals are also worth a try. The brewery's basement is home to the **Brew Ha Ha Comedy Club** (☑ 860-525-1600; http://citysteam.biz; 942 Main St; ticket prices vary; ⊙ show times vary), where you can yuk it up with visiting comedians from New York and Boston. There's plenty of great food to soak up the ale too.

☆ Entertainment

Check out CTNow (www.ctnow.com) for weekly entertainment listings.

Bushnell　CONCERT VENUE
(☑ 860-987-5900; www.bushnell.org; 166 Capitol Ave; ticket prices vary; ⊙ box office 10am-5pm Mon-Fri, to 2pm Sat) Hosting over 500 events a year, Bushnell plays a major role in the state's cultural life. This landmark historic building is the go to for most ballet, symphony, opera and chamber-music performances.

Hartford Symphony　CLASSICAL MUSIC
(☑ 860-244-2999; www.hartfordsymphony.org; ticket prices vary) The well-respected Hartford Symphony stages performances in the Bushnell all year-round.

NEW BRITAIN

Not technically a part of the Connecticut River Valley, and not really a suburb of Hartford either, New Britain (pop 73,000) is hard to situate and easy to miss. Indeed, this small formerly industrial city has seen better days. Even so, the city's truly wonderful art museum is reason enough to visit.

Moved to its present, modern premises in 2003 in honor of its centenary, the impressive yet little-known **New Britain Museum of American Art** (☑860-229-0257; www.nbmaa.org; 56 Lexington St; adult/child/student $15/free/10; ☺11am-5pm Sun-Wed & Fri, 11am-8pm Thu, 10am-5pm Sat) houses a standout collection of strictly American works, the first of its kind in the country. In 2015 the museum unveiled the state-of-the art Chase Building and all but doubled the size of its collection in recent years. Its works are presented and contextualized according to 'schools' – the Hudson River School, the Ash Can School and the American Scene Painters, for example – giving a fantastic overview of the development of modern American art. The collection features some outstanding pieces, including Thomas Benton's stunning *Arts of Life* murals painted at the height of the Great Depression.

Hungry? Stop in at **Capitol Lunch** (☑860-229-8237; www.capitollunch.com; 510 Main St; hot dogs $1.90, meals from $5; ☺10am-8pm Mon-Sat, 11am-6pm Sun) for some of the best hot dogs you'll find anywhere. Going strong for over 80 years, this is no gourmet sausage shop, but get the famous dog with mustard, onions and secret homemade sauce and you'll see immediately what all the fuss is about.

For something totally different and authentic, check out **Avery's Beverages** (☑860-224-0830; www.averysoda.com; 520 Corbin Ave; ☺8:30am-5:30pm Tue-Fri, to 3pm Sat, hours vary Mon); its 30-plus flavors of sodas and seltzers (including the hysterical 'Totally Gross' soda range) are still made with 1950s technology in the original red barn where it all started back in 1904. The water is pure well and the sugar is pure cane – no high-fructose corn syrup here.

Real Art Ways CINEMA

(RAW; ☑860-232-1006; www.realartways.org; 56 Arbor St; ticket prices vary; ☺gallery 2-10pm Tue-Thu & Sun, 2-11pm Fri & Sat) FREE Contemporary media works find an outlet at this consistently offbeat and adventurous gallery/cinema/performance space/lounge. Sip wine or beer as you watch a hot doco, listen to an all-female chamber-rock quintet or contemplate performance art. Networkers will love talking the talk with Hartford's art community at the **Creative Cocktail Hour**, held on the third Thursday of every month ($10, 6pm to 10pm).

Aetna Theater CINEMA

(☑860-278-2670; www.thewadsworth.org; 600 Main St; adult/senior & student $9/8; ☺Jun-Sep) Within the Wadsworth Atheneum (p245), this handsome art-deco theater shows independent and art films sporadically throughout the year.

Hartford Stage THEATER

(☑860-527-5151; www.hartfordstage.org; 50 Church St; ticket prices vary; ☺box office noon-5pm Mon-Fri) Staging around six major productions and one or two summer productions each season, this respected theater attracts recognized actors to Hartford. Plays include

classic dramas and provocative new works. Venturi & Rauch designed the striking theater building of red brick with darker red zig-zag details.

ℹ Information

Greater Hartford Welcome Center (☑860-244-0253; www.letsgoarts.org/welcomecenter; 100 Pearl St; ☺9am-5pm Mon-Fri) The bulk of tourist services can be found at this centrally located office.

ℹ Getting There & Away

Centrally located **Union Station** (www.amtrak.com; 1 Union Pl) is the city's transportation hub. Catch trains, airport shuttles, intercity buses and taxis from here.

AIR

Bradley International Airport (p434) is in Windsor Locks. The Bradley Flyer connects the airport with downtown Hartford ($1.50, 30 minutes, hourly).

CAR & MOTORCYCLE

By car, interstates connect Hartford to Boston (102 miles), New Haven (36 miles), New York (117 miles) and Providence (71 miles).

TRAIN

Amtrak (p244) trains connect Hartford to Boston (from $52, four hours via New Haven) and New York's Penn Station (from $33, two hours 45 minutes).

ⓘ Getting Around

BUS

Connecticut Transit (p244) operates citywide bus services. A general all-day bus pass costs $3.25.

TAXI

For cabs, check the taxi stand outside Union Station, or call **Yellow Cab Co** (☑ 860-666-6666; www.theyellowcab.com). Uber (www.uber.com) and Lyft (www.lyft.com) ride-sharing services also operate in and around Hartford.

CONNECTICUT RIVER VALLEY

The Connecticut River, New England's longest, flows southwards 410 miles from its humble source at Fourth Connecticut Lake, just 300yd from the Canadian border. It forms the state boundary between Vermont and New Hampshire, before snaking its way through Massachusetts and Connecticut until it meets the Atlantic at Long Island Sound. Mercifully, it escaped the bustle of industry and commerce that marred many of the northeast's rivers.

Today, well-preserved historic towns grace the river's banks, notably Old Lyme, Essex, Ivoryton, Chester and East Haddam. Together, they enchant visitors with gracious country inns, fine dining, train rides and river excursions that allow authentic glimpses into provincial life on the Connecticut.

East Haddam

☑ 860 / POP 9150

Surrounded by the Seven Sisters hills, East Haddam is a quiet, pretty town on the banks of the Connecticut River. You'll find a handful of worthwhile attractions in town and some great spots to picnic in the surrounding countryside.

The town came into the spotlight at the turn of the 20th century on account of two of its more flamboyant residents, actor William Hooker Gillette (of *Sherlock Holmes* fame) and wealthy local banker and merchant William Goodspeed. Goodspeed's phi-

lanthropy indirectly led to the formation of a company which wrote and produced more than a dozen Broadway musicals and as many Tony Award–winning shows.

With residents like Gillette and Goodspeed, East Haddam became a regular stopover on the summer circuit for New Yorkers, who travelled up on Goodspeed's steamship. These days, it's a sweet, sleepy town which will most interest history and nature buffs.

◉ Sights

Gillette Castle   CASTLE, PARK

(☑ 860-526-2336; www.ct.gov/dep/gillettecastle; 67 River Rd; adult/child $6/2; ◉ castle 10am-4:30pm late May–mid-Oct, grounds 8am-dusk year-round; ℗) Built in 1919 by actor William Hooker Gillette, who made his fortune playing Sherlock Holmes, this gaudy, medieval-style 'castle' is an eccentric turreted mansion made of fieldstone. Looming on one of the Seven Sisters hills above East Haddam, the folly is modeled on the medieval castles of Germany's Rhineland and the views from its terraces are spectacular. The surrounding 125 acres are a designated state park.

🛏 Sleeping

★ Boardman House Inn   B&B $$

(☑ 860-873-9233; www.boardmanhouse.com; 8 Norwich Rd; r from $199-269; ℗ ❄ 🛜) If you're in town for the opera, make a weekend of it and stay at the elegant, hard-to-fault Boardman House Inn: book the light-filled garden suite if you can. The house is a spectacular 1860 Second Empire mansion with a deep porch, tall French windows and a rose-filled garden.

☆ Entertainment

Goodspeed Opera House   THEATRE

(☑ 860-873-8668; www.goodspeed.org; 6 Main St; tickets $45-70; ◉ performances Wed-Sun Apr-Dec) The classic Goodspeed Opera House is an 1876 Victorian music hall known as 'the birthplace of the American musical' and still produces a full schedule of shows: *Man of La Mancha* and *Annie* premiered here before going on to national fame. It's worth a look at the fascinating riverfront building even if you aren't able to catch a performance.

ⓘ Getting There & Away

East Haddam is almost midway between Hartford (28 miles) and Old Lyme (21 miles) by car, including an optional ride on the historical vehicle-friendly Chester–Hadlyme Ferry (p252), when it's running.

Chester

📞 860 / POP 3840

Cupped in the valley of Pattaconk Brook, Chester is a placid riverside village with a general store, post office, library and a few shops accounting for most of the action.

🍴 Eating

When in the area, it's worth planning a meal in one of Chester's handful of noteworthy restaurants.

Good Elephant Bistro   VIETNAMESE, FRENCH $$
(📞 860-526-5301; www.goodelephantcafe.com; 59 Main St; meals $17-28; ⊙5-9pm Tue-Sun) In 2016 Chester's lauded L&E French bistro merged with the Good Elephant to expand its repertoire of contemporary French cuisine with aromatic French-Vietnamese dishes. It works. Come on Sunday for Vietnamese street food, Tuesday for an Asian twist on burger night, and any other night for foie gras, fresh seafood bursting with herbs and spices, and atmosphere aplenty.

★ River Tavern   BISTRO $$$
(📞 860-526-9417;   www.rivertavernrestaurant.com; 23 Main St; meals $20-34; ⊙11:30am-2:30pm & 5-9:30pm) This popular wood-accented bistro with a bar and dining-room menu dishes up impeccable food with a variety of inflections. The menu changes, but if it's in season you should definitely order shad, caught from the Connecticut River. Save room for Toshi's made-to-order date pudding with dark rum caramel sauce – order ahead.

🛍 Shopping

Chester is a popular spot for day-trippers who enjoy browsing the handful of quaint antique shops and boutiques.

❶ Getting There & Away

By car, Chester is a short diversion off I-95 between New Haven (35 miles) and New London (26 miles). From Hartford (30 miles), take I-91 south and pick up scenic CT 9, which runs right through town.

In summer, you can cross the Connecticut River on the car and pedestrian Chester–Hadlyme Ferry (p252).

Connecticut River Valley

CONNECTICUT ESSEX

Essex

📞 860 / POP 6700

Tree-lined Essex, established in 1635, stands as the chief town of the Connecticut River Valley region. It's worth a visit if only to gawk at the beautiful, well-preserved Federal-period houses, legacies of rum and tobacco fortunes made in the 19th century. The town also has a strong following with steam rail and riverboat enthusiasts.

◉ Sights & Activities

★ Essex Steam Train & Riverboat Ride
STEAM TRAIN

(📞860-767-0103; www.essexsteamtrain.com; 1 Railroad Ave; adult/child $19/10, incl cruise $29/19; ⊙May-Oct, dates vary; 🚃) This wildly popular attraction features a steam locomotive and antique carriages. The journey travels six scenic miles to Deep River, where you can cruise to the Goodspeed Opera House (p250) in East Haddam, before returning to Essex via train. The round-trip train ride takes about an hour; with the riverboat ride it's 2½ hours.

🛏 Sleeping

Griswold Inn
INN $$

(📞860-767-1776; www.griswoldinn.com; 36 Main St; d/ste from $155/200; P🐾) The landmark Griswold Inn is one of the oldest continually operating inns in the country and has been Essex's physical and social centerpiece since 1776. The inn's buffet-style Hunt Breakfast (served 11am to 1pm Sunday) is a tradition dating to the War of 1812, when British soldiers occupying Essex demanded to be fed.

CHESTER–HADLYME FERRY

In summer, you can cross the Connecticut River on the historic Chester–Hadlyme Ferry (www.ctvisit.com/listings/chesterhadlyme-ferry; car/pedestrian $5/2; ⊙7am-6:45pm Mon-Fri, 10:30am-5pm Sat & Sun Apr-Nov). A service has been operating here (seasonally) since 1769, making it one of the oldest continuously operating ferry services in the US. The five-minute river crossing on the *Selden III* affords great views of Gillette Castle (p250) and deposits passengers at the foot of the castle in East Haddam. In the opposite direction it's a fun way to link up with the Essex Steam Train, which runs between Chester and Essex.

---

❶ Getting There & Away

By road, from scenic CT 9 you'll come into the town center and eventually find yourself deposited onto Main St.

Old Lyme

📞 860 / POP 7600

Near the mouth of the Connecticut River and perched on the smaller Lieutenant River, Old Lyme was home to some 60 sea captains in the 19th century. Since the early 20th century, however, Old Lyme has been known as the center of the Lyme Art Colony, which cultivated the nascent American Impressionist movement. Numerous artists, including William Chadwick, Childe Hassam, Willard Metcalfe and Henry Ward Ranger, came here to paint, staying in the mansion of local art patron Florence Griswold.

Worth a look-in if you're nearby, Old Lyme is a pleasant town with some pretty historic buildings, which will appeal most to folks with a particular interest in American art.

◉ Sights

Florence Griswold Museum
MUSEUM

(📞860-434-4452; florencegriswoldmuseum.org; 96 Lyme St; adult/child $10/free; ⊙10am-5pm Tue-Sat, 1-5pm Sun; P) The 'home of American Impressionism,' the Florence Griswold Museum exhibits 6000 works with solid collections of American Impressionist and Barbizon paintings, as well as sculpture and decorative arts. Her house, which her artist friends decorated with murals (often in lieu of paying rent), is now the Florence Griswold Museum. The estate consists of her Georgian-style house, the Krieble Gallery, the Chadwick studio and Griswold's beloved gardens.

🛏 Sleeping

★ Bee & Thistle Inn
INN $$

(📞860-434-1667; www.beeandthistleinn.com; 100 Lyme St; r from $109-219; P🐾) Occupying a handsome, Dutch Colonial farmhouse dating to 1756, this classy establishment has beautiful well-tended gardens that stretch down to the Lieutenant River. Most of its 11 plush, well-appointed rooms feature abundant antiques and a canopy or four-poster bed.

❶ Getting There & Away

Accessible by road, Old Lyme is just off I-95, between New Haven (34 miles) and New London (16 miles).

HAMMONASSET BEACH STATE PARK

Though not off the beaten path by any means, the two full miles of flat, sandy beach at Hammonasset Beach State Park (☑203-245-2785; www.ct.gov/deep/hammonasset; 1288 Boston Post Rd; residents $9-13, nonresidents $15-22; ☉8am-sunset; ℙ), located midway between Old Lyme and New Haven, nicely accommodates summer crowds. Backed by pines, the 1100-acre sanctuary offers superb swimming, excellent facilities (including showers) and a long wooden boardwalk.

Stroll all the way to Meigs Point at the tip of the peninsula and visit the Meigs Point Nature Center (☉10am-4pm Tue-Sat) before heading out on a trail that meanders through saltwater marshes for excellent bird-watching.

Hammonasset Beach State Park Campground (☑203-245-1817; www.ct.gov/deep/hammonasset; 1288 Boston Post Rd; campsites residents/nonresidents $20/30, with electric hook-up $35/45, cabins $70/80; ℙ🐾) offers Connecticut's only beach camping and, despite its 558 sites, is often full in high summer. Rustic cabins are available. Reserve sites and cabins well in advance.

EAST OF THE CONNECTICUT RIVER

The southeastern corner of Connecticut is home to the state's number-one tourist attraction and the country's largest maritime museum, Mystic Seaport. Built on the site of a former shipbuilding yard in 1929, the museum celebrates the area's seafaring heritage when fishermen, whalers and clipper-ship engineers broke world speed records and manufactured gunboats and warships for the Civil War.

To the west of Mystic, you'll find the submarine capital of the USA, Groton, where General Dynamics built WWII subs, and across the Thames River, New London. To the east is the historic fishing village of Stonington, extending along a narrow mile-long peninsula into the sea. It's one of the most charming seaside villages in New England, where Connecticut's only remaining commercial fleet operates and yachties come ashore in summer to enjoy the charming restaurants on Water St.

New London

☑ 860 / POP 27,545

During its golden age in the mid-19th century, New London, then home to some 200 whaling vessels, was one of the largest whaling centers in the US and one of the wealthiest port cities. In 1858 the discovery of crude oil in Pennsylvania sent the value of whale oil plummeting and began a long period of decline for the city, from which it has never fully recovered. Even so, New London retains strong links with its seafaring past (the US Coast Guard Academy and US Naval Submarine Base are here) and its downtown is listed on the National Register of Historic Places.

Despite lacking the sanitized tourism push of nearby Mystic and Stonington, remnants of New London's glorious and opulent times are still evident throughout the city, making it one of Connecticut's most surprising destinations for those interested in history, architecture and urban sociology.

◎ Sights

New London is a bit of a sprawl. A good place to start is to hit the Visitor Center at the Historic Waterfront District where you can pick up the excellent walking tour produced by The New London Historic Society. It's also available online (www.newlondon landmarks.org). Several blocks back from the waterfront, on Huntington St, Whale Oil Row features four white mansions (Nos 105, 111, 117 and 119) built for whaling merchants in 1830. More historic houses line Starr St, between Eugene O'Neill Dr and Washington St. Although intrepid explorers will enjoy driving around neighborhood backstreets where the fine architecture-in-decline seems endless, there are some gritty areas where it's best to keep your wits about you.

Hygienic Art   GALLERY
(☑860-443-8001; www.hygienic.org; 79 Bank St; price varies for some exhibitions; ☉11am-3pm Tue-Thu, to 6pm Fri & Sat, from noon Sun) FREE Done up in a Greek Revival style replete with a sculpture garden, mural plaza, fountains and a large performance area, this not-for-profit art space hosts poetry readings, film screenings, a summer concert series and an

WORTH A TRIP

THE QUIET CORNER

Wedged between the Quinebaug and Shetucket Rivers valley, Connecticut's Quiet Corner is known locally as 'the last green valley' between Boston and Washington. The 12 miles of CT 169 between Brooklyn and Woodstock induce sighs of contentment and frequent pullovers. To get to CT 169 from New London, take I-395 north; from Stonington take CT 2 through Norwich.

From **Norwich** pick up CT 169 to **Canterbury**, where the **Prudence Crandall House Museum** (☑860-546-7800; friendsofprudencecrandallmuseum.org; 1 South Canterbury Rd, Canterbury; adult/child $6/free; ☺10am-4pm Thu-Sun May-Nov) records the heroic attempt of a Baptist schoolmistress to offer the daughters of free African American farmers an equal education in 1832. She was arrested for her efforts. Continue on to bucolic **Brooklyn** and consider dining at the fabulous **Golden Lamb Buttery** (☑860-774-4423; www.thegoldenlamb.com; 499 Wolf Den Rd, Brooklyn; mains lunch $12-17, prix-fixe dinner menu $75; ☺noon-2.30pm Thu-Sat, 7pm sitting Fri & Sat; 🅿 🐴) 🍴, where you can enjoy a farm-to-table lunch or award-winning, atmosphere-aplenty prix-fixe four-course dinner (7pm, Friday to Saturday only) with a hayride thrown in.

In **Pomfret**, quaint accommodation at **Chickadee Cottage** (☑806-963-0587; 70 Averill Rd, Pomfret Center; cottages $175-210; 🅿 🐕) allows for further exploration of the region. Homemade ice creams from **We-Li-Kit Ice Cream** (☑860-974-1095; www.welikit. com; 728 Hampton Rd, Pomfret Center; scoops from $3.50; ☺11am-8pm Apr-Oct; 🐕) round off perfect summer days: there's a bunch of wacky and wonderful flavors to choose from.

Detour to **Abington** for wine tastings and scenic dining amid the vineyards of **Sharpe Hill** (☑860-974-3549; http://sharpehill.com; 108 Wade Rd, Pomfret; tastings $10-15; ☺11am-5pm Fri-Sun). Arguably Connecticut's finest vineyard, its wines have been awarded over 250 international medals. Take a walk through the vines before sitting down to a gourmet locavore meal at the vineyard's restaurant. That is, if you phoned ahead well in advance – lunch and dinner hours vary and reservations are essential.

End your tour in **Woodstock** in the flourishing gardens of the **Roseland Cottage-Bowen House** (☑860-928-4074; www.historicnewengland.org; 556 Rte 169; adult/student $10/5; ☺11am-5pm Wed-Sun Jun 1-Oct 15), a colorful and unusual 1846 Gothic Revival–style mansion, meticulously maintained by the wonderful people at Historic New England. Follow up with English tea and scones at **Mrs Bridge's Pantry** (☑860-963-7040; 292 Rte 169, South Woodstock; items $4.50, tea service $14.50; ☺11am-5pm; 🐕), then stock up on blueberries and apples at the old-fashioned **Woodstock Orchards** (☑860-928-2225; 494 CT 169, Woodstock; ☺9am-6pm).

For further information on the Quiet Corner, take a look at the Northeast Connecticut Visitor Guide (www.visitnect.com).

annual art show attracting nearly 500 artists. The gardens and amphitheater are open during daylight hours. It's also the starting point for the **New London Mural Walk**, a self-directed tour highlighting 16 colorful murals and other large-scale installations: a great way to meet the city.

Fort Trumbull State Park FORT

(☑860-444-7591; www.ct.gov/deep/forttrumbull; 90 Walbach St; tours adult/child $6/2; ☺park 8am-sunset, fort 9am-5pm Wed-Sun mid-May–Columbus Day; 🅿) **FREE** The best view of New London is to be had from the enormous Fort Trumbull, which has stood at the mouth of the Thames River since 1839. It was an integral part of the coastal defense system and an early home for the US Coast Guard Acad-

emy. Now winding walking paths, a fishing pier and fort tours make it a great place to take kids.

Custom House
Maritime Museum MUSEUM

(☑860-447-2501; www.nlmaritimesociety.org; 150 Bank St; adult/child $7/5; ☺1-5pm Wed-Sun Apr-Dec, 1-5pm Thu-Sun Jan-Mar) Near the ferry terminal, this 1833 building is the oldest operating customhouse in the country, in addition to functioning as a museum. Its front door is made from the wood of the USS *Constitution*.

Monte Cristo Cottage LIBRARY, MUSEUM

(☑860-443-0051; www.theoneill.org/monte-cristo -cottage; 325 Pequot Ave; adult/senior & student

$7/5; ⊙noon-4pm Thu-Sun Jun-Aug; P) This cottage was the boyhood summer home of Eugene O'Neill, America's only Nobel Prize–winning playwright. Near Ocean Beach Park in the southern districts of the city (follow the signs), the Victorian-style house is now a research library for dramatists. Many of O'Neill's belongings are on display, including his desk. You might recognize the living room: it was the inspiration for the setting for two of O'Neill's most famous plays, *Long Day's Journey into Night* and *Ah, Wilderness!*

🏃 Activities

Ocean Beach Park BEACH
(📞860-447-3031; www.ocean-beach-park.com; 98 Neptune Ave; adult/child $6/4) At the southern end of Ocean Ave, this popular beach and amusement area has waterslides, a picnic area, miniature golf, an arcade, a swimming pool and an old-fashioned boardwalk. The parking fee ($24/28 weekdays/weekends) includes admission for everyone in your car. The pool and attractions all cost extra, but the kids will be begging not to leave.

🎉 Festivals & Events

Sailfest SAILING
(www.sailfest.org) This three-day festival in July features live entertainment, tall ships, amusement rides and fireworks over the Thames River.

🍴 Sleeping & Eating

Holiday Inn New London HOTEL $
(📞860-443-7000; www.holidayinn.com/newlon donct; 35 Governor Winthrop Blvd; ⊙d from $97; P❄🐾🛜🏊) New London's only downtown hotel received a complete renovation in 2013 that still feels fresh. Beds and showers do what they're supposed to do well, and a range of room types, including four suites, is available.

★On the Waterfront SEAFOOD $$
(📞860-444-2800; www.onthewaterfrontnl.com; 250 Pequot Ave; mains $11-28; ⊙3-9pm Tue, from noon Wed-Sun; 🐕) A spectacular lobster bisque and other delights from the deep, like pistachio-crusted salmon and Montauk-jumbo-stuffed shrimp are served up with water views from a multitude of windows. The bar is a popular spot with locals who don't like it rowdy. A diverse menu and friendly staff help to accommodate die-hard landlubbers and those with food intolerances.

🍷 Drinking & Entertainment

Part of New London's charm is its rough edges, which can also wear thin at some of the town's hard-boozing bars on the river side of Bank St. During the day, they're worth a visit for their enviable decks overlooking the river.

Dutch Tavern PUB
(📞860-442-3453; www.dutch-tavern.com; 23 Green St; ⊙noon-midnight Mon-Sat, 1-8pm Sun (Nov-Jan only)) Raise a cold one to Eugene O'Neill at the Dutch, the only surviving bar in town that the playwright frequented (though back in the day it was known as the Oak). It's a good honest throwback to an earlier age, from the tin ceiling to the century-old potato-salad recipe.

Garde Arts Center THEATER
(📞860-444-7373; www.gardearts.org; 325 State St; ⊙box office 10am-5pm Mon-Fri) The centerpiece of this arts complex is the one-of-a-kind 1472-seat Garde Theater, a former vaudeville house, built in 1926, with a restored Moroccan interior. Today, the theater presents everything from Broadway plays to operas to national music acts and film screenings.

ℹ️ Information

New London Mainstreet (📞860-444-2489; www.newlondonmainstreet.org; 147 State St; ⊙9am-5pm Mon-Fri) This downtown revitalization organization maintains a useful up-to-date website and produces a downloadable downtown map and brochure.

ℹ️ Getting There & Away

New London's transport hub is **Union Station** (www.amtrak.com; 47 Water St), which is served by Amtrak. Conveniently, the bus station is in the same building and the ferry terminal (for boats to Long Island, Block Island and Fishers Island) is next door.

BOAT

Cross Sound Ferry (📞860-443-5281; www.longislandferry.com; 2 Ferry St) operates car ferries (one way adult/child $15.75/6) and high-speed passenger ferries (one way adult/child $21.50/9) year-round between Orient Point, Long Island, NY, and New London, a 1½-hour run on the car ferry, 40 minutes on the high-speed ferry. From late June through Labor Day, ferries depart each port every hour on the hour from 7am to 9pm (last boats at 9:45pm). The 'auto and driver' fare is $55, for bicycles $5.

Fishers Island Ferry (📞860-442-0165; www.fiferry.com; 5 Waterfront Park; adult/senior &

child mid-May–mid-Sep $25/18, mid-Sep–mid-May $19/14, cars $56/40) runs cars and passengers from New London to Fishers Island, NY, several times a day year-round.

Block Island Express (☑ 860-444-4624; www.goblockisland.com; 2 Ferry St; adult/child/bike $25/12.50/10) operates summer-only services between New London and Block Island, RI.

CAR & MOTORCYCLE

The I-95 runs right through the center of town. New London's commercial district is just southwest of Union Station along Bank St. Follow Ocean Ave to reach Ocean Beach Park.

TRAIN

Amtrak (p244) trains between New York City (from $39, 2½ hours) and Boston (from $29, 1½ hours) stop at New London.

Groton

☑ 860 / POP 40,115

Just across the Thames River from New London, Groton is the proud home to the US Naval Submarine Base, the first and the largest in the country, and General Dynamics Corporation, a major naval defense contractor. Unsurprisingly, both claims to fame are vigorously off-limits to the public.

◉ Sights & Activities

Historic Ship Nautilus & Submarine Force Museum   MUSEUM
(☑ 800-343-0079; www.ussnautilus.org; 1 Crystal Lake Rd; ⊙ 9am-4pm Wed-Mon; ℗) FREE Kids love the Historic Ship Nautilus & Submarine Force Museum, home to *Nautilus,* the world's first nuclear-powered submarine and the first sub to transit the North Pole. The brief audio tour of *Nautilus* is fascinating primarily for military enthusiasts. Other museum exhibits feature working periscopes and sounds of the ocean.

★ Project Oceanology   CRUISE
(☑ 860-445-9007; www.oceanology.org; 1084 Shennecossett Rd; cruises adult/child $25/20; ⊙ reservations 9am-4pm Mon-Fri) Established by a group of teachers in the 1970s, Project Oceanology has now developed into a fully fledged marine-science program. In summer months families are invited aboard various cruises, including lighthouse expeditions, oceanographic research cruises (mid-Jun to August) and seal watches (February to March). The science cruises are the highlight, with hands-on activities, such as testing samples, trawling nets, recording data and navigation.

It is also the only organization with permission to bring visitors to **New London Ledge Lighthouse**, which features incredible views from smack-dab in the middle of Long Island Sound.

ℹ Getting There & Away

The I-95 crosses the Thames River via the Gold Star Memorial Bridge. New London is on one side, Groton the other. Mystic lies 8 miles to the east and is also accessed by I-95.

Mystic

☑ 860 / POP 4200

A skyline of masts greets you as you arrive in town on US 1. They belong to the vessels bobbing ever so slightly in the postcard-perfect harbor. There's a sense of self-satisfied calm and composure in the air – until suddenly a heart-stopping steamer whistle blows, followed by the cheerful cling of a drawbridge bell. You know you've arrived in Mystic.

From simple beginnings in the 17th century, the village of Mystic grew to become a prosperous whaling center and one of the great shipbuilding ports of the East Coast. In the mid-19th century, Mystic's shipyards launched clipper ships, gunboats and naval transport vessels, many from the George Greenman & Co Shipyard, now the site of Mystic Seaport Museum, Connecticut's largest tourist attraction.

◉ Sights & Activities

★ Mystic Seaport Museum   MUSEUM
(☑ 860-572-0711; www.mysticseaport.org; 75 Greenmanville Ave; adult/child $26/17; ⊙ 9am-5pm Apr-Oct, 10am-4pm Thu-Sun Nov-Mar; ℗🐾) More than a museum, Mystic Seaport is the re-creation of an entire New England whaling village spread over 17 acres of the former George Greenman & Co Shipyard. To re-create the past, 60 historic buildings, four tall ships and almost 500 smaller vessels are gathered along the Mystic River. Interpreters staff the site and are glad to discuss traditional crafts and trades. Most illuminating are the demonstrations on such topics as ship rescue, oystering and whaleboat launching.

Coogan Farm   FARM
(☑ 860-536-1216; www.dpnc.org; 162 Greenmanville Ave; ⊙ 9am-8pm; ℗🐾) 🌿 FREE Opened in Sep 2014, this public-access 45-acre his-

toric farm and nature center affords sweeping views of the Mystic River. Maintained by volunteers, the property features miles of walking tracks and protects two Stonington watersheds, wildlife habitats containing 10 species listed with a high conservation property, and historic farm buildings, which have been restored for educational use. A mile-long walking trail connects the farm with the **Denison Pequotsepos Nature Center** (☑ 860-536-1216; www.dpnc.org; 109 Pequotsepos Rd; ⊙ 9am-5pm; P ✦) ✎ FREE.

Mystic Aquarium
& Institute for Exploration AQUARIUM
(☑ 860-572-5955; www.mysticaquarium.org; 55 Coogan Blvd; adult/child $35/25; ⊙ 9am-5pm Apr-Aug, 9am-4pm Mar & Sep-Nov, from 10am Dec-Feb; ✦) This state-of-the-art aquarium boasts more than 6000 species of sea creatures, as well as an outdoor viewing area for watching seals and sea lions below the waterline and a penguin pavilion. The aquarium's most famous (and controversial) residents are the three beluga whales, who reside in the Arctic Coast exhibit. Animal-welfare groups claim it is debilitating to keep whales in enclosed containers.

Argia Mystic Cruises CRUISE
(☑ 860-536-0416; www.argiamystic.com; 15 Holmes St; adult/child $49/39) This outfit offers two- to three-hour daytime or sunset cruises down the Mystic River to Fishers' Island Sound on the authentic 19th-century replica schooner *Argia*.

★ Festivals & Events

Mystic Outdoor Art Festival ART
(⊙ Aug) In mid-August, Mystic hosts 300 international arts and craftspeople and attracts around 85,000 visitors.

Lobster Days FOOD & DRINK
(⊙ May) An old-fashioned lobster bake held at Mystic Seaport on Memorial Day weekend.

Antique & Classic
Boat Rendezvous PARADE
(⊙ Jul) Vintage vessels parade down a 3-mile stretch of Mystic River in late July.

FOXWOODS CASINO

Rising above the forest canopy of Great Cedar Swamp, between Norwich and Mystic, gargantuan **Foxwoods Casino** (☑ 800-369-9663; www.foxwoods.com; 350 Trolley Line Blvd, Mashantucket; ⊙ 24hr; P) is a must-see destination for those who don't have an aversion to the gambling industry. The complex features the world's largest bingo hall, nightclubs, cinemas, rides, video-game and pinball parlors for kids, world-class fine dining, casual eats, state-of-the art theatres attracting A-list performers and the impressive **Tanger Outlet Mall** (☑ 860-383-4340; www.tangeroutlet.com/foxwoods; 455 Trolley Line Blvd, Mashantucket; ⊙ 9am-9pm), a shopper's paradise.

Built on the ancestral land of the Mashantucket Pequot Tribal Nation (www.mashantucket.com), aka 'the fox people,' the casino is a remarkable symbol of the resilience of a tribe that was nearly annihilated by colonists in King Philip's 1637 war, and which then fought a long and dispiriting legal battle against attempts to declare the reservation abandoned in the 1970s and '80s. Their tenacity paid off, and in 1986 they were granted permission to open a high-stakes bingo hall. Not surprisingly, the casino and its success rejuvenated the tribe, which now numbers around 1000.

Ranging from the well-appointed to the sublime to the utterly decadent, **Foxwoods Resort** (☑ 800-369-9663; www.foxwoods.com/hotels.aspx; 50 Trolley Line Blvd, Mashantucket; d from $179-389; P ❄ ☎ ☎) boasts over 2200 guest rooms spread across five properties: the Grand Pequot Tower, Great Cedar Hotel, Fox Tower, The Villas at Foxwoods and Two Trees Inn. The range and variety of rooms is so great and pricing so variable that you'll need to scope out the website to see what tickles your fancy.

Visitors interested in the tribe behind the casino should definitely set aside a few hours to see the **Mashantucket Pequot Museum & Research Center** (☑ 800-411-9671; www.pequotmuseum.org; 110 Pequot Trail, off CT 214; adult/child $20/12; ⊙ 9am-5pm Wed-Sat). This ultramodern museum devoted to an ancient people features dioramas, films and interactive exhibits, highlighted by a very effective simulated glacial crevasse and a re-created 16th-century Pequot village. Shuttles run every 20 minutes between the museum and Foxwoods.

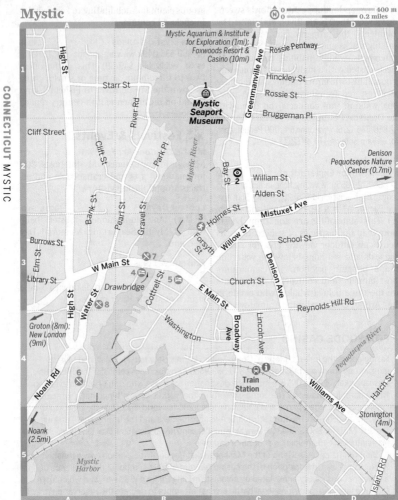

Mystic Aquarium & Institute
for Exploration (1mi);
Foxwoods Resort &
Casino (10mi)

1
Mystic
Seaport
Museum

Denison
Pequotsepos Nature
Center (0.7mi)

Groton (8mi);
New London
(9mi)

Noank
(2.5mi)

Mystic
Harbor

Train
Station

Stonington
(4mi)

Sleeping

As a bustling tourism boomtown, Mystic has an array of accommodations, the full gamut of which is listed at www.mystic.org/browse/where-to-stay. Reservations are recommended from June to August and on weekends. Outside these times, you'll enjoy a significant drop in room rates.

Whaler's Inn   INN $$
(☎860-536-1506; www.whalersinnmystic.com; 20 E Main St; d from $170; P@☎) In downtown Mystic, beside its historic drawbridge, this hotel combines an 1865 Victorian house

with a reconstructed luxury hotel from the same era (the original landmark 'Hoxie House' burned down in the 1970s) and a modern motel known as Stonington House. Seasonal packages available; these include the price of dinners and area attractions. Rates include continental breakfast, a small gym and complimentary bicycles.

★**Steamboat Inn**   INN $$$
(☎860-536-8300; www.steamboatinnmystic.com; 73 Steamboat Wharf; d from $205-260; P✳☎) Located right in the heart of downtown Mystic, the rooms of this historic inn have

wraparound water views and luxurious amenities, including two-person whirlpool tubs, cable TV, free local calls and fireplaces. Antiques lend the interior a romantic, period feel, and service is top-notch with baked goods for breakfast, complimentary bikes and boat docks.

✕ Eating

There are several places to grab a snack within Mystic Seaport Museum, but most of Mystic's restaurants are in or near the town center, close to the drawbridge. Among the town's claims to fame is Mystic Pizza, an otherwise unexceptional pizza place that shares its name with one of Julia Roberts' first films.

Mystic Drawbridge Ice Cream   ICE CREAM $
(☑ 860-572-7978; www.mysticdrawbridgeicecream. com; 2 W Main St; cones $4, panini $7.50; ⊙ 10am-9pm; ⊞) Strolling through town is best done with an ice-cream cone in hand. Some of the more quirky flavors, such as pumpkin pie and southern peach, are seasonal, but on any given day there will be something innovative to try. This perpetually buzzing parlor also serves some light fare, including panini, salads and quiche.

★Captain Daniel Packer Inne   AMERICAN $$
(☑ 860-536-3555; www.danielpacker.com; 32 Water St; mains $14-24; ⊙ 11am-10pm) This 1754 historic house has a low-beam ceiling and creaky floorboards. On the lower pub level, you'll find regulars at the bar, a good selection of beer on tap and excellent pub grub: try the fish and chips. Upstairs, the dining room has river views and an imaginative

American menu, including petite filet mignon with Gorgonzola sauce and walnut demi-glace. Reservations recommended.

★Oyster Club   SEAFOOD $$$
(☑ 860-415-9266; www.oysterclubct.com; 13 Water St; oysters $2, lunch mains $12-18, dinner mains $18-34; ⊙ 12-3pm & 5-10pm Fri & Sat, 10am-3pm & 5-9pm Sun, 5-9pm Mon-Thu; P☢) Offering casual fine dining at its best, this is the place locals come to knock down oysters on the deck out back. Grilled lobster and pan-roasted monkfish or flounder feature alongside veal, steak and a drool-worthy burger. If oysters are an aphrodisiac, anything could happen at the bar after the daily happy hour (4pm to 6pm), when shucked oysters are a buck each.

ⓘ Information

Greater Mystic Chamber of Commerce
(☑ 860-572-9578; www.mysticchamber.org; 12 Roosevelt Ave; ⊙ 9am-4:30pm) The Chamber of Commerce preaches the official word on tourism and operates a small kiosk in the train station.

ⓘ Getting There & Away

Mystic train station (2 Roosevelt Ave) is served by Amtrak (p244) trains to New York (from $41, 2½ hours) and Boston (from $49, one to 1½ hours). It's less than a mile south of Mystic Seaport Museum.

Mystic is just south of I-95 between New London and the border between Connecticut and Rhode Island.

Stonington
☑ 860 / POP 930
Five miles east of Mystic on US 1, Stonington is Connecticut's oldest 'borough' and one of the most appealing towns on the coast. Laid out on a peninsula that juts into Long Island Sound, the town's compact footprint is scattered with photogenic 18th- and 19th-century houses, many of which were once sea captains' homes.

⊙ Sights & Activities

The best way to explore the little town is on foot. Walk down **Water Street**, which runs north–south to the tip of the peninsula, and the tiny **Du Bois beach**, then head back north on Main St (parallel to Water St), one block east.

LOCAL KNOWLEDGE

WHERE THE LOCALS EAT LOBSTER

Locals know that the best place to head for fresh, fresh seafood is the tiny fishing village of **Noank**, situated on Morgan Point between Mystic and Groton. Almost the entire village is listed on the National Register of Historic Places thanks to its 18th- and 19th-century houses and shipyards, but the real treat in Noank is its seafood shacks. In fact, the quaint marine-side lobster shack covered in rainbow-colored buoys featured in the film *Mystic Pizza* is Noank's **Ford's Lobster** (☑860-536-2842; 15 Riverview Ave, Noank; mains $12-34; ☉11.30am-9pm). Here you can sit at an outdoor bar framing the dock and devour delicious buttered lobster rolls, clam chowder and mussels in white wine. If you can't get a seat or for something even more casual, head to **Captain Scott's Lobster Dock** (☑860-439-1741; www.captscotts.com; 80 Hamilton St; mains $7-21; ☉11am-9pm May-Oct; ☝) in nearby New London.

Old Lighthouse Museum MUSEUM
(☑860-535-1440; www.stoningtonhistory.org; 7 Water St; adult/child $9/6; ☉10am-5pm Thu-Tue May-Oct) Climb the winding iron staircase of this squat, granite lighthouse for 360-degree views from the lantern room. Afterwards browse the small museum, which recounts unsuccessful British assaults on the harbor during the American Revolution and the War of 1812, as well as hosting exhibits on whaling, Native American artifacts and curios from the China trade.

Included in the Old Lighthouse Museum ticket is admission to the 16-room **Captain Nathaniel Palmer House** (☑860-535-8445; www.stoningtonhistory.org; 40 Palmer St; adult/child $9/6; ☉1-5pm Mon-Tue & Thu-Sat), one of the finest houses in town and the former home of the first American to see the continent of Antarctica (at the tender age of 21, no less).

★ **Velvet Mill** ARTS CENTER
(☑917-915-6340; www.thevelvetmill.com; 22 Bayview Ave; ☉9am-5pm; ℗) This Community Arts Center hosts weekend farmers and flea markets (10am to 1pm Saturday, 1pm to 4pm Sunday) and is a hub for local artists and small businesses, including some locavore food vendors. Be sure to take a look if you're in town.

★ **Saltwater Farm Vineyard** WINE
(☑860-415-9072; www.saltwaterfarmvineyard.com; 349 Elm St; tastings $10; ☉11am-5pm Wed, 11am-7pm Thu, 11am-3pm Fri-Sun) Housed in a striking 1930s aluminum airport hangar, Saltwater Farm is one of the newest vineyards in Connecticut. Surrounded by tidal marshes and cooled by salty coastal breezes, the Cabernet Franc, Merlot, Chardonnay and Sauvignon Blanc vintages benefit from a unique microclimate and are only sold locally. The real joy is sampling wines on terraces overlooking lush green vines and Wequetequock Cove.

Barn Island Wildlife Management Area PARK
(Palmer Neck Rd, Pawcatuk) **FREE** Canoeists, kayakers, hikers and birders come to enjoy over 300 acres of unique salt- and freshwater marshes at Barn Island. Inhabited by hundreds of species of birds, 4 miles of hiking trails snake between placid pools and reed beds and offer beautiful views over Little Narragansett Bay and Wequetequock Cove.

⨳ Sleeping

Accommodations in Stonington are quaint, pricey and popular. The best rates are found off-season and on weekdays.

Stonington Motel MOTEL $
(☑860-599-2330; www.stoningtonmotel.com; 901 Stonington Rd/US 1; d $55-70; ℗✳☎☝) This owner-run, old-school motel is Stonington's most affordable accommodation and is simple, convenient and quaint. The no-frills 13 rooms have cable TV, microwave and fridge. It's an easy and pleasant bike ride into town and is well located for Saltwater Farm and Barn Island.

★ **Inn at Stonington** INN $$$
(☑860-535-2000; www.innatstonington.com; 60 Water St; d from $205-350; ℗✳@☎) Offering an easy sophistication, this romantic inn, long lauded by those in the know, continues to stay at the top of its game. From windows overlooking Stonington Harbor you can watch the sunrise or yachties tying up at the hotel dock of an evening. Elegant, country-style rooms feature plump sofas, four-poster beds, Jacuzzis and fireplaces. Bikes, kayaks and massages are available.

✗ Eating

Stonington's handful of restaurants are within a couple blocks of each other along Water St. On Saturday mornings you'll find a farmers market at the Town Docks selling fresh local produce, including honey, vegetables and cheese. In colder months it's held at the Velvet Mill.

Noah's   CAFE **$$**
(☏860-535-3925; www.noahsfinefood.com; 113 Water St; mains $12-27; ⊗7.45am-9pm Tue-Sun; 👪) Noah's is a popular, informal place, with two small rooms topped with original stamped-tin ceilings. It's famous for its seafood (especially chowder and scallops) and pastries, like the mouthwatering apple-spice and sour-cream coffee cakes. Lunchtime is a family-friendly affair, while dinner is more formal. Book ahead at weekends.

Water St Cafe   MODERN AMERICAN **$$$**
(☏860-535-2122; www.waterstcafe.com; 143 Water St; mains $17-30; ⊗11:30am-2:30pm & 5-10pm Mon-Tue & Fri-Sun, 5-10pm daily) North of Grand St, this crimson-walled cafe set in a post-and-beam house offers a creative, modern menu. The restaurant's seafood dishes, often with Asian-influenced preparations (think black-bean roast salmon and miso-glazed halibut), are the big draw, but basics – like the shoestring fries – also stand out.

❶ Getting There & Away

The only way to reach Stonington is by road (off I-95). It's also possible to take an Amtrak (p244) train to Mystic, then catch a local **SEAT** (Southeast Area Transit; ☏860-886-2631; www.seatbus.com) bus, but services are somewhat infrequent and may not connect well.

NEW HAVEN

☏203 / POP 130,660
As you wander around Yale University's venerable campus, admiring the gorgeous faux-Gothic and Victorian architecture, it's hard to fathom New Haven's struggle to shake its reputation as a dangerous, decaying seaport.

Connecticut's second-largest city radiates out from pretty New Haven Green, laid by Puritan settlers in the 1600s. Around it, Yale's over-300-year-old accessible campus offers visitors a wealth of world-class attractions, from museums and galleries to a lively concert program and walking-tour tales of secret societies. As New Haven repositions herself as a thriving home for the arts, architecture and the human mind, the good news is tourism is on the up and crime is in decline.

While Yale may have put New Haven on the map, there's much to savor beyond campus. Well-aged dive bars, ethnic restaurants, barbecue shacks and cocktail lounges make the area almost as lively as Cambridge's Harvard Sq – but with better pizza and less ego.

◉ Sights

Most of New Haven's sights and museums cluster around its stage-set green. Due south is Long Wharf and the city's harbor, and further south still, in West Haven, is the 7.5-mile-long public beach and the Bradley Point boardwalk.

★Yale University   UNIVERSITY
(☏203-432-2300; www.yale.edu/visitor; cnr Elm & Temple Sts; ⊗visitor center 9am-4:30pm Mon-Fri, 11am-4pm Sat & Sun) FREE Each year, thousands of high-school students make pilgrimages to Yale, nursing dreams of attending the country's third-oldest university, which boasts such notable alums as Noah Webster, Eli Whitney, Samuel Morse, and Presidents William H Taft, George HW Bush, Bill Clinton and George W Bush. You don't need to share the students' ambitions in order to take a stroll around the campus, just pick up a map at the Visitor Centre (at the address listed) or join a free, one-hour guided tour.

Beinecke Rare Book
& Manuscript Library   LIBRARY
(☏203-432-2977; www.library.yale.edu/beinecke; 121 Wall St; ⊗10am-7pm Mon-Thu, 9am-5pm Fri) FREE Built in 1963, this extraordinary piece of architecture is the largest building in the world designed for the preservation of rare manuscripts. The windowless cube has walls of Danby marble which subdue the effects of light, while inside the glass stack tower displays sculptural shelves of books, including one of only 48 surviving Gutenberg Bibles (1455) and original manuscripts by Charles Dickens, Benjamin Franklin and Goethe.

New Haven Green   PARK
New Haven's spacious green has been the spiritual center of the city since its Puritan fathers designed it in 1638 as the prospective site for Christ's second coming. Since then it has held the municipal burial grounds (graves were later moved to Grove

New Haven

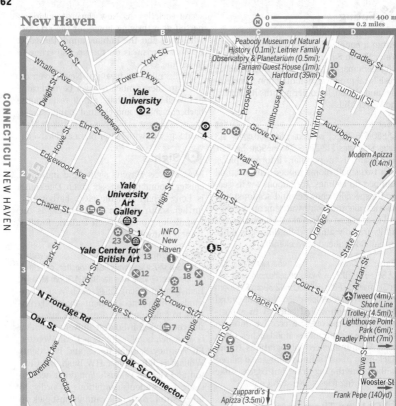

St Cemetery), several statehouses and an array of churches, three of which still stand.

★ Shore Line Trolley Museum

MUSEUM, TROLLEY

(☏ 203-467-6927; www.shorelinetrolley.org; 17 River St, East Haven; adult/child $10/6; ⊙10:30am-4:30pm daily Jun-Aug, Sat & Sun May, Sep & Oct; ⛟) For a unique take on East Haven's shoreline, take a ride on this open-sided antique trolley – the oldest continuously running suburban trolley line in the country – along 3 miles of track which takes you from River St in East Haven to Short Beach in Branford. Enjoy the museum and its beautifully maintained carriages when you're done. Bring a picnic lunch.

Lighthouse Point Park

PARK

(www.cityofnewhaven.com/parks; 2 Lighthouse Rd; ⊙7am-sunset) This pretty seaside park a few minutes' drive from Tweed New Haven Airport features the handsome 1840s Five Mile Point Lighthouse, listed on the National Register of Historic Places, and a beautiful 1916 carousel (rides 50¢) and pavilion. Parking fees apply in season (April to October).

Leitner Family Observatory & Planetarium

OBSERVATORY

(☏ 203-423-3000; http://lfop.squarespace.com; 355 Prospect St; $5; ⊙7pm & 8pm Tue Apr-Oct, 6pm & 7pm Tue Nov-Mar) A little-known attraction, Yale University's observatory hosts an hour-long planetarium show every Tuesday evening, after which the observatory's telescopes are open for viewings of planets, nebulae and star clusters.

🏃 Activities

Bishop's Orchards Winery

WINE

(☏ 203-453-2338; www.bishopsorchards.com; 1355 Boston Post Rd, Guilford; ⊙10am-7pm Mon-Sat, 11am-6pm Sun; ⛟) Bishop's Orchards Winery has been serving shoreline commu-

New Haven

nities with fresh produce since 1871. Much more than just a winery, Bishop's is also a pick-your-own farm, where berries, peaches, pears, apples and pumpkins can be picked from June through October. The rich variety of produce means the Bishop's market (open year-round) is one of the best in the area.

Bradley Point Park   BEACH
(Beach St, West Haven; ⊙9am-sunset) Bradley Point is the best family-friendly sandy beach within striking distance of New Haven. Bicycle trails and a 3.5-mile-long walkway link Bradley with Morse Beach and Sandy Point to the northeast, with views of Long Island Sound en route. Parking costs $10, or $5 after 4pm.

★☆ Festivals & Events

New Haven has a number of annual festivals, many of which include free public events. Check out Info New Haven (www.

infonewhaven.com) and Visit New Haven (www.visitnewhaven.com) for timelines of what's hot when.

International Festival of Arts & Ideas   ART
(www.artidea.org; ⊙Jun) This engaging, jam-packed festival, held in mid- to late June, feature tours, lectures, performances and master classes by artists and thinkers from around the world.

City-Wide Open Studios   ART
(www.cwos.org; ⊙Oct) One of the largest events of its kind, City-Wide Open Studios sees some of New Haven's up-and-coming talent open their doors to the public for a peek inside their workspaces.

Music on the Green   MUSIC
(www.infonewhaven.com/mog; ⊙Jul) This free outdoor concert series (mid- to late July) has presented the likes of Soul Asylum, Regina Belle, Debbie Gibson and En Vogue.

🛏 Sleeping

Area accommodations fill up – and prices rise – during the fall move-in and spring graduation weekends, or when conferences come to town. It's best to reserve well in advance if you plan to stay in town.

Hotel Duncan   HISTORIC HOTEL $
(✆203-787-1273; 1151 Chapel St; s/d $65/85; ❄🖈) Though the shine has rubbed off this antique New Haven gem – with stained carpets, unstable water pressure and exfoliating towels – it's the enduring features that some will enjoy, like the handsome lobby and the hand-operated elevator with uniformed attendant. Rooms are rented on both a long-term and overnight basis. Don't expect the earth and you might be surprised.

Check out the wall in the manager's office filled with autographed pictures of celebrity guests like Jodie Foster and Christopher Walken.

★**New Haven Hotel**   HOTEL $$
(✆800-644-6835; www.newhavenhotel.com; 229 George St; d from $169) This robust downtown hotel is both simply stylish and affordable. It's nice to see a private operator raising the bar. The hotel occupies a handsome mid-last-century brick building with bright, modern common areas, while guest rooms are airy with large windows, clean lines, dark woods and sink-into-me bedding. Reasonable rates mean it's understandably popular. Book in advance.

YALE UNIVERSITY MUSEUMS

Yale University Art Gallery (☑203-432-0600; http://artgallery.yale.edu; 1111 Chapel St; ⊙10am-5pm Tue-Fri, to 8pm Thu, 11am-5pm Sat & Sun) **FREE** This outstanding museum was architect Louis Kahn's first commission and houses the oldest university collection in the country, including masterpieces by Frans Hals, Peter Paul Rubens, Manet, Picasso and van Gogh. In addition there are displays of American silver from the 18th century and art from Africa, Asia, the pre- and post-Columbian Americas and Europe.

Yale Center for British Art (☑203-432-2800; www.ycba.yale.edu; 1080 Chapel St; ⊙10am-5pm Tue-Sat, noon-5pm Sun) **FREE** Reopened in 2016 after extensive restoration, this excellent gallery was architect Louis Kahn's last commission and is the setting for the largest collection of British art outside the UK. Spanning three centuries from the Elizabethan era to the 19th century, and arranged thematically as well as chronologically, the collection gives an unparalleled insight into British art, life and culture.

Peabody Museum of Natural History (☑203-432-5050; www.peabody.yale.edu; 170 Whitney Ave; adult/child $13/6; ⊙10am-5pm Mon-Sat, noon-5pm Sun; P ♣) It's hard not to be fascinated by this vast collection of animal, vegetable and mineral specimens, including wildlife dioramas, meteorites and minerals. The Great Hall of Dinosaurs illuminates the museum's fossil collection against the backdrop of the Pulitzer Prize–winning mural *The Age of Reptiles*.

Farnam Guest House B&B $$
(☑203-562-7121; www.farnamguesthouse.com; 616 Prospect St; r from $159; P❋🐾🛜) The Farnams have a long association with Yale as alums, donors and professors, and you can stay in their grand Georgian Colonial mansion in the best neighborhood in town. Expect old-world ambience, with Chippendale sofas, wingback chairs, Victorian antiques and plush oriental carpets. There's a Steinway grand piano in the parlor!

Study at Yale HOTEL $$$
(☑203-503-3900; www.studyatyale.com; 1157 Chapel St; r from $209; P🛜) The Study at Yale manages to evoke a mid-Century Modern sense of sophistication (call it '*Mad Men* chic') without being over the top or intimidating. Ultra-contemporary touches include in-room iPod docking stations and cardio machines with built-in TV. There's also an in-house restaurant and cafe, where you can stumble for morning snacks.

✖ Eating

The Chapel Sq area – just south of Yale's campus, between York and Church Sts – makes up a restaurant district in which cuisines from far-flung parts of the globe are represented. New Haven is also the pizza capital of New England, if not the entire East Coast. The city's most revered parlors are found in what was traditionally the city's Italian neighborhood, Wooster Sq, due east of downtown on Chapel St.

★**The Pantry** AMERICAN $
(☑203-787-0392; 2 Mechanic St; breakfast $11-24; ⊙7am-2pm Mon-Sat, 8am-3pm Sun) The secret is already out about New Haven's ah-mazing little breakfast-lunch joint. You'll most likely have to line up then rub shoulders with a bunch of hungry students (who'd probably rather we kept this one to ourselves), but persevere if you can: you won't find a better-value, more drool-worthy breakfast for miles. Take your pick: it's *all* good.

Atticus Bookstore Café CAFE $
(☑203-776-4040; www.atticusbookstorecafe.com; 1082 Chapel St; ⊙7am-9pm Tue-Sat, 8am-8pm Sun-Mon) On the fringe of the Yale campus, come here to get your bearings and mingle with the alumni over great coffee, artisan sandwiches, soup and salad, surrounded by an immaculately presented, eclectic selection of books.

★**Caseus Fromagerie & Bistro** BISTRO $$
(☑203-624-3373; www.caseusnewhaven.com; 93 Whitney Ave; mains $12-29; ⊙11:30am-2:30pm Mon-Sat plus 5:30-9pm Wed-Sat; 🍴) With a boutique cheese counter piled with locally sourced labels and a concept menu devoted to *le grand fromage,* Caseus has hit upon a winning combination. After all, what's not to like about a perfectly executed mac-and-cheese or the dangerously delicious poutine (*pommes frites,* cheese curds and velouté). There's also European-style pavement seating.

Soul de Cuba
CUBAN $$

(☑203-498-2822; www.souldecuba.com; 283 Crown St; mains $15-25; ☺11:30am-10pm) With its peach-colored walls, Afro-Caribbean soundtrack and spirit-rousing cocktails, Soul de Cuba is warm and inviting. Aside from the enormous and excellent-value Cuban sandwiches, the menu is packed with sunshine flavors from fried chicken with Spanish olives, to oxtail cooked in red wine, and red snapper simmered with tomato, cilantro and garlic.

★ZINC
MODERN AMERICAN $$$

(☑203-624-0507; www.zincfood.com; 964 Chapel St; mains $12-28; ☺noon-2:30pm & 5-9pm Tue-Fri, 5-10pm Sat & Mon) Whenever possible, this trendy bistro's ingredients hail from local organic sources, but the chef draws inspiration from all over, notably Asia and the Southwest. There's a constantly changing 'market menu,' but for the most rewarding experience, share several of the small plates for dinner, like the smoked duck nachos or the *prosciutto Americano crostini*. Reservations are advised.

Union League Café
MODERN FRENCH $$$

(☑203-562-4299; www.unionleaguecafe.com; 1032 Chapel St; mains $23-38; ☺11:30am-9:30pm Mon-Sat) An upscale French bistro in the historic Union League building. Expect a menu featuring continental classics like *cocotte de joues de veau* (organic veal cheeks with sautéed wild mushrooms; $25) along with those of nouvelle cuisine. If your budget is tight, try a sinful dessert like *crêpe soufflé au citron* (lemon crepes) washed down with a glass from the exquisite wine list.

🍷 Drinking & Nightlife

Whether you're in the mood for an artisanal cocktail in a chic setting or a local beer in an old-school dive bar, New Haven has no shortage of nightspots, and plenty of funky arts-and-drama kids, divorced professors and tomorrow's millionaires to have a drink with.

★Ordinary
COCKTAIL BAR

(☑203-907-0238; www.ordinarynewhaven.com; 990 Chapel St; ☺11:30am-2am Mon-Sat) Ordinary is anything but. It's tall, dark and handsome, ineffably stylish and a treat for the senses. Its patrons often also fall into at least one of these categories. They come for cheese boards, charcuterie and cocktails. Put on your fancy pants and join them.

116 Crown
BAR

(☑203-777-3116; www.116crown.com; 116 Crown St; ☺5pm-1am Tue-Sun) Upscale contemporary design, DJ sets, expertly mixed cocktails and an international wine list draw the style crowd to this Ninth Sq bar. Small plates and a raw bar keep you from toppling off your stool, but style this chic doesn't come cheap.

DON'T MISS

NEW HAVEN PIZZA

Pizza fiends from around the country know about New Haven's Wooster St, where Neapolitan pizza pies have been crafted in coal-fired brick ovens since the 1920s when Frank Pepe arrived in town. In 1938, Frank's nephew did a bunk and opened Sally's Apizza just down the street. These days competition has proliferated but the lines at Frank's and Sally's don't seem to get any shorter. Why not do the rounds and find a favorite for yourself:

Frank Pepe (☑203-865-5762; www.pepespizzeria.com; 157 Wooster St; pizzas from $12; ☺11am-10pm; ☑⊞) The granddaddy of the New Haven pizza scene since 1925.

Sally's Apizza (☑203-624-5271; www.sallysapizza.com; 237 Wooster St; pizzas from $7.50; ☺5-10pm Tue-Fri, to 11pm Sat & Sun) Some say Sal's spicier sauce puts his pies ahead of the competition.

Modern Apizza (☑203-776-5306; www.modernapizza.com; 874 State St; pizzas $10-20; ☺11am-11pm Tue-Sat, 3-10pm Sun) Hardly new, Modern has been slinging its Italian Bomb since 1934.

Zuppardi's Apizza (☑203-934-1949; www.zuppardisapizza.com; 179 Union Ave, West Haven; pizzas from $9; ☺11am-9pm Mon-Sat, noon-8:30pm Sun) Octogenarian Zuppardi's is in the quieter neighbourhood of West Haven.

If gluten is not your friend, don't fret! There's no surcharge for a gluten-free pie base at Modern Apizza.

BAR CLUB

(☑ 203-495-1111; www.barnightclub.com; 254 Crown St; ⊙ 11:30-1am Wed-Sun, 5pm-1am Mon-Tue) This restaurant-club-pub encompasses the Bru Room (New Haven's first brewpub), the Front Room, the video-oriented BARtropolis Room and other enclaves. Taken in toto, you're set for artisanal beer and brick-oven pizza, a free pool table, and either live music or DJs spinning almost every night of the week.

Blue State Coffee COFFEE

(☑ 203-764-2632; www.bluestatecoffee.com; 84 Wall St; ⊙ 9am-midnight; 🛜) This is the flagship store for a small New Haven chain that donates money to charities of your choice, with every purchase. Whether Blue State's popularity speaks to Yale's ideological bent or the fact that the coffee is strong and the cafe snacks tasty and affordable is hard to tell. Check the website for more information and other branch locations.

⭐ Entertainment

New Haven's after-dark culture is youthful, enthusiastic and on-the-pulse. The challenge is finding out what's the most happening gig on any given night, from acoustic coffeehouse warbling to world-class theater performances, poetry readings, plays, hip-hop slams and open-mike jams. Check CTNow (www.ctnow.com) for mainstream entertainment listings and noticeboards in cafes and on campus for the really good stuff.

⭐ Theatre & Classical Music

Yale Repertory Theatre THEATER

(☑ 203-432-1234; www.yalerep.org; 1120 Chapel St) Performing classics and new works in a converted church, this Tony-winning repertory company has mounted more than 90 world premiers. Its varied program is presented by graduate student actors from the Yale School of Drama (Meryl Streep and Sigourney Weaver are alums) as well as professionals.

Shubert Theater THEATER

(☑ 203-562-5666; www.shubert.com; 247 College St) Dubbed 'Birthplace of the Nation's Greatest Hits,' the Shubert has, since 1914, been hosting ballet and Broadway musicals on their trial runs before heading off to New York City. In recent years it has expanded its repertoire to include a broader range of events, including a series of interviews and musical performances.

New Haven Symphony Orchestra CLASSICAL MUSIC

(☑ 203-776-1444; www.newhavensymphony.org; cnr College & Grove Sts; ticket prices vary) Yale's Woolsey Hall is home to most performances by this orchestra, whose season runs from October through April. Outside season, crowds flock to the New Haven Green for the special outdoor summer concert series (featuring Beethoven, Tchaikovsky and Mendelssohn).

Long Wharf Theatre THEATER

(☑ 203-787-4282; www.longwharf.org; 222 Sargent Dr) This nonprofit regional theater mounts modern and contemporary productions, including everything from comedy troupes to the likes of Tom Stoppard and Eugene O'Neill, in a converted warehouse off I-95 (exit 46, on the waterfront).

⭐ Live Music

Café Nine LIVE MUSIC

(☑ 203-789-8281; www.cafenine.com; 250 State St; free-$20) An old-school beatnik dive with a roadhouse feel, this is the heart of New Haven's local music scene (it dubs itself the 'musician's living room'). It's an odd place where banjo-playing hippies rub shoulders with rockabillies, all in the name of good music.

Toad's Place LIVE MUSIC

(☑ 203-624-8623; www.toadsplace.com; 300 York St) Toad's is arguably New England's premier music hall, having earned its rep hosting the likes of the Rolling Stones, U2 and Bob Dylan. These days, an eclectic range of performers work the intimate stage, including They Might Be Giants and Martin & Wood.

ℹ Information

INFO New Haven (☑ 203-773-9494; www.infonewhaven.com; 1000 Chapel St; ⊙ 10am-9pm Mon-Sat, noon-5pm Sun) This downtown bureau offers maps and helpful advice.

ℹ Getting There & Away

AIR

Tweed New Haven Airport (☑ 203-466-8833; www.flytweed.com; 155 Burr St) services Philadelphia directly with connections to a global network of over 330 cities. However, flights out of airports in New York City or Hartford are significantly cheaper, and ground transportation to both cities is easy and inexpensive. **Connecticut Transit** (📞 203-624-0151; www.cttransit.com) bus G gets you to the airport ($3.25, 15 minutes). A taxi costs around $20.

BOAT

The **Bridgeport & Port Jefferson Steamboat Company** (📞 in Connecticut 888-443-3779, in Long Island 631-473-0286; www.88844ferry.com; 102 W Broadway, Port Jefferson, NY) operates its daily car ferries year-round between Bridgeport, 10 miles southwest of New Haven, and Port Jefferson on Long Island about every 1½ hours. The one-way 1½-hour voyage costs $18 for adults, $15 for seniors, and is free for children aged 12 and under. The fee for a car is $56, including the driver but not including passengers.

BUS

Peter Pan Bus Lines (p244) Connects New Haven with New York City (from $15, two hours, eight daily), Hartford (from $15, one hour, six daily) and Boston (from $15, from 3½ hours, six daily), as does Greyhound (p244). Buses depart from inside New Haven's Union Station.

Connecticut Limousine (📞 800-472-5466; www.ctlimo.com; to New York airports $70-95, to Bradley airport $49) An airport shuttle servicing Hartford's Bradley airport, New York's JFK and LaGuardia airports and New Jersey's Newark airport. Pick-up and drop off is at Union Station and select downtown New Haven hotels. Services to Newark attract a higher rate.

CAR & MOTORCYCLE

New Haven is 141 miles southwest of Boston, 36 miles south of Hartford, 75 miles from New York and 101 miles from Providence via interstate highways.

Avis, Budget and Hertz rent cars at Tweed New Haven Airport.

TRAIN

Metro-North (p244) trains make the run between **Union Station** (📞 203-773-6177; 50 Union Ave) and New York City's Grand Central Terminal (peak/off-peak $22/16.50, from one hour 50 minutes) almost every hour from 7am to midnight. On weekends, trains run about every two hours.

Shore Line East (p244) runs Commuter Connection buses that shuttle passengers from Union Station (in the evenings) and from State St Station (in the mornings) to New Haven Green. Regional services travel up the shore of Long Island Sound to Old Saybrook (45 minutes) and New London (70 minutes).

Amtrak (p244) trains run express from New York City's Penn Station to New Haven (from $31, one hour 40 minutes).

THE GOLD COAST

The southwestern corner of Connecticut, otherwise known as the Gold Coast, was once home to potato farmers and fishermen until 19th-century railroads brought New Yorkers north. With their blue-chip companies they transformed Fairfield County into one of the wealthiest regions in the USA, with the affluent town of Greenwich at its heart. Now financial firms, yacht clubs and gated communities line the shore. You must ply further north to New Canaan, Ridgefield and Redding for the original Colonial flavor of the area, although the perfectly clipped lawns and spotless clapboards are tell-tale signs that many New Yorkers also have second homes here.

Further north along the coast, Stamford, once a stage-coach stop on the New York-to-Boston post road, is the area's commercial and industrial hub, while Norwalk and Westport have quietly thriving cultural communities with radically different characters.

Westport

📞 203 / POP 26,600

Travelling south from New Haven, you enter Fairfield County via affluent Westport, dubbed 'Beverly Hills East' for its popularity as a retreat for artists, writers and film stars. Despite its links to the rich and famous, the town otherwise bears no resemblance to Beverly Hills whatsoever.

Joanne Woodward, with her late husband Paul Newman, established the well-respected Westport Country Playhouse; while Martha Stewart built her media empire from her Westport drawing room. There's a Tiffany's here for a reason.

Although there aren't any conventional tourist sights, Westport has a lovely location beside the Saugatuck River (perfect for kayaking) and a drool-worthy main street of high-end boutiques with a small-town country flavor.

⊙ Sights

★**Westport Arts Center** ARTS CENTER

(📞 203-222-7070; www.westportartscenter.org; 51 Riverside Ave; exhibits free; ⊘ 10am-5pm Mon-Thu, 10am-2pm Fri, noon-4pm Sat & Sun) The Westport Arts Center is right on the river and has a busy schedule of changing exhibits, kids classes ($12 to $65) and performances.

Westport Historical Society MUSEUM

(☑ 203-222-1424; 25 Avery Pl; ⊙ 10am-4pm Mon-Fri, from noon Sat; **P**) FREE The Westport Historical Society organizes local walks and guided tours based on a historical theme. Its headquarters, situated in the 1795 Bradley-Wheeler House, has four period rooms on permanent display and hosts various small exhibitions.

Sherwood Island State Park STATE PARK

(☑ 203-226-6983; www.ct.gov/deep/sherwood island; Sherwood Island Connector/I-95; weekdays resident/nonresident $13/22, weekends resident/non-resident $9/15; ⊙ 8am-sunset) Just south of Westport, Sherwood Island State Park features a 1.5-mile-long stretch of beach whose gentle surf and shallow waters make it ideal for families. Out of season (October to March), parking is free and dogs are permitted on the beach.

🏃 Activities

Downunder Fitness & Surf KAYAKING

(☑ 203-956-6217; www.downunderct.com/west port; 575 Riverside Ave; half-day rental from $70; ⊙ 9am-6pm) This a one-stop shop for kayaks, paddleboards, and canoe rentals and sales. You can launch off the dock just below the shop.

🍴 Eating

If neighboring Norwalk is the champion of cheap eats, then Main St, Westport, is fit for fine dining. Definitely try for a meal here if you can.

★ The Whelk SEAFOOD $$

(☑ 203-557-0902; www.thewhelkwestport.com; 575 Riverside Ave; mains $14-28; ⊙ 5-10pm Tue-Thu, noon-10pm Fri & Sat) The flagship seafood restaurant from talented chef Bill Taibe continues to turn heads with its fresh presentation of oceanic delights. There's a raw bar (oysters!), a real bar (martinis!) and a fun crew of on-the-ball chefs and servers. If you're a lover of aquatic delicacies, and like fine food without the pretense, this one is a must.

Kawa ni IZAKAYA $$

(☑ 203-557-8775; www.kawaniwestport.com; 19a Bridge Sq; dishes $6-16; ⊙ noon-11pm Tue-Sat, 4-9pm Sun; **P**) *Kawa ni* (meaning 'at the river') is a modern take on a traditional Japanese *izakaya* (pub) in the middle of Westport, offering mouthwatering, visually appealing small plates to be enjoyed with sake and beer in an intimate environment. Best with friends, you won't find your stand-

ard American-Japanese items on the menu, but lots of inventive takes on classic Japanese dishes.

The Boathouse MODERN AMERICAN $$$

(Saugatuck Rowing Club; ☑ 203-221-7475; www.saugatuckrowing.com; 521 Riverside Ave; mains $22-29; ⊙ 11:30am-3pm & 5-9pm Tue-Fri, 5-9pm Sat) Don your chinos and boaters and pop in to this waterfront favorite at the Saugatuck Rowing Club. Sip on wine, dine in the sunshine on a selection of small farmers plates and a medley of tasty starters, or go for a romantic dinner with a small menu of beautifully presented chicken, fish or steak and veal, with definite Italian influences.

☆ Entertainment

★ Westport Country Playhouse THEATRE

(☑ 203-227-4177; www.westportplayhouse.org; 254 South St; ticket prices vary; ⊙ box office noon-6pm Tue-Fri) Since its founding in 1931 this well-respected playhouse has staged hundreds of productions attracting big-name Broadway talent. It's hardly surprising when the converted former barn was given a state-of-the-art overhaul by Joanne Woodward and her late husband Paul Newman in 2003.

🛈 Getting There & Away

Westport is only accessible by road. Take US 1 east from Norwalk (4 miles).

Norwalk

☑ 203 / POP 86,500

Straddling the Norwalk River and encrusted with the salt spray of Long Island Sound, Norwalk is fiercely proud of its maritime tradition. The area supported a robust oyster-ing industry in the 18th and 19th centuries, and is still the state's top oyster producer.

The past decade saw the redevelopment of the crumbling waterfront in South Norwalk ('SoNo'), where a clutch of galleries, boutiques and restaurants opened around Washington, Main and Water Sts, but overall the town appears a little crumbly again. More development is underway, but Norwalk, although pleasant enough, isn't likely to excite and delight.

◉ Sights

Stepping Stones Museum for Children MUSEUM

(☑ 203-899-0606; www.steppingstonesmuseum. org; 303 West Ave; $15; ⊙ 10am-5pm Tue-Sun; **P**) This museum is bursting with interactive, instructive fun, from the weather cycle to gravity to the principles of conservation. The Toddler Terrain is a hit with the under-three crowd and there is a fabulous playground that is designed with mentally and physically challenged children in mind, but holds appeal for all.

Maritime Aquarium at Norwalk AQUARIUM
(☑203-852-0700; www.maritimeaquarium.org; 10 N Water St, South Norwalk; adult/child $23/16; ☺10am-5pm) This aquarium focuses on the marine life of Long Island Sound, including sand tiger sharks, loggerhead turtles and harbor seals, with daily feedings at 11:45am, 1:45pm and 3:45pm. IMAX movies are also shown throughout the day ($13/12 adult/child).

**Lockwood-Mathews
Mansion Museum** MUSEUM
(☑203-838-9799; www.lockwoodmathewsman sion.com; Mathews Park, 295 West Ave; adult/8-18yr $10/8; ☺tours 1pm, 2pm & 3pm Wed-Sun Apr-Dec; ℗) This is one of the best surviving Second Empire–style country houses in the nation, so it's no wonder the 62-room mansion was chosen as the set for the 2004 version of *The Stepford Wives*. The 2nd floor houses the Music Box Society International's permanent collection of music boxes, which you can view and listen to on the tour. Unfortunately, the site is wedged between an ugly freeway and a main road that detracts from the prettiness of the grounds.

⌕ Tours

Sheffield Island Ferry CRUISE
(☑203-838-9444; www.seaport.org; 4 North Water St; adult/child $22/5; ☺May-Sep, sailings vary) Enjoy a round-trip cruise to Sheffield Island, including a tour of its historic 1868 lighthouse, beach walks and nature trails.

✯ Festivals & Events

Oyster Festival FOOD & DRINK
(www.seaport.org; ☺Sep) Taking place in mid-September, Norwalk's oyster festival is a big deal, with skydivers, fireworks, bands and bivalves galore.

❶ Getting There & Away

Norwalk is about 32 miles southwest of New Haven on I-95.

It's possible to get from Manhattan to Norwalk in just over an hour – and be kayaking around the Norwalk Islands soon after if you're so inclined.

Take a Metro-North (p244) train from Grand Central Terminal to South Norwalk Station (peak/off-peak $15.50/11.75, one hour), which is a few minutes' walk from the 'SoNo' Harbor area.

Greenwich

☑203 / POP 62,800
In the early days, exclusive Greenwich shipped oysters and potatoes to nearby New York. The advent of passenger trains and the first cashed-up commuters saw the town become a haven for Manhattanites in search of country exclusivity.

Greenwich is perhaps best known in popular culture as the town that inspired the 1972 Ira Levin sci-fi/horror novel *The Stepford Wives,* whose protagonist, Joanna, a newcomer to a wealthy, picture-perfect Connecticut town, begins to suspect that her frighteningly submissive housewife neighbors are robots created by their husbands. Much of the eponymous 1975 film and its 2004 remake were shot in the surrounding area. It's easy to see why.

For a real glimpse of moneyed Greenwich, head across Cos Cob Harbor to the exclusive enclave of Old Greenwich, which preserves the feel of the 1800s summer colony in its shingled Victorians and neatly landscaped, 24-acre Binney Park, resplendent with ponds and tennis courts.

◉ Sights & Activities

Bruce Museum MUSEUM
(☑203-869-0376; www.brucemuseum.org; 1 Museum Dr; adult/student & senior $7/6; ☺10am-5pm Tue-Sun) One of Greenwich's wealthiest 19th-century residents, Robert Moffat Bruce was a textile tycoon who deeded his property to the city to become what is now the Bruce Museum. Its eclectic galleries serve up a bit of everything, from sculpture, photography and paintings by Impressionists from Cos Cob's art colony, to exhibits on natural science and anthropology. The Bruce is also home to a variety of traveling exhibitions.

Greenwich Point Park WALKING, SWIMMING
(Tod's Point; www.greenwichct.org; Shore Rd, Old Greenwich; day pass $6, parking $20; ☺6am-sunset) Greenwich Point Park's lush acres are lined with walking trails which sweep across the promontory leading to quiet beaches, from where, on a clear day, you can see the New York skyline. Passes (which must be displayed from May to October) are available to buy at the Greenwich Town Hall.

🛏 Sleeping & Eating

Stanton House Inn   INN $$
(☎203-869-2110; www.stantonhouseinn.com; 76
Maple Ave; d/ste from $169/239; P❉🤖✨) The
excellent-value Stanton House Inn provides
genteel country-house accommodations in
an early-1900s mansion in one of Green-
wich's best neighborhoods.

Meli-Melo   CREPERIE $$
(☎203-629-6153; www.melimelogreenwich.com;
362 Greenwich Ave; crepes $8-16; ⊙7am-10pm
Mon-Fri, 8am-10pm Sat & Sun) For a quick and
delicious bite, you can't do better than Meli-Melo. Meaning 'hodge-podge' in French,
Meli-Melo serves salads, soups and sandwiches, but its specialty is undoubtedly
buckwheat crepes. Try a wild combination
like smoked salmon, chive sauce, lemon and
daikon ($11). The French onion and French
lentil soups are, appropriately, superb.

ℹ Getting There & Away

Being only 28 miles from Grand Central Terminal, Greenwich is less than an hour by train. If
you're driving, avoid heading north for Greenwich anywhere around evening rush hour, or
south into town during the morning commute.

North of Greenwich

The only Gold Coast town without a shoreline, **New Canaan** (pop 19,800) is character-
ized by large clapboard houses, grand Georgian mansions and, unusually, one of the
most famous modern houses in the world:
the 1949 Philip Johnson Glass House.

Twelve miles further north, **Ridgefield**
(pop 24,700) serves as the poster boy for a
Norman Rockwell painting with its old Yankee charm and cultural sophistication. Tree-
lined Main St is fronted by stately 18th- and
19th-century mansions and quaint local
shops.

◉ Sights

★**Philip Johnson
Glass House**   ARCHITECTURE
(☎866-811-4111; www.theglasshouse.org; 199 Elm
St, New Canaan; tours from $25; ⊙11am-6pm
Thu-Mon May 1-Nov 30) Inspired by Mies van
der Rohe, this icon of mid-Century Modern
architecture was the home of late Pritzker
Prize–winner Philip Johnson and his art
collector partner, David Whitney. Johnson
added 13 other structures to the 47-acre site
during his life there and daily tours allow
you to explore a selection of them along

with the stunning gardens. Reservations are
highly recommended.

The Visitor's Center is conveniently located across the street from the New Canaan
train station, making an easy day trip from
NYC's Grand Central Terminal. During off-
peak hours you may need to change trains
at Stamford.

**Aldrich Contemporary
Art Museum**   MUSEUM
(☎203-438-4519; www.aldrichart.org; 258 Main St,
Ridgefield; adult/child $10/free; ⊙noon-5pm Tue-
Sun; P) Swing into the parking lot of this
spotless white clapboard mansion, which
was once the town store and is now a brilliant contemporary gallery. Photography,
sculpture, painting and mixed-media installations are displayed in cutting-edge temporary exhibitions, which have previously
featured notable names such as Cy Twom-
bly, Robert Rauschenberg, Anslem Kiefer
and Tom Sachs. Workshops for children are
held downstairs in light-filled rooms and the
museum also runs summer camps.

🛏 Sleeping

Green ROCKS Inn   B&B $$$
(☎203-894-8944; www.greenrocksinn.com; 415
Danbury Rd, Ridgefield; d/ste from $195/295;
P🅿🤖✨) ✔ Green ROCKS Inn offers eco-
friendly B&B accommodation in a striking,
shingled farmhouse. You'll find it 2 miles
north of Main St on the Danbury Rd.

ℹ Getting There & Away

You'll need a car (or a chauffeur) to explore
the area, but New Canaan is easily reached by
Metro-North (p244) from NYC's Grand Central
Terminal.

After that, public transportation options range
from limited to nonexistent.

THE HOUSATONIC VALLEY

North of the Gold Coast, the Housatonic Riv-
er Valley unfurls languidly between forest-
ed mountain peaks, picturesque ponds and
rural Colonial villages. The area is anchored
by industrial Danbury in the south, beyond
whose sprawling suburbs Connecticut's
prettiest rural landscapes line the valley's
main north–south byway, scenic US 7. The
centerpiece of the region is the Litchfield
Hills with its centuries-old farms, winding
country roads, abundant autumn fairs and
hospitable country inns.

Candlewood Lake

With a surface area of 8.4 sq miles, Candlewood Lake is the largest lake in Connecticut. Created in the 1920s with water from the Housatonic River, its shoreline is shared by the four towns of Brookfield, New Milford, Sherman and New Fairfield, and is dotted with private cottages and a smattering of country inns. It's prettiest in the spring or fall.

Visitors head to lakefront Squantz Pond State Park for picknicking, while in Brookfield and Sherman you'll find quiet vineyards with acres of gnarled grapevines lining the hillsides.

Just south of Candlewood Lake, Danbury is the closest large town to the Housatonic Valley and a good base for midrange mainstream accommodations and dining options.

◎ Sights

Squantz Pond State Park   STATE PARK
(☑ 203-312-5013; www.ct.gov/deep/squantzpond; 178 Shortwoods Rd, New Fairfield; residents $9-13, nonresidents $15-22; ☺ 8am-sunset; 🅿 🛈) On the western shore of Candlewood Lake, Squantz Pond State Park is popular with leaf-peepers, who come to amble the pretty shoreline.

❶ Getting There & Away

North of Danbury, CT 39 mostly hugs the lake's western shore. From New Milford, you can drop down on US 7 and then Candlewood Lake Rd to get back to Danbury, by the eastern shore.

Litchfield Hills

The rolling hills in the northwestern corner of Connecticut are sprinkled with lakes and dotted with forests and state parks. Historic Litchfield is the hub of the region, but lesser-known Bethlehem, Kent and Norfolk boast similarly illustrious lineages and are just as photogenic.

An intentional curb on development continues to preserve the area's rural character. Accommodations are limited. Volunteers staff a useful information booth on Litchfield's town green from June to November.

If you have your own car, there's no shortage of postcard-perfect country roads to explore in the Litchfield Hills. One particularly delightful stretch is from Cornwall Bridge taking CT 4 west and then CT 41 north to Salisbury.

ANTIQUES CAPITAL

At the southern border of the Litchfield Hills, **Woodbury** is justifiably famous as the 'antiques capital' of Connecticut, boasting over 40 dealerships and 20 stores along its historic, mile-long Main St. Woodbury Antiques Dealers Association (www.antiqueswoodbury.com) publishes an online guide. While you're in Woodbury don't forget to stop by Carole Peck's **Good News Cafe** (☑ 203-266-4663; www.good-news-cafe.com; 649 Main St S/US 6, Woodbury; mains $14-22; ☺ 11:30am-10pm Mon & Wed-Sat, noon-10pm Sun; 🅿 🛈) 🖋, a magnet for lovers of locavore cuisine who come for the inventive, seasonal menus.

Lake Waramaug

Of the plentiful lakes and ponds in the Litchfield Hills, Lake Waramaug, north of New Preston, stands out. Gracious inns dot its shoreline, parts of which are a state park.

🏃 Activities

Hopkins Vineyard   WINE
(☑ 860-868-7954; www.hopkinsvineyard.com; 25 Hopkins Rd; ☺ 10am-5pm Mon-Sat, 11am-5pm Sun Mar-Dec, 10am-5pm Fri-Sun only Jan-Mar) On the northern shore of Lake Waramaug, Hopkins Vineyard produces eminently drinkable wines from predominantly French-American hybrid grapes. Come for wine tastings with views of the lake from its bar. Call ahead during the low season.

🛏 Sleeping & Eating

Lake Waramaug State Park   CAMPGROUND
(☑ 860-868-0220;   www.ct.gov/deep/lakewaramaug; 30 Lake Waramaug Rd; campsites $17-$27) Lake Waramaug State Park has 77 campsites, both wooded and open, and many lakeside. There's a snack bar in the park and a small beach for swimming. Book well in advance.

⭐**Hopkins Inn**   INN $$
(☑ 860-868-7295; www.thehopkinsinn.com; 22 Hopkins Rd, Warren; r from $135, without bath from $125, apt from $150; 🅿 ❄ 🛈) The 19th-century Hopkins Inn boasts a well-regarded restaurant with Austrian-influenced country fare and a variety of lodging options, from simple rooms with shared bathrooms to

lake-view apartments. Whatever the season, there's something magical about sitting on the porch gazing upon Lake Waramaug and the hills beyond.

★ **Community Table** MODERN AMERICAN $$$
(☑ 860-868-9354; http://communitytablect.com; 223 Litchfield Turnpike/US 202; brunch $14-20, mains $18-32; ☺ 5-9pm Mon-Tue, noon-2pm & 5-10pm Fri & Sat, 10am-2pm & 5-9pm Sun; P) The name of this Scandinavian-inspired restaurant comes from the 300-year-old black walnut table, where you can sit down to Sunday brunch. The modern American menu is locally sourced.

ℹ Getting There & Away

Lake Waramaug is a winding 10-mile drive from Kent, to the west. It's about 14 miles from Litchfield, to the northeast, via US 202.

Bethlehem

☑ 203 / POP 3600

Bethlehem is Connecticut's 'Christmas Town' and every year thousands of visitors come for the Christmas Fair (www.ci.bethlehem.ct.us) and to have their Christmas mail hand-stamped in the village post office.

◉ Sights

Bellamy-Ferriday
House & Garden MUSEUM
(☑ 203-266-7596; www.ctlandmarks.org; 9 Main St N; adult/child $8/4; ☺ noon-4pm Thu-Sun May-Sep, noon-4pm Sat & Sun Oct) The town's religious history extends to the founding of the first theological seminary in the USA by local resident Reverend Joseph Bellamy. His home, the Bellamy-Ferriday House & Garden, a 1750s clapboard mansion, is a treasure trove of Delftware, Asian art and period furnishings. Equally exquisite is the garden, the design of latter-day owner Caroline Ferriday, who designed it to resemble an Aubusson Persian carpet, its geometrical box hedges infilled with frothing peonies, lilacs and heirloom roses.

ℹ Getting There & Away

Bethlehem is 8 miles south of Litchfield. From Danbury (30 miles), take I-84 and CT 6.

Litchfield

☑ 860 / POP 8420

Litchfield is Connecticut's best-preserved late 18th-century town and the site of the nation's first law school. The town itself converges on a long oval green, and is surrounded by lush swaths of protected land just asking to be hiked through and picnicked on.

Founded in 1719, Litchfield prospered from 1780 to 1840 on the commerce brought by stagecoaches en route between Hartford and Albany, NY. In the mid-19th century, railroads did away with the coach routes, and industrial water-powered machinery drove Litchfield's artisans out of the markets, leaving the town to languish in faded gentility. Today, farming and tourism rule the roost.

◉ Sights & Activities

A walk around town starts at the information kiosk, which doles out handy walking-tour sheets. Just north across West St is the town's **historic jail**. Stroll along North St to gawk at the well-preserved, pretty period homes, more of which can be found along South St. Set well back from the roadway across broad lawns and behind tall trees, the houses make it easy to visualize what it might once have been like here during Litchfield's golden age.

Reeve House &
Litchfield Law School HISTORIC SITE
(☑ 860-567-4501; www.litchfieldhistoricalsociety. org; 82 South St; adult/child $5/free; ☺ 11am-5pm Tue-Sat, 1-5pm Sun mid-Apr–Nov) In 1775 Tapping Reeve established the English-speaking world's first law school at his home. When attendance overwhelmed his own house, he built the meticulously preserved one-room schoolhouse in his side yard. John C Calhoun and 130 members of Congress studied here.

Litchfield History Museum MUSEUM
(☑ 860-567-4501; www.litchfieldhistoricalsociety. org; 7 South St; adult/child $5/free; ☺ 11am-5pm Tue-Sat, 1-5pm Sun mid-Apr–Nov) This museum features a small permanent collection, including a modest photographic chronicle of the town and a dress-up box with Colonial clothes for children to try on, plus some local-interest rotating exhibits. Admission is included in the ticket to Reeve House & Litchfield Law School.

Mount Tom State Park STATE PARK
(☑ 860-567-8870; www.ct.gov/deep/mounttom; US 202; resident/nonresident per car $9/15; ☺ 8am-sunset; P) The best swimming in the Litchfield Hills is at this state park, 3.5 miles west of Bantam. The not-even-1-mile 'tower trail' leads to the stone Mt Tom Tower at the summit. Fees are reduced during weekdays.

Topsmead State Forest FOREST

(☎860-567-5694; www.ct.gov/deep/topsmead; Buell Rd; ☉8am-sunset; P🚻) This forest was once the estate of Edith Morton Chase. You can visit her grand Tudor-style summer home (free guided tours are available between June and October, but hours vary, so call ahead), complete with its original furnishings. Then spread a blanket on the lawn and have a picnic while enjoying the view at 1230ft. Topsmead is 2 miles east of Litchfield.

White Memorial
Conservation Center WALKING

(☎860-567-0857; www.whitememorialcc.org; US 202; park free, museum adult/child $6/3; ☉park dawn-dusk, museum 9am-5pm Mon-Sat, noon-5pm Sun) FREE Made up of 4000 supremely serene acres, this park has two dozen trails (0.2 miles to 6 miles long) that crisscross the center, including swamp paths on a raised boardwalk. The center also manages three campgrounds and there's a small nature museum. The center is 2 miles west on US 202 from Litchfield.

🛏 Sleeping & Eating

Although your options are limited, Litchfield has the widest range of accommodations in the Hills, which, combined with its central position, makes it a logical base for exploring the region.

Litchfield Inn INN $$

(☎860-567-4503; www.litchfieldinnct.com; 432 Bantam Rd; d from $169; P➡❄🐾) Litchfield's largest lodgings feature well-appointed hotel-style rooms and a range of fantastic themed suites that are so varied you'll need to check out the website to see what tickles your fancy. Rates vary dramatically between the off and peak season. There's an excellent bar-restaurant on-site and breakfast is included.

★ Peaches 'N Cream ICE CREAM $

(☎860-496-7536; www.peachesncreamicecream. com; 632 Torrington Rd; scoops $3; ☉noon-9pm) This old-fashioned ice-cream parlor with peppermint trim on the road to Torrington has been serving up homemade ice cream for decades. Seasonal flavors include the eponymous peaches 'n cream, but also cashew cream, maple walnut and Kahlua chocolate. It also makes a neat ice-cream sandwich.

Arethusa al Tavolo MODERN AMERICAN $$$

(☎860-567-0043; www.arethusaaltavolo.com; 828 Bantam Rd, Bantam; mains $24-40; ☉5-9pm Wed-

BANTAM CINEMA

Locals know that one of the best things to do on rainy days is book in to see a film at the **Bantam Cinema** (☎860-567-1916; www.bantamcinema.com; 115 Bantam Lake Rd, Bantam). Housed in a converted red barn on the shores of Lake Bantam, it's the oldest continuously operating movie theatre in Connecticut and is a real Litchfield experience. The well-curated screenings focus on independent and foreign films, and the 'Meet the Filmmaker' series features guest directors, actors and producers, many of whom live here.

Fri, 11:30am-2pm & 5-9pm Sat & Sun; P) Belonging to a celebrated local dairy, this upscale restaurant uses the farm's dairy products and sources other ingredients locally to produce its exquisitely presented naturally flavorful dishes, like warm asparagus salad, Peking duck breast lacquered with orange blossom honey, and of course, mouthwatering desserts.

West Street Grill MODERN AMERICAN $$$

(☎860-567-3885; www.weststreetgrill.com; 43 West St; mains $25-40; ☉11:30am-9pm Wed-Sun) A Parisian-style bistro on Litchfield's historic green, this is one of the state's top restaurants. Over the years its inventive modern American cooking has earned it nods from *Gourmet* magazine and the *New York Times*. The shrimp salad with orange and fennel is delightful.

🛍 Shopping

★ Housatonic Trading Company ANTIQUES

(☎860-361-6299; www.housatonictrading.com; 920 Bantam Rd, Bantam; ☉9am-5pm Thu-Tue) Housed in a sprawling antique barn, this funky unpretentious dealer has an eclectic mix of antiques, fashion, fun stuff, furniture, books and bric-a-brac spanning decades and at reasonable prices.

❶ Getting There & Away

Litchfield lies 34 miles west of Hartford and 36 miles south of Great Barrington, MA, in the Berkshires. The town green is at the intersection of US 202 and CT 63.

No buses stop in Litchfield proper, but Peter Pan Bus Lines (p244) will get you to Torrington ($34, 2½ hours), the closest major town, from where you'll need your own wheels.

Kent

📞 860 / POP 3000

Lazing by the banks of the Housatonic River, Kent is arguably the loveliest town in the Hills, although Litchfielders would disagree. It's a popular stop for hikers on the **Appalachian Trail** (www.appalachiantrail.org), which intersects CT 341 about 2 miles northwest of town. Unlike much of the trail, the Kent section offers a mostly flat 5-mile river walk alongside the Housatonic, the longest riverside ramble of the whole trail.

During summer and fall, city folk flock to Kent's small but respected clutch of art galleries, shops and scenic countryside. Especially popular is **Kent Falls State Park**, about 5 miles north of town, where the water drops 250ft over a quarter-mile before joining up with the Housatonic River. Hike the easy trail to the top of the cascade, or just settle into a sunny picnic spot at the bottom, near the red covered bridge.

◉ Sights & Activities

Macedonia Brook State Park   STATE PARK
(📞860-927-3238; www.ct.gov/deep/macedonia brook; 159 Macedonia Brook Rd; residents/nonresidents $14/24; ⊙mid-Apr–Sep; P🐾) A wooded oasis 2 miles north of town with 51 rustic sites and pit toilets. The park offers over 80 miles of hiking trails which crest the rocky ridges of Cobble Mountain affording panoramic views of the valley against a backdrop of the Taconic and Catskill mountain ranges.

Connecticut Industrial Museum   MUSEUM
(📞860-927-0050; www.ctamachinery.com; 31 Kent Cornwall Rd; adult/child $3/1.50; ⊙10am-4pm Wed-Sun May-Oct; 🐾) Kids love this hands-on outdoor free-for-all cared for by the Connecticut Antique Machinery Association, with all manner of steam-powered locomotives, machines and demonstrations.

⊨ Sleeping & Eating

★Inn at Kent Falls   INN $$$
(📞860-927-3197; www.theinnatkentfalls.com; 107 Kent-Cornwall Rd/US 7; r $215-350; P🐾🐾) This historic, highly acclaimed inn dates back to the early 1900s. Three generous lounges with open fireplaces and a grand piano, combined with plush, 'unstuffy' guestrooms and suites that combine traditional style with modern touches, make for a home-away-from-home atmosphere. Freshly baked breads and pastries are included in the sumptuous country breakfast. In summer, guests love the outdoor pool.

Gifford's   MODERN AMERICAN $$$
(📞860-592-0262; www.giffordsrestaurant.com; 9 Maple St; mains $18-34; ⊙5-9pm Wed-Sat, 4-8pm Sun) These speciality provenders know that without fresh, top-quality ingredients you can't have truly great food. Locally sourced seasonal vegetables and meats, including free-range, golden-hued chicken and Connecticut harvested clams, all feature. Stylish contemporary interiors and a delightful covered terrace make for a memorable dining experience.

❶ Getting There & Away

Kent is 29 miles north of Danbury on US 7 and about 3 miles from the New York state line.

West Cornwall

The village of West Cornwall is just one of six Cornwall villages in Connecticut, but it is the most famous thanks to its picturesque covered bridge.

Otherwise, the area attracts nature lovers, birders and hikers who come to hike, fish and boat on the lazy **Housatonic River**.

On Labor Day weekend, in the nearby town of Goshen, you can visit the **Goshen Fair** (www.goshenfair.org), one of Connecticut's best old-fashioned fairs, with ox-pulling and wood-cutting contests.

◉ Sights

Cornwall Bridge   BRIDGE
(West Cornwall) You'll want to venture down to the river's edge to photograph this quaint covered bridge, famed for allowing the passengers of horse-drawn carriages to have a moment of sheltered canoodling, which earned it the nickname 'Kissing Bridge.'

Audubon Sharon Center   WILDLIFE RESERVE
(📞860-364-0520; http://sharon.audubon.org; 325 Cornwall Bridge Rd, Sharon; adult/child $3/1.50; ⊙9am-5pm Tue-Sat, from 1pm Sun) The Audubon Society operates the Audubon Center on Rte 4 between Cornwall Bridge and Sharon. There is a raptor aviary, which houses 16 species of birds, including a peregrine falcon, a bald eagle and a great horned owl. The center also takes in snakes, turtles and lizards that are injured and unable to survive in the wild, and household pets that can no longer be cared for. There are also eight walking trails.

Housatonic Meadows State Park
STATE PARK

(✆860-927-3238; www.ct.gov/deep/housatonic meadows; 90 CT 7 North, Sharon; ⊙8am-sunset) Housatonic Meadows State Park is famous for its 2-mile-long stretch of water set aside exclusively for fly-fishing. Its campground has 97 campsites on the banks of the Housatonic.

🏃 Activities

Housatonic River Outfitters FISHING

(✆860-672-1010; www.dryflies.com; 24 Kent Rd, Cornwall Bridge) Housatonic River Outfitters runs guided fishing trips with gourmet picnics.

Mohawk Mountain Ski Area SKIING

(✆860-672-6100; www.mohawkmtn.com; 42 Great Hollow Rd, Cornwall) In winter the Mohawk Mountain Ski Area is the largest ski resort in the state with 24 slopes and trails.

🛌 Sleeping & Eating

Cornwall Inn INN $$

(✆860-672-6884; www.cornwallinn.com; 270 Kent Rd/US 7, Cornwall Bridge; d/ste from $159/239; P🅿🛜🏊) The tranquil, 14-room historic property at Cornwall Inn consists of the six-room inn and the more rustic-flavored eight-room lodge. Fill up on straightforward country cuisine at the restaurant (meals $12 to $31), open for dinner Thursday to Sunday, which features a different fish dish each week.

ⓘ Getting There & Away

Heading south, US 7 links West Cornwall with Kent (13 miles).

Lakeville
✆860 / POP 928

A quiet and remote corner of the Litchfield Hills, the rolling farmland around Lakeville is home to millionaires and movie luminaries such as Meryl Streep, but good luck finding them in this extremely private neck of the woods.

From May to September motor races, including a series of vintage car races, take place at the venerable **Lime Rock Race Track** (www.limerock.com; 497 Lime Rock Rd; ⊙Apr-Nov). Paul Newman raced here and

thought its seven-turn, 1.5-mile track the most beautiful racing track in America.

🛌 Sleeping

⭐**Falls Village Inn** INN $$$

(✆860-824-0033; www.thefallsvillageinn.com; 33 Railroad St; d/ste $209/299; P🅿🛜) The heart and soul of one of the smallest villages in Connecticut, this inn originally served the Housatonic Railroad. Now the six rooms are styled by interior decorator Bunny Williams, and the Tap Room is a hangout for Lime Rock's racers.

🍹 Drinking

Chaiwalla TEAHOUSE

(✆860-435-9758; 1 Main St/US 44, Salisbury; items $3-10; ⊙10am-6pm Wed-Sun) Tea lovers will want to check out Mary O'Brien's shop Chaiwalla in Salisbury, which serves a variety of tea, especially unblended Darjeelings. Try Mary's famous tomato pie.

ⓘ Getting There & Away

In the far northwest corner of the state, Lakeville is 21 miles north of Kent and 24 miles northwest of Litchfield.

Norfolk
✆860, 959 / POP 1790

Norfolk's bucolic scenery and cool summers have long attracted prosperous New Yorkers. They built many of the town's fine mansions, its well-endowed Romanesque Revival library and its arts-and-crafts-style Town Hall. Today, the town is best known for its **Norfolk Music Festival** (www.norfolkmusic.org; tickets $25-100; ⊙Jul-Aug).

☆ Entertainment

Infinity Music Hall & Bistro LIVE MUSIC

(✆866-666-6306; www.infinityhall.com; 20 Greenwoods Rd W; ticket prices vary; ⊙box office 11am-9pm Wed-Sun) This beautiful beaux-arts building with its original stage brings top acoustic, blues, jazz and folks acts to Norfolk from New York and beyond.

ⓘ Getting There & Away

Norfolk is 20 miles due north of Litchfield on CT 63 and CT 262.

Vermont

POP 626,000 / ☎ 802

Best Places to Eat

➡ Revolution Kitchen (p307)

➡ Red Hen (p317)

➡ Skunk Hollow Tavern (p294)

➡ Pangaea (p286)

➡ American Flatbread (p301)

Best Places to Sleep

➡ Inn at Shelburne Farms (p305)

➡ The Grafton Inn (p282)

➡ Inn at Round Barn Farm (p300)

➡ Willard Street Inn (p305)

➡ Dorset Inn (p290)

Why Go?

Whether seen under blankets of snow, patchworks of blazing fall leaves or the exuberant greens of spring and summer, Vermont's blend of bucolic farmland, mountains and picturesque small villages make it one of America's most uniformly appealing states. Hikers, bikers, skiers and kayakers will find four-season bliss here, on the expansive waters of Lake Champlain, the award-winning Kingdom Trails Network, the 300-mile Long and Catamount Trails, and the fabled slopes of Killington, Stowe and Sugarbush.

Foodies will love it here: small farmers have made Vermont a locavore paradise, complemented by America's densest collection of craft brewers. But most of all, what sets Vermont apart is its independent spirit: the first state to endorse same-sex civil unions, the only one to elect a socialist senator in the 21st century and the only one without a McDonald's in its capital city, it remains a haven of quirky creativity unlike anyplace else in America.

When to Go
Burlington

Dec-Mar Plummet down snow-covered pistes at New England's paramount ski resorts.

Jun-Aug Kayak on Lake Champlain, climb a mountain or frolic with fireflies at a Vermont state park.

Sep-Oct Pick apples, choose pumpkins and gawk at the colors during leaf season.

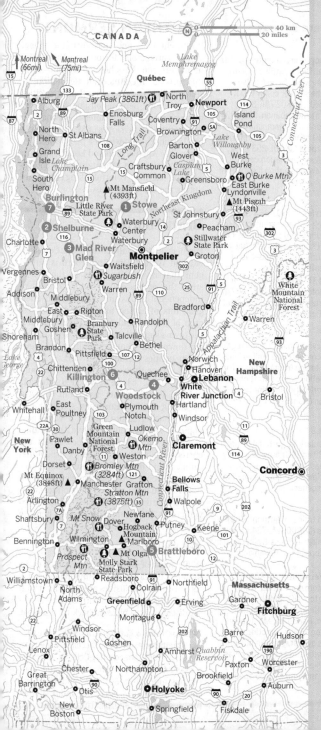

Vermont Highlights

1 **Stowe Recreation Path** (p312) Cruising Stowe's riverside path through green meadows and sculpture gardens backed by dazzling Mt Mansfield views.

2 **Shelburne Museum** (p303) Exploring a 19th-century lighthouse, a one-room schoolhouse and dozens of other historic New England buildings.

3 **Mad River Glen** (p299) Surveying your next black-diamond run or simply gawking at the foliage from the nation's sole surviving single chairlift.

4 **Billings Farm & Museum** (p292) Celebrating the apple and pumpkin harvest, making friends with pretty brown cows or hopping aboard a horse-drawn sleigh.

5 **Brattleboro Farmers Market** (p278) Catching a taste of Vermont's thriving locavore food culture.

6 **Long Trail Brewing Company** (p296) Soaking up the sun and enjoying a six-glass beer sampler on the riverside deck, just outside Killington.

7 **Church Street Marketplace** (p302) Shopping or bar-hopping your way through Burlington's multiblock pedestrian paradise.

ⓘ Getting There & Away

AIR

Vermont's major airport is in Burlington (p310), served by Continental, Delta, JetBlue, Northwest, United and US Airways. Cape Air also flies from Boston to the smaller commercial airports in **Rutland** (RUT; ☑ 802-786-8881; www.flyrutlandvt.com) and Lebanon, NH (p324), just across the Vermont/New Hampshire state line. In 2015, after a 30-year hiatus, tiny **Morrisville-Stowe State Airport** (☑ 802-253-2332, 855-359-7869; http://stoweaviation.com) began receiving Tradewind Aviation flights from White Plains, NY.

BOAT

Lake Champlain Ferries (☑ 802-864-9804; www.ferries.com; King St Dock; adult/child/car $8/3.10/30; ⊘ mid-Jun–Sep) runs ferries between Plattsburgh, NY, and Grand Isle; between Port Kent, NY, and Burlington; and between Essex, NY, and Charlotte.

The teeny-tiny **Fort Ti Ferry** (www.forttiferry. com; per car/bike/motorcycle $10/2/5; ⊘ 7am-6pm early May-Oct) runs from Larrabees Point in Shoreham, VT, to Ticonderoga Landing, NY.

BUS

Greyhound (www.greyhound.com) and **Megabus** (www.megabus.com) provide limited long-distance bus service to and from Vermont. The most convenient schedules serve Brattleboro (from Boston, New York City and points in between) and Burlington (from Boston, Montreal and New York).

CAR & MOTORCYCLE

Vermont is not particularly large, but it is mountainous. Although I-89 and I-91 provide speedy access to certain areas, the rest of the time you must plan to take it slow and enjoy the winding roads and mountain scenery.

TRAIN

Amtrak operates two trains in Vermont. The **Ethan Allen Express** (☑ 800-872-7245; www. amtrak.com/ethan-allen-express-train) departs New York City and stops in Fair Haven and Rutland.

The more scenic **Vermonter** (☑ 800-872-7245; www.amtrak.com/vermonter-train) heads from Washington, DC, and New York City to Brattleboro, Bellows Falls, Windsor, White River Junction, Randolph, Montpelier, Waterbury, Burlington–Essex Junction and St Albans. If you're a cyclist, you can buy one ticket on the *Vermonter* and get on and off as many times as you like, as long as you reserve a space for yourself and your bicycle ahead of time.

SOUTHERN VERMONT

White churches and inns surround village greens throughout historic southern Vermont, a region that's home to several towns that predate the American Revolution. In summer the roads between the three 'cities' of Brattleboro, Bennington and Manchester roll over green hills; in winter, they wind their way toward the ski slopes of Mt Snow, southern Vermont's cold-weather playground. For hikers, the Appalachian and Long Trails pass through the Green Mountain National Forest here, offering a colorful hiking experience during the fall foliage season.

Brattleboro

POP 12,000

Perched at the confluence of the Connecticut and West Rivers, Brattleboro is a little gem that reveals its facets to those who stroll the streets and prowl its dozens of independent shops and eateries. An energetic mix of ageing hippies and the latest crop of pierced and tattooed hipsters fuels the town's sophisticated eclecticism, keeping the downtown scene percolating and skewing its politics decidedly leftward.

Whetstone Brook runs through the south end of town, where a wooden stockade dubbed Fort Dummer was built in 1724, becoming the first European settlement in Vermont (theretofore largely a wilderness populated exclusively by Native Americans).

At the Old Town Hall (location of the current Main Street Gallery), celebrated thinkers and entertainers, including Oliver Wendell Holmes, Horace Greeley and Will Rogers, held forth on civic and political matters. Rudyard Kipling married a Brattleboro woman in 1892, and while living here he wrote *The Jungle Book*.

◉ Sights

While most of Brattleboro's action is easily found in the downtown commercial district, the surrounding hillsides are well salted with farms, cheesemakers and artisans, all awaiting discovery on a pleasant back-road ramble.

★**Brattleboro Farmers Market**   MARKET
(www.brattleborofarmersmarket.com; VT 9 west of I-91; ⊘ 9am-2pm Sat May-Oct) ✐ Offering a crash course in Vermont food, the market has more than 50 local vendors selling cheese, free-range beef and lamb, honey, pastries, maple syrup, fruit, veggies and

healthy snacks to nibble on as you wander. Live music and an active crafts scene round out the experience. From downtown, head west on VT 9 and continue 1.5 miles to the Creamery Bridge.

Brattleboro Museum & Art Center MUSEUM
(☏802-257-0124; www.brattleboromuseum.org; 10 Vernon St; adult/child $8/free; ☉11am-5pm Wed-Mon) Located in a 1915 railway station, this museum hosts a wealth of inventive exhibits by local artists in a variety of media. It also has a rotating multimedia exhibition program of contemporary art.

Retreat Petting Farm FARM
(☏802-490-2270; www.retreatfarm.org; 350 Linden St; barnyard $5, recreational trails free; ☉10am-4pm Wed-Sat, noon-4pm Sun late May-Aug, 10am-4pm Fri & Sat, noon-4pm Sun Sep & Oct; 🖐) 🐾 Pet, groom and say hello to over four dozen barnyard animals at this farm 1 mile north of town on VT 30. Look for the large cluster of red barns (or listen for the goats!). Out back, you can also walk, run, bike, ski or snowshoe on the farm's network of recreational trails.

Robb Family Farm FARM
(☏802-257-0163, sugar house 802-258-9087; www.robbfamilyfarm.com; 822 Ames Hill Rd; ☉10am-5:30pm Mon-Fri, to 2pm Sat; 🖐) 🐾 Run by the same family for more than a century, this 400-acre farm hosts maple-sugaring demonstrations in early spring; it also offers free sugar-house tours and sells maple products and organic beef in its gift shop year-round. From Brattleboro, follow VT 9 west to Greenleaf St, then continue 3 miles up Ames Hill Rd and look to the right.

🏃 Activities

West River Trail CYCLING
(westrivertrail.org) This lovely multipurpose trail, still partially under construction, follows 36 miles of former railway bed along the West River between Brattleboro and South Londonderry. The lower section, easily accessible just north of Brattleboro, has been open for walkers and cyclists since 2012. See the website for progress reports on the trail's completion.

Grafton Village Cheese Company FOOD
(☏802-246-2221; www.graftonvillagecheese.com; 400 Linden St/VT 30; ☉10am-6pm Sat-Thu, to 8pm Fri) Just outside Brattleboro lies the cheesemaking facility of Grafton Village Cheese Company, where you can see the sub-

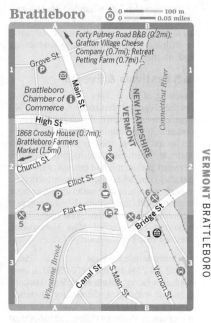

Brattleboro

lime cheddars being made (Monday through Thursday all day, and Friday till 3pm), taste and discover your favorite, and pick up a chunk to take with you. The shop also sells wine and local beer.

Vermont Canoe Touring CANOEING
(☏802-257-5008; www.vermontcanoetouring center.com; 451 Putney Rd/US 5, Veterans Memorial Bridge; canoe/kayak rental per day $50/45;

10am-6pm Mon-Sat, to 5pm Sun late May-early Sep) Rents kayaks and canoes. While away an afternoon bird-watching in the estuaries or visiting an unofficial nude sunbathing spot up the West River.

Festivals & Events

Strolling of the Heifers
PARADE

(www.strollingoftheheifers.com; early Jun;) Brattleboro's fun-spirited June celebration of community agriculture begins with flower-garlanded heifers mooing their way down Main St. Then come the bagpipes, 4H-ers, Vermont politicians, bad cow jokes from the parade's commentators, excrement-scooping superheroes (complete with capes!), antique tractors and synchronized shopping-cart performances by the local food co-op. Don't miss the crowning of Miss Ver-mooont, prettiest heifer of them all!

Marlboro Music Festival
MUSIC

(802-254-2394, box office 802-258-9331; www. marlboromusic.org; Marlboro College, Marlboro; mid-Jun–mid-Aug) A delight for chamber-music lovers, this festival is held on summer weekends at Marlboro College, 12 miles west of Brattleboro. Founded in 1951, it regularly draws big names in classical music, with performances held in an intimate 700-seat auditorium. Reserve ahead; many concerts sell out almost immediately.

Sleeping

If all you're after is a cheap sleep, there are plenty of motels on Putney Rd north of town; take exit 3 off I-91.

MAPLE SUGARING

Ranking first among states in maple-syrup production, Vermont regularly produces more than one million gallons of the sweet stuff per year – 40% of America's entire output. This is particularly impressive considering almost 40 gallons of sap must be tapped from maple trees for a mere quart of syrup. Demonstrations can be seen and samples tasted at the Robb Family Farm (p279), Shelburne Farms (p302), and dozens of other farms around Vermont during Maple Open House Weekend (vermontmaple.org/events; late Mar/early Apr), held in late March or early April, when the sap is flowing.

1868 Crosby House
B&B $$

(802-257-7145; www.crosbyhouse.com; 175 Western Ave; r incl breakfast $160-195;) Historic-house charm, beautiful Victorian gardens, trails out back and a convenient location halfway between the interstate and downtown make this a great base for exploring the Brattleboro area. Each of the three rooms and two kitchenette-equipped suites is unique, combining historic touches like a mahogany four-poster bed or slate fireplace with modern bathroom fixtures, cable TV and wi-fi.

Latchis Hotel
HOTEL $$

(802-254-6300, 800-798-6301; www.latchishotel.com; 50 Main St; r $99-190, ste $170-225, all incl breakfast;) You can't beat the location of these 30 reasonably priced rooms and suites, in the epicenter of downtown and adjacent to the historic theater of the same name. The hotel's art-deco overtones are refreshing, and wonderfully surprising for New England.

★ Forty Putney Road B&B
B&B $$$

(800-941-2413, 802-254-6268; www.fortyputneyroad.com; 192 Putney Rd; r $159-289, ste $229-329, all incl breakfast;) This sweet 1930s-vintage B&B just north of town has a glorious yard, a small cheery pub, five rooms and one luxurious suite with fireplace. Overlooking the West River estuary, it offers opportunities for walking, biking and boating right on its doorstep, and plenty of rainy-day activities, including billiards, board games, DVDs, a guest library and an indoor hot tub.

Eating

Brattleboro's eateres are mostly clustered along Main St and the streets feeding off of it, such as Eliot and High Sts. At the foot of Main St, the Brattleboro Food Co-op (802-257-0236; www.brattleborofoodcoop.com; 2 Main St; sandwiches $7-9; 7am-9pm Mon-Sat, 9am-9pm Sun) is a good spot for a snack any time of day.

Amy's Bakery Arts Cafe
BAKERY, CAFE $

(802-251-1071; 113 Main St; sandwiches, soups & salads $5-12; 7am-6pm Mon-Sat, 9am-5pm Sun;) Brattleboro's favorite bakery inspires poetic accolades for its breakfast breads, cakes, pastries and coffee with views of the Connecticut River. At lunchtime, the focus shifts to salads, soups and sandwiches, including many vegetarian options. Rotating exhibitions of art (all for sale) by local artists cover the walls.

CHEESEMAKING

Local cheesemakers have been around since Colonial times in Vermont, but it's only in the last few decades that artisanal cheese has come into vogue and become more widely available. Sheep's and goat's milk are now used in addition to cow's milk, adding variety to the traditional staples of cheddar and Colby. Vermont Cheese Council (www.vtcheese.com) lists nearly four dozen cheese producers on its online Cheese Trail map; two of the best and easiest to visit are Shelburne Farms (p302) and the Grafton Village Cheese Company (p279). Serious cheese connoisseurs can learn more about the state's smaller producers in Ellen Ecker Ogden's The Vermont Cheese Book. You'll also find a huge selection of local cheeses at places like the Brattleboro Food Co-op and City Market (p306) in Burlington.

Whetstone Station   PUB FOOD **$$**
(✒ 802-490-2354; www.whetstonestation.com; 36 Bridge St; mains $10-29; ⊙11:30am-10pm Sun-Thu, to 11pm Fri & Sat) This place is beloved for its dozen-plus craft brews on tap and excellent pub fare, but the real showstopper is its outstanding roof deck with a bird's-eye view of the Connecticut River. It's the ideal spot for a beer and a bite at sundown.

Marina Restaurant   AMERICAN **$$**
(✒802-257-7563; www.vermontmarina.com; 28 Spring Tree Rd; mains $10-28; ⊙11:30am-9pm Mon-Wed, 11:30am-10pm Thu-Sat, 10am-9pm Sun) The sublime location on the banks of the West River makes this one of Brattleboro's most pleasant places to grab a bite. The varied menu features burgers, seafood, salads, pasta and sandwiches, and there's a killer Sunday brunch. The outdoor deck is a perennial favorite for summertime sundowners. It's 1 mile north of downtown, on the west side of US 5.

★**TJ Buckley's**   AMERICAN **$$$**
(✒802-257-4922; www.tjbuckleysuptowndining. com; 132 Elliot St; mains $45; ⊙5:30-9pm Sun year-round, plus 5:30-9pm Wed mid-Jun–early Oct) 🍃 Chef-owner Michael Fuller founded this exceptional, upscale little eatery in an authentic 1927 diner over 30 years ago. Ever since, he's been offering a verbal menu of four seasonally changing items, sourced largely from local farms. Locals rave that the food here is Brattleboro's best. The diner seats just 18 souls, so reserve ahead. No credit cards.

🍷 Drinking & Nightlife

McNeill's Brewery   PUB
(✒802-254-2553; www.facebook.com/McNeills Brewery; 90 Elliot St; ⊙4pm-late Mon-Thu, 1pm-late Fri-Sun) This classic pub is inhabited by a lively, friendly local crowd. With 10 varieties, plus a few seasonal options, there's a beer for every taste here. Offerings include its namesake microbrew, McNeill's, its flagship Firehouse Amber and award-winning Pullman Porter. There's also frequent live music.

Mocha Joe's   CAFE
(✒802-257-7794; www.mochajoes.com; 82 Main St; ⊙7:30am-8pm Sun-Thu, to 9pm Fri & Sat; 🛜) Before your eyes spy this ultra-hip, subterranean space, your nose will locate the exceptionally rich brews and excellent pastries.

☆ Entertainment

Latchis Theater   CINEMA
(✒802-254-6300; http://theater.latchis.com; 50 Main St) The nicely restored, art-deco Latchis Building houses this theater, where you can see mainstream and indie films on four screens nightly, listen to live music (such as a string quartet) or catch Metropolitan Opera performances broadcast live from New York City.

ℹ Information

Brattleboro Chamber of Commerce (✒802-254-4565, 877-254-4565; www.brattle borochamber.org; 180 Main St; ⊙9am-5pm Mon-Fri) Dependable year-round source of tourist info.

ℹ Getting There & Away

While Brattleboro is very easy to get around on foot, you can call **Brattleboro Taxi** (✒802-254-6446; www.brattleborotaxi.com) for transportation beyond its limits.

BUS

Greyhound (www.greyhound.com) runs one bus daily to each of the following cities. Buses to/from NYC stop in Northampton, MA, and other New England cities en route. Check Greyhound's website for advance purchase and internet discounts.
Boston $26 to $44, 4¼ hours
New York City $31 to $60, 5¼ hours
Northampton $10 to $19, one hour
Montpelier $24 to $45, 3½ hours
Burlington $29 to $55, 1¼ hours

CAR

By car, the scenic 40-mile drive across VT 9 from Brattleboro to Bennington takes about an hour.

From Brattleboro to Northampton, MA, it's a 45-minute, 40-mile cruise down I-91.

TRAIN

Amtrak's scenic daily *Vermonter* (p278) train connects Brattleboro with points north and south, including Montpelier (from $29, 2½ hours), Burlington/Essex Junction (from $29, 3¼ hours), New York City (from $63, 5½ hours) and Washington, DC (from $96, nine hours). See Amtrak's website for details.

Around Brattleboro

Grafton

POP 680

The must-see village of Grafton is graceful, but it's not that way by accident. In the 1960s the private Windham Foundation established a restoration and preservation program for the entire village, and it has been eminently successful. The foundation's initiatives included burying all electrical and telephone lines, which helps account for Grafton's ultra-picturesque, lost-in-time appearance.

🏃 Activities

Grafton Ponds Outdoor Center OUTDOORS
(☑ 802-843-2400; www.graftonponds.com; 783 Townshend Rd) Just south of Grafton village, Grafton Ponds Outdoor Center offers year-round recreation on its network of mountain-biking, hiking and cross-country ski trails, along with canoeing, swimming, snow tubing and adventure camps for kids.

🛏 Sleeping & Eating

★**Grafton Inn** INN **$$**
(☑ 802-234-8718; www.graftoninnvermont.com; 92 Main St; r incl breakfast $159-299; 🛜) With a double porch that serves as Grafton's most picturesque landmark, this venerable inn has played host to such notable guests as Rudyard Kipling, Theodore Roosevelt and Ralph Waldo Emerson. While the original brick inn is quite formal, many of the 47 guest rooms and suites – scattered around houses within the village – are less so.

The inn has tennis courts, a sandbottomed swimming pond and crosscountry skiing trails. The dining room is New England formal and the cuisine is refined New American with a seasonal menu, while fare at the nearby cafe is lighter and more casual.

> DON'T MISS
>
> ### VERMONT LEAF PEEPS
>
> Here are a few spots to see Vermont's famous fall foliage at its best:
>
> **Mt Mansfield** Vermont's highest peak is gorgeous when draped in fall colors, especially when an early snowfall dusts the summit white. The best panoramic perspectives are from Stowe, Jeffersonville, Cambridge and Underhill. Hikers can also experience the full sweep of color from the mountaintop; one of the prettiest routes is the Sunset Ridge Trail in Underhill State Park.
>
> **Grafton** Villages don't get any cuter than Grafton, which looks like it was airlifted in from an earlier century. The white clapboard buildings are even more photogenic when contrasted against fiery leaves and a brilliant blue sky.
>
> **Lake Willoughby** The technicolor majesty of changing maples looks especially dramatic on the steep slopes surrounding this fjord-like lake in Vermont's Northeast Kingdom.
>
> **Mad River Glen** (p299) Ride the nation's last commercially operating single chair lift – the same one that whisks skiers to the mountaintop in winter – to admire spectacular panoramic views of the Mad River Valley's fall foliage.
>
> **Vermont Rte 100** A road-tripper's dream, this classic driving route through the heart of the Green Mountains shows off Vermont's farm country in its full autumnal splendor.
>
> **Merck Forest** (p287) Climb to the barn meadow at this environmental education center in southwestern Vermont for breathtaking vistas of the Taconic Mountains in bright rainbow colors.

Phelps Barn   PUB FOOD **$$**

(☑802-234-8718;   www.graftoninnvermont.com/
dining/phelps-barn; mains $11-19; ⊙4-10pm Tue-
Sun) Tucked into a historic carriage house,
the Grafton Inn's casual on-site tavern serves
light pub fare – burgers, fish and chips, *steak
frites* – and a wide range of Vermont micro-
brews. Pop in on Thursday evening, when a
burger and a pint go for $12, or on Flatbread
Fridays, when it serves pizza cooked in 'Big
Red,' the tavern's beloved pizza oven. There's
also live music every Saturday night.

❶ Getting There & Away

Grafton lies at the junction of VT 121 and VT
35, about 15 miles north of Newfane, 27 miles
north of Brattleboro and 45 miles southeast of
Manchester.

Newfane

POP 1730

Vermont is rife with pretty villages, but New-
fane is near the top of everyone's list. All the
postcard-perfect sights you'd expect in a
Vermont town are here: tall old trees, white
high-steepled churches, gracious old houses
and an adorable inn. In spring Newfane is
busy making maple sugar; in summer, the
town buzzes around its flea market; fall
lures leaf peepers; and winter brings couples
seeking cozy rooms in warm hideaways.

A short stroll exposes Newfane's core:
you'll see the stately **Congregational
Church** (1839), the **Windham County
Courthouse** (1825), built in Greek Revival
style, and a few antique shops.

Newfane is on VT 30, just 12 miles north-
west of Brattleboro, 19 miles northeast
of Wilmington and 36 miles southeast of
Manchester.

Wilmington

POP 1880

Nestled in the upper Deerfield River valley,
Wilmington is the gateway to Mt Snow, one
of New England's best ski resorts and an ex-
cellent summertime mountain-biking and
golfing spot. Many restaurants and stores
cater to families, who are the resort's main
clientele.

Wilmington was clobbered with massive
flooding during Tropical Storm Irene in Au-
gust 2011. Some downtown businesses were
wiped out completely and many more were
closed for months, but the town has rebuilt
and is back in business.

🏃 Activities

Mt Snow   SKIING

(☑800-245-7669; www.mountsnow.com; 39 Mt
Snow Rd, West Dover; lift tickets adult/child $90/70;
⊙9am-4pm Mon-Fri, from 8am Sat & Sun) South-
ern Vermont's biggest ski resort features
varied, family-friendly terrain, with 86
trails (15% beginner, 70% intermediate, 15%
expert) and 20 lifts, plus a vertical drop of
1700ft and the snowmaking ability to blan-
ket 80% of the trails. Area cross-country
routes cover more than 60 miles; other win-
ter activities nearby include tubing, snow-
mobile tours, dog sledding and sleigh rides.

Come summer, Mt Snow's Bike Park is one
of New England's best venues for lift-assisted
downhill mountain biking, and has played
host to the USA Cycling Mountain Bike
National Championships. The mountain's
3-mile introductory downhill trail, Trail 7, is
the longest of its kind in the eastern US.

To reach Mt Snow from Wilmington,
travel 10 miles north of town on VT 100.
Bus 7 (Wilmington–West Dover), operated
by MOOver (www.moover.com), offers free
hourly transport from Wilmington to the
slopes of Mt Snow year-round, with extra
services added on weekends and throughout
the ski season.

🛏 Sleeping

The Wilmington area offers a good range of
accommodations, including inns for every
budget near the town center and motels east
and west of town on VT 9. Skiers will find
a 196-room hotel, a lodge and a variety of
self-catering condos up at Mt Snow.

Old Red Mill Inn   INN **$**

(☑877-733-6455, 802-464-3700; www.oldred
mill.com; 18 N Main St; d $65-95; ☏) Squeezed
between VT 100 and the Deerfield River's
north branch, this converted sawmill in the
heart of town has simple rooms (chunky
wood furnishings, checkered bedspreads) at
bargain prices. In summer, the attached Jer-
ry's Deck Bar & Grill offers outdoor seating
with pleasant river views.

Nutmeg Country Inn   INN **$$**

(☑802-380-6101, 802-464-3907; www.thenut
megvermont.com; 153 W Main St/VT 9; r $120-190,
ste $190-255, all incl breakfast; ☏) Just west of
Wilmington, this 18th-century farmhouse
has 10 rooms and four suites with antiques
and reproduction pieces. Most luxurious is
the Grand Deluxe King Suite, with skylights
and a marble bath.

WORTH A TRIP

JAMAICA

A prime dose of rural Vermont, with a country store and several antique shops, this artsy community tucked into the evergreen forest is also home to Jamaica State Park (☑802-874-4600; www.vtstateparks.com/htm/jamaica.htm; 48 Salmon Hole Lane, Jamaica; adult/child $4/2; ☺mid-May–mid-Oct), the best place in Vermont for riverside camping. The annual Whitewater Weekend held here in late September draws kayaking enthusiasts from all over New England to pit their skills against the rampaging West River. There's good swimming right in the heart of the campground, but walkers can also head 3 miles upstream along a 19th-century railway bed to Hamilton Falls, a 50ft ribbon of water cascading into a natural swimming hole.

White House Inn   INN $$$
(☑802-464-2135; www.whitehouseinn.com; 178 VT 9; r incl breakfast $231-429; �audio☼) Perched on a hillside east of town, this white Colonial Revival mansion has great cross-country trails and 16 luxury rooms, some with Jacuzzi and fireplace. Enhancing the inn's romantic appeal are an excellent restaurant – complete with fireplace, wood paneling and views of the Deerfield Valley – and a convivial tavern.

✗ Eating

Wahoo's Eatery   AMERICAN $
(☑802-464-0110; www.wahooseatery.com; VT 9; sandwiches & salads $6-9; ☺11am-8pm mid-May–mid-Sep) 'We welcome your business and relish your buns': so reads the sign at this friendly, family-run roadside snack shack less than a mile east of Wilmington on VT 9. A long-standing local institution, it whips up quality burgers ($2 extra for grass-fed Vermont beef), along with hand-cut fries, handmade conch fritters, wraps, sandwiches, hot dogs, salads and ice cream.

Dot's   DINER $
(☑802-464-7284; www.dotsofvermont.com; 5 W Main St; lunch $4-9, dinner $5-10, dinner $14-19; ☺5:30am-8pm Sun-Thu, to 9pm Fri & Sat) Devastated by Hurricane Irene in 2011, Wilmington's venerable down-home diner was rebuilt from scratch and reopened in September 2013. Its spicy Jailhouse Chili, covered with melted cheese, is renowned throughout New

England. With a second location near the slopes in West Dover (☑802-464-6476; www.dotsofdover.com; 2 Mountain Park Plaza/VT 100, West Dover; mains $5-13; ☺6am-3pm Mon-Thu, to 8pm Fri & Sat, to 6pm Sun), it's justly popular with locals and skiers in search of cheap sustenance like steak and eggs for breakfast.

ⓘ Information

Southern Vermont Deerfield Valley Chamber of Commerce (☑802-464-8092; www.visitvermont.com; 21 W Main St; ☺9am-4pm Mon-Fri, 10am-4pm Sat & Sun) Has information on accommodations and activities.

ⓘ Getting There & Away

Wilmington sits halfway between Brattleboro and Bennington on VT 9, southern Vermont's primary east–west route; it's a winding 20-mile (half-hour) drive across the mountains to either town. Wilmington is also the southern gateway to scenic VT 100, which runs north past Haystack and Mt Snow to Killington (75 miles, 1¾ hours) and Stowe (146 miles, 3½ hours).

Bennington

POP 15,800

Bennington is a mix of historic Vermont village (Old Bennington), workaday town (Bennington proper) and college town (North Bennington). It is also home to the famous Bennington Battle Monument, which commemorates the crucial Battle of Bennington during the American Revolution. Had Colonel Seth Warner and the local 'Green Mountain Boys' not helped weaken British defenses during this battle, the colonies might well have been split.

The charming hilltop site of colonial Old Bennington is studded with 80 Georgian and Federal houses (dating from 1761 – the year Bennington was founded – to 1830). The poet Robert Frost is buried here and a museum in his old homestead pays eloquent tribute.

As Bennington is within the bounds of the Green Mountain National Forest, there are many hiking trails nearby, including the granddaddies of them all: the Appalachian and Long Trails.

◉ Sights

Old First Church   HISTORIC SITE
(www.oldfirstchurchbenn.org; cnr Monument Ave & VT 9; ☺10am-noon & 1-4pm Mon-Sat, 1-4pm Sun) **FREE** Gracing the center of Old Bennington, this historic church was built in 1805 in Palladian style. Its churchyard holds the re-

mains of five Vermont governors, numerous American Revolution soldiers and poet Robert Frost (1874–1963), the best-known, and perhaps best-loved, American poet of the 20th century, buried beneath the inscription 'I Had a Lover's Quarrel with the World.'

Bennington Museum
MUSEUM

(☑ 802-447-1571; www.benningtonmuseum.org; 75 Main St; adult/child $10/free; ◔ 10am-5pm daily Jun-Oct, closed Wed Feb-May, Nov & Dec, closed Jan) Between downtown and Old Bennington, this ever-expanding museum offers 14 galleries of ongoing and changing exhibits. It features the world's largest collections of Grandma Moses paintings and Bennington pottery, along with a rich array of Vermont paintings, decorative arts and folk art from the 18th century to the present, encompassing everything from Vermont's Gilded Age to Bennington Modernism to 'Outsider' Art. New in 2015, the Works on Paper Gallery displays prints, lithographs, photography and more by nationally recognized regional artists.

Bennington Battle Monument
HISTORIC SITE

(☑ 802-447-0550; www.benningtonbattlemonument.com; 15 Monument Circle, Old Bennington; adult/child $5/1; ◔ 9am-5pm mid-Apr–Oct) Commemorating the Battle of Bennington, a crucial American Revolutionary War battle fought near here in 1777, Vermont's loftiest structure offers an unbeatable 360-degree view of the countryside with peeks at covered bridges and across to New York. And you won't have to strain hamstrings climbing this 306ft-tall obelisk: an elevator whisks you painlessly to the top.

Robert Frost Stone House Museum
MUSEUM

(☑ 802-447-6200; www.frostfriends.org; 121 VT 7A, Shaftsbury; adult/child $6/3; ◔ 10am-5pm Wed-Sun May-Oct) When he moved his family to Shaftsbury (4 miles north of Bennington), poet Robert Frost was 46 years old and at the height of his career. This modest museum opens a window into the poet's life, with one entire room dedicated to his most famous work, 'Stopping by Woods on a Snowy Evening,' which he penned here in the 1920s.

Park-McCullough House Museum
MUSEUM

(☑ 802-442-5441; www.parkmccullough.org; 1 Park St, North Bennington; guided tour adult/child/teen $15/8/12; ◔ hourly tours 10am-3pm Fri, 10am-noon Sat May-Oct, other times by appointment, grounds dawn-dusk year-round) Just off VT 67A in North Bennington, this magnificent 35-room mansion, built in 1865, is filled with period furnishings and a fine collection of antique dolls, toys and carriages. Stroll the grounds (free of charge) during daylight hours any time of year, or visit the house on a guided tour (regularly scheduled on Fridays and Saturdays in warm weather, by appointment at other times).

🏃 Activities

Prospect Mountain Cross-Country Ski Touring Center
SKIING

(☑ 802-442-2575; www.prospectmountain.com; VT 9, Woodford; trail pass adult/child $22/17; ◔ 9am-5pm) About 7 miles east of Bennington, Prospect Mountain has more than 18 miles of groomed trails. It offers ski rentals and lessons as well as snowshoe rentals.

🛏 Sleeping

Bennington's nicest inns are on the outskirts of town, toward Old Bennington and North Bennington. Motels are spread out east and west of the center along VT 9, south on US 7, or north along US 7 and Northside Dr (VT 7A).

Greenwood Lodge & Campsites
HOSTEL, CAMPGROUND $

(☑ 802-442-2547; www.campvermont.com/greenwood; VT 9, Prospect Mountain; 2-person tent/RV site $29/38, dm $32-38, r $73-79; ◔ mid-May–late Oct; ⊛) Nestled in the Green Mountains in Woodford, this 120-acre space with three ponds is home to one of Vermont's best-sited hostels. Accommodations include 17 budget beds and 40 campsites. You'll find it easily, 8 miles east of Bennington on VT 9 at the Prospect Mountain ski area. Facilities include hot showers and a games room.

Camping on the Battenkill
CAMPGROUND $

(☑ 800-830-6663, 802-375-6663; www.campingonthebattenkillvt.com; VT 7A, Arlington; tent sites $27-33, RV sites $35-42, lean-tos $35-43; ◔ late Apr–mid-Oct) Fishing is the forte at this campground just north of Arlington, which has 100 sites split between forest, meadow and open areas. Call early to reserve the popular riverside sites. Multiday stays are required during peak periods.

Henry House
B&B $$

(☑ 802-442-7045; www.thehenryhouseinn.com; 1338 Murphy Rd, North Bennington; r incl breakfast $100-155; ⊛) Sit on the rocking chair and watch the traffic trickle across a covered bridge at this Colonial home built in 1769 by American Revolution hero William Henry. This is the real deal on 25 peaceful acres and dripping with so much original character you might expect long-gone Lieutenant Henry to walk down the hall.

Four Chimneys Inn
B&B $$$

(☎ 802-447-3500; www.fourchimneys.com; 21 West Rd/VT 9; r incl breakfast $139-329; ☜) Old Bennington's only B&B, this grand white 1910 mansion surrounded by 11 acres of manicured lawns has a variety of spacious rooms, many with fireplaces and porches. The best suite is a two-story revamped former ice house with a spiral staircase. The attached restaurant, open August to October, has seated such guests as Walt Disney, Richard Burton and Elizabeth Taylor.

✖ Eating & Drinking

Bennington's restaurants are concentrated downtown near the intersection of US 7 and VT 9. You'll find another small but appealing cluster of eateries in North Bennington, 6 miles to the northwest.

Blue Benn Diner
DINER $

(☎ 802-442-5140; 314 North St; mains $6-14; ⊙ 6am-5pm Mon & Tue, to 8pm Wed-Fri, to 4pm Sat, 7am-4pm Sun; ☞) This classic 1950s-era diner serves breakfast all day and a healthy mix of American, Asian and Mexican fare, including vegetarian options. Enhancing the retro experience are little tabletop jukeboxes where you can you play Willie Nelson's 'Moonlight in Vermont' or Cher's 'Gypsies, Tramps and Thieves' till your neighbors scream for mercy.

★ Pangaea
INTERNATIONAL $$

(☎ 802-442-7171; www.vermontfinedining.com; 1 Prospect St, North Bennington; lounge mains $8-12, restaurant mains $30; ⊙ lounge 5-10pm daily, restaurant 5-9pm Tue-Sat) Whether you opt for the tastefully decorated dining room or the intimate lounge or the small riverside terrace, you'll be served exceptional food here. The menu is full of fresh ingredients and international influences; try the Thai shrimp on organic udon noodles in a curry peanut sauce or the Herbes de Provence–rubbed Delmonico steak topped with Gorgonzola. One of Vermont's finest restaurants.

Marigold Kitchen
PIZZA $$

(☎ 802-445-4545; www.marigoldkitchen.info; 25 Main St, North Bennington; pizzas $10-22; ⊙ 5-10pm Mon-Thu, 11am-10pm Fri-Sun Apr-Oct; ☜) This homegrown neighborhood pizzeria in North Bennington makes the best pizzas in town, with your choice of stone-ground wheat-flour or gluten-free crusts and organic toppings sourced from a dozen local farms.

Madison Brewing Co Pub & Restaurant
PUB FOOD $$

(☎ 802-442-7397; www.madisonbrewingco.com; 428 Main St; mains $10-19; ⊙ 11:30am-9pm Sun-Thu, to 10pm Fri & Sat) With six to eight of its own brews on tap, this bustling two-level pub features fare ranging from sandwiches and burgers to steak, meatloaf, salads and pasta. The small upstairs deck is a popular summertime hangout.

South Street Café
CAFE

(☎ 802-442-2433; www.southstreetcafe.com; 105 South St; ⊙ 7am-6pm Mon-Thu, 7am-9pm Fri & Sat, 8am-6pm Sun; ☞) Sink into a velvet sofa and sip a cup of locally roasted joe in this inviting, high-ceilinged cafe with warm orange walls and vintage patterned tinwork. Located smack in Bennington's center at the corner of VT 9 and US 7, it's an oasis for soups, sandwiches, quiche, bakery treats and warm mugs of deliciousness.

🛍 Shopping

Bennington Potters
ARTS & CRAFTS

(☎ 800-205-8033, 802-447-7531; www.benningtonpotters.com; 324 County St; ⊙ 9:30am-6pm Mon-Sat, 10am-5pm Sun) The artisans at this factory store are maintaining Bennington's strong tradition of handmade stoneware manufacturing, which dates back to the 1700s. Take a self-guided tour through the manufacturing area, which reveals how much hand work still goes into the company's mass-produced items.

ℹ Information

Bennington Welcome Center (☎ 802-447-2456; www.bennington.com; 100 VT 279; ⊙ 7am-9pm) Bennington's spiffy new tourist office has loads of information, long hours, and free coffee and tea for motorists; it's at the highway interchange where VT 279 and US 7 meet.

ℹ Getting There & Away

Bennington is 40 miles (one hour) west of Brattleboro via VT 9, or 25 miles (30 minutes) south of Manchester via US 7.

Manchester

POP 4400

Manchester has been a fashionable resort town for almost two centuries. These days, the draw is mostly winter skiing and upscale outlet shopping (there are more than 100 shops, from Armani to Banana Republic).

MERCK FOREST & FARMLAND CENTER

Encompassing over 2700 acres of high-country meadow and forest, **Merck Forest & Farmland Center** (☑ 802-394-7836; www.merckforest.org; 3270 VT 315; ☻ visitor center 9am-4pm; ♿) is a blissful place to experience Vermont's natural beauty and agricultural heritage. The park's centerpiece is a working organic farm with animals, vegetable gardens, renewable-energy installations and a sugar house where you can watch maple syrup being produced during sugaring season. It's hidden away on a gorgeous hilltop, only 25 minutes from Manchester but a world apart from the village hustle and bustle.

The center offers a wide range of hikes, environmental education programs and such events as sheepdog trials. It also rents out cabins and tent sites, which are spread all over the property. Sales of produce and syrup, coupled with voluntary contributions, help sustain the nonprofit foundation at the heart of it all. To get here from Manchester, take VT 30 northwest 8 miles to East Rupert, then turn left on VT 315, travel 2 miles and look for signs on your left at the top of the hill.

Two families put Manchester on the map. The first was native son Franklin Orvis (1824–1900), who became a New York businessperson but returned to Manchester to establish the Equinox House Hotel (1849). Franklin's brother, Charles, founded the Orvis Company, makers of fly-fishing equipment, in 1856. The Manchester-based company now has a worldwide following.

The second family was that of Abraham Lincoln (1809–65). His wife, Mary Todd Lincoln (1818–82), and their son Robert Todd Lincoln (1843–1926), came here during the Civil War, and Robert returned to build a mansion – Hildene – a number of years later.

◉ Sights

★ **Hildene** HISTORIC SITE
(☑ 802-362-1788; www.hildene.org; 1005 Hildene Rd/VT 7A; adult/child $20/5, guided tours $7.50/2; ☻9:30am-4:30pm) Outside Manchester, the 24-room Georgian Revival mansion of Robert Todd Lincoln, son of Abraham and Mary Lincoln, is a national treasure. Lincoln family members lived here until 1975, when it was converted into a museum and filled with many of the family's personal effects and furnishings. These include the hat Abraham Lincoln probably wore when he delivered the Gettysburg Address, and remarkable brass casts of his hands, the right one swollen from shaking hands while campaigning for the presidency.

Visitors can take a self-guided tour of the mansion any time of year. Guided tours are also available (for an additional fee) from June to mid-September at 11am and 1pm, and from November to May (by reservation only) at 1pm; there are no guided tours between mid-September and October.

The museum ticket includes access to the surrounding grounds, which are home to 8 miles of **walking, skiing and snowshoeing trails**, an **observatory** with a telescope, the **Cutting and Kitchen Garden** (a pretty herb and vegetable garden), the **Hoyt Formal Garden** (an exquisite flower garden designed to resemble a stained-glass window) and an agricultural center with a **solar-powered barn** where you can see the goats that produce Hildene cheese (watch it being made here, and purchase it at the museum gift shop).

Hildene also has a packed calendar of **concerts and lectures**; check its website for up-to-date listings.

American Museum of Fly Fishing MUSEUM
(☑ 802-362-3300; www.amff.com; 4070 Main St/ VT 7A; adult/child $5/3; ☻10am-4pm Tue-Sun Jun-Oct, Tue-Sat Nov-May) This museum has perhaps the world's best display of fly-fishing equipment. This includes fly collections and rods used by Ernest Hemingway, Bing Crosby and several US presidents, including Herbert Hoover. If you can believe it, the latter penned the tome *Fishing for Fun & To Wash Your Soul*.

Southern Vermont Arts Center MUSEUM
(☑ 802-362-1405; www.svac.org; 930 Southern Vermont Arts Center Dr; ☻10am-5pm Tue-Sat, noon-5pm Sun) FREE In addition to excellent outdoor sculptures, this center's 10 galleries of classic and contemporary art feature touring shows of sculpture, paintings, prints and photography. Other attractions include walking trails, the on-site Garden Cafe, lectures and numerous musical events, including jazz concerts and the Manchester Music Festival, where classical is the focus.

🏃 Activities

Equinox Preserve
HIKING

(☏ 802-366-1400; www.equinoxpreservationtrust. org; W Union St) The Equinox Preservation Trust maintains this 914-acre woodland preserve on the eastern slopes of 3848ft Mt Equinox. Hikers will appreciate the preserve's well-signposted network of trails, the most dramatic of which is the 3.1-mile, 2840ft climb to the top of Mt Equinox via the Blue Summit Trail. Park at the W Union St trailhead, or in the gargantuan lot behind Equinox Resort.

Get trail maps at the Manchester Visitor's Center or the self-serve kiosk adjacent to the Equinox parking lot.

Appalachian Trail
HIKING, BIKING

(www.appalachiantrail.org) The Appalachian Trail passes just east of Manchester, and in this area it follows the same route as Vermont's Long Trail. Shelters pop up about every 10 miles; some are staffed from June to early October. Good day hikes include one to the summit of Bromley Mountain and another to Stratton Pond.

Stratton Mountain
SKIING

(☏ 802-297-4000, 800-787-2886; www.stratton. com; off VT 30, South Londonderry; lift ticket adult/child/teen weekend $105/76/89, weekday $89/69/79; ⊙ 9am-4pm Mon-Fri, 8:30am-4pm Sat & Sun) This all-season recreational playground, 16 miles southeast of Manchester, has 97 trails, 11 lifts (including a summit gondola), 670 acres of skiable terrain and a vertical drop of 2003ft on a 3875ft mountain. There are also over 7 miles of groomed cross-country trails. Summer activities include golf, tennis, kayaking, swimming, stand-up paddleboarding, hiking, biking and scenic gondola rides.

Bromley Mountain
SKIING

(☏ 802-824-5522, snow conditions 866-856-2201; www.bromley.com; 3984 VT 11, Peru; lift ticket adult/child/teen $73/47/63; ⊛) Approximately 5 miles east of Manchester, 3284ft Bromley Mountain is a family-oriented resort featuring 46 downhill ski runs and nine lifts. Summer attractions include the Alpine Slide (one of the world's longest), Sun Mountain Flyer (New England's longest zip line), an aerial adventure park, a climbing wall, trampolines, Vermont's longest water slide, a children's adventure park and access to the Long/Appalachian Trail.

Mt Equinox Skyline Drive
SCENIC DRIVE

(☏ 802-362-1114; www.equinoxmountain.com; VT 7A, btwn Manchester & Arlington; car & driver $15, each additional passenger $5, under 10yr free; ⊙ 9am-4pm late May-Oct) For exceptional views, climb the insanely steep 5-mile Skyline Dr, a private toll road that leads to the summit of 3848ft Mt Equinox, highest mountain in the Taconic Range; it's just off VT 7A, south of Manchester.

✹ Festivals & Events

Concerts on the Green
MUSIC

(http://visitmanchestervt.com/annual-events; Manchester Town Green, Depot St; ⊙ mid-Jul–mid-Aug) Each Tuesday evening between 6pm and 8pm from mid-July to mid-August you can catch live music performances (mainly local folk bands) alfresco at the town green.

Manchester Music Festival
MUSIC

(☏ 802-362-1956; www.mmfvt.org; ⊙ Jul & Aug) Presents an annual summer series of seven classical-music concerts at the Southern Vermont Arts Center.

🛏 Sleeping

Some of New England's stateliest old inns line the rarefied stretch of VT 7A that runs through historic Manchester village. A mile or two further north, in more down-to-earth Manchester Center, you'll find a good selection of roadside motels.

Inn at Manchester
INN $$

(☏ 802-362-1793, 800-273-1793; www.innatmanchester.com; 3967 Main St/VT 7A; r $155-245, ste $205-315, all incl breakfast; ⊛ @ 🛜 🏊) This restored inn and carriage house offers rooms and suites with comfy quilts and country furnishings, each named after a herb or flower. There's a big front porch, afternoon teas with fresh-baked goodies, an expansive backyard and comfortable common rooms, one with a wee pub.

Barnstead Inn
INN $$

(☏ 802-362-1619, reservations 800-331-1619; www.barnsteadinn.com; 349 Bonnet St; r $129-195, ste $210-310; 🛜 🏊) Barely a half-mile from Manchester Center, this converted 1830s hay barn exudes charm and is in a good location. Rooms have refrigerators and homey braided rugs, while the porch has wicker rockers for watching the world pass by.

Casablanca Motel
MOTEL, CABINS $$

(☏ 800-254-2145, 802-362-2145; www.casablancamotel.com; 5972 Main St/VT 7A; 1-room cabins

$72-209, 2-room cabins $130-250; ✳@🖤) This tidy collection of cabins on the northern fringes of town has units with microwaves, fridges and coffeemakers, each decorated in a different country theme.

Equinox RESORT $$$
(☑800-362-4747, reservations 877-854-7625; www.equinoxresort.com; 3567 Main St/VT 7A; r $299-489, ste $419-719; @🖤🏊) Manchester's most famous resort encompasses many worlds: cottages with wood-burning fireplaces, luxury town houses with full kitchens, the main house's elegant suites, and the Federal-style 1811 House's antique-filled rooms, canopied beds and oriental rugs. High-end extras abound: an 18-hole golf course, two tennis courts, a state-of-the-art fitness center, a full-service spa and endless activities, including falconry, archery and snowmobiling.

Inn at Ormsby Hill INN $$$
(☑802-362-1163, reservations 800-670-2841; www.ormsbyhill.com; 1842 Main St/VT 7A; r $205-410, ste $330-535, all incl breakfast; 🖤) Just southwest of Manchester, Ormsby Hill is arguably one of the most welcoming inns in all of New England. Fireplaces, two-person Jacuzzis, flat-screen TVs, antiques, gracious innkeepers and 2.5 acres of lawn are among the features that draw repeat guests. The inn's breakfast is without equal (from bacon-and-egg risotto to pancakes baked in the shape of a top hat).

✖️ Eating

Second Rising Bakery & Cafe BAKERY $
(☑802-768-8116; www.facebook.com/secondrisingmanchester; 32 Bonnet St; baked goods from $3, sandwiches & salads $9-11; ⊙8am-3pm Tue-Sat) Yes, the name refers to the heavenly aroma of rising dough, but it's also a nod to this beloved bakery's recent reopening. Known for years as 'The Lawyer and the Baker,' it closed in 2011 but was reborn triumphantly in 2014. You'll find everything from fresh-baked scones and cute Vermont-shaped cookies to soups, salads, sandwiches, spanakopita and salmon cakes.

Little Rooster Cafe CAFE $
(☑802-362-3496; 4645 Main St/VT 7A; dishes $5-11; ⊙7am-2pm Thu-Tue) This colorful spot serves an eclectic mix of dishes, including pan-seared salmon, roast leg of lamb, spinach salad, and focaccia sandwiches with tasty ingredients like roasted portobello mushrooms and grilled eggplant. It's also popular for its

delicious breakfast entrees, like the trademark Cock-A-Doodle-Doo (poached eggs with smoked salmon and dill-mustard-caper sauce on an English muffin).

Perfect Wife INTERNATIONAL $$
(☑802-362-2817; www.perfectwife.com; 2594 Depot St; mains tavern $12-22, restaurant $20-32; ⊙restaurant 5-10pm Thu-Sat, tavern 4pm-late Tue-Sat Sep-May, both open Mon-Sat Jun-Aug) In the hills east of town, this beloved eatery serves traditional favorites such as steak and sesame-crusted tuna alongside delicious international small plates in a cozy cobblestone-walled dining area. The adjoining Other Woman Tavern offers lower-priced pub fare and is an excellent evening hangout, with live music on Friday nights (folk, rock, blues and more).

Ye Olde Tavern AMERICAN $$$
(☑802-362-0611; www.yeoldetavern.net; 5183 Main St; mains $18-34; ⊙5-9pm) Hearthside dining at candlelit tables enhances the experience at this gracious roadside 1790s inn. The menu is wide-ranging, but the 'Yankee favorites' like traditional pot roast cooked in the tavern's own ale, New England scrod baked with Vermont cheddar, bread crumbs, sherry and lemon, and local venison (a regular Friday special) seal the deal.

🛍️ Shopping

★Northshire Bookstore BOOKS
(☑802-362-2200; www.northshire.com; 4869 Main St; ⊙10am-7pm Sun-Thu, to 9pm Fri & Sat) Forming both the geographic and the intellectual center of the Manchester community, this thriving independent bookstore is the best in Vermont, with a sprawling collection of titles on every subject imaginable (including an entire section on Vermont and New England) and an impressive array of readings and author events.

ℹ️ Information

Green Mountain National Forest Ranger Station (☑802-362-2307; www.fs.usda.gov/gmfl; 2538 Depot St, Manchester Center; ⊙8am-4:30pm Mon-Fri) Stop by for info about the Appalachian and Long Trails, trail maps and details about shorter day hikes.

Manchester and the Mountains Regional Chamber of Commerce (☑802-362-6313; www.visitmanchestervt.com; 39 Bonnet St, Manchester Center; ⊙9am-5pm Mon-Fri, 10am-2pm Sat & Sun; 🖤) Just west of the VT 30/VT 7A junction in Manchester Center, this

HIKING VERMONT'S LONG LONG TRAIL

Built between 1912 and 1930 as America's first long-distance hiking trail, the Long Trail of Vermont follows the south–north ridge of the Green Mountains for 264 miles, from Massachusetts to Canada. A little less than half of the trail is located inside the **Green Mountain National Forest** (802-747-6700; www.fs.usda.gov).

Often only 3ft wide, the trail traverses streams and forests, skirts ponds and weaves up and down mountains to bare summits like Mt Abraham, Mt Mansfield and Camel's Hump. From up top, hikers enjoy exceptional vistas, with wave after wave of hillside gently rolling back to a sea of green dotted with the occasional pasture or meadow.

Three excellent guides to the trail – *Long Trail Guide*, the *Day Hiker's Guide to Vermont* and *The Long Trail End-to-Ender's Guide* – are published by the venerable Green Mountain Club (GMC), which originally constructed the trail and still maintains it. All three guides are packed with nitty-gritty details on equipment sales and repairs, mail drops and B&Bs that provide trailhead shuttle services.

The GMC maintains more than 60 rustic lodges and lean-tos along the trail, all spaced at 5- to 7-mile intervals. Hikers can easily walk from one shelter to the next in a day, but it's imperative to bring a tent as shelters often fill up.

While the trail is wonderful for multiday excursions, it's also popular for day hikes. Call or drop by the *Green Mountain Club Visitors Center* (p315), or visit its website for information and itinerary planning advice.

spiffy new tourist office has free wi-fi, comfy armchairs and tons of brochures. The friendly staff can help visitors find rooms and provides information on local hikes.

❶ Getting There & Away

Manchester sits 25 miles (30 minutes) north of Bennington and 65 miles (1½ hours) south of Middlebury on US 7. For a more scenic (and not much slower) drive, take VT 7A to Bennington or VT 30 to Middlebury. Brattleboro is 48 miles (1¼ hours) southeast across the Green Mountains via VT 30.

Dorset

POP 2030

Six miles northwest of Manchester along VT 30, Dorset is a pristinely beautiful Vermont village, originally settled in 1768, with a stately inn (the oldest in Vermont), a lofty church and a village green. The sidewalks and many other buildings are made of creamy marble from the nearby quarry, about a mile south of the village center on VT 30. Dorset supplied much of the marble for the grand New York Public Library building and numerous other public edifices. These days the quarry is filled with water and makes a lovely place to picnic.

Dorset is best known as a summer playground for well-to-do city folks (a role it has played for over a century) and the home of a renowned theatre, the **Dorset Playhouse** (802-867-5570; www.dorsetplayers.org;

104 Cheney Rd), which draws a sophisticated audience for the annual **Dorset Theatre Festival** (www.dorsettheatrefestival.org; ⊙mid-Jun–late Aug).

🛏 Sleeping

Dorset Inn INN $$$
(802-867-5500; www.dorsetinn.com; cnr Church St & VT 30; r $165-355, ste $305-485, all incl breakfast; 🕸🐾) In business since 1796, Vermont's oldest continuously operating lodging is still going strong. Facing the village green, this traditional but updated inn has 31 renovated guest rooms. The front-porch rockers provide a nice setting for watching the comings and goings of this sleepy but upscale Vermont town. Opt for rates that include dinner, as the chef-owned restaurant is highly regarded.

🛍 Shopping

Dorset Union Store FOOD & DRINKS
(802-867-4400; www.dorsetunionstore.com; 31 Church St; ⊙7am-7pm Mon-Sat, 8am-6pm Sun) Celebrating its 200th anniversary in 2016, this classic general store facing Dorset's pretty village green sells all manner of edible Vermont items, especially high-end gourmet goodies and picnic fixings, including local cheddar cheese (of course); it also has a well-stocked wine room, a deli and a freezer full of gourmet take-and-bake treats, including its award-winning mac-and-cheese.

ⓘ Getting There & Away

Dorset is on VT 30, 7 miles (15 minutes) north of Manchester and 58 miles (1¼ hours) south of Middlebury.

Weston

POP 630

On the Green Mountains' eastern slopes, Weston is one of Vermont's most pristine towns. Built along the banks of the West River and anchored by a grassy common graced with towering maples and a bandstand, the village is home to Vermont's oldest professional theater, the Weston Playhouse, and its most famous general store, the Vermont Country Store.

☆ Entertainment

Weston Playhouse   THEATER

(✆ 802-824-5288; www.westonplayhouse.org; 703 Main St; ⊙ performances late Jun–early Sep) Vermont's oldest professional theatre, the Weston Playhouse occupies an old church on the town common and backs onto the West River. It enjoys a good reputation for musicals and drama. Before or after a show, head downstairs to the West Town Eatery, a sweet little bistro below the theater, opened in 2015 by acclaimed chefs Rogan and Abby Lechthaler.

🛍 Shopping

★ Vermont Country Store   HOMEWARES

(✆ 802-824-3184; www.vermontcountrystore.com; 657 Main St/VT 100; ⊙ 8:30am-7pm late May–mid-Oct, 9am-6pm rest of year) People come from far and wide to Weston's famed Vermont Country Store, a time warp from a simpler era when goods were made to last, and quirky products had a home. Here you'll discover taffeta slips, Tangee lipstick, three kinds of shoe stretchers with customizable bunion and corn knobs, vintage board games, clothing, personal-care items, flannel sheets and sleepwear.

ⓘ Getting There & Away

Weston is on VT 100, 19 miles northwest of Grafton and 22 miles northeast of Manchester.

CENTRAL VERMONT

Vermont's heart features some of New England's most bucolic countryside. Cows begin to outnumber people just north of Rutland (Vermont's second-largest city, with a whopping 16,500 residents). Lovers of the outdoors make frequent pilgrimages to central Vermont, especially to the resort areas of Killington, Sugarbush and Mad River Glen, which attract countless skiers and summer hikers. For those interested in indoor pleasures, antique shops and art galleries dot the back roads between picturesque covered bridges.

Woodstock & Quechee Village

POP 3050

Chartered in 1761, Woodstock has been the highly dignified seat of scenic Windsor County since 1766. Many grand houses surround the oval village green, and four of Woodstock's churches can claim bells cast by Paul Revere. Senator Jacob Collamer, a friend of Abraham Lincoln's, once observed, 'The good people of Woodstock have less incentive than others to yearn for heaven.'

Today Woodstock is still very beautiful and very wealthy. Spend some time walking around the green, surrounded by Federal and Greek Revival homes and public buildings, or along the Ottauquechee River, spanned by three covered bridges. The Rockefellers and the Rothschilds own estates in the surrounding countryside, and the well-to-do come to stay at the grand Woodstock Inn & Resort.

> **DON'T MISS**
>
> ### THE CATAMOUNT CROSS-COUNTRY SKI TRAIL
>
> Vermont's magnificent **Catamount Trail** (✆ 802-864-5794; www.catamount trail.org) 🚶 is the longest cross-country ski trail in the US, a 300-mile-long route that runs the length of Vermont. Starting in southern Vermont at Readsboro, it winds along the flanks of the Green Mountains all the way to North Troy on the Canadian border. In between lies some of the finest skiing in the east, from backcountry trails on Mt Mansfield to 11 ski touring centers – some, including Blueberry Hill (p298) and **Mountain Top Inn & Resort** (✆ 802-483-2311; www.mountaintopinn.com; 195 Mountain Top Rd, Chittenden; trail pass adult/child $22/18), offering lodging within the Green Mountain National Forest.

About five minutes' drive east of Woodstock, small, twee Quechee Village is home to Quechee Gorge – Vermont's diminutive answer to the Grand Canyon – as well as some outstanding restaurants.

◉ Sights

★ **Quechee Gorge** CANYON
(US 4, Quechee) FREE Lurking beneath US 4, less than a mile east of Quechee Village, the gorge is a 163ft-deep scar that cuts about 3000ft along a stream that you can view from a bridge or easily access by footpaths from the road. A series of well-marked, undemanding trails, none of which should take more than an hour to cover, lead down into the gorge.

Just upstream from the gorge, the tranquil waters of Dewey's Mill Pond are another lovely spot; bordered by a pretty expanse of reeds and grasses. The pond is named for AG Dewey, who set up a prosperous woollen mill here in 1869.

Billings Farm & Museum FARM
(☑802-457-2355; www.billingsfarm.org; 5302 River Rd, Woodstock; adult/child $14/8; ⊗10am-5pm daily May-Oct, to 4pm Sat & Sun Nov-Feb, closed Mar & Apr; ⊕) ⏀ A mile north of Woodstock's village green, this historic farm founded by 19th-century railroad magnate Frederick Billings delights children with hands-on activities related to old-fashioned farm life. Farm animals, including pretty cows descended from Britain's Isle of Jersey, are abundant. Family-friendly seasonal events include wagon and sleigh rides, pumpkin and apple festivals, and old-fashioned Halloween, Thanksgiving and Christmas celebrations.

Marsh-Billings-Rockefeller National Historical Park PARK
(☑802-457-3368; www.nps.gov/mabi; 54 Elm St, Woodstock; mansion tours adult/child $8/free, trails free; ⊗ visitor center 10am-5pm late May-Oct, tours 10am-4pm late May-Oct) Built around the historic home of early American conservationist George Perkins Marsh, Vermont's only national park examines the relationship between land stewardship and environmental conservation. The estate's 20 miles of trails and carriage roads are free for exploring on foot, cross-country skis or snowshoes. There's an admission fee to the mansion itself, where tours are offered every 30 minutes.

VINS Nature Center WILDLIFE RESERVE
(Vermont Institute of Natural Science; ☑802-359-5000; www.vinsweb.org; 6565 Woodstock Rd, Quechee; adult/child $13.50/11.50; ⊗10am-5pm mid-Apr–Oct, to 4pm Nov–mid-Apr; ⊕) ⏀ This

science center near Quechee houses two dozen species of raptors, ranging from the tiny, 3oz saw-whet owl to the mighty bald eagle. The birds that end up here have sustained permanent injuries that prevent them from returning to the wild. On offer are regular educational presentations and three self-guided nature trails, delightful for summer hiking and winter snowshoeing.

Sugarbush Farm FARM
(☑802-457-1757, 800-281-1757; www.sugarbush farm.com; 591 Sugarbush Farm Rd, Woodstock; ⊗9am-5pm; ⊕) FREE While this working farm at the end of a bucolic road also collects maple sap, cheddar's the king here. See how it's made and sample the 14 varieties – from the mild sage cheddar to the jalapeño and cayenne pepper variety to the prize-winning hickory and smoked cheddar. Wax-coated bars of the curd are sold and travel well.

🏃 Activities

Nordic Adventure Center SNOW SPORTS
(☑802-457-6674; www.woodstockinn.com/resort/recreation; VT 106, Woodstock; trail pass adult/child $20/15; ⊗9am-4pm mid-Dec–mid-Mar) Just south of town, this outfit rents skiing and snowshoeing equipment and has 30km of groomed touring trails, including one that takes in 1250ft Mt Tom. On full-moon nights, it leads snowshoe walks to a cabin in Marsh-Billings-Rockefeller National Historical Park.

Balloons Over New England BALLOONING
(☑800-788-5562; www.balloonsovernewengland. com; per person $275; ⊗May-Oct) While the Quechee–Woodstock general area affords no end of outdoor activities, none is likely to prove as memorable as a balloon ride. Balloons Over New England does it in style, with 'champagne' trips that last 2½ to three hours (including one hour aloft).

Suicide Six SKIING
(☑888-338-2745, 802-457-6661; www.suicide6. com/ski-area; 247 Stage Rd, South Pomfret; lift ticket adult/child weekend $68/50, midweek $30/25; ⊗mid-Dec–Mar) In 1934 Woodstockers installed the first mechanical ski tow in the USA, and skiing is still important here. Three miles north of Woodstock, this resort is known for challenging downhill runs, although the lower slopes are fine for beginners. There are 24 trails (30% beginner, 40% intermediate, 30% expert) served by two chairlifts and a J-bar. Midweek lift tickets are among the cheapest you'll find anywhere in New England.

VILLAGES FROZEN IN TIME

Many Vermont villages have a lost-in-time quality, thanks to their architectural integrity and the state's general aversion to urban sprawl. Some, like Grafton, Newfane, Woodstock and Dorset, are well-known to outsiders. Others are further off the beaten track.

Browning ton (Northeast Kingdom) This sleeping beauty 40 miles north of St Johnsbury is full of 19th-century buildings reposing under the shade of equally ancient maple trees. The **Old Stone House Museum** (✏ 802-754-2022; http://oldstonehousemuseum.org; 109 Old Stone House Rd, Brownington; adult/child $8/5; ⊙ Wed-Sun mid-May–mid-Oct, self-guided tour of grounds 11am-5pm, 1hr guided Old Stone House tour 11:30am, 1:30pm & 3:30pm) here pays tribute to educational trailblazer Alexander Twilight. The first African American college graduate in the US, he built Brownington's boarding school and ran it for decades.

Peacham (Northeast Kingdom) This idyllically sited village 15 miles southwest of St Johnsbury was originally a stop on the historic Bayley–Hazen Military Rd – intended to help Americans launch a sneak attack on the British during the Revolutionary War. These days it's just a pretty spot to admire pastoral views over the surrounding countryside.

Plymouth Notch (Central Vermont) President Calvin Coolidge's boyhood home, preserved as the **Calvin Coolidge State Historic Site** (✏ 802-672-3773; http://historicsites.vermont.gov/directory/coolidge; 3780 Rte 100A, Plymouth Notch; adult/child $9/2; ⊙ 9:30am-5pm late May–mid-Oct), looks much as it did a century ago, with a church, one-room schoolhouse, cheese factory and general store gracefully arrayed among old maples on a bucolic hillside. It's 15 miles southwest of Woodstock.

🛏 Sleeping

Woodstock and Quechee boast some of Vermont's prettiest (and priciest) inns. Even motels tend to charge top dollar in summer and fall. State parks in the area offer an economical alternative.

Quechee State Park CAMPGROUND $
(✏ 802-295-2990; www.vtstateparks.com/htm/quechee.htm; 5800 Woodstock Rd/US 4, Quechee; campsites $20-22, lean-tos $27-29; ⊙ mid-May–mid-Oct) Eight miles east of Woodstock and 3 miles west of I-89 along US 4, this 611-acre spot has 45 pine-shaded campsites and seven lean-tos a short stroll from Quechee Gorge.

The Shire HOTEL $$
(✏ 802-457-2211; www.shiremotel.com; 46 Pleasant St/US 4, Woodstock; r $129-249; 🌐🛜🏊) Set within walking distance of Woodstock's town center on US 4, this recently remodeled hotel has 44 comfortable rooms, the best of which come with fireplaces, Jacuzzis and/or decks with rockers looking out over the Ottauquechee River. Many units received new beds in 2015, all have brand-new linens, and rooms 218 and 405 have especially nice river views.

Sleep Woodstock Motel MOTEL $$
(✏ 802-332-6336; www.sleepwoodstock.com; 4324 West Woodstock Rd/US 4, Woodstock; r $88-158) Prices are generally high in the Woodstock area, so this newly remodeled motel 5 miles west of town comes as a welcome surprise. The clean, comfy rooms come with big-screen TVs, coffeemakers, minifridges and microwaves, service is attentive, and – outside of foliage season and busy holiday weekends – the nightly rate never exceeds $128.

Parker House Inn INN $$$
(✏ 800-295-6077, 802-295-6077; www.theparkerhouseinn.com; 1792 Quechee Main St, Quechee; r incl breakfast $202-311; 🌐🛜) A Victorian-style redbrick house built in 1857 for former Vermont senator Joseph Parker, this antique-laden inn has seven large guest rooms and a riverside porch. It's just 100yd from one of the Ottauquechee River's covered bridges and a waterfall. The on-site restaurant (mains $20 to $30) is excellent.

Village Inn of Woodstock INN $$$
(✏ 802-457-1255, 800-722-4571; www.villageinnofwoodstock.com; 41 Pleasant St, Woodstock; r incl breakfast $152-389; 🌐🛜) The eight guest rooms in this lovely Victorian mansion, situated on a 40-acre estate, have four-poster feather beds, down comforters, and period details like oak wainscoting and tin ceilings. Enjoy the welcoming terrace or the cozy tavern (open only to guests), with its stained-glass windows and full bar. The luscious breakfast includes granola, pastries and breads, all made on-site.

Woodstock Inn & Resort RESORT $$$

(☑888-338-2745, 802-332-6853; www.woodstock inn.com; 14 The Green, Woodstock; r $260-450; ✳☎☒) One of Vermont's most luxurious hotels, this resort has extensive grounds, a formal dining room, an 18-hole golf course, tennis courts, cross-country skiing, a fitness center, a spa and an indoor sports center. A fire blazes in the huge stone fireplace during chilly periods, enhancing the welcoming ambience. Rooms are decorated in soft, muted colors and Vermont-crafted wood furnishings.

✖ Eating

Woodstock is packed with eateries, many tending toward the upscale. If you have a picnic lunch, take it to Teagle's Landing, a tiny streamside hideaway with picnic tables just below the Central St bridge.

Mon Vert Cafe CAFE $

(☑802-457-7143; www.monvertcafe.com; 67 Central St, Woodstock; breakfast $6-13, lunch $9-11; ⊙7:30am-4:30pm Mon-Thu, to 5pm Fri & Sat, 8am-4pm Sun) Pop into this cheerful cafe for croissants, scones, and egg sandwiches in the morning or settle in on the patio for salads and panini at lunch. Enjoy the maple latte anytime. A giant chalkboard map of Vermont and New Hampshire shows the multitude of farms and food purveyors that provide the restaurant's locally sourced ingredients.

White Cottage Snack Bar AMERICAN $

(☑802-457-3455; www.whitecottagesnackbar. com; 462 Woodstock Rd, Woodstock; mains $4-17; ⊙11am-10pm early May–mid-Oct) A Woodstock institution, this glorified snack shack has been serving loyal locals fried clams, burgers and ice cream by the riverside since 1957.

★Skunk Hollow Tavern AMERICAN $$

(☑802-436-2139; www.skunkhollowtavern.com; 12 Brownsville Rd, Hartland Four Corners; mains $13-32; ⊙5pm-late Wed-Sun) Few Vermont eateries are as atmospheric as this tiny 200-year-old crossroads tavern 8 miles south of Woodstock, with worn wooden floors that ooze history. Enjoy burgers, fish-and-chips or shepherd's pie downstairs at the bar or in the more intimate space upstairs. Friday evenings, when there's live music and the band takes up half the room, are a special treat.

Worthy Kitchen PUB FOOD $$

(☑802-457-7281; www.worthyvermont.com/wor thy-kitchen; 442 E Woodstock Rd/US 4, Woodstock; mains $13-25; ⊙4-10pm Mon-Fri, 11am-10pm Sat, 10am-9pm Sun) This laid-back brewpub serving farm-to-table comfort food has become a local favorite since opening in 2013. The ever-changing menu, scrawled on giant blackboards, features daily specials, such as burgers, buttermilk fried chicken, Caesar salad or mac-and-cheese with local Plymouth cheddar, all accompanied by a frequently rotating lineup of 18 microbrews (mostly from Vermont or elsewhere in New England).

Melaza Tapas Bar & Bistro TAPAS $$

(☑802-457-7110; www.melazabistro.com; 71 Central St, Woodstock; small plates $5-15, mains $16-26; ⊙from 5:30pm Wed-Sun) Unwind here after a day of exploring with a glass of wine and an enticing mix of tropically inspired tapas and entrees. Specialties include coffee- and chili-dusted filet mignon, guava-glazed roasted pork shank and the classic Puerto Rican comfort food *arroz con pollo* (chicken with rice, fried green plantains, avocado and chipotle aioli).

★Simon Pearce Restaurant MODERN AMERICAN $$$

(☑802-295-1470; www.simonpearce.com; 1760 Quechee Main St, Quechee; lunch mains $14-18, dinner mains $22-39; ⊙11:30am-2:45pm & 5:30-9pm Mon-Sat, from 10:30am Sun) Be sure to reserve a window table overlooking the falls in Simon Pearce's dining room, which is suspended over the river in this converted brick mill. Local ingredients are used to inventive effect in such delicacies as crab and cod melt or seared chicken with roasted-corn mascarpone polenta. The restaurant's stemware is blown by hand in the adjacent glass workshop.

🛍 Shopping

Simon Pearce Glass GLASS, CERAMICS

(☑802-295-2711; www.simonpearce.com; 1760 Quechee Main St, Quechee; ⊙10am-9pm) At this exceptional studio and shop, visitors can watch artisans produce distinctive pieces of original glass.

ℹ Information

Quechee Gorge Visitors Center (☑802-295-7900; www.hartfordvtchamber.com; 5966 Woodstock Rd, Quechee; ⊙9am-5pm late May-Oct, 10am-4pm Nov-late May) Well-stocked tourist office just east of the Quechee Gorge bridge, dispensing information about Quechee and the gorge.

Woodstock Area Chamber of Commerce Welcome Center (☑888-496-6378, 802-457-3555; www.woodstockvt.com; 3 Mechanic St, Woodstock; ⊙9am-5pm daily late May–mid-Oct, 10am-4pm Mon-Fri, to 5pm Sat & Sun rest of year) Woodstock's welcome center is housed in a lovely red building on a riverside backstreet, two blocks from the village green. There's also a small information booth on the village green itself. Both places can help with accommodations.

ℹ Getting There & Away

Burlington (1¾ hours, 95 miles) is a straight shot from Woodstock via US 4 east and I-89 north. For Killington (20 miles, 30 minutes), take US 4 west.

Greyhound buses (www.greyhound.com) and Amtrak Vermonter trains (www.amtrak.com/vermonter-train) stop at nearby White River Junction. From either station, you'll need to take a taxi to Woodstock, a distance of 15 miles.

Killington Mountain

POP 810

The largest ski resort in the east, Killington spans seven mountains, dominated by 4241ft Killington Peak, the second highest in Vermont, and operates the largest snowmaking system in North America. Although upwards of 20,000 people can find lodging within 20 miles, its numerous outdoor activities are centrally located on the mountain. Officially, the mountain town is Killington Village, but all the action can be found along Killington Rd on the way up the mountain.

🏃 Activities

Killington Resort SKIING
(🖉 800-621-6867, 802-422-6200; www.killington.com; 4763 Killington Rd; lift ticket adult/teen/senior weekend $96/82/74, midweek $94/80/72)

Known as the 'Beast of the East,' Vermont's prime ski resort is enormous, yet runs efficiently enough to avoid overcrowding; it has five separate lodges, each with a different emphasis, as well as 29 lifts and 92 miles of trails. The ski season runs from November through early May, enhanced by America's largest snowmaking system.

More than 200 runs snake down Killington's seven mountains (4241ft Killington Peak, 3967ft Pico Mountain, 3800ft Skye Peak, 3610ft Ramshead Peak, 3592ft Snowdon Peak, 3295ft Bear Mountain and 2456ft Sunrise Mountain), covering 1977 acres of slopes. A quarter are considered easy, a third moderate and the rest difficult. Snowboarders will find six challenging terrain parks, including superpipes with 18ft walls.

K-1 Lodge boasts the K-1 Express Gondola, which transports up to 3000 skiers per hour in heated cars along a 2.5-mile cable and is the highest lift in Vermont. **Snowshed Lodge** is an ideal base for adults looking for lessons or refresher courses. Free-ride enthusiasts should check out **Bear Mountain Lodge** for pipe action, tree skiing or rail jibbing, not to mention the double-black-diamond Outer Limits, the longest, steepest mogul run in the east. **Ramshead Lodge** caters to children and families, as well as those looking for easier terrain, while **Skyeship Lodge** is the home of the Skyeship Gondola, a two-stage gondola with quick and direct access to Skye Peak. Each lodge has food courts, restaurants, bars and ski shops.

VERMONT KILLINGTON MOUNTAIN

DON'T MISS

COVERED BRIDGES

Vermont has more covered bridges per square mile than any state in the union. Here's a trivia-lover's guide to some of our favorites throughout the state:

Bartonsville (southern Vermont) The original 19th-century bridge here was famously swept away in Hurricane Irene's floodwaters in 2011 (search for remarkable footage on YouTube), but in classic Vermont fashion, locals rallied to have a replica reconstructed. The bridge reopened to the public in January 2013. It's 7 miles northeast of Grafton.

Northfield Falls (northern Vermont) This small town 8 miles south of Montpelier has a unique claim to fame: three covered bridges in a row! Turn west off VT 12 onto Cox Brook Rd and you'll see Station Bridge, Newell Bridge and Upper Bridge – all within a few hundred feet of each other.

Montgomery (northern Vermont) This village near the Jay Peak ski area has a whopping seven covered bridges, more than any other town in Vermont.

Windsor (central Vermont) Spanning the Connecticut River from Windsor, VT, to Cornish, NH, the 449-ft Cornish–Windsor Bridge is the longest historical covered bridge in America still open to automobile traffic.

In summer, there's mountain biking and golfing, and in fall, leaf-peepers can ride the resort's famous K-1 Express Gondola to Killington Peak for spectacular views.

Killington Mountain Bike Park
MOUNTAIN BIKING

(☑802-422-6232, 800-621-6867; 4763 Killington Rd; half-/full-day lift ticket & trail pass $34/49, half-/full-day bike rental $65/85; ⊙late Jun–mid-Oct) Killington Resort continues to build on its impressive mountain-biking infrastructure, with the opening of new trails on Snowshed Mountain. Bikers can take the Snowshed Express Quad to access the resort's newest trails for beginning and intermediate riders, or the classic 1.25-mile K-1 gondola ride to the summit of Killington Peak where 45 miles of trails await, including plenty of challenging free-ride terrain.

The Killington Bike Shop at Snowshed Lodge rents out top-quality mountain bikes.

🛏 Sleeping

Virtually everyone is here to ski, which means that Killington Resort's mountainside lodges and condos are the accommodations of choice for many. However, you'll find plenty of other options in the surrounding 'lowlands' along US 4 and VT 100, from motels to campgrounds to a historic trailside inn that has welcomed many a weary Long Trail hiker.

Killington Motel
MOTEL $$

(☑802-773-9535, reservations 800-366-0493; www.killingtonmotel.com; 1946 US 4; r incl breakfast May-Oct $72-124, Nov-Apr $78-178; ❄ 🛜) Way more welcoming than your typical motel experience, thanks to the personal attention of friendly longtime owners Stephen and Robin (and their cat Tigger), this clean, well-maintained motel just west of the VT 100/US 4 junction has some of the best rates in town. Breakfast features home-baked breads and muffins, and coffee roasted onsite in small batches by Stephen himself.

With advance notice, owners will pick up hikers from the Long Trail junction on US 4 and shuttle them to the laundromat en route to an overnight stay at the motel.

Inn at Long Trail
INN $$

(☑800-325-2540, 802-775-7181; www.innatlongtrail.com; 709 US 4; r $115-240, ste $160-280, all incl breakfast; 🛜) The first hotel built (in 1938) expressly as a ski lodge, the inn is also a temporary home to hikers pausing along the nearby Long Trail. The rustic decor makes use of tree trunks (the bar is fashioned from a single log), the rooms are simple but cozy, and suites include fireplaces.

🍴 Eating & Drinking

Killington Resort has a dozen eateries of its own, from simple cafes and pubs to a steakhouse and a farm-to-table restaurant. Several other options are spread out along Killington Rd, just below the resort.

Liquid Art Coffeehouse
INTERNATIONAL $$

(☑802-422-2787; www.liquidartvt.com/; 37 Miller Brook Rd; mains $9-26; ⊙8am-9pm Mon-Fri, from 7am Sat & Sun) Much more than a coffeehouse, Liquid Art serves everything from delicious breakfast sandwiches to 'Palette dinners' featuring gourmet dishes like kale, shiitake and sundried-tomato lasagna and apple cider and thyme-glazed mussels, plus good coffee drinks and a two-page list of specialty cocktails, all in a bright, high-ceilinged barnlike space with classic post-and-beam architecture.

Long Trail Brewing Company
BREWERY

(☑802-672-5011; www.longtrail.com; 5520 US 4 at VT 100A, Bridgewater; ⊙10am-7pm) Halfway between Killington and Woodstock, the brewer of 'Vermont's No 1 Selling Amber' draws crowds for free brewery tours and a sunny riverside deck where you can enjoy sandwiches, burgers, salads (mains $8 to $14) and, of course, beer. Order a sampler of six 4oz glasses ($8) and taste 'em all.

⭐ Entertainment

With over 25 clubs, and lively bars in many restaurants, Killington is where the après-ski scene rages. Many of these nightspots are on Killington Rd, the 4-mile-long access road to the ski resort.

McGrath's Irish Pub
LIVE MUSIC

(☑802-775-7181; www.innatlongtrail.com/McGraths_Irish_Pub.html; 709 US 4; ⊙11:30am-11pm Sun-Thu, 11:30am-1am Fri & Sat) Guinness on tap, Vermont's largest selection of Irish whiskies, and live Irish music on Friday and Saturday evenings.

Pickle Barrel
LIVE MUSIC

(☑802-422-3035; www.picklebarrelnightclub.com; 1741 Killington Rd; ⊙4pm-late Sep–mid-Apr) With four bars, three levels and two stages, this popular club showcases great rock-and-roll bands. Best of all, there's a free shuttle bus to get you home in one piece.

Wobbly Barn   LIVE MUSIC
(☑ 802-422-6171; www.wobblybarn.net; 2229 Killington Rd; ⊙ 4:30pm-late Nov–mid-Apr) This popular steakhouse doubles as an entertainment venue, with dancing, blues and rock and roll.

❶ Information

Killington Welcome Center (☑ 802-773-4181; http://killingtonpico.org; 2319 US 4; ⊙ 10am-5pm Mon-Fri, 10am-2pm Sat & Sun) General tourist information, conveniently located on US 4.

❶ Getting There & Away

To reach Killington from Burlington (1¾ hours, 95 miles) take US 7 south to VT 4 east. From Manchester, VT (70 minutes, 45 miles), take US 7 north and VT 4 east.

Middlebury

POP 8500

Standing at the nexus of several state highways, aptly named Middlebury was built along the falls of Otter Creek at the end of the 18th century. In 1800 Middlebury College was founded, and it has been synonymous with the town ever since. Poet Robert Frost (1874–1963) owned a farm in nearby Ripton and cofounded the college's renowned Bread Loaf School of English in the hills above town. The college is also famous for its summer foreign-language programs, which have been drawing linguists here for nearly a century. Middlebury's history of marble quarrying is evident in the college's architecture: many buildings are made with white marble and gray limestone.

◉ Sights

University of Vermont
Morgan Horse Farm   FARM
(☑ 802-388-2011; www.uvm.edu/morgan; 74 Battell Dr, Weybridge; adult/child/teen $5/2/4; ⊙ 9am-4pm May-Oct; ⊞) See registered Morgan horses and tour their stables at this farm 3 miles north of Middlebury. Known for their strength, agility, endurance and longevity, and named after Justin Morgan, who brought his thoroughbred Arabian colt to Vermont in 1789, these little horses became America's first native breed, useful for heavy work, carriage draft, riding and even war service.

Woodchuck Cidery   BREWERY
(☑ 802-385-3656; www.woodchuck.com/cider house; 1321 Exchange St; ⊙ 11am-6pm Wed-Fri, to 5pm Sat & Sun) Vermont's largest producer

BLUEBERRY-PICKING WITH A VIEW

About 15 miles southeast of Middlebury, an unpaved forest service road leads to one of central Vermont's best-kept secrets: the Green Mountain National Forest Blueberry Management Area. This vast hillside patch of wild blueberries is ripe (and free) for the picking between late July and early August, and the view over the surrounding mountains is fantastic. From VT 125, just east of Ripton, follow the unpaved Goshen Rd past Blueberry Hill Inn, then look for signs for the Blueberry Management Area on your left.

of hard cider offers free tastes at its state-of-the-art production facility 2 miles north of downtown Middlebury. Choose any four flavors from its current lineup of over a dozen, from classics like pear, raspberry and Amber (Woodchuck's original apple cider developed in 1991) to experimental and seasonal flavors like pumpkin, ginger and smoked apple.

Otter Creek Brewing   BREWERY
(☑ 802-388-0727; www.ottercreekbrewing.com; 793 Exchange St; ⊙ 11am-6pm) One of New England's best, this brewery makes several fine craft beers, including its trademark Backseat Berner IPA, Couch Surfer oatmeal stout and Shed Mountain Ale. Sample six beers (4oz glasses) for $8 and watch the brewers at work through viewing windows in the adjacent brewpub.

Champlain Orchards   FARM
(☑ 802-897-2777; www.champlainorchards.com; 3597 VT 74 W, Shoreham; ⊞) ✦ This century-old orchard 16 miles southwest of Middlebury sells sweet and hard cider year-round, with pick-your-own cherries, peaches, plums and berries starting in June. Its busiest season is fall, when more than 100 varieties of apples are ripe for the picking and two seasonal festivals (Harvest Festival and Ciderfest) fill the air with fiddle tunes and family fun.

🏃 Activities

Undulating with rolling hills and farms, the pastoral countryside around Middlebury makes for great cycling. Nearby Green Mountain National Forest is also home to some great ski areas.

VERMONT MIDDLEBURY

SWIMMING HOLE HEAVEN

Where do locals head when the mercury starts hitting devilish highs? One popular spot is **Bartlett Falls**, a heavenly swimming hole hidden just off the main road near Bristol, halfway between Warren and Middlebury. This gorgeous natural pool sits at the foot of a pretty waterfall, flanked by cliffs that make a popular jumping-off point for local youths. With shallow and deep sections and plenty of forested shade, it's perfect for all ages. Look for the parked cars along Lincoln Gap Rd, a half-mile east of VT 116.

Middlebury College Snow Bowl SKIING
(☑802-443-7669; www.middleburysnowbowl.com; VT 125; lift ticket Mon-Fri $35, Sat & Sun $50; ☉9am-4pm Mon-Fri, 8:30am-4pm Sat & Sun; ★) One of Vermont's most affordable, least crowded ski areas, this college-owned facility has only three lifts, but with trails for all levels, nonexistent lift lines and prices half of what you'd pay elsewhere, who's complaining? Middlebury's 'graduation on skis' takes place here each February: graduates slalom down the slopes in full valedictory regalia, their dark robes fluttering amid the snowflakes.

Rikert Nordic Center SKIING
(☑802-443-2744; www.rikertnordic.com; VT 125, Ripton; trail pass $22; ☉8:30am-4:30pm; ★) Middlebury College's cross-country ski center offers 30 miles of trails in Green Mountain National Forest, in a gorgeous mountain setting along VT 125, an easy 12-mile drive from Middlebury.

Blueberry Hill Ski Center SKIING
(☑802-247-6735; www.blueberryhillinn.com/ski. htm; 1245 Goshen-Ripton Rd, Goshen; suggested day-use donation $10; ☉9am-5pm; ★) With 50km of cross-country skiing and snowshoe trails threading through the national forest, this low-key Nordic center 15 miles southeast of Middlebury is a great place to get away from it all. Trails connect to the statewide Catamount Trail system, and the cozy Blueberry Hill Inn (singles/doubles $239/269) is right here if you decide to stay overnight.

🛏 Sleeping

Branbury State Park CAMPGROUND $
(☑802-247-5925; www.vtstateparks.com/htm/ branbury.htm; VT 53, Brandon; campsites $20-22, lean-to $27-29; ☉late May–mid-Oct; ★) Ten miles south of Middlebury on the shores of pretty Lake Dunmore, this family-friendly 69-acre park has 37 campsites and seven lean-tos. The small beach, which offers swimming and rental boats, is backed by a grassy lawn with playground and barbecue facilities. Hiking trails climb to the pretty Falls of Lana and Silver Lake in adjacent Green Mountain National Forest.

Swift House Inn INN $$
(☑866-388-9925, 802-388-9925; www.swift houseinn.com; 25 Stewart Lane; r incl breakfast $135-299; ★) Two blocks north of the town green, this grand white Federal mansion (1814) is surrounded by fine formal lawns and gardens. Luxurious standard rooms in the main house and adjacent carriage house are supplemented by suites with fireplaces, sitting areas and Jacuzzis. Other welcome luxuries include a steam room and sauna, a cozy pub, a library and a sun porch.

Waybury Inn INN $$
(☑802-388-4015, 800-348-1810; www.wayburyinn. com; 457 E Main St/VT 125, East Middlebury; r $115-210, ste $175-295, all incl breakfast; ★) A favorite of Robert Frost, this former stagecoach stop 5 miles southeast of Middlebury has a wood-paneled restaurant and sumptuous guest rooms. The inn's exterior was featured in the 1980s TV show *Newhart* (though Bob's never actually been here). Laze away a summer afternoon in the nearby swimming hole or warm yourself in the pub on a wintry evening.

Inn on the Green INN $$
(☑888-244-7512, 802-388-7512; www.innonthe green.com; 71 S Pleasant St; r incl breakfast $139-259; ❋@❋) Lovingly restored to its original stateliness, this 1803 Federal-style home has spacious rooms and suites in the main house and in an adjoining carriage house (the latter's rooms are more modern). One of its signature treats is a continental breakfast served in bed each morning.

🍴 Eating & Drinking

Middlebury is the seat of Vermont's most productive agricultural county; the local food coop on Washington St and the Marble Works farmers market (Wednesdays and Saturdays in season) both stock an impressive array of produce and cheeses from local farmers. The dozen or so restaurants downtown offer mostly American fare, with Thai, Indian and pizza thrown in for good measure.

Middlebury Bagel & Deli BAKERY $
(www.facebook.com/MiddleburyBagel; 11 Washington St; breakfasts $5-9; ⊙6am-2pm Mon-Fri, to 1pm Sat & Sun) Since 1979, the Rubright family has been showing up at 4am daily to bake some of New England's finest doughnuts and bagels. Skiers on their way to the slopes, workers en route to the job site and professors headed for class all converge here for warm-from-the-oven apple fritters, doughnuts and bagel sandwiches, along with omelets and other breakfast treats.

Storm Cafe CAFE $
(✆802-388-1063; www.thestormcafe.com; 3 Mill St; breakfast $6-15, lunch $8-13, dinner $12-29; ⊙9am-2:30pm Tue, 9am-2:30pm & 5-10pm Wed-Sat, 9am-2pm Sun) In the basement of Frog Hollow Mill, this creekside cafe serves breakfast, followed by soups, salads and sandwiches at lunchtime. In good weather, the more substantial dinner offerings are best enjoyed out on the terrace overlooking the falls of Otter Creek; some consider this to be the most imaginative menu in town.

★American Flatbread PIZZA $$
(✆802-388-3300; www.americanflatbread.com/restaurants/middlebury-vt; 137 Maple St; flatbreads $13-22; ⊙5-9pm Tue-Fri, noon-9pm Sat) 🍴 In a cavernous marble-block building with a blazing fire that keeps things cozy in winter, this is one of Middlebury's most beloved eateries. The menu is limited to farm-fresh salads and custom-made flatbreads (don't call it pizza or they'll come after you with the paddle) topped with locally sourced organic cheeses, meat and veggies, accompanied by Vermont microbrews on tap.

51 Main INTERNATIONAL $$
(✆802-388-8209; www.go51main.com; 51 Main St; mains $12-22; ⊙4pm-late Tue-Sat; 🛜) Overlooking Otter Creek, this high-ceilinged restaurant, lounge and live-music venue was started by a few Middlebury College students as a fun social space where people could dine, perform and generally hang out. It features a convivial, casual bar and serves an eclectic international menu: Brazilian shrimp stew, Texas-style barbecue and gourmet mac-and-fromage – with Vermont cheddar, of course.

Stone Leaf Teahouse TEAHOUSE
(✆802-458-0460; www.stoneleaftea.com; 111 Maple St; ⊙11am-6pm Tue-Sat) A wonderful spot for a mid-afternoon break, this peaceful oasis in MIddlebury's historic Marble Works is run by tea connoisseur John Wetzel, who direct imports fine teas from China, Japan, India, Nepal and Taiwan, and serves them in artistic little cups and teapots (which are also for sale downstairs).

ℹ Information

Addison County Chamber of Commerce
(✆802-388-7951; www.addisoncounty.com; 93 Court St; ⊙9am-5pm Mon-Fri) About half a mile south of the town green, this place dispenses information about Middlebury and the rest of Addison County.

Green Mountain National Forest District Office (✆802-388-4362; www.fs.fed.us; 1007 US 7; ⊙8am-4:30pm Mon-Fri) Drop by this ranger station 2 miles south of Middlebury for information about the many good day hikes in the region.

ℹ Getting There & Away

Middlebury is right on US 7. To get here from Burlington (50 minutes, 35 miles), take US 7 south; from Manchester (1½ hours, 65 miles), take US 7 or VT 30 north.

Mad River Valley & Sugarbush

POP 1700 (WARREN); 1720 (WAITSFIELD)

North of Killington, VT 100 is one of the finest stretches of road in the country: a bucolic mix of rolling hills, covered bridges, white steeples and fertile farmland. Here you'll find the Mad River Valley, where the pretty villages of Waitsfield and Warren nestle in the shadow of two major ski areas, Sugarbush and Mad River Glen.

For tantalizing valley perspectives, go exploring the glorious back roads on either side of VT 100. Leave the pavement behind and meander up the valley's eastern side, following Brook, E Warren, Common, North and Pony Farm Rds from Warren north to Moretown; or head west from Warren over Lincoln Gap Rd, the highest, steepest and perhaps prettiest of all the 'gap roads' that run east to west over the Green Mountains. Stop at Lincoln Gap (2424ft) for the scenic 3-mile hike up the Long Trail to Mt Abraham (4017ft), Vermont's fifth-highest peak.

🏃 Activities

★Mad River Glen SKIING
(✆802-496-3551; www.madriverglen.com; VT 17, Waitsfield; lift ticket adult/child weekend $79/63, midweek $65/60) The most rugged lift-served

ski area in the East, Mad River is also one of the quirkiest. Managed by an owner cooperative, not a major ski corporation, it largely eschews artificial snowmaking, prohibits snowboarding, and proudly continues to use America's last operating single chairlift, a vintage 1948 model! It's 6 miles west of Waitsfield.

Clearwater Sports BICYCLE RENTAL, WATER SPORTS
(☑802-496-2708; www.clearwatersports.com; 4147 Main St/VT 100, Waitsfield; ☉10am-6pm Mon-Fri, 9am-6pm Sat, 10am-5pm Sun) This friendly shop rents river-floating tubes, canoes, kayaks, stand-up paddleboards, hybrid bikes, snowshoes, rocket sleds, telemark demo gear and many other types of sports equipment. It also organizes guided kayak trips on the Winooski and Mad Rivers, along with custom tours and even yoga classes on stand-up paddleboards in a mountain lake!

Sugarbush Soaring GLIDING
(☑802-496-2290; www.sugarbushsoaring.com; 2355 Airport Rd, Warren; 15-/20-/30-/45-min rides $109/134/175/209; ☉mid-May–Oct) This outfit can take you soaring quietly through the skies, far above the mountains and river valleys, in a glider, which is kept aloft by updrafts of warm air. It's especially beautiful in early October, when central Vermont's trees are fully ablaze.

Vermont Icelandic
Horse Farm HORSEBACK RIDING
(☑802-496-7141; www.icelandichorses.com; 3061 N Fayston Rd, Waitsfield; 1-3hr rides $60-120, full day incl lunch $220, multiday treks $675-1695; ☉by appointment; ☑) Explore the scenic hills above Waitsfield on beautiful, gentle and easy-to-ride Icelandic horses. Rides range from hour-long jaunts to multiday inn-to-inn treks.

Sugarbush SKIING
(☑802-583-6300, 800-537-8427; www.sugarbush. com; 102 Forest Dr, Warren; adult/child lift ticket $93/73) Lincoln Peak (3975ft) and Mt Ellen (4083ft) are the main features of this large resort 6 miles southwest of Waitsfield. In all, 16 lifts afford skiers and snowboarders access to three terrain parks, 97 acres of woods and 111 trails, including backcountry runs like Paradise and Castlerock that hurtle through a rolling tapestry of maple, oak, birch, spruce, pine and balsam.

Summer attractions include dozens of mountain-biking trails and an 18-hole golf course.

🛏 Sleeping

Because the Sugarbush area is primarily active in the winter ski season, there are no campgrounds nearby. Many accommodations are condos ($130 to $850 per day) marketed to the ski trade. The largest selection is rented by **Sugarbush Village** (☑800-451-4326, 802-583-3000; www.sugarbushvillage.com; 145 Mountainside Dr, Warren; 1-bedroom condo per night from $137), right at the ski area.

Mad River Barn INN $$
(☑802-496-3310; www.madriverbarn.com; 2849 Mill Brook Rd/VT 17, Waitsfield; r incl breakfast $120-185; ☎☑) Built in the 1940s, this family-friendly lodge between Sugarbush and Mad River Glen ski areas was completely remodeled in 2015, using recycled materials to retain a rustic-chic effect while amping up comfort and amenities. The refurbished barn at the heart of it all houses a spacious pub with Vermont microbrews on tap, warm wood paneling and a massive stone fireplace.

Mad River Inn INN $$
(☑802-496-7900, 800-832-8278; www.madriver inn.com; Tremblay Rd, Waitsfield; r incl breakfast & afternoon tea $105-175; ✳☎) This 19th-century Victorian farmhouse surrounded by pretty gardens has seven cozy rooms and a two-room suite, complemented by a Queen Anne dining room where guests enjoy three-course breakfasts and afternoon tea by the fireside.

Waitsfield Inn INN $$
(☑802-496-3979, 800-758-3801; www.waitsfield inn.com; 5267 Main St/VT 100, Waitsfield; d incl breakfast $99-165; ☎) This converted parsonage has 12 tastefully decorated rooms as well as various nooks and dining areas to unwind in. All rooms have private bathrooms, and some have four-poster beds. The inn also offers dinner (New England comfort fare) on weekend evenings and has a tiny, on-site pub that serves home-flavored fruit vodkas (blueberry or raspberry mixed with pineapple).

★ Inn at Round Barn Farm INN $$$
(☑802-496-2276; www.roundbarninn.com; 1661 E Warren Rd, Waitsfield; r incl breakfast $175-330; ☎☑) This place gets its name from the adjacent 1910 round barn – among the few authentic examples remaining in Vermont. The decidedly upscale inn has antique-furnished rooms with mountain views, gas fireplaces, canopy beds and antiques. All overlook the meadows and mountains. In winter guests leave their shoes at the door to preserve the hardwood floors. The country-style breakfast is huge.

✖ Eating

Skiers' taverns abound in this area. Restaurants are busy in the ski season, but rather sleepy at other times. Outside of winter, call ahead to verify opening hours: they change frequently.

★**Warren Store**   SANDWICHES **$**
(📞802-496-3864; www.warrenstore.com; 284 Main St, Warren; sandwiches & light meals $5-9; ⊙8am-7pm Mon-Sat, to 6pm Sun) This atmospheric country store serves the area's best sandwiches along with delicious pastries and breakfasts. In summer, linger over coffee and the *New York Times* on the front porch, or eat on the deck overlooking the waterfall, then descend for a cool dip among river-sculpted rocks. Browsers will love the store's eclectic upstairs collection of clothing, toys and jewelry.

American Flatbread   PIZZA **$$**
(📞802-496-8856; www.americanflatbread.com/restaurants/waitsfield-vt; 46 Lareau Rd, Waitsfield; flatbread $12-22; ⊙5-9:30pm Thu-Sun) On pretty Lareau Farm between Waitsfield and Warren, this wonderful eatery keeps doing what it's been doing for two decades: baking delicious thin-crust pizza in the wood-fired oven, topped with fresh-from-the-farm meats, cheeses and veggies and homemade tomato sauce. Stay cozy in winter by the blazing pizza oven, or eat alfresco on picnic tables in summer.

Peasant   MODERN AMERICAN **$$**
(📞802-496-6856; www.peasantvt.com; 40 Bridge St, Waitsfield; mains $21-25; ⊙5:30-9pm Thu-Mon) Living up to its tagline 'a simple feast,' Peasant delivers seasonal farm-to-table treats that can vary from hearty cassoulet in the dead of winter to maple-glazed salmon with locally grown veggies in summer, all complemented by an ample choice of beer, wine and cocktails. Look for it in a cozy slate-blue house in the village center.

Mint   VEGETARIAN **$$**
(📞802-496-5514; www.mintvermont.com; 4403 Main St, Waitsfield; mains $16-20; ⊙5-8:30pm Wed-Sun; 🍴) With a short, sweet menu that's big on flavor, this stylish vegan- and vegetarian-friendly spot serves sandwiches, salads, soups and desserts: think falafel, vegetable bowls and the signature salad (spinach, arugula, pears, toasted almonds, shaved parmesan and cranberries, tossed in a mint vinaigrette). Save room for homemade desserts (tofu-pumpkin pie, anyone?) and a wide selection of loose-leaf teas.

ℹ Information

Mad River Valley Chamber of Commerce
(📞800-828-4748, 802-496-3409; www.madrivervalley.com; General Wait House, 4061 Main St/VT 100, Waitsfield; ⊙10am-2pm Mon-Fri) Staff here can assist with lodging and the latest skiing info. The Chamber also provides a 24-hour iPad information kiosk with a phone for making hotel reservations, a brochure rack and public restrooms.

ℹ Getting There & Away

From Waitsfield, take VT 100 to Stowe (40 minutes, 24 miles); for Montpelier (30 minutes, 19 miles), take VT 100B north and US 2 east.

NORTHERN VERMONT

Northern Vermont is home to the state's largest city, Burlington, and the state capital, Montpelier. Never fear, however: this area still has all of the rural charms found elsewhere. Even within Burlington, cafe-lined streets coexist with scenic paths along Lake Champlain and the Winooski River. Further north, the pastoral Northeast Kingdom offers a full range of outdoor activities, from skiing to biking, in the heart of the mountains.

Burlington

POP 42,300

Perched on the shore of Lake Champlain, Vermont's largest city would be considered tiny in most other states, but its relatively diminutive size is one of Burlington's charms. With the University of Vermont (UVM) swelling the city by 13,400 students, and a vibrant cultural and social life, Burlington has a spirited, youthful character. And when it comes to nightlife, this is Vermont's epicenter.

Due south of Burlington is Shelburne, an upscale village that's home to the one of Vermont's crown jewels, the Shelburne Museum. The village is considered more of an extension of Burlington rather than a separate suburb – people think nothing of popping down for an evening meal to one of its fine restaurants.

Burlington is less than an hour's drive from Stowe and other Green Mountain towns. In fact, the city can be used as a base for exploring much of northwestern Vermont.

Burlington

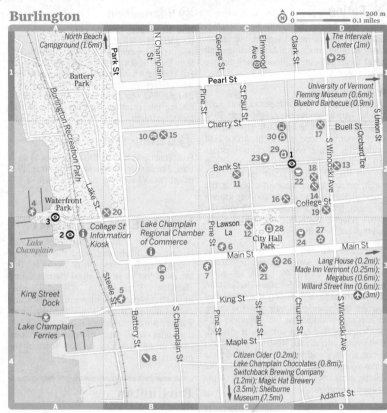

Sights

Downtown

Church Street Marketplace PEDESTRIAN MALL
(www.churchstmarketplace.com; ⊕) Burlington's
pulse can often be taken along this four-
block pedestrian zone running from Pearl to
Main Sts. When the weather's good, buskers
(now licensed by the town), food and craft
vendors, soapbox demagogues, restless students, curious tourists and kids climbing on
rocks mingle in a vibrant human parade.

Waterfront WATERFRONT
A five-minute walk from downtown, Burlington's delightfully uncommercialized waterfront is a scenic, low-key promenade with
a 7.5-mile bike path, a pier for Lake Champlain **boat trips**, the Echo aquarium and
Discovery Landing, a modern **observatory**
with a cafe that's great for watching sunset
over the lake.

**Echo Leahy Center
for Lake Champlain** AQUARIUM
(☑802-864-1848; www.echovermont.com; 1 College
St; adult/child $13.50/10.50; ⊙10am-5pm; ⊕)
This kid-friendly lakeside museum examines
the colorful past, present and future of Lake
Champlain. A multitude of aquariums wig-
gle with life, and nature-oriented displays
invite inquisitive minds and hands to splash,
poke, listen and crawl. Regular rotating exhibits focus on scientific themes – from wind
power to giant insects, and dinosaurs to ca-
davers – with plenty of hands-on activities.

South Toward Shelburne

Shelburne Farms FARM
(☑802-985-8686; www.shelburnefarms.org; 1611
Harbor Rd, Shelburne; adult/child $8/5; ⊙9am-
5pm mid-May–mid-Oct, 10am-5pm mid-Oct–mid-
May; ⊕) ⚡ In 1886 William Seward Webb
and Lila Vanderbilt Webb built themselves
a magnificent country estate on the shores

Burlington

of Lake Champlain. The 1400-acre farm, designed by landscape architect Frederick Law Olmsted (who also designed New York's Central Park and Boston's Emerald Necklace), was both a country house for the Webbs and a working farm, with stunning lakefront perspectives. The 24-bedroom English-style country manor (completed in 1899), now an inn, is surrounded by working farm buildings inspired by European romanticism.

Today, visitors to Shelburne Farms can buy some of the cheese, maple syrup, mustard and other items produced here, and – from mid-May to mid-October – hike miles of walking trails, visit the animals in the children's farmyard or take a guided 1½-hour tour ($3) from a truck-pulled open wagon. The farm is 8 miles south of Burlington, off US 7.

★Shelburne Museum   MUSEUM
(☑ 802-985-3346;   www.shelburnemuseum.org;
6000 Shelburne Rd/US 7, Shelburne; adult/child/
teen $24/12/14; ◎ 10am-5pm daily May-Dec,
10am-5pm Wed-Sun Jan-Apr; ⊞) This extraordinary 45-acre museum, 9 miles south of Burlington, showcases the priceless Americana collections of Electra Havemeyer Webb (1888–1960) and her parents – 150,000 objects in all. The mix of folk art, decora-

tive arts and more is housed in 39 historic buildings, most of them moved here from other parts of New England to ensure their preservation.

Structures include a sawmill (1786), a one-room brick schoolhouse (1840), a covered bridge (1845), a lighthouse (1871), a luxury rail coach (1890), a classic round barn (1901), a railroad station (1915), the Lake Champlain side-wheeler steamship *Ticonderoga* (1906) and a 1920s carousel. There's also an entire building (Owl Cottage) filled with books, games and activities for kids. Allow at least half a day for your visit.

Magic Hat Brewery   BREWERY
(☑ 802-658-2739; www.magichat.net; 5 Bartlett Bay Rd, South Burlington; ◎ 10am-7pm Mon-Sat Jun–mid-Oct, to 6pm Mon-Thu, to 7pm Fri & Sat mid-Oct–May, noon-5pm Sun year-round) Drink in the history of one of Vermont's most dynamic microbreweries on the fun, free, self-guided 'Artifactory' Tour (once you see the whimsical labels, this name makes perfect sense) and learn all the nuances of the beer-making process. Afterwards, sample a few experimental brews from the four dozen taps in the on-site Growler Bar, or grab a six pack to go. The brewery is located 3.5 miles south of downtown Burlington, on the west side of US 7.

Switchback Brewing Company BREWERY
(📞802-651-4114; www.switchbackvt.com; 160 Flynn Ave, Burlington; ⊙tours 1pm & 2pm Sat, tap room 11am-7pm Sun-Thu, to 8pm Fri & Sat) One of Vermont's finest microbreweries, Switchback is best known for its trademark reddish-amber ale; in 2015 it also launched a lighter-bodied Connector IPA; you'll see both on bar menus statewide, but there's nothing like getting them at the source, in the tap room in Burlington's South End. Brewery tours are offered on Saturday afternoons.

🏃 Activities

Boating

Approximately 120 miles long and 12 miles wide, **Lake Champlain** is the largest freshwater lake in the country after the Great Lakes. Consistently good wind, sheltered bays, lack of boat traffic, hundreds of islands and scenic anchorages combine to make this one of the Northeast's top boating spots.

Whistling Man Schooner Company BOATING
(📞802-598-6504; www.whistlingman.com; Burlington Community Boathouse, 1 College St, at Lake Champlain; 2hr cruises adult/child $50/35; ⊙3 trips daily, late May-early Oct) Sail around Lake Champlain with the breeze in your hair and a Vermont microbrew in your hand on the *Friend Ship*, a classic 43ft New England beauty that holds up to 17 passengers. Captains are knowledgeable about the area, and encourage passengers to bring food and drink on board. Private charters are also available (from $450 for two hours). Reserve ahead.

Spirit of Ethan Allen II CRUISE
(📞802-862-8300; www.soea.com; Burlington Community Boathouse, College St, at Lake Champlain; day cruises adult/child $20/9, sunset cruises adult/child $25/16; ⊙mid-May-mid-Oct) In addition to lunch and dinner cruises, this ship plies the lake with 1½-hour scenic, narrated day cruises at 10am, noon, 2pm and 4pm, and a 2½-hour sunset cruise at 6:30pm (earlier in fall).

Lake Champlain Paddlers' Trail BOATING
(📞802-658-1414; www.lakechamplaincommittee. org) 🛶 There's no finer way to enjoy Lake Champlain than on a multiday paddling trip on the Lake Champlain Paddlers' Trail, which provides access to over 600 overnight camping spots around the lake. Paddlers are encouraged to join the ecofriendly Lake Champlain Committee ($45 per year), for

---

DON'T MISS

BIKING YOUR WAY AROUND BURLINGTON

Burlington's core is pedestrian central. You could also spend your entire Burlington vacation on a bike – if you're staying for a number of days during the non-snowy months, consider renting a bike for your entire stay (you'll fit in well with the ever-so-green locals, who passionately use bikes as a primary mode of transport). Bike paths cover the entire city and most suburbs, and vehicles generally give cyclists plenty of breathing space.

The **Burlington Recreation Path**, a popular 7.5-mile route for walking, biking, in-line skating and general perambulating, runs along the waterfront through the Waterfront Park and promenade.

Local Motion (📞802-652-2453; www.localmotion.org; 1 Steele St; adult/tandem/child's bike per day $32/55/24; ⊙9am-6pm July & Aug, 10am-6pm May, Jun, Sept & Oct; 🚲) 🛶, a nonprofit group with its own trailside center downtown, spearheads ongoing efforts to expand bike trails and sustain existing ones. It also offers encyclopedic advice on where to cycle in the local area, along with bike rentals, maps, tours and refreshments. Highly recommended is the 12-mile **Island Line Trail**. It combines with the waterfront Burlington Recreation Path, beginning just south of the boathouse and extending onto the narrow Colchester causeway that juts 5 miles out into the lake. You can even extend your adventure at trail's end by catching Local Motion's **Island Line bike ferry** (one way/round-trip $5/8) north to the Champlain Islands; it runs from late May through early October (daily mid-June to early September, weekends rest of season).

You can also rent bikes (or in-line skates or roller-skis for that matter!) at **Ski Rack** (📞802-658-3313; www.skirack.com; 85 Main St; ⊙10am-7pm Mon-Sat, 11am-5pm Sun) and **North Star Sports** (📞802-863-3832; www.northstarsportsvt.com; 100 Main St; ⊙10am-6pm Mon-Sat, noon-5pm Sun).

which they receive an essential guidebook that details the trails, campsites and rules of the nautical road.

Diving

Throughout the 18th and 19th centuries, Lake Champlain was the site of military battles as well as a major commercial thoroughfare between the St Lawrence Seaway and the Hudson River. Over this period, many military and merchant ships, victims of cannonballs or bad weather, sank to the lake's bottom. Of the 200 wrecks discovered, nine are accessible to divers, preserved by the state of Vermont as underwater historical sites.

All divers must obtain a free permit, available at the **Burlington Community Boathouse** (☑802-865-3377; www.enjoyburlington. com; College St, at Lake Champlain; ⊙mid-May–mid-Oct); the limited permits are available on a first-come, first-served basis.

Waterfront Diving Center　　　DIVING
(☑802-865-2771, 800-283-7282; www.waterfront diving.com; 214 Battery St; ⊙9am-6:30pm Mon-Fri, 8:30am-5:30pm Sat & Sun late May–mid-Oct, shorter hours in winter) This dive shop offers rentals, charters, instruction and a full line of snorkeling, swimming, scuba and underwater-photography gear.

★ Festivals & Events

Discover Jazz Festival　　　MUSIC
(☑802-863-7992; www.discoverjazz.com; ⊙early Jun) Burlington plays host to jazz for 10 days in early June at the waterfront and various venues around town.

★Vermont Brewers Festival　　　BEER
(www.vtbrewfest.com; $35; ⊙mid-Jul) Meet Vermont's artisan craft brewers and sample their wares during this mid-July weekend event on Burlington's waterfront. Tickets go on sale two months in advance and sell out quickly.

Sleeping

Burlington's budget and midrange motels are on the outskirts of town. Many chain motels lie on Williston Rd (US 2) east of I-89 exit 14; there's another cluster along US 7 north of Burlington in Colchester (take I-89 exit 16). But the best selection is along Shelburne Rd (US 7) in South Burlington.

Burlington Hostel　　　HOSTEL $
(☑802-540-3043; www.theburlingtonhostel.com; 53 Main St, 2nd floor; dm incl breakfast weekday/weekend $40/45; ⊙May-Oct; ▣@✿) Just min-

utes from the action centers of Church St and Lake Champlain, Burlington's hostel accommodates up to 48 guests and offers both mixed and women-only dorms.

North Beach Campground　　　CAMPGROUND $
(☑802-862-0942; www.enjoyburlington.com; 60 Institute Rd; campsites $36/41; ⊙May–mid-Oct; ✿) Campers should make a beeline for this wonderful spot on Lake Champlain, with 69 tent sites on 45 wooded acres near the city center. From Burlington's downtown waterfront, follow Battery St and North Ave (VT 127) north, turning left on Institute Rd. All sites have picnic tables, fire rings, and access to hot showers, a playground, beach and bike path.

Northstar Motel　　　MOTEL $
(☑802-863-3421; www.northstarmotelvermont.com; 2427 Shelburne Rd, Shelburne; d $49-80; ✿) These are among the most convenient and reasonably priced rooms on the Shelburne Rd motel strip.

★Willard Street Inn　　　INN $$
(☑802-651-8710; www.willardstreetinn.com; 349 S Willard St; r incl breakfast $159-279; ✿) Perched on a hill within easy walking distance of UVM and the Church St Marketplace, this mansion, fusing Queen Anne and Georgian Revival styles, was built in the late 1880s. It has a fine-wood and cut-glass elegance, yet radiates a welcoming warmth. Many of the guest rooms overlook Lake Champlain.

Lang House　　　B&B $$
(☑802-652-2500; www.langhouse.com; 360 Main St; r incl breakfast $139-289; ▣@✿) This elegant B&B occupies a centrally located, tastefully restored 19th-century Victorian home and carriage house with 11 spacious rooms, some with fireplaces. Pampering touches include wine glasses and robes in each room, and sumptuous breakfasts served in an alcove-laden room decorated with old photographs of the city. Reserve ahead for one of the 3rd-floor rooms with lake views.

★Inn at Shelburne Farms　　　INN $$$
(☑802-985-8498; www.shelburnefarms.org/stay dine; 1611 Harbor Rd, Shelburne; r $270-525, without bath $160-230, cottages $270-435, guesthouses from $450; ⊙early May–mid-Oct; ✿) One of New England's top 10 places to stay, this inn, 7 miles south of Burlington off US 7, was once the summer mansion of the wealthy Webb family. It now welcomes guests, with rooms in the gracious, welcoming country manor house by the lakefront, as well as four

independent, kitchen-equipped cottages and guesthouses scattered across the property.

Relive the Webbs' opulent lifestyle by taking tea (served every afternoon), eating in the inn's fabulous restaurant (dinner mains range from $28 to $36; most of the menu is built around produce from the surrounding 1400-acre farm), or chill out playing billiards or relaxing in one of the common areas, complete with elegant, original furnishings. If you're feeling more energetic, the hiking trails, architect-designed barns and vast grounds are also worthy of several hours' exploration.

Made Inn Vermont
B&B $$$

(☑802-399-2788; www.madeinnvermont.com; 204 S Willard St; r incl breakfast $229-342) This 19th-century hillside mansion with gorgeous period features is way trendier than your typical New England B&B, thanks to the creative flair of owner Linda Wolf (a former home-stager in Santa Fe, NM). Jazzy touches include a backyard hot tub, vintage record players with a vast collection of vinyl, loaner Fender guitars and chalkboard walls where guests can express themselves creatively.

The five soundproofed rooms come with robes, slippers, HBO/Showtime and 'rock-and-roll' lighting, and there's an amazing rooftop cupola nook perfect for sipping wine, reading, eating breakfast, playing games or simply contemplating the sensational Lake Champlain views. Guests are treated to a nice selection of wines and microbrews, including Vermont's famous Heady Topper, and good strong coffee in the morning.

Hotel Vermont
HOTEL $$$

(☑802-651-0080; www.hotelvt.com; 41 Cherry St; r $199-499) Burlington's newest downtown hotel, in a LEED-certified energy-efficient building halfway between Church St and Lake Champlain, pampers guests with 125 bright modern rooms filled with high-end amenities. There's a pair of excellent on-site restaurants, and live jazz in the lobby Wednesdays, Fridays and Saturdays.

✕ Eating

A large cluster of eateries is located on and near the Church St Marketplace. But if you explore just a little bit further out, your taste buds will be richly rewarded.

★ Penny Cluse Cafe
CAFE $

(☑802-651-8834; www.pennycluse.com; 169 Cherry St; mains $9-14; ⊙6:45am-3pm Mon-Fri, 8am-3pm Sat & Sun) ✔ In the heart of down-town, one of Burlington's most popular breakfast spots serves pancakes, biscuits and gravy, breakfast burritos, omelets and tofu scrambles, along with sandwiches, fish tacos, salads and the best chile relleno you'll find east of the Mississippi. Expect an hour's wait on weekends – best bet is to put your name down, grab a coffee and take a pre-meal wander.

The Skinny Pancake
CREPERIE $

(☑802-540-0188; www.skinnypancake.com; cnr Lake & College Sts; crepes $6-13; ⊙8am-8pm Sun-Tue, to 10pm Wed & Thu, to 11pm Fri & Sat) What started as a humble Church St food cart is now a full-fledged Burlington institution, serving its delicious crepes at multiple locations, including this main branch down by the lakeshore. Regionally sourced savory crepes such as the Lumberjack (Vermont apples, ham and Cabot cheddar) share the menu with dessert classics like the Love-maker (Nutella, strawberries and whipped cream).

City Market
MARKET $

(☑802-861-9700; www.citymarket.coop; 82 S Winooski Ave; ⊙7am-11pm) ✔ If there's a food co-op heaven, it must look something like this. Burlington's gourmet natural foods grocery is chock-full of local produce and products (with over 1600 Vermont-based producers represented), a huge takeout deli section, a massive microbrew-focused beer section and a 'Hippie Cooler,' where you'll find all the tofu and tempeh you could dream of.

Stone Soup
VEGETARIAN $

(☑802-862-7616; www.stonesoupvt.com; 211 College St; buffet per lb $11, sandwiches under $10; ⊙7am-9pm Mon-Fri, 9am-9pm Sat; ⊛✔) Best known for its excellent vegetarian- and vegan-friendly buffet, this longtime local favorite also has homemade soups, sandwiches on home-baked bread, a salad bar, pastries and locally raised meats.

★ American Flatbread
PIZZA $$

(☑802-861-2999; www.americanflatbread.com/restaurants/burlington-vt; 115 St Paul St; flatbreads $14-23; ⊙11:30am-3pm & 11:30-11:30pm Mon-Fri, 11:30am-11:30pm Sat & Sun) ✔ Central downtown location, bustling atmosphere, great beers on tap from the in-house Zero Gravity microbrewery, and superb flatbread (thin-crust pizza) with locally sourced ingredients are reason enough to make this one of your first lunch or dinner stops in Burlington. Throw in an outdoor terrace in the back alleyway in warm weather, and you've got one of Vermont's finest eateries.

★Revolution Kitchen VEGAN, VEGETARIAN $$

(📞802-448-3657; www.revolutionkitchen.com; 9 Center St; mains $14-18; ⊕5-10pm Tue-Sat; 🍽️) Vegetarian fine dining? And romantic atmosphere to boot? Yep, they all come together at this cozy brick-walled restaurant that makes ample and creative use of Vermont's abundant organic produce. Asian, Mediterranean and Latin American influences abound in house favorites like Revolution Tacos, crispy seitan piccata and the Laksa Noodle Pot, and most items are (or can be adapted to be) vegan.

Leunig's Bistro FRENCH $$

(📞802-863-3759; www.leunigsbistro.com; 115 Church St; lunch mains $12-22, dinner mains $21-38; ⊕11am-10pm Mon-Thu, 11am-11pm Fri & Sat, 9am-10pm Sun) 'Live well, laugh often and love much' advises the sign over the bar at this stylish and convivial Parisian-style brasserie with an elegant, tin-ceilinged dining room. A long-standing Burlington staple, it's as much fun for the people-watching (windows face the busy Church St Marketplace) as it is for the excellent wine list and food.

A Single Pebble CHINESE $$

(📞802-865-5200; www.asinglepebble.com; 133 Bank St; mains $10-23; ⊕11:30am-1:45pm & 5-11pm; 🍽️) This spacious restaurant – the brainchild of a local chef who mastered Szechuan and Cantonese cuisine while living in China – sprawls over two adjoining

clapboard houses and offers up sumptuous MSG-free fare to the strains of traditional Chinese music. The dim sum is particularly satisfying – be sure to try the mock eel.

Daily Planet INTERNATIONAL $$

(📞802-862-9647; www.dailyplanetvt.com; 15 Center St; mains $10-25; ⊕4-9pm Sun-Thu, to 9:30pm Fri & Sat; 🛜🍽️) This long-established downtown haunt serves a changing, varied menu that ranges from apple and fennel bisque with Gorgonzola cream, to poutine (sweet-potato fries with Vermont cheddar curds, rosemary and candy cap mushroom gravy), to burgers with exotic trimmings, to pan-roasted lamb 'lollipops.' The bar stays open nightly till 2am.

Bluebird Barbecue BARBECUE $$

(📞802-448-3070; www.bluebirdbbq.com; 317 Riverside Ave; small plates $6-9, large plates $16-34; ⊕4:30-9pm Mon-Thu, to 10pm Fri, noon-10pm Sat, noon-9pm Sun) Enjoy a taste of the south in the frozen north at this barbecue joint overlooking the Winooski River north of town. Dive into huge platters of pulled pork, sausage, 15-hour brisket and barbecue ribs, and dabble in $4.50 sampler plates, accompanied by tasty sides like cornbread, buttermilk biscuits, coleslaw, braised greens and ham, mac-and-cheese or homemade bread-and-butter pickles.

Hen of the Wood GASTRONOMY $$$

(📞802-540-0534; www.henofthewood.com; 55 Cherry St; mains $22-29; ⊕restaurant 5-10pm, bar 4pm-midnight) An offshoot of Waterbury's legendary Hen of the Wood restaurant, this Burlington sister branch opened in 2013

DON'T MISS

VERMONT'S MICROBREWERIES & CIDERIES

The same easy access to fresh ingredients and commitment to local craftsmanship that defines the state's restaurants also fuel its microbreweries and cideries. With more craft breweries per capita than any other state (roughly one beermaker for every 28,000 people), Vermont pours an acclaimed and diverse array of beers and ciders.

Some of our favorite microbreweries and cider producers are listed below. Some offer free tours and/or samples; see their websites for details.

➡ Switchback Brewing Company (p304)

➡ Magic Hat Brewery (p303)

➡ Otter Creek Brewing (p297)

➡ Citizen Cider (p308)

➡ Hill Farmstead Brewery (p319)

➡ Idletyme Brewing Co (p315)

➡ Woodchuck Cidery (p297)

and has quickly become a local favorite for high-end dining. To savor its classy ambience on a smaller budget, drop by the bar for $1 oysters daily between 4pm and 5pm or 10pm and 11pm.

Trattoria Delia ITALIAN $$$
(✆802-864-5253; www.trattoriadelia.com; 152 St Paul St; mains $18-37; ⊙5-10pm) Burlington's longtime favorite for a romantic dinner, this dimly lit Italian restaurant with a large stone fireplace serves homemade pastas and specialties like *scottaditto d'agnello* (rack of lamb) or *coniglio alla griglia* (wood-grilled Vermont rabbit), coupling them with selections from its award-winning wine list.

🍸 Drinking & Nightlife

Burlington's student-fueled nightlife usually revolves around live music and mugs of beer. The city's social epicenter is Church St Marketplace (the pedestrian mall), thick with restaurants and sidewalk cafes. Late at night on summer weekends, the south end (by Main St) feels like one massive outdoor bar.

For nightlife and entertainment listings, check out *Seven Days* (www.7dvt.com), a free, energetic tabloid that tells all with a sly dash of attitude.

Citizen Cider MICROBREWERY
(✆802-497-1987; www.citizencider.com; 316 Pine St; ⊙11am-10pm Mon-Sat, to 7pm Sun) Tucked into an industrial-chic building with painted concrete floors and long wooden tables, this animated cidery is a homegrown success story, using only Vermont apples to make its ever-growing line of hard ciders. Taste test a flight of five for $7, including perennial favorites such as the crisp, classic Unified Press, or the Dirty Mayor, infused with ginger and lemon peel.

Splash at the Boathouse BAR
(✆802-658-2244; www.splashattheboathouse. com; College St, at Lake Champlain; ⊙11am-10pm mid-may–Sep) Perched atop Burlington's floating boathouse is this sometimes low-key, sometimes raucous restaurant-bar with stellar views over Lake Champlain. It serves a full menu, but that's really not the point. Come here to kick back with an evening cocktail or microbrew and watch the boats lolling about the lake, preferably at sunset when yellow and purple shadows dance across the water.

Dobra Tea TEAHOUSE
(✆802-951-2424; www.dobrateavt.com; 80 Church St; ⊙10am-10pm Sun-Wed, to 11pm Thu-Sat) This Czech-owned tearoom offers over 50 varieties – some seasonal, all hand-selected directly from their regions of origin. Sit at a table, an up-ended tea box or on cushions around a small, low pedestal.

Radio Bean BAR
(✆802-660-9346; www.facebook.com/RadioBean; 8 N Winooski Ave; ⊙8am-2am Mon-Sat, 10am-2am Sun; 🛜) This is Burlington's social hub for arts and music. Espressos, beer and wine keep things jumping, along with grilled sandwiches and baked goods. Regular live performances include jazz, acoustic music and more, both here and at the semi-attached Light Club Lamp Shop (✆802-660-9346; www.facebook.com/LightClub LampShop; 12 N Winooski Ave; ⊙7pm-2am Mon-Thu, 5pm-2am Fri-Sun). Radio Bean is also noteworthy for having cofounded The Radiator, Burlington's fabled low-power indie FM radio station (105.9).

Farmhouse Tap & Grill PUB
(✆802-859-0888; www.farmhousetg.com; 160 Bank St; ⊙11:30am-late) This place labels itself a gastropub, with over two dozen craft brews on tap (most of them Vermont-made) and a farm-to-table menu of regionally sourced food. A cozy interior 'Parlor' and an outdoor beer garden pack 'em in every night.

Half Lounge COCKTAIL BAR
(✆802-962-2188; www.facebook.com/halflounge; 136 Church St; ⊙5pm-2am Mon-Thu, from 4pm Fri, from 3pm Sat & Sun) Step downstairs to this cave-like speakeasy for cocktails, boutique wines and occasional live music. It's sophisticated and sheltered from the raucous scene that unfolds upstairs on Church St on weekend evenings. Its martini list is excellent, and it serves light tapas until the wee hours.

⭐ Entertainment

⭐ Flynn Center for the Performing Arts PERFORMING ARTS
(✆802-863-5966; www.flynncenter.org; 153 Main St) Broadway hits, music, dance and theater grace the stage at this art-deco masterpiece. Expect anything from the Khmer Arts Ensemble to Liza Minnelli.

Higher Ground LIVE MUSIC
(✆802-652-0777; www.highergroundmusic.com; 1214 Williston Rd) Two miles east of downtown, this beloved midsize live-music venue brings

DON'T MISS

VERMONT'S STATE PARKS

With more than 150,000 acres of protected land set aside in more than 50 state parks, Vermont isn't called the Green Mountain State for nothing! Finding an exceptional and often underutilized state park in Vermont is about as easy as breathing. Whether you're interested in swimming, hiking, snowshoeing, cross-country skiing, camping or fishing, you'll find plenty of places that fit the bill.

Here are some of our favorite off-the-beaten-track state-park campgrounds in Vermont:

Burton Island State Park (☑ 802-524-6353; www.vtstateparks.com/htm/burton.htm; 2714 Hathaway Point Rd, St Albans; day use adult/child $4/2; ☺ late May-early Sep; ⓐ) Only accessible by ferry, this island state park in the middle of Lake Champlain (35 miles north of Burlington) has lakeside campsites and lean-tos, walking trails, boat rentals, a cafe and a nature center.

Seyon Lodge State Park (☑ 802-584-3829; www.vtstateparks.com/htm/seyon.htm; 2967 Seyon Pond Rd, Groton; day use adult/child $4/2; ☺ late Mar–mid-Nov & late Dec–mid-Mar) The only park of its kind in Vermont, Seyon Lodge (30 miles east of Montpelier) offers private rooms in its rustic lodge on the shores of Noyes Pond and also serves meals, including three-course dinners made with locally sourced produce. There's great fly-fishing in the pond and hiking or skiing on the network of trails just outside the front door.

Jamaica State Park (p284) With campsites directly adjacent to the rushing West River, this is one of only two riverside state parks in Vermont. It's especially popular with kayakers and rafters for its annual white-water weekends in late September. It's 27 miles north of Brattleboro via VT 30.

Underhill State Park (☑ 802-899-3022; www.vtstateparks.com/htm/underhill.htm; 352 Mountain Rd, Underhill; day use adult/child $4/2; ☺ late May–mid-Oct) This teeny park on the western slopes of Mt Mansfield (25 miles northeast of Burlington) is the perfect jumping-off point for the classic climb to Vermont's highest summit via the Sunset Ridge Trail.

For complete details on all state parks, contact **Vermont State Parks** (☑ 888-409-7579; www.vtstateparks.com).

big-name acts to Burlington, along with plenty of local talent.

Nectar's　　　　　　　　　　　LIVE MUSIC
(☑ 802-658-4771; www.liveatnectars.com; 188 Main St; ☺ 7pm-2am Mon & Tue, 5pm-2am Wed-Sun) Indie darlings Phish got their start here and the joint still rocks out with the help of aspiring acts. Grab a vinyl booth or chill at the bar or dance upstairs at Club Metronome (clubmetronome.com), which hosts a slew of theme nights (every Friday is '90s night) along with larger live acts.

🏠 Shopping

Burlington Farmers' Market　　　MARKET
(www.burlingtonfarmersmarket.org; City Hall Park, St Paul St, btwn College & Main Sts; ☺ 8:30am-2pm Sat May-Oct, 10am-2pm Sat Nov-Apr) 🍃 Every Saturday from May through October, City Hall Park bursts into life with this busy farmers market; during the rest of the year, the market moves indoors to the Memorial Auditorium (250 Main St). It's enormously

popular and all vendors must grow or make precisely what they sell: expect fresh produce, prepared food, cheeses, breads, baked goods and crafts.

Outdoor Gear Exchange　　SPORTS & OUTDOORS
(☑ 802-860-0190, 888-547-4327; gearx.com; 37 Church St; ☺ 10am-7pm Mon-Sat, 11am-5pm Sun) This place rivals major outdoor-gear chains for breadth of selection, and trumps them on price for a vast array of used, closeout and even new gear and clothing. Name the outdoor pursuit and staff can probably outfit you.

Lake Champlain Chocolates　　CHOCOLATE
(☑ 802-864-1807; www.lakechamplainchocolates.com; 750 Pine St; ☺ 9am-6pm Mon-Sat, 11am-5pm Sun, hourly tours 11am-2pm Mon-Fri, tastings 11am-4pm Sat & Sun) No, you can't run through the chocolate waterfall, but Burlington's home-grown chocolate factory offers tours and tastings, plus a store where you can purchase chocolate truffles, bars, coins and gift baskets. There's also a cafe serving luscious

homemade ice cream. If all you're after is the chocolates, check out LCC's second, more conveniently located store (☑802-862-5185; www.lakechamplainchocolates.com; 65 Church St; ◷10am-9pm Mon-Thu, to 10pm Fri & Sat, 11am-8pm Sun) in Church St Marketplace.

❶ Information

BTV Information Center (☑802-863-1889; www.vermont.org; Burlington International Airport; ◷9am-midnight) This helpful office in Burlington's airport is staffed by the Lake Champlain Regional Chamber of Commerce. It keeps longer hours than the downtown branch (☑877-686-5253, 802-863-3489; www.vermont.org; 60 Main St; ◷8am-5pm Mon-Fri year-round, 9am-5pm Sat & Sun late May-early Sep).

College St Information Kiosk (College St; ◷10am-8pm daily late May-Aug, reduced hours Sep–mid-Oct) Seasonal branch of Lake Champlain Regional Chamber of Commerce, down near the lakefront.

University of Vermont Medical Center (☑802-847-0000; www.uvmhealth.org; 111 Colchester Ave; ◷24hr) Vermont's largest hospital. Has a 24-hour level 1 trauma center.

❶ Getting There & Around

AIR

A number of national carriers, including JetBlue, serve **Burlington International Airport** (BTV; ☑802-863-2874; www.btv.aero; 1200 Airport Dr, South Burlington), 3 miles east of the city center. You'll find all the major car-rental companies at the airport.

BOAT

Lake Champlain Ferries (p278) runs scenic, summer-only car ferries (one-way car and driver/adult/child/cyclist $30/8/3.10/9, 70 minutes, mid-June to September) between Burlington and Port Kent, NY.

The company also operates ferries between Charlotte, VT (south of Burlington), and Essex, NY, for as long as the lake stays unfrozen; and 24-hour, year-round service from Grand Isle, VT (north of Burlington), to Plattsburgh, NY. See the website for fare and schedule details.

BUS

Greyhound (☑802-864-6811, 800-231-2222; www.greyhound.com; 1200 Airport Dr, South Burlington) runs multiple buses daily from Burlington International Airport to Montreal, Canada (from $21, 2½ hours) and Boston (from $12, 4½ hours to 5½ hours).

Megabus (☑877-462-6342; www.megabus. com; 116 University Pl) offers bus service to Boston (from $10, four hours), Amherst, MA (from $20, 3½ hours), Hartford, CT (from $20, 4¾

hours) and New York City (from $39, 7¾ hours). Buses leave from in front of the Royall Tyler Theater on the University of Vermont campus.

Chittenden County Transportation Authority (CCTA; ☑802-864-2282; www.cctaride.org) operates its free College St shuttle bus (route 11) every 15 to 30 minutes between the UVM campus and Waterfront Park near the Burlington Boathouse, with a stop at Church St Marketplace. Local fares around Burlington are $1.25 for adults, 60¢ cents for children and seniors.

CCTA also operates buses from its Downtown Transit Center on Cherry St to destinations throughout the region. See the website for fares and schedules. There are no services on major holidays.

Burlington International Airport Route 1 (20 to 30 minutes, half-hourly, less frequent on Sunday)

Essex Junction Route 2 (40 minutes, every 15 to 30 minutes Monday to Saturday, no service Sunday)

Middlebury Routes 46 and 76

Montpelier Route 86

Shelburne Route 6

CAR & MOTORCYCLE

To get here from Boston (3½ hours, 216 miles), take I-93 to I-89. It's another 1¾ hours (95 miles) north from Burlington to Montreal.

All of Burlington's car-rental companies (Hertz, Avis, Enterprise, National, Thrifty, Budget and Alamo) are located at Burlington International Airport. The best option for Amtrak passengers arriving in Essex Junction is to take a taxi 5 miles to the airport and rent a car there. **Green Cab VT** (☑802-864-2424; www.green cabvt.com), recommended for its fuel-efficient fleet, can shuttle people from Essex Junction to the airport for about $15.

TRAIN

Amtrak's daily *Vermonter* (p278) train, which provides service as far south as New York City and Washington, DC, stops in Essex Junction, 5 miles from Burlington.

Stowe & Around

POP 4310

In a cozy valley where the West Branch River flows into Little River and mountains rise in all directions, the quintessential Vermont village of Stowe (founded in 1794) bustles quietly. The town's long-standing reputation as one of the east's classiest mountain resorts draws well-heeled urbanites from Boston, New York and beyond. A bounty of inns and eateries lines the thoroughfares leading up to Smuggler's Notch, an enchantingly narrow rock-walled pass through the Green Mountains just below Mt Mansfield (4393ft), the highest point in Vermont. More than 200 miles of cross-country ski trails, some of the finest mountain biking and downhill skiing in the east, and world-class rock- and ice-climbing make this a natural mecca for adrenaline junkies and active families.

Waterbury, on the interstate highway 10 miles south, is Stowe's gateway. Its attractions include a pair of standout restaurants, a beloved brewery and the world-renowned Ben & Jerry's ice-cream factory.

◎ Sights

Vermont Ski & Snowboard Museum   MUSEUM
(☑ 802-253-9911; www.vtssm.com; 1 S Main St, Stowe; $5; ☉ noon-5pm Wed-Sun) Located in an 1818 meeting house that was rolled to its present spot by oxen in the 1860s, this museum is an inspired tribute to skiing and snowboarding history. It holds much more than an evolution of equipment (including 75 years of Vermont ski lifts) and a chance to chuckle at what was high slope-side fashion in the 1970s. A huge screen shows ski footage so crazy that you can hardly keep your footing.

Helen Day Art Center   ARTS CENTER
(☑ 802-253-8358; www.helenday.com; 90 Pond St, Stowe; ☉ noon-5pm Wed-Sun) FREE In the heart of Stowe village, this gently provocative community art center has rotating exhibitions of traditional and avant-garde work. It also sponsors 'Exposed,' an annual town-wide outdoor sculpture show that takes place from mid-July to mid-October.

🏃 Activities

Skiing

Stowe Mountain Resort   SKIING
(☑ 802-253-3000, 888-253-4849; www.stowe.com; 5781 Mountain Rd, Stowe; lift ticket adult/child $115/95) This venerable resort encompasses two major mountains, Mt Mansfield (which has a vertical drop of 2360ft) and Spruce Peak (1550ft). It offers 116 beautiful trails, 16% of which are earmarked for beginners, 55% for middle-of-the-roadies and 29% for hardcore backcountry skiers – many of whom get their adrenaline rushes from the 'front four' runs: Starr, Goat, National and Liftline.

Smugglers' Notch Resort   SKIING
(☑ 800-419-4615, 802-332-6854; www.smuggs.com; 4323 VT 108; lift ticket adult/child $72/54; 🐾) This family-oriented resort on the

---

DON'T MISS

HIKING IN THE STOWE AREA

The Green Mountain Club (p315), 5 miles south of Stowe, was founded in 1910 to maintain the Long Trail. The club publishes some excellent hikers' materials, available here or by mail. Staff also lead guided hiking, biking, boating, skiing and snowshoeing day trips. There are several excellent day hikes around Stowe:

Moss Glen Falls (easy, 1 mile, 45 minutes) Follow VT 100 for 3 miles north of central Stowe and bear right onto Randolph Rd. Go 0.3 miles and turn right for the parking area, then walk along the obvious path to reach a deep cascade and waterfalls.

Mt Mansfield (difficult, 7 miles, five hours) Follow VT 108 west from Stowe to the Long Trail parking area, 0.7 miles past Stowe Mountain Resort ski area. Mt Mansfield is thought by some to resemble a man's profile in repose, so follow the Long Trail to the 'chin,' then go south along the summit ridge to Profanity Trail; follow that aptly named route to Taft Lodge, then take the Long Trail back down. An extremely scenic alternate route, the Sunset Ridge Trail, leads up the west side of the mountain from Underhill State Park.

Nebraska Notch (moderate, 3.2 miles, 2½ hours) Take VT 100 south of Stowe and turn west onto River Rd, which becomes Moscow Rd. Continue for 5.8 miles to the Lake Mansfield Trout Club. The trail follows an old logging road for a while and then ascends past beaver dams and grand views to join the Long Trail at Taylor Lodge.

Stowe Pinnacle (moderate, 2.8 miles, three hours) Follow VT 100 south of Stowe and turn east onto Gold Brook Rd, proceeding for 0.3 miles; cross a bridge and turn left to continue along Gold Brook Rd. About 1.6 miles later, you come to Upper Hollow Rd; turn right and go to the top of the hill, just past Pinnacle Rd, to find the small parking area on the left. The hike to Stowe Pinnacle (2651ft), a rocky outcrop offering sweeping mountain views, is short but steep.

Stowe & Around

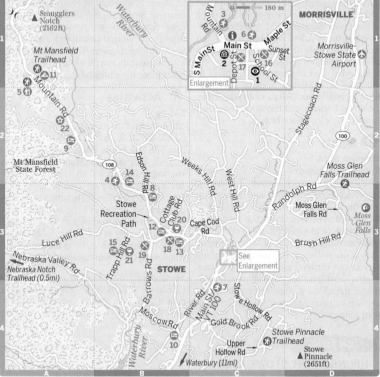

VERMONT STOWE & AROUND

west side of Smugglers' Notch is spread over Sterling (3010ft), Madonna (3640ft) and Morse (2250ft) mountains. It has incredible alpine skiing (78 trails ranging from beginner's runs at Morse to the triple black diamond Black Hole), plus 36 miles of cross-country ski and snowshoe trails, dogsled rides, a lit tubing hill and nightly family entertainment.

Trapp Family Lodge
X-Country Ski Center SKIING
(☑ 800-826-7000, 802-253-8511; www.trappfamily. com/skiing-snowshoeing.htm; 700 Trapp Hill Rd, Stowe; trail pass adult/child/teen $25/10/15) America's oldest cross-country ski center, with 37 miles of groomed trails and 62 miles of backcountry trails. One of the delights of skiing here is stopping to recharge your batteries with warm soup and hot chocolate by the fireplace at Slayton Pasture Cabin.

Walking & Cycling

★**Stowe Recreation Path** OUTDOORS
(www.stowerec.org/paths; ☺year-round; 🚴🏊)
🍃 The flat to gently rolling 5.5-mile Stowe Recreation Path, which starts from the pointy-steepled Stowe Community Church in the village center, offers a fabulous four-season escape for all ages. It rambles through woods, meadows and outdoor sculpture gardens along the West Branch of Little River, with sweeping views of Mt Mansfield unfolding in the distance.

Bike, walk, skate or ski – and swim in one of the swimming holes along the way.

Equipment Rental & Sales

AJ's Ski & Sports OUTDOORS
(☑ 800-226-6257; www.stowesports.com; 350 Mountain Rd, Stowe; ☺8am-8pm) In the village center, near the south end of the recreation path. Rents bikes, kayaks, ski and snowboard equipment.

Stowe & Around

Umiak Outdoor Outfitters OUTDOORS
(☑802-253-2317; www.umiak.com; 849 S Main St, Stowe; ⊙9am-6pm) This place rents canoes and sport kayaks, gives kayak and stand-up paddleboard lessons, and offers a variety of guided and self-guided tours on local rivers, including the Lamoille and the Winooski. In winter, it also rents snowshoes and telemark skis, and offers moonlit snowshoe tours.

Mountain Ops Outdoor Gear CYCLING
(☑802-253-4531; www.mountainopsvt.com; 4081 Mountain Rd, Stowe; ski or snowboard rental/bike rental per day $22/25) Near the north end of the recreation path. Rents bikes and skis.

🛏 Sleeping

Stowe has a wide variety of lodging, with dozens of inns, motels and B&Bs; many are along Mountain Rd. The Stowe Area Association (p316) helps with reservations.

Smugglers Notch State Park CAMPGROUND $
(☑802-253-4014; www.vtstateparks.com/htm/smugglers.htm; 6443 Mountain Rd, Stowe; campsites $20-22, lean-tos $27-29; ⊙mid-May–mid-Oct) This 35-acre park, 8 miles northwest of Stowe, is perched up on the mountainside. It has 81 tent and trailer sites, and 20 lean-tos and walk-in sites.

Inky Dinky Oinkink B&B $$
(☑802-253-3046; www.oinkink.com; 117 Adams Mill Rd, Stowe; r incl breakfast $135-155; 🛜) Artist, world traveler and animal-lover Liz Le Serviget presides over this cheerful, pet-friendly two-room B&B in pretty countryside 2 miles south of Stowe. Artwork and flowers from

her adjacent gallery and garden enliven the rooms and common areas, while home-grown veggies and berries find their way into breakfasts that may also include popovers, Swedish pancakes or lemon-ginger scones.

Arbor Inn B&B $$
(☑802-253-4772, 800-543-1293; www.arborinnstowe.com; 3214 Mountain Rd, Stowe; r $100-160, ste $130-240; @🛜🏊) This spotless, cheery space features simply furnished rooms with wood paneling; suites include extras such as wood-burning fireplaces, Jacuzzis and kitchenettes. There's a sleek yet cozy common lounge with a tiny bar, fireplace and modern art gracing the walls, a game room with a pool table and yet another fireplace, and an on-site hot tub.

Fiddler's Green Inn INN $$
(☑800-882-5346, 802-253-8124; www.fiddlersgreeninn.com; 4865 Mountain Rd, Stowe; r incl breakfast midweek/weekend $99/135; ❄) A throwback to simpler times, this unembellished 1820s farmhouse is less than a mile from the lifts and has rustic pine walls, a fieldstone fireplace and seven very simple guest rooms. The best rooms and the breakfast area overlook the river out back, within earshot of the rushing water. Guests congregate around the hearth in winter; it's all quite homey.

Stowe Motel & Snowdrift MOTEL, APARTMENT $$
(☑800-829-7629, 802-253-7629; www.stowemotel.com; 2043 Mountain Rd, Stowe; r $99-209, ste $190-250, apt $166-275; @🛜🏊) In addition to the efficiency rooms (with kitchenettes),

suites, apartment and two- to six-bedroom houses (rates highly variable; call to inquire), this motel set on a generous 16 acres offers such amenities as a tennis court, hot tubs, badminton and lawn games. You can also borrow bicycles or snowshoes to use on the recreation path.

Sun & Ski Inn   INN $$
(☑ 800-448-5223, 802-253-7159; www.sunandski inn.com; 1613 Mountain Rd, Stowe; r $109-199, ste $165-299, condo $190-340; ☜☒) A nicely landscaped inn adjacent to the river and the recreation path. The 25-room lodge has a fireplace, Jacuzzi and covered pool with retractable roof. It also rents a pair of basic two- and three-bedroom condos up the road.

Green Mountain Inn   INN $$$
(☑ 802-253-7301; www.greenmountaininn.com; 18 Main St, Stowe; r/ste/apt from $179/289/299) The Stowe Recreation Path unfurls just a few steps from the door at this 180-year-old red-brick inn, which sits in the heart of downtown Stowe. How best to relax? Settle into a rocking chair on the front porch, enjoy afternoon cookies and tea, then head to the spa. The 104 rooms are classically decorated and come in a variety of configurations.

Trapp Family Lodge   LODGE $$$
(☑ 802-253-8511, 800-826-7000; www.trapp family.com; 700 Trapp Hill Rd, Stowe; r $191-610; @☜☒☒) With wide-open fields and mountain vistas, this hilltop lodge 3km southwest of town boasts Stowe's best setting. The Austrian-style chalet, built by Maria von Trapp of *Sound of Music* fame, houses traditional lodge rooms. Alternatively, you can rent one of the modern villas or cozy guesthouses scattered across the property. The 2700-acre spread offers stupendous hiking, snowshoeing and cross-country skiing.

Topnotch at Stowe   RESORT $$$
(☑ 800-451-8686; www.topnotchresort.com; 4000 Mountain Rd, Stowe; r $255-$998; @☜☒) Stowe's most lavish resort dazzles guests with amenities: indoor and outdoor pools, tennis courts, fine dining, a skating rink, a ski touring center and a legendary spa. The stylishly modern Roost pub, with cathedral windows overlooking Mt Mansfield, was added in 2013. Accommodations range from comfortable standard rooms to immaculate two- and three-bedroom houses.

✗ Eating

Stowe offers an impressive variety of eateries for every taste and budget, spreading from the village center up Mountain Rd to the ski slopes.

Black Cap Coffee & Beer   CAFE $
(☑ 802-253-2123; www.facebook.com/BlackCap CoffeeandBeer; 144 Main St, Stowe; sandwiches $5.50-8.75; ⊙ 7am-5pm; ☜) Unwind over baked goods, sandwiches and coffee at this homey, newly refurbished cafe in the heart of the village, set in an inviting old house with armchairs, couches and a small but delightful front porch. The attached shop stocks an impressive collection of microbrews and hosts regular beer-tasting events.

DON'T MISS

BEN & JERRY'S ICE CREAM FACTORY

In 1978 Ben Cohen and Jerry Greenfield took over an abandoned gas station in Burlington and, with a modicum of training, launched the outlandish flavors that forever changed the way ice cream would be made. While a tour of **Ben & Jerry's Ice Cream Factory** (☑ 866-258-6877; www.benjerrys.com; 1281 VT 100, Waterbury; adult/child under 13yr $4/free; ⊙ 9am-9pm Jul–mid-Aug, to 7pm mid-Aug–mid-Oct, 10am-6pm mid-Oct–Jun; ⊞) is no over-the-top Willie Wonka experience, there is a campy video that follows the company's long, strange trip to corporate giant – albeit a very nice giant with an inspiring presence of community building and environmental leadership. Then you head to a special glassed-in room where you glimpse the production line in action and a staff member explains how it is done. (Note: they generally only make ice cream Monday through Friday, so if you come on the weekend you'll likely see the production-line video.) After chowing your (very teeny) free scoops, linger a while in the final hallway, which is festooned with mementos of how they've changed the world one scoop at a time. Behind the factory, a mock cemetery holds 'graves' of Cool Britannia, Holy Cannoli and other flavors that have been laid to rest. In summer, cows roam the pastures surrounding the factory. The factory is 1 mile north of I-89.

Depot Street Malt Shoppe
DINER $

(☑802-253-4269; 57 Depot St, Stowe; dishes $6-10; ⊙11am-4pm Sun & Mon, to 7pm Wed & Thu, to 8pm Fri & Sat) Burgers, fries, onion rings, chocolate sundaes, banana splits and old-fashioned malteds reign at this fun, 1950s-themed restaurant. The egg creams hit the spot in any season.

Pie-casso
PIZZA $$

(☑802-253-4411; www.piecasso.com; 1899 Mountain Rd, Stowe; mains $8-22; ⊙11am-10pm Sun-Thu, to 11pm Fri & Sat) Best known for its ample pizzas, from the sausage-and-pepperoni-laden Heart Stopper to the veggie-friendly Vienna with spinach, olives, sun-dried tomatoes and mozzarella, Pie-casso also serves everything from eggplant parmesan subs to fettuccine alfredo and penne with pesto. Gluten-free crusts using flour from nearby West Meadow Farm are also available.

★ Hen of the Wood
MODERN AMERICAN $$$

(☑802-244-7300; www.henofthewood.com; 92 Stowe St, Waterbury; mains $26-33; ⊙5-9pm Tue-Sat) ✔ Arguably the finest dining in northern Vermont, this chef-driven restaurant in Waterbury gets rave reviews for its innovative farm-to-table cuisine. Set in a historic grist mill, the ambience is as fine as the food, which features densely flavored dishes like smoked duck breast and sheep's-milk gnocchi.

The Bistro at Ten Acres
FUSION $$$

(☑802-253-6838; www.tenacreslodge.com/bistro.php; 14 Barrows Rd, Stowe; mains $19-32; ⊙5-10pm Wed-Sun) This immensely popular eatery in a plank-floored 1820s farmhouse blends cozy atmosphere with delicious food from New York–trained chef Gary Jacobson (think *steak frites,* slow-roasted duck, or lobster with bourbon-tarragon sauce and polenta). The attached bar serves a good selection of cocktails and draft beers, plus a cheaper burger-centric menu.

Michael's on the Hill
INTERNATIONAL $$$

(☑802-244-7476; www.michaelsonthehill.com; 4182 Waterbury-Stowe Rd, Waterbury Center; mains $27-43, tasting menus $45-67; ⊙5:30-9pm Wed-Mon) ✔ A 10-minute drive south of Stowe, this is one of the area's standout eateries. A seasonally changing menu built on locally sourced ingredients is served in a pair of interior dining rooms and on an intimate wraparound porch.

🍷 Drinking & Entertainment

Big resorts like Stowe Mountain Resort and Smugglers' Notch cultivate their own animated après-ski scene, as do hotel bars and other venues along Mountain Rd. There are some nice cafes in the village center, and an excellent crop of microbreweries to explore in the surrounding area.

Idletyme Brewing Co
MICROBREWERY

(☑802-253-4765; www.idletymebrewing.com; 1859 Mountain Rd, Stowe; mains $12-32; ⊙11:30am-9pm Sun-Thu, to 10pm Fri & Sat) Sip 4oz samples ($2 each) or go in for full pints at this up-and-coming microbrewery in a converted 19th-century blacksmith's shop between Stowe village and the slopes. The kitchen, under the ownership of acclaimed local restaurateur Michael Kloeti, serves burgers, bratwurst and cheese boards alongside full-fledged dinner fare: *steak frites,* duck confit, Maine crab cakes or roasted, stuffed delicata squash.

Von Trapp Brewing
MICROBREWERY

(☑802-253-0900; www.vontrappbrewing.com; Trapp Hill Rd, Stowe; ⊙7am-7pm) Since launching region-wide distribution in 2015, Von Trapp Brewing has expanded its fame among Vermont beer-lovers; drop into its tasting room and sample a flight of four 4oz glasses for $7.75. The adjacent deli and bakery serves apple strudel ($4), cinnamon rolls ($3) and sandwiches, which you can enjoy by the blazing fire in winter.

Matterhorn Bar & Grill
LIVE MUSIC

(☑802-253-8198; www.matterhornbar.com; 4969 Mountain Rd, Stowe; ⊙2pm-late Mon-Fri, 11am-late Sat & Sun) Near the top of Mountain Rd, this place starts hopping at 5pm, when skiers start hobbling off the slopes. Top draws include brick-oven pizzas and the lower-level sushi bar, which has a view of the river out back. Bands play Friday and Saturday nights during ski season.

ℹ Information

Green Mountain Club Visitors Center (☑802-244-7037; www.greenmountainclub.org; 4711 Waterbury-Stowe Rd/VT 100, Waterbury Center; ⊙9am-5pm daily mid-May–mid-Oct, 10am-5pm Mon-Fri rest of year) The Green Mountain Club maintains the 270-mile Long Trail, which runs the length of Vermont from Massachusetts to the Canadian border. Visit its office (5 miles south of Stowe) or check the website for details about the Long Trail and shorter day hikes in the region.

WORTH A TRIP

CAMEL'S HUMP

The distinctive form of Camel's Hump – the state's third-highest mountain – is a familiar image to Vermonters: its silhouette is visible on the Vermont state quarter, from suburban Burlington and along I-89. Yet it remains one of the state's wildest spots, one of the few significant Vermont peaks not developed for skiing. To get here, detour south off I-89 at Richmond (between Burlington and Waterbury), take US 2 east to Richmond's main stop light, then drive south 10 miles to Huntington Center, where you'll turn left (east) 3 miles, dead-ending at the trailhead for the 6-mile Burrows–Forest City loop to the summit. After climbing through forest, the final ascent skirts rock faces above the tree line, affording magnificent views.

Stowe Area Association (☎877-467-8693, 802-253-7321; www.gostowe.com; 51 Main St, Stowe; ⊙9am-8pm Mon-Sat, 11am-5pm Sun Jun-Oct & Jan-Mar, 9am-5pm Mon-Sat rest of year; ☎) This well-organized association with comfy couches, free wi-fi and a fireplace in winter can help plan your trip, including making reservations for rental cars and local accommodations.

⊙ Getting There & Away

AIR
In late 2015, Tradewind Aviation (www.flytradewind.com) reinstated twice-weekly commercial flights from the New York City suburb of White Plains to the newly renovated Morrisville-Stowe State Airport (p278), 7 miles north of Stowe.

CAR & MOTORCYCLE
To get to Burlington (37 miles, 45 minutes), head south on VT 100, then northwest on I-89.

TRAIN
The Amtrak *Vermonter* (p278) train stops daily at Waterbury. Some hotels and inns will arrange to pick up guests at the station. The Route 100 Commuter is the only bus service between Waterbury and Stowe, but it doesn't make good connections with Amtrak. Stowe Taxi offers taxi service.

⊙ Getting Around

BUS
GMTA (☎802-223-7287; gmtaride.org) operates a couple of useful buses for those without a vehicle.

The Mountain Road Shuttle runs every half-hour daily during ski season from Stowe village, along Mountain Rd, to the ski slopes. Pick up a schedule and list of stops at your inn or the Stowe Area Association's information office.

On weekdays, the Route 100 Commuter also offers limited service between Stowe and Waterbury, where you can connect to the Montpelier LINK Express bus to Montpelier or Burlington, operated by CCTA (p310).

TAXI
Stowe Taxi (☎802-253-9490; www.stowetaxi.com)

Montpelier & Around
POP 7755

Montpelier (mont-*peel*-yer) would qualify as nothing more than a large village in most places. But in sparsely populated Vermont it's the state capital – the smallest in the country (and the only one without a McDonald's, in case you were wondering). Surprisingly cosmopolitan for a town of 8000 residents, its two main thoroughfares – State St and Main St – make for a pleasant wander, with some nice bookstores, boutiques and eateries.

Montpelier's smaller, distinctly working-class neighbor Barre (*bear*-ee), which touts itself as the 'granite capital of the world,' is a 15-minute drive southeast of the capital.

⊙ Sights

Hope Cemetery   CEMETERY
(☎802-476-6245; www.central-vt.com/web/hope; 201 Maple Ave, Barre) Barre's cemetery, 1 mile north of US 302 on VT 14, celebrates the artistic prowess of generations of local stone carvers. The whimsical tombstones here include a man and his wife sitting up in bed holding hands, smiling for eternity; a granite cube balanced precariously on a tombstone's corner; a giant soccer ball and a small airplane. If a cemetery can ever be a work of art, this one is! It's open to the living all the time.

Rock of Ages Quarries   QUARRY
(☎general info 800-421-0166, visitors center 802-476-3119; www.rockofages.com; 560 Graniteville Rd, Graniteville; guided tours adult/child $6/2.75; ⊙guided quarry tours 9:15am-3:35pm Mon-Sat late May-Aug, daily Sep–mid-Oct, self-guided factory tours 8am-3:30pm Mon-Fri Feb–mid-Dec) The world's largest granite quarries, 4 miles southeast of Barre off I-89 exit 6, cover 50 acres, tapping a granite vein that's a whopping 6 miles long, 4 miles wide and 10 miles deep. Most

fascinating is the 35-minute guided minibus tour of the active quarry, where you can gaze down on seemingly ant-size workers in hard hats extracting massive granite blocks at the bottom of a 600ft-deep pit.

State House
HISTORIC BUILDING

(www.vtstatehouse.org; 115 State St, Montpelier; ☉ guided tours 10am-3:30pm Mon-Fri, 11am-2:30pm Sat Jul-mid-Oct, 9am-3pm Mon-Fri mid-Oct–Jun, self-guided tours year-round) FREE Montpelier's main landmark, the gold-domed capitol building, is open year-round for guided tours with volunteer guides; there are also self-guided audio tours in English, French, Spanish and German. The front doors are guarded by a massive statue of American Revolutionary hero Ethan Allen, and the base supporting the gold dome was built of granite quarried in nearby Barre in 1836.

Vermont History Museum
MUSEUM

(☑ 802-828-2291; www.vermonthistory.org/visit/vermont-history-museum; 109 State St, Montpelier; adult/child $7/5; ☉ 10am-4pm Tue-Sat) Near the Vermont State House, Montpelier's Pavilion Building houses an excellent museum that recounts Vermont's history with exhibits, films and re-creations of taverns and Native American settlements.

🛏 Sleeping

There's a surprising dearth of attractive, well-priced accommodation in Montpelier. You're better off sleeping in the Stowe area (20 miles northwest) for bucolic Vermont atmosphere, or Barre (10 miles southeast) if all you're after is a motel room.

Inn at Montpelier
INN $$

(☑ 802-223-2727; www.innatmontpelier.com; 147 Main St, Montpelier; r incl continental breakfast $190-290; ❄ 🕹) Good enough for repeat visitor Martha Stewart, this first-rate inn made up of two refurbished Federal houses sits smack in the heart of town. All the rooms are luxuriously furnished, including some deluxe units with wood-burning fireplaces; the wicker rocking chairs on the wraparound verandah make it a perfect spot to while away a lazy afternoon.

🍴 Eating

You can eat well in Montpelier, thanks to the presence of the New England Culinary Institute (NECI), one of America's finest cooking schools. Graduates often stick around town to start restaurants of their own.

★ Red Hen
BAKERY $

(☑ 802-223-5200; www.redhenbaking.com; 961b US Rte 2, Middlesex; pastries from $3; ☉ 7am-4pm Mon, to 6pm Tue-Sat, 8am-6pm Sun) One of Vermont's finest bakeries, Red Hen is well worth the 6-mile trek west of Montpelier – and a perfect breakfast stop if you're headed toward Stowe, Waterbury or Burlington. Settle into its comfy seating area over sinfully delicious sweet rolls, blueberry-studded pastries and breakfast sandwiches on hearty Mad River Grain bread, or simply grab a loaf for the road.

★ Threepenny Taproom
PUB FOOD $

(☑ 802-223-8277; www.threepennytaproom.com; 108 Main St, Montpelier; mains $10-16; ☉ 11am-late Sun-Fri, noon-late Sat) With the names of two dozen microbrews from Vermont and beyond scrawled on the blackboard every evening, this pub is a perennial late-night favorite. But it also has a fabulous lineup of snacks and light meals, including Vermont cheeses, salads, sandwiches, burgers, flatbreads and bistro classics, such as *moules frites* (mussels with French fries).

Hunger Mountain Co-op
HEALTH FOOD $

(☑ 802-223-8000; www.hungermountain.coop; 623 Stone Cutters Way, Montpelier; deli items $6-10; ☉ 8am-8pm) This terrific health-food store and deli has cafe tables overlooking the Winooski River.

NECI on Main
AMERICAN, MEDITERRANEAN $$

(☑ 802-223-3188; www.neci.edu/neci-on-main; 118 Main St, Montpelier; lunch mains $10-12, dinner mains $16-26; ☉ 11:30am-9pm Tue-Sat, 10am-2pm Sun) 🍴 NECI's multilevel signature restaurant focuses on farm-to-table locavore food. There's an open window to the kitchen, allowing you to watch student chefs at work, and a lovely outdoor patio for summer dining.

ℹ Information

Capitol Region Visitors Center (☑ 802-828-5981; 134 State St, Montpelier; ☉ 6am-5pm Mon-Fri, 9am-5pm Sat & Sun) Opposite the Vermont state capitol building.

ℹ Getting There & Away

Burlington (40 minutes, 39 miles) is an easy drive on I-89. On weekdays, you can also reach Burlington via the Montpelier LINK Express bus ($4, 1¼ hours, nine Monday to Friday) operated by CCTA (p310).

Amtrak's daily *Vermonter* (p278) train runs from Montpelier to points north and south, including Brattleboro ($29, 2½ hours) and Burlington's Essex Junction station ($12, 40 minutes). The Amtrak station is 1.7 miles southwest of downtown Montpelier, at 299 Junction Rd in the Montpelier Junction neighborhood.

Northeast Kingdom

When Senator George Aiken noted in 1949, 'this is such beautiful country up here. It ought to be called the Northeast Kingdom of Vermont,' locals were quick to take his advice. Today, the Northeast Kingdom connotes the large wedge between the Quebec and New Hampshire borders. Less spectacular than spectacularly unspoiled, the landscape is a sea of green hills dotted with farms and small villages.

Here, inconspicuous inns and dairy cows contrast with the slick resorts found elsewhere in the state; the white steeples are chipped, the barns in need of a fresh coat of paint. In a rural state known for its unpopulated setting (only Wyoming contains fewer people), the Kingdom is Vermont's equivalent to putting on its finest pastoral dress, with a few holes here and there. It's a region that doesn't put on any airs about attracting tourists, and locals speak wryly of its 'picturesque poverty.'

◉ Sights

Bread & Puppet Museum MUSEUM
(☑ 802-525-3031; www.breadandpuppet.org/museum; 753 Heights Rd, Glover; donations welcome; ⊙ 10am-6pm Jun-Oct, by appointment Nov-May) **FREE** Formed in New York City by German artist Peter Shumann in 1963, this renowned theater collective presents carnivalesque pageants, circuses, and battles of Good and Evil with gaudy masks and gigantic puppets. This unique museum consists of a two-story barn crammed with puppets and masks from the company's past performances. The high-ceilinged top floor is especially arresting, with its collection of many-headed demons, menacing generals, priests, bankers, everyday people, animals and gods (some as large as 15ft).

In July and August, performances take place at the theater's home base in Vermont. The rest of the year, Bread & Puppet is on tour. In summer, audience members are still treated to the traditional home-baked bread that gives the enterprise half its name.

The street theater of Bread & Puppet's early performances gave voice to local rent strikes and anti–Vietnam War protests as well as an epic parade down Fifth Ave in the early 1980s to protest nuclear proliferation. By then, it had moved its operation to its current home in Glover.

To get here, take I-91 to exit 24, then take a right onto VT 122 and continue 13 miles.

St Johnsbury Athenaeum MUSEUM
(☑ 802-748-8291; www.stjathenaeum.org; 1171 Main St, St Johnsbury; ⊙ 10am-5:30pm Mon, Wed & Fri, 2-7pm Tue & Thu, 10am-3pm Sat) **FREE** Home to the country's oldest art gallery still in its original form, the athenaeum was initially founded as a library by Horace Fairbanks in 1871. Comprising 9000 finely bound books of classic world literature, the library was soon complemented by the gallery, built around its crown jewel, Albert Bierstadt's 10ft-by-15ft painting, *Domes of the Yosemite*. The collection also includes other large-scale dramatic landscapes by Bierstadt's fellow Hudson River School artists, such as Asher B Durand, Worthington Whittredge and Jasper Crospey.

WORTH A TRIP

DOG MOUNTAIN

Signposted 2 miles east of St Johnsbury, captivating **Dog Mountain** (☑ 802-748-2700; www.dogmt.com; 143 Parks Rd, St Johnsbury; ⊙ 10am-5pm Mon-Sat, 11am-4pm Sun) celebrates the legacy of Vermont artist Stephen Huneck. There's an entire gallery devoted to Huneck's whimsical dog-themed artwork, but the real showstopper is the chapel next door, designed by Huneck to celebrate the enduring bond between humans and pets. Huneck's own contributions (a doggie weathervane, canine-themed stained-glass windows) are complemented by scores of photos and heartfelt writings plastered on the chapel's walls by visitors in memory of their own lost pets.

At least twice a year, Dog Mountain hosts its popular Dog Parties, where dogs are invited in for free dog biscuits, swimming, fun with Frisbees and good-natured canine competitions. Humans will appreciate the live music and superb views over the mountains of Vermont's Northeast Kingdom. See www.dogmt.com/Events.html for details.

DON'T MISS

KINGDOM TRAILS NETWORK

In 1997 a group of dedicated locals linked together 200-plus miles of single and double tracks and dirt roads to form the astounding **Kingdom Trails** (www.kingdomtrails.com; Welcome Center, 478 VT 114, East Burke in summer, Nordic Adventure Center, 2059 Darling Hill Road, Lyndonville in winter; day pass adult/child $15/7; ⊘ Welcome Center 8am-5pm Sun-Thu, 8am-6pm Fri & Sat May-Oct, Nordic Adventure Center 8:30am-4pm daily Nov-Apr; ⊕), an award-winning trail network. Passing through century-old farms and soft forest floors dusted with pine needles, it offers one of New England's best mountain-biking experiences. In winter, the trails are ideal for cross-country skiing, snowshoeing and fat biking.

Buy passes at the Kingdom Trails Welcome Center or the Nordic Adventure Center, depending on the season.

**Fairbanks Museum
& Planetarium**   MUSEUM
(✆ 802-748-2372; www.fairbanksmuseum.org; 1302 Main St, St Johnsbury; adult/child $9/7; ⊘ 9am-5pm) In 1891, when Franklin Fairbanks' collection of stuffed animals and cultural artifacts from across the globe grew too large for his home, he built the Fairbanks Museum of Natural Science. This massive stone building with a 30ft-high barrel-vaulted ceiling still displays more than half of Franklin's original collection, including a 1200lb moose, a Bengal tiger and a bizarre collection of 'mosaics' made entirely from dead bugs. The attached planetarium offers shows ($4 to $6 per person) throughout the year.

🏃 Activities

Not surprisingly, this sylvan countryside is the perfect playground for New England outdoor activities, including skiing, mountain biking and boating.

⭐ Hill Farmstead Brewery   BREWERY
(✆ 802-533-7450; www.hillfarmstead.com; 403 Hill Rd, Greensboro Bend; 4 tastes $5; ⊘ 12-5pm Wed-Sat but call to confirm, tours by appointment) The brainchild of Shaun Hill, known for his creative concoctions and uncompromising adherence to quality, this unassuming-looking brewery down a dirt road in the middle of nowhere has developed a cult following for its small-batch brews. Several beers have names based on the Hill family: for example, the hoppy Edward IPA is named after Shaun's grandfather. Another brew, Vera Mae, is made with dandelions from Hill Farmstead's own fields, which the general public is invited to come help pick!

Cabot Creamery   FOOD & DRINK
(✆ 800-837-4261; www.cabotcheese.com; 2878 Main St, Cabot; tours adult/child $3/free; ⊘ 9am-5pm mid-May–Oct, 10am-4pm Nov & Dec, 10am-

4pm Mon-Sat Jan–mid-May) Despite its nationwide distribution network, this most famous of Vermont cheese producers remains basically true to its early 20th-century roots as a New England dairy cooperative. Its half-hour tour gives you a look at the cheese-making process (not to mention high-tech machinery painted like Holsteins), after which you can pig out to your heart's content in the tasting room.

Skiing

Craftsbury Outdoor Center   SKIING
(✆ 802-586-7767; www.craftsbury.com; 535 Lost Nation Rd, Craftsbury Common; trail pass adult/child $10/5; ⊕) Cross-country skiers adore this full-service resort just outside the village of Craftsbury Common, 38 miles northwest of St Johnsbury. The 80 miles of trails roll over meadows and weave through forests of maples and firs, offering ideal skiing for all levels. In summer, the center is also a mecca for runners and boaters.

Your day pass here also grants access to the trails at **Highland Lodge** (✆ 802-533-2647; www.highlandlodge.com; Craftsbury Rd, Greensboro; trail pass adult/child $10/5) in nearby Greensboro, reachable by a daily shuttle ($5) or a 19.8km connector trail.

Burke Mountain   SKIING
(✆ 802-626-7300; http://skiburke.com; 223 Sherburne Lodge Rd, East Burke; lift ticket adult/child $64/47) Off US 5 in East Burke, Burke Mountain is relatively unknown to out-of-staters, even though nearby Burke Mountain Academy has been training Olympic skiers for decades. Locals enjoy the challenging trails and empty lift lines. Burke has 36 trails, 14 glades, three terrain parks and four lifts, including three quad chairs and one with a vertical drop of 2000ft.

In summer it's also ideal for mountain biking.

At the time of writing, the resort was transitioning to new ownership. Check the website for up-to-the-minute details.

Jay Peak
SKIING

(☑802-988-2611; www.jaypeakresort.com; 830 Jay Peak Rd, off VT 242, Jay; lift ticket adult/child $79/62; ⊛) Even when Boston is balmy, you can still expect a blizzard at Vermont's northernmost ski resort. Only 10 miles south of the Quebec border, Jay gets more snow than any other New England ski area. Easy and intermediate runs are complemented by natural off-trail terrain that offers some of America's most challenging backcountry snowboarding and skiing.

Kids love the Pump House Indoor Water-park (adult/child $39/29), where you can zip down the spine-tingling Chute or catch a wave in the Double Barrel Flowrider.

At the time of writing, the resort was transitioning to new ownership. Check the website for up-to-the-minute details.

Hiking

The stunning beauty of **Lake Willoughby** will leave even a jaded visitor in awe. The lake sits sandwiched between Mt Hor and Mt Pisgah, whose cliffs plummet more than 1000ft to the glacial waters below and create, in essence, a landlocked fjord.

The scenery is best appreciated on the hike (three hours) to the summit of **Mt Pisgah**. From West Burke, take VT 5A for 6 miles to a parking area on the left-hand side of the road, just south of Lake Willoughby. The 1.7-mile (one-way) **South Trail** begins across the highway. It's about a 35-minute drive from St Johnsbury.

Cycling

On VT 114 off I-91, East Burke is a terrific place to start a mountain-bike ride, with the vast Kingdom Trails network (p319) beckoning right at its doorstep.

Lamoille Valley Rail Trail
OUTDOORS

(☑802-229-0005; www.lvrt.org) New England's longest rail trail, still under construction, will eventually span Vermont from east to west, a distance of 93 miles. The eastern-most section of the trail, stretching from St Johnsbury to West Danville, was officially inaugurated in 2015 and is now open to ski-ers, cyclists, equestrians and snowshoers.

Long-term plans call for a network of mountain-bike routes to feed off the main trail, in accordance with special rights-of-ways granted by private landowners.

🛏 Sleeping

As elsewhere in Vermont, the Northeast Kingdom has its fair share of country inns, but you'll also find an abundance of motels at exits off I-91, especially around St Johnsbury.

Rodgers Country Inn
INN $

(☑800-729-1704, 802-525-6677; www.rodgers countryinn.com; 582 Rodgers Rd, West Glover; s/d without bath incl breakfast $65/80, cabins per week $600) Not far from the shores of Shadow Lake, Jim and Nancy Rodgers offer five guest rooms in their 1840s farmhouse, plus two independent cabins. Hang out on the front porch and read, or take a stroll on this 350-acre former dairy farm. This inn appeals to people who really want to feel what it's like to live in rural Vermont.

Inn at Mountain View Farm
INN $$

(☑802-626-9924, 800-572-4509; www.innmtn view.com; 3383 Darling Hill Rd, East Burke; r $215-245, ste $295-375, all incl breakfast & afternoon tea; ⊛🖻) Built in 1883, this spacious, elegant farmhouse is set on a hilltop with stunning views, surrounded by 440 acres that are ideal for mountain biking, cross-country skiing or simply taking a long stroll on the hillside. There's also an on-site animal sanctuary, which is a rescue center for large farm animals; guests are encouraged to visit.

Wildflower Inn
INN $$

(☑802-626-8310; www.wildflowerinn.com; 2059 Darling Hill Rd, Lyndonville; r $212-242, ste $262-452, all incl breakfast; ⊙Dec-Mar & May-Oct; 🖻🌊) This smart inn with country furnishings on a gorgeous hilltop is a favorite with families – the hayrides, mountain-bike trails, petting zoo with sheep and goats, playground, tennis courts and heaps of other on-site activities keep everyone amused.

🍴 Eating

Kingdom Taproom
PUB FOOD $

(☑802-424-1355; www.kingdomtaproom.com; 397 Railroad St, St Johnsbury; mains $8-14; ⊙4-10pm Mon-Thu, noon-midnight Fri & Sat, noon-8pm Sun) You'll find the Northeast Kingdom's largest selection of microbrews on tap at this recently opened pub in the heart of St Johnsbury. A bevy of Vermont beers such as 14th Star, Hill Farmstead, Fiddlehead and Lost Nation are offered on a rotating basis, along with mac-and-cheese, soups, salads, flatbreads and sandwiches.

Miss Lyndonville Diner DINER $

(☑802-626-9890; 686 Broad St/US 5, Lyndonville; mains $7-13; ⊙6am-8pm Mon-Thu, to 9pm
Fri & Sat, 7am-8pm Sun) Five miles north of
St Johnsbury and popular with locals, this
place offers friendly, prompt service and a
tantalizing display of pies. Large breakfasts
are cheap, as are the sandwiches, but for a
real steal try the tasty homemade dinners
like roast turkey with all the fixings.

❶ Information

St Johnsbury Welcome Center (☑802-
748-8575; www.discoverstjohnsbury.com; 51
Depot Sq; ⊙8:30am-5pm Mon-Fri, 9am-3pm
Sat, 10am-2pm Sun) Very helpful information
center, atmospherically housed in St Johnsbury's historic railway station.

❶ Getting There & Away

While St Johnsbury is easily reached by I-91 or
I-93 (a three-hour drive from Boston through
New Hampshire), the rest of the Northeast Kingdom is spread out. Use I-91 as your north–south
thoroughfare, and then use smaller routes like
VT 5A to find dramatically sited Lake Willoughby,
or VT 14 to picturesque Craftsbury Common.

To get to St Johnsbury from Montpelier (55
minutes, 38 miles), take US 2 east; from Burlington, I-89 to US 2 (1½ hours, 76 miles).

To get to Brattleboro (two hours, 122 miles),
take a straight shot south down I-91.

The only way to get around the Northeast
Kingdom is with your own wheels.

New Hampshire

POP 1.3 MILLION / ☎ 603

Best Places to Eat

➡ Black Trumpet Bistro (p329)

➡ Cider Company Restaurant (p359)

➡ Burdick Chocolate (p334)

➡ Libby's Bistro & Saalt Pub (p363)

➡ Schilling Beer Co (p354)

Best Places to Sleep

➡ Ale House Inn (p327)

➡ Snowflake Inn (p359)

➡ Omni Mt Washington Hotel & Resort (p361)

➡ The Notch Hostel (p347)

➡ Hancock Campground (p350)

Why Go?

New Hampshire bleeds jagged mountains, scenic valleys and forest-lined lakes – they lurk in every corner of this rugged state. It all begs you to embrace the outdoors, from kayaking the hidden coves of the Lakes Region to trekking the upper peaks surrounding Mt Washington. Each season yields a bounty of adrenaline and activity: skiing and snowshoeing in winter, magnificent walks and drives through autumn's fiery colors, and swimming in crisp mountain streams and berry-picking in summer. Jewel-box colonial settlements like Portsmouth buzz a sophisticated tune, while historic attraction and small-town culture live on in pristine villages like Keene and Peterborough.

But there's a relaxing whiff in the air too – you're encouraged to gaze out at a loon-filled lake, recline on a scenic railway trip or chug across a waterway on a sunset cruise – all while digging into a fried-clam platter or a lobster roll, of course.

When to Go
Concord

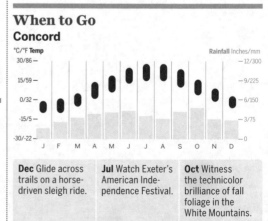

Dec Glide across trails on a horse-driven sleigh ride.

Jul Watch Exeter's American Independence Festival.

Oct Witness the technicolor brilliance of fall foliage in the White Mountains.

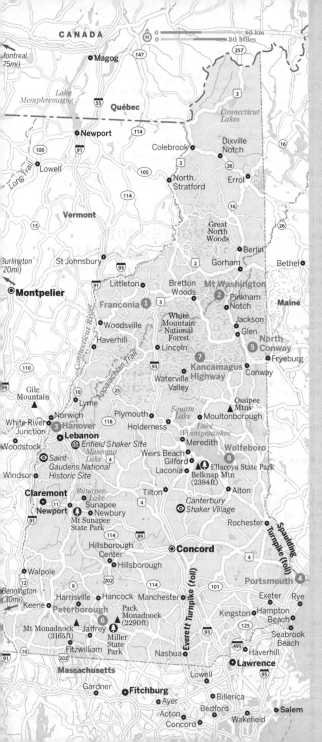

New Hampshire Highlights

1 Franconia (p353) Walking in the footsteps of Robert Frost at his former farm.

2 Mount Washington Cog Railway (p360) Trundling up the world's second-steepest railway track.

3 Hanover (p337) Taking a free walking tour of Dartmouth College and discovering renowned Mexican muralist José Clemente Orozco's riveting mural in the depths of the library.

4 Portsmouth Black Heritage Trail (p327) Getting a new perspective on New England's history.

5 North Conway (p355) Canoeing the Saco River or pitting your rock-climbing skills against the sheer granite face of Cathedral Ledge.

6 Peterborough (p333) Experiencing the creative energy of one of New England's oldest art colonies in this charming riverside town.

7 Kancamagus Highway (p349) Camping by a rushing river, surrounded by White Mountain grandeur.

8 Wolfeboro (p343) Settling into the soothing pace of lakeside living.

State Parks & Wildlife

The feather in New Hampshire's cap is the White Mountain National Forest, which covers nearly 800,000 acres in New Hampshire and Maine. Hiking trails, skiing slopes, campgrounds, swimming beaches and a few carefully controlled auto roads provide access to this gigantic natural playground.

Aside from the White Mountain National Forest, New Hampshire has a small but exceedingly well-run network of state parks, including Franconia Notch, Crawford Notch and Echo Lake, along with the entire seacoast.

ℹ Information

New Hampshire Division of Parks & Recreation (☑ 603-271-3556; www.nhstateparks. org) Offers information on New Hampshire's statewide bicycle-route system along with a very complete camping guide.

New Hampshire Division of Travel & Tourism Development (☑ 603-271-2665; www.visitnh. gov) The state tourism department provides fall foliage reports and info about ski conditions, among other things.

White Mountain National Forest (☑ 603-536-6100; www.fs.usda.gov/whitemountain) Ranger stations with information about trails and sites are scattered along major roadways throughout the national forest. Check the website for locations.

ℹ Getting There & Around

AIR

Manchester-Boston Regional Airport (☑ 603-624-6556; www.flymanchester.com) is the state's largest airport and offers direct flights to more than a dozen North American cities. The smaller **Lebanon Municipal Airport** (LEB; ☑ 603-298-8878; flyleb.com) and **Portsmouth International Airport** (www.flyportsmouthair port.com; 36 Airline Ave) serve Hanover and Portsmouth, respectively. The nearby **Portland International Jetport** (PWM; ☑ 207-874-8877; www.portlandjetport.org; 1001 Westbrook St), in Maine, is a major hub and offers additional flight options.

BUS

Concord Coach Lines (☑ 603-228-3300, 800-639-3317; www.concordcoachlines.com) operates a bus route to and from Boston's South Station and Logan International Airport, with stops in Manchester, Concord, Meredith, Conway, North Conway, Jackson, Pinkham Notch, Gorham and Berlin. Another route runs through North Woodstock/Lincoln, Franconia and Littleton.

Dartmouth Coach (☑ 603-448-2800, 800-637-0123; www.dartmouthcoach.com) offers services from Hanover, Lebanon and New London to Boston's South Station and Logan International Airport.

Vermont Translines (☑ 844-888-7267; www. vttranslines.com) runs buses from Hanover to central Vermont, with stops in Woodstock, Killington and Rutland.

CAR & MOTORCYCLE

The Blue Star (or New Hampshire) Turnpike along the seacoast, Everett (or Central) Turnpike (I-93) and Spaulding Turnpike (NH 16) are toll roads.

PORTSMOUTH & THE SEACOAST

New Hampshire's coastline stretches for just 18 miles but provides access to the captivating coastal town of Portsmouth and a length of attractive beaches, sprinkled around rocky headlands and coves. The shore along these parts has substantial commercial development, but also includes well-regulated access to its state beaches and parks.

Portsmouth

POP 21,440

Perched on the edge of the Piscataqua River, Portsmouth is one of New Hampshire's most elegant towns, with a historical center set with tree-lined streets and 18th-century colonial buildings. Despite its early importance in the maritime industry, the town has a youthful energy, with tourists and locals filling its many restaurants and cafes. Numerous museums and historic houses allow visitors a glimpse into the town's multilayered past, while its proximity to the coast brings both lobster feasts and periodic days of fog that blanket the waterfront.

Still true to its name, Portsmouth remains a working port town, and its economic vitality has been boosted by the Naval Shipyard (actually located across the river in Maine) and by the influx of high-tech companies.

◉ Sights

★**Strawbery Banke Museum**   MUSEUM
(☑ 603-433-1100; www.strawberybanke.org; 14 Hancock St; adult/child 5-17yr $20/10; ☺ 10am-5pm May-Oct) Spread across a 10-acre site, the Strawbery Banke Museum is an eclectic blend of period homes that date back to

the 1690s. Costumed guides recount tales that took place among the 40 buildings (10 furnished). Strawbery Banke includes **Pitt Tavern** (1766), a hotbed of American revolutionary sentiment, **Goodwin Mansion** (a grand 19th-century house from Portsmouth's most prosperous time) and **Abbott's Little Corner Store** (1943). The admission ticket is good for two consecutive days.

Market Square   SQUARE
(cnr Congress & Pleasant Sts) The heart of Portsmouth is this picturesque square, set neatly beneath the soaring white spire of the North Church. Within a few steps of the square are open-air cafes, colorful storefronts, and tiny galleries where banjo-playing buskers entertain the tourists and locals that drift past on warm summer nights.

Prescott Park   PARK
(www.cityofportsmouth.com/prescottpark; 105 Marcy St) Overlooking the Piscataqua River, this small, grassy park makes a pleasant setting for a picnic. More importantly, it's the leafy backdrop to the **Prescott Park Arts Festival** (www.prescottpark.org; ⊙ Jun–early Sep; 🖼️), which means free music, dance, theater and food festivals throughout June, July and August. Separate one-day music festivals showcase jazz, folk and Americana; other highlights include the clam-chowder and chili festivals.

John Paul Jones House   HISTORIC SITE
(📞 603-436-8420; www.portsmouthhistory.org/john-paul-jones-house; 43 Middle St; adult/child $6/free; ⊙ 11am-5pm May-Oct) This former boardinghouse is where America's first great naval commander resided in Portsmouth. Jones, who uttered, 'I have not yet begun to fight!' during a particularly bloody engagement with the British, is believed to have lodged here during the outfitting of the *Ranger* (1777) and the *America* (1781). The marvelous Georgian mansion with gambrel roof is now the headquarters of the Portsmouth Historical Society.

Wentworth Gardner House   HISTORIC SITE
(📞 603-436-4406; www.wentworthlear.org; 50 Mechanic St; adult/child $6/3; ⊙ 11am-4pm Thu-Mon Jun-Oct) This 1760 structure is one of the finest Georgian houses in the US. Elizabeth and Mark Hunking Wentworth were among Portsmouth's wealthiest and most prominent citizens, so no expense was spared in building this home, which was a wedding

gift for their son. Ticket price includes admission to the adjacent **Tobias Lear House** (📞 603-436-4406; www.wentworthlear.org; 50 Mechanic St; ⊙ 11am-4pm Thu-Mon Jun-Oct), a hip-roofed colonial residence that was home to the family of George Washington's private secretary.

Moffatt-Ladd House   HISTORIC SITE
(📞 603-436-7968; www.moffattladd.org; 154 Market St; adult/child $7/2.50, gardens $2; ⊙ 11am-5pm Mon-Sat, 1-5pm Sun Jun–mid-Oct) Originally built by an influential ship captain for his son, the Georgian Moffatt-Ladd House was later the home of General William Whipple, a signer of the Declaration of Independence. The 18th-century chestnut tree and the old-fashioned **gardens** behind the house are delightful.

Wentworth-Coolidge Mansion   HISTORIC SITE
(📞 603-436-6607; www.wentworthcoolidge.org; 375 Little Harbor Rd; guided tour $5; ⊙ 10am-4pm Wed-Sun late May-Aug, 10am-4pm Sat & Sun Sep–mid-Oct) This 42-room place south of the town center was home to New Hampshire's first royal governor and served as the colony's government center from 1741 to 1766. The lilacs on its grounds are descendants of the first lilacs planted in America, which were brought over from England by Governor Benning Wentworth.

Albacore Park   PARK, MUSEUM
Just north of the old town center, this park serves as a maritime museum and host to the **USS Albacore** (📞 603-436-3680; www.ussalbacore.org; 600 Market St; adult/child $7/3; ⊙ 9:30am-5pm Jun–mid-Oct, to 4pm Thu-Mon mid-Oct–May), a 205ft-long US Navy submarine, now open to the public. The *Albacore* was launched from the Portsmouth Naval Shipyard in 1953 and, with a crew of 55, it was piloted around the world for 19 years without firing a shot.

**Children's Museum
of New Hampshire**   MUSEUM
(📞 603-742-2002; www.childrens-museum.org; 6 Washington St, Dover; $10; ⊙ 10am-5pm Mon-Sat, noon-5pm Sun, closed Mon Sep-May; 🖼️) Just 12 miles north of Portsmouth, this children's museum teaches and entertains, with interactive exhibits like the Dino Detective (where kids can be a paleontologist for a day and excavate through mini digs) or climb into the Yellow Submarine (a simulated deep dive). The focus is on having fun while learning.

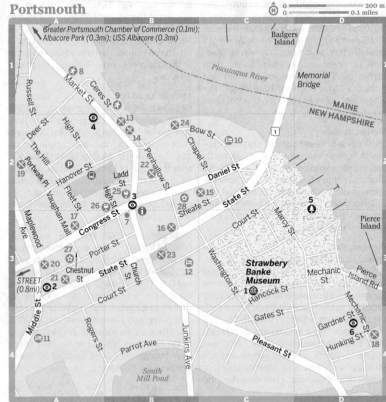

Portsmouth

Activities

Isles of Shoals Steamship Co CRUISE
(☑603-431-5500; www.islesofshoals.com; 315 Market St; adult/child from $28/18; ☝) From mid-June to October this company runs an excellent tour of the harbor and the historic Isles of Shoals aboard a replica 1900s ferry. It also offers walking tours of Star Island and party cruises featuring DJs or live bands.

Portsmouth Kayak Adventures KAYAKING
(☑603-559-1000; www.portsmouthkayak.com; 185 Wentworth Rd; tours $45-75, 3hr/half-day/full-day kayak rental $35/45/64; ☺9am-5pm) This outfitter offers a range of peaceful kayaking tours out on the harbors near Portsmouth, including a naturalist-led ecotour of Great Bay (the East Coast's second-largest estuary), sunset and full-moon tours, and a combined kayaking/yoga-on-the-beach experience. It also rents out kayaks and stand up paddleboards.

Portsmouth Harbor Cruises CRUISE
(☑800-776-0915, 603-436-8084; www.portsmouthharbor.com; 64 Ceres St; adult $14-24, child $10-17; ☺early May-late Oct) Daytime cruises on the *Heritage* explore Portsmouth harbor or the Isles of Shoals, a group of nine islands 6 miles offshore. Other options include wine and sunset cruises, and the Inland River Cruise, which heads inland through pretty tidal estuaries during the colorful fall foliage season.

Tours

In summer, choose from a variety of excellent guided walking tours of Portsmouth's historic downtown.

Harbor Trail WALKING
(☑603-436-3988; Market Sq; adult/child/teen $15/7/12; ☺1pm Thu & Sat late Jun-early Oct) This guided walking tour of the historic downtown and waterfront takes you past nine houses listed in the national register of his-

Portsmouth

toric buildings, including the Moffat-Ladd House (where a signer of the Declaration of Independence lived) and the Warner House, one of the few remaining brick mansions in the downtown area.

Portsmouth Black Heritage Trail WALKING
(☑603-436-8433; www.portsmouthhistory.org/ portsmouth-black-heritage-trail/self-guided-tour; guided tour $20; ⊙tours 2pm Sat May-early Sep) Established by dedicated volunteers in 1995, this historic trail links a series of sites connected with the African American experience in Portsmouth. Twenty-four bronze plaques commemorate nearly four centuries of black history, from the arrival of the first enslaved

people at Portsmouth's Prescott Park wharf in the 1680s to the formation of the local civil rights group Scorr in the 1960s.

Discover Portsmouth Walking Tour WALKING
(☑603-436-8433; www.portsmouthhistory.org/ take-a-tour; tour $12; ⊙10am) Sponsored by the Portsmouth Historical Society, these daily 60-minute walking tours explore the history and architecture of downtown Portsmouth.

New England Curiosities WALKING
(☑800-979-3370; www.newenglandcuriosities. com; tours $15-20) New England Curiosities runs a variety of walking tours, including its trademark 'Legends and Ghosts' tour, visiting old graveyards, an abandoned prison, the 'haunted' pubs of Portsmouth, and other locales where history and mystery collide. Call or check the website for meeting places and times.

🛌 Sleeping

Portsmouth is expensive in season. Oodles of cheaper (but less atmospheric) motels and hotels cluster at I-95 exits 5 and 6, around the Portsmouth (Interstate) traffic circle.

Inn at Strawbery Banke B&B $$
(☑603-436-7242; www.innatstrawberybanke.com; 314 Court St; r incl breakfast $125-190; ℗ 🖈) Set amid the historic buildings of Strawbery Banke, this colonial charmer has seven small but attractive rooms, each uniquely set with quilted bedspreads and brass or canopy beds.

⭐**Ale House Inn** INN $$$
(☑603-431-7760; www.alehouseinn.com; 121 Bow St; r $199-369; ℗ ❄ 🖈) This former brick warehouse for the Portsmouth Brewing Company is now Portsmouth's snazziest boutique, fusing contemporary design with comfort. Rooms are modern, with clean lines of white, flat-screen TVs and, in the suites, plush tan sofas. Deluxe rooms feature an in-room iPad. Rates include use of vintage cruising bikes.

Hotel Portsmouth INN $$$
(☑603-433-1200; www.thehotelportsmouth.com; 40 Court St; r $129-279, ste $199-359; ℗ @ 🖈) A short walk from the town center, this elegant, Queen Anne–style inn dates from 1881 and has beautiful common areas with original wood details and antiques. Its 28 large, carpeted rooms and six suites have period furnishings coupled with modern comforts; some of the larger suites have Jacuzzis.

✗ Eating

Portsmouth is a terrific foodie destination, serving up everything from lobster rolls to international street food, from quality vegetarian fare to nouvelle New England cuisine.

Moxy
TAPAS $

(☑603-319-8178; www.moxyrestaurant.com; 106 Penhallow St; tapas $8-14; ⊙5-9pm Sun-Thu, to 10pm Fri & Sat) Toto, I have a feeling we're not in Spain anymore! Yes, this cool little corner eatery specializes in *tapas* (small plates), but with a decidedly American twist. Expect anything from mini-burgers, baked beans and chili-pepper cornbread to fried clams, oysters, calamari and scallops, accompanied by excellent martinis in a cozy candlelit interior enlivened with yellow-and-olive decor and green-brick walls.

STREET
INTERNATIONAL $

(☑603-436-0860; www.streetfood360.com; 801 Islington St; mains $6-14; ⊙11:30am-9pm Mon-Sat, 10am-3pm & 4-9pm Sun) Seeking an alternative to Portsmouth's tourist-focused downtown? Head 1 mile west to this trendy international street-food haven. Locals throng industrial-chic tables and barstools in the cavernous, brightly painted interior, noshing on Asian noodles and dumplings, burgers, falafel, empanadas and key-lime tarts. The drinks menu is equally eclectic, with Thai iced tea, black cherry soda, ginger beer and local microbrews.

Colby's
BREAKFAST $

(☑603-436-3033; 105 Daniel St; mains $4-13; ⊙7am-2pm) If you get to this 28-seat eatery after 8am on the weekend, there's going to be a wait, so give 'em your name and enjoy a cup of free coffee on the patio. Once in, egg lovers can choose from a multitude of

Benedicts and omelets, along with French toast, pancakes, huevos rancheros and daily chalkboard specials.

Friendly Toast
DINER $

(☑603-430-2154; www.thefriendlytoast.com; 113 Congress St; breakfast $7-18, lunch $9-19; ⊙7am-8pm Sun-Wed, to 9pm Thu, to 2am Fri & Sat; 🛜 ☑) Fun, whimsical furnishings set the scene for filling sandwiches, omelets, Tex-Mex and vegetarian fare at this retro diner. The breakfast menu is huge and is served around the clock: good thing since weekend morning waits can be long.

Savario's
PIZZA $

(☑603-427-2919; www.facebook.com/Savarios Pizza; 238 State St; slices/calzones $1.50/3.75; ⊙11am-2pm Mon-Fri, 5-8pm Thu-Sun) Family-run for the past quarter-century, this tiny, friendly takeout pizza shop offers the cheapest lunch in town, and remains something of a Portsmouth secret – despite winning 'best in town' awards for its homemade pies and calzones.

Cure
MODERN AMERICAN $$

(☑603-427-8258; www.curerestaurantportsmouth. com; 189 State St; mains $16-34; ⊙5-9pm Sun-Thu, to 10pm Fri & Sat) Showered with accolades since opening in 2014, chef Julie Cutting's refined but cozy brick-walled restaurant makes a romantic dinner spot. The menu revolves around New England cuisine 'revisited': crispy-skinned duck breast, grilled herb-marinated lamb, beef ribs slow-braised in red wine, horseradish–sour cream mashed potatoes, crab cakes and lobster bisque, all accompanied by seasonal vegetables and a superb cocktail list.

Green Elephant
VEGETARIAN $$

(☑603-427-8344; www.greenelephantnh.com; 35 Portwalk Pl; mains $11-15; ⊙11:30am-9:30pm Sun-Wed, to 10pm Thu-Sat; ☑) Vegetarians rejoice! In 2015 the wildly popular Green Elephant bistro of Portland, ME, opened its first New Hampshire franchise in Portsmouth. The Chinese-, Malaysian- and Thai-inspired menu of curries, noodles, rice dishes and stir-fries is 100% meat-free, with plenty of steamed veggies and a plethora of vegan and gluten-free options.

Geno's
SEAFOOD $$

(☑603-427-2070; www.genoschowder.com; 177 Mechanic St; mains $7-17; ⊙11am-4pm Mon-Sat mid-Mar–Oct) For more than 40 years, this family-owned no-frills place has been a local institution for homemade chowder and lobster rolls. Its outdoor deck overlooks Portsmouth Harbor.

Surf
SEAFOOD $$

(☑603-334-9855; www.surfseafood.com; 99 Bow St; lunch $9-18, dinner $12-38; ⊙4-9pm Tue & Wed, 11am-9pm Thu & Sun, 11am-10pm Fri & Sat) We're not sure if the view of the Pisquataqua River complements the food or the food complements the view, especially at sunset at this airy restaurant. Either way, both are a satisfying way to close out the day. The seafood offerings sport some global flair, with shrimp and avocado quesadillas, haddock crepes, and shrimp vindaloo with curry sauce.

★Black Trumpet Bistro
INTERNATIONAL $$$

(☑603-431-0887; www.blacktrumpetbistro.com; 29 Ceres St; mains $21-32; ⊙5:30-9pm) With brick walls and a sophisticated ambience, this bistro serves unique combinations – anything from housemade sausages infused with cocoa beans to seared haddock with *yuzu* (an Asian citrus fruit) and miso. The full menu is also available at its wine bar upstairs, which whips up equally inventive cocktails.

Library
STEAK $$$

(☑603-431-5202; www.libraryrestaurant.com; 401 State St; mains $16-38; ⊙11:30am-9:30pm Sun-Thu, to 10:30pm Fri & Sat) In a palatial and opulent home built by a prominent judge in 1785, the Library is among New Hampshire's top steakhouses, serving juicy prime rib and rack of lamb in a dapper wood-paneled dining room.

Jumpin' Jays Fish Cafe
SEAFOOD $$$

(☑603-766-3474; www.jumpinjays.com; 150 Congress St; mains $22-31; ⊙5-9pm Sun-Thu, to 10pm Fri & Sat) This exceptional seafood cafe offers fresh catches of the day simply grilled or seared, plus unconventional twists like bouillabaisse with lemongrass and coconut or haddock Piccata (whitefish sliced and sauteed in butter, olive oil and white wine). Add a raw bar, a huge warm and cold appetizer menu, plus a buzzing modern space, and Jumpin' Jays wins on all counts.

🍸 Drinking & Nightlife

Portsmouth's drinking and nightlife scene includes a vibrant mix of cafes, brewpubs, bars and live entertainment venues, most of them clustered within a few blocks of Market Sq.

Thirsty Moose Taphouse
PUB

(www.thirstymoosetaphouse.com; 21 Congress St; ⊙11:30am-1am Mon-Sat, from 10:30am Sun) This convivial spot has more than 100 beers on tap – leaning heavily toward New England brews – and a knowledgeable staff that can walk you through them. Bites include *poutine* (a Montreal fave: fries drenched in cheese and gravy), corn dogs and a handful of salads. Downstairs in the Moose Lounge you'll find live music on weekends plus Wednesday karaoke nights.

Portsmouth Brewery
MICROBREWERY

(☑603-431-1115; www.portsmouthbrewery.com; 56 Market St; ⊙11:30am-12:30am; 🐟) Classically set with tin ceilings and exposed-brick walls, this airy brewpub serves excellent homegrown pilsners, porters and ales. Come for the beer, not for the pub fare.

☆ Entertainment

★Music Hall
PERFORMING ARTS

(☑603-436-2400; www.themusichall.org; 28 Chestnut St) For a small-town theater, this venue hosts a surprising array of performances, including dance, theater, opera and other music. Musicians, comedians and theater companies from around the country make appearances here.

Press Room
LIVE MUSIC

(☑603-431-5186; www.pressroomnh.com; 77 Daniel St; ⊙4pm-1am Sun-Thu, noon-1am Fri & Sat) Between the nightly live music (jazz to blues to folk, from 6pm to 9pm), the tasty pub fare and the wooden booths, this is one of Portsmouth's best watering holes.

Seacoast Repertory Theater
THEATER

(☑603-433-4472; www.seacoastrep.org; 125 Bow St) This theater is housed in a cool, converted building on Portsmouth's industrial riverfront and stages numerous musicals, plus the occasional comedian.

ℹ Information

Greater Portsmouth Chamber of Commerce (☑603-610-5510; www.portsmouthchamber. org; 500 Market St; ⊙9am-5pm Mon-Fri year-round, plus 10am-4pm Sat & Sun late May–mid-Oct) Also operates an information kiosk (Market Sq; ⊙10am-5pm late May–mid-Oct) in the city center at Market Sq.

ℹ Getting There & Away

AIR

In 2013 **Allegiant Air** (☑702-505-8888; www. allegiantair.com) launched commercial flights to Orlando and other Florida destinations from Portsmouth International Airport (p324), 5 miles west of downtown.

BUS

Greyhound (www.greyhound.com) runs one to two buses daily to Boston (from $10, 1¼ hours), Portland (from $9, one hour) and Bangor, ME

NEW HAMPSHIRE PORTSMOUTH

EXETER & INDEPENDENCE DAY

Exeter, founded 1638, is utterly quiet on the Fourth of July. But on the second Saturday after the 4th, this small town celebrates Independence Day two weeks after the rest of the country. The spirited American Independence Festival brings out the whole town (seemingly) dressed up in Colonial garb. The procession, led by George Washington, and the reading of the Declaration of Independence take center stage. But there are loads of other events, from Colonial cooking to militia drills to gunpowder races. Add fireworks and a night of rock and roll and you'll be reminded that re-enactments are fun.

The town's specially designated meetinghouse, unique in these parts, played a crucial role in 1774, when British governor John Wentworth dissolved the provincial assembly that met in Portsmouth in an attempt to prevent the election of a continental congress. The revolutionary councils then began to gather at the meetinghouse in Exeter, which effectively became the seat of government.

Exeter's early history is best viewed at the American Independence Museum (☑ 603-772-2622; www.independencemuseum.org; 1 Governor's Lane, Exeter; adult/child $6/3; ☺ 10am-4pm Tue-Sat May–Nov). Among the highlights of this National Landmark Property are the furnishings and possessions of the Gilman family, who lived here from 1720 to 1820, along with a document archive, including two original drafts of the US Constitution and personal correspondence of George Washington.

To reach Exeter, take I-95 to exit 2, then NH 101 west. Turn left on Portsmouth Ave/NH 10 and right on Water St.

(from $23, 4½ hours). Buses stop in front of Mainely Gourmet at 55 Hanover St.

C&J Trailways (☑ 603-430-1100; www.ridecj.com; 185 Grafton Dr) offers more frequent service to Boston from its office 5 miles west of downtown Portsmouth (off NH 33). Hourly buses run to Boston's South Station ($17, 1¾ hours) and Logan International Airport ($23, 1¼ hours). C&J also runs two to three daily buses to New York City's Port Authority bus terminal ($80, five hours).

CAR & MOTORCYCLE

Portsmouth is equidistant (57 miles) from Boston and Portland, ME. It takes roughly 1¼ hours to reach Portland and 1½ hours to Boston, both via I-95. Rush-hour and high-season traffic can easily double or triple this, however.

Hampton Beach & Around

POP 14,980

Littered with summer clam shacks, motels, fried-dough stands and arcades full of children, Hampton Beach isn't the classiest stretch of New England coastline, but it has New Hampshire's only sandy beach – a wide, inviting stretch of shore that gives pasty sun-seekers their fix. North of Hampton Beach, the tacky beach fun transitions into rolling greenswards and serpentine private drives in Rye, where oceanfront mansions and sprawling 'summer cottages' show a different side of the coastline.

◉ Sights

Rye Beaches BEACH
(🏊) As NH 1A enters Rye, parking along the road is restricted to vehicles with town parking stickers, but Jenness State Beach has a small metered parking lot that's open to the general public. Further north near Rye Harbor you're allowed to park along the roadway. Climb over the seawall of rubble and rocks to get to the gravel beach. It lacks facilities but is much less crowded than anything further south. Continuing northward, Wallis Sands State Beach has a wide sandy beach with views of the Isles of Shoals. Besides the bathhouses, there are grassy lawns for children's games, making this the top spot for families with smaller kids.

Hampton Beach State Park BEACH, PARK
(☑ 603-926-8990; www.nhstateparks.org; 160 Ocean Blvd; per vehicle $15) The beach actually begins south of the state line, on the north bank of the Merrimack River at Salisbury Beach State Reservation in Massachusetts. Take I-95 exit 56 (MA 1A) and head east to Salisbury Beach, then north along NH 1A to Hampton Beach State Park, a long stretch of sand shielded by dunes. Facilities include a promenade, bathhouses and a band shell with an amphitheater.

Seacoast Science Center SCIENCE CENTER
(☑ 603-436-8043; www.seacoastsciencecenter.org; 570 Ocean Blvd, Rye; adult/child $10/5;

⊙10am-5pm daily Mar-Oct, closed Tue-Fri Nov-Feb) Undersea videos, huge aquariums and a hands-on 'touch tank' are the highlights of this family favorite. The center hosts lots of special activities, such as trail walks, lighthouse tours and concerts.

🛏 Sleeping

Hampton Beach and – to a lesser degree – Rye have no shortage of roadside motels, scattered along NH 1A. Wherever you stay, you'll need reservations in the summer months.

🍴 Eating

All of New England's classic summer beach treats – from fried clams to soft-serve ice cream – are readily available along the waterfront.

ⓘ Information

Hampton Beach Area Chamber of Commerce (☑603-926-8717; www.hampton beach.org; 160 Ocean Blvd, Hampton Beach; ⊙10am-5pm) Offers information on tourist attractions.

ⓘ Getting There & Away

Hampton Beach is easily reached via I-95 from Portsmouth (15 miles), Boston (47 miles) and Portland, ME (66 miles). Take exit 1 if coming from the south, exit 2 if coming from the north.

MERRIMACK VALLEY

Although New Hampshire is noted more for mountains than for cities, Concord (the state's tidy capital) and Manchester (its largest city) are pleasant – if not overly exotic – places to spend a day. Both sit along the mighty Merrimack River.

Concord

POP 42,400

New Hampshire's capital is a trim and tidy city with a wide Main St dominated by the striking State House, a granite-hewed 19th-century edifice topped with a glittering dome. The stone of choice in 'the granite state' appears in other fine buildings about Concord's historical center, cut from the still-active quarries on Rattlesnake Hill, just north of town. Concord is worth an afternoon visit and also makes a good base for visiting the idyllic Canterbury Shaker village.

⊙ Sights

State House   HISTORIC BUILDING
(☑603-271-2154; www.gencourt.state.nh.us; 107 N Main St; ⊙8am-4pm Mon-Fri) **FREE** The handsome 1819 New Hampshire state capitol is the oldest such building in the US, and the state legislature still meets in the original chambers. Self-guided tour brochures point out the highlights of the building and its grounds, including the **Memorial Arch**, which commemorates those who served in the nation's wars. The capitol building's **Hall of Flags** holds 103 flags that New Hampshire military units carried into battle in various wars, including the Civil and Vietnam Wars.

McAuliffe-Shepard
Discovery Center   MUSEUM
(☑603-271-7827; www.starhop.com; 2 Institute Dr; adult/child 3-12yr $10/7; ⊙10:30am-4pm daily mid-Jun–early Sep, Fri-Sun rest of year) This science center is named after and dedicated to two New Hampshire astronauts. Christa McAuliffe was the schoolteacher chosen to be America's first teacher-astronaut – she and her fellow astronauts died in the tragic explosion of the *Challenger* spacecraft in 1986 – and Alan B Shepard was a member

---

WORTH A TRIP

CANTERBURY SHAKER VILLAGE

A traditional Shaker community from 1792, **Canterbury Shaker Village** (☑603-783-9511; www.shakers.org; 288 Shaker Rd, Canterbury; adult/child $17/8; ⊙10am-5pm mid-May–late Oct) maintains the Shaker heritage as a living-history museum. Interpreters demonstrate the Shakers' daily lives, artisans create Shaker crafts and walking trails invite pond-side strolls. The greening of America has deep roots here – for more than two centuries the Shakers' abundant gardens have been turning out vegetables, medicinal herbs and bountiful flowers the organic way.

The village is 15 miles north of Concord; take I-93 to exit 18 and follow the signs.

WORTH A TRIP

LAKE SUNAPEE

Lake Sunapee is a worthwhile detour any time of year, but especially in summer when you can enjoy the wide sandy beach and pleasant grassy lawns of **Mount Sunapee State Park** (603-763-5561; www.nhstateparks.org; 86 Beach Access Rd, Newbury; adult/child $5/2; ⊙9am-6pm late May–mid-Sep, Sat & Sun first 3 weeks of May) for hiking, picnicking, swimming and fishing. Canoes and kayaks are available for rental. From I-89 take exit 9, NH 103 to Newbury.

of NASA's elite *Mercury* corps and became America's first astronaut in 1961. Exhibits chronicle the life and story of these two icons.

🛏 Sleeping & Eating

The Centennial   HISTORIC HOTEL **$$**
(800-360-4839, 603-227-9000; www.thecentennialhotel.com; 96 Pleasant St; r $169-209, ste $229-249; P 🛜) This turn-of-the-20th-century turreted Victorian landmark has 32 luxurious rooms and suites. Stylish minimalism prevails, with subdued earth tones, deluxe bedding, trim furnishings, black-and-white artwork, and vessel-bowl sinks in the granite bathrooms. Several rooms are set in the turret, while the best have private outdoor porches. The hotel and its fine-dining, New American restaurant, the **Granite** (603-227-9005; www.graniterestaurant.com; 96 Pleasant St; lunch mains $10-18, dinner mains $16-34; ⊙7-10am, 11:30am-2:30pm & 5-9pm Mon-Thu, to 10pm Fri & Sat, 10:30am-2:30pm & 5-8pm Sun) are popular with business travelers.

ℹ Information

Greater Concord Chamber of Commerce (603-224-2508; www.concordnhchamber.com; 49 S Main St, Suite 104; ⊙8:30am-5pm Mon-Fri) Provides tourist information.

ℹ Getting There & Away

BUS
Concord Coach Lines (800-639-3317, 603-228-3300; www.concordcoachlines.com; 30 Stickney Ave) operates frequent daily buses from the Concord Transportation Center to Boston's South Station ($16, 1½ hours) and Logan International Airport ($21, 1¾ hours).

CAR & MOTORCYCLE
Concord is 68 miles north of Boston on I-93.

Manchester

POP 110,000

Once home to the world's largest textile mill – at its peak, the Amoskeag Manufacturing Company employed 17,000 people (out of a city population of 70,000) – this riverside town retains, both historically and culturally, a bit of its blue-collar roots. Exploiting the abundant water power of the Merrimack River, and stretching along its east bank for over a mile, the mill made the city into a manufacturing and commercial powerhouse from 1838 until its bankruptcy in the 1930s.

Nowadays, attracted by low taxes and a diverse workforce, the high-tech and financial industries have moved in, bringing city culture with them. The former mill is a prime symbol of successful redevelopment: the redbrick swath of structures houses a museum, an arts center, a college, restaurants and a growing array of local businesses. Manchester has opera, several orchestras, a growing gallery and dining scene, and the state's most important art museum.

◉ Sights

Currier Museum of Art   MUSEUM
(603-669-6144; www.currier.org; 150 Ash St; adult/child $12/5, incl Zimmerman House tour $20/8; ⊙11am-5pm Wed-Mon) Housing works by John Singer Sargent, Georgia O'Keeffe, Monet, Matisse and Picasso (among many others), this fine-arts museum is Manchester's greatest cultural gem. With advance reservation, museum guides also offer tours of the nearby Zimmerman House, the only Frank Lloyd Wright–designed house in New England that's open to the public.

Amoskeag Millyard Historic District   HISTORIC SITE
These former textile mills, impressive brick buildings with hundreds of tall windows, stretch along Commercial St on the Merrimack riverbank for almost 1.5 miles. Other mills face the buildings from across the river in West Manchester.

🛏 Sleeping

Despite being New Hampshire's largest metropolis, Manchester offers surprisingly uninspiring accommodations. Beyond the city's two B&Bs, big chain hotels are the norm.

Ash Street Inn   B&B **$$**
(603-668-9908; www.ashstreetinn.com; 118 Ash St; r $169-229; ❀🛜) Dating to 1885, this Victorian home has been thoughtfully renovat-

ed into a comfortable B&B. Rooms all come with top-of-the line sheets and towels, plush robes, high-speed internet and good lighting for business travelers who need to get a little work done. It's just a one-minute walk from Manchester's Currier Museum of Art.

❶ Getting There & Away

AIR

Fast growing but still not too large, Manchester-Boston Regional Airport (p324), off US 3 south of Manchester, is a civilized alternative to Boston's Logan International Airport.

BUS

Concord Coach Lines (p324) runs frequent daily buses to Logan International Airport ($18, 1½ hours) and South Station ($14, one hour) in Boston, as well as north to Concord ($5, 30 minutes). Buses depart from the Manchester Transportation Center.

CAR & MOTORCYCLE

Driving from Boston to Manchester via I-93 and the Everett Turnpike takes an hour. It's another 30 minutes from Manchester to Concord via I-93.

MONADNOCK REGION

In the southwestern corner of the state the pristine villages of Peterborough and Jaffrey Center anchor Mt Monadnock (moh-*nahd*-nock; 3165ft). 'Mountain That Stands Alone' in Algonquian, Monadnock is relatively isolated from other peaks, which means hikers to the summit are rewarded with fantastic views of the surrounding countryside. The trail, however, is anything but lonely. Monadnock is one of the most climbed mountains in the world.

Peterborough & Around

POP 6280

Picturesque Peterborough is a charming village of redbrick houses and tree-lined streets, with the idyllic Nabanusit River coursing through its historic center. Nestled between Temple Mountain and Mt Monadnock, Peterborough is a gateway to some captivating countryside, and its restaurants and B&Bs draw plenty of visitors in their own right.

Peterborough is also a thriving arts community, an impression left deeply by the nearby MacDowell Colony (www.macdowellcolony. org). Founded in the early 1900s, the country's oldest art colony has attracted a diverse and dynamic group of poets, composers, playwrights, architects, filmmakers, painters and photographers. Aaron Copland composed parts of *Appalachian Spring* at the colony; Virgil Thomson worked on *Mother of Us All;* Leonard Bernstein completed his Mass; and Thornton Wilder wrote *Our Town,* a play that was openly inspired by Peterborough. Milton Avery, James Baldwin, Barbara Tuchman and Alice Walker are among the luminaries that have passed this way.

◎ Sights

Mariposa Museum MUSEUM
(☑603-924-4555; www.mariposamuseum.org; 26 Main St, Peterborough; adult/child $6/4; ◎11am-5pm Tue-Sun; ⊞) This museum, which exhibits folk art and folklore from around the world, implores visitors to 'please touch.' It's a wonderful place for kids, who are invited to dive into the collections to try on costumes, experiment with musical instruments, play with toys and make their own art. Periodic performances feature musicians and storytellers who lead interactive performances.

Sharon Arts Center GALLERY
(☑603-836-2585; www.sharonarts.org; 30 Grove St, Peterborough; ◎10am-6pm Mon-Sat year-round, plus 11am-4pm Sun Jun-Dec) **FREE** This arts center consists of two parts: a fine-art exhibition space with a rotating array of paintings and crafts by some of the region's many artists, and a gallery-shop selling art, jewelry and pottery made by local artisans. There's a second entrance at 20-40 Depot St.

Miller State Park STATE PARK
(☑603-924-3672; www.nhstateparks.org; 13 Miller Park Rd, Peterborough; adult/child $4/2; ◎9am-5pm late May-Oct, limited access Nov-late May) New Hampshire's oldest state park, Miller revolves around Pack Monadnock, a 2290ft peak not to be confused with its better-known neighbor, Mt Monadnock. The park has three easy-to-moderate paths to the summit; you can also access the 21-mile Wapack Trail here. Miller State Park is about 4.5 miles east of Peterborough along NH 101. A self-service pay box (where you can pay the park fee by putting money in the slot) exists for days and times outside the standard hours.

🛏 Sleeping

Peterborough has a motel and a couple of B&Bs in the downtown area, with additional inns and a campground in the surrounding countryside.

WORTH A TRIP

CULINARY DETOUR: WALPOLE

Locals descend from surrounding villages to dine at the fabulous **Burdick Chocolate** (📞603-756-2882; www.burdickchocolate.com/chocolateshop-cafe-walpole.aspx; 47 Main St, Walpole; pastries from $5; ⏰7am-5pm Mon, to 8pm Tue-Thu, to 9pm Fri & Sat, 9am-5pm Sun). Originally a New York City chocolatier, Burdick relocated to this tiny gem of a New Hampshire village and opened a sophisticated cafe to showcase its desserts. Complementing these rich chocolaty indulgences, the adjacent **Restaurant at Burdick's** (📞603-756-9058; www.47mainwalpole.com/the-restaurant.html; 47 Main St, Walpole; mains $15-24; ⏰11:30am-2:30pm & 5:30-9pm Tue-Sat, 10am-2pm Sun) has a bistro-style menu of French-themed dishes, plus artisanal cheeses and top-notch wines.

Greenfield State Park   CAMPGROUND $
(📞park office 603-547-3497, reservations 603-271-3628; www.nhsstateparks.org; 133 Beach Rd, Greenfield; tent sites $25; ⏰May–Oct) Eight miles northeast of Peterborough, off NH 136, this 400-acre park has over 250 pine-shaded campsites. There's fine swimming and hiking, as well as canoe and kayak rental.

Little River Bed & Breakfast   B&B $$
(📞603-924-3280; www.littleriverbedandbreakfast.com; 184 Union St, Peterborough; r $119-149; 🛜) One mile west of the village center on the gorgeous Nubanusit River, this 19th-century farmhouse once served as housing for artists at the nearby MacDowell Colony. Innkeepers Paula and Rob Fox have converted it into a cozy B&B with four immaculate guest rooms and tasty breakfasts featuring homemade granola and muffins.

Hancock Inn   INN $$$
(📞603-525-3318, 800-525-1789; www.hancockinn.com; 33 Main St, Hancock; r incl breakfast $178-395; 🛜) New Hampshire's oldest inn has 15 rooms, each with its own unique charms. Room prices vary according to size and features: some of the coolest include dome ceilings (in rooms that used to be part of a ballroom), fireplaces and private patios. The cozy dining room is open to the public for dinner nightly.

🍴 Eating & Drinking

Nonie's   CAFE $
(📞603-924-3451; 28 Grove St, Peterborough; mains $6-12; ⏰6am-2pm Mon-Sat, 7am-1pm Sun) A long-time Peterborough favorite, Nonie's serves excellent breakfasts as well as fresh bakery items. In the summer grab a table in the tiny front garden.

Waterhouse   MODERN AMERICAN $$
(📞603-924-4001; www.waterhousenh.com; 18 Depot St, Peterborough; mains $12-25; ⏰11:30am-9pm Mon-Sat, to 2:30pm Sun; 📶) For riverside charm, step into Waterhouse's bright wood-floored dining room and grab a table beside the floor-to-ceiling windows directly overlooking the rushing Nabanusit. The lunch menu abounds in revisited American classics like BLTs, fish and chips, burgers and tuna melts, while dinner offerings expand to include steak and seafood.

Harlow's Pub   PUB
(📞603-924-6365; www.harlowspub.com; 3 School St, Peterborough; ⏰11:30am-10pm Tue, to 11pm Wed & Thu, to 1am Fri & Sat, to 9pm Sun, 4-10pm Mon) This local pub has a good selection of draft beers, including New England brews. It also serves Mexican and pub fare until 9pm, but the real reason to come here is for the convivial wooden bar and to catch live music Friday and Saturday nights.

⭐ Entertainment

Peterborough Folk Music Society   LIVE MUSIC
(📞603-827-2905; www.pfmsconcerts.org; Peterborough Players, 55 Hadley Rd, Peterborough; tickets $20-28) This active group attracts nationally known folk musicians to perform in a wonderful barn-style theater about 3.5 miles from Peterborough center. Recent shows have included the Jonathan Edwards Trio and renowned New Hampshire singer-songwriter Tom Rush.

ℹ Information

Greater Peterborough Chamber of Commerce (📞603-924-7234; www.peterboroughchamber.com; 10 Wilton Rd/NH 101, Peterborough; ⏰9am-5pm Mon-Fri year-round, 10am-2pm Sat Jun–mid-Sep)

ℹ Getting There & Away

Peterborough is at the intersection of US 202 and NH 101 (roughly one hour southwest of Concord and 15 minutes' drive northeast of Jaffrey Center). No public transportation is available.

Jaffrey & Jaffrey Center

POP 5457

Two miles due west of bigger, less-interesting Jaffrey, Jaffrey Center is a tiny, picture-perfect village of serene lanes, 18th-century homes and a dramatic white-steepled meetinghouse.

All of Jaffrey Center's sights are clustered around the village's wee historic district, located on both sides of Gilmore Pond Rd off NH 124. The most intriguing sights include the frozen-in-time Little Red School House and the Melville Academy, which houses a one-room museum of rural artifacts. Both are open from 2pm to 4pm on weekends in summer. For a deeper look at local history, wander the Old Burying Ground behind the meetinghouse. Willa Cather, a frequent visitor who wrote portions of her novels in Jaffrey (including *My Ántonia* and *One of Ours*), is buried here (a quotation from *My Ántonia* graces her tombstone). Jaffrey Town Green often hosts free concerts on Wednesday nights in July and August.

Sleeping & Eating

In Jaffrey Center, the Monadnock Inn's restaurant (Thorndike's) serves dinner five nights a week. Alternatively, head into Jaffrey (2 miles) or Peterborough (8 miles).

Monadnock Inn INN $$
(603-532-7800; www.monadnockinn.com; 379 Main St, Jaffrey Center; r incl breakfast $110-160;) Just down the road from Mt Monadnock State Park, this 11-room family-run inn has been welcoming guests for over 100 years. Rooms have a quirky, old-fashioned vibe, each with its own unique color scheme and decorative style. Beautifully maintained grounds and wide porches grace the home's exterior. The on-site Thorndike's Restaurant (mains $19 to $29) serves bistro fare.

The adjacent Parson's Pub tavern is a fun spot for a post-hike brew, accompanied by burgers or fish and chips ($9 to $12).

Sunflowers CAFE $$
(603-593-3303; www.sunflowerscatering.com; 21 Main St, Jaffrey; breakfast & lunch mains $5-14, dinner mains $12-28; 7-10:30am, 11am-2pm & 5-8pm Mon & Wed-Sat, 9am-3pm Sun) In the heart of Jaffrey, this cozy cafe with its cheerful blue and yellow facade is the perfect place to greet the day with cinnamon rolls, scones, quiches and omelets. It's just as tempting later in the day for creative salads, baked haddock dinners, steaks and gourmet mac 'n' cheese.

Kimball Farm ICE CREAM, SEAFOOD $$
(603-532-5765; www.kimballfarm.com/jaffrey; 158 Turnpike Rd/NH 124, Jaffrey; mains $6-29; 11am-10pm May-Oct) This dairy has achieved more than local fame for its sinfully creamy ice cream that comes in 40 flavors and unbelievable portion sizes – it's the perfect reward after a hike up nearby Mt Monadnock. It also serves excellent sandwiches and fried seafood, but those in the know get the famous lobster rolls.

Information

Jaffrey Chamber of Commerce (603-532-4549; www.jaffreychamber.com; 7 Main St, Jaffrey; 10am-4pm Mon-Fri) Pick up a walking-tour brochure here.

Getting There & Away

Jaffrey is at the intersection of US 202 and NH 124, while quaint Jaffrey Center is 2 miles west on NH 124. No public transportation is available.

Mt Monadnock State Park

Visible from 50 miles away in any direction, this commanding 3165ft peak is southwestern New Hampshire's spiritual vortex. The surrounding state park is an outdoor wonderland, complete with a visitor center, 12 miles of ungroomed cross-country ski trails and over 40 miles of hiking trails, 6 miles of which reach the summit.

Activities

Mt Monadnock OUTDOORS
(603-532-8862; www.nhstateparks.org; 116 Poole Rd, Jaffrey; adult/child 6-11yr $4/2) Majestic Mt Monadnock (3165ft) is the centerpiece of this popular state park between Keene and Jaffrey. Stop at the visitor center for hiking information, then set off on a scenic loop to the bare-topped summit via the White Dot and White Cross Trails (about 3½ hours round-trip). If you want to stay overnight, there's camping on-site at Gilson Pond Campground (603-532-2416; reservations 877-647-2757; 585 Dublin Rd/NH 124; tent sites $25; May-Oct).

Getting There & Away

Look for the marked park turnoff along NH 124, half a mile west of Jaffrey Center and 16 miles east of Keene. From here, it's 2 miles into the park via Dublin Rd and Poole Rd.

Keene

POP 23,400

This charming settlement of historic homes and manicured streets is a superb base for those wishing to explore the Monadnock region while staying in a classic New England town with a strong community feel.

Keene's pleasant but lively Main St is lined with oodles of non-chain shops and cozy cafes and restaurants. The street is crowned by a small, tree-filled plaza (Central Sq) with a fountain at one end. At the opposite end of Main St lies the elegant red-brick Keene State College (☑603-358-2276; www.keene.edu; 229 Main St), which accounts for almost one-quarter of the town's population and brings a bit of youth and its artistic sensibilities to the town.

🛏 Sleeping & Eating

Chain hotels and motels are big in Keene. You'll also find a handful of B&Bs.

Keene has a good mix of restaurants – including American, Italian, Mexican and Thai – largely concentrated in the Central Sq/Main St area at the heart of town.

Fairfield Inn & Suites
Keene Downtown HOTEL $$
(Lane Hotel; ☑603-357-7070; www.fairfieldinnkeene.com; 30 Main St; r $104-279, ste $129-329; ❋🔊) In a picture-perfect Main St location, this venerable century-old hotel (formerly known as the Lane Hotel) has 40 attractive rooms, each uniquely furnished in a classic style, ensuring you won't get the cookie-cutter experience. There are plenty of creature comforts (individual climate control, high-speed internet connections) and a good restaurant on the 1st floor.

Luca's Mediterranean Café ITALIAN $$
(☑603-358-3335; 10 Central Sq; lunch mains $9-14, dinner mains $15-27; ☺restaurant 11:30am-2pm Mon-Fri, 5-9pm Mon-Sat year-round, plus 5-9pm Sun May-Dec) Luca's Café serves excellent thin-crust pizzas, tasty salads and gourmet sandwiches at lunch, while dinner sees a tempting array of pastas, grilled fish and pan-seared beef tenderloin. The adjacent gourmet Italian food market (panini $7; ☺9am-7pm Mon-Sat) morphs into a casual spaghetti house each weekend.

🍷 Drinking

Prime Roast COFFEE
(www.primeroastcoffee.com; 16 Main St; ☺7am-8pm Mon-Fri, 8am-8pm Sat, 9am-5pm Sun) A coffee shop selling a bag of beans called 'Demon Roast' ain't messing around – in fact they call it 'wicked' dark. Roasting is done daily in the morning. Local artists made the tables, and the coffee is fair trade.

☆ Entertainment

Colonial Theater THEATER
(☑603-352-2033; www.thecolonial.org; 95 Main St) After 80 years, this classic Main St theater is still going strong. A diverse line-up of off-Broadway musicals, African and Eastern dance troupes, jazz ensembles, rock bands and stand-up comics graces its stage.

ℹ Getting There & Away

Greyhound (www.greyhound.com) serves Keene from Brattleboro, VT ($6 to $11, 30 to 40 minutes). Service to/from Boston ($29 to $54, 4¾ hours) is less practical due to indirect routes and lengthy transfer times. The bus stops at 67 Main St, in front of Corner News.

Keene is 20 miles west of Peterborough via NH 101 and 20 miles east of Brattleboro, VT, via NH 9.

UPPER CONNECTICUT RIVER VALLEY

The Connecticut River, New England's longest, is the boundary between New Hampshire and Vermont. The Upper Connecticut River Valley extends from Brattleboro, VT, in the south to Woodsville, NH, in the north, and includes towns on both banks. The river has long been an important byway for ex-

---

DON'T MISS

NEW HAMPSHIRE PUMPKIN FESTIVAL

One of New Hampshire's quirkiest annual gatherings, the New Hampshire Pumpkin Festival (www.facebook.com/NHPumpkinFestival; ☺Oct) on the third or fourth Saturday in October draws in thousands of visitors to admire the world's largest tower of jack-o'-lanterns. Started in 1991 by merchants in Keene, the event exploded over the years, with the town's 2003 tally of nearly 29,000 pumpkins setting a Guinness world record.

In 2014 crowds got so rowdy that Keene decided to pull the plug on the festival, prompting Laconia (p345) to step in and host the event in 2015, with plans to do the same in future years.

MOOSILAUKE RAVINE LODGE

About 50 miles north of Hanover and 15 miles west of North Woodstock, the **Moosilauke Ravine Lodge** (☑603-764-5858; http://outdoors.dartmouth.edu/services/ravine_lodge; 1 Ravine Rd, Warren; dm adult/child $35/25, linens $8, breakfast/bag lunch/dinner $9/8/16; ☺May-Oct) is a rustic lodging owned and maintained by the Dartmouth Outing Club but open to the public. The lodge is set in the midst of wooded hills and pristine countryside, and 30 miles of hiking trails connect it to the summit of Mt Moosilauke and other trailheads. (For information on hiking, regional history and trail maps visit www.mtmoosilauke.com.) Accommodations at Moosilauke are basic bunks and shared baths, but the price is right. Delicious, hearty meals are served family-style in the dining hall.

At the time of research, plans were afoot to completely rebuild the lodge between fall 2016 and spring 2017; check the website for current status.

To reach Moosilauke from Woodstock, take NH 118 west. From Hanover, take NH 10A north to NH 25. Head north on NH 25 and turn right at the junction with NH 118. Moosilauke Ravine Lodge is north of NH 118; follow the signs from the turnoff.

plorers and traders. Today it is an adventure destination for boaters and bird-watchers, canoeists and kayakers. The region's largest population center is Lebanon, while the cultural focal point is prestigious Dartmouth College in Hanover.

Hanover & Around

POP 11,300

Hanover is the quintessential New England college town. On warm days, students toss Frisbees on the wide college green fronting Georgian ivy-covered buildings, while locals and academics mingle at the laid-back cafes, restaurants and shops lining Main St. Dartmouth College has long been the town's focal point, giving the area a vibrant connection to the arts.

Dartmouth was chartered in 1769 primarily 'for the education and instruction of Youth of the Indian Tribes.' Back then, the school was located in the forests where its prospective students lived. Although teaching 'English Youth and others' was its secondary purpose, in fact, Dartmouth College graduated few Native Americans and was soon attended almost exclusively by colonists. The college's most illustrious alumnus is Daniel Webster (1782–1852), who graduated in 1801 and went on to be a prominent lawyer, US senator, secretary of state and perhaps the USA's most esteemed orator.

⊙ Sights

Dartmouth College   COLLEGE
(☑603-646-1110; www.dartmouth.edu) Hanover is all about Dartmouth College, so hit the campus. Join a free student-guided campus walking tour (☑603-646-2875; http://dartmouth.edu/visit; 6016 McNutt Hall) FREE or just pick up a map at the admissions office and head off on your own. Don't miss the **Baker Berry Library** (☑603-646-2560; http://dartmouth.edu/education/libraries; 25 N Main St; ☺8am-2am Mon-Fri, 10am-2am Sat & Sun, teatime 4pm Mon-Fri), splashed with the grand *Epic of American Civilization,* painted by the outspoken Mexican muralist José Clemente Orozco (1883–1949), who taught at Dartmouth in the 1930s.

★**Dartmouth College Green**   COLLEGE
The green is the focal point of the Dartmouth College campus, both physically and historically. Along the east side of the green, picturesque **Dartmouth Row** (College St) consists of four harmonious Georgian buildings: **Wentworth, Dartmouth, Thornton** and **Reed**. Dartmouth Hall was the original college building, constructed in 1791. Just north of Dartmouth Row, **Rollins Chapel** (College St) is a fine example of Richardsonian architecture and a peaceful place to collect your thoughts.

Sanborn House Library   NOTABLE BUILDING
(Dartmouth College) Named for Professor Edwin Sanborn, who taught for almost 50 years in Dartmouth's English department, the Sanborn House Library features ornate woodwork, plush leather chairs, and books lining the walls floor to ceiling on two levels. One of Dartmouth's most endearing traditions is the afternoon tea served here on weekdays between 4pm and 5pm – tea costs 10¢, cookies 15¢; visitors are welcome but expected to maintain a respectful silence for the benefit of the diligently toiling students.

NEW HAMPSHIRE HANOVER & AROUND

Hanover

Hanover

★ **Hood Museum of Art** MUSEUM
(☏ 603-646-2808; http://hoodmuseum.dartmouth.
edu; 6 E Wheelock St; ⊗10am-5pm Tue & Thu-Sat,
to 9pm Wed, noon-5pm Sun) FREE Shortly after
the college's founding in 1769, Dartmouth
began to acquire artifacts of artistic or historical interest. Since then the collection has
expanded to include nearly 70,000 items,
which are housed at the Hood Museum of
Art. The collection is particularly strong in
American pieces, including Native American
art. One of the highlights is a set of Assyrian
reliefs from the Palace of Ashurnasirpal that
date to the 9th century BC. Special exhibitions often feature contemporary artists. In
mid-2016 the museum initiated a $50 million
renovation and expansion project, with an
anticipated completion date of summer 2019.

Enfield Shaker Museum MUSEUM
(☏ 603-632-4346; www.shakermuseum.org; 447 NH
4A, Enfield; adult/child/youth $12/3/8; ⊗10am-
4pm Mon-Sat, noon-4pm Sun Apr-late Dec) Set in
a valley overlooking Mascoma Lake (11 miles
southeast of Dartmouth), the Enfield Shaker
site dates back to the late 18th century and
grew into a small but prosperous community of Shaker farmers and craftspeople in
the early 1800s. The museum centers on the
Great Stone Dwelling, the largest Shaker
dwelling house ever built.

★⊛ Festivals & Events

Winter Carnival FESTIVAL
(www.dartmouth.edu/~sao/events/carnival; ⊗Feb)
Each February, Dartmouth celebrates the
four-day Winter Carnival, featuring special
art shows, drama productions, concerts, an
ice-sculpture contest and other amusements.
It's organized by the Student Activities Office.

⊫ Sleeping

Hanover and neighboring Norwich, VT,
boast some wonderful historic inns, though
prices are on the high side. Less expensive
options north of town include Storrs Pond
Recreation Area and Dartmouth College's
Moosilauke Ravine Lodge; south of town,
you'll find a good selection of motels in Lebanon, NH, and White River Junction, VT.

Storrs Pond Recreation Area CAMPGROUND $
(☏ 603-643-2134; www.storrspond.org; 59 Oak Hill
Dr/NH 10; tent/RV sites $32/40; ⊗mid-May–early
Sep; ☞) In addition to 21 woodsy sites next
to a 15-acre pond, this private campground

has tennis courts and two sandy beaches for swimming. From I-89 exit 13, take NH 10 north and look for signs.

The Great Stone Dwelling HOTEL $$
(✆603-632-4346; www.shakermuseum.org/stay withus.htm; 447 NH 4A, Enfield; s/d/tr $110/135/160; ☎) This grand stone edifice – the centerpiece of the Enfield Shaker Museum – also doubles as an atmospheric lodging. On the 3rd and 4th floors are seven single rooms, 11 doubles and two triples. All are spacious and filled with natural light, with pretty wood floors, traditional Shaker furniture and wi-fi, but no air-conditioning or TV.

Norwich Inn INN $$
(✆802-649-1143; www.norwichinn.com; 325 Main St, Norwich; r $159-299; ☎) Just across the Connecticut River in Norwich, VT, this is both a historic inn and a microbrewery. Rooms in the main house are decorated with Victorian antiques and traditional country furniture, and the two adjacent buildings include modern furnishings and gas fireplaces in each room.

Hanover Inn INN $$$
(✆603-643-4300, 800-443-7024; www.hanover inn.com; 2 E Wheelock St, cnr W Wheelock & S Main Sts; r $199-549; @☎☎) Owned by Dartmouth and situated directly opposite the college green, Hanover's loveliest guesthouse has nicely appointed rooms with elegant wood furnishings. It has a wine bar and an award-winning restaurant on-site.

✖ Eating

The Skinny Pancake CREPERIE $
(✆603-277-9115; www.facebook.com/skinnypan cakehanover; 3 Lebanon St; mains $6-14; ⊙8am-11pm Sun-Tue, to midnight Wed-Sat) Already a huge hit in neighboring Vermont, this creperie made its Hanover debut in 2016, offering tempting twists on the traditional French crepe, from the Veggie Monster (cheddar, spinach, roasted peppers, caramelized onions and pesto) to the Crepedilla (with guacamole, *pico de gallo*, cheddar and chipotle sour cream). The breakfast and dessert crepes are equally awesome.

Lou's DINER $
(✆603-643-3321; www.lousrestaurant.net; 30 S Main St; mains $10-15; ⊙6am-3pm Mon-Fri, 7am-3pm Sat & Sun) A Dartmouth institution since 1947, this is Hanover's oldest establishment, always packed with students meeting for a coffee or perusing their books. From the retro tables or the Formica-topped counter, order typical diner food like eggs, sandwiches

and burgers. Breakfast is served all day, and the bakery items are highly recommended.

Candela Tapas Lounge TAPAS $$
(✆603-277-9094; www.candelatapas.com; 15 Lebanon St; tapas $8-14; ⊙5-9:30pm Tue-Thu, to 10pm Fri & Sat, to 9pm Sun) This chic spot serves classic Spanish-style tapas such as *gambas al ajillo* (shrimp sautéed in garlic, white wine, butter and lemon) or *albondigas* (meatballs), along with *tablas* (meat and cheese boards), empanadas, braised pork tacos, and Puerto Rican red beans and rice. Colorful cocktails and Mediterranean wines add to the romantic appeal.

Canoe Club Bistro BISTRO $$
(✆603-643-9660; www.canoeclub.us; 27 S Main St; lunch mains $10-16, dinner mains $12-27; ⊙11:30am-11:30pm Mon-Sat, to 10:30pm Sun) 🍴 This smart bistro and bar does excellent burgers and steaks along with more refined fare like duck breast with fig port glaze. Other enticements include superb french fries with garlic aioli and a stellar assortment of two dozen draft microbrews. There's live music six nights a week – anything from acoustic to jazz – plus a magician working the tables every Monday.

★**Morano Gelato** ICE CREAM
(✆603-643-4233; www.moranogelatohanover.com; 57 S Main St; gelato $3.25-5.50; ⊙11:30am-9:30pm Tue-Sun) Founder Morgan Morano fell head over heels for gelato while living in Florence. Next step? Import some genuine Italian equipment and launch this brilliant gelato shop in the heart of Hanover. With new batches made fresh every morning, complemented by cakes and espresso drinks, it's one of the best dessert spots in the state.

🍸 Drinking & Nightlife

Murphy's on the Green PUB
(✆603-643-4075; www.murphysonthegreen.com; 11 S Main St; ⊙4pm-12:30am Mon-Thu, 11-12:30am Fri-Sun) This classic collegiate tavern is where students and faculty meet over pints (it carries more than 10 beers on tap, including local microbrews like Long Trail Ale) and satisfying pub fare. Stained-glass windows and church-pew seating enhance the cozy atmosphere.

☆ Entertainment

Hopkins Center for the Arts PERFORMING ARTS
(✆603-646-2422; www.hop.dartmouth.edu; 4 E Wheelock St) A long way from the big-city lights of New York and Boston, Dartmouth

hosts its own entertainment at this outstanding performing-arts venue. The season brings everything from movies to live performances by international companies.

ℹ Information

Hanover Area Chamber of Commerce

(☑ 603-643-3115; www.hanoverchamber.org; 53 S Main St, Suite 208; ⊙9am-noon & 1-4pm Mon-Fri) On the 2nd floor of the Nugget Building. The chamber of commerce also maintains an information booth (⊙mid-Jun–mid-Sep) on the village green.

ℹ Getting There & Away

AIR

From Lebanon Municipal Airport (p324), 6 miles south of Hanover, **Cape Air** (☑ 800-227-3247; www.capeair.com) flies to Boston and White Plains, NY (just outside New York City).

BUS

Dartmouth Coach (p324) operates eight daily shuttles from Hanover to Boston's South Station ($28, 2¾ hours) and Logan International Airport (adult/child under 15 years $33/free, three hours), plus twice-daily service to New York City (adult/child $80/40).

Vermont Translines (p324) serves destinations in Vermont, including Woodstock ($3.50, 45 minutes), Killington ($7.50, 1¼ hours) and Rutland ($9.50, 1¾ hours).

CAR & MOTORCYCLE

From Boston to Hanover, it's a two- to three-hour drive depending on traffic; take I-93 to I-89 to I-91. From Hanover to Burlington, VT, it's an additional 1½ hours north via I-89.

ℹ Getting Around

Advance Transit (www.advancetransit.com) provides a free service to White River Junction, Lebanon, West Lebanon and Norwich. Bus stops are indicated by a blue-and-yellow AT symbol.

LAKES REGION

The Lakes Region, with an odd mix of natural beauty and commercial tawdriness, is one of New Hampshire's most popular holiday destinations. Vast Lake Winnipesaukee, the region's centerpiece, has 183 miles of coastline, more than 300 islands and excellent salmon fishing. Catch the early-morning mists off the lake and you'll understand why the Native Americans named it 'Smile of the Great Spirit.' The prettiest stretches are in the southwest corner between Glendale and Alton (on the shoreline Belknap Point Rd), and in the northeast corner between Wolfeboro and Moultonborough (on NH 109). Just to the north lie the smaller Squam Lake and Little Squam Lake.

The roads skirting the shores and connecting the lakeside towns are a riotous spread of small-town Americana: amusement arcades, go-cart tracks, clam shacks, junk-food outlets and boat docks. Even if you're just passing through, stop for a swim, a lakeside picnic or a cruise.

Meredith & Around

POP 6240

More upscale than Weirs Beach, Meredith is a lively lakeside town with a long commercial strip stretching along the shore. Its few backstreets are set with attractive colonial and Victorian homes. There are no sights per se, but it's a convenient base for exploring the Lakes Region and offers a slew of accommodations and dining options. US 3, NH 25 and NH 104 converge here.

🛏 Sleeping

White Lake State Park CAMPGROUND $

(☑ 603-323-7350; www.nhstateparks.org; 94 State Park Rd, Tamworth; tent sites with/without water views $30/25; ⊙late May–mid-Oct) This campground, 22 miles northeast of Meredith off NH 16, has 200 tent sites on over 600 acres, plus swimming and hiking trails. You'll also find some of New Hampshire's finest swimming in White Lake, a pristine glacial lake whose origins date back to the last ice age.

Meredith Inn B&B INN $$

(☑ 603-279-0000; www.meredithinn.com; 2 Waukewan St; r incl breakfast $154-229; ❋ 🖢) This delightful Victorian inn has eight rooms outfitted with antique furnishings and luxurious bedding; several rooms also have Jacuzzis, gas fireplaces or walk-out bay windows.

Tuckernuck Inn INN $$

(☑ 603-279-5521; www.thetuckernuckinn.com; 25 Red Gate Lane; r incl breakfast $169-189; ❋ 🖢) Tuckernuck has five cozy, quiet rooms (one with a fireplace) with stenciled walls and handmade quilts. From Main St, head inland along Water St, then turn right (uphill) onto Red Gate Lane.

CASTLE IN THE CLOUDS

Perched on high like a king surveying his territory, the arts-and-crafts-style **Castle in the Clouds** (☑ 603-476-5900; www.castleintheclouds.org; 455 Old Mountain Rd/NH 171, Moultonborough; adult/child $16/8; ☺ 10am-5:30pm daily early Jun-late Oct, Sat & Sun May-early Jun) wows with its stone walls and exposed-timber beams, but it's the views of lakes and valleys that draw the crowds. In autumn the kaleidoscope of rust, red and yellow beats any postcard. The 5500-acre estate features gardens, ponds and a path leading to a small waterfall. Admission includes the castle and stories about the eccentric millionaire Thomas Plant, who built it.

From late June to early September, make reservations for the Thursday-evening 'Jazz at Sunset' performances or the Monday-morning 'Walks and Talks,' about anything from geology to birds to wild food.

✗ Eating

Lakeside Deli & Grille　SANDWICHES $
(☑ 603-677-7132; www.facebook.com/Lakeside DeliGrille; 2 Pleasant St; soups & sandwiches $5-12; ☺ 11am-4pm Sun-Thu, to 8pm Fri & Sat) For a delicious lunch with prime Lake Winnipesaukee views, hit the front porch of this deli just east of downtown, beloved for its reasonably priced sandwiches, homemade soups, and fish tacos with fresh haddock and chipotle mayo.

Waterfall Cafe　CAFE $
(☑ 603-677-8631; www.millfalls.com/dine; Mill Falls Marketplace, 312 Daniel Webster Hwy/US 3; mains $5-10; ☺ 6:30am-1pm) A bright, friendly cafe on the top floor of the Mill Falls Marketplace (part of a former working mill), this cafe dishes up mainly breakfast food like omelets, buttermilk pancakes and eggs Benedict, with lunch items like salads and sandwiches. Country tables flank a spectacular wall mural depicting Lake Winnipesaukee and the surrounding rolling hills.

Lakehouse　SEAFOOD, AMERICAN $$
(☑ 603-279-5221; www.thecman.com; Church Landing, 281 Daniel Webster Hwy/US 3; lunch mains $10-19, dinner mains $21-37; ☺ 7:30-10am, 11:30am-3pm & 5-9pm Mon-Sat, 9am-2pm & 5-9pm Sun) At the Inn at Church Landing, this classy restaurant is part of the statewide 'Common Man' family of restaurants. The wide-ranging menu focuses on seafood and steaks, usually prepared with some creative international twist. Enjoy your dinner on the breezy lakeside deck.

🛍 Shopping

Mill Falls Marketplace　SHOPPING CENTER
(www.millfalls.com/shop; 312 Daniel Webster Hwy/US 3; ☺ from 10am daily) Backed by the lake and a 40ft waterfall, this restored linen mill houses a dozen shops and restaurants.

ℹ Information

Meredith Chamber of Commerce (☑ 877-279-6121, 603-279-6121; www.mereditharea chamber.com; 272 Daniel Webster Hwy/US 3; ☺ 9am-4pm Mon-Fri mid-May–mid-Oct, Mon, Wed & Fri only rest of year)

ℹ Getting There & Away

BUS

Concord Coach Lines (Concord Trailways; www.concordcoachlines.com) passes through Meredith on its twice-daily run between Boston and North Conway. Buses stop in the public parking lot at the northeast corner of US 3 and NH 25. Destinations include Concord (one-way $12, one hour), Boston's South Station (one-way $23.50, 2½ hours) and Logan International Airport (one-way $29, 2¾ hours).

CAR & MOTORCYCLE

Meredith is 40 miles north of Concord and 107 miles north of Boston. Take I-93 to exit 23, then follow NH 104 east into town.

Squam Lake

Northwest of Lake Winnipesaukee, Squam Lake is more tranquil, more tasteful and more pristine than its big sister. It is also less accessible, lacking any public beaches. Nonetheless, if you choose your lodging carefully, you can enjoy Squam Lake's natural wonders, just like Katherine Hepburn and Henry Fonda did in the 1981 film *On Golden Pond*.

With 67 miles of shoreline and 67 islands, there are plenty of opportunities for fishing, kayaking and swimming.

Holderness is the area's main town, at the southwest corner of Squam Lake. Little Squam Lake is a much smaller branch further southwest.

◉ Sights

Squam Lakes Natural
Science Center   SCIENCE CENTER
(✑603-968-7194; www.nhnature.org; 23 Science
Center Rd, off NH 113, Holderness; adult/child
$19/14, boat tours $25/21; ☺9:30am-5pm May-
Oct;) To get up close and personal with
the wildlife in the Lakes Region, visit the
Squam Lakes Natural Science Center. Four
nature paths weave through the woods
and around the marsh. The highlight is the
Gephart Trail, leading past trailside enclo-
sures that are home to various creatures, including bobcats, fishers (a kind of marten),
mountain lions and a bald eagle. Note that
last admission to the trail is at 3:30pm.

The best boat tours of Squam Lake are
run by the center; among other tours, it offers pontoon-boat cruises that observe the
loons and eagles, visit sites from On Gold-
en Pond or watch the sun set over the lake.
Combination tickets for the center and tour
are available.

Children will love the Gordon Interactive
Playscape, opened in 2015, which invites
kids to assume the role of red squirrels as
they climb, crawl, swing, balance and slide
through a series of structures, learning about
predator-prey relationships as they go.

The nearby Kirkwood Gardens, featuring
many species of New England native shrubs
and flowers, are specially designed to attract
birds and butterflies.

🏃 Activities

West Rattlesnake Mountain   WALKING
() One of New Hampshire's best family hikes, and a great sunset excursion, the
gradual 1-mile climb (450ft elevation gain)
of West Rattlesnake Mountain (1260ft)
yields spectacular views of the Lakes Region,
with Squam Lake in the foreground and
Lake Winnepesaukee in the distance. Start
at the Old Bridle Path trailhead, 4 miles
north of Squam Lake (Holderness) on NH
113; parking can be tricky in midsummer.

🛏 Sleeping

Rockywold Deephaven Camps   CABIN $$
(✑603-968-3313; www.rdcsquam.com; 18 Bacon
Rd, Holderness; per person incl full board $121-236;
) Since 1897, families have been coming
to stay at this rustic summer getaway on
Squam Lake. Cabins, cottages and lodge
rooms are available, along with three home-
cooked meals daily, and the simple pleasures
of swimming, boating, fishing and easygoing
lakeside living. Refrigeration for the entire

camp is provided by iceboxes stocked with
ice harvested from the lake each winter.

Cottage Place on Squam Lake   COTTAGE $$
(✑603-968-7116; www.cottageplaceonsquam.com;
1132 US 3, Holderness; 1-room cottages $105-175,
2-room cottages $135-265;) The cozy, com-
fortable Cottage Place fronts Squam Lake,
offering a private beach, a swimming raft
and docking space for boats. There is a wide
variety of accommodations, including standard rooms and lakefront cottages; all come
with a kitchen, many with wood-burning
fireplaces. Weekly rentals are encouraged in
summer. Pets cost $20 extra per night.

Squam Lake Inn   INN $$
(✑800-839-6205, 603-968-4417; www.squam
lakeinn.com; 28 Shepard Hill Rd, off US 3, Holder-
ness; r incl breakfast $159-249;) This
century-old Victorian farmhouse has eight
rooms, all decorated in vintage New Eng-
land style – quilts on the beds, antique fur-
nishings and a local 'Lakes' theme – with
modern touches like iPod docking stations.
Higher-priced rooms include gas fireplaces
and/or stoves. A mahogany deck and wrap-
around porch overlook woodsy grounds.

Manor on Golden Pond   B&B $$$
(✑603-968-3348, 800-545-2141; www.manoron
goldenpond.com; 31 Manor Dr, off US 3, Holderness;
r $280-410, cottages $410, ste $480, all incl break-
fast; ☺closed 1wk at Christmas & 1wk early spring
for maintenance;) This luxurious B&B is
perched on Shepard Hill, overlooking serene
Squam Lake. Elegant rooms (some with
fireplaces and Jacuzzis), gourmet breakfasts
and a lovely private beach make this one of
the lake region's finest retreats. Extra perks
include clay tennis courts, a full-service spa
and an excellent dining room. Children under 12 years are not welcome here.

🍴 Eating

Squam Lake Marketplace   SANDWICHES $
(✑603-968-8588; www.facebook.com/Squam
LakeMarketplace; 863 US 3, Holderness; meals
$7-11; ☺7am-9pm Mon-Fri, to 10pm Sat & Sun Apr-
Dec) This gourmet grocery store and bakery
serves excellent breakfast and lunch sandwiches, local homemade fudge, and other
goodies. You'll also find wines, sake, marinated meats and veggies (ready for grilling),
pasta salads and marvelous scones.

Walter's Basin   AMERICAN $$
(✑603-968-4412; www.waltersbasin.com; 859 US
3, Holderness; sandwiches $9-19.50, mains $15-26;
☺11:30am-9pm Sun-Thu, to 9:30pm Fri & Sat)

Lake trippers are encouraged to dock their boats and come in for a meal at this casual waterfront spot. Located on Little Squam Lake near the bridge, the friendly restaurant features stuffed haddock, elk meatloaf, blueberry-glazed salmon, lobster macaroni and cheese, and other comfort fare.

❶ Getting There & Away

BUS

Concord Coach Lines (☑800-639-3317, 603-228-3300; www.concordcoachlines.com) operates two daily buses from Boston to North Conway, stopping off in Center Harbor on the east side of Squam Lake. The bus stop is at Village Car Wash & Laundromat, on US 25 in Center Harbor. Destinations include Concord ($13, one hour), Boston's South Station ($24.50, 2¾ hours) and Logan International Airport ($30, three hours).

CAR & MOTORCYCLE

Holderness is 42 miles north of Concord and 109 miles north of Boston. Take I-93 to exit 24, then follow NH 25/US 3 into town, skirting the north shore of Little Squam Lake.

Wolfeboro

POP 6270

On the eastern shore of Lake Winnipesaukee, Wolfeboro is an idyllic town where children still gather around the ice-cream stand on warm summer nights and a grassy lakeside park draws young and old to weekly concerts. Named for General Wolfe, who died vanquishing Montcalm on the Plains of Abraham in Quebec, Wolfeboro (founded in 1770) claims to be 'the oldest summer resort in America.' Whether that's true or not, it's certainly the most charming, with pretty lake beaches, intriguing museums, beautiful New England architecture (from Georgian through Federal, Greek Revival and Second Empire), cozy B&Bs and a worthwhile walking trail that runs along several lakes as it leads out of town.

◉ Sights

Wright Museum   MUSEUM
(☑603-569-1212; www.wrightmuseum.org; 77 Center St; adult/child $10/6; ◉10am-4pm Mon-Sat, noon-4pm Sun May-Oct) For a Rosie-the-riveter and baked-apple-pie look at WWII, visit this museum's interactive exhibitions that feature music, documentary clips, posters and other American paraphernalia. There are also uniforms, equipment and military hardware (including a 42-ton Pershing

tank), meticulously restored by the museum. The Tuesday-evening summer lecture series (June to mid-September) is a huge draw – speakers range from authors to war refugees.

Wentworth State Beach   BEACH
(☑603-569-3699; www.nhstateparks.org; 297 Governor Wentworth Hwy/NH 109; adult/child $4/2; ◉dawn-dusk daily mid-Jun–early Sep, dawn-dusk Sat & Sun late May–mid-Jun) If your lodging or campsite does not have access to the lake, head to this small beach on the serene Wentworth Lake. Much smaller but much less developed than Winnipesaukee, Wentworth Lake offers all the same opportunities for swimming, picnicking, hiking and fishing.

Libby Museum   MUSEUM
(☑603-569-1035; www.thelibbymuseum.org; 755 N Main St/NH 109, Winter Harbor; adult/child $2/1; ◉10am-4pm Tue-Sat, noon-4pm Sun Jun-Aug, Sat & Sun only Sep–mid-Oct) At the age of 40, Dr Henry Forrest Libby, a local dentist, began collecting things. In 1912 he built a home for his collections, which later became the eccentric little Libby Museum. Starting with butterflies and moths, the amateur naturalist built up a private natural history collection. Other collections followed, including Abenaki relics and early-American farm and home implements. It lies 3 miles north of Wolfeboro.

Clark House Museum Complex   MUSEUM
(☑603-569-4997; www.wolfeborohistoricalsociety.org/clarkhouse.html; 233 S Main St; ◉10am-4pm Wed-Fri, to 2pm Sat Jul & Aug) **FREE** Wolfeboro's eclectic historical museum comprises three historic buildings: the 1778 Clark family farmhouse, an 1805 one-room schoolhouse and a replica of an old firehouse. The buildings contain relevant artifacts (such as fire engines!), furniture and the like. Admission was free when we were there, but a fee was being considered.

New Hampshire Boat Museum   MUSEUM
(☑603-569-4554; www.nhbm.org; 399 Center St; adult/child $7/3; ◉10am-4pm Mon-Sat, noon-4pm Sun late May-early Oct) Wolfeboro is an appropriate place for this boat museum. Nautical types will appreciate the collection of vintage watercraft, motors, photographs and other memorabilia.

☆ Activities

Cotton Valley Trail   WALKING
This excellent multiuse rail trail starts at Wolfeboro's information office (the former train station) and runs for 12 miles along an old railway bed. It links the towns of

NEW HAMPSHIRE WOLFEBORO

Wolfeboro, Brookfield and Wakefield and passes by two lakes, climbs through Cotton Valley, and winds through forests and fields around Brookfield.

Abenaki Ski Area
SKIING

(www.wolfeboronh.us/Pages/WolfeboroNH_Rec reation/abenaki; 390 Pine Hill Rd; lift ticket $17; ⊙ 4-7pm Wed-Fri, 11am-7pm Sat, 11am-6pm Sun) An adorable anomaly in this age of corporate-run mega-resorts, America's oldest local ski hill (opened in 1936) charges a pittance for lift tickets but comes with unexpected amenities, like modern snowmaking equipment, night skiing and a brand-new lodge. There are also 18 miles of cross-country ski trails. It's 3 miles north of town on NH 109A.

Nordic Skier Sports
SKIING, BICYCLE RENTAL

(✆603-569-3151; www.nordicskiersports.com; 47 N Main St; adult/child per day bike rental $25/15, cross-country ski rental $15/10) In the heart of town, this shop rents out bikes, skis, snowshoes, ice skates, bikes and other outdoorsy gear.

Dive Winnipesaukee
BOATING, DIVING

(✆603-569-8080; www.divewinnipesaukee.com; 4 N Main St, Wolfeboro; canoe or kayak rental per day $45; ⊙9am-7pm Mon-Sat, 8am-6pm Sun Jun-Aug, reduced hours Sep-May) For adventures in the deep blue, visit this all-purpose water-sports outfitter by the lakeside in the heart of town. It rents canoes and kayaks ($45 per day) and offers a range of diving courses in the frigid lake.

🎉 Festivals & Events

Great Waters Music Festival
MUSIC

(✆603-569-7710; www.greatwaters.org; ⊙Jun-Aug) Wolfeboro is home to the Great Waters Music Festival, where big-name artists perform everything from folk, jazz and blues to big band and Motown on the banks of Lake Winnipesaukee.

🛏 Sleeping

Wolfeboro Campground
CAMPGROUND $

(✆603-569-9881; www.wolfeborocampground. com; 61 Haines Hill Rd; tent/RV sites $28/32; ⊙late May–mid-Oct; 🛜) Off NH 28, and about 4.5 miles north of Wolfeboro's town center, this campground has 50 private, wooded sites.

Topsides B&B
B&B $$

(✆603-569-3834; www.topsidesbb.com; 209 S Main St; r incl breakfast $129-185; 🛜) A short walk to the center of town, this B&B has five elegant, classically furnished rooms with wood floors. Several have lake views.

Wolfeboro Inn
INN $$$

(✆603-569-3016; www.wolfeboroinn.com; 90 N Main St; r $199-319, ste $259-359, all incl breakfast; @🛜) The town's best-known lodging is right on the lake with a private beach. One of the region's most prestigious resorts since 1812, it has 44 rooms across a main inn and a modern annex. Rooms have modern touches like flat-screen TVs, new beds and contemporary furnishings: it feels less historic but oh-so-luxurious. Facilities include a restaurant and pub, Wolfe's Tavern (✆603-569-3016; www.wolfestavern.com; 90 N Main St; lunch mains $11-20, dinner mains $13-30; ⊙7am-9pm).

✗ Eating

Bailey's Bubble
ICE CREAM $

(✆603-569-3612; www.baileysbubble.com; 5 Railroad Ave; ice cream from $3; ⊙noon-8pm Sun-Thu, to 9pm Fri & Sat mid-May–early Sep) This old-time fave has scooped ice cream for generations of families, and is still the most popular gathering spot in the summer. There are more than 20 different flavors; feel free to mix and match, but the servings are huge!

Downtown Grille Cafe
CAFE $

(www.downtowngrillecafe.com; 33 S Main st; breakfast $3.25-7, lunch $8-12; ⊙7am-3pm) Order at the counter then head to the back patio for a great view of Lake Winn with your ham and pepper jack panini, hot pressed cubano or, our favorite, the kickin' buffalo chicken wrap with blue cheese and hot sauce. Stop by in the morning for pastries and breakfast sandwiches. Fancy coffees available too.

Nolan's Brick Oven Bistro
PIZZA $$

(✆603-515-1028; www.nolansbrickovenbistro.com; 39 N Main St; mains $10-22; ⊙11am-9pm Mon-Thu, to 11pm Fri-Sun) Delicious pizzas – cooked in the brick oven and laden with ingredients sourced from local farms – are the big draw at this popular spot a block north of the village center; but the kitchen offers a world of alternatives throughout the year, including seafood, soups, salads, wraps and even occasional sushi nights.

Wolfetrap Grill & Rawbar
SEAFOOD $$

(✆603-569-1047; www.wolfetrapgrillandrawbar. com; 19 Bay St; mains $15-26; ⊙11am-late mid-May–Sep) Nantucket meets new Hampshire at this airy eatery tucked away on Back Bay, an inlet of Lake Winnipesaukee. Inside tables are covered with parchment paper – ready for you to attack and get messy with shellfish (oysters, clams, shrimp, lobster) –

CRUISING LAKE WINNIPESAUKEE

MS Mount Washington (☑603-366-5531; www.cruisenh.com; 211 Lakeside Ave, Weirs Beach; adult/child regular cruise $30/15, Sunday brunch cruise $47/24) The classic MS *Mount Washington* steams out of Weirs Beach daily from mid-May to mid-October, making a relaxing 2½-hour scenic circuit around Lake Winnipesaukee, with regular stops in Wolfeboro and occasional visits to Alton Bay, Center Harbor and/or Meredith. Special events include the weekly champagne brunch cruise on Sundays and themed cruises (sunset dinner cruises, dance cruises, Elvis and Lobsterfest cruises) throughout summer.

MV Sophie C (☑603-366-5531; www.cruisenh.com/sophie.php; 211 Lakeside Ave, Weirs Beach; adult/child $27/13; ☉11am & 2pm Mon-Sat mid-Jun–mid-Sep) The MV *Sophie C* is a veritable floating post office. Passengers are invited to accompany this US mail boat as it delivers packages and letters to quaint ports and otherwise inaccessible island residents across four to five islands. Between mid-June and early September, its two 1½-hour runs depart six days a week from Weirs Beach.

while the deck has loungey chairs overlooking the water. The bar keeps going, as the bartenders say, 'till the wolf howls.'

Mise En Place   FRENCH, AMERICAN $$$
(☑603-569-5788; www.miseenplacenh.com; 96 Lehner St; mains $24-35; ☉5-9pm Tue-Sat May-Oct, Fri & Sat Nov-Apr) With its minimalist decoration and pleasant front patio, this is a wonderful place for dinner. Think filet mignon, roasted rack of lamb and a wide selection of seafood dishes, from lobster-and-crab risotto to sea scallops with sage butter and mushroom ravioli. Reservations advisable.

ℹ Information

Wolfeboro Chamber of Commerce Information Booth (☑800-516-5324, 603-569-2200; www.wolfeborochamber.com; 32 Central Ave; ☉10am-3pm Mon-Fri, 10am-noon Sat, longer hours late May–mid-Oct) Located inside the old train station, this small office has the scoop on local activities.

ℹ Getting There & Away

Wolfeboro is on the east side of Lake Winnipesaukee, at the intersection of NH 28 with the lakeside NH 109. From I-93, take US 3 to its intersection with NH 11. Follow this road south as it skirts the lake. Pick up NH 28 in Alton and head north.

Weirs Beach & Around

Called 'Aquedoctan' by its Native American settlers, Weirs Beach takes its English name from the weirs (enclosures for catching fish) that the first European settlers found along the small sand beach. Today Weirs Beach is the honky-tonk heart of Lake Winnipesaukee's childhood amusements, famous for video-game arcades and fried dough. The vacation scene is completed by a lakefront promenade, a public beach and a dock for small cruising ships. A water park and drive-in theater are also in the vicinity. Away from the din on the waterfront, you will notice evocative Victorian-era architecture – somewhat out of place in this capital of kitsch.

South of Weirs Beach lie **Laconia**, the largest town in the region but devoid of any real sights, and lake-hugging **Gilford**. Note that this side of the lake gets mobbed with bikers for nine days each June during Laconia Motorcycle Week (www.laconiamcweek.com), the world's oldest motorcycle rally.

☊ Activities

Belknap Mountain   HIKING
At 2384ft, Belknap Mountain is the highest peak in the Belknap range, with numerous hiking trails. The most direct route to the summit is from the Belknap Carriage Rd in Gilford. From NH 11A, take Cherry Valley Rd and follow the signs for the Belknap Fire Tower. Three marked trails lead from the parking lot to Belknap summit, a one-hour trek.

Ellacoya State Park   SWIMMING, FISHING
(☑603-293-7821; www.nhstateparks.org; 266 Scenic Rd, Gilford; adult/child $5/2; ☉9am-5pm daily mid-Jun–early Sep, Sat & Sun late May, early Jun & mid-Sep) Many lakeshore lodgings have water access, but if your place does not, head for Ellacoya, which has a 600ft-wide beach with lovely views across to the Sandwich and Ossipee Mountains. This is an excellent place for swimming, fishing and canoeing.

Winnipesaukee Scenic Railroad   TOURIST TRAIN
(☑603-745-2135; www.hoborr.com; 211 Lakeside Ave, Weirs Beach; adult/child 1hr $16/12, 2hr $18/14) The touristy Scenic Railroad offers

one- or two-hour lakeside rides aboard 1920s and '30s train cars departing from Weirs Beach and Meredith (154 Main St). The train travels to Lake Winnipesaukee's southern tip at Alton Bay before making a U-turn. Kids love the ice-cream-parlor car; for $25 (per adult or child) you can ride in the caboose.

🛏 Sleeping

Lake Winnipesaukee Motel　　MOTEL $
(☑ 603-366-5502; www.lakewinnipesaukeemotel. com; 350 Endicott St N, Weirs Beach; r $94-140, ste $120-150; ❄@🖥) Right on Lake Winn, this simple motel has cute rooms with refrigerators and microwaves.

**Proctor's
Lakehouse Cottages**　　APARTMENT $$
(☑ 603-366-5517; www.lakehousecottages.com; 1144 Weirs Blvd/US 3, Laconia; cottages $170-320, ste $170-300; 🖥🏊) This family-owned collection of cottages and suites, all with kitchens, are blissful. The more modern suites clustered in the main structure feature porches, while cottages exude old-school New England with original wood walls and rustic (but well-kept) furnishings. All have views of the lake (there's a tiny beach and deck), and every unit comes with its own lakeside grill.

Bay Side Inn　　INN $$
(☑ 603-875-5005; www.bayside-inn.com; NH 11D, Alton Bay; r $150-185; 🖥) The attractive guest rooms here sit right on the Winnipesaukee waterfront. Guests enjoy a private beach that is excellent for fishing and swimming. Motorboats (with skis) and kayaks are available for rental. Two-bedroom efficiency suites (and weekly rates) are available for longer-term guests.

Ferry Point House B&B　　B&B $$
(☑ 603-524-0087; www.ferrypointhouse.com; 100 Lower Bay Rd, Winnisquam; r $185-230, ste from $295, all incl breakfast; 🖥) Overlooking Lake Winnisquam, this picturesque Victorian B&B has 10 cozy, uniquely furnished rooms set with antiques. Rooms range in size from small to spacious; some have lake views and the largest (Lake Solitude Suite) comes with a Jacuzzi.

🍴 Eating & Drinking

Cruise the promenade for an abundance of heart-attack-inducing snack shops.

Union Diner　　DINER $
(☑ 603-524-6744; www.theuniondiner.com; 1331 Union Ave, Laconia; mains $5-10; ⊘ 6am-3pm Mon-Wed, to 8pm Thu-Sat, to 1pm Sun) Escape the waterfront hubbub at this classic American diner 3 miles south of Weirs Beach, housed in a converted 1950s railway dining car with oak-mahogany woodwork and decorative tile floors. Grab a booth or a counterside stool and treat yourself to early-bird breakfast specials or a lunch of homemade meatloaf, lobster stew, or roast turkey with stuffing and cranberry sauce. Yum!

Kellerhaus　　ICE CREAM $
(☑ 603-366-4466; www.kellerhaus.com; 259 Endicott St N/NH 3, Weirs Beach; sundaes $4-13, breakfasts $10-25; ⊘ 10am-10pm Mon-Fri, 8am-10pm Sat & Sun May-Sep, 10am-6pm Wed-Mon Oct-Apr) Welcome to the ice-cream sundae of your childhood dreams. At this Weirs Beach institution they've been making homemade ice cream for over a century, but it's the over-the-top, self-service ice-cream-sundae buffet featuring 12 toppings that packs them in. Chow down under the groovy-kitsch light fixtures next to the jukebox blaring oldies and pray your trousers will fit later.

NazBar & Grill　　BAR
(☑ 603-366-4341; www.nazbarandgrill.com; 1086 Weirs Blvd, Laconia; ⊘ late May-early Oct) This colorful lakeside bar is recommended because it's a scene. This is Weirs Beach, after all. Watch boats pull up to the dock as you sip your cocktail beside – or in – the lake. Bar fare (mains $10 to $13) includes nachos, salads, wraps and burgers.

☆ Entertainment

Weirs Drive-In　　CINEMA
(☑ 603-366-4723; weirsdrivein.com; 76 Endicott St/US 3; ⊘ 7-11pm mid-May–early Sep; 🅿) Opened in 1949 and in continual operation since then, this drive-in movie theater is a revered institution, showing summertime double features on four screens. The minimum charge per carload is $25, which covers three adults, or two adults and two kids under 12 years. Each additional person pays $5.

ⓘ Information

Lakes Region Chamber of Commerce
(☑ 603-524-5531; www.lakesregionchamber. org; 383 S Main St, Laconia; ⊘ 9am-3pm Mon-Fri) Supplies information year-round about the Laconia/Weirs Beach area.

ⓘ Getting There & Away

Weirs Beach is on the west side of Lake Winnipesaukee. From I-93 take exit 20 (from the south) or 24 (from the north) to US 3.

WHITE MOUNTAIN REGION

Covering one-quarter of New Hampshire (and part of Maine), the vast White Mountains area is a spectacular region of soaring peaks and lush valleys, and contains New England's most rugged mountains. There are numerous activities on offer, including hiking, camping, skiing and canoeing. Much of the area – 780,000 acres – is designated as the White Mountain National Forest (WMNF), thus protecting it from overdevelopment and guaranteeing its wondrous natural beauty for years to come. Keep in mind, however, that this place is popular: six million visitors flock here every year, making it the nation's second-most-visited park after the Great Smoky Mountains.

Parking at National Forest trailheads costs $3/5/20 per day/week/season. Purchase parking permits at any of the visitor centers in the area.

North Woodstock & Around

POP 2190

North Woodstock and its neighboring settlement Lincoln gather a mix of adventure seekers and drive-by sightseers en route to the Kancamagus Hwy (NH 112). North Woodstock has a busy but small-town feel with battered motels and diners lining the main street and a gurgling river running parallel to it. Nearby Lincoln has less charm, but serves as the starting point for the entertaining Hobo Railroad and two family-friendly favorites – a zip line across the Barron Mountain and an aerial park.

Sights

Lost River Gorge & Boulder Caves   CAVES, GORGE
(✆603-745-8031; www.findlostriver.com; 1712 Lost River Rd/NH 112, North Woodstock; adult/child $19/15, lantern tours per person $29; ⊙9am-5pm early May–mid-Oct; ⊞) Adventurous kids will enjoy exploring the this network of caverns and crevices formed by glaciers millions of years ago. Each cave has its own title and story, from the Bear Crawl to the Dungeon. Climbing, crawling and squeezing is required. On Saturday evenings throughout the season, plus Wednesdays and Fridays in July and August, there are guided two-hour lantern tours, which culminate with

s'mores and roasted marshmallows around the fire pit. It's 6 miles west of North Woodstock on NH 112.

Activities

Alpine Adventures   AMUSEMENT PARK
(✆603-745-9911; www.alpinezipline.com; 41 Main St/Kancamagus Hwy, Lincoln; zips from $64; ⊙9am-4pm Mon-Fri, to 5pm Sat & Sun; ⊞) Alpine Adventures offers a smorgasbord of adrenaline-charged activities: Thrillsville is an aerial park where you can clamber and fly (attached by a harness) over a hodgepodge of specially constructed bridges, cargo nets, rope ladders, zip lines, giant swings, tree houses and a freefall device, or fly in a snow tube onto a giant airbag at the new BigAirBag Stuntzone.

Hobo Railroad   TOURIST TRAIN
(✆603-745-2135; www.hoborr.com; 64 Railroad St, off Kancamagus Hwy, Lincoln; adult/child $16/12; ⊙daily mid-Jun–mid-Oct, reduced service Nov-early Jun) The Hobo is a scenic 1½-hour train ride from Lincoln south to Woodstock. Seasonal themes include foliage trains and Santa trains that follow the same route, and summers feature Sunday storybook trips, where characters like Winnie-the-Pooh and Curious George hop aboard and entertain during the ride.

Café Lafayette   TOURIST TRAIN
(✆603-745-3500; www.nhdinnertrain.com; NH 112, North Woodstock; adult/child from $80/60; ⊙mid-May–late Oct) Travel in the 1st-class dining car of the 1924 Pullman-Standard Victorian Coach while enjoying a five-course meal. The dining car has been completely and beautifully restored and decorated with dark wood, stained glass and brass fixtures. The train rides along a spur of the Boston and Maine railroad for two hours.

Pemi Valley Moose Tours   WILDLIFE
(✆603-745-2744; www.moosetoursnh.com; 136 Main St/NH 112, Lincoln; tours adult/child $30/20; ⊙May–mid-Oct) Trips with this moose-watching specialist include a 'twilight tour,' which tracks moose and other wildlife (with a 95% success rate) in a 33-passenger bus.

Sleeping

★The Notch Hostel   HOSTEL $
(✆603-348-1483; www.notchhostel.com; 324 Lost River Rd, North Woodstock; dm $30, d $60-90; ☞☒) Exactly what the North Woodstock/Lincoln area needed, this gorgeous new

White Mountains & Mt Washington Valley

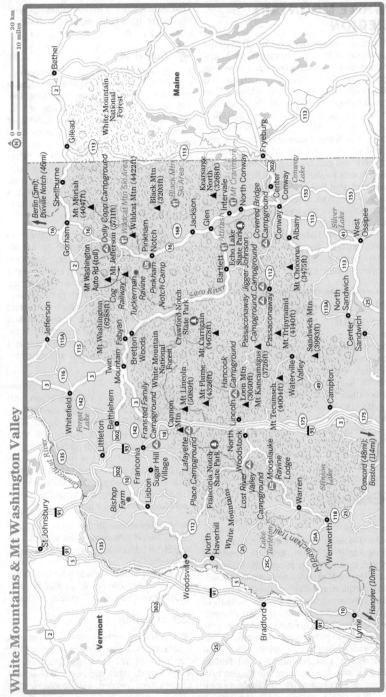

hostel, opened in 2015, is the brainchild of outdoor enthusiasts (and newlyweds) Serena and Justin. A class act all around, it welcomes guests with mutliple outdoor options, a spacious kitchen, a mountain-themed library, a newly built sauna for chilly winter nights and a cozy vibe throughout.

Lost River Valley Campground
CAMPGROUND $
(☑800-370-5678, 603-745-8321; www.lostriver.com; 951 Lost River Rd/NH 112, North Woodstock; tent/RV sites from $31/35, 1-/2-room cabins $60/70; ☺mid-May–mid-Oct) This excellent 200-acre campground (which also contains rustic honest-to-goodness log cabins with ceiling fans) is on the site of a turn-of-the-century lumber mill, and the water wheel still churns. Many of the 125 sites are on the river, which also offers fishing and hiking possibilities. There's a three-night minimum stay late June to early September (two-night minimum at other times).

Riverbank Motel & Cottages
MOTEL $
(☑603-745-3374, 800-633-5624; www.riverbankmotel.com; 183 Connector Rd, Lincoln; r & cottages $67-120; ☎❄) In a peaceful riverside setting just outside of North Woodstock, this inexpensive option has 11 motel rooms and four cottages. Accommodations are basic, though all but the cheapest rooms have small kitchen units. The cottages also have fireplaces.

Woodward's Resort
RESORT $$
(☑603-745-8141, 877-745-4888; www.woodwardsresort.com; 527 Daniel Webster Hwy/US 3, Lincoln; r $89-209; ☎❄) This 85-room resort has lovely landscaped grounds with a duck and trout pond and lots of facilities, including an on-site restaurant, a cozy pub with fireplace, a sauna and Jacuzzi, indoor and outdoor pools, and tennis and racquetball courts. Rooms are spacious, modern and attractive.

Woodstock Inn
INN $$
(☑800-321-3985, 603-745-3951; www.woodstockinnnh.com; 135 Main St/US 3, North Woodstock; r incl breakfast $96-247; ✳☎) This Victorian country inn is North Woodstock's centerpiece. It has 33 individually appointed rooms across five separate buildings (three in a cluster, two across the street), each with modern amenities but in an old-fashioned style. The on-site upscale restaurant, Woodstock Station & Microbrewery, has outdoor seating on the lovely flower-filled patio.

✖ Eating

There's no shortage of eateries around North Woodstock and Lincoln; most places serve standard American fare.

★Cascade Coffee House
CAFE $$
(☑603-745-2001; www.cascadecafenh.com; 115 Main St, North Woodstock; mains $9-14; ☺8am-7pm Mon-Fri, from 7am Sat & Sun; ☎) This creative place in the center of town serves up luscious pastries, fresh smoothies and micro-roaster coffees. At lunch, you'll also find 'wicked awesome' sandwiches, innovative salads, and homemade specials such as mac 'n' cheese or rabbit stew.

Woodstock Inn Station & Brewery
PUB FOOD $$
(☑603-745-3951; www.woodstockinnnh.com; 135 Main St/US 3, North Woodstock; mains $10-24; ☺11:30am-12:45am) Formerly a railroad station, this eatery tries to be everything to everyone. In the end, with more than 150 items, it can probably satisfy just about any food craving, but the pasta, sandwiches and burgers are the most interesting. The beer-sodden rear tavern here is one of the most happening places in this neck of the woods.

ℹ Information

Western White Mountains Chamber of Commerce (☑603-745-6621; www.lincolnwoodstock.com; 126 Main St/US 3, North Woodstock; ☺9am-5pm Mon-Fri, 11am-7pm Sat)

ℹ Getting There & Away

BUS
Concord Coach Lines (☑800-639-3317, 603-228-3300; www.concordcoachlines.com) stops in Lincoln at **Tedeschi's Food Shop** (☑603-745-3195; 36 Main St, Lincoln) on its twice-daily run between Boston and Littleton. Destinations include Concord ($16.50, 1½ hours), Boston's South Station ($28, three hours) and Logan International Airport ($31, 3¼ hours).

CAR & MOTORCYCLE
It's about 2¼ hours (140 miles) from Boston to North Woodstock/Lincoln via I-93.

Kancamagus Highway

One of New Hampshire's prettiest driving routes, the winding 35-mile Kancamagus Hwy (NH 112) between Lincoln and Conway runs right through the WMNF and

DON'T MISS

CAMPING ON THE KANCAMAGUS

The heavily wooded US Forest Service (USFS) campgrounds east of Lincoln along the Kancamagus Hwy are primitive sites (mostly with pit toilets only) but are in high demand in the warm months: if you're up for camping, this is one of the best ways to experience the Kanc. It is not possible at every campground, but advance reservations are highly recommended. Otherwise, arrive early, especially on weekends.

Hancock Campground (☑ 603-745-3816; www.icampnh.com/kancamagus-east-west/hancock-campground; Kancamagus Hwy/NH 112; tent & RV sites $24; ☺ year-round) Five miles east of Lincoln.

Passaconaway Campground (☑ 603-447-5448; www.icampnh.com/kancamagus-east-west/passaconaway; Kancamagus Hwy/NH 112; tent & RV sites $22; ☺ mid-May–mid-Oct) Fifteen miles west of North Conway.

Jigger Johnson Campground (☑ 603-447-5448; www.icampnh.com/kancamagus-east-west/jigger-johnson; Kancamagus Hwy/NH 112; tent & RV sites $24; ☺ mid-May–mid-Oct) Thirteen miles west of North Conway.

Covered Bridge Campground (☑ info 603-447-2166; reservations 877-444-6777; www.recreation.gov; Passaconaway Rd, Albany; tent sites $22; ☺ late May-early Oct)

over Kancamagus Pass (2868ft). Paved only in 1964, and still unspoiled by commercial development, the 'Kanc' offers easy access to US Forest Service (USFS) campgrounds, hiking trails and fantastic scenery.

The route is named for Chief Kancamagus ('The Fearless One'), who assumed the powers of *sagamon* (leader) of the Penacook Native American tribe around 1684. He was the final *sagamon*, succeeding his grandfather, the great Passaconaway, and his uncle Wonalancet. Kancamagus tried to maintain peace between the indigenous peoples and European explorers and settlers, but the newcomers pushed his patience past breaking point. He finally resorted to battle to rid the region of Europeans, but in 1691 he and his followers were forced to escape northward.

🏃 Activities

The WMNF is laced with excellent hiking trails of varying difficulty. For detailed trail-by-trail information, stop at any of the WMNF ranger stations or the White Mountains Attractions Association.

★ Lincoln Woods Trail   HIKING
(NH 112/Kancamagus Hwy, 5 miles east of I-93) Among the easiest and most popular trails in WMNF, the 2.9-mile, 1157ft-elevation Lincoln Woods Trail follows an abandoned railway bed to the Pemigewasset Wilderness boundary (elevation 1450ft). To reach the trailhead, follow the Kancamagus Hwy 5 miles east of I-93 and park in the Lincoln Woods Visitor Center parking lot.

Upon arrival at the Pemigewasset Wilderness boundary, you can either retrace your steps, or continue 6 miles on the easy **Wilderness Trail** to Stillwater Junction (elevation 2060ft), where you can pick up the **Cedar Brook and Hancock Notch Trails** and loop back to the Kancamagus Hwy (5.5 miles east of the Lincoln Woods trailhead parking lot).

Loon Mountain   OUTDOORS
(☑ 800-229-5666; www.loonmtn.com; 60 Loon Mountain Rd, Lincoln) In winter, this popular ski mountain near the Kancamagus Hwy's western end offers 28 miles of trails crisscrossing the 3050ft peak. Skis and snowboards are available for rental. At night the trails open up for tubing. Summer activities include gondola rides to the summit, mountain-bike rentals (adult/child $35/33 per day), a climbing wall ($10), a zip line ($27) and more.

🛏 Sleeping

Camping is the name of the game along the Kancamagus. If you're looking for indoor accommodation, head for Lincoln or Conway, at the highway's western and eastern ends, respectively.

ℹ Information

Saco Ranger District Office (☑ 603-447-5448; 33 Kancamagus Hwy, Conway; ☺ 8am-4:30pm Tue-Sun, 9am-4:30pm Mon) You can pick up WMNF brochures and hiking maps at the Saco Ranger District Office at the eastern end of the Kancamagus Hwy near Conway.

White Mountains Visitor Center (☑ National Forest 603-745-3816, visitor info 603-745-8720; www.visitwhitemountains.com; 200 Kancamagus Hwy, North Woodstock; ☺ visitor info 8:30am-5pm, National Forest desk 9am-3:30pm daily late May–Oct, Fri-Sun only rest of year) A stuffed moose (not real) sets a mood for adventure while brochures and trail maps provide details at this National Forest visitor center, east of I-93 (exit 32, between North Woodstock and Lincoln). Get all the information you need about area trails and buy a White Mountain National Forest Pass ($5 per week), which is required for extended stops at national-forest trailheads.

ⓘ Getting There & Away

To reach the Kancamagus Hwy's western starting point at Lincoln, take exit 32 off I-93 (130 miles north of Boston). For travelers coming from Maine, the highway's eastern entrance in Conway is more accessible; it's 60 miles (1½ hours) from Portland via ME 113 and US 302.

Franconia Notch State Park

Franconia Notch, a narrow gorge shaped over the eons by a wild stream cutting through craggy granite, is one of New Hampshire's most dramatic mountain passes. The Notch's many attractions include prime swimming and skiing, the dramatic hike down the Flume Gorge, and fantastic views of the Presidential Range.

The most scenic parts of the notch are protected by the narrow Franconia Notch State Park. Reduced to two lanes, I-93 (renamed the Franconia Notch Parkway) squeezes through the gorge. Services are available in Lincoln and North Woodstock to the south and in Franconia and Littleton to the north.

◉ Sights

Cannon Mountain Aerial Tramway CABLE CAR
(☑ 603-823-8800; www.cannonmt.com; 260 Tramway Dr, off I-93, exit 34B; round-trip adult/child $17/14; ☺ 9am-5pm late May–mid-Oct; ⊞) This tram shoots up the side of Cannon Mountain, offering a breathtaking view of Franconia Notch. In 1938 the first passenger aerial tramway in North America was installed on this slope. It was replaced in 1980 by the current, larger cable car, capable of carrying 80 passengers up to the summit of Cannon Mountain – a 1-mile ride with 2022ft vertical gain – in less than 10 minutes. You can also hike up the mountain and take the tramway down (adult/child $13/10).

Old Man of the Mountain Memorial Plaza HISTORIC SITE
(I-93, exit 34B) Franconia Notch was long the residence of the Old Man of the Mountain, a natural granite formation shaped like a man's face that became New Hampshire's beloved state symbol (look for his familiar profile on New Hampshire state highway signs). Sadly, the Old Man collapsed in 2003, but tourists still come to see the featureless cliff that remains. In 2013 New Hampshire opened this memorial, including granite benches, interpretive signs and stones engraved with people's memories of the Old Man.

Along the path from the parking lot to the memorial plaza you'll find a gift shop and a **museum** (I-93, exit 34B; ☺ noon-5pm Wed-Mon late May–mid-Oct) FREE displaying forensically accurate diagrams of 'the Profile's' collapse along with other tributes to the Old Man.

DON'T MISS

FLUME GORGE & THE BASIN

To see this natural wonder, take the 2-mile self-guided nature walk that includes the 800ft boardwalk through the **Flume** (☑ 603-745-8391; www.flumegorge.com; I-93, exit 34A; adult/child $16/13; ☺ 9am-5pm early May-late Oct), a natural 12ft- to 20ft-wide cleft in the granite bedrock. The granite walls tower 70ft to 90ft above you, with moss and plants growing from precarious niches and crevices. Signs along the way explain how nature formed this natural phenomenon. A nearby covered bridge is thought to be one of the oldest in the state, erected perhaps as early as the 1820s.

The Basin is a huge glacial pothole, 20ft in diameter, that was carved deep into the granite 15,000 years ago by the action of falling water and swirling stones. It offers a nice (short) walk and a cool spot to ponder one of nature's minor wonders.

🏃 Activities

The park has good hiking trails; most are relatively short, but some may be steep.

Mt Pemigewasset Trail
HIKING

(I-93, exit 34A) This trail begins at the Flume Visitor Center and climbs for 1.4 miles to the 2557ft summit of Mt Pemigewasset (Indian Head), offering excellent views. Return by the same trail or the Indian Head Trail, which joins US 3 after 1 mile. From there, it's a 1-mile walk north to the Flume Visitor Center.

Echo Lake Beach
BEACH

(☑ 603-745-8391; www.nhstateparks.org; I-93, exit 34C; adult/child $4/2; ⊙ 10am-5pm mid-Jun–mid-Sep) Despite its proximity to the highway, this little lake at the foot of Cannon Mountain is a pleasant place to pass an afternoon swimming, kayaking or canoeing (rentals from $11 per hour) in the crystal-clear waters. And many people do: the small beach gets packed, especially on weekends.

Cannon Mountain Ski Area
SKIING

(☑ 603-823-8800, snow report 603-823-7771; www.cannonmt.com; I-93, exit 34B/34C; adult/child/teen $75/53/62) Thanks to its prime Franconia Notch location, Cannon Mountain receives and retains 150in of snow annually. It has 95 runs, 24 miles of trails and New Hampshire's greatest vertical drop (2180ft). The slopes are equipped with an aerial tramway, three triple and three quad chairlifts, one double chair, a rope tow and a wonder carpet (a moving walkway for beginners).

Recreation Trail
CYCLING, WALKING

(I-93, exit 34A) For a casual walk or bike ride, you can't do better than head out to this 8-mile paved trail that wends its way along the Pemigewasset River and through the notch. Bikes are available for rental at the Franconia Sports Shop (☑ 603-823-5241; www.franconiasports.com; 334 Main St, Franconia; per day bike/Nordic skis or snowshoes/downhill skis or snowboard $25/20/30) or Cannon Mountain. Pick up the trail in front of the Flume Gorge Visitor Center.

Lonesome Lake Trail
HIKING

(I-93 btwn exit 34A & exit 34B) Departing from Lafayette Place and its campground, this trail climbs 1000ft in 1.5 miles to Lonesome Lake. Various spur trails lead further up to several summits on the Cannon Balls and Cannon Mountain (3700ft to 4180ft) and south to the Basin.

Kinsman Falls
HIKING

(I-93 btwn exit 34A & exit 34B) On the Cascade Brook, these falls are a short half-mile hike from the Basin via the Basin Cascade Trail.

Bald Mountain & Artists Bluff Trail
HIKING

(I-93, exit 34C) Just north of Echo Lake, off NH 18, this 1.5-mile loop skirts the summit of Bald Mountain (2320ft) and Artists Bluff (2368ft), with short spur trails to the summits.

🛏 Sleeping

Two AMC backcountry huts (Lonesome Lake and Greenleaf) and the Lafayette Place Campground offer the only accommodations inside the park. The best selection of motels is 5 miles south in Lincoln/North Woodstock. For inns and lodges in a more rural setting, Franconia (11 miles north of park headquarters) is your best bet.

Lafayette Place Campground
CAMPGROUND $

(☑ 877-647-2757; www.reserveamerica.com; I-93 btwn exit 34A & exit 34B; campsites $25; ⊙ mid-May–mid-Oct) This popular campground has 97 wooded tent sites that are in heavy demand in summer. Reservations are accepted for 88 of the sites. For the others, arrive early in the day and hope for the best. Many of the state park's hiking trails start here.

ℹ Information

Franconia Notch State Park Visitor Center

(☑ 603-745-8391; www.nhstateparks.org; I-93, exit 34A; ⊙ 8.30am-5pm early May–mid-Oct) Open seasonally, the state park visitor center at Flume Gorge has information about the park and surrounding area. There's also a cafeteria and gift shop.

ℹ Getting There & Away

I-93 runs right through the middle of the park. The visitor center is 135 miles north of Boston (2¼ hours without traffic).

Franconia Town & Around

POP 1100

A few miles north of the notch via I-93, Franconia is a tranquil town with splendid mountain views and a poetic attraction: Robert Frost's farm. Other nearby communities include the tiny, picturesque village of Sugar Hill (a few miles west along tranquil NH 117), and the small towns of Bethlehem (north along NH 142) and Littleton (north up I-93). The entire area is perfect

FRANCONIA'S WILDFLOWER FESTIVAL

One of New Hampshire's great unsung events is the **Celebration of Lupine** (www. facebook.com/LupineCelebration). Offering a counterpoint to the region's spectacular fall foliage season, this spring-blooming wildflower hits its colorful peak every June, carpeting the hillsides and valleys of the Franconia region with purples, blues and pinks. Framed against the mountains and dotted with butterflies, the flowers are a spectacular sight.

The lupine festival celebrates the annual bloom with garden tours, art exhibitions and concerts throughout the month. It's a big event but with a fraction of the leaf-peeping crowds. Other festival events include horse-drawn wagon rides through the lupine fields, tours of local inns, open-air markets, nighttime astronomy tours and craft shows.

for whiling away an afternoon driving down country roads, poking into antique shops, browsing farm stands and chatting up the locals at divey diners.

○ Sights

★ Frost Place   HISTORIC SITE
(☑ 603-823-5510; www.frostplace.org; 158 Ridge Rd, Franconia; adult/child $5/3; ⊘ 1-5pm Thu-Sun Jun, 1-5pm Wed-Mon Jul–mid-Sep, 10am-5pm Wed-Mon mid-Sep–mid-Oct) Robert Frost (1874–1963) was America's most renowned and best-loved poet in the mid-20th century. For several years he lived with his wife and children on a farm near Franconia, now known as Frost Place. Many of his best and most famous poems describe life on this farm and the scenery surrounding it, including 'The Road Not Taken' and 'Stopping by Woods on a Snowy Evening,' and the years spent here were some of the most productive and inspired of his life.

The farmhouse has been kept as faithful to the period as possible, with numerous exhibits of Frost memorabilia.

In the forest behind the house there is a 0.5-mile nature trail. Frost's poems are mounted on plaques in sites appropriate to the things the poems describe, and in several places the plaques have been erected at the exact spots where Frost was inspired to compose the poems. To find Frost's farm, follow NH 116 south from Franconia. After exactly a mile, turn right onto Bickford Hill Rd, then left onto unpaved Ridge Rd. It's a short distance along on the right.

Sugar Hill Sampler   MUSEUM
(☑ 603-823-8478; www.sugarhillsampler.com; 22 Sunset Hill Rd, Sugar Hill Village; ⊘ 9:30am-5pm Sat & Sun mid-Apr–mid-May, 9:30am-5pm daily mid-May–Oct, 10am-4pm daily Nov & Dec, closed Jan–mid-Apr) **FREE** It all started with a collection of heirlooms amassed by the Aldrich family over the many years they have lived

in Sugar Hill Village. Today this collection has expanded to include all sorts of local memorabilia dating from 1780, housed in an old barn built by the Aldrich ancestors themselves. There's also a store selling homemade arts and crafts and edibles.

⌂ Sleeping

Fransted Family
Campground   CAMPGROUND $
(☑ 603-823-5675; www.franstedcampground.com; 974 Profile Rd/NH 18, Franconia; tent/RV sites from $37/48; ⊘ mid-May–mid-Oct; ☢) Two miles northwest of Franconia Notch State Park, this wooded campground caters more to tenters (70 sites) than RVers (40 sites). Many sites are along a stream, and there are tons of family-friendly activities, including swimming, tubing, fishing, mini-golf and a playground.

Pinestead Farm Lodge   LODGE $
(☑ 603-823-8121; www.pinesteadfarmlodge.com; 2059 Easton Rd/NH 116, Franconia; r without bath $55-80, apt $125-150) This is a rarity in Franconia: a working farm, complete with assorted cattle, chickens, ducks and horses. Hosts Bob and Kathleen Sherburn, whose family has owned the property since 1899, rent out clean, simple rooms with shared bathroom and communal kitchen/sitting rooms. Entire apartments are also available. Visitors who come in March or April can watch maple sugaring.

Kinsman Lodge   B&B $$
(☑ 866-546-7626, 603-823-5686; www.kinsman lodge.com; 2165 Easton Rd/NH 116, Franconia; s/d without bath incl breakfast from $55/95; ☢) This lodge built in the 1860s has nine comfortable, unpretentious rooms on the 2nd floor. The 1st floor consists of cozy common areas and an inviting porch. The homemade breakfasts, with offerings such as buttermilk pancakes and luscious omelets, are superb.

★**Sugar Hill Inn**   INN $$
(☑603-823-5621, 800-548-4748; www.sugarhillinn.
com; 116 NH 117, Sugar Hill Village; r/ste incl break-
fast from $150/205; ☎) This restored 1789
farmhouse sits atop a hill that has stunning
panoramic views, especially in the fall, when
the sugar maples lining the hill are ablaze.
Sixteen acres of lawns and gardens and 14 ro-
mantic guest rooms (many with gas fireplaces
and Jacuzzis), not to mention the delectable
country breakfast, make this a top choice.

Franconia Inn   INN $$
(☑603-823-5542, 800-473-5299; www.franconia
inn.com; 1172 Easton Road/NH 116, Franconia; r/
ste incl breakfast from $129/189; ☺closed Apr–
mid-May; ☎☃) This excellent 29-room inn,
just 2 miles south of Franconia, is set on a
broad, fertile, pine-fringed river valley. You'll
find plenty of common space and well-
maintained, traditional guest rooms. The
107-acre estate offers ice skating and prime
cross-country skiing in winter, along with
hiking and horseback riding in summer.

Inn at Sunset Hill   B&B $$
(☑603-823-7244; www.innatsunsethill.com; 231
Sunset Hill Rd, Sugar Hill Village; r incl breakfast
$110-250; ☎) At this sprawling inn newly
adopted by a lovely British couple, all 30
rooms, spread across two buildings, have
lovely views of either the mountains or the
golf course next door. The pricier rooms
have Jacuzzis, fireplaces and private decks,
while simpler ones come with pretty wood
floors. There's a casual tavern serving dinner
accompanied by beers on tap.

✖ **Eating**

Many of Franconia's inns offer dining, in-
cluding the Horse & Hound Inn, Sugar Hill
Inn, Franconia Inn and the Inn at Sunset
Hill.

Polly's Pancake Parlor   AMERICAN $
(☑603-823-5575; www.pollyspancakeparlor.com;
672 NH 117, Sugar Hill Village; mains $8-13; ☺7am-
3pm daily May-Columbus Day, Thu-Sun rest of year)
Since 1938, when it began serving all-you-
can-eat breakfast fare for 50¢, this local in-
stitution 2 miles west of Franconia has been
cranking out pancakes, pancakes and more
pancakes. They're excellent, made with
home-ground flour and accompanied by
the farm's own maple syrup, eggs, sausages
and cob-smoked bacon. Sandwiches (made
with homemade bread) and quiches are also
available.

★**Schilling Beer Co**   PIZZA, PUB FOOD $$
(☑603-444-4800; www.schillingbeer.com; 18 Mill
St, Littleton; pizzas & bar snacks $10-16; ☺3-10pm
Mon-Thu, noon-11pm Fri & Sat, noon-10pm Sun) In
a historic mill by the Ammonoosuc River,
this relatively new microbrewery (opened
in 2013) serves delicious crunchy-crusted,
wood-fired pizzas along with bratwurst
and a nice selection of home brews, from
Konundrum sour pale ale to Erastus Belgian
abbey-style Tripel. The post-and-beam-style
main room, looking out at a covered bridge,
makes for a convivial setting, as does the
riverside deck.

**Cold Mountain
Cafe & Gallery**   INTERNATIONAL $$
(☑603-869-2500; www.coldmountaincafe.com;
2015 Main St, Bethlehem; sandwiches & salads
$8.50-10, dinner mains $12-21; ☺11am-3pm &
5-9pm Mon-Sat, 10am-2pm Sun May-Oct, closed
Mon Nov-Apr) Among the region's finest res-
taurants, this casual cafe and gallery has an
eclectic, changing menu, featuring gourmet
sandwiches, salads and quiches at lunch-
time, and luscious dinner options, such as
bouillabaisse, Indian-spiced lamb stew or
its signature black bean cakes. There's occa-
sional live music, from jazz to folk. Be pre-
pared to wait for your table (outside, since
the place is cozy).

☆ **Entertainment**

★**Colonial Theater**   THEATER, CINEMA
(☑603-869-3422; www.bethlehemcolonial.org;
2050 Main St, Bethlehem) This classic theater in
downtown Bethlehem is a historic place to
hear the jazz, blues and folk musicians that
pass through this little town. The venue also
serves as a cinema, showing independent
and foreign films.

🔒 **Shopping**

Lahout's   SPORTS & OUTDOORS
(☑603-444-5838; www.lahouts.com; 245 Union
St, Littleton; ☺9:30am-5:30pm Mon-Sat, 10am-
4:30pm Sun) A great place to shop for out-
door gear and clothing, Lahout's also just
happens to be America's oldest ski shop, in
business since 1920!

Harman's Cheese & Country Store   FOOD
(☑603-823-8000; www.harmanscheese.com; 1400
NH 117, Sugar Hill Village; ☺9:30am-5pm daily
May-Oct, to 4:30 Mon-Sat Nov-Apr) If you need
to pack a picnic for your hike – or if you
simply wish to stock up on New England
goodies before heading home – don't miss

NEW HAMPSHIRE LEAF PEEPS

In fall the White Mountains turn vibrant shades of crimson and gold, capped by rocky peaks. Already awesome when the trees are green, the vistas are unparalleled when the leaves turn color.

➡ The classic foliage driving tour is the **Kancamagus Highway**, a gorgeous mountain road between Lincoln and Conway.

➡ Between Lincoln and Franconia, I-93 climbs into **Franconia Notch**, where you can marvel at the colors on numerous trails.

➡ Ride the gondola up **Cannon Mountain** for lofty views of the great rainbow of colors and fantastic photo opportunities.

➡ **Crawford Notch** offers hikes for more hardy types, including one up to Mt Washington.

this country store, which stocks delicious cheddar cheese (aged for at least two years), maple syrup, apple cider (in season) and addictive spicy dill pickles.

ℹ Information

Franconia Notch Chamber of Commerce
(☑ 603-823-5661; www.franconianotch.org; 421 Main St, Franconia; ☉ 9am-5pm Tue-Sun late May–mid-Oct; ☏) Southeast of the town center.

ℹ Getting There & Away

Concord Coach Lines (☑ 800-639-3317; www.concordcoachlines.com) stops at **Macs Market** (347 Main St, Franconia). Useful routes include Boston's South Station (one way $34, 3½ hours) and Logan International Airport (one way $38, 3½ hours).

MT WASHINGTON VALLEY

Dramatic mountain scenery surrounds the tiny villages of this popular alpine destination, providing an abundance of outdoor adventures. There's great hiking, skiing, kayaking and rafting, along with idyllic activities like swimming in local creeks, overnighting in country farmhouses and simply exploring the countryside.

Mt Washington Valley stretches north from Conway, at the eastern end of the Kancamagus Hwy, and forms the eastern edge of the White Mountain range. The valley's hub is North Conway, though any of the towns along NH 16/US 302 (also called the White Mountain Hwy) can serve as a White Mountain gateway. The valley's namesake is –

of course – Mt Washington, New England's highest peak (6288ft), which towers over the valley in the northwest.

North Conway & Around

POP 2350

Gateway to mountain adventure, North Conway is a bustling one-street town lined with motor inns, camping supply stores, restaurants and other outfits designed with the traveler in mind. Although most people are just passing through, North Conway does have its charm, with a pleasant selection of restaurants, cozy cafes and nearby inns with historic allure.

◉ Sights

★**Conway Scenic Railroad** TRAIN
(☑ 800-232-5251, 603-356-5251; www.conwayscenic.com; 38 Norcross Circle; Notch Train coach/1st class/dome car $62/76/90, Valley Train coach/1st class/dome/dining car from $17/21/25.50/36.50; ☉ mid-Jun–Oct; ☗) The Notch Train, dating to 1874, offers New England's most scenic rail journey, a slow but spectacular 5½-hour out-and-back trip from North Conway to Crawford Notch. Accompanying live commentary recounts the railroad's history and folklore. Reservations are required.

The same company operates the antique steam-powered Valley Train, which makes a shorter journey through Mt Washington Valley, stopping in Conway and Bartlett. Sunset trains, dining trains and other special events are all available. Fares are reduced for kids aged 12 and under.

★**Mount Washington Observatory Weather Discovery Center** MUSEUM
(☑603-356-2137; www.mountwashington.org; 2779 White Mountain Hwy; adult/child $2/1; ⊙10am-5pm Thu-Mon) If you don't have time to drive to the summit of Mt Washington, but you think wild weather is cool, take an hour to explore this small but fascinating weather museum instead. Shoot an air cannon, interrupt a mini-tornado and learn why temperatures are so extremely cold atop Mt Washington. What happens when you push the red button inside the mock observatory shack? All we'll say is, hold on tight.

Echo Lake State Park STATE PARK
(☑603-356-2672; www.nhstateparks.org; 68 Echo Lake Rd; adult/child $4/2; ⊙9am-7pm) Two miles west of North Conway via River Rd and West Side Rd, this placid mountain lake lies at the foot of White Horse Ledge, a sheer rock wall. A scenic trail circles the lake. There is also a mile-long auto road and hiking trail leading to the 700ft-high Cathedral Ledge, with panoramic White Mountains views. Both Cathedral Ledge and nearby White Horse Ledge are excellent for rock climbing. This is also a fine spot for swimming and picnicking.

🏃 Activities

Eastern Mountain Sports Climbing School CLIMBING
(☑800-310-4504, 603-356-5433; www.emsoutdoors.com/north-conway; 1498 White Mountain Hwy; lessons & climbs per day $150-315; ⊙8:30am-5pm) This shop and climbing school sells maps and guides to the White Mountain National Forest and rents camping equipment, cross-country skis and snowshoes. Year-round, the school offers classes and tours, including one-day ascents of Mt Washington, and the grueling Presidential Range traverse. Class rates depend on how many are in a group (three maximum).

Saco Bound CANOEING
(☑603-447-2177, 888-447-2177; www.sacobound.com; 2561 E Main St/US 302, Conway; boat rentals per day $20-45; ⊙late May-early Oct) Rents out canoes, kayaks, tubes and paddleboards, and organizes guided canoe trips, from an introductory 3-mile day trip to Weston's Bridge to overnight camping excursions.

🎊 Festivals & Events

Fryeburg Fair AGRICULTURAL
(www.fryeburgfair.org; adult/child $10/free; ⊙early Oct) Just over the state border in Maine, this county fair is one of New England's largest and best-known agricultural events. Held annually in early October, the weeklong fair features harness-racing, ox-pulling, skillet-throwing, wreath-making and judging of just about every kind of farm animal you can imagine. There is also plenty of music, food and other fun. Parking costs $5.

🛏 Sleeping

White Mountain Hwy (North Conway's main thoroughfare) is lined with motels, generally of high standard. Streets just back from the main drag shelter some nice inns, while Conway (5 miles south) boasts one of New England's best-run hostels.

★**White Mountains Hostel** HOSTEL $
(☑866-902-2521; www.wmhostel.com; 36 Washington St, Conway; dm $29-31, r per person $49-69; 🛜) 🍴 Set in an early-1900s farmhouse, this gem of a hostel is just off Main St/NH 16 in Conway. Environmentally conscientious and supremely welcoming, it has five bedrooms with bunk beds and four family-size rooms, and a communal lounge and kitchen. On Saturdays, friendly owners Tim and Samara

---

DON'T MISS

AMC WHITE MOUNTAIN HUTS

The Appalachian Mountain Club (AMC; www.outdoors.org/lodging/huts) manages eight overnight huts along the Appalachian Trail in the Presidential Range. In summer and fall a small 'croo' at each hut welcomes hikers, prepares family-style meals, and shares information about conservation and natural sciences. The hut system here has been in operation for more than 125 years. If you're a hiker but not sure about backpacking, try an overnight hut trip to get your feet wet. Just pack overnight clothes, toiletries, trail snacks and water, and the croo will take care of the rest. It ain't fancy – hikers sleep in bunks in co-ed dorms with rustic bathrooms – but the views and the community? Awesome. Reservations are key.

host pay-what-you-like dinners of home-made lasagna, salad, and fresh-baked bread and cookies.

Saco River Camping Area CAMPGROUND $

(☑603-356-3360; www.sacorivercampingarea. com; 1550 White Mountain Hwy/NH 16; tent/RV sites from $39/43, huts $49; ☺May–mid-Oct; ☏☲) This riverside campground away from the highway has 140 wooded and open sites and rustic lean-tos. Canoe and kayak rental is available.

Cranmore Inn B&B $$

(☑603-356-5502; www.cranmoreinn.com; 80 Kearsarge St; r $109-329, ste $169-379, apt $249-419; ☏☲☲) The Cranmore has been operating as a country inn since 1863, and it has been known as reliably good value for much of that time. Traditional country decor predominates, meaning lots of floral and frills. In addition to standard rooms, there is a two-room suite and an apartment, and there's a hot tub on-site – perfect for post-hike sore muscles.

Cabernet Inn INN $$

(☑603-356-4704, 800-866-4704; www.cabernet inn.com; 3552 White Mountain Hwy/NH 16; r incl breakfast $99-265; ☏) This 1842 Victorian cottage is north of North Conway center, near Intervale. Each of the 11 guest rooms has antiques and queen beds, while pricier rooms also have fireplaces and/or Jacuzzis. Common spaces include two living rooms with fireplaces and a shady deck, while the large gourmet kitchen is the source of a decadent country breakfast.

Kearsarge Inn INN $$

(☑855-532-7727, 603-356-8700; www.kearsarge inn.com; 42 Seavey St; r $89-229, ste $179-309; ☏☲) Just off Main St in the heart of North Conway, this lovely inn is the perfect setting for an intimate experience near the center of town. The inn is a 'modern rendition' of the historic Kearsarge House, one of the region's first and grandest hotels. Each of the 15 rooms and one suite are spread across the main building.

Colonial Motel MOTEL $$

(☑866-356-5178, 603-356-5178; www.thecolonial motel.com; 2431 White Mountain Hwy/NH 16; r $93-167, ste $275; ☀☏☲☲) Rooms are traditional but inviting at this 26-room family-run property set back slightly from the main drag. There's a $10 fee per dog per night.

Spruce Moose Lodge LODGE $$

(☑603-356-6239, 800-600-6239; www.spruce mooselodge.com; 207 Seavey St; r $79-225, cottages $135-270; ☏) Located a five-minute walk from town, Spruce Moose has charming rooms set inside a spruce-green 1850s home. Styles vary from classic, pine-floored rooms with dark-wood furnishings to cheery, modern, carpeted quarters. There are also attractive wood-floored cottages with country charm, cozy bungalows with Jacuzzis, and two entire houses for rent (rates are highly variable; inquire for details).

✖ Eating

North Conway's unpretentious eateries cater largely to an active crowd in the mood to carbo-load and socialize after a day of outdoor adventure.

Stairway Cafe BREAKFAST $

(☑603-356-5200; www.stairwaycafe.com; 2649 White Mountain Hwy; mains $7-14; ☺7am-3pm) The all-day breakfast treats are scrumptious at this brightly decorated, six-table upstairs cafe, from blackboard specials like homemade cinnamon muffins to lobster Benedict. Omelettes come with grilled red Maine potatoes, veggie baked beans or homemade apple sauce, and there's a range of artisanal wild game sausages (try the venison-merlot-blueberry or wild boar-cranberry-shiraz varieties). Lunch offerings include burgers, wraps and salads.

Met Coffee House CAFE $

(☑603-356-2332; www.metcoffeehouse.com; 2680 White Mountain Hwy; pastries $2-4; ☺6:30am-9pm Jun-Sep, to 7pm Sun-Thu, to 9pm Fri & Sat Oct-May; ☏) Just north of Schouler Park, this small coffeehouse is the best place in town for a cup of coffee or a pastry. You can sink into a plush sofa, or grab a table out front in the summer and enjoy the passing people parade. Artwork (all for sale, mainly by local artists) decorates the walls, and baristas play an eclectic mix of world tunes and jazz.

★Moat Mountain
Smoke House & Brewing Co PUB FOOD $$

(☑603-356-6381; www.moatmountain.com; 3378 White Mountain Hwy/NH 16; mains $10-28; ☺11:30am-late) Come here for a variety of American food with a nod to southern fare: BBQ chicken and ribs, juicy burgers, luscious salads, wood-grilled pizzas, pulled-pork sliders and Creole crab cakes. Wash it down with one of the dozen-plus brews

NEW HAMPSHIRE NORTH CONWAY & AROUND

made on-site. The friendly bar is also a popular local hangout.

May Kelly's Cottage
IRISH, AMERICAN **$$**

(☑ 603-356-7005; www.maykellys.com; 3002 White Mountain Hwy; mains $9-24; ☻ 4-9pm Tue-Thu, noon-10pm Fri & Sat, noon-8pm Sun) Irish conviviality and friendliness? May Kelly's is the real deal. Local-attic decor, helpful servers, mountain views, sandwiches and hearty mains like the Ploughman's Dinner (top sirloin steak, Irish potato cake, brown bread and baked beans) make it a local favorite.

❶ Information

Mt Washington Valley Chamber of Commerce (☑ 603-356-5701, 603-356-5947; www.mtwashingtonvalley.org; 2617 White Mountain Hwy; ☻ 9am-6pm daily May-Oct, 9am-5pm Fri & Sat Nov-Apr) Tourist information just south of the town center.

❶ Getting There & Away

Concord Coach Lines (☑ 800-639-3317, 603-228-3300; www.concordcoachlines.com) offers service to Concord ($19.50, 2¼ hours), Boston's South Station ($31, four hours) and Logan International Airport ($36, 4¼ hours) on its daily run between Boston and Berlin, NH. Buses stop in North Conway at the Eastern Slope Inn (2760 Main St).

Jackson & Around

POP 816

The quintessential New England village, Jackson is home to Mt Washington Valley's premier cross-country ski center. Glen, a hamlet 3 miles south of Jackson, is a magnet for families as it's home to one of New Hampshire's most popular amusement parks, Story Land.

◉ Sights

Jackson Falls
WATERFALL

(Carter Notch Rd/NH 16B) One of the best ways to spend a sun-drenched afternoon in Jackson is to take a swim in these falls on the Wildcat River just outside of town. You'll have marvelous mountain views as you splash about. To get there, take the Carter Notch Rd/NH 16B half a mile north of town.

Story Land
AMUSEMENT PARK

(☑ 603-383-4186; www.storylandnh.com; 850 NH 16, Glen; $33; ☻ 9am-6pm daily Jul & Aug, to 5pm rest of season, Sat & Sun only late May-early Jun & Sep–mid-Oct; ⚑) This 30-acre theme and amusement park is aimed at the three- to nine-year-old crowd. The rides, activities and shows are small-scale and well done – a refreshing break from the mega-amusements in other places.

🏃 Activities

★ Jackson XC
SKIING

(Jackson Ski Touring Foundation; ☑ 603-383-9355; www.jacksonxc.org; 153 Main St, Jackson; day pass adult/child $21/10, ski/snowshoe rentals per day from $16/12) A dream destination for Nordic ski enthusiasts, Jackson XC is famous for its 93 miles of cross-country trails and knowledgeable staff. You can rent skis and showshoes, take lessons at the ski school, or test demo equipment, get your skis waxed and buy top-of-the-line gear at the on-site branch of well-regarded outfitter Gorham Bike & Ski.

Attitash
SKIING

(☑ 800-223-7669; www.attitash.com; 775 US 302, Bartlett; lift ticket adult/child/teen weekend $79/54/64, weekday $75/50/60) West of Glen, you can play and stay at Attitash. The resort's two mountains, Attitash and Bear Peak, offer a vertical drop of 1750ft; 11 lifts; and 68 ski trails (50% intermediate, 25% expert and 25% beginner). From mid-June to mid-October the resort offers horseback riding ($35 to $55), lift-assisted mountain biking ($35), zipline tours ($70) and many other activities.

Black Mountain Ski Area
SKIING

(☑ 603-383-4490, 800-475-4669; www.blackmt.com; 373 Black Mountain Rd/NH 16B, Jackson; lift ticket adult/child/teen weekends $55/38/42, weekday $40/30/35; ⚑) This ski area has a vertical drop of 1100ft. Forty trails – about equally divided between beginner, intermediate and expert slopes – are served by four lifts. This a good place for beginners and families with small children. In summer, the resort also offers horseback ($50 per hour) and pony rides ($15 per 15 minutes).

🛏 Sleeping

For the ultimate New England experience, spend the night in one of Jackson's cozy inns, nestled snugly in the valley below Mt Washington. If you'd prefer to sleep near the slopes, Attitash ski area offers everything from motel rooms to town houses to spiffy accommodations in its Grand Summit Hotel.

★ **Snowflake Inn** INN $$
(☑888-383-1020, 603-383-8259; www.thesnow
flakeinn.com; 95 Main St, Jackson; ste incl breakfast
$189-375; 🕏🖾) All of the suites at this ele-
gant inn are spacious and have fireplaces
and two-person Jacuzzis. There are plenty
of modern creature comforts, including
400-count triple sheets, flat-screen TVs and
lavish sitting areas. An on-site spa adds to
the charm. No children under 15 years.

Carter Notch Inn INN $$
(☑603-383-9630, 800-794-9434; www.carter
notchinn.com; 163 Carter Notch Rd, Jackson; r
$99-209; 🕏) Across from a golf course (that
could pass for pristine mountain pasture in
snow season), this B&B on a beautiful winding country road a mile north of Jackson has
eight rooms, no two alike. Amenities include
full country breakfasts, complimentary coffee, tea, cookies, beer and wine, a hot tub out
back and a cozy fireplace lounge. No kids
under 12 years.

Wildcat Inn & Tavern INN $$
(☑800-228-4245, 603-356-8700; www.wildcat
tavern.com; 94 Main St, Jackson; r $59-189, ste
$69-219, 6-person cottages $149-329) This cen-
trally located village lodge has a dozen
cozy rooms with antique furnishings. The
cottage – known as the 'Igloo' – sleeps up
to six people. One of Jackson's best restau-
rants, Wildcat Tavern, is on-site and offers
New England–leaning American food, with
themed evenings like lobster Tuesdays or
$26.95 dinner-for-two Wednesdays.

Wentworth INN $$$
(☑603-383-9700, 800-637-0013; www.thewent
worth.com; 1 Carter Notch Rd/NH 16B, Jackson;
r $154-428, ste $294-848; 🕏) This grand country inn is on the edge of Jackson Village,
beside a gorgeous public golf course. It's an
elegant affair, with 51 spacious rooms, a gracious lobby and dining room, and outdoor
facilities such as tennis courts. The best
rooms have fireplaces, outdoor hot tubs and
gorgeous antique furnishings.

✖ Eating

Many of Jackson's inns have excellent (and
expensive) dining rooms.

Back Country Bakery & Cafe CAFE $
(18 Black Mountain Rd, Jackson; soups & sandwiches
$5-9; ⏰8am-4pm Wed-Mon) Cheerfully decorat-
ed with orange walls and a cozy sitting area
surrounded by tree murals, this cafe in the
center of town displays a chalkboard menu
with breakfast treats on one side – granola
with Greek yogurt, pastries or breakfast sandwiches like the Attitash (egg, bacon, cheese,
peppers and spinach) – and lunch specials on
the other (sandwiches, wraps and soups).

Shovel Handle Pub PUB FOOD $$
(☑603-383-8916; www.shovelhandlepub.com;
357 Black Mountain Rd, Jackson; mains $11-26;
⏰5-9pm Wed-Fri & Sun) At this beautifully re-
stored 19th-century barn up the hill from
Jackson, delicious Yankee comfort food –
think corn chowder, lobster bisque, burg-
ers and steaks – is served alongside draft
New England microbrews. Live music two
or three times a week is icing on the cake.

★ **Cider Company
Restaurant** MODERN AMERICAN $$$
(☑603-383-9061; www.ciderconh.com; US 302,
Glen; mains $22-28; ⏰5-9pm Sun-Thu, to 10pm Fri
& Sat) Open for dinner nightly, this restaurant in an elegant 1890s farmhouse features
expertly prepared classics, such as seared
sea scallops, pan-roasted duck breast, baked
polenta and grilled hanger steak.

❶ Information

Jackson Area Chamber of Commerce
(☑603-383-9356; www.jacksonnh.com; 18
Main St, Jackson; ⏰noon-5pm Mon, 9am-5pm
Tue-Thu, 9am-noon Fri) The most helpful and
knowledgeable chamber of commerce we came
across in the entire state. Has loads of local
insight; ask here about scenic walks in the area.

❶ Getting There & Away

Jackson is 7 miles north of North Conway. Take
NH 16 and then cross the Ellis River via the historic red-covered bridge.

> ### ❶ TO THE TRAILHEAD, JEEVES!
>
> Every summer, the Appalachian Moun-
> tain Club (AMC) runs two convenient
> **Hiker Shuttles** (☑reservations 603-
> 466-2727; www.outdoors.org/lodging/lodg
> ing-shuttle.cfm; 1-way trip AMC members/
> nonmembers $19/23; ⏰daily Jun–mid-Sep,
> Sat & Sun mid-Sep–mid-Oct). The western
> route runs from AMC's Highland Center
> to the Lincoln Woods Visitor Center via
> the Zealand, Gale River, Lafayette, Liber-
> ty Spring and Old Bridle Path trailheads;
> the eastern route goes to Pinkham
> Notch via the 19 Mile Brook and Ammo-
> noosuc Ravine trailheads.

Concord Coach Lines (☑ 800-639-3317, 603-228-3300; www.concordcoachlines.com) stops at the Jackson Area Chamber of Commerce on its daily run between Boston and Berlin, NH. Destinations include Concord ($20.50, 2½ hours), Boston's South Station ($32, four hours) and Logan International Airport ($37, 4¼ hours).

Crawford Notch & Bretton Woods

This beautiful 1773ft mountain pass on the western slopes of Mt Washington is deeply rooted in New Hampshire lore. In 1826 torrential rains here triggered massive mud slides, killing the Willey family in the valley below. The dramatic incident made the newspapers and fired the imaginations of painter Thomas Cole and author Nathaniel Hawthorne. Both men used the incident for inspiration, thus unwittingly putting Crawford Notch on the tourist maps.

Even so, the area remained known mainly to locals and wealthy summer visitors who patronized the grand Mt Washington Hotel in Bretton Woods – until 1944, when President Roosevelt chose the hotel as the site of a conference to establish a post-WWII global economic order.

Today the hotel is as grand as ever, while a steady flow of visitors comes to climb Mt Washington – on foot, or aboard a steam-powered locomotive on the dramatic Mount Washington Cog Railway.

◎ Sights

★**Crawford Notch State Park**   STATE PARK
(☑ 603-374-2272; www.nhstateparks.org; 1464 US 302, Harts Location; adult/child $4/2; ☺ visitor center late May–mid-Oct, park year-round unless posted otherwise) This pretty park maintains an extensive system of hiking trails. From the Willey House visitor center, you can walk the easy 0.5-mile Pond Loop Trail, the 1-mile Sam Willey Trail and the Ripley Falls Trail, a 1-mile hike from US 302 via the Ethan Pond Trail. The trailhead for Arethusa Falls, a 1.3-mile hike, is 0.5 miles south of the Dry River Campground on US 302. Serious hikers can also tackle the much longer trek up Mt Washington.

✦ Activities

★**Mount Washington Cog Railway**   TOURIST TRAIN
(☑ 603-278-5404; www.thecog.com; 3168 Bass Station Rd; adult $68-73, child $39; ☺ daily Jun-Oct, Sat & Sun late Apr, May & Nov) Purists walk and the lazy drive, but the quaintest way to reach Mt Washington summit is via this cog railway. Since 1869 coal-fired, steam-powered locomotives have climbed this scenic 3.5-mile track up a steep mountainside trestle (three hours round-trip). Two old-fashioned steam trains run daily late May to October, supplemented by biodiesel-fueled trains late April to November. Reservations highly recommended.

The grade on the Jacob's ladder trestle is 37% – making this the second-steepest railway track in the world (after Mt Pilatus, Switzerland).

The base station is 6 miles east of US 302. Turn east in Fabyan, just northwest of the Omni Mt Washington Hotel (between Bretton Woods and Twin Mountain). Also, remember that the average temperature at the summit is 40°F in summer and the wind is always blowing, so bring a sweater and windbreaker.

Bretton Woods Ski Area   SKIING
(☑ 603-278-3320; www.brettonwoods.com; 99 Ski Area Rd, off US 302; lift ticket adult/child/teen weekends & holidays $89/53/68, weekdays $78/43/58; Nordic day pass $21/14/19) The region's largest

---

DON'T MISS

NEW ENGLAND'S LOFTIEST ATTRACTION

Housed atop Mt Washington in the Sherman Adams Summit Building, **Extreme Mt Washington** (☑ 800-706-0432; www.mountwashington.org/visit-us; Mt Washington summit; $5, free with Mt Washington Cog Railway or Auto Road ticket; ☺ variable, depending on weather), opened in 2014, gives visitors a hands-on look at Mt Washington's claim as 'home of the world's worst weather.' Exhibits show how Mt Washington Observatory scientists track climate conditions year-round despite hurricane-force winds and Arctic temperatures. Other exhibits let visitors pilot a simulated snowcat and learn how rime ice is formed. Adjacent to the museum is a lookout tower and a concession area selling souvenirs and refreshments.

ski area, Bretton Woods offers both downhill and cross-country winter skiing. The downhill area has a vertical drop of 1500ft, with 10 lifts serving 97 trails, most of which are intermediate. The resort also maintains a 60-mile network of Nordic (cross-country) ski trails that traverse open fields, wooded paths and mountain streams. Ski rental, lessons and childcare are also available.

Bretton Woods Canopy Tour　　ADVENTURE
(☑ 603-278-4947; www.brettonwoods.com; US 302; per person $89-110; ☺ tours 10am & 1:30pm year-round, plus additional times during peak periods) This four-season canopy tour sends you hiking through the woods, strolling over sky bridges and swooshing down zip lines that drop 1000ft at 30mph to tree platforms.

🛏 Sleeping

You'll rarely find a 10-mile stretch of rural road with such a widely skewed range of accommodations. Take your pick: sleep cozily in a humble tent under the stars on the east side of Crawford Notch, live it up in five-star luxury just across the mountain at the Omni Mt Washington Resort or go for one of the more moderately priced options in between.

Crawford Notch General
Store & Campground　　CAMPGROUND $
(☑ 603-374-2779; www.crawfordnotchcamping. com; 1138 US 302, Hart's Location; tent sites $36-48, cabins $78-98, yurts $68; ☺ mid-May–mid-Oct) This handy all-purpose place sells camping supplies and groceries to use at its lovely wooded sites. You'll also find small, rustic, but rather handsome wooden cabins and yurts. Some of the sites are on the Saco River, and there's good swimming right in front.

Dry River Campground　　CAMPGROUND $
(☑ info 603-374-2272, reservations 877-647-2757; www.reserveamerica.org; US 302, Harts Location; campsites $25-29; ☺ late May-early Oct) Near the southern end of Crawford Notch State Park, this quiet state-run campground has 35 tent sites with a clean bathhouse, flush toilets, showers and laundry facilities. Thirty of the sites can be reserved in advance late May to early October. Limited pre- and post-season camping is also available on a first-come, first-served basis; dates vary annually – call the info number for details.

AMC Highland Lodge　　LODGE $$
(☑ front desk 603-278-4453, reservations 603-466-2727; www.outdoors.org/lodging/lodges/highland; NH 302, Bretton Woods; per adult/child/teen r from $158/48/92, without bath from $109/48/92, all incl breakfast & dinner; ☎) This cozy Appalachian Mountain Club (AMC) lodge is set amid the splendor of Crawford Notch, an ideal base for hiking the trails crisscrossing the Presidential Range. The grounds are beautiful, rooms are basic but comfortable, meals are hearty and guests are outdoor enthusiasts. Discounts available for AMC members. The information center, open to the public, has loads of information about regional hiking.

Bretton Arms Inn　　INN $$
(☑ 603-278-3000; www.mtwashington.com; 173 Mt Washington Rd, Bretton Woods; r $149-379) People have been staying here for almost a century. On the same estate as the Omni Mt Washington Hotel, this manse was built as a grand 'summer cottage' in 1896, but it has been an inn since 1907. It offers an intimate and folksy atmosphere.

★Omni Mt Washington
Hotel & Resort　　HOTEL $$$
(☑ 603-278-1000; www.omnihotels.com; 310 Mt Washington Hotel Rd, Bretton Woods; r $149-549, ste $769-959; 🅿 @ 🛜 🐾) Open since 1902, this grand hotel maintains a sense of fun – note the moose's head overlooking the lobby and the framed local wildflowers in many of the guest rooms. Also offers 27 holes of golf, red-clay tennis courts, an equestrian center and a spa. There's a $25 daily resort fee.

ℹ Information

AMC Highland Center at Crawford Notch
(www.amc-nh.org; Crawford Notch; ☺ 24hr) Complete information about hiking, biking and camping in the area, including maps and trail guides. Daily activities and guided hikes are offered.

Crawford Depot & Visitor Center (www. outdoors.org; ☺ 9am-5pm Jun–mid-Oct) AMC's summer visitor center in Crawford Notch is housed in a historic railway depot.

Crawford Notch State Park Visitor Center
(☑ 603-374-2272; www.nhstateparks.org; ☺ 9:30am-5pm late May–mid-Oct) State park visitor center, on the historic Willey homesite.

Twin Mountain-Bretton Woods Chamber of Commerce (☑ 800-245-8946; www.twinmoun tain.org; cnr US 302 & US 3; ☺ 9am-5pm Jul & Aug, 9am-5pm Fri-Sun late Sep–mid-Oct, self-serve rest of year) Year-round info board and seasonally staffed kiosk.

ℹ Getting There & Away

From North Conway, NH, it's an easy 25-mile drive up US 302 to Crawford Notch (or 29 miles to Bretton Woods). The notch is also easily reachable from I-93. If traveling northbound on I-93, take exit 35 and continue north on US 3 to eastbound US 302. If coming south down I-93, take exit 40 and follow signs for US 302 east.

Pinkham Notch

Pinkham Notch (2032ft) is a mountain-pass area known for its wild beauty, and its useful facilities for campers and hikers make it one of the most popular and crowded activity centers in the White Mountains. Wildcat Mountain and Tuckerman Ravine offer good skiing, and an excellent system of trails provides access to the natural beauties of the Presidential Range, especially Mt Washington. For the less athletically inclined, the Mt Washington Auto Rd provides easy access to the summit.

🏃 Activities

Tuckerman Ravine   SKIING
(www.timefortuckerman.com) The cirque at this ravine on Mt Washington's southeastern flank has several ski trails for purists. What's pure about it? No lifts. You climb up the mountain, then ski down. Tuckerman is perhaps best in spring, when most ski resorts are struggling to keep their snow cover, since nature conspires to keep the ravine in shadow much of the time.

Park in the Wildcat Mountain lot for the climb up the ravine. For information about safety precautions, see the Mount Washington Avalanche Center's website (www.mountwashingtonavalanchecenter.org/information/spring-skiing).

Wildcat Ziprider   ADVENTURE SPORTS
(☑ 888-754-9453; www.skiwildcat.com/ziprider; Wildcat Mountain Resort, 542 NH 16, Pinkham Notch; Ziprider $20; ☉ 10am-5pm daily mid-Jun–early Sep, Sat & Sun mid-Sep–mid-Oct) For spectacular summertime views of Mt Washington, Wildcat Mountain resort offers a high-altitude experience. The Ziprider (like a zip line, but you are suspended from the steel cables) whizzes 70ft above the treetops, descending 2100ft at a 12% grade; the view is spectacular, though when you're flying by at 45 miles per hour, it's secondary to the adrenaline rush.

The mountain's summertime **Gondola Skyride** (www.skiwildcat.com/scenic-gondola; adult/child $15/10) offers a more tranquil and equally scenic experience.

Wildcat Mountain   SKIING
(☑ 603-466-3326, 888-754-9453; www.skiwildcat.com; 542 NH 16, Pinkham Notch; lift ticket adult/child/teen weekend $79/54/64, weekday $75/50/60) With a vertical drop of 2112ft, this ski resort midway between Jackson and Gorham tops out at 4415ft. Its 225 acres include four lifts and 48 trails for all levels, and lift tickets here grant free access to nearby Attitash Mountain Resort. The 2.75-mile Polecat Run from the summit is a treat for beginners.

Thanks to newly upgraded snowmaking equipment, the season here is one of New England's longest, starting as early as November and ending as late as May.

Mt Washington Auto Road   DRIVING
(☑ 603-466-3988; www.mountwashingtonautoroad.com; off NH 16, Gorham; car & driver $29, extra adult/child $9/7, guided tour adult/child $36/16; ☉ 7:30am-6pm mid-Jun–Aug, shorter hours mid-May–mid-Jun & Sep-late Oct) The Mt Washington Summit Rd Company operates an 8-mile-long alpine toll road from Pinkham Notch to the summit of Mt Washington. If you'd rather not drive, you can take a two-hour guided tour, which allows a full hour on the summit. In summer, one-way shuttles for hikers (adult/child $31/13) are also available. In severe weather the road may be closed (even in summer).

🛏 Sleeping & Eating

Your choices here are simple: stay at Joe Dodge Lodge in the heart of the notch, or head toward Gorham or Jackson for a wider choice of accommodations.

Joe Dodge Lodge   LODGE $
(☑ 603-466-2727; www.outdoors.org/lodging/lodges/pinkham; 361 NH 16, Pinkham Notch; r adult/child/teen incl breakfast $80/28/61, incl breakfast & dinner $105/41/78) The AMC camp at Pinkham Notch incorporates this lodge, with dorms housing more than 100 beds. Reserve bunks in advance. Discounts are available for AMC members.

Dolly Copp Campground   CAMPGROUND $
(☑ 603-466-2713, reservations 877-444-6777; www.recreation.gov; NH 16; tent & RV sites $22; ☉ mid-May–mid-Oct) On the flanks of Mt Washington, 6 miles south of Gorham, this USFS campground has 194 primitive sites, some available by advance reservation, others on a first-come, first-served basis. In 2016 the campground underwent extensive

renovations, including repaving of roads and the installation of brand-new restroom and shower facilities.

★**Libby's Bistro & Saalt Pub** INTERNATIONAL **$$**
(☑603-466-5330; www.libbysbistro.org; 111 Main St/NH 16, Gorham; mains $12-23; ☺bistro from 5-9pm Fri & Sat, pub 5-9pm Wed-Sun) A labor of love for acclaimed chef Liz Jackson, this 20-year-old bistro serves a seasonally changing, globally inspired menu that draws heavily on locally sourced ingredients; offerings run the gamut from Latin American to Middle Eastern, Vietnamese to Mediterranean. In the pub, expect more casual fare, from creative burgers to Caesar salads to mac 'n' cheese with herb-and-garlic bread crumbs.

❶ Information

Pinkham Notch Visitor Center (☑603-466-2721; www.outdoors.org/lodging/lodges/pinkham/pinkham-notch-visitor-center.cfm; 361 NH 16, Pinkham Notch; ☺6:30am-10pm May-Oct, to 9pm Nov-Apr) From its Pinkham Notch headquarters, the Appalachian Mountain Club organizes guided nature walks, canoe trips, cross-country ski and snowshoe treks, and other outdoor adventures, and operates a summer hikers' shuttle that stops at many trailheads along US 302. The *AMC White Mountain Guide,* on sale here or online from the AMC website, includes detailed maps and statistics for each trail.

The AMC maintains hikers' 'high huts' providing meals and lodging. Carter Notch Hut is located on Nineteen-Mile Brook Trail, and Lakes of the Clouds Hut is on Crawford Path. For those hiking the Appalachian Trail, the Zealand and Carter huts are open year-round.

❶ Getting There & Away

BUS

Concord Coach Lines (☑800-639-3317, 603-228-3300; www.concordcoachlines.com) stops at Pinkham Notch on its daily run between Boston and Berlin, NH. Destinations include Concord ($22.50, 2¾ hours), Boston's South Station ($34, 4¼ hours) and Logan International Airport ($39, 4½ hours). The bus stop is at the Pinkham Notch Visitor Center.

CAR & MOTORCYCLE

NH 16 runs north 11 miles from North Conway and Jackson to Pinkham Notch, then past the Wildcat Mountain ski area and Tuckerman Ravine, through the small settlement of Glen House and past the Dolly Copp Campground to Gorham and Berlin.

Great North Woods

Not too many people make it all the way up here, but New Hampshire offers three scenic routes north of the Notches and Bretton Woods. Nothing beats US 2 from the Vermont–New Hampshire state line to the Maine–New Hampshire line: the expansive but looming mountain views are unparalleled. Alternatively, if you're heading to the outposts of Maine, take NH 16 north from Gorham to Errol. This route runs parallel to the birch-lined Androscoggin River.

If you really want to get remote, follow US 3 through the Connecticut Lakes region up to New Hampshire's extreme northern tip, just below the Quebec border. This is the heart of New Hampshire's moose country. Take it slow and heed the ubiquitous signs warning of 'hundreds of collisions' – they're not joking! For a better chance of spotting a moose 'in the flesh,' consider the **moose tours** (☑877-986-6673, 603-466-3103; www.gorhammoosetours.org; 69 Main St, Gorham; adult/child $25/15; ☺variable hours) sponsored by the town of Gorham.

Maine

📖 207 / POP 1.3 MILLION

Best Places to Eat

➜ Fore Street (p377)

➜ Red's Eats (p384)

➜ Primo (p389)

➜ Five Islands Lobster Company (p383)

➜ Cabbage Island Clambakes (p386)

Best Places to Sleep

➜ Press Hotel (p376)

➜ Whitehall (p390)

➜ Recompence Shore Campground (p380)

➜ Danforth Inn (p376)

➜ NEOC Twin Pines Camp (p404)

Why Go?

With more lobsters, lighthouses and charming resort villages than you can shake a selfie stick at, Maine is New England at its most iconic. The sea looms large here, with mile upon mile of jagged sea cliffs, peaceful harbors and pebbly beaches. Eat and drink your way through food- and beer-crazed Portland, one of America's coolest small cities. Explore the historic shipbuilding villages of the Midcoast. Hike through Acadia National Park, a spectacular island of mountains and fjord-like estuaries. Let the coastal wind whip through those cobwebs and inhale the salty air. Venture into the state's inland region, a vast wilderness of pine forest and snowy peaks.

Outdoor adventurers can race white-water rapids, cycle the winding shore roads or kayak beside playful harbor seals. For slower-paced fun, there are plenty of antique shops, cozy lobster shacks, charming inns and locally brewed beer on hand.

And, oh, did we mention the lobster?

When to Go
Portland

Jun–Sep Coastal towns fill up with travelers hungry for fresh lobster.

Oct Leaf-peepers descend upon villages with cameras at the ready.

Nov–Mar Skiers and snowmobiles ride the mountain trails.

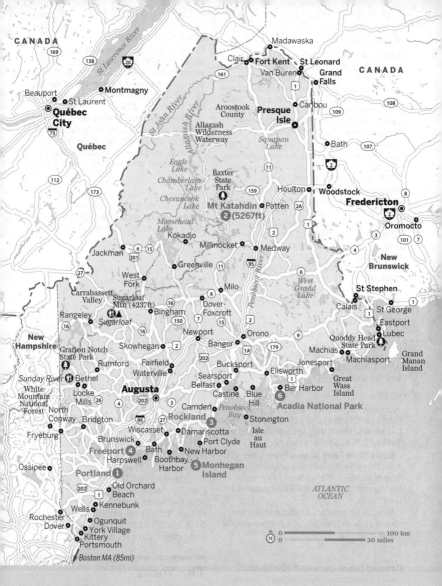

Maine Highlights

1 **Old Port District** (p373)
Exploring the cafes, bars and
galleries lining Portland's
19th-century cobblestone
backstreets.

2 **Mt Katahdin** (p403)
Bagging the end point of the
2190-mile-long Appalachian
Trail in Baxter State Park.

3 **Farnsworth Art Museum**
(p387) Exploring iconic
American art in Rockland.

4 **LL Bean** (p381) Picking
up a cozy new fleece and
preppy-chic wellies at the
flagship store in Freeport.

5 **Monhegan Island** (p386)
Painting or photographing

the windswept rocks of this
solitary isle.

6 **Acadia National Park**
(p399) Hiking up Cadillac
Mountain, then taking a
(chilly) dip in Echo Lake.

7 **Lobster Pounds** (p369)
Tying on your bib and cracking
a freshly steamed crustacean at
one of Maine's lobster shacks.

ℹ Information

Bureau of Parks & Lands (☏ 207-287-3821; www.parksandlands.com) Oversees 48 state parks and historic sites throughout the state. Details of each park are on the website, as well as activities and camping opportunities. Make campground reservations at www.campwithme.com or call 207-624-9950 (weekdays from February to mid-September only).

Maine Office of Tourism (☏ 888-624-6345; www.visitmaine.com) This is a comprehensive website, where you can also order a map and helpful brochure to be mailed to you.

Maine Tourism Association (☏ 207-623-0363; www.mainetourism.com) Runs information centers on the principal routes into the state – Calais, Fryeburg, Hampden, Houlton, Kittery, West Gardiner and Yarmouth. Each facility is generally open 9am to 5:30pm, with extended hours in summer (8am to 6pm). The website lists all chamber of commerce offices in Maine.

ℹ Getting There & Around

AIRPORTS & AIRLINES
Portland International Jetport (p434) is the state's main airport, but a number of airlines also serve **Bangor International Airport** (☏ 866-359-2264; www.flybangor.com; 287 Godfrey Blvd).

BOAT
In summer, **Bay Ferries** (☏ 877-762-7245; www.ferries.ca/thecat; ☉ mid-Jun–Sep) operates the CAT service, sailing daily between Portland and Yarmouth, Nova Scotia (six hours).

Maine State Ferry Service (www.maine.gov/mdot/ferry/) operates boats to several larger islands, mostly in the Penobscot Bay region, from terminals at Rockland, Bass Harbor and Lincolnville.

An excellent resource for all the state's ferry routes, state and privately run, is at www.exploremaine.org/ferry.

BUS
Concord Coach Lines (☏ 800-639-3317; www.concordcoachlines.com) operates daily buses between Boston (including Logan Airport) and Portland, continuing on to Midcoast Maine towns (Bath, Belfast, Brunswick, Camden, Damariscotta, Lincolnville, Rockland, Searsport and Waldoboro). There are also services connecting Boston, Portland and the inland towns of Augusta, Waterville and Bangor. Two services a day link Portland with New York City.

Greyhound (☏ 800-231-2222; www.greyhound.com) stops in Bangor, Portland, Bath, Rockland and various other towns.

CAR & MOTORCYCLE
Except for the Maine Turnpike (I-95 and I-495) and part of I-295, Maine has no fast, limited-access highways. Roads along the coast flood with traffic during the summer tourist season. As a result, you must plan for more driving time when traveling in Maine.

Note: moose are a particular danger to drivers in Maine, even as far south as Portland. They've been known to cripple a bus and walk away. Be especially watchful in spring and fall and around dusk and dawn, when the moose are most active.

TRAIN
The *Downeaster,* run by **Amtrak** (☏ 800-872-7245; www.amtrak.com), makes five trips daily between Boston and Portland (2½ hours). A couple of these services extend to Freeport and Brunswick, too.

SOUTHERN MAINE COAST

Maine's southern coast embodies the state slogan 'Vacationland,' with busy commercial strips, sandy beaches and resort towns that get packed in the summer months. Despite the crowds, there are some charming features to be found. While Kittery is a long, commercial strip mall, Ogunquit has a lovely beach and is Maine's gay mecca. Between the two lie quaint York Village and busy, populist York Beach. Beyond, the Kennebunks are small historic settlements with lavish mansions (some of which are now B&Bs) near pretty beaches and rugged coastline.

Although you'll have to use your imagination, the southern coast is deeply associated with the works of American artist Winslow Homer, who spent his summers in Prouts Neck (just south of Portland), which has some magnificent scenery.

The Yorks
POP 12,500

York Village, York Harbor, York Beach and Cape Neddick collectively make up the Yorks. York Village, the first English city chartered in North America, feels like a living history museum, with a small downtown filled with impeccably maintained historic buildings. York Harbor was developed more than a century ago as a posh summer resort and many of its grand Victorian mansions and hotels remain. York Beach has a more populist vibe, with RV parks, candy shops and arcades galore. Cape Neddick, a small, mostly residential peninsula jutting out into the sea, is home to the famous Nubble Light.

◉ Sights & Activities

Museums of Old York   MUSEUM
(☑ 207-363-1756; www.oldyork.org; visitor center 3 Lindsay Rd, York Village; 1 bldg/all bldgs adult $5/12, child $3/5; ☉ 10am-5pm Tue-Sat, 1-5pm Sun Jun-Aug, 10am-5pm Thu-Sat, 1-5pm Sun Sep–mid-Oct) York, called Agamenticus by its original Native American inhabitants, was settled by the British in 1624 and granted a charter by King Charles I in 1642. Nine of its best-preserved buildings are now cared for by the Old York Historical Society, which has turned them into individual museums. Highlights include the cells and stockades of the Old Gaol; the Emerson-Wilcox House, now a museum of decorative arts; and John Hancock Wharf, a warehouse with displays commemorating the area's maritime history.

🛏 Sleeping & Eating

Dockside Guest Quarters   INN $$
(☑ 207-363-2868, 800-270-1977; www.dockside gq.com; 22 Harris Island Rd, York Harbor; r $155-350; ☉ May-Oct; ❄ ✑) On a hill overlooking the harbor, this friendly guesthouse has been a York tradition since the 1950s. The 25 rooms and suites have a classic New England cottage feel, with white-painted furniture and crisp nautical prints. Try to snag one in the 19th-century Maine House, which has more charm than the adjacent contemporary outbuildings. There's a good restaurant on-site, too.

Inn at Tanglewood Hall   B&B $$
(☑ 207-351-1075; www.tanglewoodhall.com; 611 York St, York Harbor; r $115-245; ❄ ✑) This lovely B&B has six sweetly furnished rooms with feather beds and abundant country charm. Several rooms have gas fireplaces and private porches. The wraparound veranda of the 1880s inn provides a peaceful vantage point overlooking the gardens.

Stonewall Kitchen
Company Store & Cafe   CAFE $
(☑ 207-351-2719; www.stonewallkitchen.com/cafe; 2 Stonewall Lane, York; mains $7-20; ☉ 8am-4pm Mon-Sat, from 9am Sun) Fill up on dozens of free samples (wild blueberry jam, tapenade, caramel sauce...yum!) at the flagship store of the Stonewall Kitchen specialty foods empire, just off US 1. Or tuck into a bowl of housemade granola or a lobster Cobb salad at the excellent on-site cafe. The store is perfect for buying gifts.

> ### ⓘ SEASONAL PRICE FLUX
> Maine travel is highly seasonal. Most coastal towns slumber from fall to spring, then explode with action in summer. As a result, off-season hotel rooms can be as little as a third of their summer prices. The same principle holds for the mountain towns, only in reverse – fall and winter are high season. Portland, being the state's major city, doesn't have nearly as much price flux.

Flo's Hot Dogs   HOT DOGS $
(www.floshotdogs.com; 1359 US 1, Cape Neddick; hot dogs $2.75; ☉ 11am-3pm Thu-Tue) Flo's is a local institution: a little red roadside shack doling out steamed hot dogs for a few hours a day around lunchtime. What brings the crowds is the star ingredient: the secret-recipe relish (so popular it's now available in jars). Cash only.

Cape Neddick Lobster Pound   SEAFOOD $$
(☑ 207-363-5471; www.capeneddick.com; 60 Shore Rd, Cape Neddick; mains $15-40; ☉ noon-9pm Jun-Sep, shorter hours rest of year) In a tranquil spot overlooking the Cape Neddick River, this sunny, open dining room is popular with locals and in-the-know summer regulars. Ignore the fancy-sounding appetizers and stick with the classics – fresh-steamed lobster dripping with melted butter, washed down with local beer.

ⓘ Information

Greater York Chamber of Commerce (☑ 20 7-363-4422; www.gatewaytomaine.org/visitor; 1 Stonewall Lane, York; ☉ 9am-4pm Mon-Fri, to 1pm Sat) Helpful visitor center just off US 1.

ⓘ Getting There & Away

From Kittery, it's another 6 miles up US 1 or I-95 to York. York Harbor is about 1 mile east of York via US 1A; York Beach is 3 miles north of York via US 1A. Cape Neddick is just north of York Beach. The nearest major bus station is 10 miles away in Portsmouth, NH.

Ogunquit & Wells

POP 10,500

Known to the Abenaki tribe as 'the beautiful place by the sea,' Ogunquit is justly famous for its 3-mile sandy beach. Wide stretches of pounding surf front the Atlantic, while warm back-cove waters make an idyllic setting for a swim. In summer, the beach draws hordes of visitors from near and far, increasing the town's population exponentially.

Prior to its resort status, Ogunquit was a shipbuilding center in the 17th century. Later it became an important arts center when the Ogunquit art colony was founded in 1898. Today, Ogunquit is the northeasternmost gay and lesbian mecca in the US, adding a touch of open, San Francisco–style culture to the more conservative Maine one.

Neighboring Wells, to the northeast, is little more than an eastward continuation of Ogunquit Beach, with a long stretch of busy commercial development. Wells has good beaches, though, and many relatively inexpensive motels and campgrounds.

◉ Sights

Perkins Cove   WATERFRONT
(access from Shore Rd, Ogunquit) This picturesque inlet is dotted with sailboats and fishing boats; a narrow pedestrian bridge spans the harbor. The cove is home to a handful of attractive restaurants, art galleries and boutiques. It's a good spot come dinnertime, but also popular with ice-cream-toting day-trippers.

Ogunquit Beach   BEACH
(access from Beach St, Ogunquit) A sublime stretch of family-friendly coastline, Ogunquit Beach is only a five-minute walk along Beach St, east of US 1. Walking to the beach is a good idea in summer as the parking lot fills up early (and it costs $4 per hour to park!). The 3-mile beach fronts Ogunquit Bay to the south; on the west side of the beach are the warmer waters of the tidal Ogunquit River.

Footbridge Beach, 2 miles to the north near Wells, is actually the northern extension of Ogunquit Beach. **Little Beach**, near the small lighthouse on Marginal Way, is best reached on foot.

**Ogunquit Museum
of American Art**   MUSEUM
(☑ 207-646-4909; www.ogunquitmuseum.org; 543 Shore Rd, Ogunquit; adult/child $10/free; ⊙ 10am-5pm May-Oct) Dramatically situated overlooking the Atlantic, this petite museum houses an excellent collection of American paintings, sculptures and photographs. Standouts include paintings by Reginald Marsh, Marsden Hartley and Robert Henri, as well as the large collection of works by Maine artists.

**Wells National Estuarine
Research Reserve**   NATURE RESERVE
(☑ 207-646-1555; www.wellsreserve.org; 342 Laudholm Farm Rd, Wells; adult/child $5/1; ⊙ trails 7am-sunset, nature center 10am-4pm) 🖉 Wildlife lovers adore wandering these 2250 acres of protected coastal ecosystems, with 7 miles of hiking, snowshoeing and cross-country ski trails past woodlands, fields, wetlands, beaches and dunes. Its diverse habitats make it a particularly appealing place for bird-watching.

**Rachel Carson
National Wildlife Reserve**   NATURE RESERVE
(☑ 207-646-9226; www.fws.gov/refuge/rachel_carson; 321 Port Rd, Wells; ⊙ dawn-dusk) 🖉 **FREE**
Named after the famous environmentalist, this reserve consists of more than 14,000 acres of protected coastal areas and four trails scattered along 50 miles of shoreline. The 1-mile Carson Trail, found here at the refuge's Wells headquarters and meandering along tidal creeks and salt marshes, is by far the most popular.

🏃 Activities

★**Marginal Way**   WALKING
(access from Shore Rd, Ogunquit) Tracing the 'margin' of the sea, Ogunquit's famed mile-long footpath winds above the crashing gray waves, taking in grand sea vistas and rocky coves, allowing for some excellent real-estate admiring. The neatly paved path, fine for children and slow walkers, is dotted with restful benches. It starts south of Beach St at Shore Rd and ends near Perkins Cove.

Silverlining   CRUISE
(☑ 207-646-9800; www.silverliningsailing.com; Perkins Cove, Ogunquit; trips $40-45; ⊙ late May-Sep) Has five trips daily (including sunset) on a 42ft Hinckley sloop (single-masted sailboat), cruising the tranquil and rocky shoreline near Ogunquit. Cruises are intimate (six passengers maximum) and last 1½ to two hours.

🛌 Sleeping

★**Gazebo Inn**   B&B $$
(☑ 207-646-3733; www.gazeboinnogt.com; 572 Main St/US 1, Ogunquit; r $149-349; ❄ 🕸 🎁) This stately 1847 farmhouse and converted barn feature 14 rooms and suites – the space feels more like a boutique lodge. Rustic-chic touches abound and there's ample common space, including an inviting lounge-bar with

MAINE'S BEST LOBSTER POUNDS

Once considered a food fit only for prisoners and indentured servants, the American lobster has come a long way in the last 200 years. The tasty crustacean is now the most iconic of Maine foods; around 5000 Mainers still make their living hauling lobster traps out of the sea.

Every self-respecting coastal town from Kittery north to Calais has a lobster pound or shack not far from the local dock: these are great places to slurp thick seafood chowder and savor warm lobster rolls, or go the whole hog – tie on a bib and get cracking. They're usually low on frills but high on rustic charm, with waterfront views enjoyed from outdoor picnic tables (there is often no indoor seating; BYOB is a common policy). The term 'pound' usually implies that the establishment has a saltwater holding pen keeping lobsters alive for sale.

From south to north, here are some of our favorites (but there are dozens more):

Chauncey Creek Lobster Pier (☑207-439-1030; www.chaunceycreek.com; 16 Chauncey Creek Rd, Kittery Point; mains $7-25; ⊙11am-8pm early May-Aug, 11am-7pm Tue-Sun Sep–mid-Oct) Just out of Kittery.

Cape Neddick Lobster Pound (p367) In Cape Neddick, near York.

Nunan's Lobster Hut (p371) In Cape Porpoise, near Kennebunkport.

Harraseeket Lunch & Lobster (p380) In Freeport.

Five Islands Lobster Company (p383) In Georgetown, near Bath.

Young's Lobster Pound (p391) Just out of Belfast.

Thurston's Lobster Pound (p401) In Bass Harbor on Mount Desert Island.

For step-by-step instructions on how to crack and eat the spiny little beasts, check out the useful website of the **Gulf of Maine Research Institute** (www.gma.org/lobsters).

If you want to get closer to the lobstering process, join a lobster boat tour; they operate out of numerous coastal towns. Check out the 'How to Eat' page at www.lobster frommaine.com.

beamed ceilings. There's a lovely pool area, and a calm, mature feel (it's kid-free).

Sea Rose Suites APARTMENT $$
(☑207-646-3700; www.searosesuites.com; 214 Shore Rd, Ogunquit; 1-bedroom ste $99-335; ✴🛜⊛) This all-suite hotel sits pretty, spread over a couple of neighboring properties within walking distance of town, the beach and Perkins Cove. Suites vary in size (from one to three bedrooms) but all have a dining-lounge area and well-equipped kitchenette. Low-season rates are a good deal. There's access to an indoor and outdoor pool, fitness room and grill area.

Ogunquit Beach Inn B&B $$
(☑207-646-1112; www.ogunquitbeachinn.com; 67 School St, Ogunquit; r $129-249; ⊙May-Oct; ✴🛜) In a tidy little Craftsman-style bungalow, this gay-and-lesbian-friendly B&B has five colorful, homey rooms and chatty owners who know all about the best new bistros and bars in town. The central location makes walking to dinner a breeze.

✗ Eating

Amore Breakfast BREAKFAST $
(☑207-646-6661; www.amorebreakfast.com; 309 Shore Rd, Ogunquit; breakfast $6-16; ⊙7am-1pm Apr-Dec) When the French toast is made from lemon bread and comes stuffed with cream cheese and berries? That's *amore*. When the eggs Benedict comes with sautéed lobster or asparagus and crab? Yes, that's *amore*.

Bread & Roses BAKERY, CAFE $
(☑207-646-4227; www.breadandrosesbakery.com; 246 Main St, Ogunquit; snacks $2-10; ⊙7am-9pm Sun-Thu, to 11pm Fri & Sat Jun-Aug, shorter hours rest of year; 🗷) 🍽 Get your coffee and blueberry-scone fix at this teeny slip of a bakery in the heart of downtown Ogunquit. The cafe fare is good for a quick lunch, with dishes such as veggie burritos and organic egg-salad sandwiches. Minimal seating.

Lobster Shack SEAFOOD $$
(☑207-646-2941; www.lobster-shack.com; Perkins Cove, Ogunquit; mains $5-19; ⊙11am-9pm Apr-Oct) If you want good seafood and aren't

particular about the view, this friendly, reliable joint serves lobster in all its various incarnations, from lobster rolls to lobster in the shell, by way of chowder, steamed clams, fish tacos and even cheeseburgers.

MC Perkins Cove   MODERN AMERICAN **$$$**
(☑207-646-6263; www.mcperkinscove.com; 111 Perkins Cove Rd, Ogunquit; lunch $11-23, dinner mains $21-38; ☺11am-3:30pm & 5pm-late daily late May–mid-Oct, shorter hours rest of year) Owned by award-winning chefs Mark Gaier and Clark Frasier, MC Perkins Cove wins raves for its casual but exquisite way with local seafood. Start with Maine peekytoe crab cakes and move on to the renowned lobster mac 'n' cheese or whole fried trout. The handsome interior, all glass and burnished wood, looks right out over the Atlantic. Reservations recommended.

☆ Entertainment

Ogunquit Playhouse   THEATER
(☑207-646-5511; www.ogunquitplayhouse.org; 10 Main St/US 1, Ogunquit; tickets $47-87; ☺May-Sep; 🅰) This beloved 1933 theater wears the tag 'America's foremost summer theater.' It hosts five Broadway musicals each season. Well-known performers occasionally perform in the cast, although the productions are high quality even without them.

❶ Information

Ogunquit Chamber of Commerce (☑20 7-646-2939; www.ogunquit.org; 36 Main St/ US 1, Ogunquit; ☺9am-5pm Mon-Sat, 11am-4pm Sun Jun-Aug, shorter hours rest of year) Located on US 1, near the Ogunquit Playhouse and just south of the town's center.

❶ Getting There & Away

There's no direct bus service to Ogunquit; the nearest **Greyhound** (www.greyhound.com) stop is in Portsmouth, NH, 16 miles south.

Amtrak's **Downeaster** (www.amtrakdown easter.com) train service stops in Wells on its Portland–Boston loop.

❶ Getting Around

From late June through to Labor Day (early October), red trolleys (adult/child $2/1.50 per trip) circulate through Ogunquit (every 20 to 30 minutes, 8am to 11pm). From Labor Day to Columbus Day (mid-October), they run from 9am to 5pm. Leave the driving to them in this horribly congested town; they'll take you from the center to the beach or Perkins Cove, and all the way north through Wells.

The Kennebunks

POP 10,800

A longtime destination of moneyed East Coasters, the Kennebunks comprise the towns of Kennebunk and Kennebunkport.

Kennebunk is a modest town largely centered on US 1, with few tourist attractions beyond its lovely beaches. Just across the river, proudly waspy Kennebunkport crawls with tourists year-round. The epicenter of activity is Dock Sq, lined with cafes, art galleries and upscale boutiques selling preppy essentials (whale-print shorts, anyone?). Drive down Ocean Ave to gawk at the grand mansions and hotels overlooking the surf, including the massive compound belonging to George HW Bush, set on a protected spit of land called Walker's Point.

At the eastern terminus of School St is the charming hamlet of **Cape Porpoise**, home to some of the area's more affordable hotels and restaurants.

⦿ Sights

Seashore Trolley Museum   MUSEUM
(☑207-967-2800; www.trolleymuseum.org; 195 Log Cabin Rd, Kennebunkport; adult/child $10/7.50; ☺10am-5pm late May–mid-Oct; 🅰) On the outskirts of town, this family-friendly museum has some 250 streetcars (including one named 'Desire'), as well as antique buses and public-transit paraphernalia.

⟳ Tours

First Chance   CRUISE, WILDLIFE WATCHING
(☑207-967-5507; www.firstchancewhalewatch. com; 4 Western Ave, Lower Village; lobster tour adult/child $20/15; whale-watching tour adult/ child $48/28; ☺daily summer, weekends spring & fall) Offers a 1½-hour lobster boat cruise, taking in Kennebunkport (including Wallker's Point) from the water, and a 4½-hour whale-watching voyage (dress warm for this one!). Departure is from Kennebunk's Lower Village, just off Dock Sq.

Schooner Eleanor   CRUISE
(☑207-967-8809; www.schoonereleanor.com; Arundel Wharf, 43 Ocean Ave, Kennebunkport; cruises $45-55; ☺late May-early Oct) A splendid 55ft schooner offering two-hour sails off Kennebunkport (season and weather dependent). Bring beer, wine and snacks if you wish – especially for the 4:30pm sail.

Coastal Maine
Kayak & Bike
KAYAKING, CYCLING

(☑207-967-6065; www.coastalmainekayak.com; 8 Western Ave, Lower Village; 24hr rental bike/kayak $35/65) This operator can arrange rentals of bikes, scooters, kayaks and stand-up paddleboards (SUP), plus SUP lessons and tours, and popular guided kayaking tours ($85).

🛏 Sleeping

1802 House
B&B **$$**

(☑207-967-5632; www.1802inn.com; 15 Locke St, Kennebunkport; r $149-339; ❄🐾) In a restored 19th-century farmhouse in a quiet residential neighborhood, this B&B offers six sweet, country-style rooms and warm hospitality. All but one have their own fireplaces, making this a particularly cozy place to stay in winter.

Franciscan Guest House
GUESTHOUSE **$$**

(☑207-967-4865; www.franciscanguesthouse.com; 26 Beach Ave, Kennebunk; d $59-179, f $89-249; ❄@🐾🏊) You can almost smell the blackboard chalk inside this high-school-turned-guesthouse on the peaceful grounds of the St Anthony Monastery. Guest rooms – once classrooms – are basic and unstylish: acoustic tile, faux wood paneling, motel beds. If you don't mind getting your own sheets out of the supply closet (there's no maid service), staying here is great value and a unique experience.

Captain Fairfield Inn
B&B **$$$**

(☑207-967-4454; www.captainfairfield.com; 8 Pleasant St, Kennebunkport; r $159-499; ❄🐾) A bold, boutique mix of modern and traditional has breathed new life into this 1813 Federal mansion. No two rooms are the same, but each boasts fine linens and fireplaces. An honesty-system bar, iPads for guests and creative small-plates breakfast add a distinctively up-to-date flair.

Cabot Cove Cottages
COTTAGE **$$$**

(☑207-967-5424; www.cabotcovecottages.com; 7 S Maine St, Kennebunkport; cottages $325-695; ⊙early May–mid-Oct; ❄🐾) Set in a semicircle in a forest glade, these 16 miniature cottages look almost like fairy houses. Decor is airy and peaceful, all whitewashed walls and vintage botanical prints. Cottages range in size; all have full kitchens, though breakfast is dropped off on your doorstep each morning. Bikes, kayaks and rowboats are available for guest use.

KENNEBUNK BEACH

Kennebunkport proper has only one stretch of sand, the small **Colony Beach** on Ocean Ave, which is dominated by the Colony Hotel. But Beach Ave and Sea Rd (west of Kennebunk River and then south of the Lower Village) lead to three good public beaches: Gooch's Beach, Middle Beach and Mother's Beach, known collectively as **Kennebunk Beach**. Beach parking permits are required here from mid-June to mid-September; for non-residents they cost $20 daily, $75 weekly and $150 seasonally.

🍴 Eating

⭐Pier 77 & The Ramp
AMERICAN **$$**

(☑207-967-8500; www.pier77restaurant.com; 77 Pier Rd, Cape Porpoise Harbor; mains $14-26; ⊙11:30am-9pm) In a genius move, this Cape Porpoise gem has one menu but two faces: sit upstairs in Pier 77 if you're after a fancy(-ish) night out; downstairs in the pub if you plan to get messy over the burger. The menu is simple (hanger steak, pan-seared scallops) but well executed – and the end-of-the-world waterfront setting is ace.

⭐Nunan's Lobster Hut
SEAFOOD **$$**

(☑207-967-4362; www.nunanslobsterhut.com; 9 Mills Rd, Cape Porpoise; mains $11-29; ⊙5-10pm May–mid-Oct; 🚗) Just 2.3 miles east of Kennebunkport, Nunan's is *the* place to roll up your sleeves and flex your lobster-cracking muscles. Owners Richard and Keith Nunan still trap and cook the lobsters just like their grandfather did when he opened the restaurant in 1953. Decor is 'haute Maine fishing shack,' with wooden walls hung with ancient nets and buoys.

Bandaloop
INTERNATIONAL **$$**

(☑207-967-4994; www.bandaloop.biz; 2 Ocean Ave, Kennebunkport; small plates $8-15, mains $19-31; ⊙5-9:30pm Jun-Aug, shorter hours rest of year; 🚗) 🌿 Local, organic and deliciously innovative, Bandaloop mains run the gamut from grilled rib-eye steak to baked tofu with hemp-seed crust. For the perfect starter order the skillet steamed mussels and a Peak organic ale. Salads are truly flavorful, and the cocktails creative. Vegans and vegetarians will find joy here.

MAINE THE KENNEBUNKS

DON'T MISS

MAINE FOODIE TOURS

Hungry? And hungry for local food insight? From a lobster boat trip to a lunchtime lobster crawl or a walking tour combining art, culture and food, Maine Foodie Tours (☑207-233-7485; www.mainefoodietours.com; tours from $57) have you covered, with tours in Portland, Kennebunkport, Rockland and Bar Harbor. Departure points, timetables and tour details vary, so check what's available on the website.

Clam Shack   SEAFOOD $$

(☑207-967-3321; www.theclamshack.net; 2 Western Ave, Kennebunk; mains $5-30; ☺11am-8pm May-Oct) Standing in line at this teeny gray hut perched on stilts above the river is a time-honored Kennebunkport summer tradition. Order a box of fat, succulent fried whole-belly clams or a one-pound lobster roll ($19), which is served with your choice of mayo or melted butter. Outdoor seating only.

White Barn
Inn Restaurant   MODERN AMERICAN $$$

(☑207-967-2321; www.whitebarninn.com; 37 Beach Ave, Kennebunk; 4-course dinner $109, 9-course tasting menu $165; ☺5-10pm) One of Maine's most renowned high-end restaurants, the White Barn boasts country-elegant decor and a menu that changes weekly. Expect top-quality local seafood, meat and produce, such as Kennebunkport lobster on homemade fettuccine with cognac butter sauce, or foie-gras-crusted tenderloin of beef. Reservations are essential, as is smart attire.

❶ Information

Kennebunk-Kennebunkport Chamber of Commerce (☑207-967-0857; www.visitthekennebunks.com; 16 Water St, Kennebunk; ☺9am-4pm Mon-Fri year-round, plus 9am-3pm Sat & Sun Jun-Sep) Has a year-round visitor center in Kennebunk town.

Kennebunkport Visitor Center (☑207-967-0857; www.visitthekennebunks.com; 1 Chase Hill, Lower Village) A summertime information kiosk on Western Ave in the Lower Village, just across the bridge from Dock Sq.

❶ Getting There & Away

The Kennebunks lie halfway (28 miles from each city) between Portsmouth, NH, and Portland, ME, just off I-95 on ME 9.

There's no direct bus service to Kennebunkport; **Greyhound** (www.greyhound.com) stops in both Portland and Portsmouth.

Amtrak's **Downeaster** (www.amtrakdowneaster.com) train service stops in Wells, about 9 miles to the south, on its Boston–Portland loop.

❶ Getting Around

Bike rental is a good idea for getting around. In summer, the streets are congested and parking is pricey. There's a free parking lot in Kennebunkport at 30 North St, 0.4 miles north of Dock Sq (about an eight-minute walk).

The **Intown Trolley** (☑207-967-3686; www.intowntrolley.com; day pass adult/child $16/6; ☺hourly 10am-3pm or 4pm late May–mid-Oct) circulates through Kennebunkport, with stops at the Kennebunk beaches, the Bush compound, the Franciscan monastery and other points of interest. You can ride the entire route on a 45-minute narrated tour, or hop on and off at designated stops, including along Ocean Ave. The central stop is at 21 Ocean Ave, just around the corner from Dock Sq. The last tour leaves at 4pm in July and August, at 3pm other months.

PORTLAND

POP 66,400

Maine's largest city has capitalized on the gifts of its port history – the redbrick warehouse buildings, the Victorian shipbuilders' mansions, the narrow cobblestone streets – to become one of the hippest, most vibrant small cities in America. With a lively waterfront, excellent museums and galleries, abundant green space, and both a food culture and a brewing scene worthy of a town many times its size, it's worth much more than a quick stopover.

Set on a peninsula jutting into the grey waters of Casco Bay, Portland's always been a city of the sea. Established in 1633 as a fishing village, it grew to become New England's largest port. Today, the Old Port district is the town's historic heart, with handsomely restored brick buildings filled with cafes, shops and bars. The working wharves keep things from getting too precious or museum-like, though, as fishmongers in rubber boots mingle with well-heeled Yankee matrons.

◉ Sights

Congress St is the main thoroughfare through downtown, passing Portland's most imposing buildings: city hall, banks, churches and a few hotels. Commercial St, where many businesses are located, runs the length of the harbor. Two promenades – the upscale Western and growing-in-stature Eastern – frame downtown Portland at opposite ends of the peninsula. The West End neighborhood is home to an impressive collection of 19th-century mansions and the bulk of the city's charming B&Bs. In the east, Munjoy Hill is Portland's up-and-coming hipster enclave.

Old Port District   AREA
Handsome 19th-century brick buildings line the streets of the Old Port, with Portland's most enticing shops, pubs and restaurants located within this five-square-block district. By night, flickering gas lanterns add to the atmosphere. What to do here? Eat some fresh seafood, down a local microbrew, buy a nautical-themed T-shirt from an up-and-coming designer or peruse the local art galleries. Don't forget to wander the authentically stinky wharfs, ducking into a fishmongers to order some lobsters to ship home.

★ Fort Williams Park   PARK
(www.fortwilliams.org; 1000 Shore Rd, Cape Elizabeth; ☉ sunrise-sunset) ✔ FREE Four miles southeast of Portland on Cape Elizabeth, 90-acre Fort Williams Park is worth visiting simply for the panoramas and picnic possibilities. Stroll around the ruins of the fort, a late-19th-century artillery base, checking out the WWII bunkers and gun emplacements that still dot the rolling lawns (a German U-boat was spotted in Casco Bay in 1942). The fort actively guarded the entrance to Casco Bay until 1964. A favorite feature of the park is the **Portland Head Light** (☑20 7-799-2661; www.portlandheadlight.com; 1000 Shore Rd, Cape Elizabeth; museum adult/child $2/1; ☉ museum 10am-4pm Jun-Oct); the oldest of Maine's 52 functioning lighthouses, it was commissioned by President George Washington in 1791.

Look out for the much-loved **Bite into Maine** (www.biteintomaine.com) food truck that sets up in the park and serves delicious lobster rolls from May to October (see the website for hours).

West End   AREA
Portland's loveliest neighborhood is a hillside enclave of brick town houses, elegant gardens and stately mansions; some date from the neighborhood's founding in 1836. This is a fairly mixed community, with smaller pockets of working-class families living amid their higher-mortgage-paying neighbors. There's cultural diversity, some of Portland's best B&Bs and the scenic **Western Promenade**, a grassy pathway with fine views over the harbor, especially around sunset.

Portland Museum of Art   MUSEUM
(☑ 207-775-6148; www.portlandmuseum.org; 7 Congress Sq; adult/child $15/free, 4-8pm Fri free; ☉ 11am-6pm Sat-Wed, to 8pm Thu & Fri, closed Mon & Tue Oct-May) Founded in 1882, this well-respected museum houses an outstanding collection of American artists. Maine artists, including Winslow Homer, Edward Hopper, Louise Nevelson and Andrew Wyeth, are particularly well represented. You'll also find a few works by European masters, including Monet, Degas, Picasso and Renoir.

Portland Breakwater Light   LIGHTHOUSE
(Madison St, South Portland) Portland is graced by a handful of handsome lights, including the 1875 Portland Breakwater Light with its Corinthian columns. Dubbed the 'Bug Light' because of its tiny size, it sits in a small park in South Portland with a panoramic view of downtown across the harbor.

To reach it, cross the Casco Bay Bridge from downtown, and continue on Broadway to Breakwater Dr.

Portland Observatory   HISTORIC BUILDING
(☑ 207-774-5561; www.portlandlandmarks.org/observatory/; 138 Congress St; adult/child $10/5; ☉ 10am-5pm late May–mid-Oct) Built in 1807 atop Munjoy Hill, this seven-story brick tower was originally used to alert shipowners when their ships were heading for home. Now restored, the observatory has stunning panoramic views of Portland and its harbor. Admission includes a 45-minute **guided tour** of the observatory. From mid-July through August, special Thursday-night sunset tours offer views of the sun setting over Casco Bay (5pm to 8pm).

Children's Museum
& Theatre of Maine   MUSEUM
(☑ 207-828-1234; www.kitetails.org; 142 Free St; $10; ☉ 10am-5pm late May-early Sep, closed Mon rest of year; 📶) Kids aged zero to 10 shriek and squeal as they haul traps aboard a replica lobster boat, milk a fake cow on a model farm, or monkey around on an indoor rock-climbing wall. The highlight of this ultra-interactive, upbeat place (more a play center than a museum) might be the 3rd-floor camera obscura, where a single pinhole projects a panoramic view of downtown Portland. Lots of activities and performances, too.

Longfellow House   HISTORIC BUILDING
(☑ 207-774-1822; www.mainehistory.org; 489 Congress St; guided tour adult/child $15/3; ☉ noon-4pm May, 10:30am-4pm Mon-Sat, noon-4pm Sun Jun-Oct) The revered American poet Henry Wadsworth-Longfellow (1807–82) grew up

Central Portland

MAINE PORTLAND

in this Federal-style house, built in 1785 by his Revolutionary War–hero grandfather. The house has been impeccably restored to look as it did in the 1800s, complete with original furniture and artifacts. Admission includes the **Maine Historical Society Museum** next door, with rotating exhibits about life in Maine over the past few centuries. Ask here about historical **walking tours** (⊙1:30pm daily Jun–mid-Oct), offered by the society from June to mid-October.

Victoria Mansion   HISTORIC BUILDING
(☑207-772-4841; www.victoriamansion.org; 109 Danforth St; adult/child $15/5; ⊙10am-3:45pm Mon-Sat, 1:15-4:45pm Sun May-Oct) This Italianate palace, whose exterior would work well in a Tim Burton movie, dates back to 1860. Inside, it's sumptuously decorated with rich furniture, frescoes, paintings, carpets, gilt and exotic woods and stone. Check tour times on the website: there are guided tours twice an hour from Friday to Monday, and self-guided tours Tuesday to Thursday.

🏃 Activities

Portland Trails   WALKING, CYCLING
(www.portlandtrails.org) Thanks to the efforts of the Portland Trails conservation organization, there are some 70 miles of multi-use trails sprinkled about the Greater Portland area. One of the most popular paths is the 3.6-mile **Back Cove Trail**, which provides excellent water and city views northwest of the city center.

☞ Tours

★ **Maine Brew Bus**   BREWERY, DISTILLERY
(☑207-245-1940; www.themainebrewbus.com; 111 Commercial St; tours $55-80) Want to drink your way around Portland? We know the feeling. Hop aboard the green bus for tours and tastings at some of Portland's most beloved breweries, brewpubs and distilleries,

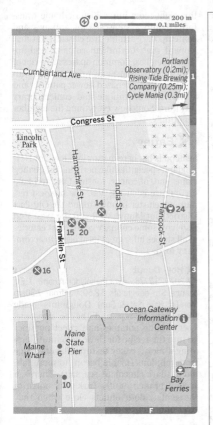

MAINE PORTLAND

Central Portland

◎ Sights

⊙ Activities, Courses & Tours

🛏 Sleeping

🍴 Eating

🍷 Drinking & Nightlife

🎭 Entertainment

🛍 Shopping

from established to up-and-coming. There's a range of departure times, itineraries and durations, all outlined on the website. Weekend events like the 'Beerunch' are particularly popular – book ahead.

Lucky Catch Lobstering   CRUISE
(☎ 207-761-0941; www.luckycatch.com; Long Wharf, 170 Commercial St; adult/child $30/18; ⊙ May-Oct) You can live the life of a lobsterman – if only for 90 minutes – as a passenger aboard the *Lucky Catch,* a commercial lobster boat. Cruises head into Casco Bay to pull up lobster traps; you can participate if you're game. Anything caught can be purchased for the wholesale price.

Casco Bay Lines   CRUISE
(☎ 207-774-7871; www.cascobaylines.com; Maine State Pier, 56 Commercial St; mailboat run adult/child $16/8) This outfit cruises the Casco Bay islands year-round, delivering mail, freight and visitors. Peaks Island, just 17 minutes from Portland, is a popular day-trip destination (round-trip $7.70) for walks or cycling; bikes can be hired on the island. There's a selection of scenic cruises, too – the three-hour mailboat run is a great way to see the sights of the bay.

Maine Island Kayak Company   KAYAKING
(☎ 207-766-2373; www.maineislandkayak.com; Peaks Island; tour from $60; ⊙ May-Nov) From its base on Peaks Island (a 17-minute cruise from downtown on the Casco Bay Lines ferry), this well-run outfitter offers fun half-day, full-day, sunset and overnight paddling trips exploring the islands of Casco Bay.

Portland Schooner Company   CRUISE
(☎ 207-766-2500; www.portlandschooner.com; Maine State Pier, 56 Commercial St; adult/child

$42/21; ⊘ May-Oct) Offers sailings aboard an elegant, early-20th-century schooner, taking in lighthouses, seals, seabirds and the rugged coastline. Feel free to bring food and drink.

⚜️ Festivals & Events

Harvest on the Harbor   FOOD & DRINK
(www.harvestontheharbor.com; ⊘ mid-Oct) A five-day feast for all the senses (but especially taste), this is Maine's premier food and wine festival. Buy tickets in advance for events such as the Lobster Chef of the Year competition, a five-course moonlight gala, or a celebration of local suds and cider.

🛏️ Sleeping

Portland has a healthy selection of midrange and upscale B&Bs, though very little at the budget end. The most idyllic accommodations are in the old town houses and grand Victorians in the West End.

For camping, head to Freeport.

West End Inn   B&B $$
(☑ 800-338-1377; www.westendbb.com; 146 Pine St; r $119-239; P ❄ 🛜) In a redbrick town house in Portland's tony Western Promenade district, this recommended six-room B&B is airy and elegant. Rooms are sunny and unfussy, with bright decor ranging from sweet florals to crisp nautical prints. The multicourse breakfast and sunny patio add appeal.

★ Press Hotel   HOTEL $$$
(☑ 207-808-8800; www.thepresshotel.com; 119 Exchange St; r $169-369; P ❄ 🛜) The Press Hotel opened in mid-2015 to widespread acclaim. It's a clever, creative conversion of the building that once housed the offices and printing plant of Maine's largest newspaper, and the press theme shines in unique details – a wall of vintage typewriters, old headlines on hallway wallpapers. Rooms are sexy, in smart navy tones, and local art adorns walls.

★ Danforth Inn   BOUTIQUE HOTEL $$$
(☑ 207-879-8755; www.danforthinn.com; 163 Danforth St; r $199-469; P ❄ 🛜) Staying at this ivy-shrouded West End boutique hotel feels like being a guest at an eccentric millionaire's mansion. Shoot pool in the wood-paneled game room (a former speakeasy) or climb into the rooftop cupola for views across Portland Harbor. The nine rooms are decorated with flair, in a sophisticated mix of antique and modern.

★ Pomegranate Inn   B&B $$$
(☑ 207-772-1006; www.pomegranateinn.com; 49 Neal St; r $159-389; ❄ 🛜) Whimsy prevails at this eight-room inn, a historic home transformed into a showcase for antiques and contemporary art: life-size classical statutes, leopard rugs, Corinthian columns and abstract sketches. Common spaces are a riot of colors and patterns; guest rooms come with hand-painted, oversized flower patterns and a wild mix of antique and contemporary furniture. Somehow everything fits together beautifully.

🍴 Eating

Seafood is big here, naturally – look for New England specialties like periwinkles, quahog clams and, of course, lobster. Cafe and bakery culture is strong, too. The buzziest restaurants cluster in and around the Old Port District, but Munjoy Hill and the West End also have some culinary gems. Most eateries of all stripes offer great local beers to accompany food.

★ Holy Donut   SWEETS $
(☑ 207-775-7776; www.theholydonut.com; 7 Exchange St; doughnuts $2.50; ⊘ from 7:30am Mon-Fri, 8am Sat & Sun) Doughnuts made from *potato*? Yep, and they're awesome. Local Maine potatoes and sweet potatoes go into the recipe for these doughnuts, creating a moist, cakey texture. Flavors range from fabulous (maple bacon) to more fabulous (dark-chocolate sea salt). There's a second branch at 194 Park Ave, north of the center. Both outlets close when they sell out of the goods.

Public Market House   FOOD HALL $
(www.publicmarkethouse.com; 28 Monument Sq; ⊘ 8am-7pm Mon-Sat, 10am-5pm Sun) A handful of fast-food stalls occupy this great market. It's the perfect place for a quick, cheap and tasty meal (soups, burritos, salads, bagels etc), with seating on the 2nd floor. The deli on the 1st floor is a good place to fill a picnic basket.

DuckFat   FAST FOOD $
(☑ 207-774-8080; www.duckfat.com; 43 Middle St; small fries $5.50, panini $11-14; ⊘ 11am-9pm Sun-Thu, to 10pm Fri & Sat) DuckFat has out-of-this-world fries. Fried in (yes) duckfat, they're shatteringly crisp, with fluffy centers. Dipping sauces (truffle ketchup, horseradish mayo etc) are good, but unnecessary. The fancy panini are also excellent, and people flock for the poutine and the milkshakes. Decor is 'hipster fast-food joint,' with a blackboard menu and a handful of bistro tables. Expect queues.

★ **Central Provisions**   MODERN AMERICAN $$
(☑ 207-805-1085;   www.central-provisions.com;
414 Fore St; lunch plates $4-15, dinner plates $5-26;
⊙ 11am-2pm & 5-10pm) Snug, redbrick Central
Provisions is Portland's latest It Girl: long
lines, media attention, and a James Beard
award for best new restaurant in 2015. An-
gle for a seat at the bar, overlooking the line
chefs in action, and choose from a masterful
small-plates menu that swings from tuna
crudo to suckling pig. Local oysters, fish and
cheeses are staples.

★ **Eventide Oyster Co**   SEAFOOD $$
(☑ 207-774-8538; www.eventideoysterco.com; 86
Middle St; small dishes $7-15;   ⊙ 11am-midnight)
Rocking seafood-lovers' worlds since opening in 2012, Eventide still has plenty of hype,
and one look at the raw bar here explains all:
fresh Maine oysters and shellfish, shucked
to order. There's an enticing menu of small
dishes, pescatorially focused but not exclusively so. The lobster roll is a must: lobster
meat and brown butter in a pork-bun-style
roll. Heaven.

Honey Paw   ASIAN $$
(☑ 207-774-8538; www.thehoneypaw.com; 78 Mid-
dle St; dishes $10-36) A new creation from the
owners of a few highly regarded restaurants
around town, hip Honey Paw has a cool
warehouse fit-out and a menu of pan-Asian
classics (Korean fried chicken, Vietnam-
ese chicken noodle soup). There's a nod to
Maine sensibilities (eg lobster wontons) and
an admirable nose-to-tail approach (eg spicy
tripe salad).

Lobster Shack at Two Lights   SEAFOOD $$
(☑ 207-799-1677; www.lobstershacktwolights.com;
225 Two Lights Rd, Cape Elizabeth; mains $5-25;
⊙ 11am-8pm Apr-Oct) Crack into a lobster dinner, lobster roll or chowder bowl at this well-
loved Cape Elizabeth seafood shack, with
killer views of the crashing Atlantic from
both indoor and outdoor seating areas. It's
about 7.5 miles south of downtown Portland.

Green Elephant   VEGETARIAN, ASIAN $$
(☑ 207-347-3111;   www.greenelephantmaine.com;
608 Congress St; mains $12-17; ⊙ 11:30am-2:30pm
& 5-9:30pm Mon-Sat, 5-9pm Sun; ☑) Even carni-
vores shouldn't miss the vegetarian fare at
this Zen-chic, Thai-inspired cafe (with lots
of vegan and gluten-free options, too). Start
with the crispy spinach wontons, then move
on to one of the stir-fry, noodle or curry fa-
vorites like tofu tikka masala or Malaysian
char kway teow (fried flat rice noodles). Save
room for the chocolate-orange mousse pie.

CULINARY PORTLAND

Portland's food scene is hot right now.
Young chefs fleeing the higher rents in
East Coast cities like New York and Bos-
ton have set up shop here, embracing
all that is fresh and local while adding
global kick, making Portland a highly
respected center of gastronomy for a
town of such a small size. Get some help
tapping into the local scene via the offer-
ings from Maine Foodie Tours (p372).

★ **Fore Street**   MODERN AMERICAN $$$
(☑ 207-775-2717; www.forestreet.biz; 288 Fore St;
small plates $12-15, mains $28-38; ⊙ 5:30-10pm Sun-
Thu, to 10:30pm Fri & Sat) Fore Street is the lauded, long-running restaurant many consider
to be the originator of today's food obsession
in Portland. Chef-owner Sam Hayward has
turned roasting into a high art: chickens turn
on spits in the open kitchen as chefs slide
iron kettles of mussels into the wood-burning
oven. Local, seasonal eating is taken very seriously and the menu changes daily.

Miyake   JAPANESE $$$
(☑ 207-871-9170;   www.miyakerestaurants.com;
468 Fore St; lunch $10-42, dinner dishes $13-18,
4-course dinner $55; ⊙ 11:30am-2pm & 5:30-9pm
Mon-Sat; ☑) This sushi bar offers some of
the freshest fish in Portland – and that's
saying a lot. Order à la carte or choose one
of chef Masa Miyake's *omakase* (chef's
choice; $38 to $70) menus, which often in-
clude local ingredients like quahog clams
or oysters. His spin on lobster is genius:
lobster meat with spicy mayonnaise in a
black sesame wrap.

Street & Co   SEAFOOD $$$
(☑ 207-775-0887; www.streetandcompany.net; 33
Wharf St; mains $24-36; ⊙ 5-10pm) A longtime
Old Port favorite for fresh seafood – grilled,
blackened, broiled, tossed with pasta. Lobster *diavolo* (in spicy tomato sauce, with pasta) for two is the house specialty (hint: don't
wear white). Reservations recommended.

Grace   MODERN AMERICAN $$$
(☑ 207-828-4422; www.restaurantgrace.com; 15
Chestnut St; mains $19-40; ⊙ 5-10pm Tue-Thu, to
10:30pm Fri & Sat) Grace is an 1850s Gothic
Revival–style Methodist church that was
closed and sold due to a declining congrega-
tion. In 2010, after a $2-million renovation
that adhered to strict historic guidelines,
it reopened as an upscale restaurant and

MAINE PORTLAND

PORTLAND BREWERY TOURS

Beer lovers will be in heaven here, as Portland is a center of microbrew culture. Here it's all about the hops, the IPA and the filtration – and the results are delicious. Several breweries are open for tours, tastings and retail purchases, making for a fun day of beer-hopping – and be sure to hop on the Maine Brew Bus (p374) to avoid having to nominate a designated driver! Note that breweries don't offer food, but brewpubs do.

Here are a few of the top places to knock back a brew or two:

Shipyard Brewing Co (☑207-761-0807; www.shipyard.com; 86 Newbury St; ☉tastings 11am-5pm Mon-Wed, to 6pm Thu-Sat, to 4pm Sun) Shipyard has grown to become Maine's largest brewer (it also brews Cap'n Eli soda). Pop by to visit its new tasting-room facilities and pick up some souvenirs at the gift store. Book well ahead for a spot on the full brewery tour, offered on Tuesday evenings ($7).

Allagash Brewing Company (☑207-878-5385; www.allagash.com; 50 Industrial Way; ☉tastings 11am-6pm) Nationally known for its Belgian-style beers, Allagash opens its doors for free tours and tastings every day (book your tour spot online; weekend tours are extremely popular). The brewery is 3.5 miles northwest of Portland's Old Port, off Forest Road. Handily, a couple of smaller breweries are just across the road from here, namely Austin Street, Foundation Brewing and Bissell Brothers.

Geary's (☑207-878-2337; www.gearybrewing.com; 38 Evergreen Dr; ☉tastings noon-7pm Thu-Sat) Call ahead to reserve a place on a tour of Maine's pioneering microbrewery (from 1986), which specializes in classic British ales. Located a few streets away from Allagash Brewing Company.

Rising Tide Brewing Company (☑207-370-2337; www.risingtidebrewing.com; 103 Fox St; ☉tastings noon-7pm Mon-Sat, to 5pm Sun) In a pocket of town growing in stature (and with a neighboring distillery), Rising Tide is well worth investigating. Locals congregate in the car park, and food trucks visit in summer, from Wednesday to Sunday. Check the website for events (food-truck attendees, live music etc). Tours are held daily at 3pm, with additional tours on Saturday at 1pm and 5pm.

If beer is your thing, it's worth doing some planning and research: Maine is home to some 70-plus microbreweries, with that number increasing frequently. There are brewers all over the state; a good resource is the online brochure and map at **Maine Beer Trail** (www.mainebrewersguild.org).

cocktail bar, where the pulpit serves as the greeter's desk and diners sit on refurbished pews beneath 27 stained-glass windows.

🍸 Drinking & Nightlife

After dinner, Wharf St transforms into one long bar, with a young, easily intoxicated crowd spilling onto the streets. Other places are along Fore St, between Union and Exchange Sts, and the northern end of Middle St. If you want something more low-key, try the West End or Munjoy Hill. Last call is 1am, so things wind down relatively early.

Back Bay Grill   BAR
(☑207-772-8833; www.backbaygrill.com; 65 Portland St; ☉5:30-9pm Mon-Thu, 5pm-late Fri & Sat) The lounge area at this swank, off-the-beaten-track restaurant is the place to go for 25-year-old scotch or fancy gin cocktails.

Great Lost Bear   PUB
(☑207-772-0300; www.greatlostbear.com; 540 Forest Ave; ☉11:30am-11:30pm Mon-Sat, noon-11pm Sun; 🛜) Decked out in Christmas lights and flea-market kitsch, this sprawling bar and restaurant is a Portland institution. Seventy-eight taps serve primarily Northeastern brews, including 40 from Maine, making the GLB one of America's best regional beer bars. Atmosphere is family friendly (at least early in the evening), with a massive menu of burgers, quesadillas and other bar nibbles.

☆ Entertainment

Portland House of Music   LIVE MUSIC
(☑207-805-0134; www.portlandhouseofmusic. com; 25 Temple St) Live music nightly, with lots of beers on tap and generally low cover charges. See what's playing online.

🛍 Shopping

The best area for shopping is around the Old Port, or in the smattering of galleries and boutiques along upper Congress St, in the so-called 'Arts District' (heading towards the West End)

Harbor Fish Market   FOOD
(📞800-370-1790; www.harborfish.com; 9 Custom House Wharf; ⏰8:30am-5:30pm Mon-Sat, 9am-4pm Sun) On Custom House Wharf, this iconic fishmonger packs lobsters to ship anywhere in the US.

🛈 Information

Ocean Gateway Information Center (📞20 7-772-5800; www.visitportland.com; 14 Ocean Gateway Pier; ⏰9am-5pm Mon-Fri, to 4pm Sat & Sun Jun-Oct, shorter hours rest of year) Located at the waterfront.

Visitor Information Booth (📞207-772-6828; www.portlandmaine.com; Tommy's Park, Exchange St; 10am-5pm Jun-Oct) Summertime info kiosk in the Old Port.

🛈 Getting There & Away

AIR

Portland International Jetport (p434) is Maine's largest and most chaotic air terminal. It's served by domestic airlines, with nonstop flights to cities in the eastern US.

BOAT

There are passenger ferries between Portland and the islands of Casco Bay, operated by Casco Bay Lines (p375).

In summer, **Bay Ferries** (📞877-762-7245; www.ferries.ca; Ocean Gateway Pier; ⏰mid-Jun–Sep) operates a fast ferry CAT service between Portland and Yarmouth, Nova Scotia (Canada), daily from mid-June to September. Journey time is six hours. Adult one-way/round-trip fares are $107/194; car passage is from $199 one way. Arrival and departure is from the Ocean Gateway Pier.

BUS

Greyhound (📞800-231-2222; www.greyhound. com; 950 Congress St) offers direct daily trips to Bangor and Boston, with connections on to the rest of the US.

Concord Coach Lines (📞800-639-3317; www.concordcoachlines.com) operates daily buses between Boston (including Logan Airport) and Portland, continuing on to Midcoast Maine towns. There are also services connecting Boston, Portland and the towns of Augusta, Waterville and Bangor. Two services a day link Portland with New York City.

CAR & MOTORCYCLE

Coming from the south, take I-95 to I-295, then exit 7 onto Franklin St, which leads down to the Old Port. To bypass Portland, simply stay on I-95.

TRAIN

The *Downeaster*, run by **Amtrak** (📞800-872-7245; www.amtrak.com; 100 Thompson's Point Rd), makes five trips daily between Boston and Portland (2½ hours). A couple of these services extend to Freeport and Brunswick, too.

🛈 Getting Around

TO/FROM THE AIRPORT

Metro bus 5 takes you to the center of town for $1.50. Taxis are about $17 to downtown.

BICYCLE

Cycling is a popular way to get around Portland. Rent bikes from **Cycle Mania** (📞207-774-2933; www.cyclemania1.com; 65 Cove St; bike rental day/week from $30/140; ⏰10am-6pm Mon-Fri, to 5pm Sat).

BUS

Portland's city bus company is the **Metro** (📞207-774-0351; www.gpmetrobus.com; fare $1.50). The main terminal is the 'Metro Pulse,' near Monument Sq. Routes serve Old Port, the Jetport, the Maine Mall, Cape Elizabeth and Falmouth, among other locations.

CAR & MOTORCYCLE

Parking is a challenge downtown; for quick visits, you can usually find a metered space (two hours maximum) in the Old Port, but rarely on Commercial St. A parking garage or lot is an easier bet; prices vary.

TAXI

Citywide rates are $1.90 for the first 0.1 mile, and $0.30 for every additional 0.1 mile. While you may get lucky and snag a taxi in the Old Port, you'll usually need to call ahead. Try **ASAP Taxi** (📞207-791-2727; www.asaptaxi.net) or **American Taxi** (📞207-749-1600).

Around Portland

Freeport
POP 7900

Nestled amid the natural beauty of Maine's rockbound coast is a town devoted almost entirely to shopping. Nearly 200 stores line the town's mile-long stretch of US 1, leading to long traffic jams during the summer. Strict zoning codes forbid the destruction of historic buildings, which is why you'll find a McDonald's housed in an 1850s Greek Revival home and an Abercrombie & Fitch outlet in a turn-of-the-20th-century library. It all adds up to a slightly eerie 'Main Street, USA' vibe.

Freeport's fame and fortune began a century ago when Leon Leonwood Bean opened a shop to sell equipment and provisions to hunters and fishermen heading north into the Maine woods. His success later brought other retailers to the area, making Freeport what it is today.

In July and August, LL Bean sponsors free Saturday-evening concerts (called Summer in the Park) in Freeport at Discovery Park.

◉ Sights

Desert of Maine   DESERT
(☑ 207-865-6962; www.desertofmaine.com; 95 Desert Rd; adult/child $12.50/6.75; ☺ 9am-5pm May–mid-Oct; ⊞) William Tuttle came to Freeport in 1797 to farm potatoes, but his deadly combination of clear-cutting and overgrazing caused enough erosion to expose the glacial desert hidden beneath the topsoil. The shifting dunes, which are 90ft deep in some areas, cover entire trees and the old farm's buildings. Admission includes a 30-minute tram tour and lots of kiddie attractions, such as gemstone hunting and a butterfly room.

Wolfe's Neck Woods State Park   STATE PARK
(☑ 207-865-4465; www.maine.gov/wolfesneck woods; 426 Wolfe's Neck Road; adult/child $6/1; ☺ 9am-sunset) Just outside Freeport, this park has 5 miles of easy hiking trails, including a scenic shoreline walk that skirts Casco Bay. To reach the park, take Bow St and turn right on Wolfe's Neck Rd.

Bradbury Mountain State Park   STATE PARK
(☑ 207-688-4712; www.maine.gov/bradburymoun tain; 528 Hallowell Rd/ME 9, Pownal; adult/child $6/1; ☺ 9am-sunset) There are several miles of forested hiking trails here, including an easy 10-minute hike to a 485ft summit. It yields a spectacular view all the way to the ocean. There's good mountain biking, and bird-watching, plus camping as well.

Eartha   LANDMARK
(www.delorme.com/about/eartha.aspx; 2 DeLorme Dr, Yarmouth; ☺ 8am-6pm Mon-Fri) FREE Geography boffins shouldn't miss a visit to the DeLorme cartographic company (now owned by Garmin) – its lofty office atrium is home to a giant rotating globe named Eartha. Eartha has a diameter of 41.5ft and has been acknowledged by Guinness World Records as the world's largest revolving and

rotating globe. The detail on it is impressive, as is the opportunity for visitors to stop by.

🏃 Activities

★**LL Bean Outdoor
Discovery School**   OUTDOORS
(☑ 888-552-3261; www.llbean.com/ods; 95 Main St) The Outdoor Discovery School offers a smorgasbord of choice, including in-store clinics (eg bike maintenance, first aid) and fantastic excursions, tours and classes – locally and across Maine. Activities range from archery to snowshoeing by way of fly-fishing and bird-watching. Sign your kids up for camp or join a fall-foliage canoe tour or a river fishing trip.

🛏 Sleeping

★**Recompence Shore
Campground**   CAMPGROUND $
(☑ 207-865-9307; www.freeportcamping.com; 134 Burnett Rd; campsites $28-52; ☺ May-Oct; ⊠) ⊿ Adjacent to the Wolfe's Neck Woods State Park, this fabulous, family-oriented, 626-acre campground has waterfront and wooded sites spread over a working saltwater farm. The farm is part of a nonprofit organization dedicated to promoting sustainable agriculture and outdoor recreation; it's open for the public to check out the animals and walk the trails.

White Cedar Inn   B&B $$
(☑ 207-865-9099; www.whitecedarinn.com; 178 Main St; r $130-209; ⊞⊠) The former home of Arctic explorer Donald MacMillan, this Victorian-era B&B is conveniently located within walking distance of the stores. It has seven homey rooms, some with brass beds and working fireplaces.

Harraseeket Inn   INN $$$
(☑ 207-865-9377; www.harraseeketinn.com; 162 Main St; r $158-310; ⊞⊠⊠⊠) This big, white clapboard inn is a Freeport tradition, with a lodge-style lobby complete with crackling fireplace and afternoon tea. While most of the 93 rooms have a classic but fresh look, the Thomas Moser Room is decked out in sleek slate and wood – stylish. The inn is a short walk from the LL Bean outlet.

🍴 Eating & Drinking

**Harraseeket Lunch
& Lobster Co**   SEAFOOD $$
(☑ 207-865-4888; www.harraseeketlunchandlob ster.com; 36 Main St, South Freeport; mains $5-30; ☺ 11am-7:45pm May-Jun & Sep-Oct, to 8:45pm Jul & Aug) Head down to the marina to feast on

lobster at this iconic red-painted seafood shack. If it's nice out, grab a picnic table – or just do like the locals and sit on the roof of your car. Come early to beat the crowds. Finish with a slice of blueberry pie. BYOB. Cash only.

Broad Arrow Tavern AMERICAN $$
(www.harraseeketinn.com; 162 Main St; mains $10-30; ⊙11:30am-10:30pm) In the Harraseeket Inn, this rustic, wood-floored charmer has a good selection of microbrews and high-end bistro fare, including steamed clams, surf 'n' turf and brick-oven pizzas. The lunch buffet (Monday to Saturday) is good value at $17.

Maine Beer Company BREWERY
(☑207-221-5711; www.mainebeercompany.com; 525 US 1; ⊙11am-7pm Mon-Sat, to 5pm Sun) The tasting room of this small, ethically minded brewery is a popular destination for beer lovers, who like both the hoppy flavors and the brewers' ideals. There are eight beers on tap, including some brewery-only releases.

🛍 Shopping

⭐**LL Bean Flagship Store** SPORTS & OUTDOORS
(☑877-755-2326; www.llbean.com; 95 Main St; ⊙24hr) A 10ft-tall Bean Boot sits outside the flagship LL Bean store. Although a hundred other stores have joined it in Freeport, the wildly popular LL Bean is still the epicenter of town and one of the most popular tourist attractions in Maine. It's part store, part outdoor-themed amusement park, with an archery range, an indoor trout pond and coffee shops.

ℹ Information

Freeport Information Center (☑207-865-1212; www.freeportusa.com; 23 Depot St; ⊙6:45pm Mon-Sat, 11:30am-1pm & 5:30-6:45pm Sun) Maintains an information center one block south of Main St, close to the train station. It also acts as the train info center.

State of Maine Information Center – Yarmouth (☑207-846-0833; www.maine tourism.com; US 1; ⊙9am-5:30pm Nov-Apr, 8am-6pm May-Oct) Facing the DeLorme cartographic company at exit 17 off the I-95, this large info center dispenses mountains of information on Freeport and all of Maine.

ℹ Getting There & Away

Freeport, 15 miles north of Portland via I-295, is a mile off the interstate on US 1. Buses do not stop in Freeport.

Amtrak (www.amtrak.com) train services link Portland and Freeport twice daily (30 to 40 minutes, $8 one way).

MIDCOAST MAINE

Carved by ancient glaciers, the coastline of Midcoast Maine is jagged and dramatic. With its wild natural beauty and down-to-earth residents, this is what many people imagine when they think of Maine – riding bikes and shopping for antiques in postcard-pretty seaside villages, taking leisurely scenic drives down the rural peninsulas, and riding the deep blue seas aboard one of the Midcoast's famous windjammers. It's a landscape that rewards slow, aimless exploration: you never know when you're going to stumble upon the next great lobster shack, lost-in-time fishing village or you-pick blueberry patch.

The English first settled this region in 1607, which coincided with the Jamestown settlement in Virginia. Unlike their southerly compatriots, though, these early settlers returned to England within a year. British colonization resumed in 1620. After suffering through the long years of the French and Indian War, the area became home to a thriving shipbuilding industry, which continues today.

Brunswick

POP 20,300

On the banks of the powerful Androscoggin River, Brunswick (settled 1628) is a handsome, well-kept town with a pretty village green and historic homes tucked along tree-lined streets. It's home to the highly respected Bowdoin College (founded 1794), which infuses the town with a lively intellectual and artistic culture.

A short drive through the city center reveals stately Federal and Greek mansions built by wealthy sea captains. Harriet Beecher Stowe wrote *Uncle Tom's Cabin* at 63 Federal St. This poignant story of a runaway slave, published in 1852, was hugely popular among people in the northern states, who saw the book as a powerful indictment against slavery.

Brunswick's green, called the Town Mall, is along Maine St. Farmers markets are set up Tuesday and Friday mornings, with free concerts Wednesday evenings in summer.

⊙ Sights

The town's main sights are all on or near the campus of Bowdoin College, with the Town Mall having a few historical diversions. Also worth seeing are the Androscoggin Falls, once a source of hydroelectric power for 18th-century sawmills.

Midcoast Maine

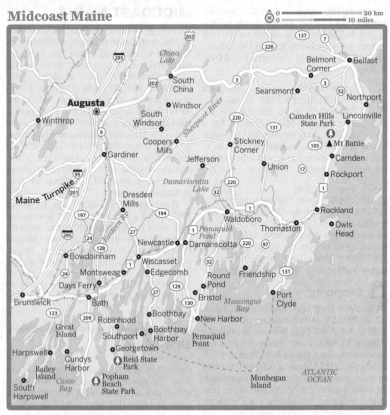

N 0 ———— 20 km
   0 ———— 10 miles

Bowdoin College COLLEGE
(☑ 207-725-3000; www.bowdoin.edu; 255 Maine St) Bowdoin, established in 1794, is one of the oldest colleges in the US and the alma mater of Henry Wadsworth Longfellow, Nathaniel Hawthorne and US president Franklin Pierce. For a tour of the handsome campus, follow the signs from Maine St to Moulton Union. **Smith Union** is the student center; there's an information desk on the mezzanine, as well as a cafe, pub, lounge and small art gallery. To find the free **museums** on campus, look for the large flagpole.

🛏 Sleeping & Eating

Brunswick Inn B&B $$
(☑ 207-729-4914; www.brunswickinnparkrow.com; 165 Park Row; r $139-259; 🛜) Overlooking Brunswick's town green, this elegant guesthouse has 16 rooms ranging from small to spacious. Each is uniquely designed in an airy, farmhouse-chic style, a mix of worn woods and modern prints. There's a self-contained garden cottage that's ideal for families. Enjoy drinks by the fire in the bar, or on the porch overlooking the Town Mall.

⭐**Tao Yuan** ASIAN $$
(☑ 207-725-9002; www.tao-yuan.me; 22 Pleasant St; dishes $7-18; ⊘ 5-9pm Tue-Sat, 4-8pm Sun) A young, lauded chef (a James Beard 'Rising Star' nominee) is behind this high-quality pan-Asian eatery, where accomplished dishes dazzle palates with fresh flavor. Small plates range from dumplings and pork buns to fresh tangy salads (the Asian slaw is a treat). Come hungry for the chef's tasting menu (15 courses for $68, or $48 on Wednesday). Reservations recommended.

🍸 Drinking & Nightlife

Frontier Cafe BAR
(☑ 207-725-5222; www.explorefrontier.com; 14 Maine St; mains $13-23; ⊘ 11am-9pm Sun & Tue-Thu, to 10pm Sat & Sun) On the 2nd floor of the colossal Fort Andross mill complex over-

looking the Androscoggin, this raw, loft-like space is part cafe, part bar, part cinema, part gallery. Arty student and professor types recline on vintage couches, sipping coffee or wine and nibbling on antipasto platters or paella. The theater features an ever-changing schedule of art-house films and live theater and music performances.

❶ Getting There & Away

Brunswick, off I-295 exit 28 or 31, is the point at which I-295 heads north and inland toward Augusta, Waterville and Bangor, and US 1 heads northeast along the coast. It's about 9 miles from Freeport and 8 miles from Bath.

Concord Coach Lines (☑ 800-639-3317; www.concordcoachlines.com) offers bus services to Bangor, Portland, Boston and a handful of Midcoast towns, departing from the **visitor center** (16 Station Ave) that's west of Maine St and close to the train station.

Bath & Around

POP 8500

Known as the 'City of Ships,' this quaint Kennebec River town was once home to more than 20 shipyards producing more than a quarter of early America's wooden sailing vessels. In Bath's 19th-century heyday, it was one of Maine's largest cities, with a bustling downtown lined with banks and grand municipal buildings. Bath-built schooners and clipper ships sailed the seven seas and the city's name was known far and wide.

Downtown, redbrick sidewalks and solid 19th-century buildings line quaint Front St, while just downhill lies a small grassy park overlooking the water. South of Bath stretch two scenic peninsulas well worth a detour: ME 209 takes you to **Phippsburg**, home to excellent beaches and a historic fort, while ME 127 runs south to **Georgetown**, terminating at a great lobster shack overlooking an island-dotted cove.

❂ Sights

★**Maine Maritime Museum**   MUSEUM
(☑ 207-443-1316; www.mainemaritimemuseum.org; 243 Washington St, Bath; adult/child $15.50/10; ☉9:30am-5pm) On the western bank of the Kennebec River, this wonderful museum preserves the Kennebec's long shipbuilding tradition with paintings, models and hands-on exhibits that tell the tale of the past 400 years of seafaring. One highlight is the remains of the *Snow Squall*, a three-mast 1851 clipper ship. The on-site 19th-century Percy

& Small Shipyard, preserved by the museum, is America's only remaining wooden-boat shipyard. There's also a life-size sculpture of the *Wyoming*, the largest wooden sailing vessel ever built.

Popham Beach State Park   STATE PARK
(☑ 207-389-1335; www.maine.gov/pophambeach; Popham Rd/ME 209, Phippsburg; adult/child $8/1; ☉9am-sunset) This 6-mile-long sandy stretch is one of the prettiest in the state, with views of offshore islands and the Kennebec and Morse Rivers framing either end. Lifeguards are on hand in July and August, but be aware that the surf is strong, with undertows and riptides. It's located off ME 209, about 14 miles south of Bath.

A few miles further along ME 209 are the ruins of **Fort Popham**, a Civil War-era fortification at the mouth of the Kennebec River.

🛏 Sleeping & Eating

Inn at Bath   B&B $$
(☑ 207-443-4294; www.innatbath.com; 969 Washington St, Bath; r $150-245; 🛜🐾) Once a shipbuilder's mansion, this stately Greek Revival home in Bath's manicured historic district has eight guest rooms done up in an appealing country style – lots of pale woods, soothing sage and green tones, and vintage botanical prints.

★**Five Islands
Lobster Company**   SEAFOOD $$
(☑ 207-371-2990; www.fiveislandslobster.com; 1447 Five Islands Rd, Georgetown; mains $6-30; ☉11:30am-7pm Sat & Sun May–mid-Oct, daily mid-Jun–early Sep) Imagine crab cakes with fresh dill-tartar sauce, golden fried clams and lobsters dripping with melted butter.

SHIPBUILDING IN BATH

More than 150 years after its shipbuilding heyday, the tradition is still very much alive here in Bath. Across US 1 from downtown, **Bath Iron Works** (founded in 1884) is still one of the largest and most active shipyards in the US, producing steel frigates, cruisers and other naval craft. Locals know to avoid driving in or out of town around 3:30pm on weekdays, when the work shift changes and the roads briefly choke with cars.

South of the shipyard, the Maine Maritime Museum is an excellent place to learn about Bath's 400-year-old shipbuilding history.

The food at this wharfside lobster shack, 13 miles southeast of Bath in the fishing hamlet of Georgetown, is a cut above average – and the view is tops. The shack is named for the islands you can see from your table. BYOB.

Solo Bistro MODERN AMERICAN **$$$**
(☑ 207-443-3373; www.solobistro.com; 128 Front St, Bath; mains $18-33; ☺ 5-10pm Wed-Sat) In a downtown storefront, Bath's most praised fine-dining restaurant has a small, seasonal menu of creative New American dishes, such as grilled octopus, miso-roasted salmon and lobster risotto. There are great-value prix-fixe deals, too (three courses for $25). The minimalist dining room could double as an IKEA showroom.

🛈 Getting There & Away

Bath is 8 miles east of Brunswick and 10 miles southwest of Wiscasset on US 1. **Concord Coach Lines** (☑ 800-639-3317; www.concord coachlines.com) offers bus service to Bangor, Portland, Boston and a number of other Midcoast towns, leaving from in front of the Mail It 4 U shipping store at 10 State Rd.

Wiscasset

POP 3700

The sign says, 'Welcome to Wiscasset, the Prettiest Village in Maine.' Others may dispute this claim, but Wiscasset's history as a major shipbuilding port in the 19th century has left it with a legacy of exceptionally beautiful houses. Set near the Sheepscot River, Wiscasset has some fine vantage points and its tidy streets are dotted with antique shops, galleries, restaurants and a few old-fashioned inns.

Like Bath, Wiscasset was a shipbuilding and maritime trading center. Great four-masted schooners carrying timber, molasses, salt, rum and cod sailed down the Sheepscot bound for England and the West Indies, a route known as the 'triangle trade.'

One caveat: as with other pretty towns astride US 1, Wiscasset has bad traffic jams in the summer (most likely due to the popularity of Red's Eats). Allow for extra time when driving through.

🛏 Sleeping & Eating

★**Squire Tarbox Inn** B&B **$$**
(☑ 207-882-7693; www.squiretarboxinn.com; 1181 Main Rd, Westport Island; r $120-199; ☺ Apr-Dec; ☎) Ten miles southwest of Wiscasset on tranquil Westport Island (connected by bridge), this 1763 farmhouse has been converted into a charmingly rustic country inn. The 11 guest rooms are sunny and old-fashioned – some with wood-burning fireplaces and beamed ceilings – and the setting is absolutely pastoral. Guests can borrow bikes or a rowboat to explore the salt marsh.

Marston House B&B **$$**
(☑ 207-882-6010; www.marstonhouse.com; 101 Main St/US 1; d $135-155; ☺ mid-May–Sep) The Marston House embodies the spirit of Wiscasset: it's an antique store with two effortlessly chic guest rooms, set in a cottage garden, with a breakfast basket delivered to your door each morning. The owners spend half the year in France, and source their inspirations – and their stock – from there.

Treats DELI, CAFE **$**
(☑ 207-882-6192; www.treatsofmaine.com; 80 Main St/US 1; mains $3-10; ☺ 8am-6pm Mon-Sat, 10am-4pm Sun) With a well-edited selection of fancy cheeses and a bakery overflowing with gorgeously browned baguettes and homemade fruit tarts, this little food store is a picnicker's heaven. Good coffee and homemade soups are worthy lures.

★**Red's Eats** SEAFOOD **$$**
(☑ 207-882-6128; www.redseatsmaine.com; 41 Water St, cnr US 1; mains $5-25; ☺ 11:30am-9pm Apr-Sep) The lines for this iconic US 1 seafood shack, just west of the downtown bridge, slow down summer traffic so much that the local government has been trying to find a solution for decades (no joke). Incredible lobster rolls, overflowing with unadorned chunks of fresh meat (and a side of either drawn butter or mayo), are what pulls 'em in.

Le Garage AMERICAN **$$**
(☑ 207-882-5409; www.legaragerestaurant.com; 15 Water St; mains $10-28; ☺ 11am-8pm Tue-Thu, to 8:30pm Fri & Sat, 9:30am-8pm Sun) This long-time bistro in an old garage overlooking Wiscasset Harbor serves upscale European and American standards – Caesar salad, seafood alfredo, char-grilled lamb – in a French country atmosphere. Creamed finnan haddie (smoked haddock, a Maine classic by way of Scotland) is the house specialty. The bar is a lovely spot for a glass of wine and a bit of people-watching.

🛈 Getting There & Away

Wiscasset is 10 miles northeast of Bath, 13 miles north of Boothbay Harbor and 23 miles south of Augusta.

Concord Coach Lines (📞 800-639-3317; www.concordcoachlines.com) stops at Huber's Market at 279 US 1 (west of downtown), with services to Bangor, Portland, Boston and a number of other Midcoast towns.

Boothbay Harbor

POP 2300

Once a beautiful little seafarers' village on a wide blue harbor, Boothbay Harbor is now an extremely popular tourist resort in the summer, when its narrow and winding streets are packed with visitors. Still, there's good reason to join the holiday masses in this picturesque place. Overlooking a pretty waterfront, large, well-kept Victorian houses crown the town's many knolls, and a wooden footbridge ambles across the harbor. From May to October, whale-watching is a major draw.

After you've strolled the waterfront along Commercial St and the business district along Todd and Townsend Aves, walk along McKown St to the top of McKown Hill for a fine view. Then, take the footbridge across the harbor to the town's East Side, where there are several huge dockside seafood restaurants.

Boothbay and East Boothbay are separate from Boothbay Harbor, the largest, busiest and prettiest of the three towns.

👁 Sights & Activities

★ Coastal Maine Botanical Gardens
GARDENS

(📞 207 633 8000; www.mainegardens.org; 132 Botanical Gardens Dr, off Barters Island Rd, Boothbay; adult/child $16/8; ⊙ 9am-5pm; 🅿) These magnificent gardens are one of the state's most popular attractions. The verdant waterfront kingdom has 270 acres, with groomed trails winding through forest, meadows and ornamental gardens blooming with both native and exotic plant species. The storybook-themed children's garden offers interactive fun, and visitors with kids in town shouldn't miss the daily story time, puppet theater or chicken-feeding (daily from mid-June to early September).

Boothbay Railway Village
MUSEUM

(📞 207-633-4727; www.railwayvillage.org; 586 Wiscasset Rd/ME 27, Boothbay; adult/child $12/6; ⊙ 10am-5pm late May–mid-Oct; 🅿) Ride the narrow-gauge steam train through this endearing village, a historic replica of an old-fashioned New England town. The 28 buildings house more than 60 antique steam- and gas-powered vehicles, as well as exhibits on turn-of-the-20th-century Maine culture. Frequent special events include craft fairs, auto shows and visits from Thomas the Tank Engine.

Boothbay Region Land Trust
HIKING

(📞 207-633-4818; www.bbrlt.org; 137 Townsend Ave) This land trust manages over 30 miles of year-round hiking trails traversing tidal coves, shoreline forest, flower meadows and salt marshes. Bird-watchers should keep their eyes peeled for great blue herons, eider ducks, herring gulls and migratory birds. Stop by the office or go online for maps and schedules of guided hikes.

🚩 Tours

Cap'n Fish's Boat Trips
BOATING

(📞 800-636-3244; www.boothbayboattrips.com; Pier 1 & 7; ⊙ Jun-Oct) Cap'n Fish offers a bumper menu of boat trips from Boothbay Harbor, from whale-watching to scenic cruising. The family-friendly 'Original' has been offered for 50 years and involves lobster-trap hauling, seal-spotting and two lighthouses (1¼ hours, adult/child $19/10).

Balmy Days Cruises
CRUISE

(📞 207-633-2284; www.balmydayscruises.com; Pier 8, 42 Commercial St; passage to Monhegan adult/child 1-way $20/10) This outfit takes day-tripping passengers to Monhegan Island (p386; 90 minutes each way, with 3¾ hours on the island); you can stay overnight and return on a later boat. There are also sailing trips to the harbor's many scenic island lighthouses (adult/child $30/20), or you can try out a two-hour mackerel-fishing excursion (adult/child $34/22).

🛏 Sleeping & Eating

Budget accommodations are few and far between in this neck of the woods. Those seeking a cheap motel may have to backtrack as far as US 1.

Topside Inn
B&B $$$

(📞 207-633-5404; www.topsideinn.com; 60 McKown St; r $159-335; ⊙ May–mid-Oct; ❋ 🤖) Atop McKown Hill, this grand mansion has Boothbay's best harbor views. Rooms are elegantly turned out in crisp nautical prints and beachy shades. Main-house rooms have more historic charm, but rooms in the two adjacent modern guesthouses are sunny and lovely, too. Enjoy the sunset from an Adirondack chair on the inn's sloping, manicured lawn. Knowledgeable, helpful hosts.

DON'T MISS

PEMAQUID POINT

Along a 3500-mile coastline famed for its natural beauty, Pemaquid Point stands out for its twisted rock formations pounded by the restless seas.

ME 130 goes from Damariscotta (northeast of Wiscasset) through the heart of the Pemaquid Peninsula (the longest on the coast of Maine) to Pemaquid Point, a major destination for its natural beauty. Artists and nature lovers from across the globe come here to record the memorable seascape in drawings, paintings and photographs.

Perched on top of the rocks in **Lighthouse Park** (📞207-677-2494; www.facebook.com/pemaquidlighthouse; 3115 Bristol Road; adult/child $2/free; ⊘sunrise-sunset) is the 11,000-candlepower Pemaquid Point Light, built in 1827. It's one of the 60-plus surviving lighthouses along the Maine coast, 57 of which are still in operation. The lighthouse-keeper's house now serves as the **Fisherman's Museum** (admission incl with park entry; ⊘10:30am-5pm May-Oct).

Newagen Seaside Inn　　　RESORT $$$
(📞800-654-5242; www.newagenseasideinn.com; 60 Newagen Colony Rd, Southport Island; r $174-335; ⊘late May–mid-Oct; ✳☂☀) A charming relic of the days when wealthy Northeastern families would descend on the summer colonies of Maine for weeks at a time, the Newagen is a world apart. On a secluded stretch of the Southport Island coast, its grand white inn and cottages are hidden beneath the pines.

Lobster Dock　　　SEAFOOD $$
(📞207-633-7120; www.thelobsterdock.com; 49 Atlantic Ave; mains $12-29; ⊘11:30am-8:30pm late May–mid-Oct) Of all the lobster joints in Boothbay Harbor, this sprawling, wooden waterfront shack is one of the best and cheapest. It serves traditional fried seafood platters, sandwiches and steamers, but whole, butter-dripping lobster is definitely the main event. Get your lobster roll ($17) warm with butter, or cold with mayo.

★**Cabbage Island Clambakes**　SEAFOOD $$$
(📞207-633-7200; www.cabbageislandclambakes. com; Pier 6, 22 Commercial St; clambake incl boat tour $62; ⊘mid-Jun–mid-Sep) A prized Maine tradition: a scenic cruise from Boothbay Harbor to the small, family-owned Cabbage Island, where a traditional clambake provides a fabulously memorable feast for diners, who can explore the island in between courses. Chow down on chowder, steamed clams, lobster and all the fixins, plus delicious blueberry cake. Lunch cruise daily, plus additional departure on weekends. Book ahead.

❶ Information

Boothbay Harbor Region Chamber of Commerce (📞207-633-2353; www.boothbay harbor.com; 192 Townsend Ave; ⊘8am-5pm Mon-Fri year-round, plus 10am-4pm Sat & Sun late May–mid-Oct) Has lots of good info on its website. It also operates a downtown **information center** (17 Commercial St) in summer.

❶ Getting There & Away

From Wiscasset, continue on US 1 for 1.5 miles and then head south on ME 27 for 11 miles through Boothbay to Boothbay Harbor.

There's no direct bus service to Boothbay Harbor. Concord Coach Lines (p366) stops in Wiscasset; you can then take a taxi. Try **Twin Village Taxi** (📞207-380-0050).

Monhegan Island

POP 69

Monhegan Island is not for the faint-hearted or the easily bored. There are no TVs, no cars, no bars and no shopping, save for a few small convenience stores. The weather is unpredictable and often foggy. The 1½-hour mail-boat ride from the mainland can be bumpy. Cell-phone coverage is spotty. The sole village remains small and very limited in its services, with almost no cars. The few unpaved roads are lined with stacks of lobster traps.

But for a world that's almost completely removed from the bustle of the 21st century, this tiny chunk of rock is a refuge. With dramatic granite cliffs, gnarled maritime forest and lush floral meadows, the island's isolated vistas have been attracting artists since the 19th century. To this day, Monhegan residents and visitors are drawn to plain living, traditional village life and peaceful contemplation.

🏃 Activities

What is there to do on Monhegan? Paint, read, hike, bird-watch, think. The island is laid out for **walking**, with 17 miles of forest and cliff-top trails, some quite overgrown. Pick up a trail map at the ferry office or at any hotel. Children, in particular, enjoy the Lobster Cove trail, with lots of rocks to climb and the wreck of a metal ship lying like a beached whale. Wander through Cathedral Woods to search for fairy houses (stones and twigs stacked to resemble tiny forest dwellings). Climb the hill for sweeping views from the base of the 19th-century granite lighthouse.

In the village, check out the working one-room schoolhouse. A number of artists open their studios to visitors during the summer months – check out the notices posted on the village Rope Shed, the unofficial community notice board.

🛏 Sleeping & Eating

★ Shining Sails
B&B $$

(☑ 207-596-0041; www.shiningsails.com; r $120-265; 🛜) Run by a friendly lobsterman and his wife, this year-round B&B has seven comfy, basic rooms, some with kitchenettes; stay upstairs for the best ocean views. The fresh blueberry muffins at breakfast are a treat. The owners also rent out various rooms and cottages throughout the island. The B&B is easy walking distance from the ferry dock.

Island Inn
INN $$$

(☑ 207-596-0371; www.islandinnmonhegan.com; r & ste $145-435; ⊘ late May–mid-Oct; 🛜) The island's most elegant digs, this Victorian mansard-roofed summer hotel has 32 simple but plush rooms and suites with crisp white linens and oriental rugs; the cheaper rooms have shared bathrooms. The wide front porch has killer views of the roiling Atlantic. The dining rooms serve three meals a day for both guests and visitors.

Fish House Fish Market
SEAFOOD $

(⊘ 11:30am-7pm late May-Sep) On Fish Beach, this fresh seafood market sells lobster rolls and chowder. Relax and eat at the nearby picnic tables.

ℹ Information

Monhegan Welcome (www.monhegan welcome.com)

ℹ Getting There & Away

You can reach Monhegan Island on passenger boats from Port Clyde, New Harbor and Booth-bay Harbor. In peak summer a day trip is possible using these services.

During high season, **Monhegan Boat Line** (☑ 207-372-8848; www.monheganboat.com; Port Clyde; round-trip adult/child $35/20) runs two or three daily trips to Monhegan Island from Port Clyde. Schedules vary according to the season; advance reservations are always a must. In winter the service operates three times a week. Parking in Port Clyde costs $7 per day.

Hardy Boat Cruise (☑ 207-677-2026; www. hardyboat.com; 132 ME 32, New Harbor; round-trip adult/child $36/20; ⊘ late May–mid-Oct) departs for Monhegan from New Harbor twice daily in summer (mid-June to September), and less frequently in spring and fall. Parking at New Harbor is $4 per day.

You can visit Monhegan on a day excursion from Boothbay Harbor in summer: Balmy Days Cruises (p385) operates a schedule that allows 3¾ hours on the island.

You can also use the boat services to travel for overnight stays.

Rockland

POP 7300

This thriving commercial port boasts a large fishing fleet and a proud year-round population that gives Rockland a vibrancy lacking in some other Midcoast towns. Main St is a window into the city's sociocultural diversity, with a jumble of working-class diners, bohemian cafes and high-end restaurants alongside galleries, old-fashioned storefronts and one of the state's best art museums, the Center for Maine Contemporary Art (CMCA). Rockland is developing a reputation as an art center, partly thanks to the CMCA's relocation here in 2016.

Settled in 1769, Rockland was once an important shipbuilding center and a transportation hub for goods moving up and down the coast. Today, tall-masted sailing ships still fill the harbor, as Rockland is a center for Maine's busy windjammer cruises (along with Camden).

Rockland is also the birthplace of poet Edna St Vincent Millay (1892–1950), who grew up in neighboring Camden.

◉ Sights

★ Farnsworth Art Museum
MUSEUM

(☑ 207-596-6457; www.farnsworthmuseum.org; 16 Museum St; adult/child $15/free; ⊘ 10am-5pm Jun-Oct, closed Mon Jan-Apr, May, Nov & Dec, plus Tue Jan-Mar) One of the country's best small regional museums, the Farnsworth houses a collection spanning 200 years of American art. Artists who have lived or worked in

Maine are the museum's definite strength – look for works by the Wyeth family (Andrew, NC and Jamie), Edward Hopper, Louise Nevelson, Rockwell Kent and Robert Indiana. Exhibits on the Wyeth family continue in the **Wyeth Center**, in a renovated church across the garden from the main museum (open in summer).

★Rockland Breakwater
Lighthouse   LIGHTHOUSE
(www.rocklandharborlights.org; Samoset Rd) Tackle the rugged stone breakwater that stretches almost 1 mile into Rockland Harbor from Jameson Point at the harbor's northern shore. Made of granite blocks, this 'walkway' – which took 18 years to build – ends at the Rockland Breakwater Lighthouse, a sweet light sitting atop a brick house, with a sweeping view of town.

While on the breakwater, watch for slippery rocks and ankle-twisting gaps between stones. Bring a sweater, and don't hike if a storm is on the horizon.

Center for Maine
Contemporary Art   GALLERY
(CMCA; ☑ 207-701-5005; www.cmcanow.org; 21 Winter St; adult/child $6/free; ⊙ 10am-6pm Tue-Sat, 1-6pm Sun) The CMCA moved from Rockport to Rockland in summer 2016, and its fabulous new home is a clever, glass-enclosed space with a sawtooth roofline, designed by Toshiko Mori. The new digs are perfect for featuring exhibitions of work by artists (both established and emerging) connected with the state of Maine, such as Alex Katz and Jonathan Borofsky.

Puffin Project Visitor Center   MUSEUM
(☑ 207-596-5566; www.projectpuffin.org; 311 Main St; by donation; ⊙ 10am-5pm Jun-Oct, closed Mon & Tue May) If birds are your bag, visit this interesting little nonprofit center, where you can learn about the National Audubon Society's success in bringing puffins and other rare Maine seabirds back to historic nesting islands in a project lasting decades. There are exhibits, souvenirs and films.

Ask here about summer **boat tours** that can take you to view the fledgling puffin colonies at Eastern Egg Rock. Different companies run trips from Boothbay Harbor, Port Clyde and New Harbor.

Maine Lighthouse Museum   MUSEUM
(☑ 207-594-3301; www.mainelighthousemuseum. org; 1 Park Dr; adult/child $8/free; ⊙ 10am-5pm Mon-Fri, to 4pm Sat & Sun Jun-Oct, 10am-4pm Thu-

Sat Nov-May; 🚸) Perched over Rockland harbor (and sharing a building with the town's visitor center), this nifty little museum features vintage Fresnel lenses, foghorns, marine instruments and ship models, with hands-on exhibits for children.

👉 Tours

Maine Windjammer Association   CRUISE
(☑ 800-807-9463; www.sailmainecoast.com; ⊙ cruises late May–mid-Oct) Although traveling by schooner largely went out of style at the dawn of the 20th century, adventurers can still explore the rugged Maine coast the old-fashioned way: aboard fast sailing ships known as windjammers. Nine of these multi-masted vessels anchor at Rockland and Camden and offer trips ranging from overnight to 11 days around Penobscot Bay and further up the coast.

🎉 Festivals & Events

Maine Lobster Festival   CULTURAL
(www.mainelobsterfestival.com; ⊙ early Aug) Lobster fanatics (and who isn't?!) won't want to miss the five-day Maine Lobster Festival, but it's not just a homage to the crusty crustacean. There's plenty of live music, parades, an art show and a fun run. Accommodation gets booked up for many miles surrounding Rockland, so book ahead.

🛏 Sleeping & Eating

There are motels stretching along US 1 between Rockland and Rockport/Camden, and some good inns close to Main St.

★Lindsey Hotel   BOUTIQUE HOTEL $$
(☑ 207-596-7950; www.lindseyhotel.com; 5 Lindsey St; r $129-249; 🐾) There's a sophisticated seafaring theme at this newly revitalized, nine-room boutique hotel on a side street just steps from Main St. The building started as a sea-captain's home but has had other incarnations; check out the 'snack vault' and the handsome oak-paneled breakfast room, or get cozy by the fire in your guest room or in the hotel library.

LimeRock Inn   B&B $$
(☑ 207-594-2257; www.limerockinn.com; 96 Limerock St; r $129-249; 🐾🐾) This eight-bedroom mansion, built in 1890 for a local congressman, has been lovingly furnished in a tasteful mix of antique and modern furniture. The sunny Island Cottage room, with views of the backyard gazebo, is our favorite.

Atlantic Baking Co
BAKERY $

(📞 207-596-0505; www.atlanticbakingco.com; 351 Main St; mains under $7; ⊙ 7am-4pm, closed Sun & Mon winter) This cheery bakery sells tasty sandwiches on fresh-made bread. Pastries, soups and salads are also available.

Suzuki Sushi Bar
JAPANESE $$

(📞 207-596-7447; www.suzukisushi.com; 419 Main St; sushi $4-9, mains $14-25; ⊙ 5-9pm Tue-Sat) The super-fresh seafood of the Maine Mid-coast is put to exquisite use at Suzuki's, which sets itself apart from many sushi bars. Firstly because the sushi chefs are women (in a field dominated by men); but also, they offer no fried food and no grilled food. Sashimi and sushi dominate the menu, though noodles and *donburi* are also available.

★ Primo
ITALIAN $$$

(📞 207-596-0770; www.primorestaurant.com; 2 Main St/ME 73; mains $32-45; ⊙ dinner Wed-Sun mid-May–Oct) 🖋 In a sprawling Victorian house a mile from downtown sits Primo, widely considered one of the best restaurants in Maine. Awarded chef Melissa Kelly has reached celebrity status for her creative ways with New England ingredients – think scallops atop local wild leek and fiddlehead ferns, or farm-raised chicken with ricotta *gnudi* (dumplings). The menu, truly a farm-to-table ode, changes daily.

❶ Information

Penobscot Bay Regional Chamber of Commerce (📞 207-596-0376; www.mainedream vacation.com; 1 Park Dr; ⊙ 9am-5pm Jun-Oct, 9am-4pm Mon-Fri Nov-May) For area information, stop into the visitor center just off Main St. It's housed in the same building as the Maine Lighthouse Museum.

❶ Getting There & Away

Cape Air (www.capeair.com) connects Rockland's Knox County Airport and Boston's Logan Airport.

Concord Coach Lines (📞 800-639-3317; www.concordcoachlines.com) runs buses to and from Boston, Portland and various other Midcoast towns, departing from the **Maine State Ferry Terminal** (517A Main St).

Camden & Rockport

POP 4850 (CAMDEN), 3330 (ROCKPORT)

Camden, with its picture-perfect harbor, framed against the mountains of Camden Hills State Park, is one of the prettiest sites in Maine. Home to the state's large and justly famed fleet of windjammers, Camden continues its historic intimacy with the sea. Most vacationers come to sail, but Camden also has galleries, fine restaurants and backstreets ideal for exploring. Pick up a walking-tour guide to the town's historic buildings at the chamber of commerce. The adjoining state park offers hiking, picnicking and camping.

Like many communities along the Maine coast, Camden has a long history of shipbuilding. The mammoth six-masted schooner *George W Wells* was built here in 1900, setting the world record for the most masts on a sailing ship.

Two miles south of Camden, the sleepy harborside town of Rockport is a much smaller and more peaceful settlement. It's known for the world-renowned Maine Media Workshops.

⊙ Sights

★ **Camden Hills State Park**
STATE PARK

(📞 207-236-3109; www.maine.gov/camdenhills; 280 Belfast Rd/US 1, Camden; adult/child $6/1; ⊙ 9am-sunset) With more than 30 miles of trails, this densely forested park is a choice place to take in the Midcoast's magic. A favorite hike is the 45-minute (half-mile) climb up 780ft **Mt Battie**, which offers exquisite views over island-dotted Penobscot Bay. Short on time or energy? You can also drive to the summit via the Mt Battie Auto Rd.

Simple trail maps are available at the park entrance, just over 1.5 miles northeast of Camden center on US 1.

☞ Tours

Like nearby Rockland, Camden offers many windjammer cruises, from two-hour trips to multiday journeys up the coast.

A number of boats depart from Camden's Town Landing or adjoining Bayview Landing, offering two-hour cruises (including sunset sails) for a similar price – check out the schedules online for **Appledore II** (📞 207-236-8353; www.appledore2.com; Bayview Landing, Camden; adult/child $45/25; ⊙ Jun-Oct), **Olad** (📞 207-236-2323; www.maineschooners. com; Public Landing, Camden; adult/child $43/33; ⊙ late May–mid-Oct) and **Surprise** (📞 207-236-4687; www.schoonersurprise.com; Public Landing, Camden; adult/child $43/33; ⊙ late May–mid-Oct). This is the quintessential Midcoast sightseeing experience.

Maine Sport
CYCLING, KAYAKING

(207-230-1284; www.mainesport.com; 24 Main St, Camden; bicycle/kayak rental per day from $26/45, sea-kayaking tours from $40; 10am-6pm Mon-Sat, to 5pm Sun) Get excellent advice on where to play in the local outdoors, plus rent gear (bikes, kayaks, stand-up paddleboards, camping equipment). You can also sign up for guided sea-kayaking, river-canoeing, or SUP tours.

Sleeping

Camden is a prime spot for summer vacationers, and a popular weekend destination year-round. For budget accommodations, try the motels along US 1, just north or south of Camden.

Camden Hills State Park
CAMPGROUND $

(207-624-9950; www.campwithme.com; 280 Belfast Rd/US 1, Camden; campsites $35-45; mid-May–mid-Oct;) The park's appealing campground has hot showers and wooded sites, some with electric hookups. There's also wi-fi. Reserve online through Maine's government reservations portal.

★ Whitehall
INN $$

(207-236-3391; www.whitehallmaine.com; 52 High St, Camden; r $109-529; May-Oct;) Whitehall was once the summer home for Camden's elite visitors (poet Edna St Vincent Millay got her start reciting verse here in 1912). New owners have breathed new life into the inn, and made it a fun, fresh and fashionable destination once more. Check out the 36 on-trend rooms, rambling porches and stylish restaurant, and you'll understand the appeal.

★ Norumbega
B&B $$$

(207-236-4646; www.norumbegainn.com; 63 High St, Camden; r & ste $199-639;) Looking like something out of a slightly creepy fairy tale, this 1886 turreted stone mansion was built to incorporate elements of the owner's favorite European castles. Today, it's Camden's poshest and most dramatically situated B&B, perched on a hill above the bay, with 11 distinctive rooms and suites.

16 Bay View
BOUTIQUE HOTEL $$$

(207-706-7990; www.16bayview.com; 16 Bay View St, Camden; r $259-419;) Gorgeous hues of bronze, gold and black bring the glamor at art-deco-infused 16 Bay View, a new, 21-room luxury boutique hotel in the center. All rooms come with private balconies, fireplaces and beautiful freestanding bathtubs.

✖ Eating & Drinking

Fresh
INTERNATIONAL $$

(207-236-7005; www.freshcamden.com; 1 Bayview Landing, Camden; mains $21-32; 11:30am-2:30pm & from 5pm Thu-Tue Jul-Aug, shorter hours rest of year) The chef-owner's menu wanders the globe at this new, well-received addition to the Camden scene, sampling techniques and flavors to spice up the fine local produce: from Brazilian fish stew to *rogan josh* curry, Black Sea moussaka to Maine lobster ravioli. Portions are sizeable, and the dining room warm and inviting.

Francine Bistro
MODERN AMERICAN $$

(207-230-0083; www.francinebistro.com; 55 Chestnut St, Camden; mains $16-29; 5:30-10pm Tue-Sat) In a cozy house on a residential downtown side street, this New American bistro is one of the Midcoast's choicest picks for a creative meal. The ever-changing menu showcases chef Brian Hill's deft ways with local ingredients - roast flounder with seaweed butter, gnocchi in duck *ragu*, smoked pork ribs with salted caramel. Everyone raves about the *steak frites*. Reservations recommended.

Lobster Pound Restaurant
SEAFOOD $$

(207-789-5550; www.lobsterpoundmaine.com; 2521 Atlantic Hwy/US 1, Lincolnville; mains $18-30; 11:30am-8pm mid-Apr–Oct;) Fresh local lobster is the name of the game at this recommended seafood joint on Lincolnville's beach, though there are plenty of other options (fishy and non-fishy). The restaurant is especially family-friendly, with a kids menu and a gift shop hawking stuffed lobsters and the like. It shares its premises with Andy's Brew Pub, with fine brews and snacks.

Drouthy Bear
PUB

(207-542-7741; www.drouthybear.com; 50 Elm St, Camden; 11am-10pm Tue-Sat) 'Drouthy' (*droo*-thee) is Scottish for 'thirsty' (thanks to poet Robert Burns' 'Tam o' Shanter'), and this cute wee pub wears its owner's Scots heritage on its sleeve, and in its long whisky list and semi-exotic food menu (from haggis to neeps and tatties, and *cranachan* for dessert). Proper afternoon tea (scones and clotted cream) is served from 2pm to 4pm.

ℹ Information

Penobscot Bay Regional Chamber of Commerce (207-236-4404; www.mainedream vacation.com; 2 Public Landing, Camden; 9am-5pm Jun-Oct, 9am-4pm Mon-Fri Nov-

May) Has an information office on the waterfront at the public landing in Camden.

❶ Getting There & Away

South of Bangor (53 miles) on US 1, Camden is 81 miles north of Portland and 77 miles southwest of Bar Harbor.

Concord Coach Lines (☎ 800-639-3317; www.concordcoachlines.com) leaves from in front of Maritime Farms (20 Commercial St/ US 1) in Rockport (next to Country Inn) for Boston, Portland, Bangor and multiple Midcoast towns.

Belfast & Searsport

POP 6700 (BELFAST), 2600 (SEARSPORT)

Just north of Camden on US 1 lies Belfast, a lively working-class town with a handsome 19th-century Main St. A pleasant seaside park and a welcome shortage of tourists make the town a worthwhile stop.

Six miles northeast, Searsport has a fine historic district with its own share of 19th-century mansions, and is home to the excellent Penobscot Marine Museum.

◎ Sights

★**Penobscot Marine Museum**　　MUSEUM
(☎ 207-548-0334; www.penobscotmarinemuseum.
org; 2 Church St/US 1, Searsport; adult/child $12/8;
◷ 10am-5pm Mon-Sat, noon-5pm Sun late May–
mid-Oct) The superb Penobscot Marine Museum houses Maine's biggest collection of mariner art and artifacts, which are spread through a number of historic buildings. There's some wonderfully evocative photography collections, and fun kid-friendly activities, too.

🛏 Sleeping & Eating

There are a number of motels along US 1 between Belfast and Searsport.

**Searsport Shores
Camping Resort**　　CAMPGROUND $
(☎ 207-548-6059; www.campocean.com; 216 W Main St/US 1, Searsport; campsites $30-92, cottages $82-148; ◷ May-Oct; 🛜) This is a special place on 40 oceanfront acres, with wooded sites: some are gold-class, with private deck; all have picnic table and fireplace. There are streamside tent areas for campers who want to get away from vehicles and RVs. Nature trails, kayak rentals, art classes, organic gardens and weekend lobster bakes add to the community feel.

★**Chase's Daily**　　VEGETARIAN $
(☎ 207-338-0555; 96 Main St, Belfast; dishes $6-14; ◷ 7am-5pm Tue-Sat, 8am-2pm Sun, plus 5:30-8pm Fri; 🖋) A true farm-to-table experience, this cafe/bakery/farmers market presents fabulous, all-vegetarian fare – plus wicked good baked treats, from cauliflower and Gruyère tarts to custard buns. The lunch menu (creative salads, soups, pasta, sandwiches) kicks in from 11am. All food utilizes produce from the Chase family farm, and in summer at around 11am the store sells its farm produce, too.

Young's Lobster Pound　　SEAFOOD $$
(☎ 207-338-1160; www.facebook.com/youngslobsterpound; 2 Fairview St, Belfast; mains $10-25; ◷ 7:30am-8pm Jun–mid-Sep, shorter hours rest of year) Choose your lobster from the pound, or order from the short, simple menu, then tuck in at the waterside picnic tables – Young's has the no-frills lobster-pound aesthetic down pat. Impressively, there's nothing deep-fried on the menu, but you can get grilled halibut or haddock, chowder, steamed mussels, and lobster in all its fabulous forms. BYOB.

❶ Getting There & Away

Belfast is 18 miles north of Camden via US 1. Searsport is a further 6 miles northeast.

Concord Coach Lines (☎ 800-639-3317; www.concordcoachlines.com) stops in both towns on its route along the coast linking Boston, Portland and Bangor.

DOWN EAST

Without question, this is quintessential Maine: as you head further and further up the coast toward Canada, the peninsulas seem to become more and more narrow, jutting further into the sea. The fishing villages seem to get smaller; the lobster pounds, closer to the water. If you make time to drive to the edge of the shore, south off US 1, let it be here.

'Down East' starts at the Penobscot River, where a bridge observatory unofficially marks the boundary. The region continues 'further Down East,' from Acadia all the way to the border with New Brunswick, Canada. Information on the region is online at www.downeastacadia.com.

Deer Isle & Stonington

POP 2000

Traveling south along ME 15, the forest opens up to reveal tranquil harbors framed against hilly islands off in the distance. This is Deer Isle – actually a collection of islands joined by causeways and connected to the mainland by a picturesque suspension bridge near Sargentville. There are few actual sights but the area is worth a drive for the idyllic views.

Stonington is a quaint settlement where lobstermen and artists live side by side. A few galleries and restaurants draw the odd traveler or two. In peak summer, it's worth investigating boat cruises and kayaking tours to get out into the natural beauty.

Boats depart from Stonington for Isle au Haut.

🛏 Sleeping & Eating

Boyce's Motel   MOTEL $
(☎207-367-2421; www.boycesmotel.com; 44 Main St, Stonington; r $49-160; 🕸) Quiet, cheap and friendly, this year-round cedar-shingle motel is a solid pick for simple, quaint rooms and cottages (some with kitchen and living room) in the heart of Stonington village. Its separate harborfront sundeck is particularly lovely.

⭐**Pilgrim's Inn**   INN $$
(☎207-348-6615; www.pilgrimsinn.com; 20 Main St, Deer Isle village; r $119-219, cottages $199-259; ⊗mid-May–mid-Oct; @🕸) Overlooking the Northwest Harbor, this handsome post-and-beam inn was built in 1793 and offers refined country charm in its 12 rooms and three cottages. Pine floors and solid-wood furnishings are common

throughout; some rooms have gas fireplaces and pretty views over the millpond. It's home to the excellent **Whale's Rib Tavern** (☎207-348-6615; meals $17-26; ⊗dinner Tue-Sat mid-May–mid-Oct).

Fisherman's Friend   SEAFOOD $$
(☎207-367-2442; www.fishermansfriendrestaurant.com; 5 Atlantic Ave, Stonington; lunch $8-20, dinner mains $11-30; ⊗11am-8pm Jun-Aug, shorter hours May, Sep & Oct) Right on the waterfront in Stonington, beside lobstermen bringing home their catch, this relaxed, friendly place has been serving up seafood since 1976. You won't go wrong picking local sea critters (crab, lobster, mussels), but there's pasta, burgers and steak for fish foes. The outdoor deck is a winner.

ℹ Information

Deer Isle–Stonington Chamber of Commerce (☎207-348-6124; www.deerislemaine.com; ⊗10am-4pm late May-early Oct) Maintains an information booth 0.25 miles south of the suspension bridge.

ℹ Getting There & Away

From Blue Hill, take ME 176 southwest for 4 miles and then head south on ME 175/15 for 9 miles to Little Deer Isle. Follow ME 15 further south to reach Deer Isle village (6 miles) and Stonington (6 miles beyond Deer Isle village).

Isle au Haut

POP 73

Much of Isle au Haut, a rocky island 6 miles long, is under the auspices of Acadia National Park. More remote than the parklands near Bar Harbor, it is not flooded with visitors in summer. If you're looking for an unspoiled, untouristed, unhyped outpost of Acadia… well, you've found it (and the boat ride over makes it that much more of an escape).

🛏 Sleeping

Duck Harbor Campground   CAMPGROUND $
(www.nps.gov/acad; tent sites $25; ⊗mid-May–mid-Oct) If you're hiking the island's 18 miles of trails, you can camp at one of the five sites here (each has a lean-to shelter). The campground is maintained by the National Park Service (NPS) and reservations are mandatory; see the website for details on applying.

Keeper's House Inn   INN $$$
(☎207-335-2990; www.keepershouse.com; Lighthouse Rd; r $325-400; ⊗late May–mid Oct) In the

Down East

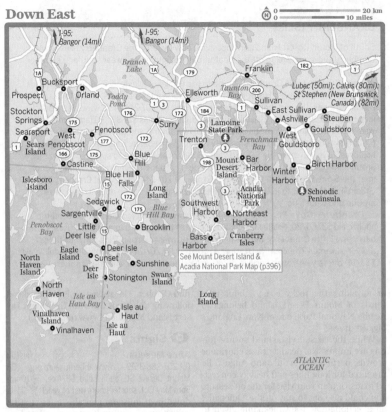

old lighthouse-keeper's house, four bright, cheerfully furnished rooms with antique furnishings and quilted bedspreads are on offer; there's also a larger cottage rented out by the week. All meals are included in the rate and are generally excellent; there's a two-night minimum stay in July and August. Bicycles and a rowboat are available for exploring the island.

Note: you're really off the grid here – it's solar power, with no TV or internet.

ⓘ Getting There & Away

Isle au Haut Boat Services (☏ 207-367-5193; www.isleauhaut.com; 37 Seabreeze Ave, Stonington; round-trip adult/child $39/19.50) operates the year-round mail-boat service, delivering people and freight between Stonington and the village settlement of Isle au Haut.

In summer, five boats a day make the 45-minute crossing from Monday through Saturday. There are fewer boats on Sundays, holidays

and during the off-season. Bicycles, kayaks and canoes (no cars) can be carried for a fee.

In July and August, a couple of services stop at the Duck Harbor Boat Landing, close to the NPS campground and park trailheads. To park your car in Stonington while visiting Isle au Haut costs $11 per day.

MOUNT DESERT ISLAND & ACADIA NATIONAL PARK

Formed by glaciers some 18,000 years ago, Mount Desert Island (MDI) is the jewel of the Down East region. It offers vast geographical variety, from freshwater lakes to dense forests, and from stark granite cliffs to voluptuous river valleys. There are many ways to experience the 108-sq-mile island's natural beauty, whether hiking the forested mountains, swimming in the secluded lakes

OFF THE BEATEN TRACK

CRANBERRY ISLES

South of Mount Desert Island and accessible only by ferry, the Cranberry Isles (www.cranberryisles.com) are an off-the-beaten-path delight and a sweet spot for a summer day trip.

The 400-acre Little Cranberry, home to the village of Islesford, is about 20 minutes offshore from Southwest Harbor. Diversions include a few galleries, a couple of summer rental cottages, the very popular **Islesford Dock** (207-244-7494; www.islesforddock.info; Islesford, Little Cranberry Island; lunch $6-18, dinner mains $12-30; ⏱ 11am-3pm & 5-9pm Wed-Sat, 10am-2pm & 5-9pm Sun mid-Jun–Sep) restaurant, and the **Islesford Market** (207-244-7667; Islesford, Little Cranberry Island; ⏱ Mon-Sat mid-Jun–early Sep, shorter hours rest of year), where the 80-odd year-rounders and 400-odd summer folk gather around like it's their own kitchen. Great Cranberry Island is even more low-key. Stop in at the **Seawich Café & Cranberry Store** (207-244-0622; Great Cranberry Island; ⏱ 8am-4pm Mon-Thu, to 1:30pm Fri, longer hours in summer) by the dock to see who's around and what's up.

Cranberry Cove Ferry (207-244-5882; www.cranberrycoveferry.com; round-trip adult/child $27.50/20; ⏱ late May–mid-Oct) carries passengers to and from Great Cranberry and Little Cranberry, departing from Southwest Harbor. Trips run four times daily in summer. The **Beal & Bunker Mailboat** (207-244-3575; round-trip adult/child $32/14) offers year-round service between Northeast Harbor and the Cranberry Isles.

or kayaking the rocky coast. About two-thirds of Mount Desert Island belongs to Acadia National Park, one of New England's biggest draws.

While the coastal vistas and spruce forests are impressive, Acadia draws enormous crowds, particularly in July and August. Be prepared for long lines and heavily congested roads, or plan your visit for the off-season. You could also opt to stay on the 'Quietside,' an affectionate and apt nickname given to the area west of the Somes Sound.

Bar Harbor

POP 5250

The agreeable hub for Acadia visits, Bar Harbor is crowded for most of the year with vacationers and visiting cruise-ship passengers. Downtown is packed with souvenir stores, ice-cream shops, cafes and bars, each advertising bigger and better happy hours, early-bird specials or two-for-one deals. The quieter residential backstreets seem to have almost as many B&Bs as private homes.

Although Bar Harbor's hustle and bustle is not for everybody, it has by far the most amenities of any town around here. Even if you stay somewhere else, you'll probably wind up here to eat dinner, grab a drink, or schedule a kayaking, sailing or rock-climbing tour.

Bar Harbor's busiest season is late June through August. There's a short lull just after Labor Day (early September); it gets busy again from foliage season, which lasts through mid-October. The season ends the weekend following Columbus Day with the Mount Desert Island Marathon (www.runmdi.org).

◎ Sights

Abbe Museum   MUSEUM
(207-288-3519; www.abbemuseum.org; 26 Mount Desert St; adult/child $8/free; ⏱ 10am-5pm May-Oct, shorter hours rest of year) 🖉 This downtown museum contains a fascinating collection of cultural artifacts related to Maine's Native American heritage. More than 50,000 objects are in the collection, including pottery, tools, combs and fishing implements spanning the last 2000 years. Contemporary pieces include finely wrought wood carvings, birch-bark containers and baskets. The museum also has a smaller, summer-only **branch** (207-288-3519; www.abbemuseum.org; ME 3 & Park Loop Rd; adult/child $3/free; ⏱ 10am-5pm late May–mid-Oct) in a lush park-like setting at Sieur de Monts Spring, inside Acadia National Park.

🏃 Activities

Bar Harbor is the base for many activities in other parts of Mount Desert Island. Tour operators lead popular hiking, climbing, kayaking and fishing excursions; keep in mind that it is often 20°F (11°C) cooler on the water than on land, so bring a jacket.

Self-guided options include countless trails geared for walking and cycling.

Bar Island Trail   WALKING
(access from Bridge St) The 157-acre island that lies directly offshore, north of Bar Harbor, can be reached on foot at low tide. For 1½ hours either side of low tide, a gravel bar is exposed, connecting the town to Bar Island. A trail continues to the summit of the island, allowing great views. It's just under 2 miles, out and back.

Shore Path   WALKING
For a picturesque view of the harbor, take a stroll along the Shore Path. This half-mile walkway, first laid down in 1880, begins near Agamont Park and continues past birch-tree-lined Grant Park, with views of the Porcupine Islands offshore and the historic mansions set back from the path. Complete the loop by returning along Wayman Lane.

☞ Tours

Lulu Lobster Boat   CRUISE
(☎207-235-2341; www.lululobsterboat.com; 55 West St; adult/child $35/20; ☺late Apr-late Oct) Brush up on your lobster knowledge while combining sightseeing and seal watching. This two-hour tour is aboard a lobster boat, hosted by Captain John (a lobster expert), and involves raising lobster traps. No kids under six permitted.

Acadian Boat Tours   WILDLIFE
(☎207-801-2300; www.acadianboattours.com; 119 Eden St; adult/child $30/18; ☺mid-May–Oct) See whales, porpoises, bald eagles, seals and more on these narrated two-hour nature cruises, which leave from northwest of the downtown area, from the dock by the Atlantic Oceanside Hotel. There are up to four departures daily in peak summer. Other boat tours are available, including sunset trips, family-friendly fishing excursions, and seabird and lighthouse cruising. See the website for full details.

Coastal Kayaking Tours   KAYAKING
(☎207-288-9605; www.acadiafun.com; 48 Cottage St; 2½/4hr tours $39/49; ☺May-Oct) Kayaking tours generally go to the islands in Frenchman Bay or the west side of Mount Desert Island, depending on which way the wind's blowing, for a four-hour adventure. Shorter (2½-hour) harbor and sunset tours are also available. The company also offers personalized kayaking tours, from family trips to multiday camping expeditions.

Downeast Windjammer Cruises   CRUISE
(☎207-288-4585; www.downeastwindjammer.com; ticket office 19 Cottage St; adult/child $39.50/29.50; ☺May-Oct) Offers two-hour cruises three times a day on the majestic, four-masted 151ft schooner *Margaret Todd*. The sunset sail is particularly popular, and you can bring snack or drinks onboard. Boats depart from the pier in front of Bar Harbor Inn.

Bar Harbor Whale Watch Co   WILDLIFE
(☎207-288-2386; www.barharborwhales.com; 1 West St; whale-watching cruise adult $59-63, child $33-35; ☺mid-May–Oct) Operates four-hour cruises that combine whale-watching and puffin-spotting, plus a number of other appealing options, including sunset whale-watching, lighthouse tours, nature cruises and lobster bakes.

Acadia Mountain Guides Climbing School   ADVENTURE, OUTDOORS
(☎207-288-8186; www.acadiamountainguides.com; 228 Main St; half-day outing $60-99) Gear up with Acadia Mountain Guides, a highly regarded and fully accredited rock-climbing school for all ages and experience levels (family climbs can be arranged). The prices depend on group size and client-to-guide ratio. You can also arrange hiking guides, and winter mountaineering.

National Park Sea Kayak Tours   KAYAKING
(☎800-347-0940; www.acadiakayak.com; 39 Cottage St; 4hr tour $52; ☺late May–mid-Oct) Four-hour kayak tours leave at various times (morning, afternoon, sunset) and explore Mount Desert Island's 'Quietside' – ie the remote west coast. Small groups of kayakers spend about 2½ to three hours on the water; transport is provided from Bar Harbor to the put-in point.

🛏 Sleeping

Bar Harbor has thousands of guest rooms, found in both cookie-cutter motels and Victorian charmers. Reservations are essential in summer; many places have a two-night minimum stay.

There is camping in the park and there are commercial campgrounds along ME 3 near Ellsworth and clustered near the entrances to the park. Numerous inexpensive motels line ME 3 from Ellsworth to Bar Harbor.

Moseley Cottage Inn & Town Motel   B&B, MOTEL $$
(☎207-288-5548; www.moseleycottage.net; 12 Atlantic Ave; B&B $175-295, motel $139-185; ❋ ☎)

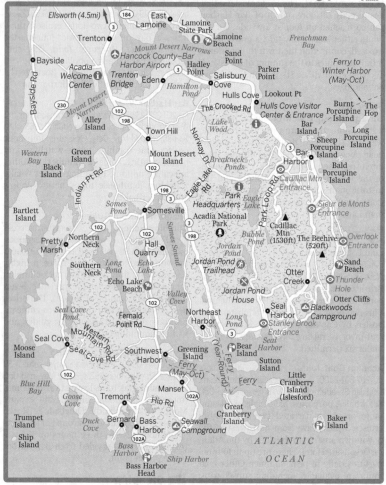

This two-faced option is down a quiet street just steps from Main St, and covers its bases very well. There are nine large, charming, antique-filled B&B rooms in a traditional 1884 inn (options with fireplace and private porch), plus a small collection of cheaper motel-style units next door. All are of a consistently high standard.

Acadia Inn
HOTEL **$$**

(207-288-3500; www.acadiainn.com; 98 Eden St; r $89-209; ☉ Apr-early Nov; ❄☎🛜⛲) This traditional 95-room hotel with helpful staff sits beside a trail leading into the park. The good-sized rooms are smart and comfortable, there's a laundry and a heated pool, and the park shuttle stops here in summer. It's a good choice if you don't mind being out of the town center.

Bar Harbor Grand Hotel
HOTEL **$$**

(207-288-5226; www.barharborgrand.com; 269 Main St; r $99-245; ☉ Apr-mid-Nov; ❄☎🛜) A replica of Bar Harbor's 19th-century Rodick House Hotel, this four-story property offers a lofty view of the town. Decor is classic, if a bit uninspired, but the staff are accommodating and the hotel is open a bit longer in the season than other local properties. Prices in

April and November are less than half the summer rate.

Aysgarth Station Inn
B&B $$

(📱207-288-9655; www.aysgarth.com; 20 Roberts Ave; r $85-170; ❄️🔊) On a quiet side street, this 1895 B&B has six cozy rooms with homey touches. Request the Tan Hill room, which is on the 3rd floor, for a view of Cadillac Mountain, or the Chatsworth room for its private deck.

★ Bass Cottage Inn
INN $$$

(📱207-288-1234; www.basscottage.com; 14 The Field; r $220-400; ⊘mid-May–Oct; ❄️🔊) If most Bar Harbor B&Bs rate about a '5' in terms of stylishness, this Gilded Age mansion deserves an '11.' The 10 light-drenched guest rooms have an elegant summer-cottage chic, all crisp white linens and understated botanical prints. Tickle the ivories at the parlor's grand piano or read a novel beneath the Tiffany stained-glass ceiling of the wood-paneled sitting room.

The location, tucked away in a hidden meadow just across the street from downtown, is Bar Harbor's best.

✕ Eating

Bar Harbor is home to countless restaurants; stroll along Rodick, Kennebec and Cottage Sts for more options.

★ Mount Desert
Island Ice Cream
ICE CREAM $

(📱207-801-4006; www.mdiic.com; 325 Main St; ice cream $4-6; ⊘mid-Apr–Oct, hours vary) A cult hit for innovative flavors like stout beer with fudge, chocolate with wasabi, and blueberry-basil sorbet, this ice-cream counter is a post-dinner must. The small, original outlet is at 7 Firefly Lane, by the Village Green.

Thrive
HEALTH FOOD $

(📱207-801-9340; www.thrivebarharbor.com; 47 Rodick St; menu items $7-10; ⊘7am-5pm) If all that fried seafood/craft beer/blueberry pie has you craving something healthy, raw and delicious, head here. Order a killer juice or smoothie or a breakfast bowl of granola or quinoa, or magic up your own nutritious creation from the salad bar.

Side Street Cafe
AMERICAN $$

(📱207-801-2591; www.sidestreetbarharbor.com; 49 Rodick St; meals $10-30; ⊘11am-10pm) At this happenin' bar and eatery, pub grub comes with the occasional twist – think build-your-own burger or loads of mac 'n' cheese fillings. Plenty of creative sandwiches, too,

like pulled pork with barbecue sauce and red-cabbage slaw. Snacks like nachos and buffalo wings go well with local brews, especially during happy hour (3pm to 6pm).

Mache Bistro
FRENCH $$

(📱207-288-0447; www.machebistro.com; 321 Main St; mains $18-32; ⊘from 5:30pm Tue-Sat May-Oct) A strong contender for Bar Harbor's best midrange restaurant, Mache serves contemporary, French-inflected fare in a stylishly renovated cottage. The changing menu highlights the local riches – think sustainably harvested scallops on fennel salad, rosemary-grilled quail, and wild blueberry trifle. Specialty cocktails add to the appeal. Reservations are suggested, but the bar is open to walk-ins.

Cafe This Way
AMERICAN $$

(📱207-288-4483; www.cafethisway.com; 14½ Mount Desert St; mains breakfast $6-17, dinner $18-28; ⊘7-11:30am & 5:30-9pm Mon-Sat, 8am-1pm & 5:30-9pm Sun May-Oct; 🌱) In a sprawling white cottage, this quirky eatery is *the* place for breakfast, with plump Maine blueberry pancakes, organic oatmeal, and eggs Benedict with smoked salmon. It also serves sophisticated dinners, such as coffee-rubbed rib-eye, sweet potato–quinoa cakes and Vietnamese noodle salad with lobster.

2 Cats
BREAKFAST $$

(📱207-288-2808; 130 Cottage St; mains $7-20; ⊘7am-1pm; 🌱) It's the most important meal of the day, so 2 Cats channels all its attention to breakfast. On weekends, crowds line up for banana pecan pancakes, smoked-trout omelets, tofu scrambles and homemade muffins at this sunny, arty little cafe. Pick up a kitty-themed gift in the gift shop.

★ Havana
LATIN AMERICAN $$$

(📱207-288-2822; www.havanamaine.com; 318 Main St; mains $25-37; ⊘from 5pm May-Oct) First things first: order a rockin' Cuba libre or mojito. Once that's done, you can take your time with the menu and the epic global wine list. Havana puts a Latin spin on dishes that highlight local produce, and the kitchen output is accomplished. Signature dishes include crab cakes, paella and a deliciously light lobster *moqueca* (stew). Reservations recommended.

🍸 Drinking & Entertainment

Atlantic Brewing Company
BREWERY

(📱207-288-2337; www.atlanticbrewing.com; 15 Knox Rd; ⊘10am-5pm) Save the ales! About 10 miles from downtown Bar Harbor, this brewery is well worth a visit – for free daily

SCHOODIC PENINSULA

Jutting into the Atlantic Ocean, the southern tip of this peninsula contains a quiet, less visited portion of Acadia National Park. The 6-mile shore drive along **Schoodic Loop Road** offers splendid views of Mount Desert Island and Cadillac Mountain. With a smooth surface and relatively gentle hills, the one-way loop road is also excellent for **cycling**.

Frazer Point has a nice little picnic area. Further along the loop, reached by a short walk from the road, you'll find **Schoodic Head**, a 400ft-high promontory with fine ocean views.

The park access road is well signposted and lies east of the small town of Winter Harbor.

To reach Winter Harbor from Bar Harbor, you need to drive back to US 1 east before turning south onto ME186. It's about an hour's drive (42 miles).

Alternatively, a **ferry** (☑ 207-288-2984; www.downeastwindjammer.com/barharbor-schoodic-ferry.html; round-trip adult/child $24/14; ⊘ late May–mid-Oct) runs in summer between the two towns; bikes are welcome aboard. Ferry times are scheduled to work in with the free **Island Explorer** (☑ 207-667-5796; www.exploreacadia.com; ⊘ late Jun–mid-Oct) shuttle (bus route 8) that operates in the Schoodic section of the national park from late June to mid-October.

---

tours (at 2pm, 3pm and 4pm, June to September) and tastings, but also for the barbecue joint set up in the garden, Mainely Meat. Do their ribs pair better with the Coal Porter or the Blueberry Ale? Taste and see.

Lompoc Café LIVE MUSIC
(☑ 207-288-9392; www.lompoccafe.com; 36 Rodick St; ⊘ 4:30-10pm mid-May–Oct) Order a glass of local pale ale and everyone's favorite mussels, then watch bluegrass, indie rock, jazz or folk musicians play on the patio of this arty cafe and bar (bands kick off at 10pm). Or down a burger and play some bocce. The venue opens occasionally over the winter for events; check its Facebook page.

Reel Pizza Cinerama CINEMA
(☑ 207-288-3811; www.reelpizza.net; 33 Kennebec Pl; tickets $6; ⊘ from 4:30pm) Sip a local microbrew and munch on pizzas ($14 to $22) with cinematic names, like The Manchurian Candidate (chicken, scallions and peanut sauce) and Hawaii 5-0 (ham and pineapple), while watching a flick on the big screen.

ⓘ Information

There are a number of options for visitor info. First for motorists is the **Acadia Welcome Center** (☑ 207-288-5103, 800-345-4617; www.acadiainfo.com; 1201 Bar Harbor Rd/ME 3, Trenton; ⊘ 9am-5pm Mon-Sat, 10am-4pm Sun late May–mid-Oct, 9am-5pm Mon-Fri mid-Apr–May & mid-Oct–Nov) as you reach Mt Desert Island (about 11 miles northwest of Bar Harbor), then the NPS-run Hulls Cove Visitor Center (p400) inside Acadia National Park.

The **Bar Harbor Chamber of Commerce** (☑ 800-345-4617, 207-288-5103; www.barharborinfo.com; cnr Main & Cottage Sts; ⊘ 8am-8pm mid-Jun–Sep, 9am-5pm Sep–mid-Jun) maintains a central year-round information office in downtown Bar Harbor.

ⓘ Getting There & Away

Cape Air (p389) connects Bar Harbor and Boston with flights year-round. The **Hancock County–Bar Harbor Airport** (www.bhbairport.com; ME 3, Trenton) is in Trenton, off ME 3, just north of the Trenton Bridge.

Getting to Bar Harbor by public transport is not easy. The only bus route to Bar Harbor is from Ellsworth, via **Downeast Transportation** (☑ 207-667-5796; www.downeasttrans.org), but it is geared to local commuters rather than travelers.

Drivers need to take ME 3 off US 1 at Ellsworth. It's about 20 miles from Ellsworth to Bar Harbor; en route you'll pass the turn-off to the Hulls Cove Visitor Center in Acadia National Park.

ⓘ Getting Around

Hiring a bike is a breeze, and a good way to avoid traffic snarls and parking problems. Another excellent option is the free shuttle system, the **Island Explorer** (www.exploreacadia.com; ⊘ late Jun–mid-Oct), which features eight routes linking hotels, inns and campgrounds to destinations within Acadia National Park.

Route maps are available at local establishments and online. Most of the routes converge on the Village Green in Bar Harbor.

Acadia National Park

The only national park in all of New England, **Acadia National Park** (✆ 207-288-3338; www.nps.gov/acad; 7-day admission per car/motorcycle $25/20, walk-ins & cyclists $12) offers unrivaled coastal beauty and activities for both leisurely hikers and adrenaline junkies.

⊙ Sights & Activities

Acadia has more than 125 miles of trails. Some are easy enough to stroll with a small child, while others require sturdy boots, full water bottles and plenty of lung power. For an easy choice, drive up Cadillac Mountain and walk the paved half-mile **Cadillac Mountain Summit Loop** for panoramic views of Frenchman Bay. It's popular with early birds at sunrise, though we think it's just as nice at the more-civilized sunset hour. A good moderate pick is the forested 2.2-mile trail to the summit of **Champlain Mountain**. The **Beehive Trail**, at less than a mile, involves clinging to iron rings bolted to the cliff face and is for the fit.

Swimmers can brave the icy (55°F, even in midsummer!) waters of **Sand Beach** or take a dip in the marginally warmer **Echo Lake**, west of Somes Sound. Both areas have lifeguard patrols in summer.

Check the park's website for a rich calendar of summertime **ranger programs** and events, from guided hikes to children's storytime to the very popular nighttime stargazing sessions on Sand Beach.

★ Jordan Pond   LAKE
On clear days, the glassy waters of this 176-acre pond reflect the image of Penobscot Mountain like a mirror. A stroll around the pond and its surrounding forests and flower meadows is one of Acadia's most popular and family-friendly activities. (Sorry, no swimming allowed.) Follow the 3-mile **self-guided nature trail** around the pond before stopping for a cuppa at the Jordan Pond House (p400).

★ Park Loop Road   SCENIC DRIVE
(www.nps.gov/acad; ☉ mid-Apr–Nov) For some visitors, driving the 27-mile Park Loop Rd is the extent of their trip to Acadia National Park. On the portion called Ocean Dr, stop at lovely **Sand Beach**, and at **Thunder Hole** for a look at the surf crashing into a cleft in the granite. The effect is most dramatic with a strong incoming tide.

Otter Cliff, not far south of Thunder Hole, is basically a wall of pink granite rising right out from the sea. This area is popular with rock climbers.

The road is largely one-way; in summer you can cover the route on the Island Explorer (p398) bus system (shuttle route 4). Note that the loop road is closed in winter, and its opening may be delayed by heavy snow.

Carriage Roads   CYCLING, HIKING
John D Rockefeller Jr, a lover of old-fashioned horse carriages, gifted Acadia with some 45 miles of crisscrossing carriage roads. Made from crushed stone, the roads are free from cars and are popular with cyclists, hikers and equestrians. Several of them fan out from Jordan Pond House (p400).

If the Jordan Pond House parking lot is too crowded, continue north to the parking area at Eagle Lake on US 233 to link to the carriage-road network.

If you're planning to explore by bike, the Bicycle Express Shuttle runs to Eagle Lake from the Bar Harbor Village Green from late June through September. Pick up a *Carriage Road User's Map* at the visitor center.

🛏 Sleeping & Eating

Most of the hotels, B&Bs and private campgrounds are in Bar Harbor. There are two great rustic campgrounds in the Mount Desert Island section of the park, with around 500 tent sites between them. Both are densely wooded but only a few minutes' walk to the ocean.

Note that reservations for the park campgrounds are handled by the National Recreation Reservation Service (NRRS; www.recreation.gov), not the park itself.

Blackwoods Campground   CAMPGROUND $
(✆ 877-444-6777; www.recreation.gov; ME 3; campsites $30; ☉ year-round) Five miles south of Bar Harbor on ME 3, year-round Blackwoods requires reservations from May to October. Flush toilets, running water, a dump station, picnic tables and fire rings are provided; paid showers and a campers supply store are a half-mile away in the village of Otter Creek. Note that the campground isn't accessed from the park's loop road.

Seawall Campground   CAMPGROUND $
(✆ 877-444-6777; www.recreation.gov; 668 Seawall Rd, Southwest Harbor; campsites $22-30; ☉ late May–Sep) Four miles south of Southwest

DON'T MISS

QUODDY HEAD STATE PARK

When the fog's not obscuring the view, the 541-acre **Quoddy Head State Park** (☎ 207-733-0911; www.maine.gov/quoddyhead; 973 S Lubec Rd, Lubec; adult/child $4/1) has darn dramatic scenery. From the parking lot, walk the **Coastal Trail**, which leads along the edge of towering, jagged cliffs. Keep an eye to the sea for migrating whales (finback, minke, humpback and right whales) swimming along the coast in the summer. The much-photographed, red-and-white candy-striped **West Quoddy Light** (1858) is the easternmost point in the US.

Harbor (about 18 miles from Bar Harbor, on the 'Quietside' of Mt Desert Island), Seawall has 200 sites (no electric hookups). There are flush toilets, running water, a dump station, picnic tables and fire rings. Paid showers and a campers store are 1 mile away. Reservations are essential.

Jordan Pond House   AMERICAN $$
(☎ 207-276-3316; www.acadiajordanpondhouse.com; Park Loop Rd; ⊙11am-9pm mid-May–mid-Oct) Afternoon tea at this lodge-like teahouse has been an Acadia tradition since the late 1800s. Steaming pots of Earl Gray come with hot popovers (hollow rolls made with egg batter) and strawberry jam. Eat outside on the broad lawn overlooking the water. The large lunch menu ranges from lobster quiche to meatloaf sandwich.

ℹ Information

Hulls Cove Visitor Center (☎ 207-288-3338; www.nps.gov/acad; ME 3; ⊙8:30am-4:30pm mid-Apr–Jun, Sep & Oct, 8am-6pm Jul & Aug) This informative center anchors the park's main Hulls Cove entrance, 3 miles northwest of Bar Harbor via ME 3. Buy your park pass and pick up maps and info. The 27-mile-long Park Loop Road (p399), which circumnavigates the eastern section of Mt Desert Island, starts near here.

When the visitor center is closed (November to mid-April), head to park headquarters, 3 miles west of Bar Harbor on ME 233, for information.

ℹ Getting There & Around

Hiring a bike in nearby Bar Harbor is a breeze, and a good way to avoid traffic snarls and parking problems.

The free shuttle system, the Island Explorer (p398), features eight routes that link hotels, inns and campgrounds to destinations within Acadia National Park. Route maps are available at local establishments and online. Most of the routes converge on the Village Green in Bar Harbor.

Northeast Harbor

Simply called 'Northeast' by locals, this fishing village is a popular getaway for the preppy East Coast yachtie set. The tiny Main St is dotted with art galleries and cafes, and the hillsides are lined with Gilded Age mansions hidden behind the trees.

◉ Sights

Asticou Azalea Garden   GARDENS
(www.gardenpreserve.org; cnr ME 3 & ME 198; suggested donation $5; ⊙dawn-dusk May-Oct) Created in 1956, this simply lovely garden is laced with paths, little shelters and ornamental Japanese-style bridges. Azaleas and rhododendrons bloom profusely from mid-May to mid-June.

⨄ Sleeping & Eating

Asticou Inn   INN $$$
(☎ 207-276-3344; www.asticou.com; 15 Peabody Dr/ME 3; r $155-380; ⊙mid-May–mid-Oct; ❋☎⊠) Guests have been arriving at this classic Maine summer hotel since the days of steamer trunks and whalebone corsets. Overlooking Northeast Harbor, the grand, gray-shingled main building has 31 sunny rooms with hardwood floors and Victorian furnishings over four stories. Also here is a restaurant, which offers sweeping views (reservations recommended).

★**Burning Tree**   MODERN AMERICAN $$
(☎ 207-288-9331; 69 Otter Creek Dr/ME 3; mains $19-30; ⊙5-10pm Wed-Mon Jun-Oct; ☑) Dine on sun-warmed greens from the backyard gardens or locally caught halibut with green peppercorns at this intimate cottage restaurant, one of the best in the region. The menu is seafood heavy and has plenty of interesting veggie options and global flavors (try the herby edamame wontons in miso). Reserve ahead. It's midway between Northeast Harbor and Bar Harbor.

ℹ Getting There & Away

Northeast Harbor can be accessed from Bar Harbor via ME 3 (12 miles).

Southwest Harbor & Bass Harbor

POP 2000

More laid-back and less affluent than Northeast Harbor, 'Southwest' is also quite tranquil. But that's a bit deceiving: it's also a major boat-building center and a commercial fishing harbor.

From the Upper Town Dock – a quarter-mile along Clark Point Rd from the flashing light in the center of town – boats venture out into Frenchman Bay to the Cranberry Isles.

◎ Sights

Bass Harbor Head Light   LIGHTHOUSE

There is only one lighthouse on Mt Desert Island; it sits in the somnolent village of Bass Harbor in the far southwest corner of the park. Built in 1858, the 36ft lighthouse still has a Fresnel lens from 1902. It's in a beautiful location that's a favorite of photographers. From the parking lot, take the short walk down wooden steps to granite boulders – this spot provides a great view of the harbor side of the lighthouse.

⨆ Sleeping & Eating

Claremont   HOTEL $$$

(☑ 207-244-5036; www.theclaremonthotel.com; Claremont Rd, Southwest Harbor; r $150-342, cottages $195-444; ☺ late May–mid-Oct; ☎) One of the island's oldest (established 1884) and most graceful hotels, the Claremont has some of the most stunning views from any guesthouse in the area, with a wraparound porch and sloping broad lawns giving way to boats bobbing in the water. Its 24 guest rooms are decorated in country-style furnishings; there are additional cottages in a variety of styles.

★**Thurston's Lobster Pound**   SEAFOOD $$

(☑ 207-244-7600; www.thurstonslobster.com; 9 Thurston Rd, Bernard; mains $10-30; ☺ 11am-9pm late May–mid-Oct) Super-fresh lobster and crab are the headliners at yellow-roofed Thurston's, overlooking Bass Harbor in Bernard. Tie on a bib and crack into a steamy, butter-dripping lobster, or a seafood-filled roll (as the menu declares, 'these guys were in the ocean when you woke up this morning'). This casual spot is rumored to be the island's best seafood shack.

❶ Getting There & Away

Reach Southwest Harbor via ME 102 (14 miles); ME 102A travels southeast of the village and runs past the national-park campground en route to Bass Harbor (7 miles).

WESTERN LAKES & MOUNTAINS

Western Maine receives far fewer visitors than the coast, which thrills the outdoorsy types who love its dense forests and solitary peaks just the way they are. While much of the land is still wilderness, there are some notable settlements. The fine old town of Bethel and the mountain setting of Rangeley are relatively accessible to city dwellers in the northeast.

In the fall, leaf peepers stream inland with their cameras and picnic baskets. In winter, skiers and snowmobiles turn the mountains into their playground. In the warmer months, the lakes and rivers, campgrounds and hiking trails draw outdoorsy types.

This is rural America at its most rustic. So bring a map and don't expect to rely on your cell phone – signals can be few and far between in these parts.

Bethel

POP 2600

An hour and a half's drive northwest of Portland, Bethel is surprisingly lively and refined for a town surrounded on all sides by deep, dark woods. Summer visitors have been coming here to escape the coastal humidity since the 1800s, and many of its fine old cottages and lodges are still operating. It's a prime spot to be during Maine's colorful fall-foliage months and during the winter ski season.

If you head west on US 2 toward New Hampshire, be sure to admire the **Shelburne birches**, a high concentration of the white-barked trees that grow between Gilead and Shelburne.

◎ Sights & Activities

Roughly 50,000 acres of the White Mountain National Forest lie inside Maine. The mountains near Bethel are home to several major ski resorts and winter is definitely the town's high season. For a dose of alpine scenery, consider a scenic drive along NH 113 from Gilead south to Stow.

Grafton Notch State Park   STATE PARK

(207-824-2912; www.maine.gov/graftonnotch; ME 26; adult/child $4/1) Sitting astride the Grafton Notch Scenic Byway within the Mahoosuc Range, this rugged park is a stunner. Carved by a glacier that retreated 12,000 years ago, the notch is a four-season playground, chock-full of waterfalls, gorges, lofty viewpoints and hiking trails, including 12 strenuous miles of the Appalachian Trail (AT; www.nps.gov/appa).

Peregrine falcons build nests in the cliffs, helping the park earn its spot on the Maine Birding Trail (www.mainebirdingtrail.com); the best viewing is May to October.

Bethel Outdoor
Adventure & Campground   KAYAKING

(207-824-4224; www.betheloutdooradventure. com; 121 Mayville Rd/US 2; kayak per day with/ without shuttle $45/32; ⏰8am-6pm mid-May– mid-Oct) Based at a bucolic riverside campground, this outfitter rents out canoes, kayaks and stand-up paddleboards. It can shuttle you upriver to the drop-off point, and you paddle back downstream. It also arranges lessons and guided trips, and fishing excursions on the river.

Sunday River Ski Resort   SKIING

(800-543-2754; www.sundayriver.com; ME 26; full-day lift ticket adult $89, child $59-69;) Six miles north of Bethel along ME 5/26, Sunday River has 135 trails spread across eight interconnected peaks, with 15 lifts. It's regarded as one of the region's best family ski destinations, with the season stretching from mid-October to April (weather permitting). There's lots of slopeside accommodation, eating and après-ski venues, and a free shuttle connection with Bethel.

There's also plenty of summer activities, including chairlift rides, ziplines, hiking, golf and a mountain-bike park.

🛏 Sleeping & Eating

Bethel Village Motel   MOTEL $

(207-824-2989; www.bethelvillagemotel.com; 88 Main St; r $60-85;) Sitting pretty on Main St, with a blue exterior and a rainbow of flowers and hanging plants, this simple, spotless old-school motel offers great-value rooms with character. It's run by a sparkling hostess, Ruthie, who has a clothing boutique downstairs.

Chapman Inn   B&B $$

(207-824-2657; www.chapmaninn.com; 2 Church St; dm $35, r $59-139;) Run by a friendly, globe-trotting retiree, this roomy downtown guesthouse has character in spades. The 10 private rooms are done up in florals and antiques, with slightly sloping floors attesting to the house's age. The cozy common space is stocked with Monopoly and other rainy-day games.

Good Food Store   SANDWICHES $

(207-824-3754; www.goodfoodbethel.com; 212 Mayville Rd/ME 26; salads & sandwiches under $8; ⏰store 9am-8pm, takeout 11am-6pm) Buy super sandwiches, salads and heat-and-eat meals at this gourmet organic market and wine shop. The homemade cookies and dried fruit are fantastic. Barbecue by Smokin' Good BBQ (www.smokingoodbarbecue. com) is sold here Thursday through Sunday, from a food trailer in the parking lot.

❶ Information

Androscoggin Ranger District (603-466-2713; ME 16, 3 miles south of Gorham) Offers information on camping in White Mountain National Forest.

Bethel Area Chamber of Commerce (207-824-2282; www.bethelmaine.com; 8 Station Pl; ⏰9am-5pm Mon-Sat, to 1pm Sun) Maintains a helpful information office in the Bethel Station building, with loads of handouts on various sights, trails and activities.

❶ Getting There & Away

Bethel lies 73 miles north of Portland, via ME 26. If you're heading into the White Mountains of New Hampshire, take US 2 west from Bethel toward Gorham, NH (22 miles) and head south to North Conway.

Rangeley Lake & Around

POP 1200

Surrounded by mountains and thick hardwood forests, the Rangeley Lake region is a marvelous year-round destination for adventurers. The gateway to the alpine scenery is the laid-back town of Rangeley, whose tidy inns and down-home restaurants make a useful base for skiing, hiking, white-water rafting and mountain biking in the nearby hills.

During the early 20th century, the lakes in this region were dotted with vast frame hotels and peopled with vacationers from Boston, New York and Philadelphia. Though most of the great hotels are gone, the reasons for coming here remain.

◉ Sights & Activities

★ Height of Land
VIEWPOINT

(ME 17) The expansive view of island-dotted Mooselookmeguntic Lake, the largest of the Rangeley Lakes, as it sweeps north toward distant mountains is astounding. Views of undeveloped forest stretch for up to 100 miles; you can even see the White Mountains in New Hampshire. The dogged Appalachian Trail runs alongside the viewpoint, and an interpretive sign shares a few details abut the 2190-mile footpath. The overlook is on ME 17, 18 miles from Rangeley.

Sugarloaf
SKIING

(☏800-843-5623, 207-237-2000; www.sugarloaf. com; 5092 Access Road, Carrabassett Valley; full-day lift ticket adult $86, child $60-70) This popular ski resort has a vertical drop of 2820ft, with 162 trails and glades, and 13 lifts, all set in Maine's second-highest peak (4237ft). It's accessed from ME 27 between the towns of Kingfield and Stratton (both have sleeping and eating options), or by ME 16 from Rangeley. The resort village complex also has lots of options.

With good conditions, the season generally lasts from mid-November to early May. Summer activities include chairlift rides, ziplines, hiking and golf.

Rangeley Lakes Trails Center
SKIING, HIKING

(☏207-864-4309; www.rangeleylakestrailscenter. com; 523 Saddleback Mountain Rd; day pass $9-19) A green yurt marks your arrival at Rangeley Lakes Trails Center, a four-season trail system covering gorgeous woodland terrain beside Saddleback Lake, which offers more than 34 miles of trails for cross-country skiing and snowshoeing during snow season. (Rental equipment is available, along with hot soup!) In summer, cross-country trails double as hiking trails, and snowshoe trails allow single-track biking.

🛏 Sleeping & Eating

Loon Lodge
INN $$

(☏207-864-5666; www.loonlodgeme.com; 16 Pickford Rd; r $110-165; 🛜) Hidden in the woods by the lake, this century-old log-cabin lodge has eight rooms, most with a backwoods-chic look, with wood-plank walls and handmade quilts (no TV). There's a formal dining room on-site, plus the intimate, friendly Pickford Pub, serving classics like burgers, fish and chips, and steak.

Rangeley Inn & Tavern
INN $$

(☏207-864-3341; www.therangeleyinn.com; 2443 Main St; r $110-230) Behind the inn's pretty powder-blue facade, you can relax by the fire and admire the mounted bear in the lobby. Rooms are simple and old-fashioned in this creaky turn-of-the-20th-century lodge, with floral wallpaper and brass beds. There's also a motel-style lodge on the property.

Forks in the Air
MODERN AMERICAN $$

(☏207-864-2883; www.forksintheair.com; 2485 Main St; small plates $9-15, mains $15-27; ⊙4-9pm) A perfect little 'mountain bistro' where the emphasis is on great local, seasonal produce, delivered in small plates (pan-roasted mussels, mac 'n' cheese) or main-sized (grilled salmon, braised short ribs). It's a hit with locals and visitors. Bookings recommended.

ℹ Information

Rangeley Lakes Chamber of Commerce
(☏207-864-5364; www.rangeleymaine.com; 6 Park Rd; ⊙10am-4pm Mon-Fri, to 2pm Sat) Offers info about restaurants, accommodation options, local trails and moose watching.

ℹ Getting There & Away

Rangeley is about 2½ hours (120 miles) north of Portland by car, on the northeast side of Rangeley Lake. From I-95, take ME 4 N.

BAXTER STATE PARK

Baxter State Park is Maine at its most primeval: the wind whips around dozens of mountain peaks, black bears root through the underbrush, and hikers go for miles without seeing another soul. Visitors can hike hundreds of miles of trails through the park, climb the sheer cliffs (this is a rock-climber's paradise), fly-fish the ponds and rivers, and spot wild animals, such as bald eagles, moose and fox-like martens. The park is most popular in the warmer months, but it's also open for winter sports like snowmobiling.

Baxter's 5267ft **Mt Katahdin** – the park's crowning glory – is Maine's tallest mountain and the northern end of the 2190-mile-long Appalachian Trail.

MAINE BAXTER STATE PARK

In order to protect the park from overuse, day-use is limited by the capacity of trailhead parking lots. Parking lots for the most popular Katahdin-access trailheads fill very early (by 6:30am) on sunny summer weekends. You'll need to reserve a space ($5) at the most popular day-use lots using the Day Use Parking Reservation (DUPR) system on the park website. Reservations can be made up to two weeks before your visit.

Sights & Activities

Baxter State Park's 200-plus miles of hiking trails range from simple strolls to the arduous climb up Mt Katahdin. For an easy day hike from the Togue Pond Gate, try the mile-long walk to Katahdin Stream Falls, or the pleasant 2-mile nature path around Daicey Pond.

Those looking to bag Mt Katahdin itself, whose summit is known as Baxter Peak, should check the weather reports, start out early, and plan on eight to 10 hours of solid uphill climbing. Katahdin hikers must reserve a parking spot at the trailhead ($5) using Baxter's website. Grab more information at the park's headquarters in Millinocket.

Sleeping

Baxter State Park Campgrounds   CAMPGROUND $
(☑207-723-5140; www.baxterstateparkauthority.com; tent sites $30, dm $11, cabins $55-130) The park has 11 campgrounds, a handful of bunkhouses and basic cabins sleeping up to six, and numerous backcountry sites ($20), including some sites with lean-tos and bunkhouses. Location, facilities and opening dates are outlined on the park website. Summer season is generally mid-May to mid-October; winter season is from December to March. Reserve your spot well in advance.

★**NEOC Twin Pines Camp**   CABIN $$
(☑800-634-7238, 207-723-5438; www.neoc.com; 30 Twin Pines Rd, Millinocket Lake, Millinocket;

4-person cabin $245-529; 🛜🐕) En route to Baxter State Park, the New England Outdoor Center offers a delectable slice of rural Maine, with creature comforts in abundance in a glorious lakeside setting. Spread over the property are 22 comfy cabins and stylish lodges with all mod cons (including full kitchen); some can sleep up to 14. Prices vary with type of accommodation and number of guests.

Eating

Restaurants, fast-food joints, supermarkets and other pre-park amenities are in Millinocket.

Within the park, there are only primitive facilities; no paved roads, no electricity. BYO everything, and pack-in and pack-out.

There are no treated water sources in the park, so bring your own or carry purifying tablets.

Information

Baxter State Park Authority Headquarters
(☑207-723-5140; www.baxterstateparkauthority.com; 64 Balsam Dr/ME 157, Millinocket; ⊗8am-4pm mid-May–mid-Oct, Mon-Fri mid-Oct–mid-May) For park information and a copy of *Windnotes*, the helpful park visitor guide, stop in at this office just beside the McDonald's in Millinocket. Rangers can help you make sense of the park's regulations.

Katahdin Area Chamber of Commerce (☑207-723-4443; www.katahdinmaine.com; 1029 Central St, Millinocket; ⊗9am-2pm Mon-Fri) Offers info on the area, including local accommodations.

Getting There & Away

Baxter's two main gates are Matagamon, in the north, and Togue Pond, in the south. Togue Pond has the park's main visitor center, where you can pick up maps and other info. It's about 18 miles from the town of Millinocket. The less popular Matagamon gate can be accessed via the town of Patten.

Understand New England

New England Today

Recalling its revolutionary roots, New England continues to claim its place as one of the nation's forward-looking and barrier-breaking regions. This is most evident in the political sphere, as controversial topics like same-sex marriage and universal health care are already old news here. A diverse economic base means that New England has fared well in recent years, as evidenced by the region's revitalized cities and increasing number of farms.

Best on Film

Jaws (1975) This cult classic was filmed on Martha's Vineyard.
On Golden Pond (1981) Won three Oscars for star performances by Henry Fonda and Katharine Hepburn in a drama set on Lake Winnipesaukee.
Good Will Hunting (1998) About a blue-collar boy from South Boston who becomes a math savant at the Massachusetts Institute of Technology.
The Cider House Rules (2000) Won Michael Caine an Academy Award for his role as a doctor in an orphanage in rural Maine.

Best in Print

Walden; Or, Life in the Woods (Henry David Thoreau; 1854) A story of the author's 26 months in a cabin on Walden Pond.
A Prayer for Owen Meany (John Irving; 1989) A novel about two friends' magical childhood in rural New Hampshire.
The Perfect Storm (Sebastian Junger; 1997) The true account of a Gloucester fishing boat lost at sea.
Olive Kitteridge (Elizabeth Strout; 2008) A Pulitzer Prize–winning book of short stories that take place in Maine.

East Coast Liberals

New England has come a long way from the theocracy it once was. Nowadays, the region is politically liberal, though a lasting strain of independent politics is evident in New England's northern states, sustained by fiscal conservatism, social libertarianism and a healthy suspicion of politics.

One of the most definitive features is the region's supportive political climate for social reformers, carrying on a legacy that includes 19th-century abolitionists, 20th-century suffragettes and 21st-century gay-rights advocates. The region has recently been at the forefront of countless 'progressive' issues, such as health care and marriage equality. The national health-care legislation enacted in 2010 was modeled after a pre-existing system of universal health care in Massachusetts. All six New England states had legalized some form of same-sex union before it was legalized at the federal level in 2015.

In 2016 the socialist from Vermont, Senator Bernie Sanders, made a noteworthy bid to become US President, running on a platform of free higher education, income equality and the separation of wealth and politics. Meanwhile, his colleague from Massachusetts, Senator Elizabeth Warren, has assumed the role of Congressional gadfly to Wall St.

Cultural Diversity

New England is becoming increasingly international – at least in the southern states. Irish, Italian and Portuguese communities have been well established in the urban areas since the 19th century. In more recent years, New England cities have continued to attract immigrants from non-European origins: you can hear Caribbean rhythms in Hartford and Springfield; smell Vietnamese and Cambodian cooking in Cambridge and Lowell; and see Brazilian flags waving in Somerville. In

Massachusetts, Connecticut and Rhode Island, roughly 15% of the population is foreign born, while one out of six residents is either Latino or Asian.

The challenges of multiculturalism were on full display in 2013, when two bombs exploded at the finish line of the Boston Marathon, killing three and injuring hundreds. Boston endured several days of confusion (including a citywide lockdown) before one alleged perpetrator was caught and another killed. They were two brothers – Chechen immigrants and Muslim extremists – who claimed to seek retribution for US killing of innocent Muslims. Recovered from the shock of the tragedy, the city went back to business – hearts were saddened but spirits never dampened.

Economic Diversity

New England has one of the healthier regional economies in the US. Tourism, education and medicine are all major players. Boston is a center for financial services, while Hartford is the country's insurance capital. The largely recession-resistant technology and biotechnology industries were spawned from local university research labs, as was the region's thriving defense industry.

The regional unemployment rate hovers around 4.4% in 2016 (just under than the national average). It's safe to say that New England has recovered from the 2008 recession, as evidenced by the packed restaurants, soaring property values and resumed development projects in cities around the region.

Rural Renewal

New England is a patchwork of farmland, yielding Massachusetts cranberries, Maine potatoes and Vermont cheeses. Some 28,000 farms blanket the region. The farmer's life is not easy, and this is highlighted by the decreasing number of family farms. But changing eating habits and environmental awareness have created new opportunities, as diners are willing to pay for food that is grown organically and locally.

Urban Renewal

Industrial and port cities around New England were built on the backs of factory workers, mill girls and sailors. Today towns like Salem, Mystic, Lowell, Providence and Portland have remade themselves as tourist destinations, building museums out of former factories, opening restaurants in old warehouses, offering cruises on canals and walks around harbors. Even in Boston, factories and warehouses now contain art galleries and studio space.

Populations are turning over in these cities. Expensive real-estate means that property is sold to the highest bidder, no matter where they come from. Many people in the old enclaves welcome newcomers, recognizing the advantages of diversity and development. But others resent being invaded by outsiders, whether immigrants or yuppies.

POPULATION: **14,680,700**

AREA: **71,992 SQ MILES**

HIGHEST POINT: **MT WASHINGTON (6288FT)**

MILES OF COASTLINE: **4965**

if New England were 100 people

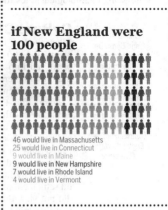

46 would live in Massachusetts
25 would live in Connecticut
9 would live in Maine
9 would live in New Hampshire
7 would live in Rhode Island
4 would live in Vermont

primary language spoken at home
(% of population)

81 English

8 Spanish

1 French

7 Other Indo-European languages

3 Asian languages

population per sq mile

NEW ENGLAND

VERMONT

RHODE ISLAND

≈ 70 people

History

When the Pilgrims landed in Plymouth back in 1620, they started something big. In the four centuries since, New England has been at the forefront of American history, instigating the War for Independence, inspiring the Transcendentalist thinkers and writers, embracing technological innovation and spurring on social change.

James Mavor and Byron Dix provide detailed, illustrated descriptions of Native American archaeological sites around New England in *Manitou: The Sacred Landscape of New England's Native Civilization*.

Culture Clash

When the first European settlers arrived in the New World, they found about 100,000 Native American inhabitants, mostly Algonquians, organized into small regional tribes. The northern tribes were solely hunter-gatherers, while the southern tribes hunted and practiced slash-and-burn agriculture, growing corn, squash and beans.

Before the English Pilgrims, the Native Americans were already acquainted with Portuguese fishermen, French fur traders, English explorers, Dutch merchants and Jesuit missionaries. The Europeans were welcomed as a source of valued manufactured goods, but they were also feared; and for good reason – in the Great Sadness of 1617, a smallpox epidemic had devastated the Native American population in the southeast. The Pilgrims were notable as the first Europeans to make a successful settlement in New England. Chief Massasoit of the Wampanoag tribe did not view this scrawny band of settlers as a threat and even hoped that they might be useful allies against his tribal rivals.

But the clash of cultures soon proved fatal to the Native American way of life. English coastal encampments spread as seemingly unoccupied lands were claimed for the king and commodity export – John Winthrop, the first governor of the Massachusetts Bay Colony, declared 'God hath hereby cleared our title to this place.' In less than a hundred years, the indigenous population was reduced by 90% due to disease, war and forced migration.

Brave New World

Seventeenth-century England was torn by religious strife. Protestants were assailed by the Catholic-leaning King James I, who vowed to 'harry them out of the country.'

TIMELINE	1497	1606–07	1614
	The Italian explorer John Cabot lands in Newfoundland and explores the coast of New England, claiming the territory for his patron, King Henry VII of England.	King James I issues a charter for the Plymouth Company to establish a settlement in the New World. The resulting Popham Colony (in present-day Maine) was abandoned after one year.	At the behest of future King Charles, Captain John Smith braves the frigid North Atlantic, makes his way from Maine to Cape Cod, maps the coastline and dubs the region 'New England.'

In 1620 the Pilgrims – led by Separatist devotee William Bradford – crossed the Atlantic to establish a community dedicated to religious austerity.

Trouble arose when the badly off-course *Mayflower* weighed anchor in Cape Cod Bay. A group of nonreligious passengers had booked their fares expecting to strike out on their own in Virginia; they threatened a mutiny when they realized they would have to spend the winter with the Separatists. The resulting Mayflower Compact brokered a deal in which both parties would have an equal say in matters of governance. Under Bradford's capable leadership, Plymouth Colony maintained a religious focus and grew modestly over the next decade. Today, you can visit a historically accurate re-creation of this first settlement at Plimoth Plantation.

In 1630 the merchant vessel *Arabella* delivered another group of Protestant Separatists, the Puritans, 50 miles north of Plymouth. The Puritans were better prepared: they were well financed, well equipped and 1000 strong, and included those of high social rank. At the head of their party, John Winthrop stood atop the Shawmut peninsula of present-day Boston and proclaimed the founding of 'a shining city on a hill.'

The Massachusetts Bay Colony was a product of the Puritan gentry's ambition to build a Christian community of personal virtue and industriousness – a community purified of pompous ceremony and official corruption, and disdainful of tyranny. Theirs was a kind of legalistic Calvinism, enforced Old Testament style. Anyone who missed church without good cause was apt to catch a whipping. Governor Winthrop constructed centralized institutions to maintain unity among the settlers, who dispersed to choice locations around the harbor and along the rivers. The General Court, an assembly of propertied men, became the principal mechanism of government. Church membership was a prerequisite for political and property rights.

The Puritan theocracy did not go unchallenged. In Boston, Anne Hutchinson started a women's Bible circle, promoting the idea of salvation through personal revelation. The popularity of this individualist-inspired view was threatening to the colony's patriarchal elders, who arrested the heretic Hutchinson and banished her to an island. One of Hutchinson's arch defenders was her brother-in-law, the Reverend John Wheelwright, who led a group to resettle in New Hampshire. This was the beginning of a trend in which independent folk, exasperated by encroachments on individual liberty by the Massachusetts state, would found their own settlements.

From his pulpit in Salem, Roger Williams sermonized for religious tolerance, separation of church and state, and respect for Native American rights. In 1636 Williams and a small group of backers founded a new

Colonial History

Pilgrim Monument (Provincetown)

Plimoth Planta-tion (Plymouth)

Mayflower II (Plymouth)

Witch House (Salem)

College Hill (Providence)

HISTORY BRAVE NEW WORLD

Governor John Winthrop sermonized from aboard the *Arabella*, 'we shall be as a city upon a hill. The eyes of all people are upon us. So that if we shall deal falsely with our God in this work…we shall be made a story and a byword throughout the world.'

1614–17	1630	1636	1675–78
In his records, Captain John Smith mentions the Massachusett Indians living around Boston Bay. Over the course of three years, three different epidemics wipe out 75% of the native population.	Led by Governor John Winthrop, Puritan settlers flee the repressive Church of England and establish the theocratic Massachusetts Bay Colony.	Freethinking theologian Roger Williams founds the colony of Rhode Island and Providence Plantations. His radical ideas include freedom of religion and separation of church and state.	Wampanoag chief King Philip terrorizes the colonists. Twenty-five towns are destroyed and thousands are killed before he is shot, ending King Philip's War.

WHO WAS FIRST?

Everyone wants to be first. Both Rhode Island and New Hampshire make claims about being the first colony to declare independence from Great Britain. But there is only one 'first.' So whose claim is legit?

The New Hampshire Provincial Government was kicked out of Portsmouth in 1774, so it moved up the road to Exeter, thus establishing the *first* independent government in the colonies. In January 1776, this local body ratified a constitution, the *first* colony to do so. But the document was explicit in 'declaring that we never sought to throw off our dependence upon Great Britain, but felt ourselves happy under Her protection while we could enjoy our constitutional rights and privileges, and that we shall rejoice if such a reconciliation between us and our parent state can be affected.' The local governance was a temporary provision, put in place until the dispute with Britain could be resolved. Not exactly a declaration of independence.

In May of that same year, still two months before the unveiling of *the* Declaration of Independence, Rhode Island issued its formal statement. With none of the stipulations and explanations of New Hampshire's constitution, Rhode Island was the first to declare outright independence.

New Hampshire finally came around six weeks later resolving 'to join with the other Colonies in declaring the thirteen United Colonies a free and independent State.'

settlement, Providence, along Narragansett Bay. The Rhode Island Colony welcomed Anne Hutchinson, declared religious freedom and made peace with the Native Americans.

Meanwhile, Bay Colony officials exiled yet another 'heretic' parson, Thomas Hooker, who suggested that nonpropertied men should not be excluded from political affairs. Hooker relocated to Hartford, amid the growing farm communities of the Connecticut River Valley.

Over time, the Puritan gentry were less effective in compelling others to embrace their vision of an ideal Christian community. The incessant pull of individual interests and the rise of a secular commercial culture proved to be the undoing of Winthrop's vision.

> Everyone knows that March 17 is St Patrick's Day, but not everyone knows it is also Evacuation Day in the greater Boston area, commemorating the day in 1776 that British troops relinquished the city of Boston after 11 months of occupation.

Cradle of Liberty

In the late 18th century, New England and the British throne clashed over the issue of taxation, exposing the conflicting strains of royal subject and personal liberty.

In 1765 the British Parliament passed the Stamp Act to finance colonial defense. Massachusetts colonists were the first to object. To safeguard colonial autonomy, local businessman Sam Adams formed the Sons of Liberty, which incited a mob to ransack the royal stamp office. The ac-

1686–89 〉	1692–93 〉	1754–63 〉	1770 〉
After the colonies openly flout trade restrictions such as the Navigation Acts, King James II establishes the Dominion of New England, instituting more rigorous controls over the colonies.	Witch hysteria in Salem sends 14 women and five men to the gallows. One man is crushed to death when he refuses to confess his guilt.	New Englanders are drawn into the French and Indian War, in which the British fought the French in the New World. The king levies taxes on the colonies to pay for war efforts.	Provoked by a local gang throwing snowballs, British troops fire into a crowd in Boston and kill five people, an incident dubbed the Boston Massacre.

tions were defended in a treatise written by a local lawyer, Sam's cousin John Adams, who cited the Magna Carta's principle of no taxation without representation. Eastern Connecticut and Rhode Island joined the protest. When New England merchants threatened a boycott of British imports, the measure was repealed.

The British government devised new revenue-raising schemes. Again, they were met with hostile noncompliance, and Boston emerged as the center of conflict. Parliament closed the Massachusetts General Assembly and dispatched two armed regiments to the city, which only inflamed local passions.

Forced underground, the Sons of Liberty set up a covert correspondence system to agitate public sentiment and coordinate strategy with sympathizers. In December 1773, the Sons of Liberty disguised themselves as Mohawks and dumped a cargo of taxable tea into the harbor. The Boston Tea Party enraged King George, whose retribution was swift and vengeful. The port was blockaded and the city placed under direct military rule.

The conflict tested the region's political loyalties. Tory sympathizers included influential merchants, manufacturers and financiers, while the rebels tended to be drawn from lesser merchants, artisans and yeoman farmers. The colonial cause was strongly supported in Rhode Island, Hartford and New Hampshire, where local assemblies voted to provide economic assistance to Boston. Aroused Providence residents even set fire to the British warship *Gaspee* when it ran aground in Narragansett Bay while chasing suspected smugglers. New Hampshire instigators seized Fort William and Mary when the panicky loyalist governor attempted to enlist more British reinforcements.

In April 1775 the British again attempted to break colonial resistance, this time arresting rebel ringleaders Sam Adams and John Hancock and seizing a secret store of gunpowder and arms. As the troops assembled, Paul Revere slipped across the river into Charlestown, where he mounted his famous steed Brown Beauty and galloped off into the night to spread the alarm. By next morning, armed local militias began converging on the area. The incident sparked a skirmish between British troops and local farmers on the Old North Bridge in Concord and the Lexington Green, leaving over a hundred dead. The inevitable had arrived: war for independence.

Other colonies soon joined ranks, heeding the advice of Boston-born Benjamin Franklin, who said, 'if we do not hang together, we will surely hang separately.' New Hampshire, Connecticut and Maine (then part of Massachusetts) wholeheartedly supported the revolutionary cause. The Green Mountain Boys, led by Ethan Allen, were a bandit gang who resisted the advances of the New York colony into northwest New England.

Revolutionary History

Freedom Trail (Boston)

Minute Man National Historic Park (Lexington)

Old North Bridge (Concord)

Fort Griswold Battlefield State Park (Groton)

Bennington Battlefield Historic Site (Bennington)

1775	**1776**	**1777**	**1787**
British troops respond to reports that colonists are stockpiling weapons. Warned by Paul Revere and William Dawes, the Minutemen confront the Redcoats in Lexington and Concord, starting the War for Independence.	Colonial leaders from 13 colonies – including Connecticut, Massachusetts, New Hampshire and Rhode Island – sign the Declaration of Independence, asserting that they are no longer a part of the British Empire.	The Republic of Vermont declares its independence, not only from Britain but also from New York. The state constitution is the first to abolish slavery and advocate universal male suffrage.	The Beverly Cotton Manufactory – the country's first cotton mill – is constructed in Beverly, MA, kicking off the industrial revolution. The era's largest mill operates for more than 40 years.

The war did not go well at first for the feisty but ill-prepared colonists, but the tide turned when the French were finally persuaded to ally with the rebellion. In 1781, the American army and French navy cornered the main British army on the Yorktown peninsula in Virginia and forced their surrender. British rule had come to an end in the American colonies.

Of Sails & Whales

New England port cities flourished during the Age of Sail. In the 17th century, the infamous 'triangular trade route' was developed, involving West Indian sugar, New England rum and West African slaves. Merchants who chose not to traffic in human cargo could still make large profits by illicitly undercutting European trade monopolies. In the late 17th century, Rhode Island provided a safe haven for pirates; indeed, Captain Kidd and Blackbeard were on a first-name basis with most Newport proprietors.

In the 18th century, Britain's stricter enforcement of trade monopolies and imposition of higher tariffs squeezed the merchants' profits. But after the American Revolution, New England merchants amassed fortunes by opening up trade routes to the Far East. Shipbuilding thrived in Massachusetts, Maine and Connecticut, and cities such as Salem, Newburyport and Portsmouth were among the richest trading cities in the world.

The whaling industry also thrived. Even today, the rich feeding grounds of Stellwagen Bank off Cape Cod attract whales to the region. In the preindustrial period, whales provided commodities, such as oil for lamps, teeth and bone for decorative scrimshaw, and other material for hoop skirts, umbrellas and perfume.

The whalers in New England were strategically placed to pursue the highly sought-after sperm whales along Atlantic migratory routes. Buzzards Bay, Nantucket Island and New Bedford were all prominent whaling centers. In the mid-19th century, New Bedford hosted a whaling fleet of over 300 ships, employing more than 10,000 people directly and indirectly, and cashing in over $12 million in profits.

Industrial Revolution

New England's industrial revolution began in Rhode Island when Quaker merchant Moses Brown contracted English mechanic Samuel Slater to construct a water-powered cotton-spinning factory. The Brown-Slater partnership was a brilliant success. Their mills sprouted up along the Blackstone River, driving a vibrant Rhode Island textile industry.

Thirty miles northwest of Boston, along the Merrimack River, a group of wealthy merchants built one of the wonders of the industrial age: a planned city of five-story red-brick factories, lining the river for nearly

Maritime History

Salem Maritime National Historic Site (Salem)

Essex Shipbuilding Museum (Essex)

New Bedford Whaling Museum (New Bedford)

Nantucket Whaling Museum (Nantucket)

Mystic Seaport Museum (Mystic)

1788	1789–1801	1820	1836
New Hampshire ratifies the US Constitution, providing the ninth and final vote needed to execute it. The new government begins operations the following year.	John Adams of Quincy, MA, serves two terms as the vice president and one term as the president of the newly independent United States of America.	Maine gains independence from Massachusetts, becoming the 23rd state to enter the Union.	With the publication of his essay Nature, Ralph Waldo Emerson introduces the philosophy of transcendentalism, which elevates intuition over doctrine and spirituality over empiricism.

a mile, driven by a network of power canals. Named for the project's deceased visionary, Francis Cabot Lowell, the city counted over 40 mills and employed over 10,000 workers; machines hummed 12 hours a day, six days a week.

This was not the grimy squalor of Manchester. Lowell was an orderly city. The workforce at first was drawn from the region's young farm women, who lived in dormitories under paternalistic supervision. The 'mill girls' were gradually replaced by cheaper Irish immigrant labor.

By the mid-19th century, steam power and metal machines had transformed New England. Railroads crisscrossed the region, hastening industrialization and urbanization. Textile mills arose along rivers in Lawrence, Nashua, Concord and Fall River. Leather works and shoemaking factories appeared near Boston. Springfield and Worcester became centers for tool and dye making, southern Connecticut manufactured machinery, and the Maine woods furnished paper mills. Even Paul Revere abandoned his silversmith shop in the North End and set up a rolling copper mill and foundry 15 miles southwest along the Neponset River.

New England Melting Pot

The rapid rise of industry led to social as well as economic changes. The second half of the 19th century brought a wave of immigrant laborers to New England, throwing the world of English-descended Whig Protestants into turmoil.

The first Irish immigrants arrived to work in the mills in the 1820s. Disparaged by native New Englanders, the Irish were considered an inferior race of delinquents, whose spoken brogue suggested that one had a 'shoe in one's mouth.' They undercut local workers in the job market and, worse yet, brought the dreaded papist religion from which the Puritans had fled. Tensions ran high, occasionally erupting in violence. In 1834, rumors of licentiousness and kidnapping led a Boston mob to torch the Ursuline Convent in present-day Somerville, MA.

A potato famine back home spurred an upsurge in Irish immigration to Boston. Between 1846 and 1856, more than 1000 new immigrants stepped off the boat per month, a human flood tide that the city was not prepared to absorb. Anti-immigrant and anti-Catholic sentiments were shrill. As a political expression of this rabid reaction, the Know Nothing Party swept into office in Massachusetts, Rhode Island and Connecticut, promising to reverse the flow of immigration, deny the newcomers political rights and mandate readings from the Protestant Bible in public school.

Subsequent groups of Italian, Portuguese, French Canadian and East European Jewish immigrants suffered similar prejudices and indignities. By the end of the 19th century, the urban landscape of New

The first naval skirmish of the Revolutionary War took place in Machiasport, ME, when drunken colonists killed an English sea captain and ransacked the royal ship that was supposed to be monitoring the lumber trade. The crown's swift response was to burn the town of Portland to the ground.

Industrial Revolution History

Slater Mill (Pawtucket)

Boott Cotton Mills Museum (Lowell)

1863	1895	1919	1945
Massachusetts native Robert Gould Shaw leads the 54th Regiment of black troops into battle in the Civil War. Colonel Shaw is killed in action and buried in a common grave next to the fallen black soldiers.	Massachusetts native WEB Du Bois becomes the first African American to earn a PhD from Harvard University. The historian becomes a tireless advocate for civil rights for blacks.	Boston police strike for the right to form a trade union; chaos reigns until the military reserve arrives. The failed strike is portrayed as a socialist scheme to destroy society.	Maine scientist Percy Spencer accidentally melts a chocolate bar in his pocket while standing in front of a magnetron. From this observation, he invents the microwave oven.

MOLASSES EXPLOSION OF 1919

For years Boston was a leader in the production and export of rum, made from West Indian sugar cane. Near the water's edge in the North End stood a storage tank for the Purity Distilling Company. On a January morning in 1919, the large tank, filled to the brim with brown molasses, suddenly began shuddering and rumbling as its bindings came undone.

The pressure caused the tank to explode, spewing two million gallons of molasses into the city like a volcano. The sweet explosion leveled surrounding tenements, knocked buildings off their foundations and wiped out a loaded freight train. Panic-stricken, man and beast fled the deadly ooze. A molasses wave surged down the streets drowning all in its sticky path. The Great Molasses Flood killed a dozen horses, 21 people and injured more than 100. The cleanup lasted nearly six months. *Dark Tide,* by journalist Stephen Puleo, provides a fascinating account of the causes and controversy surrounding this devastating explosion.

England resembled a mosaic of clannish ethnic enclaves. Sticking together became an immigrant survival strategy for finding work, housing and companionship. Neighborhoods took on the feel of the old country with familiar language, cuisine and customs. The New England melting pot was more like a stew than a puree.

In the early 20th century, when new southern and Eastern European immigrants began preaching class solidarity, they were met with renewed fury from New England's ruling elite. Labor unrest in the factories mobilized a harsh political reaction against foreigners and socialism.

Local history professor Thomas O'Connor recounts the history of an Irish enclave in South Boston: My Home Town.

Reform & Racism

The legacy of race relations in New England is marred by contradictions. Abolitionists and segregationists, reformers and racists have all left their mark.

The first slaves were delivered to Massachusetts Bay Colony from the West Indies in 1638. By 1700, roughly 400 slaves lived in Boston. In the 18th century, Rhode Island merchants played a leading role in the Atlantic slave trade, financing over 1000 slave ventures and transporting more than 100,000 Africans.

A number of New England's black slaves earned their freedom by fighting against the British in the Revolution. Crispus Attucks, a runaway slave of African and Native American descent, became a martyr by falling victim in the Boston Massacre. Salem Poor, an ex-slave who bought his freedom, was distinguished for heroism in the Battle of Bunker Hill.

In the early 19th century, New England became a center of the abolition movement. In Boston, newspaper publisher William Lloyd Garri-

1954	1960	1966	1970s
General Dynamics Shipyard in Groton, CT, launches the *Nautilus*, the world's first nuclear-powered submarine. Nuclear power means that the sub can remain submerged for much longer periods of time.	Massachusetts native John F Kennedy is elected president, ushering in the era of Camelot. As the first Irish American president and the first Catholic president, JFK makes his home state proud.	Republican Edward Brooke of Massachusetts is the first African American popularly elected to the US Senate. During two terms, Brooke is a relentless advocate for affordable housing.	Boston tries to racially integrate schools by busing students between neighborhoods, inciting violent reactions. School attendance declines dramatically, and several people are killed.

son, Unitarian minister Theodore Parker and aristocratic lawyer Wendell Phillips launched the Anti-Slavery Society to agitate public sentiment. New England provided numerous stops along the Underground Railroad, a network of safe houses that helped runaway slaves reach freedom in Canada.

The New England states still maintained their own informal patterns of racial segregation, however, with African Americans as an underclass. Although Massachusetts was the first state to elect an African American to the US Senate by popular vote in 1966, race relations were fraught. In the 1970s Boston was inflamed by racial conflict when a judge ordered the city to desegregate the schools through forced busing. The school year was marked by a series of violent incidents involving students and parents.

20th-Century Trends

The fears of the Yankee old guard were finally realized in the early 20th century when ethnic-based political machines gained control of city governments in Massachusetts, Rhode Island and Connecticut.

While the Democratic Party was originally associated with rural and radical interests, it became the political instrument of the recently arrived working poor in urban areas. Flamboyant city bosses pursued a populist and activist approach to city politics. Their administrations were steeped in public works and patronage. According to Providence boss Charlie Brayton, 'an honest voter is one who stays bought.'

The Republican Party in New England was cobbled together in the mid-19th century from the Whigs, the Know Nothings and the anti-slavery movement. In the 20th century, it became the political vehicle for the old English-descended elite, who envisioned a paternalistic and frugal government and preached self-help and sobriety.

Economically, New England experienced its share of booms and busts. The good times of the early 20th century crashed down in the Great Depression. After a brief recovery, the region began to lose its textile industry and manufacturing base to the South. With the mills shut down and the seaports quieted, the regional economy languished and its cities fell into disrepair.

But entrepreneurial spirit and technological imagination combined to revive the region, sustained by science, medicine and higher education. Boston, Providence and Hartford were buoyed by banking, finance and insurance. The biggest boost came from the technological revolution, which enabled local high-tech companies to make the Massachusetts Miracle, an economic boom in the 1980s. Even with stock-market corrections and bubble bursts, technological developments continue to reinvigorate New England.

African American History

Black Heritage Trail (Boston)

African Meeting House (Nantucket)

Oak Bluffs (Martha's Vineyard)

Harriet Beecher-Stowe Center (Hartford)

HISTORY 20TH-CENTURY TRENDS

Sarah Messer's youth in the historic Hatch house in Marshfield, Massachusetts, inspired her to write *Red House: Being a Mostly Accurate Account of New England's Oldest Continuously Lived-in House* (2004).

1980s	2000	2004	2013
Massachusetts experiences a period of economic growth. Known as the Massachusetts Miracle, the economic turnaround is fueled by the technology industry.	Vermont becomes the second state in the US (after Hawaii) to legalize same-sex civil unions, allowing many of the same benefits afforded to married couples.	Massachusetts becomes the first state in the Union to legalize same-sex marriage. The city of Cambridge becomes the first municipality to issue marriage licenses to gay and lesbian couples.	Two bombs explode at the Boston Marathon, killing three and injuring hundreds. In response to the terrorist attack, the city embraces the motto 'Boston Strong.'

New England Literature

New England's reverence for the written word arrived with the Puritans and was nurtured over the centuries by the area's universities and literary societies. Indeed, the region was the nucleus of the Golden Age of American Literature, with the nation's formative writers coming out of Boston, Concord and Hartford. This literary tradition thrives today, as writers and scholars continue to congregate in university classrooms and crowded cafes around New England.

Colonial Literature

Concord Literary Sites

....

Ralph Waldo Emerson Memorial House

....

Orchard House

....

Walden Pond

....

Old Manse

The literary tradition in New England dates to the days of Puritan settlement. As early as 1631, Anne Bradstreet was writing poetry and meditations. Shortly thereafter, Harvard College was founded (1636) and the first printing press was set up (1638), thus establishing Boston/Cambridge as an important literary center that would attract writers and scholars for generations to come.

Early colonial writings were either spiritual or historical in nature. Governor John Winthrop chronicled the foundation of Boston in his journals. Governor William Bradford, the second governor of Plymouth Colony, was the author of the primary historical reference about the Pilgrims, *Of Plimouth Plantation*. The most prolific writer was Reverend Cotton Mather (1663–1728), who wrote more than 400 books on issues of spirituality – most notably the Salem witch trials.

The Golden Age

It was during the 19th century that New England became a region renowned for its intellect. The universities had become a magnet for writers, poets and philosophers, as well as publishers and bookstores. The local literati were expounding on social issues such as slavery, women's rights and religious reawakening. Boston, Cambridge and Concord were fertile breeding grounds for ideas, nurturing the seeds of America's literary and philosophical flowering. This was the Golden Age of American literature, and New England was its nucleus.

Ralph Waldo Emerson (1803–82) promulgated his teachings from his home in Concord. He and Henry David Thoreau (1817–62) wrote compelling essays about their beliefs and their attempts to live in accordance with the mystical unity of all creation. Thoreau's notable writings included *Walden; or, Life in the Woods* (1854), which advocated a life of simplicity and living in harmony with nature, and *Civil Disobedience* (1849), a treatise well before its time.

Nathaniel Hawthorne (1804–64) traveled in this Concordian literary circle. America's first great short-story writer, Hawthorne was the author of *The Scarlet Letter* (1850) and *The House of the Seven Gables* (1851), both offering insightful commentary on Colonial culture. Louisa May Alcott (1832–88) grew up at Orchard House, also in Concord, where she wrote her largely autobiographical novel *Little Women* (1868). This classic is beloved by generations of young women.

Around this time, poet Henry Wadsworth Longfellow (1807–82) was the most illustrious resident of Cambridge, where he taught at Harvard. Longfellow often hosted his contemporaries from Concord for philosophical discussions at his home on Brattle St (now the Longfellow National Historic Site). Here he wrote poems such as 'Song of Hiawatha' and 'Paul Revere's Ride,' both cherished accounts of American lore.

Meanwhile, some of these luminaries would travel one Saturday a month to Boston to congregate with their contemporaries at the old Parker House (now the Omni Parker House hotel). Presided over by Oliver Wendell Holmes, the Saturday Club was known for its jovial atmosphere and stimulating discourse, attracting such renowned visitors as Charles Dickens. Out of these meetings was born the *Atlantic Monthly,* a literary institution that continues to showcase innovative authors and ideas.

Down the street, the Old Corner Bookstore (now a stop on the Freedom Trail) was the site of Ticknor & Fields, the first publishing house to offer author royalties. Apparently Mr Fields had a special gift for discovering new local talent; by all accounts, his bookstore was a lively meeting place for writers and readers.

All around the region, progressive writers fueled the abolitionist movement with fiery writings. William Lloyd Garrison founded the radical newspaper *The Abolitionist* on Beacon Hill. Social activist Lydia Maria Child had her privileges at the Boston Athenaeum revoked for her provocative antislavery pamphlets. Harriet Beecher Stowe (1811–96), whose influential book *Uncle Tom's Cabin* recruited thousands to the antislavery cause, was born in Litchfield, CT, and lived in Brunswick, ME, before she eventually moved to Hartford.

In 1895 WEB Du Bois (1868–1963) became the first black man to receive a PhD from Harvard University. A few years later, he wrote his seminal tract *The Souls of Black Folk,* in which he sought to influence the way blacks dealt with segregation, urging pride in African heritage.

LITERARY LIGHTS

Ralph Waldo Emerson (1803–82) Essayist with a worldwide following and believer in the mystical beauty of all creation; founder of transcendentalism.

Henry David Thoreau (1817–62) Best remembered for *Walden; or, Life in the Woods,* his journal of observations written during his solitary sojourn from 1845 to 1847 in a log cabin at Walden Pond.

Emily Dickinson (1830–86) This reclusive 'Belle of Amherst' crafted beautiful poems, mostly published after her death.

Mark Twain (Samuel Clemens; 1835–1910) Born in Missouri, Twain settled in Hartford, CT, and wrote *The Adventures of Tom Sawyer* and *The Adventures of Huckleberry Finn.*

Edith Wharton (1862–1937) This Pulitzer Prize–winning novelist's best-known work, *Ethan Frome,* paints a grim portrayal of emotional attachments on a New England farm.

Robert Frost (1874–1963) New England's signature poet, whose many books of poetry use New England themes to explore the depths of human emotions and experience.

Eugene O'Neill (1888–1953) From New London, CT, O'Neill wrote the play *A Long Day's Journey into Night.*

John Irving (b 1942) New Hampshire native writes novels set in New England, including *The World According to Garp, The Hotel New Hampshire* and *A Prayer for Owen Meany.*

Stephen King (b 1947) Maine horror novelist; wrote *Carrie* and *The Shining.*

LOWELL: THE TOWN & THE CITY

'Follow along to the center of town, the Square, where at noon everybody knows everybody else.' So Beat Generation author Jack Kerouac described his hometown of Lowell, MA, in his novel *The Town & The City*.

One of the most influential American authors of the 20th century, Jack Kerouac (1922–69) was born in Lowell at the mill town's industrial peak. He inhabited Lowell's neighborhoods, he graduated from Lowell High School and he wrote for the *Lowell Sun*. It is not surprising, then, that the author used Lowell as the setting for five of his novels that draw on his youth.

Kerouac is remembered annually during the Lowell Celebrates Kerouac (LCK) festival (p99). Aside from the festival, there are walking tours and films based on places that Kerouac wrote about and experienced.

Of course, Kerouac is most famous for his classic novel *On the Road*. With it, he became a symbol of the spirit of the open road. He eventually went to New York, where he, Allen Ginsberg and William Burroughs formed the core of the Beat Generation of writers. Nonetheless, Kerouac always maintained ties to Lowell, and he is buried in Edson Cemetery, a pilgrimage site for devotees who were inspired by his free spirit.

Banned in Boston

In the 20th century, New England continued to attract authors, poets and playwrights, but the Golden Age was over. This region was no longer the center of progressive thought and social activism that had so inspired American literature.

This shift in cultural geography was due in part to a shift in consciousness in the late 19th century. Moral crusaders and local officials promoted stringent censorship of books, films and plays that they deemed offensive or obscene. Many writers were 'banned in Boston' – a trend that contributed to that city's image as a provincial outpost instead of cultural capital. Eugene O'Neill (1888–1953) is the most celebrated example. O'Neill attended Harvard, he was a key participant in the Provincetown Players on Cape Cod and he spent the last two years of his life in Back Bay, but his experimental play *Strange Interlude* was prohibited from showing on Boston stages.

Henry James (1843–1916) grew up in Cambridge. Although he was undoubtedly influenced by his New World upbringing, he eventually emigrated to England. A prolific writer, he often commented on American society in his novels, which included *Daisy Miller* and *The Bostonians*.

The revolutionary poet ee cummings (1894–1962) was also born in Cambridge, although it was his experiences in Europe that inspired his most famous novel, *The Enormous Room*. Descended from an old New England family, TS Eliot (1888–1965) taught at Harvard for a spell, but he wrote his best work in England.

Robert Lowell (1917–77) was another Boston native who was restless in his hometown. He spent many years living in Back Bay and teaching at Boston University, where he wrote *Life Studies* and *For the Union Dead*. Encouraged by his interactions with Beat Generation poet Allen Ginsberg, Lowell became the seminal 'confessional poet.' At BU, he counted Sylvia Plath (1932–63) and Anne Sexton (1928–74) among the students he inspired before he finally moved to Manhattan.

One of the Beat Generation's defining authors, Jack Kerouac was born in Lowell, MA. His hometown features prominently in many of his novels, but he too eventually decamped to the new cultural capital to the south.

Robert Frost Sites
....
Robert Frost Stone House Museum (Shaftsbury)
....
Frost Place (Franconia)

America's favorite poet, Robert Frost (1874–1963), was an exception to this trend. He moved from California and lived on farms in Shaftsbury, VT, and Franconia, NH, where he wrote poems including 'Nothing Gold Can Stay' and 'The Road Not Taken.'

Contemporary Literature

Boston never regained its status as the hub of the literary solar system. But its rich legacy and ever-influential universities ensure that the region continues to contribute to American literature. Many of New England's most prominent writers are transplants from other cities or countries, drawn to its academic and creative institutions. John Updike (1932–2009), author of the Pulitzer Prize–winning Rabbit series, moved to Massachusetts to attend Harvard (where he was president of *Harvard Lampoon*), before settling in Ipswich, which is where he died.

Born in Ithaca, NY, David Foster Wallace (1962–2008) studied philosophy at Harvard. Although he abandoned the course and moved out of the city, his Boston-based novel, *Infinite Jest,* earned him a MacArthur Genius Award. Jhumpa Lahiri (b 1967) is a Bengali Indian American writer who studied creative writing at Boston University. Her debut collection of short stories, *Interpreter of Maladies,* won a Pulitzer Prize for Fiction in 2000. Set in Boston and surrounding neighborhoods, her works address the challenges and triumphs in the lives of her Indian American characters. Geraldine Brooks is an Australian-born writer who resides part-time on Martha's Vineyard. Several of her novels are set in New England, including *March,* which earned her a Pulitzer Prize.

Of course, New England has also fostered some homegrown contemporary talent. John Cheever (1912–82) was born in Quincy and lived in Boston. His novel, *The Wapshot Chronicle,* takes place in a Massachusetts fishing village. Born and raised in Dorchester, Dennis Lehane (b 1966) wrote *Mystic River* and *Gone, Baby Gone,* both compelling tales set in working-class Boston 'hoods, both of which were made into excellent films.

Stephen King (b 1947), author of horror novels such as *Carrie* and *The Shining,* lives and sets his novels in Maine. King is a well-known Red Sox fan, who is often sighted at home games. Also from Maine, Elizabeth Strout (b 1956) used a small coastal town as the setting for her wonderful quirky novel, *Olive Kitteridge,* which won the Pulitzer Prize for Fiction in 2009.

John Irving (b 1942) was born and raised in Exeter, NH, which serves as the setting for many of his stories, including *The World According to Garp, A Prayer for Owen Meany* and *A Widow for a Year.* In 1999 Irving won an Academy Award for his adapted screenplay of *The Cider House Rules,* which takes place in rural Maine.

Novelist Annie Proulx (b 1935), author of *The Shipping News* and *Brokeback Mountain,* was born in Connecticut and grew up in Maine. Although she lived for more than 30 years in Vermont, most of her stories are not set in New England.

New
England
Book-
stores
....

*Montague
Bookmill
(Montague)*
....

*Harvard
Bookstore
(Cambridge)*
....

*Concord
Bookshop
(Concord)*
....

*Where the
Sidewalk Ends
(Chatham)*
....

*Northshire
Bookstore
(Manchester)*
....

NEW ENGLAND LITERATURE CONTEMPORARY LITERATURE

Universities & Colleges

No single element has influenced the region as profoundly as its educational institutions. New England's colleges and universities attract scholars, scientists, philosophers and writers who thrive off and contribute to the region's evolving culture. This renewable source of cultural energy supports poetry slams, film festivals, music scenes, art galleries, coffee shops, hip clubs and Irish pubs. Take your pick from the eminent Ivies, the urban campuses, the liberal arts colleges or the edgier art and music schools.

Ivy League

New England is home to four of the eight Ivy League universities, all of which were founded before the American Revolution. They are known for academic excellence, selective admissions and Yankee elitism.

In the 1980s Yale University became known as the 'gay ivy,' after the *Wall Street Journal* published an article about homosexuality on campus. The active community at Yale originated the LGBT rallying cry 'One in Four, Maybe More.'

Yale University

Yale University is the centerpiece of the gritty city of New Haven, CT. Founded in 1701 as the Collegiate School, the university was renamed in 1718 to honor a gift from rich merchant Elihu Yale. In the 1930s Yale instituted a system of residential colleges, whereby students eat, sleep, study and play in a smaller community within the larger university. There are now 12 residential, Oxford-style colleges, each with its own distinctive style of architecture. The school is also home to the enigmatic 'Skull and Bones,' an elitist secret society of aspiring kleptomaniacs. So-called 'Bonesmen' try to outdo each other by 'crooking' valuable artifacts and objets d'art from around the university. Its alumni include presidents, senators, Supreme Court justices and other upstanding citizens.

Brown University

Brown University has lent its progressive viewpoints to Providence, RI, since 1764 (though prior to American independence, it was known as the College in the English Colony of Rhode Island and Providence Plantations). The university charter specified that religion would not be a criterion for admission – the first institution in the New World to do so.

Brown University's most esteemed faculty member is Josiah Stinkney Carberry, professor of psychoceramics (the study of cracked pots). Every Friday the 13th is known as Carberry Day, when students donate their loose change to a fund for books.

Brown has earned a reputation for refined radical-chic academics. In 1969 the university adopted the New Curriculum, which eliminated distribution requirements and allowed students to take courses without grades. In 1981 the university opened a research center devoted to sexuality and gender. The previous university president, Ruth J Simmons, was the first African American president of an Ivy League institution.

Today, the Georgian-era campus on College Hill enrolls about 6000 undergraduate students and 2000 graduate students. It is unique for its program that allows students to design their own course of study.

Dartmouth College

Dartmouth College dominates Hanover, NH, making it the quintessential New England college town. Dartmouth is unique among the Ivies for its small size, its rural setting and its emphasis on undergraduate education. Dartmouth also employs a year-round quarter system, known as the

D-Plan. The school is famed for its spirited student body and the cultlike loyalty of its alumni. To get a sense of campus culture, think William F Buckley in Birkenstocks.

Dartmouth's 270-acre Georgian-era campus is centered on a picturesque green. The university also owns huge tracts of land in the White Mountains region and in Northern New Hampshire. No surprise, then, that the university has an active outing club (which incidentally maintains portions of the Appalachian Trail).

In 2005 a group of Dartmouth Frisbee players converted a school bus to run on waste vegetable oil. For more than a decade, the so-called Big Green Bus spent its summers traveling the country and hosting events to promote sustainability and environmental awareness.

Harvard University

A slew of superlatives accompany the name of this venerable institution in Cambridge, MA. It is America's oldest university, founded in 1636. It has by far the largest endowment, measuring $36.4 billion in 2016. It is often first in the list of national universities, according to *US News & World Report*. Harvard is actually comprised of 10 independent schools dedicated to the study of medicine, dentistry, law, business, divinity, design, education, public health, arts and science, and public policy, in addition to the traditional Faculty of Arts and Sciences.

Harvard Yard is the heart and soul of the university campus, with buildings dating back to its founding. But the university continues to expand in all directions. Most recently, Harvard has acquired extensive land across the river in Allston, with intentions of converting this working-class residential area into a satellite campus with a science center, sporting facilities and more.

Boston & Cambridge Institutions

More than 50 institutions of higher education are located in Boston (too many to mention here). About a dozen smaller schools are located in the Fenway, while the residential areas west of the center (Brighton and Allston) have been dubbed the 'student ghetto.'

Massachusetts Institute of Technology

On the north bank of the Charles River, the Massachusetts Institute of Technology (MIT) offers a completely novel perspective on Cambridge academia: proudly nerdy and not so tweedy as Harvard. It excels in science, design and engineering. MIT seems to pride itself on being offbeat. Wander into a courtyard and you might find it is graced with a sculpture by Henry Moore or Alexander Calder; or you might just as well find a Ping-Pong table or a trampoline. In recent years, it seems the university has taken this irreverence to a new level, as a recent frenzy of building has resulted in some of the most architecturally unusual and intriguing structures you'll find on either side of the river.

Boston University

Boston University (BU) is a massive urban campus sprawling west of Kenmore Sq. BU enrolls about 30,000 undergraduate and graduate students in all fields of study. The special collections of BU's Mugar Memorial Library include 20th-century archives that balance pop culture and scholarly appeal. Peruse the rotating exhibits and you might find papers from Arthur Fiedler's collection, the archives of Douglas Fairbanks, Jr, or the correspondence of BU alumnus Dr Martin Luther King, Jr.

Dartmouth alum Chris Miller wrote the film *National Lampoon's Animal House* based on his fraternity days.

In 2003 a couple of Harvard computer-science students hacked into university computers to copy students' photographs and publish them online. Although their site was shut down by Harvard officials, the students were inspired to found Facebook. See how the story unfolds in the film *The Social Network*.

UNIVERSITIES & COLLEGES BOSTON & CAMBRIDGE INSTITUTIONS

A WALK ACROSS THE HARVARD BRIDGE

The Harvard Bridge – from Back Bay in Boston to Massachusetts Institute of Technology (MIT) in Cambridge – is the longest bridge across the Charles River. It is not too long to walk, but it is long enough to do some wondering while you walk. You might wonder, for example, why the bridge that leads into the heart of MIT is named the Harvard Bridge.

According to legend, the state offered to name the bridge after Cambridge's second university. But the brainiac engineers at MIT analyzed the plans for construction and found the bridge was structurally unsound. Not wanting the MIT moniker associated with a faulty feat of engineering, it was suggested that the bridge better be named for the neighboring university up the river. That the bridge subsequently needed to be rebuilt validated the superior brainpower of MIT.

That is only a legend, however (one invented by an MIT student, no doubt). The fact is that the Harvard Bridge was first constructed in 1891 and MIT only moved to its current location in 1916. The bridge was rebuilt in the 1980s to modernize and expand it, but the original name has stuck, at least officially. Most Bostonians actually refer to this bridge as the 'Mass Ave bridge' because, frankly, it makes more sense.

By now, walking across the bridge, perhaps you have reached the halfway point: 'Halfway to Hell' reads the scrawled graffiti. What is this graffiti anyway? What is a 'smoot'?

A smoot is an obscure unit of measurement that was used to measure the distance of the Harvard Bridge, first in 1958 and every year since. One smoot is approximately 5ft, 7in, the height of Oliver R Smoot, who was a pledge of the MIT fraternity Lambda Chi Alpha in 1958. He was the shortest pledge that year. And, yes, his physical person was actually used for all the measurements that year.

And now that you have reached the other side of the river, surely you are wondering exactly how long this bridge is. We can't speak for Harvard students, but certainly every MIT student knows that the Harvard Bridge is 364.4 smoots plus one ear.

Boston College

Not to be confused with BU, Boston College (BC) could not be more different. BC is situated between Brighton in Boston and Chestnut Hill in the tony suburb of Newton; the attractive campus is recognizable by its neo-Gothic towers. It is home to the nation's largest Jesuit community. Its Catholic influence makes it more socially conservative and more social-service oriented than other universities. Visitors to the campus will find a good art museum and excellent Irish and Catholic ephemera collections in the library. Aside from the vibrant undergraduate population, it has a strong education program and an excellent law school. Its basketball and football teams are usually high in national rankings.

University Art Collections

Hood Museum of Art, Dartmouth College (Hanover)

Museum of Art, RISD (Providence)

Yale Center for British Art (New Haven)

Harvard Art Museum (Cambridge)

Liberal Arts Colleges

The small, private liberal arts college is a New England social institution. Dedicated to a well-rounded traditional curriculum, these schools are known for first-rate instruction, high-income tuition and upper-class pretension. The schools place an emphasis on the undergraduate classroom, where corduroy-clad professors are more likely to be inspiring teachers than prolific researchers. Their cozy campuses are nestled amid white steeples and red barns in the rolling New England countryside. Mandatory for all first-year students: *Plato's Republic,* rugby shirt and lacrosse stick.

Little Ivies

The 'Little Ivies' are a self-anointed collection of a dozen elite liberal arts colleges, 10 of which are found in New England: Amherst, Williams and Tufts in Massachusetts; Connecticut College, Trinity and Wesleyan in Connecticut; Middlebury in Vermont; and Bowdoin, Bates and Colby in

Maine. From this select cohort, Williams and Amherst annually battle it out for top spot on the *US News & World Report* ranking of Best Liberal Arts Colleges (currently numbered 1 and 2, respectively).

Seven Sisters

Massachusetts is also home to four of the Seven Sisters, elite undergraduate women's colleges, founded in the days when the Ivy League was still a boys-only club. Mount Holyoke and Smith College are situated in the state's hippie-chic central Pioneer Valley; Wellesley is found in a posh Boston suburb of the same name; and Radcliffe is in Cambridge next to Harvard, to which it now officially belongs.

Art & Music Schools

Rhode Island School of Design

In a league of its own, the Rhode Island School of Design (RISD) boasts many famous graduates who have become pop-culture path cutters, such as musician David Byrne and his fellow members of Talking Heads, graffiti artist and designer Shepard Fairey, and animation expert Seth MacFarlane. The concentration of creativity at RISD makes this Providence neighborhood among the edgiest and artiest in all New England.

MassArt

More formally known as the Massachusetts College of Art, this is the country's first and only four-year independent public art college. In 1873 state leaders decided the new textile mills in Lowell and Lawrence needed a steady stream of designers, so they established MassArt in Boston to educate some. With thousands of square feet of exhibition space on campus, there's always some thought-provoking or sense-stimulating exhibits to see.

Berklee College of Music

Housed in and around the Back Bay in Boston, Berklee is an internationally renowned school for contemporary music, especially jazz. The school was founded in 1945 by Lawrence Berk (the Lee came from his son's first name). Created as an alternative to the classical agenda and stuffy attitude of traditional music schools, Berk taught courses in composition and arrangement for popular music. Not big on musical theory, Berk emphasized learning by playing. His system was a big success and the school flourished. Among Berklee's Grammy-laden alumni are jazz musicians Gary Burton, Al Di Meola, Keith Jarrett and Diana Krall; pop and rock artists Quincy Jones, Donald Fagen and John Mayer; and film composer Howard Shore.

Emerson College

Founded in 1880, Emerson is a liberal arts college that specializes in communications and the performing arts. Located in Boston's theater district, the college operates the Cutler Majestic Theater and the Paramount Theater, and its students run Boston's coolest radio station, WERS. Emerson celebs include Norman Lear, Jay Leno and 'the Fonz.'

The Williams College class of 1887 were the first students in America to wear caps and gowns at their graduation. The college copied the tradition from Oxford University in order to avoid an embarrassing discrepancy in the dress of rich and poor students.

Rhode Island School of Design (RISD) was founded when a local women's group had $1675 left over in their fund for Rhode Island's exhibit at the 1876 Centennial Exhibition. Some sources claim the competing proposal for the funds was for a drinking fountain in the local park.

Outdoor Activities

New England offers unlimited opportunities to enjoy the great outdoors. The White Mountains, the Green Mountains and the Berkshires are high points for skiing and hiking. Thousands of miles of coastline entice travelers with sailing, sea kayaking and whale-watching, while glacial lakes and pretty ponds invite swimming, canoeing and fishing.

Hiking

You can't go wrong when deciding which rearing peaks deserve the effort of lugging your knapsack, backpack or climbing gear.

The White Mountains in New Hampshire throw back some of the foulest weather on record, but still draw everyone from day-hikers to multiday technical mountaineers. Pick a trail along the Kancamagus Hwy (p350) or around Crawford (p360) or Pinkham Notch (p362).

New Hampshire's utterly accessible Mt Monadnock (p335) is a 'beginners' mountain,' a relatively easy climb up a bald granite batholith. Much less traveled, Moosilauke Ravine Lodge (p337) offers great views, few crowds and miles of trails.

Maine's sublime Mt Katahdin (p403) remains practically untouched by tourism. Those who make it across the infamous Knife Edge will remember the experience for life. Acadia National Park (p392) and Grafton Notch State Park (p402) have miles of groomed trails for all skill levels.

Vermont's Green Mountains are seamed with hiking trails, particularly Vermont's own end-to-ender, the Long Trail, with both easy and challenging hikes. Many excellent trails radiate out of the Stowe area (p311), which also sports world-class ice climbing.

The highest peak in Massachusetts, Mt Greylock makes an excellent goal in the Berkshires, but there are scores of lesser hiking trails in the region's many state parks.

New England Mountain Bike Association (www.nemba.org) is a wealth of information about places to ride, trail conditions and ways to connect with other riders.

Cycling

See Boston by bike from the Charles River Bike Path (p57). Or, follow part of Paul Revere's midnight ride from Boston to Lexington on the Minuteman Commuter Bikeway (p92).

On Cape Cod in Massachusetts, tool around the Cape Cod Canal (p127), the Shining Sea Bikeway (p130), the Cape Cod Rail Trail (p137) or the Cape Cod National Seashore (p150) bike paths. In the Pioneer Valley, the Norwottuck Rail Trail (p186) connects Amherst and Northampton, while the Ashuwillticook Rail Trail (p204) follows the Hoosic River from Pittsfield to Adams in the Berkshires.

In Rhode Island, take a spin on the beautiful 14.5-mile East Bay Bike Path (p214), which follows the waterfront out of Providence and weaves past picnic-worthy state parks.

The Burlington Recreation Path (p304) follows the shore of Lake Champlain for 7.5 miles of smooth riding. It links up with the 12-mile Island Line Trail that takes cyclists out to the Colchester causeway.

Islands are particularly well-suited for great cycling. Rent wheels for the quaint roads of Block Island (p236), RI; for the carriage roads of Mt Desert Island (p393), ME; for the beachy trails of Nantucket (p157) and Martha's Vineyard (p165), MA; and for the long loop around Isleboro, ME.

Swimming

The ocean never really heats up in New England, but that doesn't stop hordes of hardy Yankees from spilling onto the beaches and into the sea on hot summer days. Protected from the Arctic currents, Rhode Island's beaches tend to be the warmest, particularly at Block Island (p236) and Newport (p226). Beaches on Cape Cod, Nantucket and Martha's Vineyard (p124) are stunningly beautiful and the water is tolerably cold.

On the North Shore of Massachusetts, Plum Island offers a nice combination of dunes, a wide beach and a wildlife refuge (p114) harboring more than 800 species of plants and wildlife. In Ipswich, Crane Beach (p112) is a wonderful, pristine stretch of sand in the heart of a wildlife refuge, with trails traversing its dunes. Bring your surfboard and hang ten at Good Harbor Beach (p108) and Long Beach (p110) on Cape Ann.

New Hampshire's short coastline is hemmed in with condos, but Rye Beach (p330) is an old favorite. Maine has a scattering of coastal beaches with icy water, including Ogunquit (p367), Kennebunkport (p370) and Bar Harbor (p394).

Rangeley Lake (p402) in Maine and Lake Winnipesaukee (p345) in New Hampshire are two of New England's largest inland lakes that are ideal for a dip: the former is quite isolated, but the latter is bursting with resorts, shops and services.

Sailing

For maritime sails, options are wonderfully varied. Pluck lobster from their traps on a boat out of Portland (p375), Boothbay Harbor (p385) or Bar Harbor (p395), ME. Hop aboard a research vessel out of Norwalk (p268), CT, and learn about the inhabitants of the sea. Inherit the wind aboard a windjammer out of Camden (p389), ME, or a 19th-century-style schooner in Mystic (p256), CT.

APPALACHIAN TRAIL

Every year, thousands of ambitious souls endeavor to hike the complete 2179 miles of the Appalachian Trail (AT). Everyone has their own reasons for taking on this challenge, but almost all hikers share at least one goal: a life-changing experience. How could it not be that? Half a year carrying your life on your back – facing the harshest weather conditions and the most grueling physical challenges – is bound to affect you somewhere deep inside.

Such extreme challenges are not for everybody. Indeed, when the AT was dreamed up, it was never intended to be hiked all in one go. Rather, it was meant to connect various mountain communities where people could go to refresh and rejuvenate. As for refreshing and rejuvenating, the trail has been a smashing success: it's estimated that two to three million visitors hike a portion of the trail every year, inhaling the fresh air, admiring the spectacular scenery and partaking of the great outdoors.

New England offers myriad opportunities to do just that. Even if you don't have five to seven months to spare for a thru-hike, you can still challenge yourself: every New England state but Rhode Island offers access to the AT; New Hampshire and Maine contain portions that are considered among the most difficult of the entire AT. New England also offers some of the most amazing vistas and remote wilderness along the trail. So load up your backpack and take a hike – even if it's just for the day.

RESOURCES

➡ *AMC White Mountain Guide* (2012) features the most complete trail information for hiking in New Hampshire.

➡ *Hiking Maine* (2015) offers maps and trail information for 72 hikes in the northernmost New England state.

➡ Rails-to-Trails (www.railtrails.org) details the (mostly) flat railroad beds that have been converted to hiking and cycling trails, including nearly 250 in New England.

➡ Vermont Outdoor Guide Association (www.voga.org) features outfitters and guides and offers other info about hiking, cycling, camping, dog sledding and more.

Trained sailors can take out their own boat on the **Boston Harbor** (617-242-3821; www.courageoussailing.org; Pier 4; per hour sailboat rental/lesson $15/45; noon-sunset Mon-Fri, 10am-sunset Sat & Sun Jun-Oct; 93 from Haymarket, Inner Harbor Ferry from Long Wharf, North Station) or in the Charles River Basin (p57). The sailing capital of New England is undoubtedly Newport (p221), RI, where there are endless opportunities to sail – whether you want to do the work or have somebody else do it for you!

Skiing & Snowboarding

New England has no shortage of snow. And there is no better way to enjoy it than to strap on some skis. These days, downhill skiing takes all forms, including free-heeling, telemarking and snowboarding. Vermont is arguably ski central in New England. Killington (p295) ski area is known throughout New England for its extensive snowmaking apparatuses and its steep mogul field. Mad River Glen (p299) is a rough-and-ready spot that refuses admittance to boarders. For beginner and intermediate skiers, Abenaki Ski Area (p344) in New Hampshire is one of the sweetest, family-style resorts in the region, while Jiminy Peak (p200) is the best resort in the Berkshires. Maine is home to the massive Sunday River Ski Resort (p402), with slopes on eight peaks, as well as Sugarloaf (p403) resort, sitting on the slopes of the state's second-highest mountain (4237ft).

If the gravity of the situation makes you nervous, you might prefer Nordic skiing. Stowe (p310), VT, hosts the largest connected cross-country ski trail network in the East. Located in the wooded hills of the Northeast Kingdom, Craftsbury Outdoor Center (p319) sports 80 miles of groomed and ungroomed trails for your exploration, while Jackson XC (p358) is famous for its 93 miles of trails and well-informed staff.

When Henry David Thoreau was 40 years old, he took a canoe trip in the remote Maine woods. He recorded his observations and meditations in a volume called *Canoeing in the Wilderness*.

Survival Guide

Directory A–Z

Accommodations

New England provides an array of accommodations, but truly inexpensive options are rare. Reservations are recommended, especially in high season.

➡ **B&Bs** Intimate, family-run guesthouses are often contained in historic or architecturally interesting homes. Properties range widely, from economical to luxurious.

➡ **Camping** The most basic campgrounds have bathing facilities and electricity/water hook-ups, while others offer more extensive recreational facilities.

➡ **Hotels** Found mainly in cities, hotels include run-of-the-mill chains, historic properties and stylish boutique hotels.

➡ **Roadside motels** What they lack in style, they make up for in convenience and cost. Often offer the best value for budget and midrange travelers.

SLEEPING PRICE RANGES

The following price ranges refer to a double room with bathroom in high season. Unless otherwise indicated, breakfast is not included. Rates do not include taxes, which cost 5.2% to 12% depending on the state.

$ less than $100

$$ $100–250

$$$ more than $250

B&Bs

Accommodations in New England vary from small B&Bs to rambling old inns that have sheltered travelers for several centuries. Accommodations and amenities can vary widely, from the very simple to the luxurious (and prices vary accordingly). Many inns require a minimum stay of two or three nights on weekends, and advance reservations or bills paid by check or in cash (not by credit card). Some inns do not welcome children under a certain age.

Many B&Bs are booked through agencies, such as **Inns of New England** (www.innsofnewengland.com), which books B&Bs and inns in all five New England states.

Camping & Holiday Parks

With few exceptions, you'll have to camp in established campgrounds (there's no bivouacking on the side of the road). Make reservations well in advance (especially in July and August) for the best chance of getting a site. Most campgrounds are open from mid-May to mid-October.

Rough camping is occasionally permitted in the Green Mountain National Forest or the White Mountain National Forest, but it must be at established sites. State park sites usually offer services like flush toilets, hot showers and dump stations for RVs. Campsites at these places cost between $15 and $30. Private campgrounds are usually more expensive ($25 to $40) and less spacious than state parks, but they often boast recreational facilities like playgrounds, swimming pools, game rooms and miniature golf.

The following resources provide camping information:

Connecticut Department of Environmental Protection (☑860-424-3000; www.ct.gov/dep) Has a large section on outdoor recreation in Connecticut.

Maine Bureau of Parks and Land (☑207-287-3821; www.parksandlands.com) Offers camping in 12 state parks.

Massachusetts Department of Conservation and Recreation (☑617-626-1250; www.mass.gov/eea) Offers camping in 29 state parks.

Rhode Island Division of Parks & Recreation (☑401-222-2632; www.riparks.com) For a listing of all of Rhode Island's state beaches.

Vermont State Parks (☎888-409-7579; www.vtstateparks.com) Complete camping and parks information.

Cottages, Cabins & Condos

Cottages and cabins are generally found on Cape Cod, Nantucket, Martha's Vineyard and in New England's woods. They are two- or three-room vacation bungalows with basic furnishings, bathroom and kitchen. Rates vary greatly, from $80 to $700 per night, depending upon the location, season and size.

Efficiencies

An 'efficiency,' in New England parlance, is a room in a hotel, motel or inn with cooking and dining facilities: stove, sink, refrigerator, dining table and chairs, cooking utensils and tableware. Efficiency units are located throughout New England. They cost slightly more than standard rooms.

Hostels

Hosteling isn't as well developed in New England as it is in other parts of the world. But some prime destinations, including Boston, Cape Cod, Bar Harbor, Martha's Vineyard and Nantucket, have hostels that allow you to stay in $150-per-night destinations for $30 to $60 per night.

US citizens/residents can join **Hostelling International USA** (☎240-650-2100; www.hiusa.org). Non-US residents should buy a HI membership in their home countries. If you are not a member, you can still stay in US hostels for a slightly higher rate.

Hotels & Resorts

New England hotels, mostly found in cities, are generally large and lavish, except for a few 'boutique' hotels (which are small and understatedly lavish). Resorts often offer a wide variety of guest activities, such as golf, horseback riding, skiing and water sports. Prices range from $100 and up per night.

Motels

Motels, located on the highway or on the outskirts of most cities, range from 10-room places in need of a fresh coat of paint to resort-style facilities. Prices cost $65 to $150. Motels offer standard accommodations: a room with a private entrance, private bathroom, cable TV, heat and air-con. Some have small refrigerators, and many provide a simple breakfast, often at no extra charge.

Children

Traveling within New England with children presents no destination-specific problems. In fact, parents will probably find that New England offers a great variety of educational and entertaining ways to keep their kiddies busy. They will also find that most facilities – including hotels and restaurants – welcome families with children. Look for the family-friendly icon (🖼) in the listings for particularly welcoming spots.

Many restaurants have children's menus with significantly lower prices. High chairs are usually available, but it pays to inquire ahead of time. Roadside stands pepper rural New England, offering kid-friendly fare like fried fish or fish sticks, burgers, fries, chicken fingers and other small plates – most also include a kids' plate.

Children are not welcome at many smaller B&Bs and inns (even if they do not say so outright); make sure you inquire before booking. In motels and hotels, children under 17 or 18 years are usually free when sharing a room with their parents. Cots and roll-away beds are often available (sometimes for an additional fee) in hotels and resorts. Campgrounds are fantastic choices for families with kids – many are situated on waterways or lakes and offer family activities (tube rental, swimming, kayaking etc). For those who don't want to rough it, many campgrounds also offer simple cabins to rent.

Most car-rental companies lease child safety seats, but they don't always have them on hand; reserve in advance if you can. Rest stops generally have changing stations for parents' convenience. Most public transportation (bus, train etc) offers half-price tickets or reduced fares for children.

Customs Regulations

Each visitor is allowed to bring 1L of liquor and 200 cigarettes duty free into the US, but you must be at least 21 years old to possess the former and 18 years old to possess the latter. In addition, each traveler is permitted to bring gift merchandise up to the value of $100 into the US without incurring any duty.

Discount Cards

Many museums and other attractions offer discounts to college students with a valid university ID. Travelers aged 50 years and older can also receive rate cuts and benefits,

BOOK YOUR STAY ONLINE

For more accommodations reviews by Lonely Planet authors, check out http://lonelyplanet.com/hotels/. You'll find independent reviews, as well as recommendations on the best places to stay. Best of all, you can book online.

especially members of the American Association of Retired Persons (www.aarp.org). AAA members (www.aaa.com) are also eligible for many discounts at sights and hotels.

There are several programs that offer discounts to Boston-area attractions:

City Pass (www.citypass.com)
Smart Destinations (www.smartdestinations.com)

Electricity

120V/60Hz

Food

Eating in New England is a treat, whether feasting on fresh seafood, munching berries from the bush or dining at one of the region's top, chef-driven restaurants.

The finest dining and most innovative cooking takes place in New England's cities, especially Boston, Portland, Providence and Burlington. At high-end restaurants, reservations for dinner are usually recommended, especially during peak tourist seasons and on weekends. Reservations are not usually needed for lunch.

Except in the most rural areas or the smallest towns, vegetarians will have no problem finding animal-free eats. Other dietary restrictions are also usually accommodated.

New England is America's seafood capital, home of the mighty cod and the boiled lobster. Here are some of the region's seafood staples:

➡ **Chowder** A thick, cream-based soup that is chock-full of clams or fish.

➡ **Oysters** Normally served raw on the half-shell. Sweetest are Wellfleet oysters from Cape Cod.

➡ **Steamers** Steamed clams served in a bucket of briny broth.

➡ **Lobster roll** Eliminate the work of eating a lobster. Lobster meat, usually with a touch of mayo, is served on a lightly toasted roll.

➡ **Clambake** A meal of steamed lobster, clams and corn on the cob.

➡ **Scrod** Could be any white-fleshed fish. Often broiled or fried and served with french fries in the classic fish-and-chips combo.

GLBTI Travelers

Out and active gay communities are visible across New England, especially in cities such as Boston, Portland, New Haven and Burlington, which have substantial LGBT populations. Provincetown, MA, and Ogunquit, ME, are gay meccas, especially in summer. Northampton, MA, and Burlington, VT, also have lively queer communities.

Insurance

Travelers should protect themselves in case of theft, illness or car accidents. Your regular home owners' insurance, auto insurance and health insurance may offer certain coverage while traveling but be sure to check your policies. Worldwide travel insurance is available at www.lonelyplanet.com/travel-insurance. You can buy, extend and claim online anytime – even if you're already on the road.

Internet Access

Many hotels, restaurants and public spaces offer wireless access for free or for a small fee. Cybercafes and libraries offer inexpensive online computer access. If you bring a laptop with you from outside the US, it's worth investing in a universal AC and plug adapter.

Legal Matters

The minimum age for drinking alcoholic beverages is 21. You'll need a government-issued photo ID (such as a passport or US driver's license). Stiff fines, jail time and penalties can be incurred if you are caught driving under the influence of alcohol or providing alcohol to minors.

Money

ATMs & Cash

Automatic teller machines (ATMs) are ubiquitous in towns throughout New England. Most banks in New England charge at least $2 per withdrawal. The Cirrus and Plus systems both have extensive ATM networks that will give cash advances on major credit cards and allow cash withdrawals with affiliated ATM cards.

If you're carrying foreign currency, it can be exchanged for US dollars at Logan International Airport in Boston. Many banks do not change currency, so stock up on dollars when there's an opportunity to do so.

Credit Cards

Major credit cards are widely accepted throughout New England, including at car-rental agencies and at most hotels, restaurants, gas stations, grocery stores and tour operators. However, some restaurants and B&Bs – particularly those handled through rental agencies – do not accept credit cards. We have noted in our reviews when this is the case.

Visa and MasterCard are the most common credit cards. American Express and Discover are sometimes not accepted.

Currency

The dollar ($; commonly called a buck) is divided into 100 cents (¢). Coins come in denominations of one cent (penny), five cents (nickel), 10 cents (dime), 25 cents (quarter) and the rare 50-cent piece (half dollar). Notes come in denominations of one, five, 10, 20, 50 and 100 dollars.

Tipping

Many service providers depend on tips for their livelihoods, so tip generously for good service.

➡ **Baggage carriers** $1 per bag

➡ **Housekeeping** $2 to $5 per day, $5 to $10 per week

➡ **Servers and bartenders** 15% to 20%

➡ **Taxi drivers** 15%

➡ **Tour guides** $5 to $10 for a one-hour tour

Opening Hours

The following is a general guideline for operating hours. Shorter hours may apply during low seasons, when some venues close completely. Seasonal variations are noted in the listings.

Banks and offices 9am or 10am–5pm or 6pm Monday to Friday; sometimes 9am–noon Saturday

Bars and pubs 5pm–midnight, some until 2am

Restaurants Breakfast 6am–10am, lunch 11:30am–2:30pm, dinner 5pm–10pm daily

Shops 9am–7pm Monday to Saturday; some open noon–5pm Sunday, or until evening in tourist areas

Post

No matter how much people like to complain, the **US postal service** (USPS; ☏800-275-8777; www.usps.com) is extremely reliable for the price. If you have the correct postage, drop your mail into any blue mailbox. However, to send a package weighing 16oz or more, you must bring it to a post office.

Post offices are generally open from 8am to 5pm weekdays and 9am to 3pm on Saturday, but it all depends on the branch.

Public Holidays

New Year's Day January 1

Martin Luther King Jr Day Third Monday of January

Presidents' Day Third Monday of February

Easter In March or April

Patriots' Day Third Monday of April (Maine and Massachusetts only)

Memorial Day Last Monday of May

Independence Day July 4

Labor Day First Monday of September

Columbus Day Second Monday of October

Veterans Day November 11

Thanksgiving Fourth Thursday of November

Christmas Day December 25

Safe Travel

You're unlikely to come across any major problems while traveling in New England. Most of the region enjoys high standards of living, and tourists are usually well taken care of.

Driving Hazards

New England driving can be tricky, particularly in big cities, where narrow streets, clogged traffic and illogical street layouts can make unfamiliar drivers miserable. New England drivers are notoriously impatient. Beware the 'Boston left,' where the first left-turning vehicle jumps out in front of oncoming traffic.

Outdoor Hazards

Outdoor activities, from beach-going to mountain-hiking, can be dangerous anywhere in the world. Pay attention to weather and water conditions before setting out on any sort of adventure.

➡ The White Mountains are notorious for strong winds and wild weather, but conditions can be dangerous on any of the New England mountain trails. Inquire about weather conditions with rangers before setting out.

➡ Always stay on marked trails and do not disturb wildlife while hiking.

→ In recent years, shark sightings have not been uncommon off Cape Cod, and beaches may close for that reason. Not all public beaches are guarded, so inquire about riptides and other dangers before swimming at area beaches.

Weather

It snows a lot in New England. If you're visiting between December and March, there's a good chance you'll experience a major snow storm, possibly impeding your progress until roads are plowed.

Telephone

Always dial '1' before toll-free (800, 888 etc) and domestic long-distance numbers. Remember that some toll-free numbers may only work within the region or from the US mainland.

All phone numbers in the US consist of a three-digit area code followed by a seven-digit local number. You now must dial 1 plus all 10 digits for local and long-distance calls in most areas, particularly in Eastern Massachusetts.

Pay phones aren't as readily found at shopping centers, gas stations and other public places now that cell phones are more prevalent, but keep your eyes peeled and you'll find them. Calls made within town are local and cost 50¢.

To make direct international calls, dial ☑011 plus the country code plus the area code plus the number. (An exception is calls made to Canada, where you dial 1 plus the area code plus the number. International rates apply to Canada.) For international operator assistance, dial ☑0.

If you're calling New England from abroad, the international country code for the US is 1. All calls to New England are then followed by the area code and the seven-digit local number.

Mobile Phones

The US uses a variety of cell-phone systems, and most are incompatible with the GSM 900/1800 standard used throughout Europe and Asia. Check with your cellular service provider before departure about using your phone in New England.

Verizon has the most extensive cellular network in New England, but Cingular and Sprint also have decent coverage. Once you get up into the mountains and off the main interstates in Vermont, New Hampshire and Maine, cell-phone reception is often downright nonexistent. Forget about using it on hiking trails.

Phonecards

These private prepaid cards are available from convenience stores, supermarkets and pharmacies. Cards sold by major telecommunications companies like AT&T may offer better deals than upstart companies.

Time

New England is on US Eastern Standard Time (GMT+5). New England observes daylight saving time, which involves setting clocks ahead one hour on the second Sunday in March and back one hour on the first Sunday in November.

Toilets

Most parks, beaches and other public places offer public toilets, although they are not common in big cities. There is no public mandate stating that restaurants, hotels or public sites must open their doors to those in need, but you can usually find relief at information centers, libraries, museums and larger hotels.

Americans have many names for public toilet facilities, but the most common names are 'restroom,' 'bathroom' or 'ladies'/men's room.' Of course, you can just ask for the 'toilet.'

Tourist Information

State Tourist Offices

Connecticut Office of Tourism (☑888-288-4748; www.ctvisit. com)

Greater Boston Convention & Visitors Bureau (GBCVB; ☑888-733-2678; www.boston usa.com)

Maine Office of Tourism (☑888-624-6345; www.visit maine.com)

Massachusetts Office of Travel & Tourism (☑617-973-8500; www.massvacation.com)

New Hampshire Division of Travel & Tourism (☑603-271-2665; www.visitnh.gov)

Rhode Island Tourism Division (☑800-556-2484; www. visitrhodeisland.com)

Vermont Division of Tourism (☑800-837-6668; www. vermontvacation.com)

Chambers of Commerce

Often associated with convention and visitors' bureaus (CVBs), these are membership organizations for local businesses including hotels, restaurants and shops. Although they often provide maps, lodging recommendations and other useful information, they focus on establishments that are members of the chamber.

A local chamber of commerce often maintains an information booth at the entrance to town or in the town center, often open only during tourist seasons.

Travelers with Disabilities

Travel within New England is becoming less difficult for people with disabilities, but it's still not easy. Public buildings are now required by law to be wheelchair accessible and also to have appropriate restroom facilities. Public transportation services must be made accessible to all, and telephone companies are required to provide relay operators for the hearing impaired. Many banks provide ATM instructions in Braille, curb ramps are common, many busy intersections have audible crossing signals, and most chain hotels have suites for guests with disabilities.

Mobility International USA (☑541-343-1284; www.miusa.org) advises travelers with disabilities on mobility issues and runs educational international exchange programs.

Download Lonely Planet's free Accessible Travel guide from http://lptravel.to/AccessibleTravel.

Visas

Citizens of many countries are eligible for the Visa Waiver Program, which requires prior approval via Electronic System for Travel Authorization (ESTA).

Visa Waiver Program

The US has a Visa Waiver Program in which citizens of certain countries may enter the US for stays of 90 days or less without first obtaining a US visa. This list is subject to continual re-examination and bureaucratic rejigging. For an up-to-date list of countries included in the program, see the US Department of State website (http://travel.state.gov). Under the program you must have a round-trip ticket (or onward ticket to any foreign destination) that is non-refundable in the US and you will not be allowed to extend your stay beyond 90 days.

To participate in the Visa Waiver Program, travelers are required to have a passport that is machine readable. Also, your passport should be valid for at least six months longer than your intended stay.

Electronic System for Travel Authorization

Since January 2009 the US has had the Electronic System for Travel Authorization (ESTA), a system that has been implemented to mitigate security risks concerning those who travel to the US by air or sea (this does not apply to those entering by land, such as via Canada). This pre-authorization system applies to citizens of all countries that fall under the Visa Waiver Program. This process requires that you register specific information online, prior to entering the US.

Information required includes details like your name, current address and passport information, including the number and expiration date, and details about any communicable diseases you may carry (including HIV). It is recommended that you fill out the online form as early as possible, and at least 72 hours prior to departure. You will receive one of three responses:

➡ 'Authorization Approved' usually comes within minutes; most applicants can expect to receive this response.

➡ 'Authorization Pending' means you should go back online to check the status within roughly 72 hours.

➡ 'Travel not Authorized' indicates that your application is not approved and you will need to apply for a visa.

Once approved, registration is valid for two years, but note that if you renew your passport or change your name, you will need to re-register. The cost is $14. The entire process is stored electronically and linked to your passport, but it is recommended that you bring a printout of the ESTA approval just to be safe. If you don't have access to the internet, ask your travel agent, who can apply on your behalf.

Visa Applications

Documentation required for visa applications:

➡ A recent photo (50.8mm by 50.8mm).

➡ Documents of financial stability and/or guarantees from a US resident are sometimes required, particularly for those from developing countries.

➡ Visa applicants may be required to 'demonstrate binding obligations' that will ensure their return home. Because of this requirement, those planning to travel through other countries before arriving in the US are generally better off applying for their US visa while they are still in their home country rather than while on the road.

The validity period for a US visitor visa depends on your home country. The actual length of time you'll be allowed to stay in the US is determined by the Bureau of Citizenship and Immigration Services at the port of entry.

As with the Visa Waiver Program, your passport should be valid for at least six months longer than your intended stay.

Transportation

GETTING THERE & AWAY

While the two most common ways to reach New England are by air and car, you can also get here easily by train and bus. Boston is the region's hub for air travel, but some international travelers fly into New York City to do some sightseeing before heading up to New England. Flights, cars and tours can be booked online at lonelyplanet.com/bookings.

Air

Because of New England's location on the densely populated US Atlantic seaboard between New York and eastern Canada, air travelers have a number of ways to approach the region.

Airports & Airlines

The major gateway to the region is Boston's **Logan International Airport**

(✆800-235-6426; www.mass port.com/logan), which offers many direct, nonstop flights from major airports in the US and abroad.

Depending on where you will be doing the bulk of your exploring, several other airports in the region receive national and international flights. It's also feasible to fly into one of New York's major airports.

Bangor International Airport (✆866-359-2264; www.flyban gor.com; 287 Godfrey Blvd) Bangor International Airport in Maine is served by regional carriers associated with Continental, Delta and US Airways.

Bradley International Airport (BDL;✆860-292-2000; www. bradleyairport.com; Windsor Locks) Bradley International Airport, 12 miles north of Hartford in Windsor Locks (I-91 exit 40), is served by American Airlines, Southwest Airlines, Delta, JetBlue and US Airways.

Burlington International Airport (BTV;✆802-863-2874;

www.btv.aero; 1200 Airport Dr, South Burlington) Vermont's major airport.

Green Airport (✆888-268-7222; www.pvdairport.com; 2000 Post Road, Warwick) Located 20 minutes south of Providence, RI.

Manchester-Boston Regional Airport (✆603-624-6556; www.flymanchester.com) A quiet alternative to Logan, Manchester Airport is just 55 miles north of Boston in New Hampshire.

Portland International Jetport (PWM;✆207-874-8877; www. portlandjetport.org; 1001 Westbrook St) Serves coastal Maine.

Land

Border Crossings

Sharing a border with Canada, Vermont has 15 places to cross, while Maine has 24. Generally, crossing the US–Canadian border is straightforward, though the

---

CLIMATE CHANGE & TRAVEL

Every form of transport that relies on carbon-based fuel generates CO_2, the main cause of human-induced climate change. Modern travel is dependent on airplanes, which might use less fuel per mile per person than most cars but travel much greater distances. The altitude at which aircraft emit gases (including CO_2) and particles also contributes to their climate change impact. Many websites offer 'carbon calculators' that allow people to estimate the carbon emissions generated by their journey and, for those who wish to do so, to offset the impact of the greenhouse gases emitted with contributions to portfolios of climate-friendly initiatives throughout the world. Lonely Planet offsets the carbon footprint of all staff and author travel.

length of the lines can be a hassle. All travelers entering the USA are required to carry passports, including citizens of Canada and the USA.

Bus

You can get to New England by bus from all parts of the US and Canada, but the trip will be long and may not be much less expensive than a discounted flight. Bus companies usually offer special promotional fares.

Greyhound (☑800-231-2222, international customer service 214-849-8100; www.greyhound.com) The national bus line, serving all major cities in the USA.

Peter Pan Bus (☑800-343-9999; www.peterpanbus.com) The regional bus company, serving 54 destinations in the northeast, as far north as Concord, NH, and as far south as Washington, DC, as well as into western Massachusetts.

Go Bus (www.gobuses.com; Alewife Brook Pkwy; 1 way $18-42; ☎; Ⓣ Alewife), **Lucky Star Bus** (www.luckystarbus.com; South Station; 1 way $25; ☎) and **Megabus** (www.megabus.com; South Station; 1 way $10-30; ☎) offer inexpensive bus fares between New York City and Boston.

Car & Motorcycle

Interstate highways crisscross New England and offer forest, farm and mountain scenery, once you are clear of urban areas and the I-95 corridor between Boston and New York. These interstate highways connect the region to New York; Washington, DC; Montreal; and points west.

Hitchhiking

Hitchhiking is never entirely safe, and we don't recommend it. Travelers who hitchhike should understand that they are taking a small but potentially serious risk.

Crossing the US–Canadian border can be a challenge for

hitchhikers. Most drivers will not want to take the risk or endure the hassle of transporting a stranger across the border. It is possible to cross the border on foot, although border guards are likely to be suspicious: expect extensive interrogation. Non-US citizens will likely be requested to prove their means (ie access to money) and plan to exit the country (ie return ticket).

Hitchhiking is legal in all six New England states, as well as neighboring New York, as long as you stay off the traveled part of the road or on the shoulder. On interstate highways, hitchhiking is restricted to on-ramps.

According to Hitchwiki (www.hitchwiki.org), all six states rank as 'easy' on the Ease of Hitchhiking map, as does New York. Vermont is cited as the easiest place to thumb a ride in the entire country.

Train

Amtrak (☑800-872-7245; www.amtrak.com) is the main rail passenger service in the US. Services along the Northeast Corridor (connecting Boston, Providence, Hartford and New Haven with New York and Washington, DC) are some of the most frequent in Amtrak's system. Amtrak's high-speed *Acela Express* makes the trip from New York City to Boston in three hours.

Other Amtrak services to New England:

➡ The *Ethan Allen* is an express train linking New York City and Albany to Rutland, VT.

➡ The *Vermonter* runs from Washington, DC, and New York City, through New Haven and Hartford in Connecticut, Springfield and Amherst in Massachusetts, and then on to St Albans in Vermont.

➡ The *Lake Shore Limited* departs from Boston, stopping at Worcester, Springfield and Pittsfield

before crossing into New York and continuing west. Connecticut is also served by commuter trains from New York City, operated by **Metro-North** (☑212-878-7000, 877-690-5116; www.mta.info) and **Shore Line East** (☑800-255-7433; www.shorelineeast.com).

Sea

Bay Ferries (Map p374; ☑877-762-7245; www.ferries.ca; Ocean Gateway Pier; ☺mid-Jun–Sep) Operates the summertime CAT service, sailing daily between Portland, ME, and Yarmouth, Nova Scotia (six hours).

Bridgeport & Port Jefferson Steamboat Company (☑in Connecticut 888-443-3779, in Long Island 631-473-0286; www.88844ferry.com; 102 W Broadway, Port Jefferson, NY) Daily ferry between Long Island and Connecticut.

Cross Sound Ferry (☑860-443-5281; www.longislandferry.com; 2 Ferry St) Year-round ferry from Orient Point on Long Island to New London, CT.

Fishers Island Ferry (☑860-442-0165; www.fiferry.com; 5 Waterfront Park; adult/senior & child mid-May–mid-Sep $25/18, mid-Sep–mid-May $19/14, cars $56/40) Year-round ferry between New London, CT, and Fishers Island, NY.

Fort Ti Ferry (www.forttiferry.com; per car/bike/motorcycle $10/2/5; ☺7am-6pm early May-Oct) Runs from Shoreham, VT, to Ticonderoga Landing, NY, from May through October.

Lake Champlain Ferries (Map p302; ☑802-864-9804; www.ferries.com; King St Dock; adult/child/car $8/3.10/30; ☺mid-Jun–Sep) Runs from Burlington, VT, to New York State, traversing the lake.

Seastreak (☑800-262-8743; www.seastreak.com) High-speed ferry service connecting Martha's Vineyard to Highlands, NJ, and New York City (six hours) on weekends in season.

GETTING AROUND

Air

Flying can be an efficient way to reach the islands and other more distant corners of New England. The flights are short, airplanes are small, and weather is a critical factor in the safety and reliability of flights. Buy tickets directly from the airlines for the cheapest fares.

Airlines in New England

Regional and commuter airlines connect New England's cities and resorts with Boston and New York City.

There are several regional airlines, especially serving Cape Cod and the islands:

Cape Air (✆800-227-3247; www.flycapeair.com) Flights to several New England destinations, including Cape Cod, Martha's Vineyard and Nantucket.

Nantucket Air (✆508-771-6944, 800-227-3247; www.nantucketairlines.com) Flights to Nantucket from Boston, New York and Providence.

New England Airlines (✆800-243-2460; www.block-island.com/nea; 56 Airport Rd, Westerly; one way/round-trip $54/99) Very short flights to Block Island from mainland Rhode Island.

Bicycle

Cycling is a popular New England sport and means of transportation on both city streets and country roads. Several of the larger cities have systems of bike paths that make bike travel easier and more pleasant. Disused railroad rights-of-way have also been turned into bike trails that are perfect for bicycle touring (p424).

Bicycle rentals are available in most New England cities, towns and resorts at reasonable prices (often $20 to $35 per day).

Boat

Regular ferry services ply the coast, servicing islands up and down the coast:

Bay State Cruise Company (www.boston-ptown.com; Commonwealth Pier, Seaport Blvd; round-trip adult/child $88/65; ▣SL1, SL2, ⊤South Station) Boston to Provincetown.

Block Island Express (✆860-444-4624; www.goblockisland.com; 2 Ferry St; adult/child/bike $25/12.50/10) From New London.

Block Island Ferry (Map p238; ✆401-783-4613; www.blockislandferry.com) From Newport and Point Judith.

Falmouth–Edgartown Ferry (✆508-548-9400; www.falmouthedgartownferry.com; one-way adult/child/bike $25/15/5; ☉late May–early Sep) Shuttles between Cape Cod and Martha's Vineyard.

Hy-Line Cruises (✆508-778-2600; www.hylinecruises.com; Ocean St Dock) From Hyannis to Nantucket and Martha's Vineyard.

Island Queen (✆508-548-4800; www.islandqueen.com; 75 Falmouth Heights Rd, Falmouth Harbor; ☉round-trip adult/child/bike $20/10/8) Between Falmouth on Cape Cod and Oak Bluffs on Martha's Vineyard.

Maine State Ferry Service (www.maine.gov/mdot/ferry/) Runs ferries around Penobscot Bay from terminals at Rockland, Bass Harbor and Lincolnville.

Provincetown Ferry (Map p38; www.bostonharborcruises.com; 1 Long Wharf; round-trip adult/child $88/65; ☉May-Oct; ⊤Aquarium) From Boston.

Salem Ferry (Map p38; www.salemferry.com; Central Wharf; round-trip adult/child $45/35; ☉7am-7pm Mon-Fri, 8am-8pm Sat & Sun May-Oct; ⊤Aquarium) From Boston.

Seastreak (✆800-262-8743; www.seastreak.com) Operates from New Bedford to Martha's Vineyard and Nantucket.

Steamship Authority (✆508-477-8600; www.steamshipauthority.com; South St Dock) Hyannis to Nantucket; Woods Hole to Martha's Vineyard.

Bus

Buses go to more places than airplanes or trains, but the routes still bypass some prime destinations, especially in rural places.

The national bus company, Greyhound, as well as Peter Pan, provides service to and within New England. Regional carriers that ply routes within New England include the following:

C&J Trailways (✆800-258-7111; www.ridecj.com) Provides daily service between Boston and Newburyport, MA, as well as Portsmouth and Dover, NH.

Concord Coach Lines (Concord Trailways; ✆800-639-3317; www.concordcoachlines.com) Covers routes from Boston to New Hampshire (Concord, Manchester, Conway and Berlin) and Maine (Portland, Mid-Coast, Bangor and Augusta).

Dartmouth Coach (✆603-448-2800, 800-637-0123; www.dartmouthcoach.com) Servicing Hanover, Lebanon and New London from Boston.

Plymouth & Brockton Street Railway Co (✆508-746-0378; www.p-b.com) Provides frequent service to the South Shore and to most towns on Cape Cod, including Hyannis and Provincetown.

Car & Motorcycle

Yes, driving is really the best way to see New England. But heads up: New England drivers are aggressive, speedy and unpredictable, particularly around Boston and other cities. You have been warned. Traffic jams are common in urban areas.

Municipalities control parking by signs on the street, stating explicitly where you may or may not park. A yellow line or yellow-painted curb means that no parking is allowed there.

Driving Licenses

An International Driving Permit (IDP), obtained before you leave home, is only necessary if your regular license is not in English.

Fuel

Gas stations are ubiquitous and many are open 24 hours a day. Small-town stations may be open only from 7am to 8pm or 9pm. Gas prices were around $2.30 to $2.50 per US gallon at the time of research.

At some stations, you must pay before you pump; at others, you may pump before you pay. More modern pumps have credit/debit card terminals built into them, so you can pay with plastic right at the pump. At 'full service' stations, an attendant will pump your gas for you; no tip is expected.

Hire

Rental cars are readily available. With advance reservations for a small car, the daily rate with unlimited mileage is about $60, while typical weekly rates are $300 to $600. Rates for midsize cars are often only a tad higher. Dropping off the car at a different location from where you picked it up usually incurs an additional fee. It always pays to shop around between rental companies.

Having a major credit card greatly simplifies the rental process. Without one, some agencies simply will not rent vehicles, while others require prepayment, a deposit slightly higher than the cost of your rental, pay stubs, proof of round-trip airfare and more.

The following companies operate in New England:

Alamo (📞844-341-8645; www.alamo.com)

Avis (📞800-633-3469; www.avis.com)

Budget (📞800-218-7992; www.budget.com)

Dollar (📞800-800-3665; www.dollar.com)

Enterprise (📞844-362-0812; www.enterprise.com)

Hertz (📞800-654-3131; www.hertz.com)

National (📞877-222-9058; www.nationalcar.com)

Rent-A-Wreck (📞877-877-0700; www.rentawreck.com) Rents out cars that may have more wear and tear than your typical rental vehicle, but are actually far from wrecks.

Thrifty (📞800-847-4389; www.thrifty.com)

Insurance

Should you have an accident, liability insurance covers the people and property that you have hit. For damage to the actual rental vehicle, a collision damage waiver (CDW) is available for about $10 a day. If you have collision coverage on your vehicle at home, it might cover damages to car rentals; inquire before departing. Additionally, some credit cards offer reimbursement coverage for collision damages if you rent the car with that credit card; again, check before departing. Most credit card coverage isn't valid for rentals of more than 15 days or for 'exotic' models, such as 4WD Jeeps and vans.

Road Hazards

New England roads are very good – even the hard-packed dirt roads that crisscross Vermont. Some roads across northern mountain passes in Vermont, New Hampshire and Maine are closed during the winter, but good signage gives you plenty of warning.

Road Rules

Driving laws are different in each of the New England states, but most require the use of safety belts. In every state, children under four years of age must be placed in a child safety seat secured by a seat belt. Most states require motorcycle riders to wear helmets whenever they ride.

The maximum speed limit on most New England inter-

states is 65mph, but some have a limit of 55mph. On undivided highways, the speed limit will vary from 30mph to 55mph. Police enforce speed limits by patrolling in police cruisers and in unmarked cars. Fines can cost upwards of $350 in Connecticut, and it's similarly expensive in other states.

Local Transportation

City buses and the T (the subway/underground system in Boston) provide useful transportation within the larger cities and to some suburbs. Resort areas also tend to have regional bus lines.

Taxis and Uber are common in the largest cities, but in smaller cities and towns you will probably have to telephone a cab to pick you up. Shuttles may take travelers from their hotel to the airport.

Train

For train travel within New England, Amtrak operates the *Downeaster*, which runs from Boston's North Station to Brunswick, ME; stops along the way include Exeter, NH, as well as Portland and Freeport, ME. Amtrak (p435) offers several other services connecting New England destinations to each other and to other states.

Other regional train services:

MBTA Commuter Rail (📞800-392-6100; www.mbta.com) Boston's commuter rail travels west to Concord and Lowell, north to Salem, Rockport, Gloucester and Newburyport, and south to Plymouth and Providence.

Metro-North (📞212-878-7000, 877-690-5116; www.mta.info) From New York City to New Haven.

Shore Line East (📞800-255-7433; www.shorelineeast.com) Connecticut's service along the Long Island Sound.

Behind the Scenes

SEND US YOUR FEEDBACK

We love to hear from travelers – your comments keep us on our toes and help make our books better. Our well-traveled team reads every word on what you loved or loathed about this book. Although we cannot reply individually to your submissions, we always guarantee that your feedback goes straight to the appropriate authors, in time for the next edition. Each person who sends us information is thanked in the next edition – the most useful submissions are rewarded with a selection of digital PDF chapters.

Visit **lonelyplanet.com/contact** to submit your updates and suggestions or to ask for help. Our award-winning website also features inspirational travel stories, news and discussions.

Note: We may edit, reproduce and incorporate your comments in Lonely Planet products such as guidebooks, websites and digital products, so let us know if you don't want your comments reproduced or your name acknowledged. For a copy of our privacy policy visit lonelyplanet.com/privacy.

OUR READERS

Many thanks to the travelers who used the last edition and wrote to us with helpful hints, useful advice and interesting anecdotes:
Cathelijne Augustijn, Christina Jacobi, David Callow, Doreen Nicol, Katherine Davis-Young, Sheela O Regan

WRITER THANKS

Gregor Clark

Thanks to all the generous New Englanders who helped with this project, especially Katherine Quinn, Sarah Pope and Margo Whitcomb. Love and special thanks to Gaen, Meigan and Chloe for helping me explore this beautiful region and always sharing my excitement for the road less traveled.

Carolyn Bain

My warmest thanks to all the chatty innkeepers, bartenders and barflies I had the good fortune to spend time with – who else would you ask for tips on the region's best beach/trail/lobster roll/craft brew etc? Sincerest thanks to the people of Nantucket for welcoming me back into your fold and embracing my nostalgia – especially to Roselyne Hatch and Tania Jones. Special mention goes to Emily Golin, Carla Tracy, Thomas Masters, and Kimberly and Barry Hunter for their kindnesses.

Mara Vorhees

Thanks to friends and neighbors who have taught me so much about New England over the years. I am grateful to my faithful travel companions, Shay and Van: it's always more fun to travel – though more difficult to write – when you're along for the ride. And thank you, Jerz, for going along with the sunrise thing, all 19 times (and counting).

Benedict Walker

Massive thanks to the ever-delightful Rebecca Warren for taking me on and for your patience and guidance along the way. Huge hugs to my twin in the Big Apple, Lyndal Hunt, for your love and hospitality; to my buddy Peter Falso in Newport for fun and laughs; to my always-awesome pals Heather, Pete and Wendy; and to the master architect, Tom Zook, for your friendship, knowledge and support. Finally, thanks Mum: I love you to the moon and back.

ACKNOWLEDGEMENTS

Climate map data adapted from Peel MC, Finlayson BL & McMahon TA (2007) 'Updated World Map of the Köppen-Geiger Climate Classification', *Hydrology and Earth System Sciences*, 11, 1633–44.

Cover photograph: New England during the fall, Libby Zhang/500px ©

THIS BOOK

This 8th edition of Lonely Planet's *New England* guidebook was researched and written by Gregor Clark, Carolyn Bain, Mara Vorhees and Benedict Walker. The previous edition was written by Mara Vorhees, Gregor Clark, Ned Friary, Paula Hardy and Caroline Sieg. This guidebook was produced by the following:

Destination Editor Rebecca Warren

Product Editors Carolyn Boicos, Kate Chapman, Kate Mathews

Senior Cartographer Alison Lyall

Book Designer Wendy Wright

Assisting Editors Sarah Bailey, Michelle Bennett, Samantha Forge, Ali Lemer, Rosie Nicholson, Kristin Odijk, Charlotte Orr, Victoria Smith

Assisting Cartographer Julie Dodkins

Cover Researcher Naomi Parker

Thanks to Amy Irvine, Andi Jones, Claire Naylor, Karyn Noble, Tony Wheeler, Dora Whitaker

Index

Map Legend

Sights

- Beach
- Bird Sanctuary
- Buddhist
- Castle/Palace
- Christian
- Confucian
- Hindu
- Islamic
- Jain
- Jewish
- Monument
- Museum/Gallery/Historic Building
- Ruin
- Shinto
- Sikh
- Taoist
- Winery/Vineyard
- Zoo/Wildlife Sanctuary
- Other Sight

Activities, Courses & Tours

- Bodysurfing
- Diving
- Canoeing/Kayaking
- Course/Tour
- Sento Hot Baths/Onsen
- Skiing
- Snorkeling
- Surfing
- Swimming/Pool
- Walking
- Windsurfing
- Other Activity

Sleeping

- Sleeping
- Camping

Eating

- Eating

Drinking & Nightlife

- Drinking & Nightlife
- Cafe

Entertainment

- Entertainment

Shopping

- Shopping

Information

- Bank
- Embassy/Consulate
- Hospital/Medical
- Internet
- Police
- Post Office
- Telephone
- Toilet
- Tourist Information
- Other Information

Geographic

- Beach
- Gate
- Hut/Shelter
- Lighthouse
- Lookout
- Mountain/Volcano
- Oasis
- Park
- Pass
- Picnic Area
- Waterfall

Population

- Capital (National)
- Capital (State/Province)
- City/Large Town
- Town/Village

Transport

- Airport
- BART station
- Border crossing
- Boston T station
- Bus
- Cable car/Funicular
- Cycling
- Ferry
- Metro/Muni station
- Monorail
- Parking
- Petrol station
- Subway/SkyTrain station
- Taxi
- Train station/Railway
- Tram
- Underground station
- Other Transport

Routes

- Tollway
- Freeway
- Primary
- Secondary
- Tertiary
- Lane
- Unsealed road
- Road under construction
- Plaza/Mall
- Steps
- Tunnel
- Pedestrian overpass
- Walking Tour
- Walking Tour detour
- Path/Walking Trail

Boundaries

- International
- State/Province
- Disputed
- Regional/Suburb
- Marine Park
- Cliff
- Wall

Hydrography

- River, Creek
- Intermittent River
- Canal
- Water
- Dry/Salt/Intermittent Lake
- Reef

Areas

- Airport/Runway
- Beach/Desert
- Cemetery (Christian)
- Cemetery (Other)
- Glacier
- Mudflat
- Park/Forest
- Sight (Building)
- Sportsground
- Swamp/Mangrove

Note: Not all symbols displayed above appear on the maps in this book

OUR STORY

A beat-up old car, a few dollars in the pocket and a sense of adventure. In 1972 that's all Tony and Maureen Wheeler needed for the trip of a lifetime – across Europe and Asia overland to Australia. It took several months, and at the end – broke but inspired – they sat at their kitchen table writing and stapling together their first travel guide, *Across Asia on the Cheap*. Within a week they'd sold 1500 copies. Lonely Planet was born.

Today, Lonely Planet has offices in Franklin, London, Melbourne, Oakland, Dublin, Beijing and Delhi, with more than 600 staff and writers. We share Tony's belief that 'a great guidebook should do three things: inform, educate and amuse'.

OUR WRITERS

Gregor Clark

Vermont, New Hampshire Gregor Clark has been exploring New England's back roads since childhood, when he rode bikes through Cape Cod's dunes, skated on frozen ponds in northwestern Connecticut and saw his first shooting star in Vermont's Green Mountains. A lifelong polyglot with an insatiable curiosity for what lies around the next bend, Gregor has contributed to over three dozen Lonely Planet guides, with an emphasis on North America, Latin America and Europe. He lives with his wife and daughters in Middlebury, VT.

Read more about Gregor at:
https://auth.lonelyplanet.com/profiles/gregorclark

Carolyn Bain

Cape Cod, Nantucket & Martha's Vineyard; Maine Australian-born Carolyn worked a glorious season on Nantucket a decade or so back – and like countless visitors before her, she fell in love with Cape Cod at first sight. Sand dunes and salt spray, history and wholesomeness, cozy inns and seafood feasts: this was (and still is) the USA at its most charming. On this trip, Maine made an awesome adjunct, and she relished the chance to go beyond lighthouses and lobsters to uncover craft brews, moose trails and road-tripping nirvana.

Read more about Carolyn at:
https://auth.lonelyplanet.com/profiles/carolynbain

Mara Vorhees

Boston, Around Boston, Central Massachusetts & the Berkshires Born and raised in St Clair Shores, Michigan, Mara traveled the world (if not the universe) before settling in the Hub. The pen-wielding traveler covers destinations as diverse as Belize and Russia, as well as her home in New England. She lives in a pink house in Somerville, MA, with her husband, two kiddies and two kitties. Mara also wrote the Plan Your Trip, Understand and Survival Guide sections.

Read more about Mara at:
https://auth.lonelyplanet.com/profiles/mvorhees

Benedict Walker

Rhode Island, Connecticut Born in Newcastle, Australia, Ben holds notions of the beach core to his idea of self, though he's traveled hundreds of thousands of kilometers from the sandy shores of home. Ben was given his first Lonely Planet guide *(Japan)* when he was 12. Two decades later, he'd write chapters for the same publication: a dream come true. A communications graduate and travel agent by trade, Ben whittled away his twenties gallivanting around the globe. He thinks the best thing about travel isn't as much about where you go as who you meet: living vicariously through the stories of kind strangers enriches one's own experience. Ben has also written and directed a play, and toured Australia managing the travel logistics for top-billing music festivals.

Read more about Benedict at:
https://auth.lonelyplanet.com/profiles/benedictwalker

Published by Lonely Planet Global Limited
CRN 554153
8th edition – Mar 2017
ISBN 978 1 78657 324 7
© Lonely Planet 2017   Photographs © as indicated 2017
10 9 8 7 6 5 4 3 2 1
Printed in China